University Follies

JEWISH ROOTS IN A JESUIT UNIVERSITY

PAUL WARREN

ISBN 979-8-35093-340-6

JANET WARREN (1954–2023)

Without her love, this story could not have been told.

No one you have been and no place you have gone ever leaves you.

—Bruce Springsteen

The struggle itself toward the heights is enough to fill one man's heart. One must imagine Sisyphus happy.

—Albert Camus

Bernard loved the valleys, Benedict the mountains; Francis the towns, Ignatius loved great cities.

—Old Jesuit Proverb

Contents

Author's Note

The chronological order and substance of some of the recollections have been altered by imperfect memory, the passage of time, and the occasional use of artistic license. Dialogues with students, professors, deans, and presidents with whom I worked capture the essence of exchanges rather than *verbatim* recordings. Tales contained in this work, thus, might be considered in the same manner as lithographs of paintings of Picasso and Miro that carry the notation, *after a work by . . .*

Names of the majority of university characters have been changed to protect the innocent and not-so-innocent; names of presidents, provosts, family, and a nationally recognized school reformer have not: Presidents, provosts, and school reformers cut a public swath too broad to be covered by pseudonyms. Family will understand.

One

So It Began

It was in a dark, smoke-filled Fado house hidden in narrow cob-blestone streets of the Alfama district of Lisbon where I first sensed that my career as dean at Boston University would be drawing to a close. I had been at my best earlier in the day as I delivered an invited presentation from the Portuguese minister of education for educators selected to staff Portugal's first Normal Schools for the training of teachers. I would pause every few paragraphs as I worked from a paper I had prepared in Boston to permit a translator to convey my message to attendees not universally proficient in English. The luxury of the unexpected time had provided an opportunity for me to elaborate on thoughts and insert humor into the emerging script at the risk of producing a work which in length would rival Eugene O'Neil's *Long Day's Journey.* True to the history of my theatre family, I was seduced by the opportunity to play the lead actor in my own production. Compliments from the minister and applause from the audience on delivery of my closing words left me on a high that can only be felt by an actor receiving rave notices for a leading role. The high only lasted until that Fado evening in the Alfama with Jon, special assistant to the Boston University president, and his wife who had joined my wife, Janet, and me on the US AID sponsored trip.

A briny fragrance of sea and age drifted down damp narrow caverns between ancient mortar dwellings as a Portuguese American graduate student in Boston who had assisted my School of Education receive the grant from US AID led the four of us through a maze of cobblestone streets to a Fado bar of his choice. Save for an occasional streetlamp and light from a window to break the night's dark, the district was hardly different from that of 1775 when an earthquake had leveled Lisbon leaving only the Alfama intact. Once the bar of our guide's choice was located and we were seated, he wished us a good evening, left directions for return to our hotel, and departed to join friends.

The hum of muted Portuguese conversation and unfamiliar sweet fragrance of a hovering blanket of cigarette smoke from closely clustered tables reminded us that we were foreigners in a sea of locals. When a waiter drifted to our table, asked in English what we would like to drink, and glasses of Campari were soon set before us, any discomfort quickly dissolved. We had time for a first Campari and follow-up before the hum of conversation in the room abruptly faded when a wraith of a woman, black shawl over her shoulders, emerged from behind a black velvet curtain into the haze of smoke. Proximity to one another and guests at other tables evaporated. We sat alone in cigarette smoke, candle-light, and silence.

Mournful laments filled the space for the next hour. We were consumed by the haunting melody and singer's plaintive words—not one of which we understood. Mesmerized, we were lost in our private thoughts and emotions. We sat silently swallowed in a wave of melancholy until broken by the waiter's "Another Campari," following the final lament of the set. On a nod of consent and the waiter's departure, Jon dulled by earlier drinks, couldn't wait to lean across the table and slur, "Paul, I learned more from the minister's remarks in twenty minutes this morning than I learned from your day-long presentation." The evening drew to close with silence and emotions of another order.

Less than a year later, any doubt as to the imminent end of tenure as dean ended. I had found joy and a sense of accomplishment over the years in the facilitation of projects and programs to assist underserved populations whether as a teacher in the New York City public high schools, administrator or staff on urban government and university projects in the South and New York, or professor and dean at Boston University That was until John Silber, the controversial Boston University president decided that his university would respond to the opportunity to "adopt" the Chelsea Public Schools.

Chelsea schools in the 1960s were buried in the poverty and decline of a city of approximately 35,000 residents shoe-horned into less than two and a half miles directly across the Mystic River from Boston. Chelsea schools, historically a gateway for immigrants, were a case study in failure with only half of its students, mostly from low-income families, graduating from high school. The opportunity to enter into a Boston University–Chelsea Public School partnership in which the university would be responsible for the day-to day management of the schools was too great for Silber to resist. I was soon to find out that the opportunity was also too great for him, a skeptic of education as a field of study, to trust a dean of a school of education to play a major role in the project.

After only a few meetings as member of the University team of administrators with little or no professional experience in public education selected by Silber and his special assistant, Jon, who had drawn my Portugal Fado evening to an abrupt end, it became clear that my advice wasn't wanted. There was no receptivity to recommendations drawn from my years of experience with underperforming public schools and lower-income students. With each succeeding meeting of the committee, I felt more and more like a student whose observations fail to capture the attention of a professor than the dean of a school of education. It was time to negotiate my retirement.

At least some momentary pleasure was provided by a bittersweet moment with President Silber before my departure. At a friendly farewell meeting requested by the president to thank me for my years as dean, I was asked what I thought about his appointing a National Endowment for the Humanities officer in D.C. and former New England public school superintendent to manage the Chelsea project and serve as dean of the School of Education. I couldn't resist responding with sparkle and a smile, "John, I know Peter. He received his doctorate from the School of Education a few years ago. We must have done a great job." The president who had frequently criticized the School of Education and its too frequent hiring of its own graduates acknowledged my "Gotcha" with a slowly stretching grin. I'm not sure my response answered his question, but in 1988, a year after my resignation, Boston University formally "adopted" the Chelsea schools with significant foundation, state, and City of Chelsea financial support—and Peter was named as dean.

After almost twenty years of service, the past seven as dean, I looked forward to an extended escape in our summer Vermont home followed by a sabbatical leave for the upcoming academic year. There would be time for Janet and me to relax and travel free from the day-to-day distractions and tensions that went along with my responsibilities as dean. I wasn't sure I wanted to be a dean again—anywhere. All I knew for certain was that my past work with education colleagues seeking to make a difference for populations who had gotten the short end of the stick had been rewarding.

Landscape projects, fly fishing, writing, and evenings with friends in the Green Mountains of Vermont over an extended summer provided a healthy antidote to simmering anger that I carried from my final year at Boston University. But summer suddenly morphed into a vibrant symphony of fall color and it was time to return to Boston. Alone during the day in our Boston loft with Janet back at work, I had to begin to seriously consider post-sabbatical plans. Writing projects became secondary to conversations with colleagues, work on a professional portfolio, and detection of career possibilities in Boston and New England. Autumn, too soon, was swallowed by December winds. Janet and I found ourselves deep into winter with career plans for the next year not much clearer.

One February Sunday morning, relaxed in the warmth of our Fort Point Channel former Molasses factory loft, stretched out in a comfortable couch, conscious of the hiss of sleet on our windows and whistling gusts of winds outside, and leafing lazily through the pages of the *Chronicle of Higher Education*, the announcement "Search: Dean School of Education, University of San Francisco" caught my attention. The temptation of a San Francisco winter escape should I be invited to interview was great. I wasn't totally surprised that the announcement's prominent celebration of the institution as "San Francisco's *Catholic and Jesuit* University" triggered memories of how early suspicion of Catholics and Catholicism had crept into my life. Maybe I should apply anyhow.

* * *

I had felt so "grown up" at "ten" in 1948 when my mother asked me to walk alone with my younger sister Jennifer on the fifteen-minute walk from our duplex in Greenwich Village to progressive Little Red Schoolhouse on Bleecker Street. The southwest corner of Washington Square Park exited to MacDougal Street, where once one block down, row houses formerly noble homes on one side, were now partitioned into apartments occupied primarily by Italian-American residents. Small shops, coffee houses, and hang-out bars across the narrow street were shut. The early morning sun that had bathed the park was lost in shadows. The street was asleep. Its pulse would pick up later in the day when folksingers, writers, jazz musicians, and local residents and tourists would bring the neighborhood to life. Rienzi's The San Remo and smaller coffee shops, The Blue Note, and hang-out bars would be packed. But now, all was quiet.

Jennifer and I walked alone on the sidewalk until we passed a cluster of children roughly our age whose school uniforms let us know that they were on their way to Our Lady of Pompeii, just across 6th Avenue from our Little Red. We stopped to watch the cluster of girls in ironed white blouses and plaid skirts, boys not far behind in dark blue long pants and mandatory white shirts and ties. We didn't acknowledge them and they ignored us. We were school neighbors but aside from an occasional after-school exchange of words, we never talked with one another. I was only ten years old and I already suspected there was something different about Catholics. I was sure if I could quietly sneak into Our Lady of Pompeii, I would observe our uniformed passers-by seated at desks anchored to the floor, disciplined not to speak until requested by a nun who oversaw the silence. I was sure Bible readings, cursive writing, rote learning, and raps of a ruler on student knuckles filled the day. I assumed at the front of every room hung a cross with statues of saints nearby. We worshipped our own god at Little Red but it was the progressive educator, John Dewey.

Memories triggered by the *Chronicle* announcement were not limited to innocent childhood walks. Years later, when I was a senior at Stuyvesant High School, I recall walking home from school one afternoon, pedestrians and storefronts invisible. I was on a mission: get home as quickly as possible. I couldn't wait to tell my mother of the meeting with New York's Cardinal Spellman.

Classmates and I, imprisoned in our bolted-down, graffiti-etched seat-desk classroom desks, had spent the period with the Cardinal whom our sociology course instructor had somehow managed to have visit the class as a guest. Visits of a rabbi and minister earlier in the term had contributed to discussions on the influence of religion in New York City history. But to be visited by a Cardinal. That was something special. I only vaguely remember the discussion about the role of Catholicism in the life of Irish and Italian immigrants who emigrated to the city and the prejudice they experienced as a result of their faith, but I vividly remember arriving home that afternoon and the response of my mother to my proudly sharing an autograph the Cardinal had given to class members.

Murmurings of Ms. Kidwell's guinea pigs behind the wooden door of her first-floor residence and laboratory welcomed me as I rapidly climbed the creaking steps to our second-floor flat. A lot had changed for my sister,

Jennifer and me since my dad died my freshman year. There was no longer a smiling doorman to greet us or any small-talk with Tom, the elevator operator, as I took the elevator to our duplex apartment. I unlocked the well-worn wooden door to the apartment and followed the long hallway with its creaking floors to the kitchen where I suspected Mom would be nursing a cup of coffee.

I still recall the framed photograph of my dad sitting on the leather-topped desk squeezed next to my mother's bed as I passed through her alcove bedroom. Photographs of Broadway, Off-Broadway, and national tour productions in which she had performed covered the walls and kept her theatre memories alive. True to form, she was seated at the kitchen table, sipping her coffee with the requisite Marlboro cigarette resting in an ashtray and the daily crossword puzzle waiting completion before her. Age had blurred the lines of her once-prominent cheekbones and dulled her striking beauty, but her large frame, red hair still long enough to be pulled back over her broad shoulders, and the commanding voice still made the statement, "I'm here."

"How was school today, dear?"

"Cardinal Spellman visited our class today. Look what I got."

I proudly placed the autographed study sheet from class on the table next to the emerging crossword puzzle. Mom slowly put on her reading glasses, picked up the study sheet, seemed to read it forever, and returned it to the table without saying a word. I wasn't prepared for silence. I certainly wasn't prepared for the words to follow.

"May I vomit on it?" she finally erupted.

I should have remembered that Cardinal Spellman had a special friendship with Roy Cohen, then-closeted legal counsel to Senator McCarthy. I should have remembered the roles Roy Cohen, Cardinal Spellman, and the Catholic Church played in support of Joseph McCarthy's search for Communists and gays that had badly scarred the lives of close family friends. Howard, a Tony winning Broadway set designer had been forced to design department store window displays rather than Broadway sets to support his family. John, a Broadway director, save an occasional summer stock job, couldn't find work. His companion, Bill, had been fired from a Decca Records executive position and eventually found work in a Brooklyn flower shop.

I'm still not sure what contributed to the reaction of me and my sister to Lady of Pompeii students we had passed on our way to Little Red. But I have little doubt what had triggered my mother's response to the Cardinal's autograph: the unholy trinity of McCarthy, Cohen, and the Church.

The *Chronicle* announcement awakened ghosts from my past but it also provided a catalyst for us to talk about the part religion had played in our quite different childhoods. I didn't know much more about Janet's religious childhood than she had grown up as a member of a religious Jewish family, had a bat mitzvah, and attended synagogue as a child; she knew little more about mine than that I was the son of an Episcopalian mother disowned by her family for marrying a Jew, neither attended synagogue or church, and considered myself an agnostic. The true religious conversation between the two of us had taken place over our wedding ceremony plans not so long ago—and Janet's desire for a rabbi to perform the services.

Should I apply? There was agreement. There was little to lose by indicating an interest in the position. Should I be invited to visit the university, it would serve as a dress rehearsal for future opportunities—and might even help me decide whether I wanted to be a dean again. A not unimportant additional benefit might be that it would provide an opportunity for me to confront the religious ghosts that intruded on my sense of who I am and what I believe. I also had to admit, relief from New England cabin fever, albeit short, would be unequivocal.

A week later, I submitted a letter of interest and vita. A few weeks later, I was invited by the University of San Francisco Search Committee to visit the campus. The Nor'easter had long gone to sea, but winter still lingered. The position of dean in a Catholic university across the country far from my children and family friends was the last thing I had in mind for a new job, but it was reassuring to be wanted. I looked forward to my university meetings. I looked forward to visiting a city I had loved as a conference attendee and tourist.

Two

Confessions

The roar of back-thrust and bounce of the 707 on San Francisco airport tarmac jolted me from a half sleep. Timing the extraction of my carry-on from the overhead compartment and folding into the impatient line of tired passengers in the aisle waiting to exit took precedence over university thoughts. Strategic placement secured, suitcase in hand, it wasn't long before I flowed into the terminal along with other passengers. A fireplug of a man in suit and tie, wearing tasseled highly polished loafers and waving a USF placard, couldn't be missed amidst the casually dressed greeters. As we approached one another, he broadcast with the gusto of introduction of professional wrestling combatants, "Al Kagen, chair of the University Search Committee, it's good to meet you in person. Welcome to San Francisco." We shared a firm handshake and with my reciprocal, "It's good to be here," suitcase in hand, we set off double-time to the airport parking garage. It felt good to stretch my legs after the long flight as I kept up with the man who had extended the invitation for my visit to the university.

He placed my suitcase in the trunk of his recent model Toyota convertible, opened the passenger door for me, and trotted around the car's rear to join me in the obvious new car aroma. With almost a simultaneous lowering of the convertible's hood, turn of the ignition key, and pronouncement, "Let's enjoy the ride to the city," we were off. Foot heavy on the pedal as he maneuvered through the maze of roadways leading from the airport to merge onto Route 101 toward "The City," Al's transformation from academic title holder to tour guide once on the freeway was immediate: landmark identification, geographical features, weather patterns, all rolled from his mouth like those of a tour bus guide I had listened to years earlier on a visit as a tourist to ' The City.' Car top down, I was transfixed by stars that shone only to disappear in the dark sky before reappearing through chains of fog in the temperate weather. I was immersed in a new world. This was a far cry from Boston. Once we entered the city proper, Al assumed the role of Assistant Vice President for Labor Relations. A *Readers' Digest* history of university-union relations poured forth as we wound through deserted streets until we reached the Stanyan, a small hotel on a street bordering Golden Gate Park, walking distance from Lone Mountain and the university. The Stanyan was to be my home for the next two nights. Al accompanied me into its dusky reception area and with confirmation of my reservation by an unenthusiastic receptionist, a shake of hands, and a wish for good luck, he exited for his trip home to Marin. I was alone.

The grinding of a sanitation truck, slam of empty garbage cans on morning pick-up run and screaming seagulls fighting over scraps of garbage woke me too soon from a restless sleep. There was solace in knowing that it was already 9:00 back in Boston and I had time to freshen up with a shower and take advantage of Mr. Coffee before I pulled myself together to go down to the lobby. I felt rejuvenated as I took a seat at a chair and table in a cozy corner with a second cup of coffee downstairs and pulled the typewritten agenda for the day from a glossy green and yellow folder—the University's colors, left with me by Al. I was no less puzzled by the agenda this morning than I had been when I had given it a cursory reading before going to sleep. The first appointment was with the University president, Father President Lo Schiavo. And, I was on my own to walk to the university and find his office. That wasn't the way searches were carried out in Boston.

Towering spires of St. Ignatius Church that were visible long before I reached the university campus provided a North Star for my walk. Several blocks later, a parched lawn plaza bordered by adjoining buildings was suspiciously like urban campuses I had visited over years as professor and dean. The impressive spired Gothic church left little doubt I had found the Jesuit University campus. On entering the plaza, the words *Pro Urbe et Universitate* carved in granite above the entryway to a dominating structure in the constellation of buildings left little doubt I had located the administration offices.

The maze of hallways that branched out from the entryway to the building reminded me of my attempt not so long ago on a trip to New York City to negotiate corridors from one subway line to another to reach a destination when visiting the city—save the silence and polished floors of my current search. After a flight of steps and a few wrong turns, the words Office of the President on a door identical to other doors strung down the corridor provided relief. On entering, I hoped I was in the right office. I couldn't be sure. There was no one to greet visitors. The reception area was empty. Fortunately, a lean turnip of a priest dressed in uniform must have heard the door open and drifted toward me from an adjoining office. With a firm handshake and warm smile, Father Jack, with whom I had previously spoken many times on the phone, introduced himself and greeted me as if we were long lost friends. He was to be my escort to Father President.

Father President, John LoSchiavo, S.J. (Society of Jesus) in form fitting, tailored, and crisply ironed priest's uniform slowly rose from behind his desk, bare except for a lonely telephone, as we entered his office. Father Jack with a formal, "Father President, Dean Warren," succinctly introduced me and with a departing friendly nod, followed by a silent about-face, he drifted from the office. I was left alone with Father President. With a prayer-like wave of his large hands, Father President invited me to take a seat on an antiseptic couch in his Spartan office. His conditioned athlete's frame seemed to morph to over six feet as he approached and settled down on the couch next to me. He pivoted his torso toward me, adjusted his wire-rim glasses on his dominant nose, and smiled broadly, revealing large, ivory-white teeth. I was uncomfortable. I had never before sat so close to a priest. My distinct impression that the same person who designed the church pew must have designed the couch didn't help matters. And to boot, I was unsure whether to address my couch-mate as Father, President, Father President, or John. Fortunately, concern over nomenclature immediately evaporated on Father's opening words, "Paul, we're proud of our Catholic and Jesuit heritage and take the Jesuit commitment to social justice seriously."

I certainly didn't need to address him as Father President. A polite, but informal "Father," would be appropriate. But Father's openers had a way to go before I would have a chance to comment. The social justice introduction gained momentum.

He continued, "Our students take the commitment to social justice seriously. I bet you didn't know the university had a football team that became known as the team that was 'undefeated, untied, and uninvited.'" He would have won that bet. I had no idea the university had had such a team. I also had no idea how the history of a football team might relate to a university's social justice mission. I would soon learn that in 1950, the University of San Francisco had fielded the nation's first National Collegiate Athletic Association racially integrated football team and that the team, ranked among the nation's top college teams, and although undefeated, hadn't been initially invited to a bowl game. Controversy over the failure of a bowl invitation to USF ultimately led to an Orange Bowl invitation being extended. As late as 1950, teams with African-American athletes weren't invited to compete in bowl games.

Preamble to the story provided, Father's voice became stronger, his eyes sparkled, and he slammed his hand down on his knee with a clap of pride, "The team was invited on the condition that the university leave its two black players at home. Team players refused the invitation." The link between the university social justice mission and football had been established. I was impressed. I was aware football plays a major social, financial, and recognition role for many universities, but this was the first time I had heard a president speak of football as the primary conveyor of university mission.

Father wasn't finished. He abruptly jumped to the topic of USF basketball. Other than providing "let me-make-you-comfortable small-talk," I couldn't guess what compelled Father to turn to a tale of basketball.

"Paul, you must know of Bill Russell and K. C. Jones." I finally had a chance to say something. "Father, you can't live in Boston and not know of K. C. Jones. He is the coach of the Celtics," I replied with a smile. "And Bill Russell is worshipped in Boston. He retired a year after I moved to the city." At least I had a chance to establish some basketball *bona fides*. There was no point to share that I wasn't much of a basketball fan, and if asked to claim allegiance to a team, I would have named the Knicks—a vestige of New York roots and fellow Princetonian, Bill Bradley's contributions to the team. Father proceeded to inform me that Bill Russell and K. C. Jones were basketball stars at the University of San Francisco who brought two NCAA titles to the university in the mid-1950s. This time, notation of the team's accomplishments was followed by a slow nodding of his head as he took me into his confidence. He was to speak of justice of quite another variety.

"You may already know, I had to discontinue university basketball in 1982."

I had no idea of Father's suspension of USF basketball and only vaguely remembered occasional televised USF basketball feats while I was finishing high school. He got right to the point.

"There were too many infractions inconsistent with the university's obligation of moral leadership and its leadership role in the city for me to permit the program to continue."

Father provided no detail about the nature of infractions but shared with me the anger of many university trustees at his decision and confessed that there were probably some still angry at him for the decision, despite the reinstatement of the university basketball program a few years later. I'm glad I hadn't asked him to elaborate on factors that led to his decision. I later learned that the program had been suspended in 1982 after probation penalties from the NCAA in 1979–80 and 1980–81 for illegal player recruitment and payments to some all-star players by an over enthusiastic alumnus. Coupled with NCAA sanctions in 1981 and student charges of rape against a star player settled with a plea of guilty to assault, Father really hadn't had much of a choice.

I felt some relief when Father redirected his attention from football and basketball to academic and budget issues. Those are the things about which presidents usually speak when talking of university health and are most important to academics seeking appointments. Relief, however, was short-lived. Confessions of previous University proximity to bankruptcy, lingering professor anger, faculty union grievances, and trustee concern over cost over-runs for the construction of a state-of-the art health and recreation center were presented more in the manner of a supplicant seeking priestly pardon than a president seeking to influence a potential dean. Impressions of physical fitness and confidence first conveyed by his solid frame, form-fitting, crisply ironed priest's uniform and mission driven leadership were fading.

Father glanced at his watch and confessed, "I've gone on too long, Tell me about yourself." It was about time. Where should I begin? Father helped answer the question when he picked up my resume and commented, "I notice from your resume, you were a high school teacher in New York City before you became a professor and dean in Boston."

I admitted that I never anticipated substitute teaching assignments to fill time between television commercials would lead to full time teaching in a New York City public high school. In my wildest dreams, I never imagined that an invitation from a New York University professor while I took courses prerequisite to a permanent NYC teaching license to become a teaching fellow and matriculate for my PhD would lead to a career in higher education.

Emotions that had flowed through Father's tale of the university's 1950 football team had impressed me. His emotion and words carried more weight than a formal statement of commitment to social justice. I also knew he had been a high school teacher and headmaster before becoming a university president. He had my resume. I gambled that empathy with my social justice *bona fides* earned as high school teacher, professor, and administrator would carry most weight in this setting. And this morning would be the only opportunity I would get to tell a university president a story I saved for student orientation meetings with students or skeptics who questioned why anyone might want to teach in an inner-city school. I told Father the story of Alfred, a student I had taught at Haaren High School, a non-exam, upper Manhattan west-side public school attended primarily by Black and Puerto Rican students from low-income families.

Alfred had faced odds confronted by too many New York City public school children: a run-down physical structure, worn textbooks that had circulated through classes for years, older teachers who reminisced about "better days," and novice teachers who struggled in their new assignments. One day on a walk down a street in Greenwich Village a few years after I had left Haaren to become a teaching fellow and instructor at NYU, the words, "Mr. Warren, Mr. Warren," shouted from somewhere behind a back-up of cars waiting for the traffic light to change at 10th Street and Broadway caught my attention.

"Mr. Warren, Mr. Warren." The call came again. Then, in front of the cars with motors revving and exhaust pouring out as they waited for the green light, a young Black man in a deep blue doorman's uniform with dirty gold epaulets dancing on his shoulders, dashed across the street to join me. Safety of the sidewalk reached, a little out of breath, he adjusted the visor of his cap that had gone awry from the sprint and panted, "Mr. Warren, do you remember me?" His face was vaguely familiar. I think he sensed my tentativeness.

"Mr. Warren, I'm Alfred Tyson. I was in your English class at Haaren High School."

"Of course, of course, I remember you," I half-lied and asked how he was doing.

"Don't let this uniform fool you, Mr. Warren. I'm going to community college," he proudly boasted. It seemed important for him to add, "I'm only doing this to make money to pay tuition."

Alfred extended his hand and I grasped it in both of mine. It was half shake, half job well done—for both of us. "Mr. Warren, I still remember that English class on poetry." I didn't need words of thanks. His smile said it all. I sometimes missed teaching high school students.

Father was also smiling as I finished my story. He picked my resume up from the coffee table next to the couch.

"I notice you worked in Roxbury when you were a professor in Boston. Tell me more about that experience?" I couldn't have had a better cue to build on my leadership in a U.S. Department of Education–funded project relevant to his university's social justice mission.

Anger of Boston's Black community over the failure of the Boston School Committee to support any meaningful reform in the city's schools had contributed to state authorization for an independent school in Roxbury free from Committee oversight. I recounted for Father how a faculty colleague and I who had worked together on education projects while doctoral students in New York and were both newcomers to Boston had been impressed by the director of a Roxbury independent school shortly after our arrival. After many visits to the school and meetings with Roxbury education leaders, a significant training proposal developed by the two of us to support a Boston University program to work with the independent school to prepare community residents to serve as para-professionals and ultimately become certified Boston teachers was approved by the U.S. Department of Education. Background to the project shared, I got to my tale.

"Father, I have to tell you about a day at that school in Roxbury that I will never forget," I prefaced before getting to a dramatic telling of the story. Why should my actor mother, sister, and uncle be the only ones in the family to perform?

"Paul, get down flat on the seat. I don't want anyone to see you. And I certainly don't want anyone to see me sneaking your poor white ass out of here," Judy quietly directed me as she negotiated her beat-up car through pot-marked Roxbury streets the evening Martin Luther King was assassinated.

Father's eyes and silence betrayed that he was with me. I had an audience. I embellished on how it had just gotten dark when I folded myself into a fetal position on the rear seat of Judy's car outside "Black" Highland Park Free school in Roxbury for my safe return to my "white" university. I still recall the fright from angry voices and the smell of acrid smoke from burning tires as we left. I assured Father I hadn't needed Judy's admonition to "keep my white ass down." It was disorienting to be transported forbidden to look out the car window. I was glad it was a Black Roxbury resident driving the car.

Father sat straight up in his couch corner, back erect. He was still with me. I finished the story by sharing the relief I felt when angry voices were replaced by the normal sounds of city traffic.

"When Judy, over her shoulder, gave me an all-clear signal, 'Paul, we're crossing the overpass on Mass Avenue, you can sit up now,' I knew we had made it to 'white' Boston."

Performance over, I posed a question and proffered an observation relevant to the concept of social justice.

"Father, if such fear could be generated in a white man in Boston, what must it feel like to be a Black resident in a white community in a time of racial unrest?"

The trip from a small community school in Roxbury to the safety of an office and colleagues at Boston University, not more than a mile away, was a short one—geographically. I wondered whether Judy was as intimidated on my side of town as I had been when on the other side of the overpass. I never learned the answer to my question. Long after the car ride, our paths diverged; Judy's deeper into the Black community and mine to the then white community of university administrators.

"It was a terrible time. It was a terrible time," Father softly murmured before he changed gears. "Have you ever worked in a university with a union?"

I was caught off balance. I had planned to use my answer to his question about the Roxbury project as a stepping stone to talk about contributions I had made to the development of programs to serve minority and underserved populations, secure grant awards and foster the introduction of an Early Childhood Center in the School of Education while dean in Boston. I had hoped my Roxbury dialogue would lead to discussion about relationships I might establish between the USF School of Education and city's schools, public or Catholic, or assistance the school might provide to Bay Area schools. Had I placed too much faith in the power of my stories?

Father's anger at his unionized faculty erupted before I had a chance to respond to his question. He recounted how faculty a few years earlier after calling a strike had hired a biplane to buzz Market Street trailing the banner "USF is Unfair to Faculty" when he was Grand Marshal for a Columbus Day parade. He was critical of the naivete of professors who chanted "books not bricks" as they protested construction of Koret, the new health and recreation center.

Had I ever worked in a university with a union? This wasn't the time for me to share my sympathy with Boston professors during the contentious introduction of a short-lived union prompted by the authoritarian and temperamental leadership of the university president. I evaded a direct answer to Father's question by highlighting how as an associate dean, I had maintained respect of professors and administration through contentious years starting in 1975 noting BU professors' effort to unionize, legal challenges from Silber, a court mandate, establishment of a union, negotiations with administration, a 1979 faculty strike, and ultimately a union contract. I also noted the U.S. Supreme Court in 1980, however, had ruled faculty in private universities can be considered management and thus don't have the right to unionize. Boston professors had only won a Pyrrhic victory for faculty. I hadn't answered Father's question but he seemed satisfied—and, I suspected, jealous of Silber's ultimate victory.

Father looked at his watch. "Goodness, now I'm really late for a meeting. I have to go." Our meeting was over too soon after it had begun. I worried that I hadn't had enough time to make a favorable impression on the president.

As we rose and as something of an afterthought, a religious bookend to our conversation, he assured me, "Paul, we celebrate God and provide an academic home for people of all nationalities, of all faiths: Catholic, Protestant, or Jewish—and people without any religious affiliation. We even have a Judaic Studies program." I don't know whether Father knew of my religious affiliation, or lack thereof, but it was reassuring to know that people of all faiths and nationalities were welcomed at the University—although I suspected some were more welcome than others.

"Where are you off to next?" he asked as we left his office together. When I told him it was with the School of Education professors, Father's response of "Good luck," delivered with a smile and a sparkle in his eyes suggested he knew something I didn't.

Three

A Cauldron of Professors

I stood alone on top of the hill San Franciscans call Lone Mountain, home for the School of Education, one hundred and three steps up from Lower Campus and the Office of the President. A cold washcloth fog muffled the sighs of a far-off foghorn in San Francisco Bay. A sprawling turret-like structure was buried in the gray damp, but I had no idea of the next steps to locate the School in the sprawl until a figure in long skirt, wool wrap cloaked over shoulder, and hair disheveled from the moist dank emerged out of nowhere. Sensing my quandary in this Macbethian setting, she asked if she could help. When I shared my dilemma, she raised a cloaked arm and without a word, cloak slipping from shoulder, pointed a finger toward the far end of a fog-shrouded structure before she drifted off. Less than a hundred yards in the direction designated by the enshrouded passerby, I could make out the figure of someone standing alone in the dusk light of an entryway, words in gilt gold letters, *Rossi Wing*, painted on plate glass above the entry to the School of Education.

"Dr. Warren, welcome," a tall, weathered, bespectacled man in Harris Tweed greeted me on my entry. The lanky interceptor in tweed embraced my hand, one hand beneath, one above, in the manner a vise embraces a piece of wood, and continued without taking a breath, "Dr. Hubert Roberts, call me Hubert, chairman of the School Faculty Council, School representative to the university union, the University Faculty Association."

I fished a tired issue out of my pocket to wipe off my misted glasses and commented on the fog as I reciprocated with, "It's good to be here." Hubert wasn't interested in weather conditions or my sentiments. "Follow me, the faculty looks forward to meeting with you," he directed as he rotated toward a stairwell I hadn't even noticed. It was a challenge to keep up with him as he descended, passed an empty academic department reception station, and brusquely opened a frosted glass door, entrance to a conference room.

If real estate curb appeal had an academic equivalent, my remark to Hubert would have been, "This isn't what I had in mind. Let's move on." Time-worn chairs that could have been Goodwill hand-me-downs or discards from upgraded classrooms were scattered on stained wall-to-wall carpeting along the room's perimeter. I couldn't help but wonder whether the small clusters of professors surrounded by chairs, coffee cups in hand, waiting our arrival, were as discouraged by the surroundings as I was. Hubert led me to a cluster in conversation, succinctly introduced me, and departed. Everyone seemed a little uncomfortable. I was thankful the inquiry of a cluster member as to whether I would like a cup of coffee introduced a sense of informality. As she departed to get my coffee from a large urn on a near-by fold-up table on which drips of coffee were absorbing a tray of limp pastries and a round robin of introductions began, I began to feel more comfortable. We balanced coffee cups and pastries as the professors shared academic department membership and provided an occasional comment on their professional interest. Unfortunately, there wasn't enough time to move from introductions to conversation before Hubert's voice rumbled through the room, more of an order than a request, "Will everyone be seated." As if on command, the cluster dissolved with polite smiles and a chorus of "It's been nice to talk with you." Something wasn't right.

Hubert immediately filled the vacuum left by the dissembling cluster with his return and I stood uncertain as to my next move. With a gesture of his heavily veined hand, he directed me to follow him. Again, I found myself anxious to keep up with him as he selected a chair, pulled it next to a location I'm sure he had carefully chosen, and gently ordered, "Have a seat."

The two of us sat silently as professors dragged their chairs to form a ragged circle spun off of Hubert's strategic placement. Laggards to the forming circle were just sitting down when Hubert twisted his frame toward me and without words of welcome or introduction to the assembling professors, asked me to introduce myself. I had barely recovered from my first impression of the room or abbreviated cluster introductions. I wasn't prepared for a sudden transition from small-talk to presenter.

I have always taken pride in my ability to speak extemporaneously, but Hubert's invitation presented a challenge of another order. The challenge was compounded by the fact that I had not interviewed for a job since I had been considered for dean at Boston University—and that had been ten years ago and with professors I knew. Now here, I was in an institution of which I knew little, where I knew no one, and I was not even sure I wanted the job. But I had experience as a dean. I had pride. In less than twenty-four hours in San Francisco, I had discovered a host of clues about USF dynamics to complement the homework I had done before leaving Boston. I would rise to Hubert's challenge.

I thanked the gathered professors for the invitation to visit the university and shared a few inane observations about San Francisco fog and Boston snow flurries as something of a "get to know you" warm-up. I had no clue how much of a presentation Hubert wanted, but the centrality of the concept social justice to the Jesuit mission, so consistent with values that had shaped my family life and professional career had just been reinforced by my meeting with the university president. I had a theme to guide my presentation.

"I've just come from a good meeting with Father President," I opened. That was a mistake. What I had conceived as a courteous, appropriate opening protocol was not received as such. Mention of the president's name transformed a set of modestly attentive cluster of seated professors to grimaced bobbing-head dolls. I was learning too quickly what might have been behind Father President's wish for "good luck" upon leaving his office. I would need to learn what contributed to the bobbing-head doll syndrome before the day was over. Now was not the time. I moved on.

Rather than jumping to my professional chronology, which, I trusted, the professors who had reviewed my vita were familiar, I chose to focus on my personal background and professional priorities. I felt these elements would provide a better sense of my fit with what I already felt was central to the university mission—and consistent with San Francisco political leanings.

I confessed I was lucky to have attended a small, progressive school in Greenwich Village through the eighth grade and grow up in a socially conscious, politically liberal family. I couldn't resist throwing in a reference to my family's theatrical roots before adding with a smile that I had escaped a career in theater but hadn't strayed too far from those roots: teaching had permitted me to write the script, play a leading role, and hope for good reviews from my audience. Service as university dean had provided an opportunity to be a co-producer. My whimsical metaphor caught their attention.

I admitted that I strayed from my family's liberal social and political roots when, to my mother's dismay, I accepted a scholarship from Princeton University for my undergraduate work but was granted forgiveness when I graduated with my social and political values intact. The climate in the room changed, even my bobbing-head dolls were engaged, when I shared my surprise that an invitation from an NYC public high school, in which I had been a substitute teacher, evolved to full time "permanent sub" to a career in higher education. I was beginning to feel more comfortable. It became easier to trace a line that connected my life as a teacher in NYC schools to dean in Boston.

I told of how at Haaren, I had witnessed first-hand the plight of poor and minority children caught in one of these schools but also been lucky to get the chance to know that rewards really didn't get much better than when you reach one of these students. I let the assembled professors know this was a message that needs to be conveyed to prospective teachers.

I shared how I had enjoyed the theatrics of capturing a class's attention during my years as a high school teacher in Manhattan but it hadn't taken me long to realize that Jonathan Kozol's coining of the phrase, "death at an early age," when writing about Boston public elementary schools, with modification in grade level, applied to many students in New York's non-exam public high schools.

Why did I leave Haaren? Day after day in my private classroom, it became more and more evident that there was only so much I could do as a classroom teacher to address larger problems faced by urban public schools. When I was thrown a lifeline by an NYU professor to be a teaching fellow and matriculate for a doctoral degree, I took it. The degree would provide an opportunity to make a difference beyond the boundaries of my classroom teaching.

Project work in Brooklyn's Ocean Hill-Brownsville District, and in the South Bronx on foundation plus federal government supported projects as well as consultant assignments in Georgia, Mississippi, and Alabama while studying for my doctorate at NYU opened a new world. I quickly learned resistance to change compounded by racial and economic struggle was far more intense than abstractions conveyed in books and journals. Awareness of challenges faced by struggling schools was to remain part of my life.

I confessed that no one who has grown up in New York's Greenwich Village can ever conceive of leaving the city. I was no different. I was naïve. University appointments for fresh PhD recipients in New York City are limited. When Boston University made me an offer difficult to refuse, I accepted.

Boston provided a host of new learnings. I quickly learned what Kozol was talking about; the impact of racism and front-page dramatics of the Boston School Committee on school reform was dramatic. A tale of Boston University prejudice took the group's level of interest up a notch. I elaborated.

A colleague and I with fresh doctoral degrees from NYU had been excited to receive funding from the U.S. Department of Education for a pilot program to prepare community residents to become teachers in a largely Black, independent elementary school in Roxbury a year after our assistant professor appointments. But with the introductory words of our accomplishment by the School of Education dean, "The number of adult Black students who will be enrolled in the School will pose challenges," to the gathered full faculty, we knew we had our work cut out for us. Those were hardly the words of congratulations or support we had expected to receive on the multi-year major grant award. There were knowing nods from a good number in the gathering. I trusted that the professors were sympathetic with my observation rather than the dean's dilemma. I wasn't sure my audience was sympathetic my transition from professor and project director to assistant dean and director of graduate studies at the university less than two years after we got the Roxbury program off the ground.

I did admit, however, social unrest on the Boston campus and in the United States, following the Kent State Massacre, rather than university and community work in Boston, had contributed to my appointment as assistant dean by the older, conservative School dean; promotion of a young liberal, professor who didn't threaten more conservative professors to assistant dean would strengthen his reputation with younger professors. I hoped to gain some sympathy when I mused, "In retrospect, I don't know whether his action was a promotion or demotion." The addendum earned a few smiles but after Father President's disparagement of the union and

Hubert's pride in his union position, I had expected a more enthusiastic response to the confession of desertion from faculty ranks.

The first step on the administrative ladder from assistant to associate and then one president, one dean, and eleven years later to appointment as dean of the Boston University School of Education by President John R. Silber had been taken.

I had no clue from Hubert on when to turn the meeting over to professors. And I wasn't confident that unraveling my dean's journey would hold their interest—or mine. Professors had my resume. They could trace my chronology from assistant dean to dean. I'm sure they had concerns they wanted me to address. I decided it was time to turn the meeting over to them.

"You must have questions you would like to ask."

Hubert was the first in the ring. He had worn a set smile, arms folded across his chest, throughout my presentation. If it were not for the metronome-like lean back, lean forward, front legs off floor, front legs on floor maneuvering of his chair, he could have been mistaken for a figure in Truffaut's Wax Museum. Had he only been biding time until I was silent?

"Dr. Warren, have you worked with a unionized faculty?" He took a beat and then added, "What do you think of unions in higher education?" His questions had obviously been drawn up long before I arrived. He wanted everyone, including me, to remember that he was the School representative to the University Faculty Association, union shop for full-time University professors.

There was little doubt his sentiments on the importance of professors' union on campus were quite different from those of Father President. It had only taken a short drive from the airport, a meeting with the University president, and greeting by Hubert for me to sense that the faculty union was a driving force on campus. A tactful Labor-sympathetic reply would be politically wise. Boston University (BU) history shaped my response.

BU professors had called for a common strike in 1979 when I was associate dean. I had witnessed too many presidential vetoes of professor promotion and tenure recommendations, unilateral appointments of professors and administrators at inflated salaries, arbitrary approval of professor pay raises, and diatribes directed at "left wing" professors and students who protested the war in Viet Nam to not have sympathy with professor efforts to form a union. I shared with Hubert, that despite my management position, I had often privately met with individual professors to assist them on strike-related personal concerns.

It was important that professors knew I shared BU professors' celebration at the announcement of one of Silber's rare defeats when after three weeks of faculty strikes, he was forced to recognize the union and a union contract was signed. But they also had to know that one year after union recognition, the U.S. Supreme Court ruled that the faculty at private universities were not to be protected to unionize under the terms of the National Labor Relations Act of 1935, and when BU contract expired in 1982, the union was declassified. I took pride in my quiet support of professors during those years and applauded many of the protocols created by the brief life of the union during my tenure as dean from 1981 to 1988.

I concluded my response to Hubert with the observation, "It appears many of the protocols the BU faculty fought for are already in place at USF. You are lucky," and added, "What do I think of unions in higher education? Authoritarian, arbitrary behavior of management in a university calls for the presence of unions."

This was neither the time nor the setting for me to share my concern that an adversarial climate I already sensed at USF created by unionization might be as demoralizing as that which had been precipitated by Boston University's controversial authoritarian president.

My words resonated with pale, razor-mustached former dean Professor Dante who I recognized from a photograph still carried in the

USF Catalogue—despite the fact that he had stepped down from the position more than a year ago. He shared some disturbing University history.

"Dean, when a meeting between a committee of USF professors elected to discuss the grievances with the university president over a freeze on faculty salaries in 1975 ended with our president's advice, 'If you don't like it, you can go to collective bargaining. That's precisely what we did."

Dante paused, seemingly to ponder over the wisdom of words to follow, "I'm not sure relations between the faculty, certainly School of Education professors, and the president are much better today than they were between the president and faculty in 1975. I'm not even sure the School of Education would exist today if it weren't for the tuition we generated. Why do you think I stepped down as dean?"

A professor in crumpled gray pin-striped suit and off-centered tie, slight in frame with wispy gray hair, jumped up from his seat at Dante's rhetorical question. "Let me introduce myself. I'm Professor David. I was the first dean of the School. Dean, you don't mind if I call you dean; after all, you were one in Boston?" A curious question, I suppose to demonstrate sensitivity before he proceeded to confirm his Alpha credential with a nod directed at former dean Dante. Dante acknowledged the nod with a smile that reminded me of Jack Nicholson in *The Joker.*

David proceeded to remind me, and his colleagues, how as the first dean, he was responsible for the multicultural faculty seated before me. Having reminded the faculty of his self-ascribed status as the School's founding father, and recruitment of many of the already tenured professors, he shifted to his success working with the University Administration to establish the School of Education in 1972 and the introduction of School doctoral programs three years later. I wondered whether his words were offered to calm the vitriol of Dante's earlier comments or blow his own horn. *Bona fides* established, David finally asked a question, "Why would anyone want to be a dean a second time?"

"Sometimes I ask myself the same question." I laughed and acknowledged the challenges and frustrations that come along with the job while assuring him that the feelings of accomplishment drawn from fostering new programs far outweighed the financial and political challenges that come along with the job. I smiled and apologized to the faculty in advance for building on a metaphor I had shared earlier regarding my love for teaching.

"David, a dean is a socially sensitive producer. It's his or her job to identify scripts of artistic merit or social consequence, cast the actors, and mount a production that will garner good reviews and find an audience. Why would I want to be a dean again? I grew up in a show business family, David. I'm a producer at heart." With a response of "Touché," David sat down. I didn't share with the professors that this wasn't the first time I had used versions of the metaphor to respond to questions about the joy I had experienced as a teacher and as a dean.

A striking Black woman, with dashiki cast over her shoulder, wasn't interested in metaphors and rose from her seat the moment David sat down.

"Dr. Warren, Professor Emilia, Department of Multicultural Education." She paused. "Dr. Warren, I noticed you have worked in Ocean Hill, Brownsville, and the South Bronx while you lived in New York and in Roxbury while in Boston." She paused again before asking, "Do you think a white man can help white professors and white students learn how to teach Black children?"

The slow cadence and intensity of Professor Emilia's delivery suggested this was far more than a "devil's advocate" question. She stood regal and silent as she surveyed me and her colleagues waiting for a response. The question was as much directed to professors as it was to me. She wasn't, however, looking to them for an answer. I understood the provocative delivery of her question. A Black woman who, I was pretty sure, was one of the only two Black professors at the time on School faculty of approximately thirty full-time professors and member of an academic department in the School with a specific multicultural and social justice mission had reason to be skeptical.

I acknowledged the challenge posed by Emilia's question and shared my conviction that schools that served primarily Black students would be more effective with a significantly greater number of Black teachers. I was aware I didn't provide a definitive answer to her question when I suggested that my experiences in New York and Boston convinced me good white teachers could reach Black students and good Black teachers could reach white students, and shared my experiences at the Roxbury independent school. When I happened to mention the name of Martin Luther King in the context of speaking about the school in Roxbury, Professor David, now half-asleep, eyelids at half-mast after his earlier introduction, came to life and waved for attention. He rose not waiting for Hubert's acknowledgement. On David's ascendancy, Professor Emilia slowly surveyed her colleagues and with a sigh of resignation sat down. I suspected there was no way a white man could have satisfactorily responded to Emilia's question.

David bloviated, "I marched in Selma along with Martin Luther King, Hosea Williams, John Lewis, and thousands of others." Emilia sighed more loudly from her seat to be sure that all would hear. Glances of resignation darted from one professor to another. Obviously, this wasn't the first time David had trumpeted his civil rights *bona fides* and relationship to Dr. King.

A long-time veteran of faculty differences and idiosyncrasies, David was oblivious to professors' response to his testimony to self and casually pulled up the sleeve of his jacket to view his watch.

"Dean, I'm sorry, I have to leave for another meeting," and on reaching the door, dropped a soft aside over his shoulder, "Oh and, Dean, I'm from New York too." On his departure, a sister in black-and-white nun's habit rose from a string of two priests and herself, seated next to one another.

"Dean, welcome. I'm Sister Rachel John, chairperson for the Catholic Educational Leadership Department and director of ICEL, Institute for Catholic Educational Leadership," and added with a Cheshire cat smile that swallowed her face, "It's only fair to let you know that I'm also a Dominican in a sea of Jesuit warriors."

Warm smiles of two priests seated at her side, the elder in uniform, the younger in Hawaiian shirt with priest's collar, made it clear, Jesuit or Dominican, she was the Catholic matriarch in the School. They glowed in her presence. Sister rose from her seat, opened a book placed conspicuously on the arm of her chair, and slowly turned its pages to find a quote obviously selected for the occasion.

"Dr. Warren, let me read a paragraph from *To Teach as Jesus Did.*" She slowly read the paragraph to make sure I heard every word. "What are your thoughts?" she asked.

I don't remember the precise words of the reading but I do recall the message: Catholic schools have a responsibility to convey a message of peace and justice. I was being let off easy. She could have chosen, I'm sure, a selection that could have called for a response that revealed my knowledge of the teachings of the Prophets or Jesus. I'm afraid my knowledge of Christian teachings didn't go much deeper than words of Christmas carols or memory remnants of securing "chapel credits" at Princeton while an undergraduate. But questions of peace and justice were at the core of my Little Red School House experience and central to my family's political life as I grew up in the Village. Personal and professional life in New York and Boston provided a foundation from which I could craft a response. From somewhere deep in my academic past, I excavated the title of a book by a progressive educator. I recall the precise opening words of my response.

"Sister, George Counts, a contemporary of John Dewey wrote a book, *Dare the Schools Build a New Social Order*. I would ask, 'Dare the schools teach for a world of peace and justice.'" Taking a cue from earlier professor comments, I suggested that a response to that dare might start with the study of events that led to the civil rights acts of the mid-1960s or crusade of Martin Luther King, a response that would be buried in the "woke" mind-set of the 2020s.

Sister nodded with what I hoped was a nod of affirmation and followed up, "Share with us your thoughts on what it means to be working in a Catholic university."

I wasn't going to get away with a totally secular response to *Teaching as Jesus Did.* In preparation for my trip to San Francisco, I had anticipated someone would ask me about my comfort with the University's Catholic and Jesuit identity. Homework on the life of St. Ignatius paid off.

"One would be hard put to find a better model to guide a Catholic university than the work of St. Ignatius with the poor in the slums of Rome." I elaborated on the life of Ignatius, his role in the founding of the Society of Jesuits, and his influence reflected in the number of Jesuit schools and universities throughout the world. I tied his work in the slums of Rome to earlier discussion of my work in urban depressed areas before I concluded, "If this university were to have only an infinitesimal degree of the impact on the life of the poor in our cities as had the work of St. Ignatius, we could all celebrate." Sister's smile broadened as she stage-whispered, "Thank you," and sat down.

Hubert nodded to a professor who I noticed had been sharing quiet asides earlier with a woman professor at his side during David's and Dante's silent *alpha* exchanges.

"Dean, I'm Sol. Welcome. Let me ask you some academic questions, if no one objects." The tone of his voice suggested his question was more a comment on the nature of the previous questions of his colleagues than a question to me.

Any tenseness I felt over an academic grilling was relieved by Sol's warm smile, NYC dialect, and welcoming words that included reference to his experience as a cab driver while a graduate student in Boston. There was an instant sympatico. Point made to colleagues, no objections received, questions of an academic nature flowed.

"Dean, why did you select Talcott Parsons' social system model to analyze the implementation of Boston desegregation's plan?" "Dean, what criteria did you use for measuring the outcomes of your Teacher Corps and Boston University projects?" "Dean . . ." There were more questions I don't recall.

Sol had not only carefully read my resume, but he had also reviewed my only published book. I don't doubt that issues of social justice were of concern to him but he was more interested in scholarship. I was thankful for his questions. It provided an opportunity to share my experiences as Associate Dean for Research and Development and administrator for several federal projects, and to share with professors my knowledge of U.S. education policy development and education change acquired through frequent trips to D.C. while Boston University dean and writing of the book, *The Dynamics of Funding.*

We had a lively back and forth before Hubert's voice suddenly intruded, "Sol, we need to move on." Sol had other thoughts.

"For shit's sake, Dr. Roberts, I drove all the way in from Novato to talk with the candidate but if your goddamn union watch says it's time to move on, I guess it's time to move on."

Sol glowered at Hubert. Hubert glared back. I sat silently, a witness to a standoff I didn't fully understand. Face flushed, four legs of his chair now planted firmly on the floor, Hubert broke the staring contest. "We have a timeline and I'm running this meeting." The woman professor at Sol's side whispered to him softly. Sol apologetically looked at me and with a "what are you going to do" shrug of shoulders, added, "Thank you, dean."

With an announcement of "It's almost 11:30, we need to move on," Hubert declared the meeting over. He rose from his chair. I hesitatingly rose from mine. I was unprepared for the abrupt ending but I also hadn't been prepared for the abrupt opening. Hubert led me out of the tired conference room without any opportunity for casual talk with individual professors.

Our destination was the Lone Mountain Cafeteria. If not for Formica tables scattered on a linoleum floor, a Clorox suggestive scent of sanitizers and mélange of odors from foods in an aisle of stainless-steel receptacles, the cafeteria could be mistaken for a tired gymnasium. Hubert confirmed the time for my next meeting with the School Search Committee, provided directions to locate the "View Room," site for the meeting, and pointed toward the aisle of foods and with a perfunctory "It's been good meeting you," departed into the maze of dark corridors that we had traveled to the cafeteria.

It had been quite a morning. Here, I now sat alone with my wilted chef's salad and mug of coffee in gymnasium ambience waiting for the next act more than an hour away. Had I made a mistake in accepting the invitation to visit San Francisco?

Four
Sea Change

Hesitant sun bathed the campus. Cotton candy wisps of clouds, Pacific stragglers from fog's retreat, scooted across a now blue sky. The dank gray of morning was no more as I departed the cafeteria for the View Room for my meeting with the School Search Committee. Set against a cerulean blue sky background, the panorama of downtown city structures from the fourth floor room was a welcome change from the morning's closeted, tired conference room. It augured well for a change from the earlier Hubert production.

"Welcome, you can call me Sister K," a young woman with a soft Irish brogue, smile, and firm handshake rose to greet me as I entered the room. "Come join us." She welcomed and pulled out a chair for me to take a seat among the half dozen professors seated around a table. "How's everything going?" she asked, in a tone that suggested interest in the colleagues' behavior as much as my comfort. I'm not sure she was looking for an answer. Quite a change from Hubert's brusque welcome. I quickly learned that professors were as much interested in telling me about themselves as my history. I particularly recall the laments of two professors, one who felt under-appreciated by her peers, the other under-appreciated by University central administration.

Sister's brogue acquired a cutting edge as she shared her umbrage at "Weekend warriors," a title she granted professors who taught on alternate weekends to part-time students in contrast to Teacher Education professors who taught and supervised younger full-time School students who planned to teach in Bay Area classrooms. She wanted to be sure that I knew teachers were the true disciples of the School's mission.

The certainty and mischievous of her presentation left little doubt that wisdom rather than fear of intimidation had contributed to her silence at the morning's meeting. Celebration of the School's Teacher Education program had been buried in the morning bluster of veteran tenured professors who taught courses in the School's weekend doctoral programs. Not unlike schools and universities across the county, School of Education, teacher certification programs often rank low on the institution's status totem pole. Sister K didn't feel that way.

A Uriah Heep of a professor who I didn't recall being present at the morning meeting had gripes of another variety. I strained as I listened to his low decibel, monotone follow-up to Sister's "Weekend warrior" assignation. Lack of appreciation for his department's program that provided certification for marriage and family counselors was obviously painful. "Dean, the University only appreciates us because of the amount of tuition income our students generate for the University." His observation was consistent with Dante's comment earlier today on beleaguered presidential support for the School.

I made the mistake to quip, "With all those graduates, I suppose divorce must be virtually non-existent in the Bay Area." Sometimes my sense of humor gets in my way. That was a mistake. I should have known better. I already knew many professors, to the point of paranoia, were sensitive to administrator comments of every variety.

Concerns gave way to gentle back and forth, as I shared frustrations and accomplishments in Boston and the half dozen professors shared their frustrations and accomplishments in San Francisco. Unlike this morning, frustrations were accompanied by evidence of pride. The ambience in the room evolved to one of camaraderie as time passed. More than anything else, professors wanted someone to listen to them; professors wanted someone with whom they could talk. And maybe I was such a person.

I had a lot to think about after our meeting concluded as I walked back to the Stanyan to take a brief break before dinner. Priority over the concern about the Catholic mission of the University had diminished during the day but the relationship between Management and Labor was troublesome. The afternoon had been relaxing but it would be naïve to not recognize the host of academic and political challenges that would be present for any new dean. I looked forward to dinner with department chairpersons but I first needed a quick nap and shower.

Verdant vines hung on an enclosing wooden fence, silverware reflected rays of setting sun, and the professors were casually talking with one another in the twilight of the outdoor patio as former dean Dante led me into the patio to join chairpersons at the Magic Flute, a Sacramento Street restaurant, a short drive from the hotel and the campus. Such a dinner setting in March wouldn't be possible "back East."

We were more of colleagues than applicants and critics as appetizers, entrees, and wine seamlessly folded into comfortable talk about life in San Francisco and my history in Boston. I found myself more a raconteur of Boston University tales under Silber than a candidate asked to rise to the challenges posed by the San Francisco president. I didn't learn much about the professors' research and writings that evening, nor they of my academic contributions, but I did learn that many of my hosts were avid readers of *The Chronicle of Higher Education* and familiar with the exploits of Boston University's president.

The timeless flow of conversation, drinking, and eating was broken when the waiter asked, "Coffee, anyone?" Hands rose briskly as heavy strands of fog scud across a rising moon and fog began to reclaim the city. Propane heat lamps were no match for the cold breath of oncoming night. The saline dampness of the Pacific displaced the earlier twilight warmth. When I noticed Sister Rachel John, our hostess for the evening, covertly glance at her watch, I hoped it was a signal for moving on. Barely had

Sister's wrist returned to her lap, that David, with a final sip of coffee, placed his cup on the saucer and with Godfather-like voice, commanded as much as asked, "Paul, why don't you come with me? I'll give you a lift to your hotel." My wish had been granted. David didn't wait for Sister to sign the tab or for me to finish my coffee. He rose from the table and extended his hand for me to join him. It was an offer I couldn't refuse.

I felt cheated as I rose to be whisked from the patio. I would have liked to have had the opportunity to share some closing observations with the chairpersons drawn from my day's visits, or at least convey thanks for dinner and the relaxed evening. But I couldn't very well ask David to wait a few minutes. I was to shortly learn that he had some private observations he was anxious to share with me.

I stood silently by the door to his aging Honda parked directly across from *The Magic Flute* as he redistributed old mail, empty coffee cups, and very possibly, a few forgotten student papers to the rear seat to carve out space for me to enter. Once he had cleared a nest on the front passenger seat for me to sit down, he gestured for me to enter and gently closed the passenger door before he circled to join me in the car. With both of us now seated, I presumed ready to take off, David stared silently out the front window for a few beats before he slowly inserted the ignition key. Once the key was inserted, he leaned back and rested his hands on his lap. It was obvious he wasn't in a rush to pull out. I was tempted to ask him if he felt alright. I'm glad I held back because it was only moments before he spoke.

"Paul, I have to tell you, there was an elephant in the room this morning," he almost whispered. I was relieved David wanted to talk about such elephants. I had sat in on many group meetings with candidates for university positions over the years but I had never witnessed a public display of such tension between professors or hostility toward university officers as I had that morning.

"You should know, scars of past University union-management battles have been aggravated by the process that's being followed in looking for a new dean." David paused just long enough for me to be perplexed by his observation before he continued, "There has been conflict between Labor and Management at every step of the search. The meeting was scheduled at a time chosen by management, and was boycotted by many professors. And the composition of the University Search Committee wasn't approved by the faculty." He waited for a reaction. I sat silently. And the matter wasn't helped by the fact that one of the committee's co-chairs, Vice President Al who had picked me up at the airport, represented management during the faculty strike a few years ago. He isn't trusted by faculty or respected by the other deans."

Once the message was delivered, David turned the ignition key. He had not planned his observation to be a topic for discussion. We were on our way back to the hotel. I looked forward to a good night's sleep. I hoped tomorrow's meetings with University officers or "Management" would help me understand more about "the elephant in the room."

Five

Them

The same cold, gray cotton fog and muffled street sounds greeted me on my too-early morning awakening as my first morning in the city. Street noise complemented by adjustment to Pacific Coast Time and intruding thoughts of the past day that had awakened me, however, permitted a warm shower, CNN distraction, and coffee in my room before descending to the hotel lobby to meet with the dean of the School of Management. Today, I would be escorted rather than walking alone to the campus. I looked forward to breakfast with other school and college deans on campus and later appointments with University officers, or "Them" as referred to by School faculty.

A second cup of coffee at my side, reading the morning's *San Francisco Chronicle* in a dark corner of the lobby lounge, provided a sense of the luxury close to what I felt on Sunday mornings in our Boston loft when I would routinely bury myself in the pages of the *New York Sunday Times* seated in an over-stuffed chair, cup of coffee on a side table. A tap on the shoulder and announcement, "Dean Warren, Samuel Walton, dean of the School of Management, call me Sam," broke my reverie and brought me back to the Stanyan lobby.

Freshly pressed, pin-stripe suit tailored to his large frame, strands of thinning gray hair brushed back over his shining dome, Sam had arrived to take me to breakfast. He was a casting agent's image of a business school dean. I rose and with warm handshakes and a "Let's go" from Sam, we were off. As we departed the lobby, I was peppered with questions.

"Did the concierge help you when you arrived?"

"How was your room?"

"How was the bed?"

I couldn't resist wondering whether his questions reflected personal concern or the professional interest one might anticipate from a dean of a school with a hotel management program.

Sam's highly polished Lexus was parked at the hotel entrance. This morning, there was no need to check street names against directions or wander halls to locate my final destination, and I felt like an arriving dignitary as I departed from his car at the University only minutes away and he escorted me to the Administration building. Sam guided me through the same maze of darkened corridors I had negotiated the day before, but this time, I was led to a door that carried a bronze nameplate: Hall of Honor. He opened the door, rested his hand lightly on my shoulder to guide my entrance as we entered a mahogany-paneled, albeit windowless, room. Not the image of a Hall of Honor one might have expected. I don't know whether grade inflation was a University concern but it clearly suffered from title inflation. But I did have to give the University some credit. A bouquet of bacon drifted from covered food trays that sat on a white crisply ironed tablecloth. Silverware embraced porcelain plates on a long dining table. Coffee cups sat on white saucers carefully placed on a mahogany side table. An ambience of honor had been created. I couldn't help harbor the thought that crisply ironed tablecloths and silverware on a mahogany table were to Management what a dripping coffee urn and soggy pastry on a card table were to Labor.

Deans were congenially talking with one another as we entered. Without prompting from Sam, a chorus of "Come on in" and "Welcome" greeted me before any formal introduction. It wasn't long before we leisurely drifted from casual conversations to pick up plates from the table, turn to trays of scrambled eggs, bacon, and sausage, and toast waiting for harvest, and seated ourselves at the table that prompted a recollection of *The Last Supper*. I had no illusion that the deans were prophets but camaraderie and discussion as we enjoyed breakfast and lingered over coffee left an impression of wise men, and one woman. We as easily could have been professional colleagues and friends who had not seen one another for a long time relaxing at a professional conference as a quorum gathered to interview a potential dean. We shared hopes, challenges, and frustrations: I, those I had experienced at BU; they, those they faced at USF. They were as anxious to share challenges and frustrations of their life at the University as they were to delve into my qualifications. A theme of USF potential sacrificed by day-to-day administration demands, union interference, and outright incompetence emerged as we shared experiences.

What seemed of greatest import to the deans was that I was an "outsider," someone who had fought some of the same battles as they had and who could bring a fresh perspective to problem-solving. They were looking for help. They were optimistic deans could make a difference. 10:00 a.m. The appointed hour for Sam to usher me to the first station in my applicant whirl with University vice presidents came too soon.

I was passed off from one vice president to another, a baton passed from one runner to another, in an interview relay until the day's race from station to station was to conclude with dinner with Assistant Vice President Father Jack. Dean Sam's appearance at the door of my final meeting at the end of the day to escort me to Father Jack's office announced that the relay was over. The sharing of thoughts and anecdotes with vice presidents provided a few new insights, but for them, as with the deans whom I had met earlier in the day, the allure of an "outsider" was evident. I was ready for a change of pace.

"Father will be with you in a few minutes," Samuel assured me as he left me in the vacant anteroom to Father's office to return to his more deanly duties. I thought I detected the faint fragrance of myrrh in the sanitary empty room, or perhaps the bouquet was just my imagination. Whatever, the fragrance was less seductive than the morning's bacon. A religious cross on the wall triggered thoughts of a story told to me by my Uncle Jacob, once a matinee idol and respected actor in the Yiddish theater, as I sat waiting for Father Jack's emergence in the empty silence.

Years ago, Jacob and I had been seated in his small high-rise studio apartment in Manhattan where he now lived alone. He was in his eighties, only a frail shadow of his theatre days. I was interviewing him for my senior thesis, *The Profession of the Actor,* as a sociology major at Princeton.

Jacob, like my father, had been born in Russia. He told the story of watching a clown in a touring circus bring laughter and tears to the small town crowd in which he lived when he was only fourteen years old and confessed, "I knew immediately I wanted to be like him and join this magical group."

The following day, he had gone to the circus producer's building address he had cajoled from a stage hand after the show. As Jacob stepped into the dark entryway of the apartment building in which the producer lived, paint peeling from hallway walls, he had second thoughts of continuing. But he wanted to join the circus troupe. He climbed the tread-worn stairs to the second floor and walked down a dusky corridor looking for the correct door number.

I still recall, almost word for word, Jacob's description of what followed. He hadn't lost his ability to mesmerize. He was still an actor; I was his audience.

"I could make out the apartment number I had been given. I knocked softly. Then more loudly. I stood alone in the dark hallway. Maybe no one was at home." Jacob waited several beats before continuing, "Then the door slowly opened. The figure of a large man dressed in a black robe with a large gold cross dangling from a chain around his neck stood right in front me." Jacob paused again before he dramatically delivered the closing line, "The man was a Russian Orthodox priest. I was a Jew."

Jacob was invited to join the circus and went on tour with the group. He would later become a member of the Russian Repertory Theatre, emigrate to the United States, and become a recognized actor in Yiddish theatre and on Broadway. And now, here I was, only half Jewish, but all skeptic, waiting to meet a man in clerical garb with a cross on his office wall to ask for a job. If Jacob were still alive, we might have had a good laugh.

Thoughts of Jacob ended with the entry of Father Jack, his lay assistant at his side, into the waiting room only a few minutes later.

"Paul, I don't think you've formally met Bede. She keeps everything under control in my office," Father introduced his sidekick.

Bede smiled and offered a warm "Welcome" before handing Father a single sheet of paper. "All the information you requested is there, Father."

Father skim-read the sheet, looked directly at me, and smiled "Shall We?" We were off. Bede smiled at Father and then almost conspiratorially at me as we departed. I wonder whether she, like Father President, knew something I didn't.

Father, one eye on Bede's sheet, the other on car license numbers, strode down the line of parked Toyotas lined up in the twilight of the underground Jesuit Community garage as in a National Rental Car commercial. "Here we are," he finally stopped abruptly. Bede's sheet had done its job, but only so far.

"I'll need your help with directions." Father handed the directions to me and added, "I haven't been to the Majestic Hotel restaurant before but I understand it's good."

He haltingly navigated the car across major intersections, making abrupt left or right hand turns as I recited Bede's directions until with a right on Sutter Street, the Majestic Hotel was visible. Front wheels of the Camry squealed against the curb as Father lurched to a stop in front of the hotel five feet beyond the designated drop-off point for valet parking.

"Not a bad job," he mumbled as he gave the car keys to the obviously unnerved valet. I couldn't help but think there might be a God, and that he, or she, took special joy in protecting his or her children, especially elderly priests. I now understood Bede's conspiratorial smile.

Father and I wandered into a low-lit, mirrored oak bar room off the hotel's main lobby. Neither of us knew where the dining room was located, and there was no concierge to provide guidance. Plush red fabric chairs pulled up to an imposing bar were impressive. Was the interior design prompted by memories of days of San Francisco Gold Rush and the 49ers? Fortunately, through half-open heavy velveteen drapes at one end of the bar, I could make out an adjoining dining room.

A maître d'hôtel evidently caught off-guard by our early arrival time emerged from the bar's permanent twilight to lead us through the parted drapes down the steps to the dining area. The room glowed in filtered late afternoon light from large-paned street-level windows. Fresh flowers sat in crystal vases. The room was a still-life awaiting an Impressionist's palette of oils. Father was more relaxed now that he wasn't driving and we had emerged from the dusky bar.

"Quite nice," Father murmured to nobody in particular as we were led to our table.

"Would you care for a cocktail?" he asked before we had time to place napkins on our laps. It was the first time I had heard the word *cocktail* since I had arrived in San Francisco two days ago. Wine reigns in the Bay Area. But I forgot, Father was an Angeleno.

Much of our talk over dinner was friendly palaver, but there was also talk of things Jesuit, of things Jewish, of things about which I needed information, on subjects difficult to discuss in an office setting. One exchange remains vivid. I asked, "Father, will the fact that I'm more Jewish than any other religion and my wife is Jewish make it difficult for me to fit into the USF community?" It wouldn't have been wise for me to share my doubts about the very existence of God or the historical failures of religion to foster peace and justice. Father's wistful observation was comforting.

"Paul, I'm sure you're aware that the number of men in the Jesuit Order has been shrinking for many years. Maybe it's part of God's plan. Maybe it's God's way of saying it's time for lay men and women, men and women of other faiths, men like you, to help convey the message of the Jesuits and St. Ignatius." Cocktail talk set the table for a commendable and relaxed meal.

Salmon, a California staple, complemented with waiter-recommended Viognier, a varietal unfamiliar to "back East" me, and sourdough bread was seductive. There was enough substance to conversation to provide a better sense of the University's mission. We talked about San Francisco's receptivity to outsiders as I sipped my coffee, he his tea; he still an Angelino, me still a New Yorker, even if I lived in Boston. I wasn't ready for our time together to end when he exclaimed, "My, it's already 9:00. It's been a long day for you, and I'm usually in bed not much later than this. I'll drop you off at your hotel."

As I watched Father drive off alone into the night after dropping me off at the Stanyan, I found comfort in my earlier evening thought that there might be a God who took special joy in protecting his or her children, especially elderly priests. I had enjoyed my final evening in San Francisco. I wasn't prepared for the postscript provided by Professor David on the early morning car ride to SFO and flight back to Boston.

Before I had time to buckle my seatbelt, Professor David, the designated driver for my return to SFO asked, "How was dinner with Father Jack last night?" His question was more than polite protocol; he was fishing. We both knew that. No response beyond a polite "It was enjoyable" was really expected.

"Where did you eat?" David asked. We were now on safer ground.

"At the Majestic Hotel."

"At the Majestic Hotel?"

From the expression on David's face, I could tell once again that there was something I didn't know. And I expected, neither did Father.

"Yes, on Gough and Sutter Street."

"Do you know anything about that hotel's history?"

"No, I don't."

David chuckled, and then lowered his voice. Did his hushed voice signal the information to be shared was confidential?

"The Majestic was a thriving brothel for gay men until it was renovated several years ago."

We both laughed. The irony of having a final interview dinner for a position in a Catholic and Jesuit institution in a former gay brothel with an unaware Jesuit vice president merited a good chuckle. There was clearly a collection of secrets around here of which one couldn't be aware until he or she had been a member of the community for a while.

Six

Meditation

When the plane finally set down at Logan, wind-driven flakes of wet snow were plastering Boston. The spring-like morning breezes and filtered sun of early morning departure from SFO were seasons ago as I stood on line among arrivals waiting for a cab. Fortunately, it wasn't long before I was able to fold myself into the back seat of an available cab free from the penetrating cold. When the winter-stained, tiled interior of the Sumner tunnel emptied into the controlled chaos of Boston's North End, it felt good to know that it would only be a matter of minutes before I would be back in the warmth and quiet of our brick and beam loft just across Fort Point Channel.

The monotonous drone of the plane's jets and six hours to sit alone on the trip back to Boston had provided a perfect setting to mull over my San Francisco adventure, but by the time of landing, I had reworked my visit to a point of exhaustion. Ghosts of Catholic prejudice that had accompanied me on my trip west had still peaked their heads but were of the socially conscientious Casper variety rather than the invasive variety that had intruded the life of my mother and our family friends. My ghosts may not have been slain, but they were mortally wounded. So be it, if the two Fathers wore their feelings of social justice on their sleeve and if the catalyst for Sister Jean's and Sister K's social justice teachings were the teachings of Jesus.

Words of the *Collective Bargaining Agreement* at USF seemed to carry more weight than those of the Bible, and influence of the union seemed to carry more power than the teachings of the prophets for many professors, including Jesuits. I don't know whether University history, professor personality, administrator attitude, or contract text contributed more to this sorry state of affairs, but there was no question that the union was more than an elephant in the room; it was a beast that sucked the life out of the room. With apologies to Shakespeare, "The university was such stuff as unions are made of and was rounded with grievances."

Odds for success of a dean at the University would call for a gambler who bet on long shots. I felt wiser for my introduction to the Jesuit world; a socially conscious role in higher education was what I was seeking but I was also glad the primary goal for my trip hadn't been to secure a job. Janet and I had a lot to talk about.

The cast of Fathers and professors set against the backdrop of San Francisco and shadow of Saint Ignatius Church provided rich fodder for dinner time conversations for weeks after my return. Yearnings, frustrations, and anger of the players I had met were the stuff of which tragi-comedies are written. We enjoyed playing the role of theater critics as we extracted themes, analyzed characters, and traced events of my San Francisco days. A final scene conveying a move to San Francisco wasn't part of the script. But all our conversations were all in March.

It was now April. Career options at other universities had slowly petered out. Why hadn't I heard anything from Father Jack for a month? Had I failed to impress professors and administrators with whom I had met? I was convinced I made a good impression, but not unimportantly, my ego had now taken a hit. Consideration of a move from New England hadn't been an agenda item when I accepted the invitation to visit but . . . A phone call late one May afternoon shook things up.

"Paul, it's Father Jack," the caller greeted me on my answering the phone, and with barely a moment for me to reciprocate, continued, "Paul, I'd like you to join the University." Janet and I no longer bathed in the luxury of playing San Francisco theatre critic. I was caught off guard. We had made the decision to spend another year at Boston University and revisit plans for the future as the year played out.

I quickly pulled myself together and reminded Father that when I left after my earlier visit, I had told him I would need a chance for Janet and me to visit San Francisco together if I were asked to become dean. There was too much at stake with a possible move across country for me to not talk more with School professors and get a better sense of the University and San Francisco before taking such a leap. The warmth of his succinct invitation cooled. I guessed blessings from a Father aren't usually declined. Father remembered our conversation and arrangements were made to visit the University.

I was off again to San Francisco; this time, Janet was with me. Meetings with professors I had earlier met were warm; professors who had not met with me earlier were welcoming. In the course of an informational meeting between Janet and an alumni director at another San Francisco university, the director on being informed that we were considering a move to San Francisco mentioned that he knew a woman vacating her flat with a picture book view of the Golden Gate Bridge.

"Would you be interested?" he asked Janet, adding the woman knows Father Lo Schiavo well and attends Mass at St. Ignatius. Janet jumped at the news. She may not have found a potential job but she had found a matchmaker.

True to the matchmaker's word, the adoration of the flat owner for the University president gushed over as we met. The flat's large dining room picture window bridge framed the San Francisco Bridge and the Bay as in a chamber of commerce photograph. If I was convinced there was a God, I would have no hesitation in crediting divine intervention for the unfolding scenario.

The next morning, I informed Father Jack at a farewell breakfast at an upscale bistro in Haight-Ashbury that I had been impressed by people with whom I had visited during our visit, Janet and I had gotten a better feel of the city, and we had located a possible place to live before I added, "Jack, there are a few contract adjustments I would like you to follow up on, and Janet and I would like a couple of days to talk at home before we decide to make a move across the country."

I'm sure Father would have preferred a definitive, "I accept" before we departed from breakfast, but he was satisfied with, "We'll talk over the phone within forty-eight hours after we return to Boston." Janet and I digested more than talked about our San Francisco trip on our return flight. We mulled privately rather than with one another. We would save conversation for when we were back in Boston.

We were bushed and it was well past dinnertime when we entered our loft. A good night's sleep would be more beneficial than conversation. Talk would have to wait. The trip back to San Francisco had been seductive but we couldn't help worrying that we might be acting too quickly if we were to take Father Jack up on the offer. Might we be making a mistake for want of a New England alternative?

I was surprised as we wrestled with the question of "to go, or not to go" over the next two days, how seldom the ghost of Catholicism entered our conversation. We spent hours rehashing the academic and political challenges as well as professional implications of moving to a "less" academically prestigious university and family disruptions that a move to the West Coast would entail. I have to admit, however, I did once wander back to recollections of my first meeting with Father President. Janet had listened patiently as I recalled how the presence of the cross hanging on the wall of his office and his priestly dress had faded and how comfortable I had felt as we shared his tales of pride and frustration, and we proceeded to talk about our professional lives and social justice. I'm afraid I waxed into a mix of nostalgia and romanticism when I conjectured that Father would have felt comfortable talking with Little Red School House teachers on matters of race and justice, as long as all stayed away from discussion of unions.

When I had concluded one nostalgic trip with, "He would have felt comfortable sitting with classmates and me as ribbons of light from an old film projector cut the dusk of the school's assembly room and we watched a grainy black and white film and listened to Frank Sinatra sing "The House I Live In,"

'A name, a map, or a flag I see / A certain word, democracy
That's America to me . . .
The children in the playground / the faces I see /All races and religions
That's America to me.'"

Janet pulled me back from the cliff of nostalgia with a few brief words, "Hon, we have to make a decision." We moved on.

Despite the University's flaws and Catholic auspice, the invitation from USF became more and more attractive as conversations flowed. A move to a physically beautiful city with a liberal history and more temperate climate to a university with a strong social justice mission might provide a healthy change. We were ready to escape New England winters and the conservative politics and academic preciousness of Boston University. We reasoned that if we were to live in San Francisco for only a few years, we could enjoy the Bay Area free from the politics of BU and find time to travel in a part of the country with which we were unfamiliar. And if we rented our Boston loft, we would always have a home, friends, and children from my first marriage "back East" to return to in a few years, should we wish. It would be worth placing a bet on a long shot.

Father Jack and I spoke a few days later, and he conveyed the president's approval of contract adjustments I had requested. The warmth and sincerity conveyed in his, "I look forward to working with you," made it easy for me to respond, "Father, I look forward to joining you."

Janet and I would soon be moving to California, religious ghosts and all, leaving much behind and not sure of what was to come.

Seven
This Isn't Boston

Bits of litter caught in whirlpools of hot air chased one another as I climbed the one hundred and three winding steps up the hill called Lone Mountain to my office for my first day as dean in San Francisco. Two priests, in full apparel, deep in conversation were oblivious to my presence as they passed on their way down to the lower campus. The fragrance of the dry straw drought-seared campus was foreign after lush New England summers, but the sunny morning was a welcome change from the washcloth fog and muffled sighs of a distant foghorn on my March interview. But I felt alone and far from the world I knew.

The cold marble floors and dusky entryway to the School of Education were no less gloomy than what I remembered from my fog-saturated interview visit. A summer academic ghost city of empty partitioned cubicles for staff and assistant deans sat behind a heavy steel door, a literal and figurative firewall between administration and professors. I paused to greet Dorothy, my predecessor's secretary, before I entered my frosted glass cordoned corner office. At least someone was at work. My "Good to see you," produced only a murmured "Good morning," before her eyes retreated to the safety of her computer screen. I hoped future greetings of staff would be more welcoming.

Three neatly stacked piles of paper, cover sheets in large font boldface, waiting my arrival sat on an oversized desktop—*Correspondence*, *School Summer Credit Hour Generation*, and *Fall Admissions*—statistics in the latter two piles, the fiscal lifeblood of the University. An envelope marked *Confidential* from the Office of the Academic Vice President sat conspicuously alone. There was no clue that within a matter of weeks, I would witness a Marx Brothers–like performance of a trio of Labor–Management damaged professors, receive shower confessions from a naked University president, mediate a controversy over Christmas tree condoms, and be seduced by a Sister with a Cheshire cat smile. Years as dean in Boston hadn't prepared me for such a cornucopia of challenges.

Correspondence marked *Confidential* from a higher ranked university officer always gets top priority. A hand-written note from Academic Vice President Father Jack with whom I had negotiated my contract welcoming me to the University was a nice touch. Hand-written scribbles on an attached memo were not as welcoming.

"There will be a Special Meeting of the Council of Deans two weeks from today to discuss the academic year budget." I had learned years ago that it's never good news when deans are asked to attend a special meeting with higher administration officers to discuss budget, even if the request is handwritten. Little time was going to be wasted in my introduction to University budget decision-making.

It took a few stabs for me to master the buttons on my many-buttoned phone before I connected to Dorothy's extension and asked her to join me. It was only moments before she crept into my office, lowered herself on a chair, and looked down at her lap like an errant schoolchild called into a principal's office rather than an assistant to the dean. I tried to make her feel important.

"I need your help. I can't find a School of Education Annual Report."

"Dean, there aren't any," she sheepishly replied. Maybe the document had a different title in San Francisco.

"Are there materials we share with potential students and University colleagues to give them a sense of who we are and what we've accomplished?"

"The University Catalogue is on the shelf behind your desk," Dorothy replied with a sudden sense of confidence.

She wasn't getting what I was looking for. Deans at universities where I had previously worked had all left written trail markers touting the accomplishments of their school or college, and indirectly themselves. Dorothy was having difficulty identifying any such trail markers here. I wondered whether I had become a member of a community that solely relied on the oral tradition to transmit its culture. Universities, by culture and history, have always revered the written word.

Dorothy sensed my befuddlement and tried to be helpful. "*The Collective Bargaining Agreement between the University of San Francisco Faculty Association and the Trustees* is on your coffee table." One of the many takeaways from my job interview with professors had been how central the *Agreement* was to university life. I had already carefully read the accretion of words in the document accumulated over time of collective bargaining negotiations over the years to govern Labor versus Management contests. They provided little information about School or University mission or program, save for notation of the University's Jesuit and Catholic roots.

I thanked Dorothy and told her she had been helpful, the first of many white lies I would tell during my tenure as dean, before she slinked from my territory to the safety of her cubicle.

Lodged in the staff of schools and universities in which I had worked over the years, I could usually find an inconspicuous respected senior staff member, content in her or his role, unencumbered by political baggage, who was familiar with ghosts in the institution's closet. Assistant deans don't meet those criteria. They have too much at stake with the arrival of a new dean.

Located in the pool of staff offices outside my offices, Zoe was such an individual. It hadn't taken me long to learn that during Zoe's many years at the University, she had held virtually every staff administrative title, except dean. She knew the whereabouts of every University or School shoal with the potential to sink a new dean. She knew the location of every sail, line, or piece of equipment necessary to keep my School afloat.

"Zoe, can you give me some time when you have a minute?" I asked one morning as I passed her cubicle on the way to my office.

Before there was time to hang up my sport jacket, she was at my door, clipboard and legal pad and pen in hand. I rose from behind my desk and waved her in as I moved to a coffee table with comfortable chairs. Brightly patterned heavy wool socks–stuffed Birkenstock sandals shouted out as she joined me. With her "so sixties" Birkenstocks complemented by long dull brown hair which had probably never seen the inside of beauty parlor, pale face free of make-up, thick rimmed glasses, and costume of a wrinkled deep blue windbreaker hanging over generic slacks, I suspected she must once have been a Haight-Ashbury or Berkeley flower child.

"Dean, how can I help you?"

"Let's start with take a seat." Zoe sat down, placed the legal pad on her lap, and was poised to take notes.

"Let's just talk. You won't need your pen. Tell me about your job."

"Dean, it's my job to make you look good. I see myself as the woman behind the scenes. I don't want to be out front."

With such deference to Management, the unfair suspicion of her former flower child history was shattered. And with her desire for privacy, I must admit, a potential dilemma was resolved: I wouldn't need to worry about first impressions her dress might make on outside visitors to the school.

"Zoe, I need advice on priorities for the next few weeks before fall classes begin. Share some of your thoughts with me. For openers, where do I start?"

She didn't hesitate as she enumerated a daunting array of tasks that needed to be completed before fall classes began. I had to give her credit. She certainly was not intimidated by a first meeting with the dean.

"Dean, I'm sure you're a better problem solver than stenographer," she noted on my fumbling efforts to take notes and sensitively asked me to put down my pen.

It took less than fifteen minutes to conclude that a host of housekeeping chores demanded attention before I could tackle academic and social justice priorities that had convinced me the University might be worth taking a shot. What I remember most vividly were the words of advice Zoe shared hesitatingly as she prepared to leave my office.

"I know I shouldn't be saying this Dean, but be careful of former deans and associate deans who are still professors. There are several of them on the faculty and they can be just plain old mean." I wasn't sure how to respond. She continued, "They know the *Collective Bargaining Agreement* almost word for word. You'll need to know the agreement cold. And there are a few union hot shots on the faculty who won't hesitate to file a grievance every time there's a disagreement." My search for a captain was over but I wasn't prepared for her prescience or imminence of her "hot shot" prophesy.

Less than a week later, heated voices of male professors in the reception area invaded my office space. Amidst the cacophony of words, I could make out the voice of Professor Hubert, School guide on my initial visit to campus and School union representative. Moments later, my phone rang. Dorothy's plaintive voice was muffled by the background barking of professors. To leave her alone at the mercy of Professor Hubert and his band of angry men would constitute cruel and inhuman punishment. She didn't need to ask. Help was needed.

"Dorothy, tell them I'll see them."

An apex of a triangle of professors led by Professor Hubert, gray-white crew-cut Gary wearing heavy-set framed glasses trailed on his left, sway-backed corpulent Walther on his right, stormed into my office before I got the phone speaker back in the cradle. The vacuum left by Hubert's charge sucked them into the office. My grumpy old men moved from the base points of the human triangle to form a line-up in front of my desk.

"Dean, we need to speak with you," barked Professor Hubert.

"Yes," seconded Gary firmly.

"Yes," echoed Walther.

"We don't want to file a grievance but it may be necessary," Gary, obviously the aggrieved party, jumped back in.

What was it with these professors and their Marx Brothers' repartee? Save Hubert, I had previously only exchanged pleasantries with them and here they were, already talking grievance. I had to hand it to them, however. They had caught my attention. Gary stepped forward. He was to be the featured performer following the trio's warm-up banter. He pulled a carefully folded piece of paper from his shirt pocket.

"Dean, you sent me this memorandum. Let me read it to you." With the speed and inflection of a cop reciting Miranda rights, he proceeded.

Dear Gary, I've just finished reading Higher Education Reform. It's a well-written document and does a good job of critiquing the legislative initiatives of the period treated. You should feel good about your role as First Reader. From a personal perspective, I wish Peter's final chapter had more fully treated the long-term impact of the legislation. The study of educational reform is of particular interest to me.

Good work!

Reading finished, Gary dropped the memo on my desk and stepped back into the line-up. He said nothing. He just stared at me. What was going on? Why was everybody so angry? I gave my memo a quick second reading but I couldn't figure out what all the turmoil was about. I gave it back to Gary.

"How can I—"

Gary jumped in before I finished the sentence, "Dean, I want the memo removed from your files."

"Yes," seconded Hubert.

"Yes," echoed Walther.

I explained to the trio that during my first weeks on campus, I had read a sampling of doctoral dissertations to give me a better sense of student work and Peter's dissertation had caught my attention. It treated a topic in which I had particular research interest.

"Dean, I appreciate your reasoning," Gary responded softly but firmly, "but I want the memo removed from my file along with copies from the files of Hubert and Walther who are also members of Peter's dissertation committee." Hubert stepped forward.

"If Gary's request is denied, I'll have him file a grievance."

"Dean. We're serious," Gary added. Silent Walther nodded in agreement. There was no doubt they were serious, but I was still at a loss as to what they were serious about. Hubert was back.

"Dean, the dean that follows you might want to use your memorandum to reprimand Gary. Remember that faculty outlast deans here," his last words an addendum to make sure I understood the seriousness of the matter—and was aware of the short tenure of deans.

I reassured sensitive Gary, bellicose Hubert, and silent Walther of the honorable intent of my comment and pledged to have copies of my memo removed from their files. Assurance delivered, Hubert responded with an affectless "thank you" and led Gary and Walther out of my office in single file.

If I had been familiar with the concept of "Ham and egg justice," later shared with me by Parsa, my experienced assistant dean, an Iranian-American woman in a man's Jesuit world, I would have better understood my visitors' pique.

As Parsa had explained the concept, "The chicken and the pig are expected to contribute to the human diet. The chicken can meet this expectation by laying an egg and moving on; the pig doesn't have this luxury. There is nothing that he can leave behind without sacrificing his life."

I guess Gary had been the pig in the equation. I wasn't aware that he had recently been badly wounded by a denial of his application for promotion and feared that my comment in his file might incite a mortal shot from a dean to follow. I was never sure who was the chicken.

The sudden visit by my trio of gruntled professors was the finishing touch to the days of tackling the inventory of administrative chores shared by Zoe. I expected there would be many more such days before I could get to my agenda. I badly needed a break.

I had laughed to myself when Father Jack first told me that free membership in Koret, the newly completed university health center, would be granted with my appointment as dean. Health club membership had seemed "so California." But after my administrative and union baptism of fire, I was ready to find out how "so California" Koret was.

Underwater lights of an Olympic size pool visible through a large plate glass window provided a turquoise hue to the water a floor below as I proceeded from the Koret entrance turnstyle. I hadn't imagined how "so California" the Center was. Lingering aftertaste from unsolved challenges and frustration at my union professors would dissolve once I immersed myself in the water below. Secular baptism in the waters would work wonders. I was too soon reminded that I was no longer the competitive swimmer I had been when I was younger, but thoughts of the day dissolved after a few laps. Laps completed, the healthy tiredness felt good. I was ready to celebrate my accomplishment with a hot shower.

Jets of water ricocheted off my back as I closed my eyes and drifted into a standing dream undisturbed by University characters when through the wash of the running water, I heard a masked call, "Paul, Paul." The call was repeated and the voice was familiar. It was that of Father President John, lather streaming down his body, standing beneath the showerhead next to mine. I had never before stood naked next to a college president, let alone a priest.

"It's good to see you here," Father garbled through the flow. I wouldn't feel comfortable responding, "It's good to see you too."

Rather, I garbled, "Quite an impressive facility. Now I know why you fought so hard for it."

"You can't know all the challenges we faced in building Koret?"

Father's rhetorical question begged a response. A new dean doesn't ignore the invitation of a president who wants to share his thoughts.

"No, I don't."

Father launched into a far more detailed account of the trials of Koret construction than he had shared with me during my job interview. I would give an occasional nod as obstacle followed obstacle, issue an "uh, huh" from time to time, and once in a while, provide a sympathetic "No!" His litany of Koret confessions came to a sudden end with the application of shampoo and messaging of his thinning hair under the shower head. But shampoo applied and rinsed, he had another tale to tell.

He shook his head in exasperation and asked of no one, "How did the University, a Catholic University, end up with an improved telephone system in which individual numbers carry the prefix '666,' numbers of the Devil?" Quite a leap from his Koret confessions. My University education was continuing. I hadn't equated the numbers "666" with the numbers of the Devil and wasn't aware the installation of the new system with the prefix "666" occurred under the president's watch. Father was implicitly seeking forgiveness for a lack of oversight.

Skin on my fingers was beginning to shrivel. Father must have sensed that he had rambled on for too long, or was experiencing the same shriveling. He turned off his shower. I was relieved. It wouldn't be necessary for me to be the one to end our conversation. He reprised the story of asbestos discovery and resultant soaring costs for Koret construction as we proceeded to pick up towels to dry off. Like any good story teller, he had been holding back on the punch line.

"Dean, of course, if it had been Stanford, they would have discovered oil rather than asbestos!"

I'm sure Father had gotten a lot of mileage from that line, but I had to give him credit. I was glad he had stuck to his guns as challenges to the construction of Koret mounted. I planned to spend a lot of time at the Center.

There was no "Good morning," no "It was good talking with you," on a morning call I received the next day from Father. There was only, "Paul, have you followed up on last year's Counseling Department Christmas Party?"

I was caught off guard. A few days after my arrival on campus, Father had made an off-the-cuff reference to Christmas-past condom decorations hung on a Christmas tree in my School. I had let his comment slide as it didn't seem of consequence or suggest follow-up. I should have known better: the wedding of condoms and Christmas on a Catholic University campus can be volatile. Now, I had a delicate challenge: how to honor Father's implicit directive without School professors and Ducky, the administrative assistant who coordinated the celebration, labeling me the "dean of condom control"? I had to find a way to meet with Ducky privately, hoping to contain my mission; I would also need to find a way to share the president's concerns with Ducky without feeling foolish. The opportunity to discretely meet presented itself less than a week later.

Ducky was shuffling papers on his desk as I passed the Counseling Department reception area on my way to lunch. There were no signs of professors in the warren of offices adjoining his station. I pounced.

"How are you doing?" I asked, an opener to small-talk before I introduced what had brought me to his station. I girded myself to casually introduce the topic of the department's Christmas party, being aware that a question about a holiday party close to a year ago didn't fit with the flow of casual conversation. The moment I mentioned the word "Christmas," Ducky knew I was uncomfortable. He grinned. He didn't say a word. He wasn't going to let me off the hook. He let me hang in silence. What dean wouldn't feel uncomfortable talking with a secretary named Ducky about condoms on a Christmas tree?

"Oh, has Father President spoken with you?" he finally broke the silence. I sheepishly nodded. Ducky was one up. It was now his show. He exuberantly continued, "Dean, we had a wonderful party. There was cider. There was wine. Professors brought food. They were even civil to one another, and to their students. The office was loaded with ornaments." Ducky was having fun. He wasn't going to make this easy for me. I'm convinced he wanted me to say the word "condom." I obliged.

"Ducky, was the department's Christmas tree last year decorated with condoms?" I was embarrassed; he was emboldened.

"Oh, Dean, it was quite a tree." He rose from his chair. He opened his arms to form a wide open-ended circle and stood on tiptoes, circled arms reaching for the ceiling. "Oh Dean, it was a big, big one."

His eyes were those of a mischievous child telling a dirty joke. I tried to keep a straight face.

"And, Dean, the decorations were so colorful. Condoms, like icicles, hung from the branches. Dean, you should have seen the colors, and tasted the flavors: red, green, blue; cinnamon, spearmint, peppermint." Ducky suddenly became deferential. Variety of colors and flavors shared, he decided playtime was over.

"Yes, Dean. At last year's Christmas party, I decorated the department Christmas tree with condoms. You don't need to talk with people in the Castro, or for that matter Jesuits, to know the impact of AIDS. I thought it appropriate that a Counseling Department acknowledge the AIDS crisis and use the Christmas season as an opportunity to urge safe sex."

"Thanks, Ducky. This is helpful." I wasn't sure of what else to say. He had a point—of sorts. Safe sex and Christmas celebration, however, aren't good bedfellows in a Jesuit university with a Social Justice mission—even if the university is located in San Francisco.

Ducky relaxed once he had delivered the social justice and health message but he couldn't maintain his serious deportment.

"Dean, do you have a request for any special colors or flavors for this year's tree?" He obviously didn't appreciate the intensity of Father President's interest.

"Ducky, there's political protection and there's health protection. Pay attention to both," I rejoined before I left the office. Immediately, I felt a bit stodgy.

Condom control fortunately had faded from Father President's list of priorities. It took much longer for Ducky to stop reminding me of the condoms of Christmas past.

Opening weeks were providing challenges for which no dean, regardless of experience, could have been prepared. I certainly wasn't prepared to jump from the challenge of Christmas condoms to a Sister's identification of a priest as a sex object to justify open student enrollment in his workshop.

The morning after my meeting with Ducky, I asked Sister Rachel with her Cheshire Cat smile to join me in my office to address student over-enrollment in a summer workshop scheduled by her Catholic School Leadership Institute.

"Dean, you called. I'm here." Sister bustled into my office and sat down with a flourish. I got to the point.

"Sister, more than forty students, well over the listed cap, have registered for the Graziano workshop. Some students will need to be asked to drop the workshop or enroll for another one." Sister's smile immediately morphed from beatific to tormented frown. She wasn't happy with the news. She rustled down in her chair.

"Dearie, you just don't understand."

I must have missed something. I wanted her on my team and offered what I thought would be a generous solution to the problem: authorization for a second section of the workshop with my budget rather than that of her institute covering the expense for an additional instructor.

"Dearie, you still don't understand," Sister glowered. She swallowed any remnant of a smile on her face and placed both arms firmly on the arms of her chair. My angelic Cheshire cat was now a mother protecting her young. She sensed I was vulnerable after my initial retreat and took the offense. She shifted her heavy frame to the front of the chair seat, feet firmly planted on the floor.

"Dean, let me paint a picture for you. The classroom is hushed. Vibrations of anticipation can be felt in the filled-to-capacity room as Father wearing a black academic gown enters. He strides to the rostrum. His gown flows from his six-foot frame. His almond brown eyes sit deep in his sharp-featured, sun-tanned, craggy face as he assays the mostly female class. He exudes mystery—and not just that of the Church." Sister's Cheshire smile was back. She knew she had me on the run. "Dean, you can't cap enrollment."

Concluding argument presented, Sister's voice lowered as she leaned toward me. I was about to be made privy to something important.

"Dearie, do you know students refer to him as 'Father What-a-Waste'?"

I didn't and Sister wasn't about to elaborate. I was left to wonder whether it was priestly vows of celibacy that triggered this response from his students or something else? It didn't matter. If Father was half the professor Sister made him out to be and students flocked to his workshop, I would honor her request to leave enrollment open. Let there be one hundred students in his workshop; let his voice rumble like thunder down the halls. More professors' voices should so rumble while students listen in awe.

Mission accomplished, Sister rose from her seat with a reassuring, "Dearie, I knew you would understand," and left my office. I could now get back to attacking the pile of papers on my desk before the day came to an end.

On campus now for less than three weeks, I had received a preview of School life from Zoe, viewed a traveling morality play from aggrieved professors, received confessions from Father President, mediated a dispute over Christmas condoms, and heard a tale of a priestly mystery from Sister Rachel. And I had yet to attend the urgent budget meeting scheduled by the Academic Vice President.

* * *

I slowly walked down from the School's lookout post on the hilltop to lower campus after a weekend break from campus. San Francisco early morning glow bathed the hillside. It was a "good to be alive" morning. I looked forward to meeting with fellow deans and the AVP even though the agenda provided some worry.

The hallways of the Administration building were as dark, cold, and uninviting as I had remembered. Like a rat in a maze, I circled the network of corridors until I observed a 3 × 5 index card with *Deans Meeting, 10:00,* typewritten and slipped into a frame on the door frame. I hesitatingly opened the door to witness Father President standing alone at the head of a long highly polished wooden conference table. I didn't know he would be joining us. Half-filled coffee cups, dirty silverware, and empty sugar wrappers littered the tabletop. As I approached the table, sour odor from an opened container of Half n' Half betrayed its age.

Father's "Good Morning" greeting was as much a sigh of resignation as welcome. He nodded toward the debris. "And these people work for me," he lamented, a lament he shared in muted voice with the entry of each succeeding dean. I was truly in another world. Boston University's President John would cry, "Off with their heads," and heads would fall, whether it be that of a window cleaner leaving streaked windows, a chef preparing too-moist scrambled eggs for a parent morning buffet, or a construction worker failing to correctly grout bricks.

It was only moments before I, along with deans, most of whom I had not seen since March, was sharing welcomes and engaging in small-talk as we casually assisted the president to pick up the leavings of his staff. This was obviously not the first time the deans had participated in such clean-up experiences. This was truly a different university. And the morning had only begun.

Several minutes after the scheduled time for the beginning of the meeting, Father Jack burst into the room, cheeks red from exertion. He apologized for being late and invited us all to take seats and quickly pulled a chair up next to Father President already seated at the head of the table. Two senior University officers, I was pretty sure, the only Catholics in the room, now lodged at the table's point of power signaled that business was about to begin. I miscalculated. Father Jack sat silent. No one spoke. Might there be blessings before such meetings, I wondered. I wasn't prepared for Father's words.

"Let me catch my breath. I just got in from El Salvador last night." We were silent. "Sometimes it's hard to be an American when you witness what's being done in our country's name to suppress the poor," he paused. His face was flushed. His voice trembled as he continued, "Words don't convey the poverty of the country, or the violence of the military who with our government's support is suppressing these people." He paused again.

"The monstrosity of it all. The monstrosity of it all. Sometimes it's hard to think of forgiveness."

Jack was silent. We sat not quite knowing how to respond.

"I apologize," he provided a form of closure.

Apology wasn't needed. His words provided a sea-change from Boston University of far greater import than the failings of University maintenance staff. BU president, John Silber, also a member of the Kissinger Commission, had supported the Salvador military in the name of fighting communism. I was far closer to my political roots in this religious institution than I had been at the university I had left behind.

Father turned the meeting over to Father President. Father President placed his elbows on the table, slowly folded one arm over the other, and leaned forward. The special meeting was underway.

"As you're aware, we're facing some financial difficulties. Enrollments last term didn't meet projections and it appears that there will be a shortfall again this term. Father Jack will distribute the papers."

Father Jack placed individual sheets of budget printouts he had brought with him in front of each dean as he walked the table's perimeter. Deans promptly buried themselves in enrollment and credit hour figures specific to their school or college.

I was lost in a maze of seemingly unconnected figures in a format new to me. Fellow newcomer, Dean Joel of the Law School, looked up from his printout, our eyes met, pupils skyward. Whispers were exchanged between two deans who, I was to learn later, presided over colleges with significant drops in projected tuition income. Dean Samuel, Management School dean who had been around longer than the rest of us, broke the study hall silence.

"Father President, what do you want deans to do with these figures?" It was obvious this was not the first time he had participated in such an exercise.

“I’m asking all schools to provide my office with a four percent savings for the upcoming year by the end of the week. Any questions?” Father President shot back.

He pushed his chair back, “Sam, Father Jack will take it from here.” Direction given to his vice president, he stood and left the meeting.

This wasn’t the same Father President I had met on my first visit; this wasn’t the same Father President who had shared thoughts as we showered side by side. Nor was it the same Father lost in the litter of his staff just moments ago.

Knowing smiles of veteran deans said it all. We would each go back to our schools and colleges and give Father President and Father Jack the numbers they wanted.

“Any questions?” Father Jack asked. There were none.

“Good. Let’s take off our sandals and shake out the dust.” Shake out the dust we would.

I didn’t know where he got that “take off our sandals” line. It must be some religious reference. Maybe it was a special Jesuit call to arms. Then again, maybe it was just about heat and dust; they certainly had plenty of that on campus.

Eight
A Living Theater

"Don't get caught up in the weeds," a Boston colleague advised me shortly after I informed him that I had accepted the offer to be dean in San Francisco. Although I considered his advice somewhat gratuitous at the time, having been the dean of his school for eight years, he was right on. When I found myself after less than a month in San Francisco, caught up in the weeds of my own doing, I wished I had remembered his advice.

Vincent, vice president of Buildings and Grounds, self-proclaimed "Space Czar" held the keys to all that was worth being locked on campus and had easy access to all University offices and responsibility for all things that leave physical footprints presidents cherish: landscape, building renovation, new construction, and plant maintenance. Heavily bespectacled and soft-spoken in his late forties, Vincent had impressed me at a welcome lunch as a conscientious and reasonable gentleman—and a fine weaver of tales. We had enjoyed one another's company. It was time for a second lunch, this time, my treat.

Owner and receptionist Phil's generous smile, firm shake of hand on arrival reserved for male University officers, coupled with a robust announcement for all diners to hear, "Gentlemen, I have a table especially for the two of you on the patio," as we entered The Magic Flute made us feel wanted and important. My interview dinner with department chairpersons on their backyard patio seemed so long ago.

Vincent and I shared University gossip and relished in stories of earlier university life on the east coast. Idiosyncrasies of university life brought an added dimension to dining. Too soon, only a few stray leaves and olive pits from our salads remained on our plates; only crumbs of the crusty garlic bread remained in the breadbasket. Glasses of wine were almost empty. It was time for me to get to the hidden agenda for my lunch invitation.

"Vincent, the School's foyer reminds me of the plant in the *Little House of Horrors* that takes delight in devouring visitors. No, on second thought," I added, "it's more reminiscent of Sartre's *No Exit.*" I had learned at our earlier lunch that Vincent liked the theatre; theatre references would appeal. To drive the point home, I invoked to the little white lie strategy present in deans' inventories.

"We expect visitors from the State Department of Education within the next few weeks to discuss a pending accreditation review. I really need your help." I admit I used some artistic license; the pending visit was several months away.

Vincent was sensitive to my problem and promised specs for work to be done later in the month. Courtesy couched in theatrical reference, coupled with fear of public external sanction, was working. But not well enough. I needed immediate action. I needed to generate fear. I evoked the specter of union action knowing we lived and worked in a union University in a union city and that Vincent daily interacted with more unions than any one manager can handle: custodians, landscapers, carpenters, painters, and electricians.

"Would it be alright if a hypothetical painter and hypothetical carpenter assistant stole into the School's entryway in the dark of night and with paint and roller, hammer and saw, made the entryway look more inviting?" Vincent knew where I was coming from, or more accurately, from where the painter and carpenter might be coming. His silence and broad smile said it all. I continued, "Everyone would be happy, no one would be offended. I would have the entry cleaned up and you wouldn't have to deal with a charge of hiring scab labor. It would just be one of those mysteries."

I wasn't prepared for his response, "I hear you, Paul," and with a laugh that caught the attention of diners at the next table, crowed, "After all, this university is built on the biggest mystery of them all."

He let his words of wisdom take hold before continuing, "If you can intercept the phantom painter and his assistant, perhaps I can get the job done next week. I'll find a way to push costs off to the next fiscal year's budget."

The School entryway was painted the following week and the walls were covered with expensive fabric, not to my taste, but a lot more attractive than the previous brown sheets of Luana paneling. It had been a most enjoyable and productive lunch.

One morning, not long after the lobby work had been completed, I found myself softly singing a jingle as I approached the School, "I'm the little union label and I'm proud as proud can be, to be sown on every garment at the Howard Factory." Years ago as a young child, I would often covertly listen to the Barry Gray radio show on WMCA before I fell asleep in my darkened bedroom, parents still awake in our Greenwich Village living room. The periodic interrupting promo lyrics for Howard Clothes must have been stored somewhere in the deep recesses of my mind for all these years, awaiting the stimulus of Vincent and San Francisco.

The late labor leader Harry Bridges, who called San Francisco his "City," would have appreciated a manager recalling a labor jingle. He would have been ecstatic if he had witnessed a manager extort a fellow manager's fear of unions. He wouldn't have noticed my postponement of academic tasks in the weeds.

Thank goodness, Janet who was still in Boston baby-sitting our furniture until the arrival of the movers, would be joining me next week. There was so much to talk about that couldn't be conveyed by nightly telephone calls or email. And the fall semester hadn't yet begun. On August

25, I received a call on my personal line at the office: "Hi Hon, I made it." I never realized how welcome a phone call could be.

A few days after Janet's arrival, undergraduates returned to San Francisco. Clusters of luggage rested outside lower campus dormitories; sound systems blasted through open dorm windows; lines of students queued everywhere for almost everything. Parents of undergraduates, separated from their once-were-children, wandered aimlessly as their progeny engaged in the rites of university fall. And professors were back—that is, on lower campus.

The San Francisco University semester opening ambience was not unlike that of colleges and universities across the nation—except for that of the School of Education. The School sat alone on top of Lone Mountain, a hill set aside from other University schools and colleges, save one. We sat alone by schedule: most School classes were scheduled on Friday evenings and Saturdays. We sat alone by student profile: the mean age of the older, working professionals enrolled in our graduate programs was close to forty—and most were part-time students. The energy of the opening week on lower campus had waned by the time of the following Saturday registration for the School of Education students for our first "Teaching Weekend."

I stood, coffee cup in hand, looking out the picture window from my office recently renovated by Vincent's work crew—no longer just a corner cubicle sheltered by frosted glass. It was 7:00 a.m. Early morning fog was mesmerizing as it drifted through the branches of the Jack Pines and Redwoods outside my window until human figures, one by one emerged from the murk. Their emergence prompted memory of a movie scene from the film *Field of Dreams* that I had recently viewed in which Shoeless Joe Jackson and Black Sox teammates emerge from the cornfields of Iowa. The ritual of fall registration was about to begin. Thoughts of Shoeless Joe Jackson and cornfields didn't last long.

At precisely 7:30 a.m., Gabriella, a young staff member barely out of college herself, left the warren of School Administration offices to open building doors and greet the by-now roiling students queued outside. Doors open, students poured through the entryway like bluefish driving schools of menhaden up on the beaches in Montauk when I was a young. Funneled into a "holding room," students were assigned group numbers in preparation to be called to register for classes and pay tuition bills.

I crept from my office to the nearby open floor space cleared and set up for student registration. It was quite a spectacle to observe. A uniformed security officer in cobalt blue, pistol on hip, stood silently by the steel door entry to the Office of the Deans. Moments later, a file of students started to stream through the open steel barrier to the Office of the Deans before merging into a line, reminiscent of Boston morning cars merging into the Callahan Tunnel as they enter the city. A string of tables gathered for the occasion with staff seated on one side to process class registration and tuition payment was positioned for their arrival.

The officer in blue stood silently as checks were transmitted by students in exchange for class registration cards. Upon registration of the last student, Gabriella harvested the tuition checks and with the officer in blue alongside, departed to the Bursar's Office. Registration tables were quickly folded, staff departed, and students were off to their first class sessions. It had been less than an hour since I stood gazing out my window at the fog-shrouded pines.

I returned to my office to bask in the quiet of the impressive, apparently successful morning to nurse my bottomless cup of coffee, compile a "to do" list for the upcoming week, and review notes for an afternoon presentation to students. A heated exchange of voices outside my half-open office door less than a half-hour later broke the peace. Something was not sitting right with somebody.

Looking up from my desk, I noticed shadows cast on my frosted glass wall similar to those that might be left by two birds in a mating dance. Something was unfolding outside my office. I had to investigate. I didn't expect to discover a University security officer in too snug uniform, partnered with an agitated woman, face marked with cherry-red blotches of anger, crossing accelerated crab-like back and forth in a modern dance routine. With my appearance, the dance slowed.

"Excuse me, Dean," whispered the officer.

"I want to file a complaint," screeched the woman.

"Excuse me, Dean," now more pronounced from the officer.

"I want to file . . ." several decibels higher from the woman.

The salvo picked up, steps quickened. Side to side, the two figures slid back and forth. The officer's stomach threatened to break loose from the confines of his shirt. He finally managed to throw out a full sentence.

"Excuse me, Dean, this woman has a complaint she would like to file against one of your professors."

"Dean, I want to file a complaint against one of your professors," cherry-red faced bobbing partner echoed. I knew there would be new challenges at the University but . . . I took advantage of a lull in the dance to ask the unlikely partners to join me in my office where we might sit and talk rather than slide and screech.

The couple raced for the two chairs. Lieutenant Grasso, nametag prominently pinned on the fat-challenged uniform, opened the conversation.

"Dean, this woman, Cathy Carson, wishes to file a complaint against one of your professors."

"Dean, I want to file a complaint against one of your professors," Cathy echoed again as she jumped up from her chair. We weren't making much progress.

"Cathy, now slowly, let's start from the top," I pleaded. She sat down.

"Dean, I work for the College of Professional Studies and one of your professors is meeting with students in a classroom scheduled for use by our college." We were now making some progress. "I entered the classroom to inform him that he was in the wrong classroom." Cathy rose from her chair.

"Dean, please stand up." I obliged. She jumped across to where I was standing, dug fingers into my jacket shoulder, and started to twist my upper torso while she pushed me toward the door. "Dean, he shoved me out like this." I was sure there was no malice meant by her demonstration. Lieutenant Grasso was not so sure.

He jumped to his feet, "Just a minute, just a minute. Let's calm it."

Cathy stepped back and sat down again. She continued to share details of her confrontation with my professor, my Professor Hubert. Why, of all people, did it have to be Professor Hubert of the engulfing handshake and pained grin? Professor Hubert, leader of the three wise men to my office, Professor Hubert, union representative for the School?

The more I tried to calm things down, the more questions I asked, the more Cathy's agitation increased. Red blotches merged into a scarlet mass. Lieutenant Grasso was too busy tucking in his shirt and fastening popped buttons to make any progress. I told my dancers we could only resolve matters with Professor Hubert present. Cathy wanted none of that. I told the two of them I would go to Hubert's classroom and inform him of Cathy's charges and reminded them that the due process must be honored for all parties. I assured them I would immediately follow up on the complaint. Assurances lowered room temperature; Cathy and the Lieutenant kept their distance as they exited far more quietly than they had entered.

I mastered the maze to School classrooms in an adjoining building, located the room identified as the scene of the crime, knocked gently on the door, and slowly opened it. I hoped I was doing the right thing, Fireplug Al, Vice President for Labor and consultant for all such events, wasn't on campus. I would need to rely on experience and a beginner's knowledge of the *Collective Bargaining Agreement.*

Professor Hubert, in his trusted Harris tweed jacket, half-sat on a desk corner, legs angled to the floor. I entered the room and softly asked him to join me outside the classroom for a minute.

The hallway was empty. There we were, the two of us standing alone, face-to-face. The space empty of students now took on the aura of a midnight Grand Central Station passageway. Neither of us were comfortable.

"Hubert, I just met with a young woman and a Public Safety officer." As I summarized the meeting, he stood silently chewing his lower lip. He said nothing. He only stared and chewed. He wasn't making things easy. I needed to break his trance.

"Hubert, the matter is a sensitive one. You should probably speak with the Faculty Association representative as soon as possible." His face coloration progressed from pale skin tone to flush crimson. Now I had two crimson-faced individuals on the warpath.

A fine spray shot from his mouth, "Dean, that woman interrupted my class. A classroom is a professor's castle and she invaded my castle." He leaned toward me, placed his face closer to mine, and hissed his earlier pronouncement in case I missed it, "A classroom is a professor's castle." I wasn't here to talk about castles or be sprayed on. I needed to restore some semblance of calm.

"Hubert, I don't know exactly what happened. I just know that a very angry woman entered my office and made a serious charge. I need to be sure everybody is treated fairly."

Hubert's face coloration returned; his blood pressure must have lowered. He provided me with his version of the morning's events. There were some differences of opinion as to who had said what to whom, who had said what first, and the manner in which Cathy had been escorted from the room. At least, there was agreement that the event had occurred; there would be a starting point from which to proceed.

"Dean, I want to speak to my Association representative immediately. Should I excuse my class?" He had no interest in continuing our conversation, for he was Labor and I was Management. I told him I'd be willing to meet with the class for the remaining hour.

"Do what you must do. I need to leave." He rapidly disappeared around a corner in the silent, empty hallway.

I met with students, told them to take a class break, and that I would be back in five minutes and rushed back to my office to call Lieutenant Grasso to bring him up to date and ask him to share the information with Ms. Carson.

When I returned to the classroom, students who had been casually talking returned to their seats. Now it was my turn to sit on the corner of the desk, legs angled to the floor. Without getting into detail, I explained that there had been a misunderstanding between a University staff person and their professor about assignment to the classroom in which they had been meeting. We talked casually about what has just passed for a brief period and they were sensitive as to how there might have been some misunderstandings. They were sympathetic to the importance of the due process but they wanted to talk more about the program in which they were enrolled than in what had just occurred. It was nice to work with adult students.

We all left the classroom a little wiser. Two things were clear: a six-foot-plus male professor needs to be extremely careful when he asks a five-foot-plus female to leave a classroom, and that I did not need to be an expert on the *Collective Bargaining Agreement* to expect the episode to spawn a grievance.

The first day of classes for the fall semester came to an end late that afternoon after my orientation meeting with students. Early morning coffee, emergence of students from Lone Mountain flora, the bustle of registration, the dance of Lieutenant Grasso and Cathy, and the spray of Professor Hubert seemed light years ago when I left for home. I had truly been provided a front row seat for my introduction to the living theater of the School of Education "Teaching Weekend." I couldn't wait to get to our Divisadero flat, have a glass of wine with Janet, and talk about the day's events.

Nine

Life Is a Cabernet

On October 17, 1989, 5:06 p.m., Janet and I became true San Franciscans. There wasn't a cloud in the azure blue sky. The temperature hung at eighty degrees Fahrenheit. The opportunity to slip out early from a ceremonial signing of the *Trustees of the University, University of San Francisco Faculty Association Collective Bargaining Agreement*, the University's secular equivalent to the New Testament, and get home early couldn't be resisted. It was too nice a day to linger and make small talk with colleagues more interested in the buffet table than the make-believe love-making between Management and Labor as officers signed the new *Agreement* at the far end of the room.

Glasses of wine in hand, seated at our dining room table, we gazed out the picture window that framed the vermillion orange towers of the Golden Gate Bridge. A containership, backlit by the slowly sinking sun, glided beneath the bridge into the Bay. In the late afternoon haze, Marina tile roofs on stucco homes below gave a sense of the Mediterranean. San Francisco was at its most seductive. It was hard to believe I had been in "the City" for close to two months. Janet and I were beginning to savor our new world. We toasted to our health. Life was good. Until . . .

Our cat, Avril, awoke from a late afternoon nap and, bolted by us out of the dining room, tore down the hallway and dove beneath the living room couch. As he disappeared beneath the couch, our hallway floor started to roll, lazy waves in a gentle sea. Avril was having no "catmare." Paintings swayed on hanging wires; dishes rattled in the kitchen; a glass shattered on the bathroom tile floor. A television screen in the adjoining den that only moments ago displayed a Giants–A's World Series game went black.

Janet and I quickly moved beneath the nearest doorframe. Wasn't that what people were supposed to do in a moment such as this? The house released a human moan as wooden beams stretched on a rolling foundation. Car alarms emitted discordant cries from the street. We were in the midst of an atonal symphony. Then suddenly, there was silence—the dead silence that only follows catastrophe. In the pause provided by the stillness, eruptions of flame shooting through the billows of dust and smoke from the Marina District masked our earlier Bay view. The heat of that mid-October day suddenly became oppressive. The afternoon moment of savoring had ended.

Only moments later, we were drawn to the sound of voices from Divisadero Street at the far end of our flat. Standing in the middle of the street, we witnessed neighbors with whom we had previously only exchanged a courteous "Good morning" or "It's a beautiful day" talking with one another. A queue had formed in front of a man who with a car phone in his shiny black Porsche was enabling residents to reach friends and family outside the Bay Area. We rushed down our front steps to become a member of the congregation. We needed support. These people knew how to cope. They had obviously been through this before. This was all new to us.

We didn't learn until the next day that we had been caught in an earthquake, titled Loma Prieta, name of the shifting Tectonic plate that had caused all the damage. In Marblehead, it had taken the "Blizzard of '76" and twenty-six inches of snow to drive people to the street to talk with one another; Loma Prieta with seismic reading of 6.9 accomplished a similar end in San Francisco.

I knew an introduction to the San Francisco community of priests and professors would pose challenges. I knew unfamiliar names and parables drawn from the New Testament would be common in the Jesuit Community parlance. I never expected that familiarity with the terms *Loma Prieta, San Andreas Fault, Richter scale, tectonic plates, tremblers,* and *after-shocks* would be fundamental to Bay Area conversation. But neither had I suspected that the terms ôenology, *varietal, tannic level,* or *vintage year* absent from the "back East" talk would be fundamental.

The Bay Area is a playing field for oenologists. Knowledge of vineyard locations and wineries, varietals and vintage years, alcohol and tannic levels, wine tasting protocol and wine-speak are social imperatives. It didn't take me long to know that I would need to learn wine-speak if I were to negotiate on a level playing field with colleagues and fully engage with friends. Talk of the good Martini or Manhattan would need to be held for trips back to Boston or New York.

Shortly after Janet's arrival, Marin-tanned Sol whose words had strongly flavored my first meeting with the faculty in the spring and his calming partner, Sheba, both New York expatriates, took the two of us under their wings. Unwittingly but willingly, we became students in their Bay Life cultural program. Science of Oenology, prerequisite for acceptance in Bay Area social circles, was our first course. Sol knew varietals, vintage years, and the location of out-of-the-way wineries; he could have served as an oenology coach for Paul Giamatti in *Sideway*s. Sheba possessed the grace prerequisite to teach social skills to enrich wine-speak; she could have served as wine etiquette coach for Martha Stewart. Janet and I couldn't have had better mentors.

A sense of normalcy after Loma Prieta had returned to campus life. A pre-Prieta planned reception Janet and I had planned to celebrate the fall semester with professors in our Divisadero flat would take place as scheduled.

Late fall afternoon, sun slanted through our living room windows. Janet and I bathed in the autumnal warmth and conversation hum of relaxing professors. The living room was full. There was a gentle hum of conversation, and we had overcome the embarrassment of scheduling the reception for a Sunday on which the San Francisco 49ers were playing at Candlestick Park. Everyone was comfortable even if it had required adjustments in the Sunday afternoon 49er worship plans for some. I was enjoying sharing my newly acquired oenology prowess with School colleagues.

"Cabernet, Pinot, or Zinfandel?" "Chardonnay or Sauvignon Blanc?" I inquired as guests settled in. I had made progress in wine-speak. For the rare person who didn't drink wine, Janet would toss in, "We also have Perrier." No one with a sense of sophistication in San Francisco drank tap water.

I was talking with one of our professors when I noticed two empty wine bottles on the living room side table, our make-shift wine bar, and excused myself to pick up the bottles and walk down the flat's long center hallway to the kitchen to get more wine. Sol stood in the kitchen doorway, placement timed for my arrival, I'm sure. He held high two bottles of Cabernet I had bought for the reception, one in each hand.

"I can't believe you bought this stuff," he proclaimed and laughed as I passed him to enter the kitchen.

He followed alongside and, with gusto, inverted the bottles of Cabernet I had earlier uncorked into the sink and turned toward me as the last belch of red wine imploded on the white porcelain and circled down the drain. His brown eyes laughed; a broad smile etched his tanned face. I didn't know what to say or do. I just stood there and watched and listened as a final gurgle of the wine circled down the drain, leaving a red Rorschach image on the sink bottom.

"Dean, life is too short for bad wine," he pronounced deadpan. "You still have a lot to learn." I smiled awkwardly. I wasn't aware Sol and Sheba had decided our faculty reception would serve as an oenology lab test.

"Sheba," Sol called down the hallway. "Sheba," he barked a second time. She emerged from the warmth of the living room, swooped up a large brown bag, evidently deposited in a corner when she and Sol had first entered our flat, and strode to join us. She placed the bag carefully on the kitchen counter and, one by one, lifted out bottles of wine. Sheba seductively introduced each bottle as she placed it on the counter.

"'87 Cabernet from William Hill.

"'85 Zin from Rafanelli, and you should like this '87 Cain's Cuvee."

Bottles presented, she turned to Sol and handed him a bottle opener she had brought for this special lesson. She didn't want any cork in the wine that might result from a novice's uncorking with an inappropriate opener.

"Hon, would you do the honors? I'm going back to the living room."

Evening's lesson over, wine uncorked, Sol and I returned to the living room, bottles in hand.

Sol and Sheba's wine apprenticeship introduced Janet and me to the important role of wine in Bay Area social discourse. But it hadn't alerted me to the part wine played in selected School social rites. My education in things oenological was to continue a few mornings later.

Sister Rachel, snowy white owl in nun's dress, was my new instructor. Dominican in a Jesuit university, she swooped into my office. I hadn't finished my first cup of morning coffee before her landing. Sister's broad Cheshire smile signaled pure pleasure.

With a flirtatious blinking of eyes, lilting voice, and smile, she approached my desk.

"Dean, are you familiar with the churchly axiom 'presumed permission'?" I warily informed her I wasn't. My knowledge was about to be increased, but at a cost.

"Well, Dean, it's sort of like the axiom 'It's better to apologize than ask for permission.'" I got the drift. Sister now hovered over her prey.

"Dean, there are times when it's better to proceed on the assumption that there will be support for your actions rather than do nothing until you get permission." The drift was now a riptide. I was about to be swept under. "You know the women professors meet a few times a year for dinner?"

I nodded that I was aware of the tradition. "Last night, we had our dinner to celebrate the beginning of the School year. It was wonderful. It was just wonderful." Sister was luminescent.

"Professor Rebecca asked me at dinner if the dean was treating for wine, and I replied, 'I'm sure he would if he were asked.'" Sister paused a second. Her grin now broadened. She popped the question.

"Dean, I'm asking you, would you treat the ladies to wine?" I hesitated. Her smile morphed into "I gotcha." I was to be her early morning mouse. She knew she had me.

"Of course," I slowly replied. She was two for two; she had already celebrated her Father What-a-Waste conquest.

How could I have said "no" to a request couched in such charm? Question asked, answer sought received, Sister relaxed her talons. I was to be saved for a future meal. She turned to leave but came to a brief halt before she left the office. Sister was familiar with university ways. There was one technicality.

"Oh, Dean. I saved the full receipt for the dinner. I'm leaving it with Dorothy in case you need it to process payment. Thanks again. The ladies will appreciate your help."

I was giving little away in this transaction and gaining a great deal: female professors' goodwill in exchange for a couple of bottles of wine. Later in the day, I looked at the receipt left by Sister. No wonder it had been a wonderful dinner. The women banqueters had selected several bottles of an older vintage of a pricey varietal to celebrate the occasion.

Was it worth pursuing my surprise at the cost of the wine with Sister? I sought advice from a former dean of the School who had been a member of the Society of Jesuits until he married his secretary.

On sharing my quandary he commented, "*De minimus not curat preator*," translated, "The magistrate does not consider trifles." Sister's wine selection was such a trifle.

Early morning surprises were becoming a specialty of the house. I wasn't prepared for a surprise of another cultural order a few weeks later. Barely seated at my desk, the personal call line on my phone broke the silence. I picked up the receiver.

"Paul, Father Jack." Until this morning, I had never spoken directly with Father on the call from his office without assistant Bede's introduction, "Father would like to speak with you," before he got on the phone.

"It's important I see you as soon as possible. Can you come down to my office?" There was no "Good morning" salutation.

"My calendar is open until 9:30. Can you join me?" Can you join me becomes a rhetorical question when posed by a superior university officer. Something extraordinary must be brewing—and I suspected it wasn't coffee. The luxury of getting to my office before staff arrived and catching up on paperwork without interruption, coffee cup at hand, was not to be.

Father silently welcomed me to his office with a sweep of his hand and proceeded to his desk. Bede wasn't in yet. "Have a seat." He gestured for me to sit down on his couch as he seated himself at his desk. His face was fixed as a wax mask. He didn't say anything. He wasn't the most garrulous individual, but total silence?

"Paul," Father hesitated before proceeding. He seemed uncomfortable. I didn't know how to help him. "Paul," he started again. I would have to wait until he identified whatever obstacle made it difficult for him to deliver his message. He looked down at his feet. He looked up at me, still hesitant to continue. He couldn't put it off any longer.

"Paul, I got a telephone call last night that troubles me." Father hesitated before he followed up on the oblique opener. Now I was troubled.

"I got a call from someone in the San Francisco community who said they would 'out you' if you didn't come out of the closet." I laughed nervously.

"What closet, Father?" I was being cute. Too cute. I knew full well what was on his mind. Father wisely chose not to respond to my clumsy humor.

"He said if you don't come out of the closet, he would share the information with Father President and the University Board of Trustees."

Once Father delivered the message, he seemed more relaxed. He had done his part. The ball was now in my court. I let his words sink in. I was taken aback. I shook my head slowly and forced a half-laugh, a laugh of bewilderment, before I responded.

"Father, I have been called many things in my life. And I suppose once or twice, a womanizer. But coming out of the closet is a new one."

Father placed both hands on his desk, his shoulders dropped. He looked me straight in the eyes. He was silent. I filled the silence.

"No, Father, I'm not gay."

He replied, as if seeking an apology, "I hope you understand I have nothing against gays, but I felt obligated to share the contents of the phone call with you. I don't want to be surprised by a public outing and have to explain the situation to our Board of Trustees. Paul, please understand I had to ask the question."

With his asking of the question, Father had carried out his responsibility. Our meeting was over. He walked with me to the door from his office, placed his hand on my shoulder, and asked in the manner of a close friend, "If you have any information that might help me understand why someone would have made this phone call, please feel free to share it with me."

As something of a postscript, in my final year at the University, I learned of a gay priest with the name *Paul Warren* who lived in the Bay Area and was under review to serve on the University Board of Trustees.

Sharing that information with Father Jack might have shed some light on the events of that morning; but Father was no longer at the University.

So many things were different in the Bay Area than in New England; smells of Pacific salt winds and straw-blanketed hills replaced the briny smells of the Boston Atlantic and pine bouquet of New England forests. The dry, dusty, and religious ambience of the San Francisco campus was a far cry from the urban and secular ambience of the Boston University campus. And professor–management history could complicate dean–professor relationships in a manner not present back East. But the greatest difference of all was the omnipresence of the Church and its Jesuit warriors.

I learned a lot during my beginning months at the University but I had yet to become well acquainted with members of the Jesuit Community, the Community with a capital "C" that provided the University its special *gravitas.*

Ten

Jesuit Warriors

A large portrait of a beatific Jesus front and center in the entry to Ignatian Hall presided over the space as I approached the receptionist to inform her that Father Gregory was expecting me and we would be having lunch together in the Jesuit Community dining room. One call from the receptionist, and Father one of the grand old men of the Jesuit Community, aided by a cane and stooped under the weight of accumulating years, shortly emerged from a corridor into the hushed silence of the reception area. His handshake was strong and welcoming. "Let's go eat."

I walked at his side as we slowly passed back through the windowless corridor from which he had just emerged toward the dining room. We ambled down the freshly waxed floors with side doors open to silent cookie-cutter, cross-on-wall empty resident rooms. The ambience was more hospital than sacred. Several hundred feet and two turns later, sunlight from an interior open patio poured in through large windows. Father pulled open a heavy wooden door across from the patio. A new world awaited.

Priests silhouetted against diffused window light in an ornate, wood-paneled, dimly lit room circled slowly, trays in hand, around a food-laden, stainless steel center island, slowly dipping stainless steel serving spoons into stainless steel containers of meats, vegetables, salads, and condiments in a ritual-like manner. Father picked up a tray, handed it to me as we approached the island, and inserted me into the feeding circle. With an "I'll get a table," he was off.

Once in line, I understood the slow, meditative movement of the priests. There were difficult choices to be made: veal cutlet or roast beef;

chicken or eggplant fricassee; lasagna or spaghetti. There were hard-boiled eggs, pickled beets, chickpeas, cottage cheese. There was lettuce, Iceberg or Romaine; fruit, cocktail or fresh. Quite an offering for men of abstinence. I drifted along the perimeter of the island with the string of priests as I harvested my lunch. Harvest finished, Father returned, put his arm on my shoulder, and pointed to our table. He had already completed his sweep of the counter having long ago mastered the art of priestly buffet selection.

I removed the plates from my tray and placed them on the table and sat down. Father took a deep inhale of his coffee, set his cup down carefully, and wiped his lips. Before I had time to take my first bite, my tutorial in Jesuit history began.

"Let me tell you about St. Ignatius of Loyola: Ignacio Lopez de Loyola. He was an iconoclast who didn't suffer fools lightly. And he wasn't shy about showing his displeasure with erratic behaviors of men of the cloth." From what I already knew of Father, he could as easily have been describing himself.

"St. Ignatius was a man given to the follies of the world until he was hit by a cannonball and his leg was blown off at Pamplona." Father paused for a moment. "Never underestimate the power of a cannonball."

He laughed. He enjoyed his own humor. He was a master of timing and delivery. He repeated, in case I missed the drama of the event, "One shot from a cannon put motions in place that would give birth to the Jesuit order."

I was aware of the link between the shooting of Archduke Francis Ferdinand and World War I, the sinking of the USS Maine and the Spanish–American War; and Japan's bombing of Pearl Harbor and America's entry into World War II. But Ignacio Lopez de Loyola, Basque nobleman with a shattered leg as precursor to the Jesuit order? Of that I knew nothing.

Father continued, "Ignatius was recuperating in Loyola when out of boredom, he turned to the only two books available in the residence: a biography of Jesus and *Flos Sanctorum*, a chronicle of the lives of saints." The words *Flos Sanctorum* rolled off the tip of Father's tongue. I would have studied Latin rather than French if I had suspected my career path would have led me to a Jesuit university.

"Reading these two works, Ignatius began to realize there was more to life than jousting on the field of battle or partaking of perks that come with being a nobleman."

Father took another forkful of salad, another calculated pause, and provided a saintly smile, before he added, "Ignatius found lasting joy to be found in testing himself against the rigors of the saints." I had done enough homework to know of St. Ignatius but certainly hadn't done enough. The tale of Ignatius wasn't finished.

"Ignatius spent the last years of life in Rome, inspired by the vision embodied in the *Spiritual Exercises*. Now a teacher and worker among the poor in the city, he dedicated his life to writing the *Constitution* that celebrated the centrality of philosophy and theology as well as the importance of the humanities to the life of the Jesuit." With one more sip of coffee, Father concluded, "He established guiding principles and priorities for Jesuit educators and Jesuit schools."

Courtesy and personal comfort demanded I interrupt. "Father, your food is getting cold. Please."

He took a few bites while I tried to let him know that I knew something of St. Ignatius, primarily his work with the urban poor. Lesson over, Father's energy was redirected to consuming the now cold food on his plate. It was a perfect time for me to take a break from his tutorial, and I excused myself to get some coffee. I wasn't prepared for another lesson on my return. Father put his fork down and wiped his lips again.

"Paul," Father opened, "there was to be no temporal remuneration for any Jesuit professors." I sat silently. Father took a few final bites from his now tepid lunch, slowly chewed, and swallowed.

He pushed aside his plate and in case I missed it, repeated, "Paul, there was to be no temporal remuneration for any Jesuit professors." I was still at a loss as to the import of his latest contribution to my knowledge of Jesuit spirituality and scholarship. Father knew precisely where he was going.

"And you wonder why there's a faculty union at the University?" Father nodded to affirm the wisdom of his observation. He had moved from the sixteenth to the twentieth century, from Ignacio to University politics in little over an hour. He certainly knew how to cover Jesuit territory—even if greatly simplified for the likes of me.

"Would you like some more coffee?" Father asked. We rose together to refill our cups. The circling priests had dined and departed. He chortled as we returned to our table, "There's one more story I want to tell you. This will be a short one, I promise."

"I had a very good friend, a Jesuit priest also, who died a few years ago. He was frightened and sought solace from me as death approached. I tried to help him as he trembled on his deathbed and urged him to look to the love of the Lord and the Lord's forgiving embrace. His trembling continued unabated. I tried to reassure him of the peace he would find in God's kingdom but alas, with no success. 'Father, you don't understand,' my dying priest friend croaked, 'It's not the Lord of whom I'm afraid, it's St. Ignatius and the Jesuits.'"

With the delivery of the punch line, Father rose from the table. "It was good to get to know you. I enjoyed it. I'll walk you back out." I don't know how much better he knew me but I know we enjoyed our lunch together.

Father wasn't the only priest anxious with twists of joy to serve newly arrived non-Catholic deans tales of Jesuits. Joel, dean of the School of Law, and I had become friends during our opening months at the University. We had much in common: he was Jewish, as was I, well, sort of. He was a newcomer to Jesuit and Catholic education, as was I. He had arrived on campus the last day of July; I had arrived the first day of August. We had shared impressions, asked questions of one another, and laughed a lot as we were introduced to an academic world in which the Jesuit was king.

Unwittingly one afternoon, we found ourselves playing straight men to Father Jerome. We had arrived together for a Faculty Assembly meeting—a rare occasion at the University when professors and administrators, as often referred to as Labor and Management, met as a group. Joel and I mingled with professors and fellow deans until it was time to take our seats. Moments after we sat down, I leaned over to whisper something to Joel as we waited for the meeting to begin. Unfortunately, the ear to which I had gently directed my words was not that of Joel, it was that of portly Father Jerome. Some mystical power must have been present for Father to insert himself between the two of us without our knowledge. I apologized. Father laughed and extended a hand to Joel, then me. "My privilege, deans." His welcome to both of us was too warm; his smile too broad to suggest that his placement between us was accidental.

Father's reputation had preceded him. He was one of those Jesuits who oozed authority, a man of measured words, provocative questions and crisp-humor, all spiced with quotes from scripture. He turned to say something to Joel as I embarrassedly sat back after my previously misdirected words. His eyes darted back to me, then to Joel, then to me again. It was rare, I'm sure, that Father got the opportunity to simultaneously capture the attention of two deans, especially two deans not of Christian persuasion. His rich voice wove a web around the two of us.

"Do you realize there are no Jesuits in Hell?" Father rhetorically asked Joel before turning to ask the same question of me. Joel and I almost simultaneously gave the response of the straight man.

"No, Father. We didn't. Why are there no Jesuits in Hell?" I didn't have a clue as to the answer. I suspect neither did Joel, although we both knew there were enough priestly transgressions to justify assignment to stations down below. Father looked at me; Father looked at Joel. He waited the appropriate number of beats before he stung, timing second only to that of Jack Benny.

"The Devil long ago issued an edict that prohibited Jesuits from entering his domain. The reasoning was really quite understandable." Father's voice dropped to imitate the voice of the Devil, "This is one place where I will not tolerate the Jesuit's incessant asking of questions or telling others what to do." Father's reputation for straight-faced delivery of one-liners validated, he turned to the front of the room. The meeting was about to begin.

After only a few months on campus, I already had some sympathy with the Devil's edict: incessant questions of Jesuit officers could be maddening. As for the accuracy of Father's observation about Jesuits' banishment from Hell, I would leave that judgment to a Jesuit. Maybe Father Gregory could help.

The twinkle-in-eye, tongue-in-cheek, laugh-at-oneself humor of the Jesuit often was an antidote to the solemnity of the Church—or the tedium of some University formal events. I never appreciated this quality more than at Janet's and my first University Alumni dinner.

Few university events go on as long, or mean as little to attendees—save university officers hoping to receive financial pledges in return for recognition of alumni and proud families of recipients, as alumni award dinners. The University of San Francisco Alumni Awards Dinner at the Fairmont, grand dame of San Francisco hotels, was no exception.

Prelude to the annual, long evening of food, wine, and awards, priests splendid in their black suits and white collars mingled with University officers, professors, staff, and guests aglow in tuxedos and cocktail dress in the Fairmont reception lounge. Professional colleagues who seldom socialized with one another extended enthusiastic greetings, and deans small-talked with guests they would probably never see again. Students selected to serve as ushers, only the most photogenic and most personable, wandered through the crowd until it was time to announce the entry to the banquet room. With the opening of banquet room doors, students herded guests, as border collies herd sheep, into the ornate room.

Janet and I broke away from the flowing herd when we sighted the table that carried the same number as the card presented to us on arrival. Similarly numbered guests shortly joined us. Janet and I surveyed the room. We couldn't believe how little time it had taken to convert the churning reception to seated banqueters. One seat remained vacant at our table; given the hour, it was probably reserved for a guest who wouldn't be attending. We didn't know a soul at our table. We would need help if we were to survive the evening.

We simultaneously noticed Father Dominick trailing a final pulse of guests as they were guided into the banquet room. Salvation was in reach. I jumped from my seat to intercept him. I needed to capture this teller of tales and custodian of University mission, before he landed at another table.

"Father, won't you join us?"

"What a nice offer. To what do I owe the privilege of being asked to sit at the dean's table? And with his beautiful wife?" he added with a wink at Janet. "Just give me a moment to say hello to Father President."

I didn't tell him the table was neither "the dean's table" nor that Janet and I didn't know a soul at the table. And certainly not that my invitation stemmed from the need for relief from the long evening that awaited.

True to his word, it was only moments before Father returned. I pulled out his chair. He would be a buffer between seated strangers and us. Tonight, we would consider Father Dominic of pursed lips and wagging tongue our special guest. His lofty title, vice president for Mission, had never detracted from the pleasure he got from telling evocative tales.

Waiters snatched earlier placed appetizer plates moments after diners had settled; they dove over shoulders to retrieve entrée plates the moment plates emptied. Dessert plates were dealt like cards on the table on retrieval of the last entrée. Cards dealt, coffee cups filled, the formal program began.

Pro forma, award recipients bounced to the podium on invite. Testimonials were read, plaques were presented, and honoree words of gratitude to family and University were extended. Award recipients shared University memories probably meaningful to them and close friends, but probably meaningless to the hundred-plus banqueters. And the stories went on, and on, and on.

Father Dominic, Janet, and I exchanged glances. Where was the Master of Ceremonies with the hook to pull speakers off the platform? But with Father Dominic seated next to us and a bottle of Cabernet guarded from other guests, we would get through it. Ramblings of award recipients faded to background noise as Father's tales played on our private main stage.

"Let me tell you about this winter break's Caribbean cruise," Father didn't need any encouragement. His flock for a one-week Caribbean cruise had truly been an unholy one. With great relish, he expounded passenger peccadillos on rum punch sated evenings. "And Janet," he laughed, "my mornings were filled with morning-after confessions." Father may have been seated at "the dean's table" but Janet was his favorite.

Once confessions had been received, Father assured us that he reserved the afternoons for sunbathing. He closed his Caribbean tale with an assurance to Janet, "Despite all the debauchery around me, I had time to think of things spiritual as we sailed from port to port." We were distracted by Father's tales of the Jesuit Community spring retreats in alumni estates overlooking the Pacific with dinner pre-prandials in lush living rooms and soaks in infinity pools nestled in straw-colored rolling hills.

Just when we thought Dominic's inventory of tales was over, he launched into ecstatic remembrances of a retreat during the past summer at a Jesuit retreat in Oaxaca with native gourmet meals and infinite varieties of fine Mexican tequila. Our tales of summer travels \paled in comparison.

With the clattering retrieval of dessert plates and coffee cups by hotel staff, the evening was finally drawing to a close. Father Dominic took a last bite of strawberry shortcake and a final sip of coffee before an overzealous waiter pulled his plate from the table. He wiped whipped cream from his pursed lips and carefully placed the napkin on his lap and leaned toward Janet, face close to her as in telling a secret, or making a confession, and with eyes half shut, smile tightly stretched, *sotto voce* asked, "If this be poverty, I bet you're wondering what must be chastity?" Father Dominic didn't wait for an answer. He rose from the table and was quickly lost among the departing guests.

It wasn't only priests' anecdotes, formal ceremonies, or the bells of St. Ignatius that contributed to the Jesuit ambience of the University. Opportunities to partake in the Jesuit world were abundant. Few programs better articulated mission, history, challenges, and the humor of Jesuit presence than University symposiums and seminars.

Early one afternoon, seated peacefully alone in the Lone Mountain cafeteria having lunch, absorbed in a *San Francisco Chronicle* tale of the indulgences of Mayor Willie Brown, a tap on my shoulder jarred my escape from the office. It was "Godfather" Professor David. He had a knack for rising out of nowhere.

"Dean, are you going to this afternoon's Jesuit Symposium seminar, 'With Whom and About What Do They Talk'? It's at four o'clock. Will I see you there?"

"It's already on my calendar," I lied. Earlier in the week, I had considered attending, but this morning, when I noticed that my late afternoon calendar was open with no fog expected later in the day, I thought I'd leave work early. Why had I told Godfather that the event was on my calendar? I consoled myself reasoning that I might find it interesting. I couldn't resist being curious about what does go on behind the walls of the Jesuit Community. Do they talk about God? Do they talk about the Pope? Do they talk about the Church? Do they rehearse homilies? Or do they for the most part talk about University matters and share gossip about members of the University community like all of us? Perhaps, the seminar would provide some answers. And if the session didn't enlighten, I would still earn goodwill points from Jesuit officers for my attendance.

At 4:00 p.m., the heavily curtained, wood-paneled room was crowded. Front rows were filled with Catholics who took pride in the display of Catholicity: white-haired Caucasian men in priest's apparel and a smattering of nuns wearing habits—and Godfather David. Seated in the middle rows were practicing Catholics and church-going Protestants, including Professor Hubert. Low-profile Protestants, Jews, and skeptics curious about the Jesuit brand of Catholicism sat in rows at the rear of the room; here were seated most of the deans. Arrogant New York expatriate, Jewish Marin Sol, sat in the last row. His stiff posture shouted, "Show me." Godfather in the front rows was supplicant, Hubert in the middle was needy, and Sol holding up the rear was defiant. We sat together but apart, waiting for the program to begin.

Time-touched Father Anthony, the rotund and balding variety of Jesuit, shuffled to the podium. He carefully rested his paper on the platform in front of him. He wasn't ready to read from the manuscript until he informally provided the audience with a synopsis of things to come.

"I will be drawing parallels between the persecution suffered by Jesuits at the hands of others and that suffered by the Jews, the Irish, the Gypsies, or Roma. And I will talk a bit about the historical tensions between Rome and the Jesuits." This wasn't what I expected, but it could be interesting.

Godfather leaned forward in his front row seat; reference to Jews must have caught his attention. Professor Hubert sat up straight; tension between the Vatican and the Jesuits must have piqued his interest. Professor Sol's eyes fixed on Father Anthony, parallels between the persecution of Jews and Catholics were probably of particular interest. How could audience members, sacred or lay, not pay attention? If these were the issues about which Jesuits talked, it might be worth joining the conversation.

Once Father oriented the audience, he slowly adjusted his eyeglasses to rest mid-point on the bridge of his nose and turned attention to the manuscript before him. He regularly looked up over the top of his glasses as he read the text to gaze at the audience; he wanted to be sure that points had connected. Raptness of attendees confirmed, he would give a nod of appreciation and return to the written word. He knew how to work an audience.

We were captured by his tales of the suppression of Catholics in Europe and the United States, battles between the Vatican and the Jesuits, Jesuit sheltering of Jews during the Holocaust, and Catholic inclusion in Hitler's net of "inferiors" along with Jews and Roma. Father's scholarly, sobering message seduced the assembly in less than an hour. He could have recruited an army of Catholics, Protestants, Jews, Skeptics, and Agnostics from the gathering to join him in a march for social justice.

We didn't learn much that afternoon about what went on behind the walls of the Jesuit Community, or about what and with whom the Jesuits talked, but we did learn a great deal about the Jesuit's place in world history. I was glad Godfather had trapped me into attending.

Travails of the Church, title of the following month's symposium seminar, had caught my attention, for tales of Church travail and hypocrisy had peppered my growing up years. I had conspicuously placed the date and time for the meeting in my calendar on learning it's title. The title had also caught the attention of others; the room was filled to capacity, same seating pattern from front to rear present in the previous presentation: Jesuit, Catholic, Protestant, Jew, Agnostics and an Atheist or two.

Father George, the afternoon's speaker, was the lean and wiry variety of Jesuit. His words of introduction immediately caught the group's attention, "I would like to share with you some of the miscalculations and outright mistakes we have made in the name of the Lord." Fidgeting in the front rows, stillness in the middle rows, and rapt attention in the rear recorded the audience's level of religiosity and comfort.

"I would like to share some of the challenges faced by our pastors in developing countries." Fidgeting faded, stillness spread to the rear rows. It was less dangerous to catalogue transgressions in someone else's backyard far, far away when there was so much to talk about closer to home.

Anecdotes of well-intended but misguided efforts of priests and pastors in developing countries filled the hour. We were left with quite an inventory of miscalculations, indiscretions, arrogance, and just plain stupid mistakes. Father George's openness was refreshing. He closed his presentation with a stab at humor.

"Think of it, when people fall, more often than not, they fall forward. The nice thing is that when you get up, you realize you're one step ahead." He paused for a moment and then added, "When we fall, we get up, blame the Bishop, Cardinal, or Pope, and keep on going."

Father's final stab of humor fell short for many. While his closing comment brought wide smiles to those in the front rows, uncomfortable chortles were audible in the rear rows for priests hadn't always fallen forward. The "Blame it on the Bishop, Cardinal, or Pope" punch line, albeit in jest, was not sensitive to unfolding revelations of priests' sexual transgressions with children of their flock.

Whatever concerns an individual, religious or lay, might raise with issues treated in the Jesuit seminars and colloquia, there was little question that the Jesuit with *bon mot* and crafted script, mischievous smile, and glimmer in the eye knew how to market his product.

Eleven

School Divas

Was it the Bay Area lifestyle, California sunshine, shifting tec-tonic plates, that created so many divas on the School of Education faculty, I wondered. I suspect all of these West Coast elements contributed to their presence, but I had little doubt that the history of the University and the presence of the faculty union were the driving forces in the creation of so many divas on the School faculty.

The School harbored a cluster of professors who suffering from aggravated self-import didn't hesitate to share their import with whomever might listen—or declare war on those not sympathetic. There were others with religious or racial identities that led administrators to swoon or became apoplectic on the mention of their name, and some who emanated a professorial rockstar glow with student groupies following beatifically in their wake.

Divas Sister Katrina, affectionately known as Sister K and Sister Rachel, with her Cheshire smile, emanated a golden glow that was made all the more seductive by virtue of their straddling the academic–religious cusp. The *chutzpah* of wine-savvy Diva Sol, pronouncements of Godfather, and theatrics of Hubert during my first year at the University, paled when set against the charm, wiles, and influence of Divas Sister K and Sister Rachel with her Cheshire smile.

Sister K was Little Red Riding Hood with an Irish brogue; when she was good, she was very, very good. Within months of my arrival, Sister K as Director of Teacher Education, demonstrated how very, very good she could be. Jesuit Community priests, School of Education professors,

California State Department of Education officers, and I, all fell prey to her powers.

College program accreditation review experiences, whether as professor or dean, whether in New York or Boston, had left me with the impression that visitations of accreditation committees, regardless of university or program visited, give birth to out-of-ordinary behavior: presidents and provosts vow undying support for programs of which they know little, professors praise colleagues with whom they have seldom worked, faculty commend deans of whom they aren't necessarily fond, and students rally around professors despite reservations. Sister K's master casting and direction of players to perform in the School of Education Teacher Credential Program, California Commission for Teacher Education Accreditation Review, didn't change my impression of the accreditation ritual.

During my first week on campus, Zoe, my newly discovered captain of Deans' Office, staff had alerted me to a pending California Commission accreditation review. I knew little about the Commission, less about California accreditation standards, and nothing of the hoops we would need to pass through to secure Commission blessing. The more I learned of the challenge, the more inclined I was to ask for a year's extension for the visit. I would have to donate months to participate in a ritual designed to validate "what has been" rather than seek "what might be." I had been invited to the University to shepherd "what might be," not "what had been." I would plead the new dean's arrival from out of state and lack of familiarity with the California standards. That was until Sister K wove her web. After only a few meetings with Sister, with her green eyes and Irish brogue, I began to suspect that the only thing she couldn't do was sing *Somewhere Over the Rainbow*. She had been meeting, lunching, and wooing Commission members in Sacramento for at least a year before my arrival. She had memorized Commission Standards. She had secured the allegiance of University Arts and Science faculty as well as Education colleagues. After a second or third meeting with Sister in my office, I once again found myself prey to the seduction of the School Sisters.

"Dean, the visit will provide a chance for me to shine and for you to revel in the glow." How could I to say no to such an opportunity?

Sister's update on visit planning one autumn afternoon removed any self-doubt about my earlier capitulation.

"Dean, I've spoken with Father Jack. He has set up an account for me to hire an assistant." She drew me in with her Irish smile. "You know Father Jack can't say no to a pushy Sister."

I was delighted with Sister's success but wished she had told me of her meetings with Father. I understood she was Catholic and had a direct line to higher authorities, possibly the highest of all. But she was also a professor who reported to me, and I was dean who reported directly to the academic vice president. When I told Sister that I would have appreciated her touching base with me prior to meeting with Father Jack, she turned on her charm: blue-green eyes slowly blinked, warm smile broadened, and brogue thickened. Her voice became throaty; her Eartha Kitt purr soothed. She patted my forearm in the manner that my younger sister would rub a horse's nose before giving it a cube of sugar when I was a child. Sister held many cubes of sugar.

"Dean, come, come. Don't be upset. You know I can play Father Jack like a violin." There wasn't much I could say beyond "Full speed ahead." She had gotten much more from Father Jack than I could have ever.

Sister kept me up to date on visit preparations: School documents were complete; subject area specialists were actively involved; Arts and Science faculty were active contributors. Any doubt as to the preparation for the visit evaporated when she concluded a meeting with the information, "Dean, we've scheduled student rehearsals for testimony to State examiners next week. Would you like to attend?" I politely declined the invitation, indicating I had full confidence in her planning and the students' performances.

Any thought I might be in control of Sister's accreditation venture evaporated when I approved her request to treat professors with whom she had worked to dinner at an up-scale Sacramento Street restaurant to which I wasn't invited. Everything was relative. It was easy to justify expenditures requested by Sister K after my previous approval of the fine wine purchase for female professors at the request of Sister Rachel, her Sister on the cusp.

Sister's brogue became more pronounced, her pale blue-green eyes beseeched, her smile became more fetching, and her suit more tailored with the arrival of the Commission Site Visit Team to campus. All the actors in her credential validation play performed convincingly. Never had I witnessed a better production of the rites of accreditation. I remember the exact words of congratulations shared with me by the chair of the State Visit Team in the privacy of my office before his return to Sacramento.

"Dean, that Sister of yours is quite a crackerjack. She's developed a real apostolate of learning. You, she, and your faculty are to be commended."

I would have to do some homework on his "apostolate of learning" reference. I didn't recall that term being among Commission standards.

With the ritual of accreditation in the rearview mirror, I now had time to get to academic priorities. I was developing a better understanding of the fears and hopes of professors as well as strengths and weaknesses of individual programs. I was becoming sensitive to the waltz of Jesuits and the pulse of the Bay Area. It was the right time for a faculty "retreat." Strange title for an event designed to move an institution forward.

I hoped an overnight stay at a tailored, landscaped religious retreat on "the Peninsula" would provide a bucolic setting in which professors could forget tensions of University campus life and put aside conflicting personal agendas. Looking back, the two days on the peninsula represented something of a honeymoon in which the marriage was never consummated.

Professors enjoyed one another's company, the accommodations were comfortable, landscaped grounds were alluring, and professors left the retreat with a warm and fuzzy feeling of success and a draft mission statement confirming a marriage of ideas. When cars pulled out the second afternoon for their return to the City, there was no "Just Married" sign and throwing of rice but everyone was happy—almost everyone. I didn't see how we could do all things for all people, all of the time. On second thought, evidently, neither did professors. The Peninsula marriage was soon in trouble.

A few weeks after return to campus, I was pleased to be invited as guest to a School Faculty Association Meeting (terms of the *Collective Bargaining Agreement* only permit deans to attend faculty meetings at the invite of professors). The invitation signaled goodwill; we would be moving on. I was unprepared, however, for the diva theatrics that would bury efforts to convert Mission Statement words to deeds.

I sat quietly, albeit a little comfortable, in a corner of the room as "guest" at the invitation of the faculty over whom I presided. Only a few moments into the discussion of one of the Peninsula Retreat–approved recommendations, an increase in School programs to support Bay Area elementary and high school program development efforts, I found myself witness to war between humanities and basic research professors. Such wars are not uncommon in schools of education, but this afternoon, the performance of the diva generals contributed an added theatrical dimension.

Multi-ringed, multi-braceleted Professor Thomasina, warrior for basic research, wearing the carefully fitted suit of the statistician, stood in one corner of the academic ring. Professor Emilia, warrior for the Humanities, also wearing tailored suit, but with dashiki slung over shoulder, sat in the audience, not yet called to the ring.

Thomasina was finishing a review of recent articles on the positive impact of teaching reading to pre-kindergarten children with implications for how School professors might work with local schools. Her bracelets jangled as she gestured to emphasize points; her heavily jeweled hands reflected and discharged rays of sunlight from side windows of the Faculty Lounge as she dropped numbers to justify findings. I vividly remember the setting and the ambience but I don't remember the specific words or precise numbers, but her presentation went something like this.

"Seventeen hundred students participated in the Illinois study. Reading readiness was significantly higher for 94 percent of the sample at a .05 level of significance."

A laser beam of light shot from one of her rings as the sun again caught its movement.

"Two thousand six hundred and sixty-three students participated in the Tennessee study with 83 percent of the sample showing significant reading gains at a .05 level of significance."

A shrapnel of light from one of her bracelets bounced off the audience.

Professor Thomasina peppered professors with levels of significance, numbers of children, numbers of teachers, amounts of gain—and rays of light. She was oblivious to everything but the numbers and the sun-paled summaries of her PowerPoint presentation when a basso cry from the far corner of the room arrested the attack of numbers.

"ENOUGH." Professor Emilia rose from the huddled mass of professors seated around her. She grew taller and more imposing as she rose.

"Excuse me, excuse me," Emilia repeated to be sure that everyone had heard.

Assured of the attention of colleagues, she carved a path through seated professors to the front of the gathering. Colleagues sat silently. She entered the ring. Once she reached the desired vantage point, she stopped abruptly as if a piece of tape had been placed on the floor to mark the precise location for maximum effect. She slowly pirouetted to face the audience. She glared at Professor Thomasina. She didn't utter a word. Her eyes danced from Thomasina to the audience, audience to Thomasina. Save for the darting of her eyes, she could be mistaken for a regal statue as she stood silently in place. She held center stage. Emilia had commanded and received full attention from both camps. Professor Thomasina retreated to her corner.

The shaft of sunlight from the window now rested squarely on Emilia, as if to signal the coming of a message from on high. In soft basso, she broke the silence with her customary prelude to commentary, "My, my, my." She paused. Professors were still silent. They waited for the follow-up. Emilia stood frozen a few more moments. Appropriate number of moments passed.

"My, my, my," she encored and added, "such big numbers to describe such small children."

The gathered professors waited for more. There was to be no more. Emilia stood motionless. The room was still wrapped in silence. Emilia glanced from one side of the room to another, nodded affirmatively, and shared a smile of conquest. "Thank you," she concluded. That was it. Nothing else was said. She had made her point. There was no need for more words: eight little words said it all. Regally, slowly, she left the ring to return to her seat among Humanity colleagues. The voice of the humanities had spoken.

Thomasina stood alone in the vacuum left by Emilia's departure. She chirped "Thank you" to the faculty and chicken-stepped from the front of the room to a vacant chair in the midst of the gathering. Emilia now sat erect and silent in her seat. Murmurings of professors dissipated to silence. No one appeared to know where to go next. Sister Rachel, facilitator for the session, finally broke the tension.

"I thank you all for attending. I'll accept a motion to adjourn."

"I so move," murmured Thomasina. Professors leaped up from their seats. It was time to go. Small talk, as if nothing out of the ordinary had happened, rustled through the room as they drifted off to return to their offices. Godfather, among the last to leave the room, caught my attention. With a whimsical smile, he reminded me of words he had shared with me months ago: "Remember St. Jude?"

I was quickly learning that neither retreat pledges, professor assurances of support, nor Jesuit goodwill was a match for the power of divas. I needed to get to know the School's students better; I needed to change the metrics. I need to recruit them in the battle for change.

I had hosted several special events, spoken at many student orientation programs, met with student government representatives and occasionally with classes as a guest speaker at the invite of a professor during my first year at the University, but with the exception of occasional meetings with students on private grievances, I didn't know a great deal more about the student body than the information conveyed through statistics: age, occupation, level of education, program of admission, and number of credits accumulated. Only when one of my assistant deans called on me to resolve a gripe that couldn't be resolved, did I get a real sense of personal student concerns and challenges faced by the School. I needed to take the initiative if I were to insert them into the mix of decision-makers.

Invitations from my office for *Breakfast with the Dean* in the School's aptly named View Room were sent out to Graduate Student Council members. An informal breakfast, me alone with students on a fall Saturday morning before classes, I reasoned, might provide an opportunity to get a sense of who they were, their gripes, and what they wanted. And as a bonus, if I could insert them into the mix of decision-makers, perhaps they might aid as a catalyst for change.

San Francisco Bay was visible through the towering Jack Pine treetops. The downtown San Francisco skyline was profiled in the early morning sun. Eggs, bacon, and oatmeal steamed in silver holders; an aroma of bacon drifted through the room. Croissants and rolls nestled in a large linen napkin; a white linen tablecloth covered Formica tabletops, their classroom origin concealed to create an ersatz banquet table.

It was refreshing to be alone with students free from my desk in a comfortable setting. We engaged in small talk as we filled plates with selections from fruit trays, warming pans of eggs, bacon, and sausage, and poured coffee from a silver urn. This morning, there were no Labor–Management or professor–student divides. Plates filled, we slowly drifted to seats around our ornately set table.

I made a stab at humor and assured the students that this wasn't where administrators had breakfast every morning. There were a few gracious chuckles. From the lukewarm reception, I knew I'd be better off if I gave guests time to take full advantage of their breakfast choices free from dean humor.

Plates close to empty, it was time for me to get to the morning's agenda. I thanked the students for joining me at this early hour and assured them that I recognized many had classes to get to once our meeting was over, or previous plans, and assured them that I wouldn't take it personally if they had to leave early prior to what I hoped was my planned provocative open-ended observation planned to catch their attention.

"Sometimes I suspect the School's programs aren't much different from what they were ten years ago—and maybe longer." I waited for response. The opener caught the attention of a few, but there was silence. There was more interest in finishing up breakfast, or talking with neighbors. My attempt at provocation had been a bust. I threw a direct question.

"What changes would you like to see in the School?" Only one response would be needed for others to follow. Janet had always counseled me not to jump into the void on receiving silence after a question. I was relieved when a student bailed me out.

"Conflicts in scheduling don't permit me to take the courses I want."

Others quickly joined:

"Tuition is too high."

"I can never get to see my advisor."

"Dean, some of the courses are dated."

The responses didn't surprise me, but these were not the types of help I was seeking. I had posed a question hopefully that would generate responses more important than an inventory of the obvious. I didn't need to sponsor a breakfast to gather these insights. The volley of student complaints was of the variety voiced day after day, year after year, on campuses across the nation. I was sympathetic to their observations, but there were no clues as to how they might stimulate change.

First volley of responses over, there was a pause. This time, I wouldn't fill the silence with another question. I would wait until someone threw me a line I could build on. Michael, a community college instructor and athletic coach in quest of a doctoral degree, threw out a lifeline.

"How many of you have seen *Field of Dreams*?" he asked the gathering.

I didn't know where he was going, but I would wait see if his fellow students took the hook. They certainly hadn't taken mine. A few students nodded affirmatively, others garbled a response through sips of coffee or final bites of pastry. There were nibbles but no running with the line. I needed help. I repeated Michael's question for the group. It was Michael who bailed me out.

"Well," Michael beamed as he turned to me to share a moral from *Field of Dreams.*

"Build it, Dean, they will come." Alice who had been paying more attention to croissant and marmalade than the conversation asked, "Build what?"

Michael was on a metaphor role, "We need to build a new stadium, we need to create a new identity, we need to attract new players. Build it. Students will come."

Michael was either a baseball fan still hurting from San Francisco's debacle at the hands of Loma Prieta and the Oakland A's—or a movie buff. It was too bad that students like Michael were only temporary members of the University community. Like the Michaels (or Michelles) in universities across the country, he would pay tuition, collect credits, receive a diploma, and move on, while professors would collect their checks and remain. I could use a few more Michaels. Students began to run with Michael's *Field of Dreams* metaphor and pose questions worth pursuing:

"What does it mean to be a Jesuit and Catholic University?"

"Is the University's peace and social justice mission more than a mantra?"

"Do we have special responsibilities toward the less fortunate?"

"How can moral obligations and service roles connect to our academic goals?"

"Can students hold a job and be academically challenged at the same time?"

"How can courses be kept up to date?"

"How can the School help me?"

I wish I could have gotten my professors to devote their full energy to selfless, creative extended responses to questions of this order.

We didn't build any new programs, attract any new players, or build any new stadiums that morning, but the students were enthusiastic, the conversation was optimistic. We were working together as the morning unfolded. It was exciting. Before we adjourned, students to class or outside obligations, me to my office, we agreed to form a student task force to work with faculty and associate deans to accept the challenge of bringing the newly adapted School Mission Statement to life. We would follow up on responses triggered by Michael's *Field of Dreams.* All that remained for me to do was to capture the dreams, build a team, and draw an audience. No small charge but one well worth pursuing.

It had taken me two years, but the pieces were finally in place to permit me to focus on program development. I was beginning to understand what made a Jesuit a Jesuit and to appreciate the Jesuits' contribution to the ambience of University. I was getting a sense of the history that contributed to tension between Labor and Management. I was beginning to appreciate the fears that contributed to the growth and the staying power of the diva. And most University officers and professors were pleased with my efforts to strengthen the academic reputation of the School and make it a more comfortable environment in which to work and study. I was now ready to build my field of dreams. Until Father John announced his decision to step down as University President.

Twelve

Promise and Retreat

Reverberations from the of the announcement of the resigna-tion of Father President John I roiling through campus had barely calmed before names of selected Jesuit, faculty, and management representatives along with those of University trustees were announced to constitute a President Search Committee. Its charge: deliberate, pursue, and land a new University President. The promptness of Committee appointment tempted deans to suspect that there might have been a committee-in-waiting; we certainly weren't sure what had contributed to Father President's decision to retire or how committee members were selected. There was no doubt, however, that Jesuit warriors would lead the charge; and once a president was discovered in the bull rushes and blessed by these warriors, the candidate's name would be presented to the full Search Committee and University trustees for confirmation.

The Committee's mission was eased by the endangered species designation created by the diminishing pool of presidential-qualified Jesuits. The search was focused, short, and successful. The announcement of the new president's election was transmitted via email: *The Board of Trustees is proud to announce the appointment of Father John Schlegel, S.J., as the twenty-sixth president of the University of San Francisco. Father Schlegel currently serves as Provost at Marquette University and will be joining USF full time at the end of the current academic year. He will be on campus regularly prior to his relocation to San Francisco.*

White smoke rising over the Jesuit Community Residence to signal John II's appointment would have been so much more regal than an e-mail communication. But smoke, or no smoke, we had a new Father President.

University members swarmed, like worker bees on discovery of a queen bee with the announcement of the election of Father Schlegel as our new president. The common denominator: one administrator wanted to appear more important to the University mission than the next; one professor wanted to appear more worthy of scholarly recognition than the next. All wanted to be the first to catch the attention of the queen bee. Community members were sucked into a social and political vortex of self-aggrandizement. Vice presidents and deans regularly transmitted documents celebrating accomplishments to the Office of the President. Announcements belched forth from the Public Relations Office; Alumni and Dean of Student offices forwarded flyers celebrating special events. A few professors even forwarded mission-relevant or scholarly publications. We were all so self-congratulatory in the hope that Father President would notice us. To borrow words from the musical, *Hamilton,* the smash hit that opened on Broadway long after Father President had come and gone, "We all wanted to be in the room where it happens."

It wasn't very long after the email message of John II's appointment that I received a telephone call from Father Jack.

"Are you available to meet with Father Schlegel next Tuesday?" There was no need for me to check my calendar. Earlier appointments or meetings can always be rescheduled. It's not every day a dean gets the opportunity to converse with an incoming president. I would be there along with the other deans.

Tuesday arrived quickly. Deans pulled chairs to form a half-circle to huddle uncomfortably in the corner of a large conference room designed for grand meetings—certainly not for the small huddle we had created. We sat quietly awaiting Father President's arrival. It was only moments before our new leader entered and glided across a long stretch of floor to join us. A tall, lean, well-conditioned man, cloaked in black apparel with a pencil-straight stance and glide of stride, he reminded me of a Bolshoi Ballet

Cossack dancer. The tanning salon rust of his face accented his steel gray eyes, and carefully combed white hair framed a high forehead. In his crisp priestly garb, he slid into a chair left vacant for him. Back still straight as a pencil, clasped tan hands placed on lap, knees perpendicular to the floor, a confident, single word "Hello" danced from his mouth. We collectively mumbled, "Welcome."

Comfortably seated, Father continued, "I'm glad to be here. I've been a Provost and a professor and I look forward to working with you." His opening words might appear bland to an outsider but they were important to us. He had immediately drawn a line of distinction between his university experience and that of Father President John I. He, unlike John I, was experienced in the academic ways of universities. He wanted to be sure we knew it.

"Tell me. What are the major challenges you face?"

Saul, dean of the College of Arts and Sciences, true to form, led off. He wanted to be sure that John II appreciated that the liberal arts were the centerpiece of a Jesuit university; *ipso facto,* he was dean of the University's most important college. Dean Samuel immediately followed Saul's lead. His school had import of another type. He dropped names of influential University trustee graduates of the School of Management. *Ipso facto*, he was dean of the University's most important school for gift donors. And he couldn't help throw in his previous Stanford affiliation, a play for academic validation. Saul and Samuel were quick on the draw in the quest for presidential blessing. Other deans held back. There was time for us to more subtly share our importance to the University. We were wrong.

Conversation had just begun to get underway when Ingrid, the confident, carefully tailored assistant from the President's office, silently slipped into the room and slow-walked to John II's side. With a deferential "Excuse me" to the group, she whispered into Father's ear. There was a brief exchange of murmurs. With another "Excuse me" to the deans,

Ingrid silently exited, only to return in a few minutes. There were more murmurs between her and Father, before with another "Excuse me," she was off again. Father President was distracted. Saul and Samuel were frustrated. There had been no response from Father President to their opening comments. The rest of us were plain puzzled.

"Where were we?" Father asked.

Saul picked up the thread of conversation. Samuel sat poised to elaborate on Saul's elaboration. But Ingrid was back again. There was another round of whispers followed by an "Excuse me," this time from Father, as Ingrid departed one more time. We sat silently. What was going on between blond Ingrid and copper-tan Father? Father's veneer of control was chipping. He let us in on the conversations.

"There appears to be some confusion." We already sensed that. "The University has scheduled my press conference for 2:30 p.m. and my flight back to Minnesota is at one o'clock."

We were tempted to respond, "You ain't seen nothing yet," or "You'll need to get used to it," but empathy at this point would have served no purpose.

"I'm afraid I have to leave you to get this matter straightened out." His bronze plaster mask permitted only a painful smile. "There will be more opportunities for us to talk in the future."

Father rose and with a roller skate Cossack glide and one more "Excuse me," exited the conference room. Our introduction meeting with Father President was over. I couldn't help but think that after this morning's display of University planning, he must wonder whether all the president's men and all the president's women at this University could put the University back together again. That was the last we saw of Father until he was installed as president in the Fall.

There certainly didn't appear to be any second-guessing on Father President John II's decision to join the University as he spoke months later at the Fall Installation services in St. Ignatius Church and trumpeted to the gathered University community members and dignitaries, "The campus of the University should serve as a beacon on a hilltop," and conveyed the social service and multicultural goals he had set for his years as University President.

I wish I had known that September Installation morn, that the hilltop of which he was speaking was that from which my School would soon be evicted. I never expected that a handsome, expensively designed office complex would be carved out from my School's former home to house Father President and Father President's successors, supporting officials, and their staffs. I never suspected that the University beacon would shine from my former home on the hilltop.

True to his Installation words, *Pro urbe et universitate* carved in stone above the former central administration offices became more than an engraving; community service and multiculturalism became University mantras. The social justice theme of the Jesuit Community was celebrated. Father President was to be more than a king of bricks and mortar, of trees and flowers. More than a year after his arrival, he invited me to meet alone with him.

"Have a seat, dean," Father welcomed me to his office. There was no smile. With his gray eyes, ochre tan, and crisply ironed priest's apparel, he remained seated behind the barricade of his desk.

"How are things going with the School?" he asked.

I shared students' participation as interns in a Mission Affordable Housing Project and identified new collaborative programs with the San Francisco Public Schools, a project with a local Catholic elementary school serving largely Black lower income children, and professor collaborations with human service agencies. I also didn't miss the opportunity to inform him of higher academic admission standards established by the School.

His invitation signaled to me he must have already sensed a fit between School goals and the University mission.

"Paul, I'd like you to give me a proposal that builds on the School's outreach programs in the City. I want you to help extend service opportunities for University undergraduates and your School to work more closely with the College of Arts and Sciences. I wish he had asked earlier for my School to join him in his urban mission.

"John, I'll get you a proposal within a month," I replied.

We talked briefly about what he had in mind; I shared some thoughts I had in mind. There wasn't a need for extended discussion. He was pleased. I was pleased. This was the kind of challenge I was glad to confront. I had new leverage to pursue my urban priorities.

On return to my office, I did what deans have done forever: I appointed a faculty task force, including student membership, a by-product of my Dean's Student Breakfast, and scheduled private meetings with professors whose support would be important for the program. I included, "Update to President Proposal Request" as a regular agenda item for bi-weekly meetings with department chairpersons. I called a Special Meeting with chairpersons and proposed a follow-up School retreat. With anticipated chairperson and faculty approval, I expected a proposal would shortly be in Father President's hands. Pieces for a significant urban program were falling into place; a proposal was in the making. Or so I thought.

Chairpersons were seated one morning when I entered the paneled chapel, now conference room, in the renovated high school on Turk Street, the School's new home upon eviction from Lone Mountain. The agenda for this morning's meeting: School Response to the President's Proposal Request.

I was a few minutes late for my own meeting. When I entered the room, I immediately noticed that the seating arrangement of professors around the conference table was different than usual; colleagues who usually sat together were separated. Sister Rachel was perched at one end of the table. Professor Dante, pale predecessor as dean, sat at the other. Strategic end positions had been claimed by two of my divas.

A chair at mid-table was unoccupied, obviously left vacant for me. With a smile and "I'm sorry I'm late," I took my seat. Not a word was forthcoming from my colleagues. Something was awry.

"Dean," Sister Rachel finally broke the silence. Where was her beatific smile?

"Yes, Sister," I innocently responded.

"Dean," Sister repeated as her bifocals dropped to the tip of her nose and she peered over the rim at the gathered group, "I would like to add an item to this morning's agenda. It's a top priority matter and needs to be discussed before we talk about Father President's request and the materials you've shared with us."

I didn't have the foggiest idea from where she was coming—from wherever, it didn't bode well. Dante, from the other end of the table, steely eyes squinted, voice heavy with cold, added before Sister's last word fell, "And, Dean. If the problem isn't solved, there'll be no discussion of the President's request for an urban service proposal from the School." All eyes were focused on Dante. "None of us will be able to find a parking spot; none of us will be able to join you in developing a proposal."

I was caught in the cross fire of a Sister–Dante pincer attack. Sister's agenda request was a call to battle; Professor Dante's words were those of the enforcer. Other chairpersons didn't say a word. "Faculty Parking" had stolen my agenda. I quickly surrendered. I had to accept Sister's proposal for change of agenda. We would discuss specifics that precipitated the Sister–Dante attack before getting to the School proposal. Sister opened the salvo.

"Dean, when I arrived this morning at 7:30, University ground crew were painting out lines that had previously demarcated two parking spaces."

Fellow chairpersons were rapt. We were now talking serious stuff. "And I went outside again just before our meeting to check what was happening." She paused to maximize the impact of her discovery. "Dean, spaces previously designated for cars now contain bicycle stands with a sign, 'For bicycles only.'"

Professor Dante squinted a smile as Sister exclaimed the horror of it all. Dante's smile evolved to a sneer. It was his turn again.

"Dean, were you contacted about this change?"

"Nope." I shook my head.

"Why not? You've got to stay on top of things," he admonished.

"Yes," Sister softly echoed from the other end of the table. "You need to stay on top of things." There was no "dearie" in her admonishment. Chairpersons had me in full retreat. I was pinned down as the troops fired away.

"Public Safety doesn't enforce parking regulations."

"I can't get a spot after 9:00 a.m."

"I pay for parking and can't find a spot near the School."

"We're never told what's going on."

More than an hour later—so much for proposal discussion—the meeting came to an end. On departure, Dante wanted to make it clear that I understood the severity of the transgression.

"Dean, you know that removal of School parking spaces constitutes a change in working conditions. We might be forced to file a grievance." Clearly, no residual forgiveness or charity was evident in the former chapel.

I knew that parking trumped most other agenda items on urban campuses across the nation, but I should have been more forceful in getting my chairpersons back to the original agenda. I was no further along in developing a response to Father President's challenge than I had been before we met. I settled for chairperson's agreement to attend a second Special Meeting, one week later.

Parking tempers had calmed when we met the following week to discuss the proposal. There was reasonable consensus on program features, but chairpersons wanted the opportunity for all professors to be familiar with the document and follow-up plans before pledging their support and requested a morning "retreat," this time on campus rather than at a bucolic setting. I was skeptical about the "retreat" nomenclature for a single-morning, on-campus meeting, but the faculty needed to "buy in" to the proposal if it were to have any chance at success—and I was being held hostage by my chairpersons.

Sister proposed a qualified, senior doctoral student serve as facilitator for the meeting. Dante seconded the motion. If I were to serve as facilitator for the meeting, the Chairs reasoned that professors would feel jammed by Management; if I were to name a professor, they felt he or she would be cast as a shill for me. The power of the past to trump personal relationships was discouraging but if chairpersons so reasoned, I would go along. I didn't have much of a choice. The chairperson of the Counseling Department knew the perfect person; colleagues were pleased. I was worried.

Two weeks later, 9:30 a.m., professors milled with morning pastries, coffee cups in hand, in a large sterile meeting room tucked away among Lone Mountain classrooms as they waited for the event to begin. Fog-softened light drifted through the meeting room windows, creating a dreamlike atmosphere. Eleanor, the selected student facilitator emerged from the milling professors and ambled over to me.

"Hi, Dean. We've never formally met but I've heard a lot about you. I'm excited for the chance to work with your faculty."

Eleanor was a big woman. Heavy-rimmed tortoise-shell glasses added to the bulk of her round face. A white Catholic school blouse that would have looked better on a child restrained her upper torso. A long deep purple flannel skirt hung loosely over her ample hips. Fragrance of washing machine detergent wafted from her garments. Birkenstock sandals snuck out from beneath her billowing skirt. I knew judgements on appearance were dangerous, and politically inappropriate, but now I was really worried.

"Dean, is it about time to begin?" I was relieved.

With a soft, "I'm ready," I nodded "Yes," and Eleanor meandered back into the congregation of professors.

"Will you all form one large circle?" It was only moments before Eleanor's voice floated up from some placement in the congregation. She and I may have been ready to begin but no one paid any notice.

"Please form one large circle," she repeated, her school marm voice now ramped up several decibels. Professors begrudgingly drifted into an erratic circle. Eleanor rumbled from one side of the slowly forming circle to the other.

"Come on in, come on in," she beseeched the resistant flock. Once a circle of sorts emerged, she buoyantly and enthusiastically enunciated "Good Morning" in elementary school teacher talk, emphasis on crisp "G" and "M," as she slowly flowed to the center of the group.

"Good morning," professors sheepishly responded.

"Good Morning, say it as if you mean it," she bellowed.

"Good Morning," a few professors mumbled.

My face felt hot. I could feel perspiration in my armpits. Planted in the center of the ragged circle, Eleanor chirped brightly to the now silent participants, "We're all going to participate in a warm-up exercise." She looked in my direction. I tried to shrink back into a corner—to no avail. "Come on, Dean, join us." I reluctantly joined the circle. I was beyond pain. I tried to hide myself behind one of my professors as Eleanor pulled a ball of twine from her skirt pocket, the biggest skirt pocket I had ever seen.

"I'm going to roll this ball of twine to one of you," she informed the group now murmuring among one another. "When you receive the ball, you'll share something with the group that brings you joy. Hold the string that has unraveled from the ball as it traveled to you in one hand, the ball in the other. After sharing what brings you joy, roll the ball to someone else in the circle. Any questions?" There were none.

Unraveling of the morning began with the first roll of that ball. The thinning ball created a spider web of twine in the center of the circle as it rolled from professor to professor. I was transfixed by the pattern. I backed out of the circle. I didn't want to be the recipient of what remained of the now shapeless ball. I wouldn't have known what to say to my circled colleagues other than "I'm sorry." I now suspected how a fly must feel when caught in sticky silk filament spun by a spider. A fly in the web, however, would shortly be put out of its misery.

The seemingly endless warm-up over, Elizabeth with help from Sister presided over a large group discussion while I sat quietly among the professors, available, should there be questions of me. There were none. Professors just wanted the chance to air their concerns about the potential impact of the proposal on faculty load and decision-making authority of the College of Arts and Science in a collaborative program with the School of Education. There was little discussion of the substance of the proposal; there were few recommendations for changes. The meeting ended with slow, disinterested nods of support from professors.

Chairpersons meeting the next day at the scheduled follow-up meeting gave a quiet endorsement. "Have it proofread, send it to Father President, and let's see what happens," Dante directed.

None of us could have anticipated that almost simultaneously with the transmittal of our proposal to the Office of the President, Father President would be buffeted with a string of San Francisco surprises that would consume his time and take precedence over the review of the School's submittal. Nothing of substance ever emanated from our efforts. I couldn't help recall Godfather's periodic references to St. Jude.

Thirteen

City of Indulgences

Deans weren't even aware that there was a phone in the seminar room when it's staccato ringing brought conversation at a Council of Deans meeting to an abrupt halt. Discussion of student enrollment figures, tuition income, and budget projections would hold. Father Jack, presiding over the meeting, turned the attention to his assistant, Bede, and without a word, the request was transparent: "Please get it." His loyal assistant slowly rose from her seat to answer the call. We silently eavesdropped.

"Father, it's for you," Bede announced for all to hear. It was now Father's turn, obviously aggravated at the interruption, to rise from the table and take the previously inconspicuous phone from Bede. Any message that called Father away from the table must be important. We were sure his conversation would be far more interesting than the discussion of enrollment numbers.

"Uh huh, uh huh, uh huh. I'll tell Joel. Uh huh, uh huh." Father's deferential "uh huhs" signaled that he was talking to a superior. And there was only one superior on campus: Father President. Brief conversation over, Father firmly returned the receiver to the base and exclaimed for all to hear, It's those damn Sisters! They're back again."

"Damn Sisters," he muttered once more as returned to the table. We were curious but we were amused. That was quite a pair of exclamations from a priest about fellow Religious. With his second "Damn sisters," Father looked squarely at Joel, the quiet, calm dean of the Law School. Father sighed; Joel sighed. They were obviously more informed than the rest of us.

"Joel, please join me in the hall."

"Excuse me," Father apologized as he left the room, Joel in his wake. As Joel followed Father from the room, he looked back over his shoulder to the fellow deans and shook his head slowly in silent apology to colleagues for the mystery of his exit. Father returned in less than five minutes, without Joel. He took his seat at the table. and with a "Let's get back to our discussion," we returned to the landscape of enrollment figures, tuition income, and budget.

Father wasn't volunteering any attention on the "Damn Sisters" and we weren't ready to ask any questions. Full disclosure would need to wait. He rapidly moved us from one agenda item to the next. He was preoccupied; we were curious. We would need to follow-up later on our own. We adjourned well before the scheduled time.

I noticed a copy of the student newspaper, *The Fog Horn*, resting on a hallway chair as we left the room. The headline in bold type across the top of the first page read, "Sisters of Perpetual Indulgence Giving Out Condoms." Placed immediately beneath the headline, a photograph captured a statuesque nun with pronounced five o'clock shadow standing on the steps of the School of Law. If any of us had read the student newspaper prior to our Deans Meeting, we might have understood Father's "Damn Sisters" exclamation and Joel's dispatch.

Not so long ago, I had learned of the challenge condoms on campus present for this Catholic University, but I never anticipated nuns would take the offense in University condom wars. I couldn't wait to call Joel when I returned to my office.

"Joel, what are you and Father's beloved Sisters up to?" I asked the minute I got to my desk. He didn't appreciate my humor. That wasn't like Joel. He must be up to his neck in perpetual indulgence. He brought me up-to-date.

"Our Student Council passed a resolution that claims that the University in seeking to deny Sisters of Perpetual Indulgence access to campus, and the right to distribute condoms violates constitutional freedoms of speech and assembly." He laughed as he added, "They might as well have cited religious and gender preference violations while they were at it."

Joel had more to tell. "A meeting with Father President is scheduled for later this afternoon. *The San Francisco Chronicle* plans to follow-up on the *Foghorn* story. I'm meeting with the Law School Student Council this evening."

One street theater performance had tossed the dean of the School of Law into a mix of issues that could keep U.S. Supreme Court members busy for quite a while. I was glad I dropped out of law school in New York many years ago after only one day of attendance. The Joels of the world could far better handle questions of constitutionality implicit in conflicts between the Church, the University, and the Sisters of Perpetual Indulgence generated by the Sisters' theatrical production than I.

The heady mix of drag queens and condom distribution resting on a bed of Church dogma was irresistible to the press; its power to distract deans and presidents from their academic charge was great. Only in San Francisco on a Catholic university campus would gender-free men with an affinity for wearing nuns' habits garner such press.

I'm sure Joel drew little comfort from knowing that his fellow deans would be looking over his shoulder enjoying some good laughs as the drama unfolded—even if they had to save their mirth for private moments.

When as a nightcap to his condom dealing Sisters, I learned that Father President had to cope with the discovery that one of his assistant vice presidents had a thriving side career as a porno star, I suspected the School's proposal might have fallen prey to competing time demands on Father President. San Francisco was truly a city of indulgences.

Tab was pleasant, well-dressed, and outgoing. He was also a University officer and a regular morning visitor to the Koret Health Center when John II took office. As I would dress from my early morning Master Swimmer transition to University Dean it was impossible not to witness Tab's performance as he prepared for transition from early morning workout at Koret to University Assistant Vice President. He would slowly parade from locker to distant scale, towel over shoulder, nipple rings, and six-pack abdomen on display. Weight once confirmed, he would about-face, take a long loving look at himself in a mirror and slowly amble back to his locker to dress for VP responsibilities. I never suspected that his Koret routine could have served as a movie trailer for his extra-University film work.

At a *Magic Flute* lunch conversation with space czar Vincent, my University "Deep Throat" and now friend, I learned awareness of Tab's anatomical features went far beyond the confines of the Koret locker room. Tab held campus-wide recognition as a porno star with films available in now-extinct video store triple X backrooms with pirated copies in University student dormitories.

Our meal finished, Vincent and I were relaxed as we sipped our glasses of chardonnay and most diners had left the courtyard.

"Paul, let me tell you the story of Father President and Tab." Vincent was looking forward to this moment. He loved storytelling. *Sotto Voce,* careful to shield words from any remaining diners, he began.

"Father President faces quite a dilemma: what to do with the discovery that an officer in his administration is a porno star?"

Without much thought, I casually responded, "It seems pretty straightforward. Three words: 'You are fired,' would seem to resolve the problem. Tab's film career shouldn't pose too great a dilemma for Father." I was so naïve.

Vincent continued, "When Father President learned about Tab's film appearances, he called him into his office to inform him that he had received reports of his porno career from students. Tab showed no remorse.

In fact, he was proud of his film success. And he was well prepared for his meeting with Father President."

Vincent's demeanor changed as he conjectured Tab's response to Father President's complaint. He assumed the part as an actor cast to play Tab. I was worried the enthusiasm of his performance might carry over to a far table.

"'Father President, my roles in the films were performed when I wasn't on duty at the University. The Bill of Rights guarantees freedom of expression, and film is a legitimate form of such expression.'"

Vincent paused to conjecture that Father must have been taken aback by Tab's lack of contriteness. He chortled as he returned to his roles as *raconteur* and porno star.

"'Father, there were no University pennants on the walls, no University tattoos on appendages, no involvement of University students, no references to any University affiliation. I have the right to pursue a film career separate from my University assignment.'"

Vincent, now playing the part of *raconteur*, inserted an aside direction, "Tab is about to up the ante." Back to the role of Tab, he continued,

"'If you fire me from the University on the basis of my acting in porno films, I will sue the University for violation of my rights of free speech. While I'm at it, I will claim that as a gay man, I'm a victim of gender discrimination and sexual harassment.'"

Raconteur Vincent delivered the final line, crow's feet lines emanating from his laughing eyes. "Case rests." The lunch show was over.

Tab's case presented a conundrum. If Tab remained at the University, there was little question that his student fan base would grow and University whispers would go public. If he sued, the San Francisco community, the Jesuit Community, University trustees, and the Catholic Church would all be caught up in a cyclone of verbiage. *Chronicle* headlines, press releases, and very possibly costly litigation would swirl. And with the unfolding tales of priestly sexual impropriety carried in newspapers across the country, front-page coverage of the story of Tab and Father John II in San Francisco newspapers might lead to AP coverage. A potential lead sentence to an article, "*The action takes place in a Catholic and Jesuit University in the City of San Francisco*," would provide all the spice necessary to attract a national audience.

John II well played the cards with which he was dealt. Tab was given a special assignment at the University, an all too familiar administrative remedy for wayward Catholics, and I understand that he continued to receive a University paycheck for a while before his name disappeared from University personnel rosters and he silently faded into the larger San Francisco community. There are a few cities other than San Francisco in which the tale could have played out as richly.

Sacred-secular tensions faded with the movement of Sisters of Perpetual Indulgence to another location and the retreat of Tab into the heart of the City. It wasn't too long, however, before tension of another order reminded the deans they were members of a Catholic and Jesuit academic community.

Father President John II and Father Jack were seated center stage as deans straggled into the room for a Council of Deans meeting. Agenda: Undergraduate General Education Requirements. Deans had proposed curriculum changes at a previous Council meeting that would incorporate objectives currently included in the required religion courses for undergraduates into the redesigned humanity courses. We were aware that our recommendations dealt with a sensitive issue at the core of the University's religious mission and had asked Father Jack to share our recommendations with Father President before we took formal action. We weren't surprised when Father President asked to meet with us. With apologies to the late Edward Albee, we never suspected that our meeting with Father President would see us cast as guests in a game of *Get the Deans*.

Father Jack and Father President had arrived in the meeting room and were seated together at the head of the table before we entered. There were no nods of welcome as we individually drifted into the room. Furtive looks were passed from one dean to another as each of us took our seat. The silence was suffocating. There was no question about who held the power.

All deans finally present, Father Jack opened the meeting, "Father President, the deans have discussed at some length a proposal for a change in student General Education requirements and recommended topics currently covered in discrete required religion courses be folded into revised humanities courses. They feel the proposed changes will provide undergraduates greater flexibility in their programs and relate the study of religion more effectively to the study of humanities. They also believe that increased program flexibility brought about by the change will make the University more attractive to incoming freshmen and transfer students."

Father Jack had done a good job of summarizing our earlier discussion. He also evidently knew what was to follow his opening prologue. We didn't. He turned toward Father President and delivered a line clearly crafted long before this morning's meeting.

"Father, share concerns with the deans that you shared with me." Father President's uptake was immediate. His message was unambiguous.

"This is a Catholic institution. The current undergraduate requirement for religious study is consistent with the University's mission. Neither the trustees nor I could assent to the recommendations you discussed."

Now we knew why Father President had asked to join the Council meeting. Now we knew why Father Jack had delivered his lines as if drawn from a teleprompter. For all of his support of deans, Father Jack was also an emissary for Father President.

"Is there additional information you wish to share with me or Father Jack?" Father President dared, looking directly at us.

We reiterated our support for the University mission and elaborated on the academic program points shared by Father Jack. We confirmed our sensitivity to the place of humanities and religion in a Jesuit University. And we stressed the potential appeal of the new curriculum for prospective freshmen and transfer students currently squeezed into a Procrustean bed of University undergraduate requirements.

Father President sat silently, a visible pulse above his jawbone being the only movement in his frozen face as we spoke. We would have had more success selling popcorn at a movie house than ideas in this hothouse.

Our thoughts shared, Father President rose with a "Thank you" and glided toward the door without a word. He stopped abruptly at the doorframe and turned back to the group. He looked Father Jack in the eye—we were no longer part of the discussion and turned to depart the room.

The proposal never made it past Father Jack. It never made it to Father President—and it never made it to the Board of Trustees.

Aftertaste left by the chastisement by Father President at our perceived stray from the University's religious roots was shortly to be removed by laughter that I derived from a well-intended celebration, I am sure, of Father's University multicultural mission.

San Francisco celebrates its multicultural population every chance it gets: Cinquo deMayo, Gay Pride Day, Cesar Chavez Day, Chinese New Year. The University's celebration of multiculturalism, however, wasn't limited to City-declared days of recognition. Under Father John II's flag of multiculturalism, the University sponsored its own Multicultural Services Day. A pig barbecue, for reasons I never understood, was the centerpiece for this year's University celebration of its private holiday.

Fire engine siren screams penetrated my office as I tried to continue a phone conversation. When the bleat of car horns outside my window joined the symphony and I could hear the screech of metal on metal as staff raised windows, I apologized to the caller and hung up the phone. I had to see what was going on. The School's street-side location brought us closer to City life, but today's excitement had little to do with urban identity. Talk of passers-by on the street intruded through open windows in the outer office.

Captain Zoe panted as she entered my office, "Dean, Dean, smoke is rolling down the hill." She was out of breath having just returned from a run down the hallway to the School's hillside entrance to find out what all the commotion was about. "Come with me. Come with me."

We arrived in time to hear the whining of additional sirens as two fire trucks roared off Turk Street. They wound up the steep and winding driveway to Father President's kingdom above us on the hilltop. A haze of thick blue-gray smoke blanketed the hillside and swallowed the red trucks as sirens haltingly wound down. There was silence for only a moment before muddled voices and raucous laughter penetrated the acrid haze. Then like a stream of disturbed multicolored carpenter ants, young men in Hawaiian shirts, closely followed by men and women in U.S. Army fatigues erupted from the haze of smoke and flowed down the hillside. The Hawaiian-shirted students and fatigue-clothed ROTC soldiers-to-be scattered in every direction as they approached street level. The smoke, colors, and bustle reminded me of the final burst of color and cheer at the conclusion of July 4th Boston Symphony celebrations by the Charles. The only thing missing was the 1812 Overture.

I felt the need to say something intelligent to puzzled staff and students who had now gathered around me, but I didn't have the faintest idea of what was going on. I couldn't stand and gape, fascinating as events might be. With a whisper to Zoe, I left for my office to call Father Jack. Maybe he could help. He wasn't in the office but I reached his assistant, Bede.

She interrupted before I could finish my first sentence, "Paul, we know. We know. We're getting calls from community residents. We're getting calls from students in the dorm—and even Father President was in our office just a few minutes ago."

"Bede, can you give me just a brief idea of what's happening so I can tell my staff and students something," I implored. She laughed.

"Paul, try to keep a straight face when you tell them the Vice-President for Student Affairs sponsored a pig roast for students to celebrate Multicultural Services Day."

"A pig roast for Multicultural Services Day?" I quizzingly responded. "I'm missing something."

"I'm just a messenger," Bede laughed, and paused before she continued, "Monica forgot a few things. She didn't get a permit from the fire department. She didn't inform the ROTC Office in whose backyard the pit would be dug. She didn't tell Father President. And, of course, nobody told the neighbors that there would be a barbecue."

I chuckled before pleading, "Bede, give me some help. How do I share this info in twenty-five words or less with my staff and students?"

"That's why we named you dean, Paul," she replied. She had the final laugh.

Fourteen

Season's Greetings

The fragrance of pine boughs greeted me as I opened our Broderick Street front door. The bouquet of hallway pine awakened memories of "back East" winter holidays. It was good to get home. The University's early Christmas party had been festive, but too true to the recipe of countless university food service holiday parties for me to linger. Successfully spearing my quota of shrimp in the expanding queue of toothpick shrimpers, I had briefly milled with colleagues, glass of eggnog in hand, extending "Happy Holidays" wishes, careful to reserve "Merry Christmas" greetings to priests, before I made an early exit.

"You've got some mail from the president's office. I brought it upstairs," Janet shouted down the stairwell as I entered the foyer of our house.

"It's probably an invite to some black-tie event to which we don't want to go," I mumbled as I climbed the stairs to our second-floor living room. Christmas season in San Francisco was prime time for black-tie extravagances of every variety. John II and City society basked in such events. I opened the envelope and pulled out a card: a white dove with the greeting *Shalom* drifting across a pale blue sky greeted me.

"Hon, take a look at this." Beneath the printed "Happy Chanukah" message carried on the flip side to the card's cover, there was a handwritten note from Father President written in medical doctor script. "Best to you and Janet at this special time of year."

"That's nice—that's thoughtful," Janet smiled before she added, "Is it a first for you?" It wasn't, but beyond the Chanukah cards I had received from Janet and her parents, it probably was only the second or third time I had received such greetings.

"You should thank John," Janet added more seriously. She was right. I probably should say something to Father President even if I rarely celebrated Chanukah.

"Should I also tell Father President that other than the cards I've gotten from you and your parents, this is the first Chanukah card I've ever received?" I flippantly responded.

"That's a good question." Janet chuckled as she left the living room. I needed help. At this moment, it wasn't going to come from her.

We talked a bit about John's card at dinner that night and agreed that I should acknowledge his thoughtfulness and maybe tell him a little about my religious background. When Janet asked me a few weeks later whether I had spoken with Father and thanked him for the card, I admitted that I had never gotten around to it and elaborated that there was no real need for me to meet with him.

"Most officers, if not all, know I'm not Catholic; many also know I'm not Protestant. Therefore, I'm sure most, including Father President, conclude, I'm Jewish."

Janet wasn't satisfied with my response. I had provided a poor excuse rather than rationale for not talking with Father President.

When a Chanukah card from Father President arrived the following December, by default, I had made a decision. After no "thanks" from me or conversation the previous year, I couldn't now tell Father President that I hadn't celebrated Chanukah until after Janet and I were married. Year three, the card came. Year four, the card came . . .

On the announcement that Father President would be leaving the University to assume the presidency at another university some years later, I was tempted to confess to him my tale of Chanukah and his cards. He might have gotten a laugh from it. But he might not have been happy that after silently receiving his cards for close to a decade, I had waited until he was prepared to leave to tell him that I was only sort of Jewish. Once Father departed for his Midwest presidency, leaving what he believed to be his Chanukah-celebrating dean behind, the cards no longer came. My silence really didn't make much of a difference after all.

Christmas always, Chanukah sometimes, are special times on University campuses: classrooms are empty, holiday parties are over, faculty offices are vacant, and hallways are silent. Professors and students have retreated for family visits or vacation getaways.

This winter was no different. December's crystal clear, black-blue early night descended on the city as I walked from my Broderick Street home to the University. Ornament-clad trees, and an occasional Menorah, glowed behind resident windows as dusk wrapped holiday homes.

Janet was in Florida to celebrate Chanukah with her family. I would use my free time to catch up on office paperwork. It would be nice to be able to leave thoughts of the University behind when I escaped to meet post-Florida Janet in Boston and then drive with her to our Vermont home for the holidays.

I was making progress in reducing the paper piles on my desk. Only the review of department chairpersons' course schedules for spring term remained. There was one hitch: an asterisk was placed on the schedule coversheet next to the name of one of the chairpersons. A note from Associate Dean Parsa paper-clipped to the sheet assured me that Hermione, chairperson with asterisk, would submit her department's schedule separately before she left for the holidays. I double-checked the correspondence on my desk; Hermione's schedule was nowhere to be found.

I would call her at home. Maybe I could catch her even if Christmas was only a few days away. I was lucky. Apologetically she told me in the rush of pulling things together before she left for the holidays that she had forgotten to drop her department's course schedule off in my office. "It's sitting on my desk top and you should have no problem seeing it." I thanked

Hermione and wished her a merry Christmas. I would retrieve the document and soon be off.

The quiet darkness of the corridor bordering professor offices that ran the length of the floor above mine was soothing. The turn of my key, the mousetrap slap of the cylinder in the front door lock, cut the silence. Ambient light from holiday-ready homes across Turk Street shed a pale light through the glass panel doors and professor offices that faced the street. This Friday before Christmas, not a creature was stirring . . . well, almost.

Searching for a light switch, I played my hands over the wall adjoining the entryway. Before I could locate the panel, I heard soft voices and a giggle from one of the offices.

"Hello," I inquired quizzically. "Hello, is anyone there?" I repeated. There were no more soft voices, no more giggles.

"Hello?" I repeated a third time and started to walk down the corridor. There was the soft sound of a gently closing door at the far end of the strip of offices. It was now silent. I about-faced and returned to Hermione's office. The materials were where she said they would be. I had the information I needed to finish up.

The soft voices, giggles, and a gently closing door just heard on my class schedule retrieval triggered memories of a Christmas-time experience while I was dean in Boston years ago. As in San Francisco, most professors had left the university for the holidays. On entering a suite of darkened offices to retrieve a professor friend's attaché case he had forgotten at the office, I had noticed an office in which a faint light glowed behind its frosted glass divider. On approaching to see whether a light had inadvertently been left on, there through a half-open door, stood Professor Adam behind his desk, shirt half-tucked in, buttons and button-hole misaligned, pot belly peeking through openings.

"I'm finishing up some work, Dean," he stuttered. In a corner of his office, a pair of ballet slippers lay on the floor. Adam appeared to be alone but . . . I knew he wasn't a dance aficionado, slippers or no slippers. I remember the only words I could muster were, "Excuse me. Have a good holiday," before I sheepishly turned and left the suite.

I was glad I neither saw an Adam, nor ballerina slippers in the string of professors' offices upstairs in San Francisco. But I would have enjoyed sharing a San Francisco Adam story this Christmas with my friends back East.

Holidays in the snow-covered Green Mountains, fragrance of spruce and balsam, time with my children, families and friends, and alone time with Janet free from university conversation, provided a much-needed change of pace. It was not until it was time to start pulling things together to return to San Francisco that thoughts of University challenges intruded on the nights of sound sleep.

A Deans' Council Meeting on my post-Christmas return to the University after my Vermont escape prompted me to consider that there might be a greater power that looks over things Jesuit. Following my Christmas tour of the darkened corridor of Hermione's colleagues, was it a coincidence that the meeting had a single agenda item: faculty–student relationships? Secular irony or Jesuit power, the agenda provided quite a postscript to my December tour and generated interesting conversation.

Labor Relations VP Fireplug Al wrapped in an Oxford button-down pink shirt, too tight a suit, and a red tie that shouted "look at me" sat quietly next to Father Yves, University counsel, in full clerical dress, as we entered the room. Father Jack had appointed Fireplug Al and Father Yves as discussion facilitators. He must have reasoned that a duet of a Labor/Management and Legal/Godly players were best suited to facilitate a discussion of student–faculty relations of extra-curricular personal nature.

Al opened the meeting with bravado and an air of confidence reserved for people who find truth either in the words of the Bible or the text of the *University Collective Bargaining Agreement.* Citing section and paragraph in the manner a priest cites scripture, he held up the little green booklet for all to see that contained the *University–Faculty Association Collective Bargaining Agreement* and recited, "The *Collective Bargaining Agreement* prohibits, and here I quote 'romantic relationships between faculty and students.'"

Father Yves, University counsel, religious and legal credentials in place, picked up where Al left off and reminded us, "Deans carry both a moral and a legal responsibility to assure that every step has been taken to prevent romantic relationships between professors and students." Yves's counsel provided, Al returned to the Management–Labor scripture he had just shared.

"Let me point out, the article that cites romantic relationships between faculty and students is distinct from, and supplementary to, any article that addresses the topic of sexual harassment." Yves was back in, "And may I add, any legal statute in the Commonwealth of California."

Al and Yves had quite a duet going. Fireplug Al was talking *Agreement;* Father Yves was talking law. Father Jack sat silently as his guardians of morality, law, and *Agreement* steered the meeting. I'm not sure Father appreciated the irony of a womanizing University Labor officer and a gay Jesuit University attorney in a relationship with a Jesuit professor serving as moderators for today's consideration of romantic relationships. The deans certainly did.

The admonitions of our twin guardians of morality failed to immediately generate discussion. It was difficult to tell whether we were being admonished or asked for advice. When you're not sure of the message that's being delivered, it's difficult to identify appropriate questions or provide germane observations. Saul, never hesitant to speak and whose marriage to his wife grew out of a classroom romantic relationship prior to his arrival at the University, finally broke the silence.

"How do we differentiate between sexual and romantic relationships?"

Saul was stirring up the waters. He knew, I'm sure, that was the last question our unlikely twin navigators of sexual and romantic seas would have chosen as a catalyst to generate discussion. Yves looked at Al; Al shrugged his shoulders. They didn't know how to handle the question. With Saul's opener, a game plan was born. Deans were ready to pose questions to discomfort our leaders of contract and morality.

"Do we proceed differently if the graduate student is also a staff member?" Samuel, recently married to one of his staff, a former graduate student, asked.

"Does the article apply to consenting adults?" I followed. More than one of my professors had romanced, married, and even divorced their adult students.

"Is romance limited to male-female relationships?" Dean Phillip of Nursing directed to Yves, his turquoise ring slowly tapping the table.

I wish our leaders had picked up on Saul's original question. I couldn't let it be forgotten and couldn't resist playing with words, "Are you asking us to become romance detectives?" Aware that if the reply was affirmative, I would need to sleuth the after-class behavior of so many of my professors that I would have little time to pursue things academic.

Conversation continued as Fireplug Al, Father Yves, and deans played out their parts, all aware of the ironies underlying the dialogues. And we never talked about sexual harassment. It was quite a morning.

I felt sorry for Father Jack who had sat silently at the table, unaware of the not-so-hidden agenda playing out in the deans' interaction with Al and Yves. He had asked the two of them to chair the meeting in the hope of assisting us to monitor the human condition. He couldn't have known that all of the participants in the discussion at one time or another in their lives could have been judged as less than paragons of sexual or romantic virtue. For certain, he wasn't familiar with my recollection of the story of Adam and the ballerina slippers triggered by my walk down the darkened halls of my School only weeks earlier.

Fifteen
Dueling Principles

It was just after 8:00 a.m. when the light on my phone's base signaling "private line" intruded on an early morning office paper shuffling. It was too early for professors to be at the University. It must be Janet. When I had rushed off to work from home, our conversation about dinner plans with friends for the evening had been left unfinished.

"Hi, Hon," I distractedly mumbled as I picked up the receiver. There was no reciprocating "Hi, Hon."

"Paul, this is John." I should have learned by now to wait for a caller to identify him or herself before making assumptions about who is at the other end of the line. Father President found no humor in my "Hi Hon" greeting. On the lighter side, I'm sure this was the first time he had received such a salutation from one of his deans. There was to be no lighter side.

"Paul, I need to talk to you about your latest faculty appointment recommendation." I had an idea of what might be on his mind but I waited for him to continue. I wasn't going to risk another "Hi, Hon" miscalculation.

"Yes, Father," I responded deferentially.

"I know it's your business and I shouldn't be intruding but . . ." I was tempted to interrupt Father and affirm the wisdom of his observation but thought better of it. He continued, "I'm not sure you were totally honest with Father Jack in your recommendation for the appointment of Rebecca Feinstein."

I was caught off guard. I was used to a president's questions about a professor candidate's academic credentials; Boston University's Silber or one of his minions from time-to-time questioned forwarded appointment recommendations but to be questioned on honesty with a superior officer was a first.

"John, I need more information. Help me." I bought time. I needed to find a way to respond to his indictment without transforming our conversation to confrontation.

"Paul, it's my understanding that O'Sullivan was the first choice of the Search Committee." Father was right but . . . I had recommended an accomplished Berkeley PhD graduate, Rebecca Feinstein, already an assistant professor at another university, rather than one of our own doctoral candidates, Kevin O'Sullivan. I wasn't totally surprised at Father President's interest in the recommendation. For the past several months, Father Francis, Jesuit Community member and professor in my School, also Doctoral adviser for Kevin, had made a point to keep me updated on Kevin's progress toward finishing his studies and his hope to join our faculty. Father Francis was likely the Iago whispering in the ear of the president.

"John, let me share the information with you that I shared with Father Jack," I responded. His silence was a signal to proceed.

"Names of two finalists for the position were provided to me by the School Search Committee; one already an assistant professor at New Mexico University; the other a doctoral student currently completing his degree with us."

I summarized qualifications of the two finalists and shared in detail a conversation I had with Father Jack even before I had transmitted my formal recommendation to him, including sharing with him the whisper and wink of the Search Committee Chair, "We really like O' Sullivan," as she left my office consultation on the Committee's recommendation.

There was silence on the other end of the line. Something else must be on John's mind. I'm sure he knew which candidate was Jewish and which was Catholic. I hoped that wasn't what was driving his interrogation. I'm sure he also knew University policy calls for faculty search committees to submit two nominees for appointment to a dean without indication of preference with the dean authorized to forward the name of the candidate he or she feels best qualified of the two to fill the position.

"Paul," Father finally responded, "it's my understanding that you were not totally honest with Father Jack." He was back to the question of my honesty. The tenor of our discussion changed. I'm proud I didn't respond to Father President's bait with a wild thrashing of the waters. I slowly and carefully repeated the steps I had taken in forwarding Feinstein's recommendation, including details of my conversation with Father Jack. I also reminded Father President of O' Sullivan's close friendship with Father Francis. I bordered on crossing the line between discussion and confrontation when I succumbed to the temptation to throw in a reminder of his concern about the University appointing its own graduates to faculty positions. Then I crossed the line.

"John, you may disagree with me on my appointment recommendation, but you should have spoken with Jack before calling me."

Father couldn't let the conversation end with one of his deans providing unsolicited advice. His somber voice absorbed anger, "Paul, I appreciate your sharing the qualifications of the two candidates with me but you know there is also such a thing as University mission." This time I took the bait.

"John, I'm well aware of the importance of the University's Jesuit mission." I let the words sink in and added, "I'm also aware of its traditional academic mission."

I don't remember whether it was Father President or I who hung up first. But I remember I was angry. I was more angered by Father questioning my honesty on the basis of information from an anonymous individual than questioning my recommendation. Too many family friends while I was in high school during the McCarthy years had been permanently scarred by unsubstantiated charges from unnamed individuals to let that transgression go unnoticed. Father President John was no Joseph McCarthy, but action on the basis of information provided by unidentified individuals is dangerous, whether in a university or the halls of Congress.

The day had barely begun and I already needed to let off steam. "I called Janet and shared the essence of my discussion with Father President including my "Hi, Hon" greeting. We both laughed at the salutation; we both worried over the substance. But I felt better. Never underestimate the healing power of a loving wife. We both agreed we would need to talk later at some length.

Unwittingly, Janet had provided a remedy for my president-induced morning angst when she followed up on the unfinished dinner plan's discussion that had preceded my rush off to the office. We would be having dinner with friends that evening at a bistro in Portrero Hill, formerly a blue collar and artists' neighborhood, currently under siege by gentrification. A Portrero Hill bistro was a perfect choice. I needed a real change of pace—as far away from the University as possible. I looked forward to dinner with Alice, a former Bostonian, to whom I had transmitted the doctoral degree diploma at a Boston University graduation while I was dean years ago and was now a good family friend and education consultant and researcher in the Bay Area. Alice would be joining us with her most recent beau, Leon from Oakland, who we had never met.

Janet and I arrived early at the bistro. It reminded me of a dark Greenwich Village pub of the 1960s with its long bar and adjoining small-tired tables on a floor of small, weathered tiles. It was already a hub of activity for locals. Conversation at the bar wafted through the intimate space. It was a bistro, but this was San Francisco. Although whiskey bottles lined the walls behind the bar, glasses of wine held by standees and bottles of wine on the tables of diners betrayed the invasion of the gentry. Janet and I were escorted to seats at a table by a large window and absorbed the ambience while we waited for Alice and Leon.

It wasn't long before we observed an older purple Jaguar convertible pull up to the curb just down the street and a hefty, wispy-bearded driver exit and cross over to open the passenger's door. Demure Alice emerged, the bulky man, obviously Leon, took her hand as she navigated the curbside. In moments, they joined us.

We rose to greet them as they approached our table. Leon's welcome handshake swallowed my hand; Alice's gentle hug was restorative. We shared broad smiles of introduction as we all sat down. Greeting small talk was just advancing beyond the "It's good to meet you" and "How was traffic on the Bay Bridge?" stage before a waiter, menus in hand, drifted in our direction. Leon wasn't ready to study a menu. There were priorities.

"A bottle of Cabernet please," he demanded as much as requested, vineyard of which I don't recall the name noted.

Wine was to become a river on which appetizers and entrees flowed for the evening and served as a lubricant for monologues of Leon. This wasn't to be an evening for conversation with Janet, Alice, and I catching up on events of our San Francisco life. It was an evening for monologues. I could as easily have been seated at the Village Vanguard in Greenwich Village listening to a bigger-than-life storyteller.

Alice had told Janet that Leon was a character from Oakland before we had gotten together but neither of us ever guessed that he was something of an unreconstructed Marxist. He was more than a Marxist. From appetizer to entrée to dessert, he regaled us with tales of Labor, Oakland, and San Francisco waterfronts. Well into the evening, at some point between entrée and dessert, Leon ordered a second bottle of wine. It must have been of a different varietal with higher alcohol content: tales of Labor were immediately replaced by declarations of his love for demure Alice who protested gently, although, I suspect, basked in the aura of love from her Marxist in the purple Jaguar convertible.

By evening's end, the morning confrontation with Father President had faded into the fog in the same manner that Leon's purple Jaguar had as he and Alice returned to Oakland in their purple Jaguar. Dinner in Portrero bistro with Leon and Alice in the town that Labor leader Harry Bridges called his own, provided a fitting coda for the day.

Anger at Father President was less jolting after Portrero soliloquys from my wine guzzling, lovelorn Marxist, but the wound still festered the morning after. Father had crossed a line when he accused me of dishonesty based on the claim of an anonymous third party. It demanded a formal response. On return to my office the next day I called Father Jack. I had to meet with him.

It was comfortable sitting alone with Father in his office. He nodded his assent to my request that our discussion be off the record before I shared my concerns.

"Jack, Father President's accusation brought me back to the horror of the McCarthy years. I need to record my concern over our conversation in writing."

Jack wanted to know more about my experiences during those years. I couldn't resist sharing with him the memory of my mother and I sitting together at the death knoll for McCarthy before I spoke about my plan to formally respond to the President's implicit, if not direct, charges.

"It was April 1954, a little less than a year after the death of my father. I remember the Army-McCarthy Hearings flickering live in black and white on our twelve-inch television screen in the living room. My mother and I were drawn to the screen like moths to light. The thirtieth day of the Hearings, Joseph Welch, attorney for the Army, challenged Roy Cohn, chief counsel for the Committee 'before the sun goes down,' to provide the United States Attorney General with the list of 130 communists or subversives he had previously waved before the prosecuting attorney."

Jack was following every word. I continued, "Senator McCarthy rose from his seat to speak. My mother, seated on the couch next to me, knew drama when she saw it. We were transfixed. When McCarthy advised Welch to check on a junior attorney in his Boston office if he was so concerned about persons aiding the Communist Party, Welch sat silently and looked directly at McCarthy. I remember the lingering silence. Welch had timed his answer for maximum impact. Slowly and calmly, he took center stage.

"Until this moment, Senator, I never really gauged your cruelty or recklessness."

McCarthy resumed the attack.

Welch interrupted, *"Have you no sense of decency, sir, at long last have you no sense of decency?"*

"Give it to him. Give it to him," my mother bellowed. That afternoon, a new hero was added to my life and McCarthy had been mortally wounded."

As something of addendum to the tale, I let Jack know the scars left by the McCarthy years were to haunt my mother and intrude on my life for years to follow before I got to the point for my asking to meet with him.

"Jack, I want my exchange with the president to be on record. I don't want to risk, no matter how small, scars from President Schlegel's accusation to leave a mark on my life akin to the scar my mother's friends bore by virtue of McCarthy's accusations."

Jack nodded and responded, "Just let me see the letter before you send it. I want to be sure your selection of words doesn't accidentally stir up already troubled waters."

Father had shown personal support for his deans on many earlier occasions. I trusted him and shared the letter with him the next day. With recommendation for one or two grammatical edits and advice to remove an exclamation point, he gave his blessing. Edits made, I had a work study student hand carry my epistle to Father President's office, "CONFIDENTIAL" in upper case blazed across the face of the envelope.

Weeks later, on returning from lunch, a large envelope from the Office of the President, marked "CONFIDENTIAL" in upper case letters, rested conspicuously on my desk top. I anxiously opened it. A handwritten note within obviously hastily scratched out on a pink "For Your Information" page torn from a memo pad let me down.

"There must have been a breakdown in communication. We should talk, John."

We never did talk. The "breakdown in communication" just sat there, an unspoken distrust floating in the room at most of my meetings with John II as long as he served as University president. He was too proud to ask for a meeting. I was too stubborn to request one. Our silences said more than words could ever convey.

The quite different challenges posed by the "Hi, hon" presidential stand-off, and Marxist in a purple Cadillac evening, were to be topped off a few days later by a plea from Professor Eugene, my latest diva mired in the hubris of his fellow divas in the School's Department of Multicultural Education. Variety may be the spice of life, it may also be the thing of which deanships are made.

"Brother, these bitches are tough!" Professor Eugene announced as he catapulted into my office at 9:00 a.m., right on schedule. No "Good morning" or "Hello," only "Those bitches are tough." I knew some of Eugene's Multicultural colleagues could be difficult, but I had no idea they were that unsettling.

Without a break in verbal stride, Eugene pirouetted and sat down at my office table.

He pulled a heavily creased page from the collection of papers not quite captured by his three-ring binder.

"Look at this! Look at this!" The page contained a listing of classes offered by his department accompanied by names of professors assigned to teach them.

"Eugene, I don't fully understand. Help me."

"Courses I'm scheduled to teach are not there. Dean, I need help. I need help. I'm dealing with a group of divas."

I'd known that for years and even shared with Eugene the challenge he would face before I had asked him to join the faculty little more than a year earlier. Eugene needed to let off more steam before I had a chance to respond.

"Dean. Professors Fiametta, Emilia, and Ida are divas in their own culture! They cultivate their own students. They go to their own conferences. They talk their own special languages. They don't talk with one another. They're hardly ever here. And there are no courses for me." He was on a roll. The stacatto beat of his heavy gold ring kept cadence on the hardwood surface of the table as he switched to rap.

Emilia only wants to work with Af-ri-can-amer-i-cans
Fiametta only works with Lat-in-os, and
Ida only works with Fil-i-pin-os."
Players identified, he proceeded,
What do I do? What do I do?
I'm Black and I'm new! I'm Black and I'm new!
There's none for me, it's all for those three. There's none for me.
It's all for those three.

He was doing a good job of capturing the behavior of this Multicultural trio and the dilemma of a male professor dropped into a pool of veteran matriarchs. He was also giving an impressive audition for a featured role in my cast of divas. I had no illusion that I could break down the walls that separated one Multicultural professor's fiefdom from another but I could at least remedy Eugene's immediate problem and add his teaching assignment to the course schedule.

There was a not-so-subtle irony to Eugene's plight: his Multicultural colleagues had built walls to distance cultures from cultures, themselves from one another, and students of different ethnicity or race from one another. Multicultural divas had become Pied Pipers for students of their own kind.

I assured Eugene that I heard him and could remedy the course assignment problem. For the moment, I could only extend sympathy for his isolation—a pretty poor response to his larger concerns.

"Oh, Emilia, oh, Faimetta, oh, Ida. Oh, Dean, you said it." Eugene raised his eyes to the ceiling on assurance that I would resolve the scheduling problem. He jumped up from his seat and laughed. I was glad he could find humor in his plight.

"I'm off. There are students to meet if I can get them before they fall into the clutches of the divas—and if I can find courses to teach. Till later, alligator."

Eugene bounced out of my office. He had it relatively easy. There were only three divas with whom he had to deal. If I were to succeed, I had to find a way to harness the energies of so many more.

Father President's umbrage, Leon's vows of labor and love, and the rap of struggling Eugene were all distractions from the program review and development goals. Frustration changed to hope only a few weeks later when I received a phone call from my Sister with the Cheshire cat smile.

"Dean, I've got some good news for you," Sister informed me. "Faculty have supported my request for a retreat to discuss the School Task Force proposals you shared with us."

I was finally in reach of making a significant impact on the School's academic identity. After several years of work with chairpersons, faculty committees, and students, the faculty was ready to act on proposals to restructure School programs and sharpen the mission of the School. Her conditions for support were simple.

"If you'll pay the fee for Dean Connie from Spokane to facilitate the meeting and costs associated with an off-campus retreat, I'll work with you to develop the agenda for the meeting."

Faculty must have forgiven or forgotten the retreat with the twine lady; that was a relief. A location for the retreat was secured, a date was set, an agenda was developed, and working proposals were sent to Dean Connie. I would pick her up at SFO.

Sixteen

Disciples of Different Orders

It was good to see Dean Connie again, attaché case slung over her broad shoulders, as she maneuvered the velvet ropes guiding her into the SFO terminal upon arrival from Spokane. She and I had worked together on an earlier successful retreat with faculty, and I looked forward to the next few days.

"Paul, I'm starved. Let's have dinner at a nice restaurant. We can go over materials I've brought for tomorrow's meeting after we've eaten," she suggested, as we shared travel and professional niceties on our hike to the airport garage. Connie had her priorities in order. Working papers may have been in her attaché case, but it was food first, then work. I wasn't surprised. I had already made a reservation for the two of us to have dinner at *Café Kati*, then a welcoming, slightly offbeat restaurant, on a slightly offbeat street, off of pre-upscale Fillmore Street.

We folded the discussion of challenges to be faced the next morning into the enjoyment of creative dishes presented from *Café Kati's* kitchen along with a good bottle of wine. Too soon, it was time to leave the comforting restaurant. Time passes quickly in the company of good service, conversation, food, and wine, but we had a lot in front of us for the next day. I drove Connie to the Stanyan where she would be staying for the night and accompanied her to the reception desk before she ascended to her room through the same tired, dimly lit lounge in which I had eaten breakfast on my first visit to the University. With simultaneous, "See you in the mornings," she climbed the stairs to her room. Tonight, unlike years ago, it was my turn to disappear into the fog. I would pick her up in the morning.

San Francisco Bay glimmered beneath the Golden Gate Bridge as Connie and I crossed over to the Marin Headlands, my '87 BMW ragtop down. Rust ochre towers of the bridge glowed. The morning fog had pulled back early to reveal an azure blue sky; cool air streamed over us in the warm early morning sun; it was a postcard perfect San Francisco morning.

Diamond sparkles of the Bay behind, we entered the warmth of Marin and shortly arrived at Dominican College, home for the day's retreat. If it weren't for the majestic redwoods and the bouquet of Bay and Eucalyptus, we could as easily have been on a rural New England campus. Connie and I were the first to arrive. We luxuriated in the silence and warmth of Marin and the richness of Peet's French Roast as we waited for professors to arrive. Too soon they intruded on our quiet. The mood of camaraderie as they greeted us was comforting; the gentle hum of conversation in the reception area bode well for the day. When rays of sun emerged over the hilltop shading the room and bathed us all in its golden glow, I knew it was going to be a good day.

The hour hand on the wall clock read 9:30, time to get down to work. Connie gently guided the professors toward an adjoining conference room in which chairs had previously been set up for our arrival. Voices of informal chatter softened as seats were selected and Connie strode to the front of the gathering.

"Good morning. It's good to be back with you," Connie purred. Soft, staggered smiling "Good mornings" were returned. All was in order. It was now her show. From here on in, I could take a back seat—and become a nervous participant-observer.

She quickly got down to business. "We've set a firm closure time for the meeting. We'll be ending promptly at 3:00 p.m." There were collective murmurs of relief. Professors were happy; this would not be one of those retreats that drag on endlessly. Connie added, "We won't be able to go beyond 3:00 because Dean Warren and I have to catch a flight to Chicago to attend a meeting with other Jesuit school of education deans."

"Hallelujah," exclaimed Father Professor Thomas, loud enough for all to hear and bright enough in Hawaiian shirt to leave an impression. Connie ignored Thomas's celebratory obstinacy.

"By the end of the meeting, I'm confident we'll have come to a decision on a revised organization structure for the School that helps it build on its strengths."

Connie's announcement of the day's goal didn't play as well as her opener. Dante whispered to Hubert, loud enough for neighboring professors and Connie to hear, "I'll believe it when I see it," as he and Hubert exchanged conspiratorial grins. Connie didn't bite. She asked a few professors in the front row to help hand out the materials she and I had discussed at length before her arrival: two alternative reorganization proposals for the School along with accompanying narrative that summarized deliberations and decisions that had led to their development.

"Give them a quick review and raise any questions you might have. We'll have opportunity later to discuss them at length," she directed. After allotting time for summary review, she asked, "Any thoughts?" There was no response.

Connie filled the silence with an explanation of how she had used School Task Force proposals forwarded to her by me to develop the handouts. There was still silence. I don't know how she felt at the moment but I was getting that same queasy feeling I had when that ball of yarn was first rolled from professor to professor at our last retreat.

Connie wasn't going to extract response from the professors in the manner a dentist extracts a tooth. The action would only create pain. The meeting needed to proceed. She gave marching orders for the balance of the morning.

"We'll meet in small groups until 11:00 with randomly assigned group members. I'm asking each group to select a representative to report their group's recommendations to all of us before we break for lunch. Any questions?" Silence again. My queasy feeling was mounting. Numbers to assign group membership were read off: "One, two, three, four, five; one, two, three, four, five . . ." Professor group assignments completed, there was a scuffling of chairs and drone of voices as groups proceeded to five designated meeting rooms. After the earlier silence, suddenly there was all this life.

I needed to get a better sense of group climate. It certainly wasn't early morning's golden glow. I wandered the halls, peeked in doors of meeting rooms, and sat in briefly on some discussions. Professors curiously silent or absent from previous planning meetings on campus were actively leading too many discussion groups. Divas who had lost their voices at this morning's opening session were leading others. My Sisters at the cusp were celebrating their programs.

One of Eugene's divas, seldom on campus, prominent at national professional meetings and loved by her bilingual apostolate, sketched a giant sunflower on poster paper, each petal a School program extending from a multicultural stamen. Her magic marker was a baton as she conducted her multicultural symphony.

Sister K's lilting brogue mesmerized her group as she recited the catechism: "Teacher education is at the core of the School's mission." There were no petals, but if there had been, Teacher Education would have been the receptacle.

Down the hall, Sister Rachel's Venn diagram of concentric circles placed the School's Catholic Education Program at the center—a contributor to other programs and central to the mission of a Catholic university. No flower, same anatomy.

School organization structures that blossomed on poster boards hung from walls were all new to me. What had happened to all our preparatory work? Conversations between previously antagonist professors bridged historical, social, and intellectual divides. And to make matters worse, tenured professors had risen to protect their turf. Connie and I would suffer the collateral damage.

The meeting hemorrhaged to a close at 3:00. It didn't end with a bang or a whimper. *Bang* and *whimper* were too gentle words to describe the events of the day that had started so seductively. Carnage was everywhere: collections of construction paper that contained recommendations lay crumpled on meeting room floors; diagrams and notes torn from poster board pads hung Scotch-taped to the walls.

Connie and I were in full retreat as we pulled out of the Dominican campus parking lot to drive to SFO. We had been routed. That boulder kept rolling down the hill just when I thought I had made it. St. Jude trumped Sisyphus. California weather had been at its best today. We had not.

I pushed my foot down on the gas pedal to accelerate as we raced down Route 101. I didn't feel like talking; neither did Connie. I don't know whether I was relieved to be leaving on a plane that would whisk me away from today's rout or sorry that I couldn't hang around and try to alleviate the pain and salvage parts of the proposal. Connie, too, was upset. But she would be returning to her deanship in Spokane and wouldn't have to deal with the fall-out from today's meeting while professors would be waiting for me in San Francisco on my return from Chicago.

My office was littered with artifacts from our Marin debacle on my return. Poster board scratchings covered my coffee tabletop; pink "Please call" slips filled a shiny clip on my desktop; meeting notices and faculty appointments for the week filled my calendar book. When I leafed through the collected "Please call" slips, I came across a note from my new assistant, Catherine.

"Mr. Kohl called. He just learned you were in San Francisco. Please call." The phone number carried a California prefix.

I had first met Herb, a noted educator, activist, writer, and social gadfly, when I was dean at Boston University and he was a visiting professor at Harvard. I had tried to secure an appointment for him in President John Silber's conservative castle, only to be told by one of the University president's administrators, "There's no more space in the University for soft social scientists of the Left." Over a period of years, our paths had crossed often enough for us to maintain a distanced friendship, but with the passage of time, we had lost track of one another. Clean-up and recovery could wait. I needed an uplift after the Marin debacle. I would return his call immediately.

Herb's soft voice with a touch of New York City dialect at the other end of the line was soothing. Conversation flowed with the warmth of childhood friends on return to a high school reunion. It was as if we had spoken yesterday. We needed to talk some more, a lot more, and agreed to meet the following week at a Herb-selected diner in San Rafael, midpoint between his Point Arena home on the coast north of the city and the University.

I took a few wrong turns before I located the small diner tucked in between larger buildings on a San Rafael side-street saved for the moment from rehabilitation fitting with the city's gentrification. The slam of the diner's closing screen door announced my arrival. Herb sat alone at a corner table, glass of water and open book sitting on the Formica tabletop in front of him. He looked a little older, a little more disheveled, and a little smaller than I remembered him. I'm sure I looked a little older, a little grayer, and a little more lined to him. He slowly stood to greet me. We gave one another a gentleman's embrace before we sat down.

I have no memory of what we ordered. Neither, I suspect, does Herb. We recalled old meetings, shared paths taken since Boston, reminded ourselves of professional frustrations and accomplishments, and spoke at some length of the sad state of public education, particularly in the urban centers of our country in which schools were as much prisons as seedbeds for curiosity for children of low-income, often families of color. In those couple of hours together, we talked about issues I wish professors back on campus spent more time on. Lunch was drawing to a close, the few other diners were gone, and clean-up preliminary to its closing was obvious. I couldn't help but think that there must be some way our conversation could continue; our meeting had to be more than simply a break for a trip of social nostalgia. I hope Herb felt the same way. As we rose to leave, I made a first tentative move.

"Herb, I'd like to find some way in which we could work together again." I hesitated, "Are you interested?" He paused a moment. Smiled.

"It might be fun." He then tacked on a sentence to bring ecstasy to any dean with a strained budget who seeks to add a prominent educator to his team, "You know, I don't need a tenure line position."

I could think of no more upbeat way in which we could have said goodbye.

Memories of Marin and my restless faculty faded as I drove back to the City. Serendipity had just dealt me a good hand. I was preoccupied with thoughts of this Don Quixote who relished tilting at education windmills coming to the University. He could help jumpstart my sputtering urban agenda. He could be a confidante with whom I could share frustrations. He was an old school Progressive. He had Jewish New York roots. He would be a friend. I would find a way for him to join me. After all, I was the dean and I worked in a university committed to social justice, and social justice was what Herb was all about. I would push that boulder up the hill one more time.

I knew I would face some conflict and experience some sleepless nights in pursuit of an appointment for Herb. Father Jack would be resistant, collective bargaining terms would be tested, some professors would be threatened, and my unilateral decision-making would be questioned. To boot, the introduction of one more diva to the pool of School waters could only add to the turbulence. But to not take advantage of his call and our being on the same coast would constitute educational malfeasance. I would wait, however, to formally seek an appointment for Herb until after spring graduation rites, not much more than a month away. Free from term-end activity, Father Jack would be more relaxed and faculty would be in their summer mode.

Allusions to the Marin debacle popped up from time to time on my return from Chicago, but the event had evidently been less traumatic for professors than it had been for me. We were well into University springtime. Spring term was drawing to an end, summer escapes were imminent, and graduation loomed. Life focused on final class sessions, academic assignment capstones, graduation list compilation, commencement speaker recruitment, and commencement ceremony plans. Everything was pretty much under control in the School. That was until the first week in May.

Less than two weeks before commencement, I was notified that a family emergency would make it impossible for the scheduled School commencement speaker to be present. There was little time to identify, secure, and announce an alternate to celebrate the accomplishments of our graduates, but fortunately the professional network of a School professor came to the rescue and an alternate speaker was secured. As no faculty meeting was scheduled prior to commencement, I informed the professors by memorandum of our good fortune. The memo was brief and to the point:

I am pleased to inform you that Dr. Price Cobbs, internationally recognized psychiatrist who practices in the Bay Area, will be the commencement speaker for the School of Education at the upcoming graduation ceremony. Dr. Cobbs's many publications include "The Jesus Bag" and "Black Rage."

The selection and announcement of commencement speakers for the School had seldom energized professors or created much discussion. I never thought response to the announcement, albeit by memo, of this year's speaker, a solid scholar, a practicing psychiatrist, and author respected by Bay Area colleagues, would be any different. I soon learned otherwise. The memorandum hadn't been distributed for much more than an hour before Catherine was on my intercom line.

"Dean, there's a message on my phone that must have come in while I was at lunch." She sounded troubled. "It's from Father Francis. I think you should come and listen to it. You have to hear his tone of voice."

The message must truly have been something out of the ordinary. Never before had Catherine invited me to listen to a telephone message on her line. I joined her at her desk. She recovered the message and handed me the phone. If the caller's tone of voice had been any colder, the phone arm would be covered with hoar frost.

"This is Father Francis. It's urgent that Dean Warren call me as soon as possible. I need to talk with him about the graduation speaker."

Father's words shot from the speaker were delivered in the manner, I suspect, he reserved for admonishing wayward boys when he was a Catholic high school disciplinarian. I must have done something terribly wrong. I excused myself, returned to the privacy of my office, and closed the door. This wouldn't be a routine return of call.

Father must have been sitting at his desk, looming over the phone, waiting for my call. Before the end of the first ring, he was at the other end of the line.

"Father here," a monotone, sober acknowledgement greeted me.

"Father, it's . . ." I got no further.

"Dean, I received your memo about the graduation speaker. Have you read what this man wrote?" His steeled voice suggested I had not. He repeated, "Have you read what this man wrote?" volume up a notch.

"Yes, I have," I replied, rather curtly, I'm afraid.

"I hope you know what you're doing, Dean. *The Jesus Bag* is filled with four-letter words." I was silent. "Dean, there's no need to tear scabs off old wounds," Father intoned, in obvious reference to Cobbs's late 1960s' book that tackled racism in the church.

"Dean, I hope you know what you're doing," he barked again. I held the receiver away from my ear. This was serious. Father Francis, strong of mind but deferential to protocol, had always been most courteous when we spoke.

"Father," I responded in what I hoped was a calm, deanly manner, "I had lunch with Dr. Cobbs a few days ago. I'm convinced he is a reasonable man, sensitive to the importance of graduation speeches." I then made the mistake of sharing an additional thought.

"Father, I don't think a commencement address, the last formal interaction of the School with students in its graduating class, would suffer from encouraging students to think about some sensitive issues."

I should have known better than sermonize one who lives by the sermon. My response clearly wasn't the response Father was expecting.

"Dean, I hope you know what you're doing," he now snarled. "Excuse me, I have to meet with some students." The sound of the dial tone was piercing. I'm confident no students were waiting for his immediate attention.

On graduation day, I didn't relax until Dr. Cobbs's address drew to a close. He had worked from a carefully developed manuscript; insights were impressive, challenges compelling, and there were no inciting expletives. After the procession of deans and professors had exited from St. Ignatius Church at the end of the ceremony to proceed to the graduation reception, several graduates had approached me to request copies of the address—a request I had not previously received for a commencement speaker's presentation.

Father Francis suddenly appeared at my side on my way down the hillside to join the professors and faculty at the reception. He was out of breath from his effort to catch up to me. He placed his arm on my shoulder and looked me straight in the eye.

"Good job." That was all he said before he fell back to the colleague with whom he had been talking. That afternoon, Father Francis' words were almost as meaningful as Dr. Cobbs' powerful contribution.

I, however, have a confession to make about that graduation ceremony. Father Francis' initial heated concern about my selection of the speaker prompted me to take extraordinary steps to reduce chances for tension between members of the Jesuit Community and my School.

After my terse phone conversation with Father, I immediately called Dean Jerome of the University library. Jerome had arrived at the University following life as administrator in Boston. We had delighted in sharing Boston stories, enjoying one another's humor, and had developed a close relationship since his arrival. I had shared with him my telephone conversation with Father and had confessed, "Jerome it has been a long time since I've read Cobbs' works. I do remember there was some pretty strong language. I need your help. Would you check to see whether the library has *Black Rage* and *The Jesus Bag*?"

I waited while Jerome checked to determine whether the books were in the library's listings.

"Paul, we have one copy of each of the books."

"Please check them out for me. I'll have Catherine pick them up right away." The motives behind my request were not entirely academic.

I re-read Cobbs' work before our graduation ceremony. The Church seen through his lens in *The Jesus Bag* took quite a beating and the language of *Black Rage* was stronger than I remembered. I had to admit to myself that I could understand why the works might have offended Father. But this wasn't the 1960s and the University is an academic institution, not a church. I held on to the publications.

I still question the propriety of my keeping University library copies of these works in my office until after graduation. If a student had removed a book from the library with the intent of preventing someone else to read the work, I might have requested some form of discipline. I still try to convince myself, not entirely successfully, that I was protecting freedom of speech and the exchange of ideas, fully aware that I, by securing the only University copies of *The Jesus Bag* and *Black Rage*, had assured that these writings were not shared with the Jesuit Community.

Once graduation ceremonies were over, and the academic year behind us, the pulse of University life slowed and everybody was more relaxed. And for all the year's frustrations, there were things for which I was thankful: Rebecca Feinstein had been appointed, professors had forgotten the Marin retreat, prickly Father Francis was at peace with my choice of Dr. Cobbs, and Don Quixote from Point Arena waited on the horizon. I was prepared to push that boulder up the hill.

Seventeen

Quixote Arrives

My Don Quixote was seated on his horse just over the horizon in Point Arena waiting for a call from me to join in my urban quest at the University but Father Jack, No. 2 pencil in hand, was more interested in budget numbers than in Quixote's arrival. He was neither familiar with the social justice jousts nor the writings of the accomplished progressive educator. He knew nothing of reformer Herb other than my testimony. I better appreciated the story Father Jerome told of the priest's fear of dying and going to heaven for all the questions the Father asked: Is this a full-time appointment? Is this an administration or faculty position? How long is the commitment? From what accounts are you transferring money? Is there faculty approval? It felt I was seated in his office forever before Father begrudgingly approved my request for the transfer of funds from one School budget line to another with the caveat and comment, "For this one time only, Paul. Herb needs us more than we need him."

I forgave Father for his misguided assessment of the relative needs of Herb and the University. No dean has ever accomplished anything by contesting an immediate superior's magnification of the reputation of his institution. We needed Herb more than he needed us, even though I suspected his appointment might pose greater challenges for me than Father's judgment. Dante was first in line to confirm my prognosis.

"You know Herb was big in Berkeley in the 1960s," seeped from Dante's thin, razor-thin, moustache-accented lips as we passed in the hallway the day following my notice to the faculty of Herb's appointment. Ash-gray, cold eyes peered at me from slits in his gray-pink baby skin face. He gave a smile of the "I gotcha" variety.

"Do you know why Herb left Berkeley?" Dante wasn't looking for a response. We were both aware of Herb's scuffles with school management due to his advocacy for activist students in the 1960s. Dante had more to share.

"You know, Herb doesn't have his doctorate, and the Collective Bargaining Agreement prohibits hiring a professor without a doctorate."

"Herb will report directly to me as a Research Associate and Project Director. The Agreement permits Management to teach individual courses," I immediately shot back. I had anticipated that objection. It was my turn to give the "I gotcha" smile.

Dante recognized my slight-of-hand for he too had been a dean of the School: Herb would be a scholar in Management dress. I also suspected Dante wasn't happy that there was now one more diva in the pool—especially one with national stature and who's a friend of the dean. Every new diva in the pool gave him less swimming room.

"Good luck," Dante tossed over his shoulder as we parted, tone of voice more a challenge to duel than a wish for success.

Less than a week later, Catherine apologetically announced as she entered my office, "A student whose name is Susan says it's urgent that she meet with you; she doesn't want to meet with Dean Parsa."

"Let me talk with her." When a student indicates that meeting with an associate dean won't do, it usually is in regard to a particularly sensitive issue, often one of sexual harassment.

"Dean, thank you for seeing me," Susan spoke softly as she entered my office.

"Have a seat," I gestured toward my coffee table and joined her. She just looked down at the table; she didn't look me in the eye. I tried to make her more comfortable.

"Would you like some coffee?"

"No, thanks." She nervously wrung her hands before raising her head.

"Dean, I need to share something with you that was said by one of my professors." She hesitated and was obviously uncomfortable before she proceeded. "Dean, what I'm sharing with you can't leave this office. The professor is my doctoral advisor and . . ." I assured Susan that our conversation was confidential—unless she wanted to initiate a formal grievance which requires I adhere to "due process" protocols.

She reiterated, "I don't want our conversation shared with anyone," and assured me she wasn't filing a grievance.

"Dean, my professor warned students in class not to attend public forums scheduled by Herb Kohl or to take any classes with him and stated, 'What does Herb know about teaching Black children? He's not Black,' and scoffed, 'Or his wife who writes all his books.'" This was a tale of harassment of an order different from what I had anticipated. There are clearly delineated protocols to address questions of sexual harassment, but there were no collective bargaining road maps to guide me on follow-up to this professional and personal transgression.

I wasn't totally surprised when Susan shared the name of the professor. I had overheard Professor Emilia make a comment to the same effect when she left the faculty meeting at which I had shared the contribution I thought Herb's appointment would make to the School's urban and social justice initiatives.

I thanked Susan for sharing her concern, shared my disappointment at the professor's unprofessional behavior, and again assured her that our discussion would remain confidential.

Susan may have felt a little better than when we first sat down to talk, but I certainly didn't. Personal discretion aside, a professional code of behavior had been violated by one of my professors. Yes, Herb didn't have a doctorate, and yes, he wasn't Black, but he had national recognition and a record of publication and work in schools that most of my professors should envy. I needed to find a way to sensitively address Emilia's transgression without involving Susan.

I decided to wait a while before I formally confronted Emilia. An immediate private follow-up would only raise her hackles, possibly implicate Susan, and further complicate Herb's reception by faculty that went far deeper than concern about degrees completed, color of skin, or budget encumbrance. I had little doubt that jealousy, collective bargaining fundamentalism, and Herb's hubris rested at its core.

Not long after my meeting with Susan, I found myself caught in the web of an Emilia experience of quite a different nature, which unexpectedly led to an opportunity to share Susan's observation.

Father President had asked selected administrators and professors to join him in his hilltop castle to discuss a matter of some urgency. The University was in jeopardy of losing a major foundation award of close to one million dollars to support discrete programs and actions central to the proclaimed University multicultural mission delineated in the foundation-funded proposal. Appointment of additional professors of color was one of those promised actions. One year after receipt of foundation funds, there were few new professors of color at the University. The foundation was concerned; the University was frightened. Father President John II needed help—in a big way.

Cups of dark coffee in white presidential china sat half-empty in front of previously seated University deans and officers when Father President took his seat at the head of the long cherrywood table. He brought his hands together in prayer position and rested them conspicuously on the tabletop, paused, and welcomed the gathering. Moments into the opening remarks, a knock on the conference room door interrupted Father. Heads of seated participants turned as the door slowly opened. There stood Ingrid, Father President's well-groomed, blond assistant next to statuesque, Black, fashionably late, Professor Emilia.

"Father President, Dr. Emilia is here," Ingrid announced. I didn't know Emilia had been invited to the meeting, but I wasn't totally surprised. Shortly after John II's arrival, it became clear that several University professors who vehemently waved the flag of multiculturalism had special access to the president; Dr. Emilia was one of them. I had learned soon after arrival at the University to accept Sisters' and priests' expedited access to Father President or Father Jack without the deans' knowledge but was slow in learning of special access for lay professors who conspicuously waved the multicultural flag. I had learned long ago, however, regardless of the institution of higher education, that anointed professors with direct access to a university president can complicate a dean's decision-making.

"Emilia, I'm glad you could join us," suddenly, deferential Father President welcomed my diva. There had been no such warm reception for the rest of us. "I assume most of you know Dr. Emilia," he added uncertainly.

Most heads nodded positively. A few attendees who had not previously met our latest guest, stood to introduce themselves. Emilia stood regally in the doorway. Her dark brown eyes would fix on a single attendee, hold one moment, and then move to the next as they acknowleged her presence and she theirs, a visual metronome. Her eyes held a few moments longer on administrators in clerical garb; priests caught in her gaze smiled meekly and gave a second nod of welcome. Professor Emilia had elevated the art of silently commanding attention to a science. The round of introductions and welcomes was almost complete when the door to Father President's conference room swung open again. Vice President Holden rushed into the room, camel hair coat open, vested pin-stripe suit revealed. His "back East" prep school roots showed.

"I'm sorry. I'm late. The traffic on the Bay Bridge . . ."

Our meeting was now quite wonderous. It was bordering on a circus scene in which clowns keep popping out of a small car. This wasn't a circus, and these weren't clowns but the dynamic created by the popping up of surprise players was not dissimilar.

Holden broke the metronomic trance cast by Emilia. She stepped aside to let him proceed to the table and take a seat. Emilia's welcome had been interrupted. She wasn't ready to sit down. She took a step back, the door frame becoming a portrait frame, and slowly lifted the draped coat from her arm and handed it to Ingrid. Free from her coat, Emilia was ready to join us. Before pulling her chair up to the table, she cleared her throat and cleared it once again. She now had the attention of all.

With a sense of timing that would have made any stand-up comedian proud, she broke the silence, "My, my, my." Her signatory prefatory words triggered a memory of Tommy Lee Jones's "Oh my, oh my, oh my," as he observed the train wreck in the film, *The Fugitive.* We had a train wreck of our own unfolding here. Emilia wasn't finished.

"All these Jesuits and a camel's hair coat." The priests smiled. The vice president blushed. "And where are the Black folk?"

The portrait painted by Emilia was remarkably gentle. Those few words, "and where are the Black folk," said it all. There was nothing like a quick stroke of her verbal brush to get things going.

Things got going, but not very far. We reiterated the need for more vigorous recruitment outreaches, identified additional University incentives, and recommended broader faculty involvement to attract professors of color. I'm not sure we accomplished a great deal.

After the meeting was over, Emilia and I walked together down the hill from Father President's complex. We talked casually about the meeting before I asked her if she would join me for a few moments when we got to the School. Seated in my office, we talked at greater length about the challenges Father President faced in his multicultural quest over a cup of coffee before I found a pretext to throw in a "by the way" transition words to introduce the essence of Susan's observation. I tried to engage Emilia with a preamble that would, hopefully, precipitate constructive conversation.

"There may be some misunderstanding . . ."

Her dark brown eyes glowered; she was suspicious.

Careful to mask my source, I repeated, "There may have been some misunderstanding," before I shared concern about professors sharing opinions of other professors' ability or qualifications with students and the comments that she may have shared with students about Herb Kohl.

Emilia immediately rose from her chair. Her statuesque frame intimidated and with a smirk, dared, "Come, come, Dean." There was no Emilia trademark, "my, my, my." "Come, come, Dean," she repeated and added, "I can't be bothered by claims like that."

I wasn't totally surprised at Emilia's umbrage but couldn't help being discouraged. Here we had just come from a meeting that indirectly touched on the question of stereotyping as a function of race, and she had denigrated the contributions of one of our professors largely on the color of his skin.

"Good afternoon, Dean." Our meeting was over. Emilia smugly left my office.

I had my hands full. With the indifference of Father Clark, the umbrage of Dante, the racism of Emilia, and only a handful of professor "hurrahs" on Herb's appointment, I had painted myself into something of a corner with my slight-of-hand appointment. The enthusiasm of deans at other University schools and colleges on my initiative didn't carry much weight with my professors. I needed to find a way to help Herb, the School, and myself.

I had a strategy. I reasoned if I were to facilitate Herb, my prophet for social justice, and fellow prophet Father Thomas who sought to empower the poor through his project with Mexican- Americans in the Mission District of San Francisco to collaborate, Herb would become less of a pariah, and Father Thomas and would get greater recognition. And Herb would be visibly linked to the University's Jesuit social justice. I would be forgiven my personal relationship with Herb. "Lunch on the House," courtesy of the dean, for the two of them would be the first small step to accomplish these ends. I called Herb to ask him to join me in my office.

"Herb, Father President talks about social justice. Father Thomas talks about social justice. And you have a record of social activism and writing that gives life to the concept." Herb was silent. He sensed where I was going.

"It would be a *mitzvah* if you and Thomas could find a way to work together." Herb knew when I threw around my limited knowledge of Yiddish that this was no simple challenge. He gave me a resigned smile of "Go on, go on."

I continued, "If the two of you can work together, Father will get some much-needed support, Jesuit colleagues will be grateful, and the School's social justice initiatives will get greater visibility." I didn't share with Herb a hidden agenda: University acknowledgement of his importance.

Herb sat silently. He knew enough of Father's work and disposition to know that I wasn't presenting him with the opportunity of a lifetime. When I told him I would treat the two of them to lunch, Herb's nod of head and emotionless eyes translated, "If you really want me to, Dean, I'll do it." I hadn't expected an enthusiastic reception to the idea. I asked Herb to give Father a call. We would talk again after he had lunch with Thomas.

A few days after the "Save Father Thomas–Help Herb" lunch, I got a call from Herb asking to meet with me. My calendar was open. Moments after putting the receiver down, Herb was at my doorway. To arrive at my office so quickly, he must have slid down the stair railing. He blew in and shut the door with just short of a slam.

"I've never seen anything like it," he blustered even before he took a seat.

"I've never seen anything like it," he repeated in case I didn't hear or underestimated the importance of his words of wonderment. He stretched back on the chair, raised his eyebrows, and combed his fingers through his hair. He had a look of puzzlement, the look a cat gives when it swats its plaything under a piece of furniture and isn't able to reach it. I had no idea what triggered his bewilderment.

"Paul, it was one of the strangest meetings I've experienced in all my years." I wasn't prepared for his story.

"Thomas and I had lunch together. He didn't really want to talk about his work in the Mission. I'm not sure he knew what he wanted to talk about other than how I could help him get some of his writing published," Herb hesitated. "We couldn't get a coherent discussion going. He was under the weather." Translated, I suspect, Thomas who many knew had a too-fond relationship with tequila had had too much to drink. Maybe I was being unfair; maybe Herb's *hubris* had overwhelmed him. But more likely, Thomas with a glass or two of wine, or favorite tequila under his belt, had just been plain ornery. I didn't have a chance to probe before the story took a new twist.

"After lunch, we went back to the seminar room next to my office to talk about what might be the next steps. I wasn't hopeful but I knew my assignment. Thomas was slurring some of his words and returned to "Do you know a publisher" talk, when out of nowhere, some Catholic higher-up I'd never previously met entered the room. He wasn't a professor. I don't know who or what he was. But he was someone important."

I sat silently while Herb paused to catch his breath. I had previously participated in conversations with a frustrated or angry Herb but this interaction was different. He was flustered rather than angry. Calmed down, he continued, "He asked if he could meet with Father Thomas in private. Thomas slowly stood up, like a boy who had just been caught stealing a chocolate bar from a candy store. Without a word, the two of them left the room with only nods of farewell. And, Paul, no one ever returned." No wonder Herb was bewildered.

"Herb, thanks anyway. I appreciate your effort. Let me see what I can find out. I'll give you a call to let you know what's happening."

There was no answer on Father Thomas's office phone when I called. There was no answer when I called his Jesuit Community residence. His department chair didn't know Father's whereabouts. I didn't reveal Herb's meeting with Thomas but the outcome of Father's meeting with the mystery Jesuit was important; Father was scheduled to teach classes later in the week. I would have to call Father Jack, as much in his role as a member of the Jesuit Community as in his role as an academic officer. I wasn't prepared for Father's response to my sleuthing.

"Paul, Father Thomas will be taking a leave for the rest of the term." I could have told Father Jack that leaves needed to be approved by the dean. I could have asked him why I wasn't informed. I could have asked him the reason for Father Thomas's leave. But I didn't. We both knew Thomas had a battle with the bottle and it was evident that a Church veil of protection from indiscretion had been cast.

I did ask him whether I should contact the department chairperson to inform him that Thomas needed to take a sudden leave of absence.

As I look back at the silent evacuation of Father Thomas from the classroom, I'm thankful that his indiscretion hadn't been more serious. But if the mildest of indiscretions receive such clandestine treatment, I couldn't help but suspect that more serious offenses of the Church might be hidden behind blackout shades that shut out all light. With apologies to the earlier Jesuit Seminar speaker, I knew when priests fell, they didn't always fall forward. Shortly before I stepped down as dean some years later, the *Boston Globe, Spotlight Team* investigative report of sexual misconduct of priests confirmed that suspicion.

Eighteen
Schools, Students, and Smiles

The mischievous gleam in Sister K's eyes and lilt of her uplifting Irish brogue was missing as she dropped herself into the chair. The *persona* of the Irish Little Red Riding Hood of the School's director of the Teacher Education was absent.

"Dean, I have some bad news to share with you. I have to go to Houston. I'm being called back to my home order."

"For how long," I asked. I knew she periodically traveled there to visit her Order. The pause before her reply provided a clue that I wouldn't like the news she was about to share.

"Mother Superior has been talking with me for quite a while about the possibility of my returning to Houston. My Order has asked me to join them several times over the past few years but I've been able to get them to postpone. They've just asked me to head up a major training and evaluation effort for the Church. Dean, I just can't say no to this opportunity."

We had worked closely together for too long for her not to pick up my disappointment. Sister tried to lighten things up a bit, "I guess, when the Order calls, you come, even if it is Houston."

Sister knew I would miss her. The School would miss her. The wedding of Irish charm, Catholic religiosity, and in-your-face self-confidence she brought to the University was a dynamic force. And anticipation about the whirlpool of divas who might want to add the title "Director of Teacher Education" to their resume left in the vacuum left by her departure was disconcerting. I also would personally miss the opportunities Sister had provided for me to meet and talk with our students preparing to become teachers. Her enthusiasm and optimism provided a bridge for me to connect to prospective and veteran teachers.

Nina, a veteran San Francisco teacher who was supervisor for some of Sister K's students, was one of those teachers. I first met Nina at a Fairmont Hotel–supported beginning-of-the-school-year reception for beginning and experienced teachers in the San Francisco public schools.

Holding a glass of a too-sweet punch in one hand, wilted celery stalk in the other, I strained to hear Nina's frail voice in the crowd. Softly but with enthusiasm, she was sharing the joy she got from reaching students at San Francisco's Thurgood Marshall High School in Bayview, a gritty, struggling part of the City. Her excitement was soft but evident; her concerns were clear but politic. Challenges she confronted as a creative teacher in a bureaucratic, political, large city system were many. I was reminded of both the celebrations and the frustrations of my years in the early 1960s as a teacher at Haaran High School in Manhattan. We could have talked on and on. But Nina wanted to meet with colleagues she had not seen since summer, and I needed to circulate. As we drifted apart, she extended an inviation, "Dean, come visit my classroom."

That evening at dinner with Janet, I shared how impressed I had been by Nina, this slight, soft-spoken white woman who despite all challenges was flourishing in a Bayview public school that served, or underserved, primarily poor Black students. Janet immediately picked up on the joy Nina's tales had brought me and the memories they had evoked about my "up" moments, as well as moments of frustration, years ago as a teacher in New York.

"Nina Kopf is on the phone," Catherine notified me little more than a month after the Fairmont reception. I hadn't forgotten my conversation with Nina. Charisma or no charisma, she had left an impression. Catherine put the call through.

"Dean, remember me? I met you at the SFUSD teachers' reception. I'm working with one of your student teachers. Are you going to take me up on the invitation to visit my classroom?"

"Name the time and I'll be there." It would be a nice change of pace from the office and I liked to visit City schools. Whether I left excited or dismayed on the departure from these visits, they made it impossible for me to forget why I was here.

Thurgood Marshall sat like a jail deposited on a small hilltop in the midst of small, tired houses. I weaved my old BMW convertible up the driveway and parked as close to the school as possible. The neighborhood seemed on lockdown. No one was on the streets; it was strangely silent. It was a long way from Lone Mountain and Pacific Heights to Bayview. I was white. I was driving a BMW. I was a little uncomfortable.

I crossed a small burnt-out strip of grass separating the school from the cracking asphalt and after a few futile tries to open locked side doors, I located one that was unlocked and strained to pull it open. Mission accomplished, student monitors seated at the door-side greeted me or, more accurately, intercepted me and escorted me to the principal's office. As I walked down the hallway, dark in man-made twilight, student guards at my side, I couldn't help but wonder why must it be this way. Too many city schools I had visited—New York, Boston, or San Francisco—had an atmosphere more like a prison than a palace of learning.

Three elderly ladies, barricaded behind a forbidding counter in a large, sprawling room, were pushing papers and monitoring telephones as we entered the office. A lone teacher pulled papers from a cross-hatched mailbox on the wall. With the student monitors at my side, I introduced myself to one of the elderly women who was leaning over the counter. Her call to a back office triggered the exit of a late middle-aged man with creased face, wrinkled white shirt, too-thin a tie, and sallow complexion, marks of a beat-up school veteran. He skirted around the end of the counter barricade, thanked, and dismissed my guards.

"Good morning, I'm Mr. Horn. Assistant principal. How can I help you?"

"Hi, I'm Paul Warren from USF."

"Oh, Dean Warren. It's good to meet you." His face thawed from its morning frost. "My name is Anthony, call me Tony. You're here to see Ms. Kopf. She told me you would be coming. I'll take you to her room. Follow me."

There was no small talk as we left command central. A piercing Klaxon horn-fire siren hybrid reverberated through the school as we entered the hallway. "That's the end of homeroom," Tony explained.

Students poured out from classrooms, torrents pouring through the hallways. Teachers stood in doorways, white overseers as mostly Black students streamed to their first class. We stood together at the office doorway waiting for the torrent to subside as the students peeled off into classrooms. Torrent spent, Tony double-timed down the corridor to Nina's room. I had to pick up my pace to keep up.

Room reached, Tony opened the classroom door, leaned in, and announced, "Ms. Kopf, your visitor is here." Before I could thank him, he was off on another errand.

"Dean, welcome, give me a moment," Nina acknowledged without a break to the rhythm of attendance-taking as she pushed cards around in a book to match student with seat reminiscent of the manner I had pushed "Delaney Cards" as a New York City public school teacher.

"Dean Warren from the University of San Francisco will be visiting us today," she announced to the class and gestured for me to take a seat. I walked quietly to the back of the room, found an empty chair, and sat down. I didn't see our student teacher. Nina's voice was soft—as I remembered.

"James you're late," she quietly noted and smiled as James, a six foot-plus Black student entered a moment later through the classroom door.

He murmured, "I'm sorry," and quietly took his seat.

I couldn't make out what two students close to me at the rear of the room were saying, but they were obviously not happy with one another and weren't shy about letting their differences be known. Nina fixed her eyes on the two combatants and gently commanded, "Please." One word did it. Wrangling stopped. The two students opened their workbooks. A few moments later, Nina shared the day's plans with the class.

"Today we'll continue our work on the concept of displacement. I've set up four workstations and I will count off numbers for team assignment. Each team will carry out three experiments: one team member will be responsible for setting up the equipment, a second will read directions for each step of the experiment, a third will carry out the directions, and a fourth member will take notes. Responsibilities will alternate as you move from one experiment station to another. Any questions?" There were none. Nina knew what she was doing. Students knew what she was doing. I was lost in the logistics of it all.

"James, start with number one." Students immediately sounded numbers designating team membership. Nina set the class in motion.

"Group Number One, come pick up the equipment and lab worksheets; the rest of you to your workstations."

Students fell into their groups with greater speed and less fuss than professors at my School retreats. Nina circulated from group to group as her budding scientists carried out the experiments. The students were as steeped in the scientific method as I had been as a student at Stuyvesant High School in New York City. Nina signaled for me to join her as she looked over their shoulders.

I hadn't studied physics since I survived high school physics—with the help of a tutor. I hadn't even accepted it as a discipline of personal interest until my son became a physics teacher. And here I was, watching students who carried the label "culturally deprived," participating with confidence in physics experiments. Nina of small frame, soft voice, and pale white skin had reached these young men and women of color. For close to ninety minutes, students in Nina's class were true scientists.

Nina and I talked for a few minutes after class was over. "Cathy, the student teacher, called in sick this morning. I'm sorry I didn't get a chance to call and tell you."

"Don't worry. I'm glad you didn't. It was good to see a real teacher at work."

"I did good, didn't I?"

She smiled. I smiled. There was no need for me to answer. My smile said it all. She had answered Professor Emilia's question, "Can a white person teach Black students?"

The drive back to the University seemed far shorter than the one to Thurgood Marshall. Maybe, after all, what I was doing was worthwhile. Maybe I wouldn't need to adopt St. Jude as my patron saint. I didn't care what Godfather said. I wished more of my professors understood that support for the development of hundreds of Ninas in the City was central to the mission of our School.

Meetings with teachers like Sister K's supervising teacher Nina lifted my spirits; my meeting with Julia, a student of Sister K and a teacher-to-be at a reception for Teacher Education students, was more enigmatic.

Julia strode purposefully through the huddling students to shake my hand. She broadcast exuberance. The confidently extended hand with a broad smile announced, "Hi. I'm Julia." I took her hand; her grip was strong. Her eyes met mine. "Dean, it's good to finally meet you. I've often heard your name during the year but we've never had a chance to meet." Our grasp broke.

I smiled and shared, "It's good to meet you."

Was it her firm handshake, high cheekbones, sparkling eyes, or her Julia Roberts smile that held my attention? She certainly wasn't cast in the same mold as Nina.

"Dean, I'm a tutor in President Clinton's *America Reads* program. Some of the students I work with at Taft Middle School are a real challenge. But, wow! It's the real thing. I can't wait to have a class of my own."

Julia bubbled like a freshly poured glass of champagne. If there were more students with the exuberance of Julia and the skills of Nina, there was hope for our schools.

She enthused as she talked about her student teaching experiences. She was a magnet that drew other students as we talked—or rather Julia performed and I attended. I was soon aware that I was but one attendee in the midst of an audience of teachers-to-be gathered for Julia's performance.

"Dean. Let me tell you about what happened last week. I'm used to sexist behavior—and you know the schools are sexist." She wasn't asking a question. There was something to be said for her observation but . . . this was not the time for me to interject.

She continued, "Let me give you an example. Eduardo is a seventh grader who I've been working with at Taft. He's pretty bright. But some days he's there, others he's not—if you know what I mean." Julie gave me a conspiratorial wink, making sure it was appreciated by her audience.

"Well, last week, he wasn't there. Or not really. He was sound asleep at his desk; his head was buried in his arms, the book the class was reading splayed open on his desk. I went over to him." She paused, surveyed the gathering to be sure that everyone was attentive, and proceeded, "I gently tapped him on the shoulder, 'Eduardo, let's see if we can find out together what happened,' and turned the book right side up." Her enunciation had become crisper, her pace of presentation had slowed. The audience hung on every word. Julia was evolving into a diva before her time.

"Eduardo slowly raised his head and muttered 'Why?'"

"'Reading can be fun, first of all. And, Eduardo, it's needed for any job,' I told him."

"'Let me help you, teach,' Eduardo grunted. 'I won't need to read. I'll have a secretary do that for me. Real men don't read.'" Students, metal filings to Julia's magnet, boisterously laughed.

"Can you believe that? Can you believe that? Talk about sexism," she bellowed.

Before I had a chance to comment on her grand finale, a handsome young man entered the room and proceeded to the outer rim of metal filings drawn by Julia's magnetism.

"John, I'll be right there," she shouted over the heads of her fans and, with a polite, "Excuse me, Dean, it's been a pleasure meeting you but I have to go," was off. The show was over.

I continued to talk with the dwindling reception crowd but it wasn't the same. I wish I could have talked with Julia a little more about her experience with Eduardo, about the mission of the School, about my experiences in schools. After lifting me up, she had gently let me down. Maybe she wouldn't be like Nina. I suddenly felt very old, a little pedantic, and perhaps sexist.

* * *

Enigmas generated by students take several forms. Dean Jim, the newly appointed dean of the School of Nursing, introduced me to a new one when he placed his hand on my shoulder and softly asked as deans drifted away from a concluded Council meeting, "Can I have a minute? I need some advice."

Jim's legs had incessantly nervously twitched, his eyes fixed on the window rather than colleagues during our meeting. He had been silent throughout—with us in body only. He was clearly distracted about something. We spent much more than a minute together in the silence of the dean-vacated room.

"Paul, a student in my school is enrolled in a practicum at St. Mary Hospital and his field supervisor wants me to change the student's placement site." In teacher and nurse preparation programs, relations between on-campus professors and part-time field supervisors of students can be sensitive. I needed to know more. I asked Jim if he had spoken with the supervisor.

"The supervisor isn't really the problem. The student is going through some personal changes that are causing a problem," Jim continued.

"Let me use fictitious names. The supervisor doesn't know whether to address the student as John or Florence. She now addresses him or her as John or Florence depending on the clothing he or she wears on a given day." Jim had an interesting dilemma.

"I've met with his, or her, field supervisor several times. We've had good conversations." Jim seemed to be handling the problem pretty well. Something was still missing.

"Is there a problem other than the 'his' or 'her' designation?"

"Paul, you've got it, but you've missed it." He was exasperated. I was puzzled.

"One day *he* goes into the hospital dressed as John, the next day *she* goes into the hospital dressed as Florence. On the days he's in the male mode, he insists on being called John by the patients; on the days she's in the female mode, she insists on being called Florence by the patients. The patients are thrown for a loop."

It wasn't the relationship with the supervisor that was the problem. It was not the John to Florence gender change that was the problem, it was the inconsistency of it all. Now I got it. I gave Jim advice I'm sure he didn't need.

"You or the supervisor meet with John or Florence, whoever he or she is on the given day with one simple request: Whatever gender you plan to adopt in the field is your business. We have only one requirement. Don't change your gender from day-to-day, the patients are wrestling with enough, as it is."

The remedy was so clear. Jim just needed someone with whom he could talk. The student opted for Florence. The field supervisor was comfortable, the patients forgot John, and Florence completed her practicum assignment with a glowing report from her supervisor.

A few months later, Jim and I were seated next to one another at graduation ceremonies as Florence crossed the stage to receive her diploma from Father President. Jim leaned toward me and whispered, "There she goes, our Florence Nightingale," as she received her diploma. It was nice to celebrate small victories. There weren't enough of them.

Challenges posed by student behavior could take so many forms. Fleeting occasional thoughts on the fantasy of how nice it would be if a university diploma could serve as a warranty for the use of logic and professional behavior abruptly came to an end after conversations with Aaron Pushkin, one of our School's not-so-recent graduates.

Catherine knocked softly on my door before opening it and entering the office. This was so unlike her; she always called on the phone when my door was closed. Something out of the usual must have been unfolding. She softly closed the door.

"Dean, I know you told me not to bother you, but you need to speak to the man waiting by my desk. He has Gabriella in tears, and now he's shouting at me. We don't know what to do." I was right that something out of the ordinary was stirring up staff.

"Let me talk to him," I responded without hesitation. Catherine's nodding, "thank you, thank you" as she turned to leave wasn't needed. Within seconds of our departure, a hurricane blew into my office. Even before it made landfall, I was reconciled to the fact that this was going to be one of those situations in which very little goes right.

"Dean, I'm Aaron Pushkin. Pushkin spelled P-U-S-H-K-I-N like in the Russian author." I had to give Aaron credit; his introduction certainly caught my attention.

"Thanks for talking to me, Dean, but let me warn you. I'm angry."

No such warning was needed. Froth sprayed from his mouth with the enunciation of each consonant. His lips quivered. His hands rapidly went from clenched to open, open to clenched, and I had no idea what had brought him here. He continued before I had a chance to utter a word.

"Dean, I took a course from Dr. Reuther a little while ago and I can assure you I did all the make-up work to remove the 'Incomplete' for the course. I've just discovered that my transcript now shows an 'F' for the course. A salary raise from my school system is being held up."

"Slow down, slow down," I urged.

"The University's mistake for not giving me credit for the course with Dr. Reuther that would give me thirty credits above the master's degree will cost me five hundred dollars a year." His speech slowed. He now spoke too slowly. I could have as well been an angry child being chastised by a parent to retain self-control as a dean being chastised by a student. If Pushkin were a radiator, his steam valve would still be in danger of blowing off.

"What are you going to do about it?" he demanded. I tried to remain calm and informed him that unfortunately Dr. Reuther had died a year ago.

Aaron tossed aside an "I'm sorry," before he added, "I know Dr. Reuther is dead, Dean. That's why I came to see you."

I was sure I could address the problem that brought Aaron to my office; I had no illusion I could address his self-control or personal relations skills. I asked him to give Catherine the title and number of the course in question, the date when he took it, and a telephone number at which we could reach him. I assured him that we would follow up on the matter and get back to him within twenty-four hours. He was mollified by the assurance and volunteered, "Dean, I believe I took the course right at the beginning of my program, approximately six years ago."

I was tempted to say, "What took you so long to notice this problem? It would have been easier to resolve with Dr. Reuther alive." But there had already been enough drama.

I repeated my request for him to give the relevant information to Catherine and assured him that we would follow-up on the problem and be in touch with him tomorrow. Aaron thanked me and left my office. There was no smile but his anger had diminished.

The next morning, Gabriella proudly greeted me and triumphantly waved a grade transmittal form.

"Dean, we've located the problem with Aaron Pushkin's transcript. Dr. Reuther submitted a grade change form to our office a year after class grades were sent to the registrar. But I don't think it was forwarded to the registrar. His 'Inc.' was automatically changed to an 'F' after a year. All copies of the form are in Mr. Pushkin's file in our office." Her smile let me know how much easier she had made life for all of us.

"I've sent a copy of the form to the registrar with a note of explanation. It was easy, Dean." Happy endings are always gratifying. As promised, I gave Aaron a call.

"Aaron. We've solved the problem. Professor Reuther must have been late in entering a grade change form for you. We found the form with all copies lodged in your folder. My office must not have transmitted a copy to the registrar's office and Inc. notations automatically change to an 'F' after a year. I apologize. We've contacted the registrar's office. "The 'F' has been removed and a grade has been entered."

I told him we would overnight mail an updated transcript to him as soon as Catherine confirms his current address." I expected a "thanks," or some acknowledgement of our rapid follow-up.

Rather, he asked, “Dean, what was my grade for the course?”

“You received a B+. The grade has already been entered on your transcript.” Aaron didn’t waste a moment in responding.

“A ‘B+’? I expected an ‘A.’ How do I file for a change of grade?”

I sighed, “Aaron, give me a break,” and hung up. He never filed a petition for a grade change and we never heard from him again.

Nineteen

A Jesuit Goy and a Mitzvah

Latin pronouncements, religious references, and biblical cita-tions were tools in the arsenal of the Jesuit Community. They were also tools in the arsenal of Sister Rachel, a Dominican, Godfather David, a Jew; and Vincent, the Protestant space czar. I have to admit, on occasion, I used Yiddish and Torah references as a tool in my arsenal. I figured, why not use weapons at the University which had worked so well for me in other settings.

I never fully understood the references to the Latin term, *Ratio Studiorum,* a collection of regulations for Jesuit school officials and teachers adopted in 1599 often cited in Jesuit speaker presentations. The presentations usually provided clues to the term's importance, but I needed more than clues if I were to feel comfortable in my Jesuit environment. I needed a religious tutor. I called rehabilitated Father Thomas who was delighted to have his secular dean call him for religious instruction.

"Let's meet for lunch at Loyola House, you'll be my guest," he replied without hesitation when I shared my request for *Ratio* instruction.

Loyola House, the recently constructed new Jesuit Community home with its commanding views of the City couldn't have been a better place to talk of things Catholic and Jesuit. With Father and me seated by a window with downtown San Francisco buildings etched against cerulean blue sky for our view, napkin on lap, food gathered from the buffet for our meal, I was ready for my instruction to begin.

"Paul, the *Ratio* guides the behavior of Jesuits in their schools and provides directives or rules to help teachers and administrators," Father paused. He took a bite, and continued, "Let me give you an example. The

Ratio stipulates that the Jesuit shall resort to corporal punishment only as a last resort. Should such punishment be necessary, the *Ratio* also stipulates that a Jesuit shall not administer it." I laughed. He seemed perplexed.

"Thomas, that reminds me of an experience I had many, many years ago when I was a counselor in an Orthodox Jewish camp." He raised his heavy eyebrows, lowered his five o'clock shadowed chin to his chest, and gazed at me over the rim of his glasses. He said nothing. His implicit interest was an invitation for me to share my camp counselor story. I put my silverware down. The tale merited full attention.

"Camp Monroe was, and still may be, an Orthodox Jewish summer camp in the Catskills. After many previous summers as a camp counselor, I had planned to do something other than be a camp counselor this particular summer, but somehow I never got around to deciding what that "other" might be. Suddenly, it was late May and I didn't have a summer job. I had never spent a summer in the city; this would not be my first. By default, I'd made the decision to find a job as a camp counselor, one more time, even if hiring summer camp counselors had finished for most camps. Camp Monroe, however, was still interviewing.

When I accepted an offer from Camp Monroe, I hadn't given much thought to what life as a counselor might be like in a Jewish Orthodox camp. Probably because all I really cared about was to get out of New York City for the summer. I was soon to learn that the *Halakhah,* sort of a Jewish *Ratio,* provided guidelines for behavior as a counselor at the camp." I didn't tell Father that I was only previously aware of the *Halakhah* by virtue of a course on the Jewish religion I had taken while at Princeton.

Father was attentive but silent. I had expected some response to my *Ratio-Halakhah* analogy, a raised eyebrow if not a question to urge me on. Father seemed relaxed. I was having fun and was in no rush to get back to my office. I continued, "My first night at camp, I was struggling to get my six-year-olds ready for bed after their long trip from New York City.

It was getting dark. They were hyperactive, nervous, and maybe a little frightened. I was nervous—and a little frightened. I had expected to be a counselor for older campers but on arrival at the camp, learned that I had been reassigned to a cabin for six-year-olds. Camp was a new experience for them; six-year-old care and Jewish Orthodox life were new experiences for me."

The show-business side of my life kicked in; my delivery became more animated, more dramatic, more image-evoking.

"Red-headed, hysterical Martin was tangled in his underpants, a stream of urine running down his legs, a pool forming around one soaked sneaker. I couldn't extricate him from his warm, wet pants. An odor of sour eucalyptus drifted from his body into the cabin. His hysteria was mounting. It was now country dark, not New York dark. I pulled the string to turn on a single naked low wattage bulb that swung on a frayed electrical cord hanging from the ceiling. Almost simultaneously with the lighting of the bulb, there was a wailing at the cabin door, 'You created energy. You created energy.' Dimly lit in the doorway, I could make out the features of a stooped-over short woman. More calmly this time, she repeated, 'You created energy. You created energy. Don't do anything. I'll get the custodian to turn off the light.'" I reminded Father as an aside, the Orthodox Jew is forbidden to create energy on the Sabbath that begins at Friday sundown. She must have assumed I was Jewish.

"Father, that woman's call for non-Jewish help, for the *Shabbos Goy*, in turning off the light was not unlike the Jesuit call for the non-Jesuit enforcer." Father got the analogy.

He had a sense of humor and observed, "We should have coined the phrase Jesuit Goy. It's so succinct. It says it all—*Jesuit Goy*." We both laughed.

"One man's *Ratio* is another man's *Halakhah*," I responded.

We had milked the *Ratio-Halakhah* parallel for all it was worth and were enjoying ourselves. With our newfound insight, we got up to get coffee and dessert. Good company and a great view of the City called for a second cup—and a second story—when we returned to our table.

"Father, Jesuits know the power of the Latin phrase but Jews know the power of the Yiddish phrase," I opined after my first sip.

"Go on. I'm game," he encouraged, with a smile bordering on resignation. I had always enjoyed telling the tale of my introduction to local politics. Both our cups now on the table. I began.

"While living in Marblehead, in a moment of weakness before I moved to Boston, I agreed to let my name be inserted as a write-in candidate for School Committee. After a couple of weeks of door-to-door canvassing, street-corner sign-carrying, and requisite acceptance of a League of Women's invitation to participate in a panel discussion, the Chairman of the town Board of Selectmen and local Temple President, Arnold, asked if I wished to speak to the congregation of his synagogue. I accepted." No political candidate turns down an opportunity to speak to an assembled congregation of any faith.

"I had presented what I'm afraid approached a full-fledged stump speech to the packed auditorium following Arnold's introduction as facilitator and returned to my seat next to him. He rose from his seat on the stage and asked, 'Questions from the audience?' An over anxious member of the congregation who was to confuse question-asking with pronouncement-making stood up. His flow of pronouncements was picking up momentum; there was no question in sight. Arnold sat quietly. He wasn't going to come to my rescue and interrupt a synagogue member. It was evident I would need to save myself. I seized the opportunity when a grandiose declaration of schools' responsibility to society that would have even made John Dewey blush boomed from the speaker's mouth." Time for throwing in my political punch line and analogy to the Jesuit use of Latin terms had arrived.

"That would be a *mitzvah*," I exclaimed in decibel level to match that of the speaker. When I returned to my seat on the hall's stage, I leaned over to Arnold and whispered, 'When was the last time there was a school committee member in Marblehead who could say, "It would be a *mitzvah*?"' 'Are you Jewish?' asked Arnold. I winked."

I provided Father with an epilogue of sorts. During the weeks between the meeting at the synagogue and election day, Arnold and his friends in the congregation must have spread the word of my *mitzvah* pronouncement. I carried 90 percent of the vote of the predominantly Jewish Clifton precinct and hence became the first write-in candidate in the long history of Marblehead to be elected to the School Committee. And all because of a wink and a *mitzvah*.

The dining room was now empty, save for Father Thomas and me. Neither of us, I'm sure, had expected lunch to go on for so long or to wander so far from the *Ratio*. I was a little wiser for my luncheon with Father on things Catholic and Jesuit; he was a little wiser on things Jewish and Orthodox.

It was only one week later when Father's reference to *Deuteronomy* as a reference for the wisdom he was to share outperformed my citation of the Halakhah. Professors and associate deans were all horse-shoed into the corral of an architect's seating banquette designed for *Architectural Forum* publication at the meeting I had called. The School's mission statement and undergirding programs, I'm afraid, still promised all things to all people. Without clear definition and priorities, marketing was hampered, and with little prospect of budget increases, we risked being placed in a Procrustean bed in which all programs would be equally short, equally long, and equally dead.

My opening remarks to the assembly of professors were buried in a bed of silence. There wasn't a murmur of assent or dissent; there wasn't even a nod or shaking of heads. I snuck a look up at the clock on the wall.

Ten minutes had passed and there were fifty to go. I was out there on my own. If I was to survive the balance of the hour, I needed to catch my professors' attention. I put the "PowerPoint" presentation that was catching few professors' attention on hold. I stepped away from the computer. Maybe if I interjected some humor, the meeting would come to life. My "It would be a mitzvah" moment in Marblehead had made a difference; use of lexicon derived from my Jewish roots might help me now. All I needed was to get to one Jewish professor to respond. If I could evoke a response from one Jew, there would be a response from another. And then the Catholics and the Protestants would join in; it would be like my *Ratio* moment with Father Thomas. I called on my Jewish-root strategy.

"The question implicit in the School's mission statement that calls for an answer is analogous to the question posed at a family Passover dinner: 'Why is this night different from any other night?'"

There was silence. I had expected a few chuckles at least from my Jewish colleagues. I tossed out a clue to help, "Why is this School different from any other school?" Again, there was no pick up. I felt instant empathy with a family friend who on retirement as a lawyer chose stand-up comedy as a second career.

Standing at the front of the room, enveloped in silence, I remembered some advice from my psychologist wife, "Don't be afraid of silence. Don't fill it with your words. Wait for a response." Janet was right. Finally, somebody took the hook. Relief, albeit short-lived, came from an unexpected source. Father Thomas, recent lunch partner familiar with my Jewish tale telling, rose to the offering like a trout rises to a fly.

"Why is this School different from any other school? I can answer that question. It's as stated in *Deuteronomy*."

Relief was short-lived. I didn't know *Deuteronomy*. I didn't have the foggiest idea about what Father was talking as he went on and on. Obviously, neither did many professors. I didn't anticipate that his *Deuteronomy* observation was to serve as a preamble for his delivery of a homily that was more at home at Sunday morning services than at a university faculty meeting. I squirmed while Father and *Deuteronomy* hijacked my meeting. After what seemed like an eternity of *Deuteronomy* from Father, my Passover analogy was long gone. Any inclination that professors might have had to discuss the program focus had been squelched. I should have asked the question, "Why should this faculty meeting be different from any other faculty meeting?"

Goals set for the faculty meeting were not realized that painful afternoon, but I did learn something. If I were to semantically joust with religious references in this university, I needed to be prepared to parry with readings from the Bible as well as terms drawn from the Torah, Haggadah, or Halakhah.

Early the next morning in the calm prior to staff and professor arrival, I had time to think of the previous day's meeting. There was no question that my hope to talk about program change had failed miserably. But it was more than the failure of humor or religious readings and citations to stimulate discussion that worried me. One couldn't have been a dean as long as I had to not worry about the accumulation of unanswered, or perhaps unanswerable, questions that had accumulated over my years as San Francisco dean. Why had parking anxiety side-tracked a new program initiative? Why had program reformulation proposals led to a rout in Marin? Why had there been such strong resistance to my appointment of a nationally recognized education activist? As I mulled over those questions, I recalled an observation made by an educator years ago when I was studying for my doctorate.

"Trying to change a curriculum is not unlike trying to move a cemetery; you don't know how many friends the dead have until you try to move them." He was right on.

Twenty

Dilemmas of a Different Order

I never thought I would be witness to a display as grand as the roaring fire engines and smoke-shrouded exodus from Monica's Multicultural Day roast until I witnessed the fireworks between Grand Monica and Petite Betty as I sat innocently in the reception room waiting to meet with Assistant Vice President Monica. The wait for my scheduled meeting with Monica was now longer than many I had experienced in doctors' offices. I had already skimmed through *The Foghorn*, read a few articles in *Jesuit*, the Society of Jesus monthly, the only reception area reading materials. I was up to date on University and Jesuit happenings but that wasn't the purpose for my visit.

I was about to rise to schedule an alternate meeting time with Monica's secretary, when from behind the closed door to Monica's office, a cry of anger cut through the silence. Curiosity prevailed. I would wait a little longer. Moments later, Monica's clearly identifiable voice, an octave and decibel level higher than usual, saturated the reception room as the door to her office burst open. She stood in the doorway, face-to-face with Petite Betty.

"I've had it with this university. This is a Catholic university. This is supposed to be a place that not only preaches morality but demands moral behavior," Petite Betty stormed. Monica, emotions under full control, slowly delivered a traditional administrator retort to her crimson-flushed combatant.

"I'm sorry, we'll look into the matter." That wasn't good enough for Petite Betty.

"I gave you my daughter, confident that you would look out for her," she retorted. She wasn't calmed by Monica's calm commitment to look into the matter, and as she approached the door to leave the reception area, she stammered, "The dormitory is nothing but a brothel with a chapel and you dare to call it a co-ed dorm?" She took a few more steps, halted, and sputtered, "I call it a brothel with a chapel." Petite Betty was poised for her grand exit.

Unperturbed, Monica softly and knowingly replied, "Excuse me, excuse me, Mrs. Robinson. You're wrong. We receive federal funds."

"What's that got to do with anything?" blurted Petite Betty. I had some sympathy with her. Where was Monica going?

"Mrs. Robinson," Monica replied to the now apoplectic parent, "Federal law mandates the separation of church and state. The University has received Federal fund support for a long time. The government neither funds chapels nor brothels. We are regularly audited." I wasn't prepared for Monica's religious twist.

Both combatants had now gone over the edge. Petite Betty was distressed by the sexual activity in her daughter's dorm room; Grand Monica talked of church-government relationship. And I had been introduced to a novel application of the principle of church-state separation. I have little doubt that lawyers would enjoy serving either as defense or prosecution attorneys in a case of *Monica v. Robinson* or *Robinson v. Monica.*

"Thank you for nothing," Petite Betty exclaimed as she swung the door open and stormed out of the reception room into the hallway. The game of wordplay had ended.

Lawyers would have appreciated quite a different challenge suggested by a story shared with me by Holden, Vice President for Development, the man in the camel's hair coat who had interrupted Professor Emilia' s grand entrance to Father President's emergency meeting.

I had felt a twinge of envy as I climbed the hill to meet with Holden who worked alongside Father President in the president's mountain perch, my School's former home. Renovation of my old School fit for Father President and his minions complete, Father was now in the final stages of one more building project: the construction of Loyola House, a new Jesuit Community home.

The new Jesuit home was near completion. The architect's planning and detail of the structure conveyed care, love, good taste—and cash. The splendor of the new facility had already been noticed by the larger Jesuit world and the assignment to San Francisco had suddenly become appealing to younger Jesuits; the young have always preferred castles to infirmaries, tomorrow to yesterday.

The odor of fresh lumber and Spackle was still evident as I passed through my School's former remodeled entryway. A refinished teal blue elevator with an interior more reminiscent of Florida than California slowly rose to Holden's floor. The doors slowly and silently opened to reveal vacant office cubicles bathed in sunlight lining the aisle to his office. I had entered an academic ghost town, and it wasn't even a University Friday afternoon.

Through an open door at the end of the corridor, I could see Holden standing with his office door open. Noting my approach, he turned from a window from which he had been viewing the new construction, John II's Jesuit Community *Relais & Chateaux.* My arrival had interrupted his reverie.

"Where is everyone?" I asked upon entering his office. He didn't answer, or rather I didn't recognize his lack of a direct response as an answer.

"Take a look out my window," Holden offered with a sigh and returned to viewing the almost finished Loyola House with me now at his side. The building made quite a statement: views of the Marin Headlands to the north, cross-hatched city streets to the east. A courtyard with a fountain and surrounding plantings complemented by religious statuary set in antiqued walls almost directly below Holden's window provided a warming touch.

I observed with a chuckle, "It's quite something—it's not medieval Italy but it looks as if it's been here forever. A home like that could even make someone like me reverent," I joked. There was no acknowledgment of my attempt at humor. I hadn't appreciated that Holden's "Take a look out my window" was prelude to his answering my opening question, "Where are all the people?" My attempt at humor had interrupted his answer.

"Let me tell you about the cost of instant antiquity," he continued. "Two days ago, men clothed in what looked like space suits, began sandblasting all of the concrete courtyard walls. A patina of antiquity appeared right before my eyes. Each passing minute, a decade was added to the age of the walls. With each hour of sandblasting, we went forward into the past." Holden was showing signs of emergence from his tightly wound New England cocoon.

"Where is everybody?" I asked again. I wasn't prepared for his answer.

"No one gave thought to where the dust from the sandblasting would go. I'm sure they didn't expect that most of it would end up in our offices. This place sounded like an infirmary—coughing, sneezing, rashes, running eyes—one staff member even developed chest pain." As if divulging an inside secret, he added, "I don't know whether it was compassion or a fear of legal action that led the Administration to give all staff in the building a week off." The mystery of the building's silence was solved but I never learned whether the fear of lawyers or empathy had led to the floor's vacant offices.

"What about the Fathers who already live in the Castle?" I asked. "They couldn't take a vacation."

"Oh, they have God. I guess they figure they won't need legal counsel."

Pinstripe Vice President Holden's observations were New England sedate in comparison to the histrionics of Grand Monica and Petite Betty.

But this wasn't the same Holden who had been intimidated by Professor Emilia in the president's office, the staid, pin-striped, church-going New Englander in the camel's hair coat I thought I knew.

The new Loyola House on upper campus along with the spires of time-honored St. Ignatius Church on lower campus physically contributed to the Jesuit aura of spirituality. The distinguished social activist Father Drinan's visit from Boston provided a glimpse into the very human dimension of Jesuit life.

Father Drinan, professor and social activist at Jesuit Boston College and former congressman from Boston, recognized nationally for his protest of the Vietnam War, had been invited by the University as a guest in a Distinguished Speakers Program to share thoughts with the University community and local residents. I looked forward to seeing him again as many Boston University professors and I, certainly not John Silber, had met him and applauded the work of the activist professor at neighboring Boston College.

The bandbox Gershwin Theater (name later dropped due to differences between Gershwin family representatives and Father President) located in the School of Education was packed. Attendees for the event had come from far beyond the walls of the University campus—testimony to Father Drinan's moral stature and Jesuit presence in the Bay Area.

Father with his lean and wiry frame, slowly approached the podium and rested a manuscript on the lectern. Hands firmly planted on the podium, he surveyed the house. His eyes, lighthouse reflectors, swung slowly from port to starboard, starboard to port. He made eye contact, one by one by one, with attendees seated in the front rows. Once he was assured of full attention, he rested his forearms and elbows on the podium and struck a conversational pose. He was relaxed. He was no longer frail. It was now time for him to warm up the audience; he would get to the heart of his presentation once he had secured ownership of the audience. He'd chosen a whimsical anecdote as the lure to reel us all in. I don't remember the tale's precise wording but it went something like this:

On my last visit to San Francisco, after sitting for hours at SFO waiting to board my delayed flight to return me to snowbound Boston, I was informed by the airline that equipment would not be available for the flight due to blizzard conditions back East. No flights would be leaving for Boston until the next morning. I was also told arrangements had been made with a nearby motel to put up passengers for the night.

Far from home, no time set for the next day's departure, and alone at the hotel, I felt down. Magazine selections in the room were hardly distracting, news on television depressing, and evening programming insipid. I turned to the Gideon's Bible that still could be found in the top bedside drawer of many an airport hotel or motel. What reading would bring me the greatest comfort? Probably one of the psalms. I thumbed through the titles. Ah, there's one. The psalm was particularly lyrical; the words were calming and gave a sense of comfort. I buried myself in the reading and within moments, had forgotten the lousy hotel room in which I'd been put up for the night and the uncertainty of tomorrow—and then as I came to the end of the reading, there was a hand-written notation in the margin, 'If you're still lonely call (650) . . .'"

Father paused before continuing. He knew how to deliver a punch line, how to work an audience. "*It wouldn't be appropriate for me to give you the full number.*"

There was muted laughter; there were warm smiles. Father's intellect and political stature were complemented by a sense of humor. The audience was his.

When I now recall Father's presentation, the man I had met and whose political convictions I had strongly supported while I was in Boston, I don't know whether to feel angry, or just plain sad. I would like to still be able to laugh upon remembering the lead-in to his presentation that afternoon but so much has changed for the Church and the Catholic community since he spoke. Today, Father's tale of *Gideon's Bible* would generate uncomfortable murmurs rather than the warm laughter of that afternoon. The work and words of honorable men of God such as Father Drinan have been rendered suspect, their contributions to creating a more just world stained by the behavior of some of his colleagues.

In his whimsical introduction, Father Drinan, a man whose stature and commitment to social justice I had recognized and admired for years back in Boston, inadvertently triggered the memory of a personal ethical question of quite different order and significance I had not so long ago generated by my own behavior.

There were few restaurants or bistros close enough to the University for regular off-campus lunch visits of professors and staff. Too often, Hilltop Café seated on a hilltop that goes by the name Lone Mountain, was the destination for professor, staff, and student upper campus lunch. Hilltop Café, provided with its toney name shortly after the arrival of Father President John II, had a distinctive ambience. A scent of disinfectant mingled with vapors of fast food in stainless steel trays; salads in plastic containers burrowed beneath glass shelves carrying tired baked goods; large stainless steel cylinders belched thick yogurt. And high carbohydrate chips of every variety rested next to the cash register to capture last minute impulses.

Too often, I would take a lunch break from my office and read the newspaper, a cup of yogurt or a salad on a tray before me, with diners at neighboring tables hunched over worn plastic trays loaded with fast food nation offerings.

Manny, supervisor of the cafe, nevertheless took pride in his work and tried to keep students, staff, and professors happy. He also loved to keep deans happy. I had to give him credit. I was convinced that of all his deans, I was his favorite. I never suspected, however, my status as Manny's "favorite" would create a major ethical dilemma.

"Mmm, that's good," I commented to Professor Godfather one lunchtime as we slid our trays down the stainless steel shelf after sampling the cafe's *peanut butter* yogurt. It was a pleasant change from the perfumed *Peach Nectar* mass that usually swirled from the spigot. I hadn't noticed Manny, like a mother duck guarding her ducklings, looking over the food line.

"Dean, you like peanut butter yogurt?" He obviously had overheard my "Mmm." His smile broadened as he emerged from behind the counter. His cheeks rose to meet his eyes. I nodded affirmatively and continued my conversation with Godfather as we slid our trays toward the cashier.

"Dean, it's good to see you, we have your yogurt," Manny greeted me at my next Café lunch. "Dean, it's good to see you, we have . . ." was to become an early afternoon mantra chanted by Manny lunch after lunch, day after day, as the yogurt machine streamed its peanut butter yogurt. I never witnessed anyone other than me pull down the *peanut butter* lever. But the stainless steel cow that dispersed the life-supporting yogurt now always carried the tag *Peanut butter. Peanut Butter* displaced *Peach Nectar*. It displaced *Blueberry Swirl*. It displaced *Orange Chocolate*. There were no more specials. Student choice was limited to *Vanilla*, *Chocolate*, or *Peanut Butter*. Students had become hostage to my *peanut butter* preference.

Pleasure provided by my *peanut butter* fix faded as weeks passed but I was caught in a web of privilege and good intention. Just when I was ready to inform Manny and free myself from his web, he spun another silken strand.

"Dean, the peanut butter yogurt is on us." He wanted to make me happy. How could I break the news to him of my desire to break my fix after weeks of his beneficence? I resorted to the white lie.

"Manny," I informed him one afternoon a few days later as I pulled down the lever for *vanilla*, "The doctor thinks I might have an allergy to peanuts."

"It's not serious?" he softly inquired.

"No, thanks. Everything is under control."

Only days later, that peanut butter yogurt, ceased to be a staple. *Peach Nectar*, *Blueberry Swirl*, and *Orange Chocolate* swirled once again.

As something of a postscript to the story, I must admit that there was part of me that liked Manny's special treatment. I liked having my ego massaged by his favors—and flavors. Everyone, especially deans, enjoy special treatment from time to time. But to honor a dean's tastes at the expense of students posed something of an ethical question. I would need to be more sensitive to the potential for the growth of ethical issues from the grant of small favors.

Ethical questions whimsically generated by Manny's behavior and by Father Drinan's anecdote, although of quite different order, paled in magnitude when set against the dissonance created by the horror of September 11, 2001.

Conflagration of the Twin Towers sent shockwaves of horror and brought life in San Francisco to a temporary standstill. Geological shockwaves the scale of Loma Prieta in California have a long history. Save Pearl Harbor, political shockwaves in America the scale of 9/11 have no history. One week later, Herb was in my office. Teaching and success of a project to attract teachers for teaching in Boston and Oakland was shielding him from the criticism of colleagues.

"Paul, I'm trying to have my classes for the next few weeks provide a safe environment in which students can safely exchange dangerous ideas and thoughts. Why don't you sit in on a class next week?"

The University community singed by the smoldering flames of hatred was trying to deal with issues that seldom enter classrooms. It was a time of raw emotion. If ever there was a need for a safe place in which to exchange dangerous ideas and confront emotional issues of right and wrong, it was now. I accepted Herb's invitation.

Herb's class had already begun when I entered the room. On the wall hung poster boards with photographs depicting man at his worst: flaming World Trade Center towers, an Israeli bus engulfed in flames, Israeli tanks in Gaza, children cowering in the rubble of bombed out buildings in Palestine. Herb had never shied away from taking on tough issues—and often in a most provocative manner.

"I've asked the dean to join us today." He off-handedly introduced me to the students and invited me to take a seat.

Students were seated in two distinct clusters of chairs, distinctly separated from one another. I wondered whether the placement of students in the distinct clusters was a result of assignment or political and cultural antagonism? Would I risk making a political statement if I chose to sit in one cluster rather than another? I slinked into a chair at the side of the room, hopefully, neutral territory. Herb set the discussion in motion.

"Let's pick up where we left off last time. We had been discussing the concept of *Intifada*. Ahmed, why don't you lead off?"

The discussion didn't merely take off. It erupted with the velocity and heat of a space launch: Sharon and Arafat, Zionism and Judaism, Jew and Muslim, Palestine and Israel, terrorism and war, *Intifada* and Crusades, persecution and prejudice. No topic was off-limits as students fueled the fire. I was frightened that exchanges would leave scars from which they would never recover as they stumbled through mine fields of fear and prejudice. I wondered whether with such great heat, it would be possible to separate the emotional from the intellectual or reach new understandings.

Herb would occasionally redirect discussion, or calmly with little apparent emotion, interject a question to calm the waters of hate. As a questioning Jew himself, and arbiter of tough questions for years, maybe he could help the students negotiate this minefield. Anger was spilled. Stereotypes were tested. Politically loaded solutions were floated. Blame was assigned.

As the class progressed, it became clearer and clearer that the battlefield would not quieten this week or next week, this month or next month, this year or for years to come. The planted political explosives were too powerful. I was absorbed in the release of heat rather than impressed by the acquisition of new knowledge. At the particular moment in history, I'm not sure it could, or should, have been any different.

When Herb took advantage of a brief lull in the spilling of sentiments and almost apologetically informed the class, "We need to call it quits for this evening," I settled for the hope that today's exercise, with Herb's low-key leadership, might help students, at least for the time being, to establish a beachhead for reason and a way to relieve emotional pressure. I was relieved, the clustering of chairs, at least for today, didn't seem to reflect ideological divides.

Dangerous ideas had been tested in a relatively safe environment but I'm not sure any beachheads had been established. I know Herb's closing comment "We need to call it quits" disappointed me. There was so much more he could have said in closing. But I immediately learned that Herb hadn't quite called it quits.

"Dean," he pivoted his chair, "Any thoughts? Why don't you bring us to a close?" I was certain students weren't waiting for words from the dean, and I certainly wasn't waiting to say something to the students. But it wasn't possible to sit in Herb's classroom this afternoon and not have thoughts to share.

"Herb, I don't know whether I can do justice to this evening's discussion—or capture the range of thought and pains shared."

Herb sat silently looking at me. I was buying time. I pulled thoughts together as we all sat silently. Fortunately, a small piece I had written for the graduate student newsletter a week ago about 9/11 came to mind. I found my voice, deanly but personal, romantic but sad. I shared thoughts contained in that newsletter.

"When my kids passed through their adolescent years, they dubbed everything 'awesome': this song was 'awesome'; that party was 'awesome'; that movie was 'awesome.' Everything was 'awesome.' Well, I've seen very few things in life that I would call awesome."

Herb appeared troubled. I sensed the class was getting restless. They must be thinking, "What is he talking about?" I wasn't worried. I knew where I was going.

"At one point during your discussion, I recalled a personal moment I had in Jerusalem about fifteen years ago. One of the few truly awesome moments I have experienced took place one late afternoon as I stood across from the Wailing Wall. The ancient city glowed gold in the dry heat. There before me I saw Orthodox Jews, dressed in black, tallis over their shoulders, davening before the wall. I heard chants of the call to evening Muslim prayer drifting over the wall from neighboring mosques. And at some point, the peeling of bells from Christian churches contributed to the cacophony. It all seemed so steeped in history. For all the religious battles over the years, everything seemed so peaceful. 'That was awesome.' Maybe there really was one God I thought; he was just worshipped in different ways." I paused and waited for the words to sink in before I softly, almost as an after-thought, reminisced, "That afternoon in Jerusalem seems so long ago."

There was deep silence in the classroom. Nobody left their seats to leave. I didn't know whether my comments had been helpful but I knew I had been honest, albeit a bit theatrical.

Herb nodded, "We're finished for this afternoon." The class filed quietly out of the room.

Twenty-One

Rainforests and Rumors

Father President John II, shortly after his arrival as University President, placed a bet on Father President John I: appointment of the former president as University Chancellor would increase gift giving to the University. He bet Catholic celebrants who knew him affectionately as 'Father Lo' coupled with the recognition and respect of the San Francisco community made him a natural for the position.

President Father John I while as president, seldom met with deans as a group and when he did, he invariably carried news calling for a painful remedy to be administered. Father Jack would invariably be left to pick up the pieces and put in place steps for remediation whether it be budget cutting, addressing a trustee grievance, or resolving a student complaint logged in the president's office. Deans respected John I as an institutional figurehead and burdened overseer rather than academic leader or ally. Our first thought on learning of John I's appointment was how relieved he must be to no longer have to put up with budget shortfalls, union snipes, trustee questions—or deans.

It had been more than a year since Father John II's appointment as president when the agenda for the Council of Deans' Meeting carried one item: University Development Campaign. Father Chancellor John, in his capacity as chancellor, would be meeting with the Council.

Father John was seated alongside Father Jack, casually talking with one another as we entered the room for the Council Meeting. John greeted each dean with a smile and a "Join us," as he or she arrived, quite a contrast in atmosphere from my first Deans' Council Meeting with Father at which his lamentation of custodial staff service preceded a directive for budget cuts to be overseen by Father Jack.

We all chatted with one another as if we were old friends as we sat around the table before getting to the morning's agenda. Conversation flowed freely and our new chancellor was relaxed. His pronounced change in persona and appearance tempted the thought that the notion of eternal youth might not be all that absurd. He had become "Father Lo" also to the deans. My concern that the interrogation Father might receive at this meeting from some deans who had always been critical when he wore the presidential crown faded. That was until we got to the business of the agenda and he gave deans an assignment.

"I want you to meet individually with professors in your schools and ask them for a contribution to the University campaign," he requested less than ten minutes into the discussion of fund raising. Deans knew they would be expected to contribute to the campaign but none of us had anticipated personal solicitation of our professors.

Saul, dean of Arts and Sciences, wasn't shy about voicing his discomfort. Why should the dynamics of this meeting be any different from those long ago when Father was president and Saul union steward prior to his desertion from the ranks of Labor to join Management.

"Father, I won't do it. We can't ask for contributions without noting who gives and who doesn't, who is generous and who is tight-fisted." Saul consciously glanced at the dean of the School of Law before he added, "There may also be legal implications." The dean nodded affirmatively. He didn't need say anything. Opinions of attorneys, verbal or non-verbal, always carried extra weight when discussing Labor–Management affairs at the University. Saul was emboldened.

"John, how can I evaluate the performance of my professors and not be vulnerable to claims of bias when I have a record of how much money they have contributed to the University?" Question asked and implicitly answered with the attorney dean's earlier nod, Saul continued, "I won't go to professors, ask them to make a donation, and require that they share how much they're prepared to give the University."

Labor Relations Fireplug Al, emboldened by Saul's ultimatum added, "And, Father, there may also be collective bargaining implications. If deans request and log individual professor donations, they may open themselves to grievances. I'll look into it."

With the validation for Saul's concerns from a lawyer and implicit confirmation from the VP for Labor Relations, observations of deans whipped across the table like a roll of BBs in the back of a pick-up truck. One pronouncement led to another; momentum picked up. Saul's South African dialect became more clipped as he ticked off items of concern. "Ticking" quickly converted to diatribe.

Saul now in diatribe mode, we noticed a percussive "knock, knock, knock" on the table top as Father John's knuckles tapped in calibration to the beat of Saul's pronouncements. With Saul's acceleration of listing problems, the pace and force of Father's knuckle tapping picked up—his hand rose and fell, a vertical metronome. Saul's recitation finally slowed. Father's metronome, in turn, slowed. We were all transfixed by this strange duet as Saul's emotion moderated and Father's beat steadied. Had Father's metronome distracted him? Then in the manner of someone with greater authority addressing one with less, Father slowly dropped two words, "Saul, Saul." Saul's litany of concerns ceased. There was momentary silence. In the sudden calm, Father stage-whispered again, "Saul, Saul." All eyes turned to Father.

"Saul, this is why we appointed you dean. We wanted you inside the tent pissing out rather than as union steward outside pissing in." That was all Father said. There was no reference to objections raised by Saul. There was no anger, no confrontation, only Father's soft, white-toothed smile. He chuckled at his own sense of humor. This was a far different Father than the Father President we knew with a temper and willingness to show it.

We had seldom seen Saul at a loss for words. His face glowed pink. Father continued to sit quietly and smile. A soft smile beats florid cheeks in any contest. Saul was gracious, a trait he seldom revealed in public.

"*Touché*," he muttered and smiled.

Saul and the deans ended up the winners that morning. We were to be asked to write a letter to professors requesting their participation in the campaign; they were to send their contributions directly to the Development Office. We would neither be collectors nor accountants. Of equal import, we all left the meeting with a smile on our faces.

The deans and Chancellor Father John found comfort in exchanges in the intimate setting provided by a seminar room. Fellow deans and I found comfort of a different order in an address delivered by Father Greeley, noted scholar, sociologist, and detective story writer, in a public forum housed in the now School of Education—no longer the Gershwin Theater.

It wasn't until well into the reign of John II that I truly appreciated the comfort and mystery of Catholicism for followers of the faith. Father Greeley had been invited by Sister Rachel to speak at a University forum; I wish he had visited the University earlier.

Students, professors, and administrators, Catholic and non-Catholic, religious and lay, sat quietly waiting for Father Greeley's presentation. Not a seat in the theater was empty. Murmurs of anticipation provided white noise as Sister carefully negotiated the stairs to the stage. Father Greeley, a well-preserved, lithe priest followed the slow-stepping, stolid Sister. Sister approached the lectern as Father took a seat. Her radiance bathed the audience; her Cheshire smile was visible from the last row of the orchestra. Murmurs were stilled. She carefully lifted the lanyard-held glasses resting on the bib of her habit to her eyes and basked in the moment like a sleeping cat on a sun-washed pillow. She purred Father's churchly and scholarly credits with the audience before she concluded, "Father has been around a long time and has raised many an eyebrow. Some Religious have even gone so far as to call him a Jesuit's Jesuit, a gadfly of the Catholic church. Please join me in welcoming Father Greeley."

Sister stood radiant at the lectern glowing in the aura of the moment. This was her moment too. I suspect she didn't want to leave center stage, but with Father approaching, she had no alternative.

Father stood alone at the podium. Sharp white light from a spotlight danced off his silver hair. His slightly stooped figure cast a crisp shadow on the stage.

"I'm here to provide an antidote to beige Catholicism; Catholicism devoid of all color," he announced. There was a momentary pause. He surveyed the audience, eyes fixed on one row, then the next, and then the next. He was no longer addressing a crowd, he was speaking to each of us individually.

"I'm here to talk about stories of color rather than dialectics."

He had captured the attention of the house—skeptics and all. He didn't need to use a catchy phrase or humorous opener.

"I'm here to talk about a rainforest of metaphors. I'm here to celebrate the saints, the statues, the festive holy days, the Madonna, the Cross, the rosary." As he proceeded, tales of the prophets and rituals of the Church came to life. The bells and smells of ceremony figuratively drifted through the audience.

"I want to share this rainforest of metaphors with people who sit on the outside looking in. I want to share this rainforest with people who would bring logic to every encounter rather than celebrate faith."

He was talking to professors who insisted on bringing logic to every encounter. He was talking to me. I didn't care whether it was the first or the tenth time he had delivered the same lines, or whether his presentation had been field-tested and revised hundreds of times. Symbols, statues, and ceremonies became so much more than the worship of idols that I as a child had been convinced took place on Sundays behind the heavy doors of the Church of Our Lady of Pompeii.

Father held the audience in his hands. We were all now part of his world of colors. How could we not celebrate imagination? How could we not celebrate stories of the Church, even if we were neither religious nor members of the Church? I would have to give more thought to the proposition that logic should inform all behavior.

Father was caught up in his own rainforest. Time was irrelevant until Sister caught his attention with a half-raised arm signal and nod that translated as, "It's time to draw remarks to a close." When Sister gives a signal, the recipient responds. We could have all sat longer and basked in the glow from his tales, but Sister had a schedule to honor and Father a reception to attend. It was time to leave his rainforest. I don't remember how long we were mesmerized by Father, but I know when his presentation came to a close, I was left with the same feeling of uplift and regret I often experience on finishing a good novel. And I had left some of my skepticism at the theater's front door.

The rainforest of metaphors provided a rainbow of colors, but like all rainbows, the wonder is ephemeral, the arch breaks down, the colors fade, and the last ray of light refracts through the last drop of water. In the cold light of my office, the rainbow was no longer. But I couldn't help wondering that if there was a way to expose teachers to Father Greeley's rainbow, they might bring its magic to the classroom. My job would be so much more rewarding if I could take credit for the development of "teachers of the rainbow" and wipe out beige thinking.

One early morning, the smallest of happenings nurtured in the rich soil of Father Greeley's Catholic rainforest lightened up my day. I was leafing through mail sitting in the "in box" that sits on Catherine's desk when outside my office, my new associate dean, Father Matthew, not his usually pale self, flung open the door of the reception area to the deans' offices and with a pronounced bounce to his step, rapidly strode rather than ambled down the boulevard between staff cubicles toward my office. There was color in his usually pallid cheeks. He exuded after-shower freshness. The rich soil of an out-of-state Jesuit conference coupled with the break from the University for a few days had worked wonders.

"Morning, Paul." His voice was clear, his delivery brisk, as he approached Catherine's desk. There was no sign of the allergies that often plagued him. He was happy. It was good to have him back. It felt good to start the day on an up note.

Mary, his assistant, papers in hand for him to read, darted from her cubicle into the center aisle on Father's arrival. She was suddenly a football lineman ready to prevent Father from entering his office.

"Father, everybody's looking for you." There was no break in Father's stride. He slipped around Mary. He was suddenly a fullback twisting off a pending tackle. He pirouetted, forward motion unaffected. Mary repeated more stridently, "Father, everyone is looking for you." Clear of the tackle, door to his office reached, Father Matthew stopped for a second. I expected him to go into an end zone dance before he entered.

"Mary, that's what they said about Jesus." In the event I missed the exchange, he cast a broad smile in my direction. "That's what they said about Jesus. Get it?" He entered his office and closed the door behind him.

Mary stood silently by her station, papers still in hand. Her scowl slowly evolved into a smile. She would just have to wait to deliver her messages until Father Matthew was ready to see her. Father safely in his office, I returned to mine.

You didn't need to appreciate Jesus or wander in Father Greeley's rainforest to appreciate Father Matthew's humor that morning. His springtime pirouette into his office was to be a preamble to matters of far greater importance than a relaxed chancellor, the flora and fauna of Father Greeley's rainforest, or Father Matthew's bounce.

Janet and I longed for the warmth of hazy, sunny days as we counted the days until our Vermont summer escape while raw winds and cold, damp fog off the Bay crept into every nook and cranny of life and the sun only made an occasional late afternoon appearance before fog and night reclaimed ownership. San Francisco summer weather was different from that of "back East." But University summer was, in many respects, the same as "back East" university summers. With a sampling of professors teaching only a course or two before promptly leaving campus, faculty committees not meeting, administrators serially on vacation and not convening as a group, no one is regularly in touch with one another. There are no reliability checks. Summer is the prime growing season for university rumors. This summer's San Francisco University rumor was consequential and pervasive.

During the spring semester, word-of-mouth reports of John II's visits to other Jesuit campuses looking to fill vacated president positions entered dean conversations. By summer, third person, unsubstantiated reports of Father President's frequent visits were common knowledge. There was no question, Father John II planned to leave his San Francisco kingdom.

Visible accomplishments, years in position, and egocentrism often tempt university presidents to seek appointment at another university of greater status. Father President met all these personal criteria—landscaping projects with eye-catching flora were obvious; executive office, academic construction, and renovation projects dotted the campus. And Loyola House, the new castle for the Jesuit Community, insurance for Father President's place in the University pantheon of presidents was close to completion. He had also presided over the University's evolution from a sleepy backwater of Jesuit and Catholic higher education to a more dynamic academic institution. One additional factor contributed to Father President's wanderlust: he had played all his academic cards. He needed to find another University campus on which to weave his spell before he tripped over his vanity and restless deans reclaimed their academic prerogatives.

Day after day, the University was enveloped in the cold summertime fog that moved inland off the Pacific. What better weather and season could there be to hunker down and feed on rumor? "Insider" reports of receptions Father had received at universities he had visited provided the grist for conjecture. Where would Father go? Would it be Georgetown? Notre Dame? Boston College? Holy Cross? Each insight from an individual dean into a possible new kingdom for Father served as testimony to that dean's connections.

"Paul, did you hear that Father John is a finalist at Georgetown?" Dean Phillip of the jade ring asked on returning from a conference of health educators in the District of Columbia. "They have a medical school, you know."

Soft-spoken Dean Jerome of the Library on return from a librarians' conference in New England observed, "Father John is looking at Holy Cross," to which Dean Saul of Arts and Sciences responded, "It's hidden in the woods somewhere near Worcester. Can you imagine him being chauffeured in a stretch limo to Boston to mix with Boston Society?"

Dean Saul, a few days later, off-handedly and privately informed me, "Father's going to be offered the presidency at Creighton." Saul's air of certainty evoked credibility. He must have spoken to someone in the know. He continued, "It's in his home diocese, his mother lives there, he has friends there, and Creighton has a Med School as well as an ugly campus in need of beautification—and God knows, Paul, with Georgetown and Holy Cross out of the picture, John is running out of options."

Saul's reputation as a dean with access to insider information was validated a week later when Wise Jim, our new Provost, notified deans individually by phone that Father President had accepted an invitation extended by the Creighton University Board of Trustees to serve as president. Well-connected Saul, to no one's surprise, won the "Where's John Going?" award.

Wise Jim asked us to keep the information confidential until public announcement of Father's departure from the University later in the day. Request or no request, I felt compelled to personally tell my associate deans of Father President's planned departure—after all, there would be a public announcement in only a matter of hours. It's difficult to keep a matter "confidential" from close trusted colleagues if no harm is apparent in discretely sharing the information.

I stuck my head in the offices of my associate deans and asked them both to join me in my office. Parsa and Matthew, as if fused at the hip, joined me in a matter of minutes. They shared a nervous look with one another as they sat down, the look of the cat that had just swallowed the canary. They knew that something was up. I pulled a chair up to the table at which they were seated. I got right to the point.

"I've just spoken with Wise Jim. Father President has accepted the position of President of Creighton University." Please keep the information confidential until the Provost notifies the University community later this afternoon."

Parsa smiled. Father Matthew of little affect and quick wit was true to form.

"Paul, I already saw the white smoke rise over the Nebraska horizon." Saul wasn't the only one with connections. I shouldn't have been surprised. As a member of the Jesuit Community, Matthew was privy to inside information and accorded privileges that go along with membership in the Society of Jesus. Dean Saul may have had his connections with the Board of Trustees, Father Matthew had his with a higher authority.

As promised, later that afternoon, Wise Jim circulated an email to the University community that announced Father John II had been selected as president of Creighton University. Father John II, S.J., the third President John for whom I had worked during my years as dean in Boston and San Francisco, would be moving on.

Twenty-Two

Palms and Farewell

The deans could as easily have been described as a family of children called together to learn of their father's divorce as professional colleagues when they were called together by Father President to share a personal farewell. Maybe it was my own long-ago divorce from my first wife or conversations with psychologist wife, Janet, that triggered my farewell analogy. The deans harbored variations of the questions that a child upon first learning of his parents' separation might ask: "Why are you leaving us?" "Why are you moving so far away?" "Will you miss us?" But there was a major difference: we already knew the answers to these questions and we wouldn't plead, "We love you," or "Please stay." We were confident that we wouldn't miss one another. Divorce might be a good thing for both Father and his children.

There was a library hush to the room as we sat around the conference table and waited for Father to join us. Some of us reviewed mail, others finished up memos, and some talked quietly to one another. Dean Saul, normally intrusive, clip-worded, and antagonistic, floated no filler comments—for a while. Five minutes passed and there was still no Father President. Saul couldn't tolerate the silence any longer. He had never lost his anger at Father John II for telling him that the search for the position of Provost open on Father Jack's retirement, now filled by Wise Jim, would be limited to members of the Jesuit Community and then proceed to appoint a Provost who wasn't a Jesuit.

"Why is John wasting all our time by calling us here? We know why he's moving. He's bored. He has no friends. His choices for relocation are running out—and Creighton is located in his home diocese."

Wise Jim broke off his quiet conversation with Samuel at the other end of the table and focused his eyes on Saul. Saul wasn't distracted by Jim's silent message to calm down.

He repeated for emphasis, "Creighton is the only University at which he has friends," before adding, "it has a medical school and a dismal looking campus. Father will be able to build new buildings and be a landscape gardener while he basks in the status of a university with a Med school."

Emboldened by his colleague's comments, Dean Samuel in his hand-tailored Hong Kong suit, not breaking Saul's cadence, picked up on the frustration, "We've been waiting now for over ten minutes. Father isn't even here to tell us what we already know. I had to cancel an important appointment to be here," and asked to no one in particular, "How much time do students have to wait for a late professor to show up before leaving the classroom?"

Samuel knew we wouldn't walk out. Wise Jim's stare passed from Saul to Samuel. His children were acting up. Jim didn't utter a word. His look said it all: control yourself.

Jim couldn't have timed his silent admonition better. Father President's lanky frame filled the doorway. Jim's cautionary stare softened as Father entered the room in full Bolshoi glide. Jim pulled out a chair next to him from under the table for Father, and Father briskly slid sideways into the seat, slowly pulled the chair up, placed both hands flat on the tabletop, and smiled as we all sat silently.

Father's "Good morning," more an obligatory prelude to what was to follow than a warm greeting, broke the silence. The deans softly echoed a rote "Good morning" that young children might provide in response to a "Good morning" from a Catholic elementary school teacher. "Good mornings" exchanged, Father President lifted his hands from the table, leaned back slowly, and punched out a single sentence. He was looking for laughs; he was tired of playing the straight man.

"I figured I had better take the job if I wanted to be buried at home."

I wasn't prepared for Father's opener—nor, I suspect, were the rest of us. When a fifty- year-old-or-so man or woman in apparent good health speaks of burial, even in jest, one has to be respectful—or worried. Father's sense of humor either missed the target or the prognosis for his health wasn't good. We couldn't have known at the time that Father would, in 2015, die of cancer in Omaha. Sometimes, reality trumps humor.

"Have you picked out your plot?" embittered Saul politely, asked *sans* smile. Father President didn't take the bait. No words were needed; a cold stare sufficed. Father moved on. He outlined factors that had led to his decision—along with a healthy list of his contributions to the University during his reign. Once his soliloquy of accomplishments ended, he added, "As you know, Nebraska, in many ways, is home to me." Put more simply, he wanted to be with friends. There was little more for him to do here, and he had grown tired of his company.

This was neither the place nor the time to ask Father about relations with his current University family even if we were confident that family problems had contributed to his decision to call it quits. It must be hard for any university president to explain to colleagues with whom he has worked for many years as to why he has chosen to leave one university presidency for another. And from San Francisco to Omaha?

I had to hand it to Father President though. For all the behind-the-curtain-talk about his presidency, there was little question that the University's outward face to neighbors and prospective students was far more appealing than when he had arrived. And I understood why he, and most university presidents, feel compelled to construct physical edifices. They stand as visible, eternal monuments to their presidency once they are gone. Academic markers, unlike structural edifices, crumble more rapidly and are often lost in the dust of time.

One morning not long after our deans' meeting with John II , "deep throat" Vincent's tale of Father's final days at the University was to leave a more lasting impression on me than our farewell gathering with Father, and it provided a fitting sense of closure.

"Paul, got a minute?" Vincent asked as he peeked his head into my office. He knew I always had a minute for him. After all, he was my University "deep throat," I his favorite audience. He took special joy in keeping me informed of the flurry of John II's departing campus beautification gifts. I waved him in.

"May I close the door?" When he closed the door before I had a chance to respond it was a sure sign that he had special information to share. I wasn't to be disappointed this morning. He sat down at my coffee table and started with today's scoop before I had time to join him.

"Paul, you know the palm trees Father President planted on top of Lone Mountain at the entry to upper campus?" he asked. How could I have not? Two columns of a dozen one-hundred-foot Canary Island palms seemed to have risen almost overnight during the final term of John II's reign and now bordered the path to the upper campus complex of executive offices. With tightly wrapped fronds around their trunks, they resembled steeples of a Russian Orthodox Church, or lines of palms pictured on Hollywood postcards.

"You know they're the talk of the campus. *The Foghorn* wants to know how many students' tuition it took to plant the trees. The union wants to know how much money ear-marked for the purchase of trees could have gone to professors' salary increases. And native San Franciscans want to know what the University is doing planting palm trees in San Francisco—palms are so Los Angeles."

Vincent's thick, heavy-rimmed glasses couldn't hide the mirth of his eyes. He chortled as he listed a litany of complaints from University members and San Franciscans. He was wound up. He interrupted his itinerary of information with a sip of water.

"Go on," I urged. There was no need for me to ask him to continue.

"My ground crew was working round the clock to get those trees planted before the announcement of Father President's resignation was made. They were assigned 24/7 to the task." Vincent took another sip of water. He was milking the story for every drop. I was now set up for the punch line.

"And after the job was done, do you know how the staff in my office referred to the project?"

I played the straight man, "No, I don't. Tell me." How else could I have replied?

"They refer to it as Father's last erection."

Vincent's chortle became a guffaw. I couldn't help counter, "and it's certainly quite a magnificent one." We snickered like two children enjoying an off-color joke. "I'll deny having made the last comment if the words travel out of this office, priests already have enough trouble," I finished. Vincent laughed. We knew we spoke inappropriately—but in full confidence.

"Well, I'm off." Vincent pushed back his chair and rushed out of the office. There was business that called for his attention. He couldn't have been gone for more than fifteen minutes when my personal line rang. It was Catherine.

"Paul, your friend wants to speak with you. He says it'll be brief." I wondered what could he want.

"Put him through."

"Paul, I forgot to answer your question about why the fronds of the palms are bound." Vincent sounded rushed. "They need to remain bound for forty days and forty nights after transplanting to retain moisture necessary for their survival."

I had forgotten that I had even asked him why the fronds of the newly planted trees were wrapped in twine to create phallic spires. I had always been impressed with Vincent's commitment to his job and detail; today's follow up was beyond the call of duty.

"Paul, I'm serious! The fronds need to be wound for forty days and forty nights." The tale got richer.

"Do you know the names of the two workmen who supervised the transplants?"

I wasn't sure how his latest question related to the biblical, botanical, or anatomical information he had previously shared but I played the role of the straight man one more time.

"Okay, Vincent. I'm game. What are they?"

"Jesus and Moses," he bounced back. Vincent could have been a borscht belt comedian. "I'm not making the story up, Paul. It's true."

I'm not sure I believed Vincent's latest addendum. But he was having so much fun with the story. What purpose would it serve to share my doubts? Come to think of it, I was left with a sense of ecumenical calm knowing that Jesus and Moses had toiled hours to transplant those trees that could have just as easily been in Bethlehem—or Los Angeles.

Twenty-Three

A Torch Is Passed

"Only Jesuits need apply," might as well have been the lead sentence to the University's search announcement for an heir to the throne of John II. The pool of potential Jesuit university presidents in the nation was rapidly evaporating and the University's history was too tumultuous to permit it to be among the first to appoint a president without S.J. pedigree.

When the Presidential Search Committee discovered an academically qualified member of the Society of Jesus who lived and worked less than one hundred miles south of the City in Palo Alto, there was little question as to where to cast the first fly. The challenge became one of landing the Jesuit from Santa Clara. Christ the fisherman couldn't have done a better job.

Father Steve Privett, S.J., Provost of Santa Clara University, was selected as the twenty-seventh president of the University. Bantamweight, socially conscious Father Steve, with a reputation for calling things as he saw them unfettered by social or political niceties, would be at the helm of the University in September 2000. A new phase in the life of the University was about to begin.

The tenor of University conversation following the announcement of Father Steve's selection and pending arrival changed abruptly. Personal opinions of Father John's stewardship of the University viewed through a rearview mirror were replaced by more careful, investigative conversations, albeit shaped by self-interest. The road on the trip we would all be asked to travel would undoubtedly be different from the one we had just traveled and have implications for our schools and colleges—and potentially our jobs.

Daniel, recent enthusiastic Berkeley-bred dean of the School of Law, proud of his Judaism and Jerome, soft-spoken, Black, Boston College émigre, dean of the University Library, and I had a lot to talk about with our new president only miles and months away. Lunch away from the University campus before my summer retreat to Vermont would be good for all of us.

There wasn't a whisper of a cloud in the rich blue sky. The Farallon Islands, twenty-plus miles offshore, stood crisply etched against the horizon as we exited Jerome's new Plymouth Cruiser and walked down Sacramento Street to *The Magic Flute*. It was one of those rare hot, dry summer days when fog takes a vacation from the City.

Phil, *The Magic Flute's* ebullient host, announced on our entry for all diners to hear, "The deans are with us. Dr. Warren, Dr. Daniel, Dr. Jerome. A pleasure to serve you. Do you wish a seat inside or in the courtyard?"

He knew what our answer would be on this sun-warmed day but he had to ask the question for all to hear. I suspect each of us enjoyed the attention. An attentive host and friendly colleagues with most professors away for summer breaks provided an ideal climate to savor a leisurely lunch.

Father Privett wouldn't be moving to the City from his rose-gardened, sequestered Santa Clara campus until fall, but he was the main course. We batted around so many questions, few for which we had clear answers. No matter. On an afternoon like this, seated outside in the courtyard, there was no rush; there was plenty of time for conjecture. Why would Father want to come from the country to the City? Why would he want to come to a University lower on the academic pecking order than Santa Clara? And, most importantly, what impact might his appointment have on our lives?

"Paul, do you know anything about Steve's history with professional schools?" Daniel asked. I did not.

"What happened to the School of Education at Santa Clara?" asked Jerome. I wasn't sure but I knew Father had actively participated in a Santa

Clara project that worked with children in East Palo Alto; poverty was to East Palo Alto as wealth was to Palo Alto.

"I don't know anything about the Santa Clara library," Jerome mused. "Do you think he'll bring any of his staff from Santa Clara?" We didn't have the foggiest idea.

"Are there any clues about how he feels about non-Catholic officers in a Jesuit and Catholic university?" Daniel asked, almost apologetically. Here we sat, a religious Jew, a non-practicing Protestant, and a half-Jew skeptic, contemplating a question inappropriate in any other setting. We all knew what the formal answer had to be, but . . .

We shared snippets of Santa Clara Father Steve lore that had been picked up by detective work of fellow deans:

"He's not shy about letting his opinions be known."

"He doesn't have time for armchair scholars."

"He doesn't suffer fools."

"He takes the theme of social justice seriously."

"He practices what he preaches. . . ."

We didn't have enough information to confirm the accuracy of the lore, but we had little doubt that we would find out soon after his arrival.

Daniel, Jerome, and I stretched back and talked, and talked, and. . . . We were in no position to draw any conclusions as what life might be like under Father Steve's reign without more homework, but we suspected it would be far different than that in the reigns of John I and II. It really didn't make a difference at this moment. We three were friends playing Privett *20 Questions* as we shared bits and pieces of Father Steve's history and sipped our Chardonnay in the San Francisco sun.

Lunch slowly wound to an end. None of us felt compelled to leave our courtyard roost. There was no mail requiring immediate answer. There were no memos to be sent. Work on reports to be written could wait until tomorrow. But as the courtyard emptied and our waiter's interest turned to the preparation of set-ups for dinner, we knew it was time to go.

We beat the approaching meter maid to the car, red panel of *expired* dropping as we arrived, and quickly piled into Jerome's retro Cruiser. To passers-by, we must have looked like actors in an old gangster film fleeing from the police. Race with meter maid won, safely ensconced in the rear seat, I relaxed.

It seemed only minutes before Jerome pulled into my School's parking lot off Turk Street to drop me off and he and Daniel proceeded to their lower campus offices. I had been relaxed sitting in the back seat, comfortable as the mild air passed over the half-open window. I wished the trip back to campus had taken longer.

"Have a good break, Paul. Don't worry. Remember you've got friends here," Jerome laughed as I fumbled for the rear door handle.

I was prompted to respond, "What's with the 'don't worry, remember you've got good friends here' farewell salutation?" Did he know something I didn't?

Door handle mastered, two feet on the ground, I gently closed the door. I didn't want to leave. Daniel echoed Jerome's "You've got friends here" farewell as Jerome put his foot down on the gas pedal and burst into a rendition of *Who could ask for anything more?* that would make Gershwin turn over in his grave. "You've got music, you've got clout, with the support of a Black man and a Jew, you can't go wrong, who could ask for anything more?" As the car swung out the parking lot onto Turk Street, I could hear the two of them laughing as they drove off.

True San Francisco summer returned to the City the next day. It didn't matter. Plane reservations had been made a month earlier. Janet and I would be off to a month of Vermont summer in a few days.

Our month in the country always seemed too short. Too soon after we would acclimate to the Vermont change of pace, being with old friends and family and true summer weather, thunderstorms and all, thoughts of our San Francisco professional lives would begin to intrude. Father Steve would be arriving in less than a month after my return to campus. When I found myself waking up at night to mull over challenges I would face on my return to the City, I knew Vermont time was running out; the elusive Rainbow assumed mythic qualities, safe from my flies and nymphs for another year.

Behavior patterns of University staff on my return this year were not significantly different from those I had experienced on the arrival of Father President John II years ago. Vice presidents were maneuvering for attention, deans were forwarding materials to impress the incoming president, and professors were wondering whether a new president would make any difference in their lives. And I guess priests prayed a lot. The only University community members not caught up in the "here comes the president" storm, ironically but not unsurprisingly, were students.

Welcoming events for Father President Steve Privett, S.J., followed time-honored University protocols for the installation of a new president. The pomp and ritual of new university presidential welcomes I had experienced over my close to forty years in higher education had always impressed me, but looking back on these ceremonies, they left little or no emotional impact. Such was not the case with the Inaugural Mass that concluded the installation of Father President Privett. The emotional impact of that fall afternoon still resonates.

The elections of John F. Kennedy in 1960 and of Barack Obama in 2008 promised new hope and boded change for the country; Father Privett's Inauguration Mass promised new hope and boded change in University climate. "Ask not what your country can do for you," Kennedy had beseeched in 1960 as laser white sun reflected off a fresh snowfall, steam from his breath visible in the frigid cold; "Yes, we can," Barack Obama had assured as he spoke exhilarated by the diversity and size of the crowds. Both president's inaugurations had brought tears to my eyes. So did the Inauguration Mass of the University's new president.

The procession of white robed priests emerged from the dimly lit vestibule at the rear of St. Ignatius Church and proceeded toward University officers seated in the Sanctuary. Chords of the large organ reverberated through the gothic structure as celebrants flowed down the red carpet center aisle. Held high at the head of the line of priests, oversize banners carried portraits of the six priests slain by the Salvadoran military in El Salvador. Slowly like an incoming tide, the procession moved toward us. Late afternoon ribbons of light caught motes of airborne dust. The portraits glowed as they caught rays of the autumn sun as it streamed through the church's stained-glass windows. The martyrs came to life; they almost breathed.

I hadn't known much about the Martyrs of El Salvador before coming to the University. I vaguely recalled that there had been priests killed in El Salvador sometime in the late 1980s—but their deaths were only dim footnotes in political discussions at Boston University. Their murders then seemed so far away and so distant to my life. It was so different this afternoon.

The procession mounted the platform. The white albs of the priests contrasted with the black academic gowns and multicolor hoods of seated University officers. Father President rose and approached the podium. The Mass began.

"In celebrating the death of these eight, labeled subversives murdered by the Salvadoran government for speaking out against the oppression of the poor, I constantly remind myself not to idealize them in death beyond what they were in life: a cook and her daughter, college administrators, teachers—people like you and me."

Father Steve had worked with the priests in their efforts to help refugees in Salvador's Chalatenango Province fight the ravages of poverty and escape the military; Boston University President Silber had worked with the Kissinger Commission to validate the role of the same military in Salvador. President Father Steve and his Jesuit predecessors had supported rebel efforts to help the poor; President Silber had supported efforts to defeat the rebels.

"This is the stuff of God's kingdom. Their lives and deaths speak of a wisdom and eloquence that far outstrips the mindless violence of their murderers."

I was far from my childhood home in Greenwich Village in so many ways, but as I sat on the stage, swept up in the social justice banners and rainforest of the Catholic religion, in some strange way, I had come home. I, a child of Jewish and Episcopalian parents, brought up in a home that questioned the existence of God, once a young man in a family in which Catholicism took a beating, now found myself wrapped in the mystery and humanity of this Catholic Mass.

Father Steve didn't pass the torch to a new generation that afternoon but his presence and message signaled a new day for the University. He dramatically broadcast the ethical and service dimensions of his religion and the cry for social justice as he held up the Jesuit torch for all to see. I don't remember all the words of Father's homily but I do remember the glory of that afternoon: man and religion were at their best. When the Jesuits were good, they were very, very good. They truly knew how to celebrate their rainbow.

I found new hope in Father President's public dedication to the theme of social justice. My efforts to sharpen and vitalize the urban mission for my School which had oft-times met with indifference or resistance would be reinforced. Herb's new Center for Teaching and Social Justice with its pilot program to attract socially conscious teachers for struggling Bay Area schools, the recent federal AmeriCorps contract to recruit and support aspiring teachers who reflect the ethnic and racial makeup of urban schools, and our collaboration with Teach for America to attract outstanding liberal arts graduates to teach in urban schools would have a new ally.

I was either a cockeyed optimist or naïve—or both. Unfortunately, hope faded and progress stumbled as collective bargaining protocols coupled with endemic human and institutional resistance to change not unique to this university made their power known.

Twenty-Four
Pain and Promotion

**Promotion and tenure action decisions should carry *High Fire* ***Danger* notices. Professors have morphed into squirrels as they gather nuts of accomplishment stored over the years to include in their application; applications are subsequently packaged and sent to outside readers for review. Months later, on the basis of reviews from outside readers, school or college professor colleagues sitting in committee, and upon recommendation of the dean and university committees and officers, notices of approval or rejection are finally communicated to the applicant. It's no wonder small fires can escalate to infernos when an application for promotion or tenure is denied. I still bear scars from such fires.

In the University of San Francisco, collective bargaining protocols provided a dry undercover awaiting only a spark to ignite a firestorm. Denial of a professor promotion or tenure application usually generated grievance and arbitration actions. My challenge was to bring such fires under control while advocates for the denied professor assembled and professors sympathetic to my recommendation remained silent.

I couldn't help but contemplate the irony that April, the month that marks the solemnity of Good Friday and the celebration of Easter, is the month stipulated by the University *Collective Bargaining Agreement* in this Catholic institution for applicant notification of action. And of course, with apologies to T. S. Eliot, April can also be the cruelest month. I quickly learned of the vulnerability of California to wildfires. I was slower to learn how long fires of tenure or promotion rejection can linger.

The glow from graduation ceremonies in St. Ignatius Church still lingered as clusters of graduates and their families slowly wandered into the gymnasium for post-graduation celebration with friends, families, and professors. Dressed up with tablecloth-covered tables, trays of refreshments, pitchers of punch, urns of coffee, and a brown-papered floor to protect its wood surface, I suspect, the gym, save for a few coats of paint, was little changed from the days when Bill Russell and K. C. Jones cavorted on its hardwood floor.

Proud students in graduation robes, parents or spouses in spring dress or slacks n' jackets signaled, "We've made it." Professors in casual attire with robe over shoulder signaled, "We've made it." Spouse, parent, and child exuberance celebrated, "We've all made it."

It wasn't long before the arriving clusters of celebrants blended into an assembly of accomplishment and joy. Only minutes ago worn and barren, the gymnasium was now vibrant with the hum of conversation and peals of laughter. It was too important a day to question whether coffee, cake, and punch in a gymnasium was the best the University could provide to celebrate the occasion after students' expenditure of tens of thousands of tuition dollars.

Gatherings of smiling professors, graduates, and parents dotted the room. I mingled among the proud graduates, families, and welcoming professors. Children of older graduates beamed next to their proud parents. An occasional, "Dean, I'd like you to meet . . ." was extended by a graduate, and I would be drawn into a celebratory conversation with family members. It was a heady time to be a dean.

I drifted toward a student for whom I had been a member of his dissertation committee who was exuberantly enjoying the company of my Marin professors, Sol and Sheba. The graduate's older parents were laughing, his wife was proudly smiling, his boisterous children hung on to their dad's graduation robe. Before I reached the joyous band, a voice of authority intruded, "Dean Warren, Dean Warren." I stopped. A fashionably dressed, imposing woman, probably in her early forties, approached.

"Dean Warren, you are Dean Warren, aren't you?" she asked rhetorically as she squared off in front of me.

I nodded and offered a perplexed "Yes." I was fixed in her stare. There was no immediate response, only glower. I repeated "Yes" again and added, "Can I help you?"

"Let me look at you," my inquisitor stepped back. Her eyes swept from foot to head, head to foot. "So you're Dean Warren," she repeated.

I needed to say something. I needed to assert myself, however weakly, to break the freeze. "Can I help you?" I asked again, looking into her cold eyes and frozen face. Her eyes bored straight into mine. I had no idea what she might hope to see there.

"So you're Dean Warren," she repeated slowly this time. Then added, "So you're the bastard who wouldn't promote my mother."

Message delivered, Emilia's daughter turned and drifted back into the crowd of celebrants. I felt something like a boxer must feel after being hit by a punch to the head that arrives from nowhere. The glow of the celebration had lost some of its luster. The ghost of a past promotion decision had done its job. Smoldering embers and long-lasting scars remained for Emilia's daughter long after the blaze ignited by my denial of her mother's promotion request and failed arbitration. I couldn't wait for my summer escape from the University.

The month in Vermont became more and more important to me as years passed. I coveted clearing encroaching hardtack, building stone walls, and tending a vegetable garden under the warm sun. I luxuriated in the sounds of northeast summer: the violin of crickets, the occasional cry of a crow, the rustle of poplar and maple leaves. Clearing underbrush one afternoon, Janet's call broke my summertime trance.

"Paul, Catherine's on the phone. She says it's important she talk with you." I reluctantly put down the scythe, pulled off my work gloves, and slowly returned to the house.

"I'm sorry," Janet whispered as she handed me the phone. My monotone "Hello" to Catherine reflected my mood.

"Dean, I'm sorry to bother you but eight cartons of materials marked, *Confidential, For the Dean's eyes only*, have been delivered to your office by Professor Judy. What should I do with them?" We were not even into August and the *Collective Bargaining Agreement* didn't require a professor's application for promotion and tenure be received by the dean until September 15. I couldn't have cared less what Catherine did with them at that moment and told her to pile the boxes in a corner of my office. I would get to them in two weeks when I returned to San Francisco. I'm afraid my irritation at Professor Judy's early delivery and Catherine's interruption was conveyed in my brisk, "Thanks for calling," before I hung up. I should have been gentler with Catherine. She was doing her job and it was the compulsive Judy who had broken the spell of that summer afternoon.

Back in San Francisco two weeks later, I marveled at the cubic footage consumed by the pile of Judy's cartons as they sat waiting my review. She had built a cardboard monument to herself. She was a squirrel for all seasons. I wasn't totally surprised. Over the years, she had notified me of every book in progress, article under review, article pending publication, paper read, public presentation made, and invitation to talk to any University group about anything. She must have reasoned that she would be granted tenure on the basis of quantity if not quality.

I was only into box three of Judy's cache when there was a knock on my half-open office and Associate Dean Parsa entered. She had helped me keep the School on track since the day I arrived and didn't need to wait for permission to enter.

"How's it going, big fella?" Parsa liked to build me up when she sensed I was being pulled down. She could see I was drowning in the undertow of this tenure application.

"Do you mind?" she asked rhetorically as she pulled over a chair to join me in the midst of the ring of academic accretions. "How's it going, big fella?" she asked again. I gave a smile bordering on grimace. There was no need for me to say anything. Parsa deserved more than my silence.

"Do you know the distinction between the optimist and the pessimist?" I asked. Before she could respond, I continued, "Let me share a tale to which I was first introduced many, many years ago in a book, *There Must be a Pony*."

"I've got time if you've got time. Go ahead." Parsa sat back in the chair. I proceeded.

"It was Christmas and a father had made a special effort to provide his children, one a pessimist, the other an optimist, with special gifts. He led his children to two rooms in which the gifts sat. The pessimist was shown a room filled with gifts of all shapes, sizes, and colors. He turned to his father and whined, 'I bet there's nothing in here that I like.' Father then led the optimist to another room. The room was filled with horse manure. The son turned to his dad and joyously exclaimed, 'With all this shit, there must be a pony,' and began to shovel away."

"Paul, let me share a hunch with you. You're still looking for the pony." Parsa knew my dilemma. "Dig away, my optimistic dean," she encouraged.

"Thanks." I smiled as she gingerly navigated her way out from my office through the collection of corrugated cardboard stalls. I appreciated the break Parsa provided and her departing salutation but I wasn't her "optimistic dean."

I never did find a pony in Professor Judy's boxes but I did find a sampling of materials I could package for external reviewers. Hermeneutics, her area of research, title derived from Hermes, a Greek god and messenger for Zeus, ironically failed to deliver her message to academic colleagues and University reviewers.

The rejection of Judy's tenure application resulted in a full-throated battle cry consistent with the rules of war contained in the University's *Collective Bargaining Agreement.* Judy, Union president, Union lawyer, University lawyer, University vice president, professor witnesses, and I, all became combatants in a battle played out on the fields of grievance and arbitration until an arbitrator's ruling was rendered more than a year after hearings began.

I felt relief rather than joy on learning of the arbitrator's decision to not approve Judy's tenure application. I was vindicated. No pony had been found in her cartons of material. I never anticipated the collateral damage wrought by the recommendation to deny Professor Judy's application.

It was unfortunate that Professor Judy's mandatory tenure review year was the same as that of Professor Job. Job was the antithesis of Judy.

He was open; she was secretive. He was trusting; she was suspicious. He was straightforward; she was calculating. He was modest; she was full of self.

There had been an instant *simpatico* when I first interviewed Job and recommended his appointment as an assistant professor in the School. He was a transplant from "back East" with years of classroom teaching in Vermont. He had worked with San Francisco city schools as part of his responsibilities with a local-based, federally funded regional research center. As we had conversed during his job interview and he spoke of his teaching, his soft voice and warm dark eyes conveyed care. I had no question that he would be a valuable asset to the School.

As years ran up to the mandatory time for Job's tenure review, however, I was getting worried. His obvious caring was being undermined by intrusive family tragedies. Papers promised yesterday were unfinished tomorrow; student reviews of teaching had slipped. Teachers in a collaborative program with a neighboring middle school had begun to lose faith in his leadership. Too much talent and good intent was going to waste.

I needed to find a way to buy time for Job to permit healing. Review of his tenure application at this particular time would be dangerous. I was confident that the mandated tenure review timetable contained in the *Agreement* needed to be finessed if he was to remain at the University.

When I asked Job to join me in my office to share my concerns about his tenure application, I thought I had found a way to throw him a lifeline, although I knew this would still be one of those delicate meetings in which I had to share a decision I wished I didn't have to make. I quickly got to the point.

"Job, I want you to stay at the University." I hesitated before I added, "But I'm not going to be able to recommend you for tenure." He didn't say a word as we sat across from one another. He was making me squirm. It should have been the other way around.

"Job," I repeated. "I want you to stay at the University. I'm sure I can get you a three- year assignment, half-time professor, and half-time project director that will enable you to continue your work with City schools." He was still silent; he showed no emotion. I added, "The appointment would also give you time to build your research and writing record that has been hurt by the family pressures you're facing."

I tried to be supportive. I repeated I wanted him to stay at the School.

I added, "Most importantly, Job, the mandatory tenure review clock will stop and there will be no denial of a tenure review application." I was filling space and time with my words. He still sat without a word."

"Job, once I transmit a recommendation for promotion and tenure denial, decision-making processes are mandated by terms of the *Agreement* and the two of us will be cast in adversarial roles. Any degree of freedom I have to develop an alternative solution to enable you to stay here will vanish. There will only be an 'up' or 'down' on your application."

Job's downcast eyes showed hurt. His silence poorly masked his disappointment. I had let him down. He rose from the chair, still without a word, and proceeded to leave.

"Give some thought to the proposal," I pleaded as he approached the door. Our eyes didn't meet as he left my office. He was distracted by distress, I by discomfort.

A few days after Job and I had danced around the prickly pear of tenure, Dante blew into my office. His skin was paler than usual, gray-blue eyes colder than ever. He wore a cloak of pallid malevolence. I soon learned that there was a stiletto hidden beneath his cloak.

"Job told me about his meeting with you. You're making a big mistake."

I shared with Dante the factors that had influenced my action and the essence of my offer to Job that would enable him to remain at the University.

"Off the record, Dante," *en confidence* as current dean to former dean, I continued, "If I try to make a case for Job's tenure on the basis of his teaching evaluations and publication record, there's no way in the world that Judy, who I will not be recommending for tenure, and whose paper credentials are stronger than those of Job, will not grieve my decision citing gender and ethnicity prejudice and I have little doubt that an arbitrator would rule in her favor."

I thought Dante with his years as a dean, and privately a vocal critic of Judy, would understand my reasoning. He smiled a cold smile. His pencil-line moustache seated on his upper lip, registered for warm smile, flatlined. I continued, "Dante, I'm trying to find a way to keep Job here but I can't risk the cost to the School of Judy being granted tenure. As a former dean, you should appreciate the stakes." Dante got up abruptly from the chair. He admonished one more time, "Paul, you're making a big mistake," and departed.

He was right, I was making a mistake, a big mistake, but not the mistake he had in mind. I should have known the words *en confidence* meant little to Dante.

Once former dean Dante picked up the torch for Job, my relationship with Job deteriorated. Discussions between us suddenly were guarded, eyes never met when we talked. We courteously but silently passed one another in School hallways. Seldom during my many years as dean had I felt so uncomfortable.

Dante was to rise through the murkiness of cigarette smoke and alcohol haze, exhumed by him and two of his professor colleagues in an office he had been assigned as a reward for his assistance in the relocation of the School from Lone Mountain, to become Job's mentor and ambassador. I was never sure whether it was Job's adoption of the wrong peer group for counsel or the peer group's adoption of Job as *cause celebre* that contributed to his rejection of my offer.

Job had a stroke shortly after the notice of the University denial of his application for promotion and tenure; he filed a grievance but appeal and arbitration hearings were not possible due to his poor health. A year after my retirement, I learned that extended discussions with University Administration had led to a settlement with Job that included his receiving University health insurance coverage. I never saw Job again.

No time in my years as dean had the pain of promotion and tenure review been as great: the animus of Dante killed respect; the distrust of Job hurt. The failing health of Job and family members' illness was tragic. The loss of friendship with a sensitive colleague is still painful.

Twenty-Five

Brambles and Anomalies

I was caught in the flames of an impenetrable bramble of the Jesuit world when a routine protocol for promotion unpredictably set off a fire alarm and ensuing brush fire took more than a month to extinguish. In the closing years of John II's reign, I had secured approval to appoint an additional associate dean to assist me and was lucky to find a qualified individual in our midst.

Professor Patrick was a personable, young, handsome, well-organized professor who had helped bring order to a dysfunctional academic department in the School. He carried the enthusiastic endorsement of department colleagues and was respected and liked by students. I felt some guilt asking him to leave the classroom to join me but I was confident the School would benefit by his service in the deans' office.

I did recognize there might be a glitch: Patrick was gay and proud of being gay—and this was a Catholic University. Conscious of the Church's official sensitivity on the question of sexual orientation, I wanted to be sure of Father Jack's support before proceeding. Although I had not fared too well in my earlier Feinstein–O'Sullivan smooth-the-waters meeting with Father prior to the submittal of a formal recommendation, I still believed it would be helpful to meet informally with Father talk about my recommendation and scheduled a meeting.

Seated in Father's office, I shared Patrick's academic and professional qualifications that had led to my planned recommendation before I finally added, "Father, you may have one concern." His interest piqued; he engaged me like a dog waiting for a biscuit from his master.

"Father, you know he's gay?" I couldn't immediately read his reaction. There was no immediate response. His lips were the first, and only part of his body, to move.

"You said Patrick has the support of faculty? You said he has the support of the School Search Committee?"

I reiterated that the Search Committee unanimously supported my recommendation along with professors in his department—as long as the department got authorization to search for a professor replacement. Jack was silent. Was there something he was thinking but not saying? After what I was sure were seconds, rather than minutes, he responded, "Forward the papers for Patrick's appointment to me." Worry that my recommendation for Patrick might create a dilemma for Father was calmed.

Patrick and I had never talked about his being gay. He knew I knew he was gay and we knew that Father Jack knew he was gay. But we also knew there were a few professors in the School who were not comfortable with his sexual orientation, including Father Francis, the crusty, old Jesuit School professor who never hesitated to share his views on School personnel decisions with members of the Jesuit Community. I was proud of Father Jack. He might be open to criticism from Father Francis and some of his more conservative Community colleagues.

From here on in, Patrick's appointment would be smooth sailing. He would soon be joining me as an associate dean. I forwarded the papers for Patrick's appointment to Father Jack. A few weeks later, there was a call on my private line. Bede was on the phone.

"Paul, Father Jack would like to speak with you." I was switched to his inner office. As I spoke with him, there was a resonance to my words I hadn't noticed before in phone conversations with him. He quickly got to the point.

"Paul, would you give me a full write-up of the comparison between Patrick and the runner-up candidate for the position of associate dean."

Why would he be making this request now? Was he on speaker phone? Was someone else in his office listening to our conversation; that might explain the resonance on the phone. I was afraid something to which I wasn't privy was unfolding. I recalled years ago, Sister Rachel telling me that Father Francis was dismayed when Patrick, comfortably gay, had been first appointed as a professor in the School. Had my recommendation to promote Patrick been brought to the attention of conservative Jesuit Community members?

I gave Father Jack his write-up. I inflated Patrick's appropriateness for the position; I deflated the qualities of the runner-up. I sang Patrick's praises. My response was hand-delivered to Father, "For the Provost's Eyes," blazoned on the envelope.

Days passed. Previously accessible Father was elusive. Weeks passed. There was still no word from him. It was now mid-May, Patrick was calling me regularly, too regularly, asking about the status of his appointment. Did he, too, know something I didn't? Graduation Day arrived and it had now been almost a month since my recommendation for Patrick's appointment had been transmitted.

University graduation ceremonies provided opportunities for gowned vice presidents, deans, and other University officers whose paths don't regularly cross to mingle with one another. As we milled and small-talked in the dusky hallway of a classroom building waiting for the Graduation procession to begin, I found myself standing next to Father Yves, the quietly gay University counsel.

Father asked, "How are things going, Paul?" as two lines formed to emerge into the bright sun toward St. Ignatius Church.

"No complaints. The only hitch is I'm waiting word on one of my appointment recommendations," I replied. I was thrown by Father's response.

"I know, we're meeting with outside counsel tomorrow to discuss that case," he whispered and gave me a wink. Did his wink signify something? Why had advice of outside legal counsel been sought? Could Patrick's appointment have become a "case"?

The Marshall signaled for the procession to commence. Father Yves fell back in his parallel line. There was no chance to follow-up as the paired lines of assembled officers left the building and glided in full plumage across the lawn to enter St. Ignatius Church, throb of the organ pumping out *Pomp and Circumstance.*

One week after graduation, I received a telephone call of thanks from Patrick. He had received a letter from the Provost: *We are pleased to inform you of your appointment as Associate Dean in the School of Education.*

I hadn't been officially informed of any meeting with lawyers - and hadn't been informed of conclusions reached. It wasn't the first time I had felt the loneliness of a dean shut out of the decision-making process by higher-ups in the Jesuit Community. I needed to meet with Father Jack again. I needed some answers.

Stillness hung in the room, one week later, as I entered his office and sat down. There was no need for palaver.

"Father, I need to talk to you about Patrick's appointment." Father knew why I was there.

"It's not that Patrick is gay, Paul." He hesitated for a moment. Something was making him feel uncomfortable. "You probably don't know that Patrick left the seminary when he was studying to become a priest." I didn't. "And he didn't leave alone; he left with another seminarian who is now his companion." I didn't know that either.

I was relieved. Well, sort of. Something more universal than Catholic conservatism or Patrick's sexual orientation had been playing out; blatant hypocrisy was the culprit. Patrick had jilted the Church for another lover. His eloping with a fellow Jesuit-to-be must have stirred up quite an array of emotions: betrayal, distrust, ingratitude, and perhaps green-eyed jealousy. I will never know. I will also never know what precipitated the delays in processing Patrick's appointment. But I wouldn't be surprised to learn that Father Francis was the Iago lurking in the shadows.

Thoughts of Patrick's appointment faded when Janet and I escaped to Vermont for our summer vacation. That was until I picked up an Express Mail letter at our small-town post office, peeled off the strip from the emblazoned envelope, and carefully extracted the enclosure: the cover of the *Bay Guardian* Sunday magazine section. Beneath a bold caption, "The New American Family," on the full page in color, cover of the *Guardian*, was a photograph of Patrick, his companion, and their young, adopted daughter.

"Thanks, Patrick," was scribbled in its bottom corner.

I vividly recall moments of anger emanating from my failure to support promotion and tenure recommendations. Memories of polite "thank you" or a brief kiss on the cheek from those whom I had successfully recommended promotion or tenure have faded. Patrick's handwritten note of thanks has not. Neither has Professor Eugene's graceful acceptance of tenure denial. Recall of Eugene's application for promotion, like review of Patrick's, still elicits a melancholic smile from another time.

Professor Eugene dropped scholarly references at the slightest provocation. He carried academic credentials from both sides of the Atlantic and was African-American. I had celebrated the opportunity to appoint Eugene five years earlier as an assistant professor in my too white, too tenured School. And he was a showman who could charm, with a capitol "C." Even my mother-in-law, who had been verbally seduced in a most decorous manner by Eugene at a faculty reception for professors at our home while visiting from Florida years earlier, regularly asked about him months after her visit.

It was early summer. He and I were discussing his pending promotion and tenure application as his mandatory date for review approached.

"Eugene, how's it going?" I asked. This would be the last time we could talk about promotion and tenure as gentlemen on a problem-solving mission. From now on, collective bargaining protocols necessitated he, Labor, and I, Management, only talk "on record" until a decision to tenure or not to tenure has been reached.

"I'm pulling together the pieces, Dean. A secretary is cleaning up some articles to be submitted for publication. I'm finishing up my major book. I'm cataloguing my service contributions. I'm collecting my teaching materials. Don't worry, my man."

I did worry. I didn't want to lose Eugene but I had listened to much talk and seen few products from him over the years. He could tell a story as well as the best but. . . . There wouldn't be much help I could offer after today other than reminding him of *Agreement* regulations that govern tenure review. I reminded him, "Eugene, the *Collective Bargaining Agreement* mandates that the application for promotion and tenure be received by the dean by September 15th with a two-week period for the applicant to add additional materials that may not have accompanied the application, should the dean request." I added for emphasis, "I won't be able to grant any time extensions even if I want to."

"Don't worry, my man, my materials will all be there," he replied to assure me, and possibly convince himself, that there was nothing to worry about. Eugene and I spent a pleasant hour together but I was certain there was a lot to worry about.

As conversation wound down, Eugene gathered his notebooks and collection of papers he had brought to my office to share. Loose pages fluttered to the floor. He leaned over quickly to catch them and bumped into the binder notebook we had been reviewing. Its rings snapped open. More pages, freed from constraint, slid from the table to the floor. Printed and handwritten materials now strewn across the table and the floor of my office acquired a life of their own as they eluded our grasp. After some effort, papers recovered and placed back within the notebook covers, Eugene half-skipped out of my office.

"Relax, my man. It's all under control," he tossed over his shoulder as he departed.

September 15, the day ordained by the *Agreement* for applications to be submitted, an application cover page, *Name of applicant, Actions Requested* filled entered, rested in the in-basket outside my office. I was relieved. Boxes of materials to support his application must be in my office. No boxes were in sight when I entered. Eugene had lifted me up only to let me down. I called him at home.

"Eugene, I've got the cover page for your tenure review but I don't have the rest of your application." I tried to convey a sense of nonchalant confidence to suggest that I thought his materials were in his office waiting for delivery to mine.

"Don't worry, Dean, the *Collective Bargaining Agreement* provides the dean with two weeks to review the candidate's application. If it isn't complete, the dean is to notify the candidate; the candidate then has two weeks to complete the application." Eugene was either quoting from the *Agreement*, had consulted a union officer, or had committed my spring message to memory. I had never received such a literal reading of the promotion and tenure clause. Eugene was right. His cover page did carry the title, *Candidate's Application*. Technically, I guess, I had received an application consistent with *Collective Bargaining* text. I hoped the rest of his materials would follow in two weeks.

Two weeks later, a strange collection of papers with an affixed handwritten note rested on my desk upon my arrival to the office.

"Dean, I know the application is still not complete but the *Agreement* permits you to transmit papers that constitute an incomplete application to the School Promotion and Tenure Review Committee."

The *Agreement* was silent on whether or not to forward an incomplete application for further review. Labor VP Fireplug Al had regularly reminded deans that if the *Agreement* is silent or a clause of the *Agreement* is incomprehensible, "management prerogative" prevails. I called Al to share my uncertainty as to the next steps. His reaction was predictable.

"Paul, inform the Committee that you're not in receipt of a complete application; thus there is nothing to transmit." Al loved confrontation. As Assistant Vice President for Labor, it could be argued that his job rested on the presence of conflict. I wasn't sure what I would gain by not forwarding Eugene's application at this point. Al replied, "I hear you, Paul, just remember I'm here to serve the deans." I needed more than words of loyalty. I sought Father Jack's advice.

"Be careful, Paul. Don't needlessly stir things up. Transmit his application. Let faculty make the determination as to the status and quality of the application." True to form, Father sought accommodation. It was not by accident that he had moved the University back from the brink of Labor-Management war as Academic Vice President the year before I arrived as dean. I took Father's advice. I would rely on the School Promotion and Tenure Committee judgement on application status rather than Management semantic ruling on the term *application.*

Eugene's application was forwarded to the University Promotion and Tenure Committee carrying its rejection by the School Promotion and Tenure Committee. Again, it was rejected. My subsequent recommendation to deny Eugene's tenure request to deans composed as a University Merit Committee was as brief as possible. I just wanted the guillotine to fall quickly.

During the weeks that followed the University notification of rejection of his application, there was not a peep from anyone. Even Eugene seemed comfortable when I had notified him of the University's action.

"That's cool, man. That's alright. I'm fine." Unlike other cases in which I had denied a professor's application, there would be no drawn-out process of appeal and arbitration. Eugene wasn't interested in pyrotechnics.

Eugene faded quietly from the School after the University notice of tenure denial. There were no requests from him for recommendations and little news of where he would be going or what he would be doing. Quite a while after his departure, I learned he was heading up an educational venture with a school in southern California. I hoped he was doing well; there are so many ways education could benefit from the skills of a showman.

Twenty-Six
Birdy and Homer

For all the hope generated by Father President Steve's dedica-tion to the theme of social justice on his arrival, I had been around too long to not be aware that hope is vulnerable to reality and institutions resistant to change. Perhaps that was why I remember so vividly those rare moments when I knew a few words of mine made an observable, here-and-now, incontrovertible difference.

Many months after Father Steve's arrival, I along with Herb and his Center for Teaching and Social Justice were still sailing into the winds of resistance when I received a message from the San Francisco Superintendent of Schools. He wished to meet with Herb and me as soon as possible to discuss a project.

I had to contact Herb immediately. His telephone extension was busy, busy, busy. I couldn't wait any longer for him to get off the phone. I needed to reach him. With a quick "I'll be back in a few minutes" to Catherine, I left my office, mounted the flight of stairs, two steps at a time, and walked double-time across the freshly waxed floor toward Herb's corner asylum. Here in his corner office with an adjoining workstation for his private assistant, Gil, Herb had created a private sanctuary for his students and a few professor colleagues.

Gil, hand cupped over receiver, voice barely above a whisper, was deep in conversation when I entered and stood silently by his desk. I didn't want to interrupt but needed his attention.

"I've got to go, the Dean is here," he whispered to the person at the other end of the line. Gil must be using Herb's line; that explained the busy,

busy, busy when I tried to get through. He gently rested the phone arm in its cradle.

"I didn't mean to interrupt," I foolishly apologized, for that's what I intended.

"No problem."

"Is Herb around? The superintendent of Schools wants to see us."

I could see from where I stood that Herb wasn't in his office, although his presence certainly was: tiny statuaries and academic manipulanda sat carefully on his windowsill, protest posters were taped to office walls, bookshelves were filled to capacity, and cubes of student papers rested on his desk.

"Let me check down the hall," Gil replied as he slowly got up from his seat. With Charlie Chaplin steps, he was off down an adjoining corridor, backbone to a string of professor offices. He returned in moments, "Dean, you must have just missed him."

I would have to wait to contact the superintendent. As I turned to return to my office, I spotted a newcomer at Gil's workstation and paused.

"Is there anything else, Dean?" Gil asked.

"Gil, are congratulations owed to you for the new addition to the office?" I asked in jest. Deans don't always need to behave as kings, or queens, or assistants as subjects. Gil was at a loss to answer until he followed my eyes fixed on a lone, tattered goldfish, gold-white stomach distended, tail down, suspended in cloudy water in a vessel not much larger than a large glass soup bowl.

"Oh, that. Herb and I thought the office could use a bit more life. His name is Birdy."

I couldn't resist commenting, "The last time I saw a goldfish stand on his tail like that was when I was a kid. I killed it with over-feeding and dirty water. I hope Birdy is luckier." Gil forced a laugh. Observation shared,

I had to go, leaving his poor piscatorial specimen struggling for oxygen as he or she fought for life.

On crossing paths over the weeks that followed, I would ask Gil with tongue in cheek, mischief in eye, "How's Birdy?" He would smile but he seldom said a word. About three weeks later, I got a call from Gil.

"Dean, Herb would like to speak to you." He transferred me to Herb.

"Paul, can you come up to my office?" He wasn't posing a question. I, Pancho, had no choice but to join my Don Quixote. He may have located more windmills at which to tilt.

Herb stood in the hallway by the entry to his sanctuary. "Come with me," he gently commanded. His usual amble took on a George W. Texas strut; he chugged forward with a sense of purpose and determination seldom exhibited by professors. Was there a new display for his Center? Had he been the recipient of an award? Was he angry at somebody—or something? Was somebody angry with him?

Gil was standing at attention as we entered Herb's domain. I wasn't prepared for the significance of the moment about to unfold. With a broad smile and extended index finger, Gil pointed toward his workstation. "Dean, look." A brand new ten-gallon-plus aquarium sat on the shelf separating Gil from the rest of the professorial world. In it swam Birdy with purpose as he or she navigated fresh plant life and circled a red castle resting on blue sand. Today was a good day for Gil—and for me—and most assuredly for Birdy. My earlier observation on the health of Birdy and his living environment had made a difference.

I was disappointed to later learn from Herb that the aquarium had been purchased and placed to help shield Herb and Gil's corner office from professor neighbors rather than as a humanitarian, or piscatorial, act to aid Birdy prompted by my earlier conversation with Gil.

Birdy's exotic new home provided a momentary blush of progress but I had no illusion that everything was falling in place. Herb was a lightning rod that drew the volatile energy of professors who found comfort in their Procrustean beds. I was inured to Professor Emilia with her dismissal of Herb as a Honky who sought to work with Black children and gray-pink Dante's asides created by Herb's access to the dean. Professor Michael posed a challenge of quite a different order.

Creative but anal compulsive Professor Michael who glowed in the classroom couldn't resist the opportunity to fill the vacuum left by the departure of Houston-claimed, brogue-buoyed Sister K. The title Director of Teacher Education sounded good to him; the position sounded right to his wife, also a University administrator. Professor Michael, Director of Teacher Education, sounded good to me too, although I suspected the attraction of the position for Michael and his wife was enhanced by the thought it might serve as a stepping stone to his deanship on my retirement. His potential ambition didn't matter to me if he could bring the same order to the Teacher Education program he had brought to other elements of his professional life. We would all be winners.

Tension between ego-driven compulsive Michael and ego-driven cock-sure Herb that followed my appointment of Michael as Director of Teacher Education didn't surprise me. Erratic phone calls, angry emails, casual comments, and barbs between the two of them became everyday distractions that sucked the air from my deanship. For all our sakes, I needed to meet with them to see whether some form of truce could be negotiated and, therefore, asked them to join me in my office.

Michael, in crisply pressed slacks, silk shirt with French cuffs, fresh-cut gelled hair standing at attention, sat on one side of the table. Reformer Herb, in seasoned Harris tweed jacket, slacks for which a crease was only a memory, disheveled hair at ease, sat silently at the other. Before I completed my first sentence, Michael interrupted to stake out his turf.

"There is one set of California Commission Standards to which the Teacher Education program must conform; courses taught for students in classes in Herb's pilot program don't meet these standards. There's really not much to discuss."

Verdict on Herb's program rendered, Michael turned his torso forty-five degrees; his eyes focused on my office wall. He had checked out of the meeting. His behavior reminded me of a mutt named Homer I once owned who when confronted by a bigger dog would stare fixedly into a corner, confident that if he looked into the corner long enough, the bigger dog would disappear. Michael was now my mutt, Herb, my bigger dog. Herb was not about to disappear.

"I'm familiar with the State standards and all my students will meet those standards. It's my business how I get there. When have you visited my classes, Michael?" Herb responded before provocatively adding, "When have you spoken with my students?" Herb looked to me for support. I didn't want to take sides at this point. I said nothing.

Primarily for Michael's knowledge, Herb filled the silence with a citation of his personal accomplishments, the names of progressive educators who had walked his walk, and failures of traditional teacher education programs, and reminded him of the School's commitment to the University's social justice mission.

Michael was transfixed by the wall. His eyes remained glued on its white emptiness. Herb's eyes were fixed on me. If eyes could speak, their message would be, "Say something, Dean." We all sat uncomfortably. Seldom had I sat with two people who said so much, in so few words, in so short time—and heard so little. I was failing miserably in my role as mediator. There was now only suffocating silence. Minutes seemed like hours. It was obvious that no agreement on a cease-fire between compulsive Michael and confident Herb would be reached in this room at this time. I needed to end the meeting before I became collateral damage in the war of egos.

"I'll get back to you," I muttered, not having the foggiest idea of when or what I might say when I get back to them. With my poorly veiled invitation to leave, Michael and Herb pushed back their chairs without a word to one another or me, stood, and filed from my office, making sure there was enough distance between them to preclude eye contact or an opportunity to exchange words. I stood feeling very much alone and quite incompetent as they departed.

There was never reconciliation between the two of them. Michael and Herb continued to throw barbs at one another until the day I left the University. Herb's students continued to be his students, the others, by default, Teacher Education program students whose professors reported to Michael. Michael never became dean and Herb left the University a year after my departure.

Twenty-Seven
Made in the Vatican

The ornamentation of Ducky's Christmas tree, invasion of the Sisters of Immaculate Conception, Grand Monica and Petite Betty's dormitory debate, gay Patrick's appointment review, and Father President John II's confrontation with Porno Tab, all had one feature in common. They all carried the label: *Made in San Francisco.*

Ex Corde Ecclesiastes, a Promulgation issued by Pope John Paul in late summer 1990 was different. It carried the label: *Made in Rome.* Vatican initiated *Ex Corde* represented action of the Catholic Church to establish universal academic instruction criteria for Catholic universities. The potential for Vatican infiltration of University life generated quite a different dynamic on University life than perceived individual transgressions.

Catholic universities and the nation's press were closely monitoring the progress of *Ex Corde* and its primary goal: maintenance of the Catholicity of Catholic colleges. The goal of *Ex Corde* was clear and understandable—even to non-Catholics. Its potential impact on the academic ethos of the Catholic university was less clear. *Ex Corde* called for courses in Catholic religion to only be taught by Catholic theologians and for professors in theology departments to take oaths of allegiance to the Church. Could *Ex Corde* open the door to the delegation of university academic decision-making to the Vatican? Although the pronouncements would have no immediate effect on my School's professors and most other University professors, once the Church was permitted to establish criteria for professorial qualifications or assignments in any school or academic department of a Catholic university, the question of what other boundaries between the Church and the University might be compromised had to be asked. If today's target was a religion department, might tomorrows be history? biology? Or education?

Unfortunately, the fear of the extension of religious intrusion to broader fields of study, and even public education, doesn't call for as great a leap as one might imagine. Walls between the Church and public education, science, and religion, assured with the 1925 Scopes Trial ruling, are increasingly threatened by actions of State Boards of Education, local school committees, and most recently vocal neo-conservatives across the nation. If it is possible for Church–State walls to crumble in the public school community, professor concern of Church–Academic walls falling in a private Catholic college or university is easily understood. It was no wonder *Ex Corde* attracted so much attention on the University campus.

When I was a School Committee member in Marblehead, issues of school closing, principal appointment or dismissal, and hockey coach contract renewal or release drew the greatest attention and largest attendance. While professor or dean at New York University or Boston University, budget cutbacks, president censure, or collective bargaining meetings drew the largest audiences. The common denominator for these quite different meetings and topics was self-interest. The same common denominator held for *Ex Corde.* A "standing room only" crowd of priests and professors of all faiths—and no faith at all—were assembled in the conference room to listen to a panel of priests, Father Steve as moderator, discuss the Papal *Promulgation.*

Ex Corde prompted many questions of self-interest. Might the *Promulgation* affect the welcome and status of the non-Catholic on a Catholic campus? Might it influence professor recruitment? Might it interfere in professor assignments? Might it affect a school's curriculum? Might it affect faculty research agendas? Might it affect student enrollment? And perhaps of most immediate concern for some professors at this Catholic and Jesuit university, might it threaten my job?

Father President Steve, sensitive to the ripples, or waves, cast by *Ex Corde* had called a University-wide meeting to allay professorial concerns. Soft murmurings passed from professor to professor in the audience as panelists took their seats. Father President garbed in religious apparel, rather than his usual California-casual with priest's collar over secular dress, laughed as he shared private comments with fellow Jesuit Community priests before he moved to take his place among the panelists.

Father's opening words to the now hushed audience painted a picture of the Church as a complex, political, and very human institution sensitive not only to the words of scripture but to the needs of its various audiences. Father's scholarly disposition showed. He was speaking like a true Jesuit. His remarks concluded with an observation and implicit charge to university officials.

"Ultimately the question is whether the Catholic university can be ecumenical and supportive of free academic inquiry safe from the challenges of Ex Corde."

There wasn't a sound in the room. Father's rhetorical question and charge set the tone for the meeting and revealed his hand. In a prepared, carefully worded presentation, he had taken the initiative, in true Jesuit gadfly form and in a most politically sensitive manner, to implicitly allay professorial concerns created by *Ex Corde*.

"Questions to the panelists are invited," Father encouraged once the last Jesuit panelist had spoken. He was anxious to make the setting more comfortable for professors. Panel members sat silently while they waited for someone to muster enough courage to publicly float a question about the sensitive issue. Father was not one to tolerate silence while waiting for a response.

Etched in my brain as deeply as Father's opening words or panel contributions is the response of Father Gregory, a panelist, who had regaled me years ago with Jesuit stories in the old Jesuit Community dining room, to break the silence on Father Steve's invitation questions. On silence from the audience, Father President turned to Father Gregory.

"Let me ask a question to get the discussion going. Father, what are the chances for *Ex Corde* requiring oaths of loyalty to the Church for faculty and administrators?"

With eyeglasses precariously balanced on the bridge of his nose, cherubic smile and jowls extending over his clerical collar, Father Gregory was a definite candidate for sainthood and a respected figure known by almost all on campus. The elderly priest's hands had a slight tremble as he wrapped his fingers tightly around a glass of water and took a sip.

Father's smile acknowledged that he had been thrown a softball question. He slowly lowered the glass of water from his lips to the table; words flowed slowly but smoothly on a firm current. He was suddenly ten years younger.

"I've been around a while." He paused, took a deep breath, slowly lifted the glass of water to his lips again, and sipped deeply. He slowly placed the glass back on the table. Father Gregory was both priest and performer.

"I've seen a lot and heard a lot." He paused to let his time-accorded wisdom be appreciated before he continued, "The Pope and the cardinals are infallible as long as they are alive. When they're dead, it's all up for grabs." He let those words sink in before concluding his reply, "The timing of *Ex Corde's* dissemination and its slow evolution tell me a lot; the age of the Pope and the ages of the cardinals also tell me a lot."

He didn't need to say anything more. One needn't have been Catholic to find relief in Father Gregory's words.

The vacuum of silence broken, a young, prematurely gray, well-manicured, up and coming new Jesuit Community resident in the palace on the hill, popped up from his seat in the audience. It was more comfortable for a priest than a lay member to ask the first question from the audience.

"In light of the document's status, how would you proceed?" the young priest directed a question to Father Gregory.

Without a moment's hesitation, Father responded, "Creativity and patience; creativity and procrastination," and took another sip of water, eyes over the rim of the glass fixed on the young priest, before he slowly returned the glass to the table. He elaborated on his earlier response to the president's question, "When push comes to shove in Rome, don't underestimate the power of the American dollar."

With his latest and evidently closing words of wisdom, Father Gregory once again picked up his now almost empty glass of water, downed the balance as if it was a shot of whiskey, and slammed the empty glass down on the table. The verdict had been delivered without words drawn from religious scripture.

Father President Steve must have felt it was time for a touch of priestly and Jesuit presidential reverence. He brought the assembly of priests and professors back to the safer territory of a Catholic university's mission and reminded the audience, "We can't forget that the open discussion, the airing of differences, and respect for the Church and the spiritual rest at the core of a Catholic University's being." Reminded of game rules, it became comfortable to speak.

Professors threw questions and panelists responded. Both lay and religious were reminded, as if there ever were any doubt that there is the Vatican and there is the University of San Francisco; and although Vatican's God and the University's God are the same, Vatican and University policies and priorities are discrete and not identical.

As discussion continued, questions for those unfamiliar with Church ways focused more on Church norms and folkways than on self-interest and safety. Tension in the room had been reduced by earlier words of Father Steve and Father Gregory. We had become participants in an academic seminar on the Catholic Church and were wiser for our attendance. Jesuit or secular, conservative or liberal, we were far more comfortable than when we had arrived; neither a Pope's pronouncement, College of Cardinals verdict, nor a Bishop's vigor would jeopardize any of our careers. And I was reminded that creativity and patience are powerful tools for survival.

Twenty-Eight
It's Time to Go

The boulder kept falling back down the hill. The quest for last-ing School reform had become more existential. I would too often wake up from a sound sleep long before sunrise, steal into my home office, scribble reminders for the next day's tasks, and then return to bed knowing that attempts to fall back to sleep would be futile. Something greater than disappointment, reaching Medicare age, or thoughts of mortality, or health challenges prompted my decision to retire. I was tired of my job. I was tired of pushing the boulder up the hill. It was time to trade in the title *Dean* for that of *Professor Emeritus.*

When a "Hello" or "Good morning" from an *emeritus* professor sticking his head into my office on a visit to the School became a prelude to conversation beyond a polite, reciprocal "Good morning" or "How are you," I knew I had entered a new stage of my deanship. Even some *emeriti* with whom I had seldom spoken prior to retirement became regular visitors. Maybe they were lonely. Maybe they were frightened that their thoughts were now of little consequence. I mused, *Had they become academic Willy Lomans riding on a smile and a shoeshine?* I worried, might I become like them on retirement? I couldn't summarily dismiss their outreach, when they implicitly invited conversation. I accepted. I couldn't bury my head in office, paper-pushing with and respond, "I'm sorry, I'm up to my neck."

Former Faculty Council chair and protagonist, Professor *Emeritus* Hubert was one of those Willy Lomans. On days scheduled for meetings of his department, he made it a point to get to the School early, stick his head in my open door, cross the transom, and drift into my office adorned in the same weathered tweed jacket he had worn for the past decade.

"Have you got a minute?" he would warmly ask. He would smile, enter the office, and approach my desk.

"How's it going, Dean?"

"Pretty good, Hubert. And you?"

"Mind if I have some of your coffee?"

"Help yourself."

"I've lost seven pounds. Are you taking care of yourself?"

"I'm keeping up my swimming and watching what I eat."

"We can't be too careful, you know."

With use of the pronoun *we*, Hubert proclaimed the two of us, fellow survivors of open- heart surgery, comrades. At that time, only I knew I was preparing to shortly join him as an *emeritus* in the fraternity of brothers in the house of the retired.

"I have to get to my department's meeting," he would announce, give me a crunching handshake, turn, and leave to fill his personal cup from the Mister Coffee that sat just outside my office. I suspected his regular attendance at department meetings, permitted by virtue of collective bargaining designated privileges for *retired* faculty, was to allay fear that he may be forgotten. Cup filled, he would stride off down the boulevard of staff cubicles on his way to the meeting, coffee slopping over the cup's rim.

The newfound cordiality between the two of us, I'm sure, left professors and staff who had been witness to our earlier wars aghast. But maybe I was naïve. Perhaps the trail of sugar crystals and Creamora powder left around Mister Coffee in his wake as he left for his department meeting rather than representing collateral damage of friendly dialogue was analogous to that of a dog marking his territory.

Hubert, unwittingly, I'm sure, had opted for the part of Willie Loman. Godfather David, in contrast, who had provided the harrowing late night drive to the Stanyan Hotel during my interview visit to the University, had opted to model the part of the race car driver portrayed by Paul Newman in the film, *Winning*. Godfather was no Paul Newman but. . . . No invitation sought, no notice needed following retirement, he would frequently stop by my office when on campus.

I had not seen Godfather for a few months before this morning's meeting. His thinning white bird's nest hair was gone; in its place a shining, freshly shaved dome emerged from the collar of his hallmark-wrinkled suit. A new *persona* had evolved during his out-of-the-ordinary absence from my door frame.

"How do you like it?" he asked, while he sensuously ran his hands over his new dome as if polishing an apple.

"It looks great," I replied. I didn't have the heart to tell him that flakes of dandruff from somewhere somehow still found a way to rest on the shoulders of his dark suit jacket.

"I'm driving at Sears Raceway," he announced with pride. I only knew of the raceway as a result of Janet and me being caught in too many traffic jams as we passed its entranceway on our return to San Francisco after a Sonoma Summer Sunday.

"I'm impressed. Have a seat." My welcome was an invitation for David to tell me a tale of his conversion.

"Dean, there's the foot on the gas pedal, the jump of the RPMs, the roar of the exhaust; the smell of burning fuel, the car coming to life, the thrill of high speed."

He was tripping over his words as he enthused over his new world. His excitement was contagious. I wish he had been as excited about teaching and energizing students.

Sears Raceway, not the University, now fueled Godfather's need for recognition. I wasn't totally surprised. He always had had some venture cooking on the side. I was encouraged he found excitement at the Raceway: emeriti professors, or deans, needn't become a Willie Loman on retirement. Anticipation of the jump in RPMs, the roar of the exhaust, and the smell of burning fuel at the raceway had replaced his curiosity about the School and life of former colleagues.

I couldn't live the life of a Willie Loman professor seeking acknowledgement nor a Paul Newman race-car driver seeking excitement in the dust of Sears Raceway. And I didn't wish to remain as a professor, living in the shadow of a new dean like so many of the School's former dean professors, once I stepped down from the deanship. I didn't know for certain what I wanted to do, but I knew what I didn't want to do.

Janet and I had always assumed I would retire before her, but we hadn't talked in any detail about retirement. The subject was now no longer an abstraction. We spent many evenings talking about what retirement might look like for both of us. We both knew it was time for me to retire when I shared with her that I could summarize the conversation with almost every professor who entered my office before we spoke and predict virtually any response to recommendations I might make. Janet's value as a psychologist and sensitivity as wife became clearer and clearer as we talked. She listened and questioned. She heard the frustration I shared in endlessly pushing the boulder up the hill, only to have it roll back to the base. She also reminded me of the sense of accomplishment and joy I had felt when I shared those brief times when the boulder stood for a while at the top of the hill before rolling back down. But we agreed that the day-to-day wear was getting me down. Janet didn't want to have Sisyphus as a husband; I didn't have the appetite to play the Sisyphean dean.

We had a lot to talk about. I was divesting from a career while Janet had just finished investing in one. After her hours of study culminating in a doctoral degree and American Psychological Association Psychology licensure as a psychologist and employment at Kaiser Permanente, I would *de facto* be imposing retirement on her, should we leave San Francisco.

Evenings were devoted to personal questions, to questions about the life we chose to live rather than the job I chose to pursue. Questions of the order: "How would you feel leaving Kaiser?" "How might we feel if we moved from San Francisco? "Where might we live?" We had a lot to discuss. Fortunately, no outside force was setting a timeline nor forcing decision-making as had been the case in Boston. We were in charge of our own decision-making; we shouldn't have been surprised to discover that in many ways, freedom raised greater issues and posed greater challenges. We needed to immerse ourselves in "How would you feel if . . . questions." The search for answers to questions of that nature called for soul searching and denied simple answers.

We reminisced about our early years in San Francisco and recalled our successful search for autumn leaves on side streets to remind us of the Northeast. We remembered the mystical white horse in the Mendocino fog after our first Thanksgiving restaurant dinner when we knew no one well enough in the Bay Area with whom to celebrate the holiday together. Things were so different now; we didn't need to look at our calendar to realize how much time we spent with close friends we had acquired since that first autumn. We wondered if the fact that so many of them had moved to San Francisco from somewhere else had made it easier for friendships to grow more rapidly here than in staid New England? And as we talked and absorbed the warmth and familiarity of our living space and furnishings we had accumulated while in the City, we knew our house had become a home; it was now part of who we were. We would be losing part of who we were if were to move back East and leave our San Francisco home and our friends behind. But. . . .

Northeast roots were strong. Summer and winter vacations we had spent at our Vermont house were magical. Vermont's Green Mountains, the glow of fall foliage, and alabaster white of the first winter snow were inviting. Memories of earlier years when the Vermont house had been built, of my children when they were young, of old friendships, provided a strong dose of nostalgia for me. And if we were to move "back East," I would be closer to my children, now young adults, my son a Pied Piper of a high school physics teacher on Boston's North Shore and my daughter, a gifted budding artist living on Martha's Vineyard. And, I would only be little more than a four-hour drive from Greenwich Village—my real home. As we talked and reminisced, it became clear there was more "I" than "us" in our deliberation. I had to ask myself, was I lobbying for Janet once again to be a "following wife" and follow me back East as she had when she followed me to San Francisco? I had a lot more to think about. We had a lot more to talk about. We needed more time.

One decision, however, did emanate from our early conversations: I would formally inform the University of my plans to retire as dean. Once plans for retirement were finalized, we could return to the question of whether to remain in San Francisco or move back East.

If universities, like the Kwakiutls who once sent the elderly at a designated age off on an ice flow, comrades waving as the current carried them to sea, had an analogous ritual to celebrate the moving on of a dean, life would have been simpler. But there are no such analogs in universities—or in "advanced" societies.

The challenge of questions to be answered once the decision to retire was reached was almost as daunting as those prior to making the decision. Do I share the decision with colleagues and close friends prior to negotiating a formal retirement agreement? What information do I share with colleagues and friends during the negotiation of retirement terms? And in what order do I share information with close colleagues, professors-at-large, and staff when terms of retirement have been finalized?

Protocols governing announcement of professor promotion, tenure, or retirement were clearly established. There were no such protocols for informing colleagues and the broader faculty of retirement after thirteen years of service. I would have to rely on personal judgement. Where do I start?

I owed reformer Herb early notice of my retirement thoughts. We were more than just colleagues and I had brought him here without formal faculty consent or a previously approved position. He was on a non-tenure line appointment, and with limited advocacy from colleagues, would be vulnerable once I departed. I asked him to join me for lunch.

Architectural lines of buildings and the City skyline were as sharp as a razor's edge as we proceeded to lunch in *The Magic Flute* where maître d'hôtel Phil, true to form, buoyantly greeted us and led us to a courtyard table.

I waited for the resolution of a Herb versus hamburger and roll tussle, catsup erupting from the roll, hamburger seeking to escape the roll's hold, before getting to my agenda item. His placement of the now formless bun and remaining hamburger on his plate provided the pause for which I had been waiting.

"Herb, I haven't set any date yet but I've been a dean for a long time, probably too long. I need a change." He poured more carbonated water in his glass of white wine, took a sip, and slowly placed the glass back on the table.

"I'm not surprised. You've been dean for too many years for me to be surprised. No one stays too long as a dean if they want to maintain their sanity." He wanted more information: "What's the timing? This spring? The year after?" My answer wasn't totally honest.

"I don't really know." I shrugged. "You can be sure I'll let you know before I announce a final decision."

We both knew I had provided protection for his run at the University. We also knew things would be more complicated for him once I left. But I think we both felt better when we finally left our courtyard retreat. As we passed through the now empty-inside dining area on our way to the street, I added, "It's off the record, Herb."

He gave me an, "I thought you should know better nod," accompanied by a roll of his eyes. He was right. Over his years at the University, we had spent too much time on projects to slay sacred cows, engaged in too many slights-of-hand to avoid union scrutiny, and participated too many times in School and University internal wars for me to harbor any doubt about his confidentiality.

Herb rested at one end of my dean-professor trust continuum, former dean Dante at the other.

"Paul, how about a quick lunch?" Dante asked one day as he passed my office on a cloudy and damp afternoon. My calendar was light. It would be good to get out of the office for an hour or so. It was Dante's invite; Dante had his favorite lunch spots.

I felt comfortable as we huddled at a beer-lubricated lunch in a warm Geary Street Irish pub on the cold, damp afternoon. Despite confrontations over the years, a residue of simpatico between us remained. Probably because Dante, too, had once been a dean of the School and we had worked closely in managing the relocation of the School from Lone Mountain to our current location. I broached thoughts of my retirement with Dante. To this day, I'm not sure why. It was a mistake.

We were relaxed. The pub made good Shepherd's Pie; a second draft beer was perfect. We lingered as we shared tales of University gossip. It was a nice break from shuffling papers on my desk until Dante wanted to know more about my retirement thoughts. University small talk quickly evolved into cross examination. It was time to get back to the office.

The walk across Geary, up Stanyan to Turk to the School seemed longer, the afternoon wind colder, the atmosphere danker than when we left my office for the pub. Other than the complain about the weather, we said little until Dante paused as we reached the entry to the School. He couldn't help dropping a foreboding farewell after a most relaxing break, "Paul, I'm going to do everything in my power to get tenure for Job. You've made a grave mistake." We entered the School and went separate ways to our offices. I forgot to thank Dante for lunch.

Twenty-Nine

Point of No Return

Lone Mountain felt more of a mountain than hill as I climbed to Wise Jim's office at the peak. The two of us had reached a point of diminishing returns upon negotiation of retirement returns through memoranda, telephone, and email. It was time to bring closure in person.

Seated on a couch for visitors tucked into a quiet sun-bathed cube of space designated as reception area for the complex of University central administration academic offices, I waited to meet with Jim. I felt a little like when I had sat outside the principal's office at Stuyvesant High School waiting to meet with the principal. The circumstances and hushed setting were far different but there was the same feeling of isolation as I waited for a verdict to be delivered by a superior. This time, rather than waiting for a reprimand, however, I was waiting to play *Antique Road Show* with academic pieces, Wise Jim the appraiser, and I the guest, to see how much my retirement was worth.

It wasn't long before Jim ambled down the short corridor from his office to greet me. "Come on in," he warmly welcomed. As we walked side by side, I felt more comfortable. I knew why I was here; he knew why I was here. We both understood what I requested in exchange for turning in my deanship and tenure.

I sat down on one love seat, my usual perch in his office, Jim on the other, cattie-corner to mine. He crossed his legs, leaned back, and placed one arm on the seatback; the other rested on the couch seat cushion, a white sheet of paper flat beneath his hand. Shadows that danced on a wall as sunlight passed through swaying pine boughs outside his office evoked the same calm I derived from gazing at the drift of cloud-cast shadows on a clear day across Vermont mountains. I was relaxed.

"What a day," I exclaimed. "It doesn't get much better than this."

"It's been a dry winter. We could use some rain," Jim responded. We were both dancing around what we knew had to be discussed.

"How's Janet doing?" I assumed he was talking about her career as a psychologist rather than any reaction to my decision to retire.

"She's doing well. And your son?"

I was talking about his son's career as an aspiring news reporter.

We were no closer to starting the discussion we knew we needed to have than when I had entered his office. Our friendly banter continued for a few more minutes before Jim picked up the page resting beneath his hand on the couch. I could make out that it was the memo I had sent him confirming retirement points about which we had previously talked. We had parried courtesies long enough.

"Let's review the major points of your proposal to prevent any misunderstanding when I pass it by Father Steve," Jim directed. It was time to get to business.

There were no surprises, as point by point, he noted requests we had touched on in earlier discussions and memoranda exchange addressing questions, the type of which in one form or another, directly or indirectly, any administrator asks a professor and, I suspect, any dean who seeks to trade in tenure for retirement asks of a superior.

"How long a sabbatical do you want?"

"How did you calculate the salary you requested for the sabbatical year?"

"When do you want your resignation to take effect?"

And for a dean, particularly, at this institution, "Do you plan to remain as a professor?

We were comfortable as conversation flowed from point to point and I shared the reasoning behind my requests. In some cases, simple confirmation of my notes were needed; others were more sensitive and deserved fuller discussion. We bounced through areas of agreement. We talked about sensitive areas without rancor. We made real progress. Wise Jim was a good listener. When Jim said, "I'll share your proposal with Father Steve," the tone of his voice said it all: a deal had been struck. He stood and extended a hand of congratulation. I stood and extended mine. Our meeting had concluded.

As I left his office and walked down the corridor to leave the building, I heard Jim's door close behind me. He had moved on to other business. I felt as I did when I completed the first lap at my early morning Master's swim sessions at Koret: the water temperature hadn't been too cold, the drill for the hour wasn't too difficult, and I felt better for the exercise. A few days later, I received a telephone call from Jim.

"Father President has approved your request. I'll be getting you a formal letter. Congratulations."

It was official. I put the phone arm back on the receiver. I couldn't go back now. The afternoon sun streamed through my office window, the hum of traffic, crickets of the city, was soothing. All was quiet in the outer offices. I was at peace with the decision. Let the grand romp to retirement begin. I asked Catherine to track Janet down at Kaiser-Permanente.

"Is everything alright, Hon?" Janet asked. "Catherine had me pulled from a meeting with a client. She said it's important I talk to you."

"Everything's fine. Father Steve has approved my retirement." There was a moment of silence.

"That's great." I think Janet meant it.

"They agreed to all the terms," I added.

"We need to celebrate." I hope she meant it. "We can talk tonight. I have a client waiting; talk to you later." It seemed there was a vacuum of silence, and then she added, "Hon, you should feel good. Congratulations," before we hung up. I think she meant it.

I was at peace with my decision to retire but there was lingering uncertainty. Or maybe, I was just nervous. Maybe I was frightened that after over twenty years of service as a dean in Boston and San Francisco, I might suffer the same malaise some prisoners experience that lead to their return to prison when set free from twenty-plus years of incarceration. Recidivism, however, wasn't an option for sixty-five-year-old retiring deans.

I had a responsibility to first inform Associate Dean Patrick before the decision went public. So different in temperament, interest, and responsibilities from Herb, he, too, was appointed without protection of the union or safety of tenure. My decision to retire would indirectly contribute to professional uncertainty once I departed. Both would be vulnerable to the vicissitudes of my successor. Patrick's friendship with Father Steve prior to Father's ascendancy to University President, and the recent retirement of conservative Father Francis, might make his membership in the University community more secure, but a new dean could shake things up.

I left the safety of my office and ambled to the half-open door of Patrick's office. He was meeting with my Cheshire Sister. I whispered, "Have you got a minute after talking with Sister?" Neither my presence nor whisper caught Patrick's attention; caught in Sister's spell, he neither heard nor saw me. I would need to intrude and fully opened the door.

"Sister, Patrick, excuse me." Sister stopped talking. Patrick sat quietly, still under Sister's trance.

"Patrick, would you stop by my office when you and Sister are finished?" I apologetically asked.

"We'll be finished soon, dearie," Sister assured me. She had spoken for the two of them and I withdrew to my office. Less than five minutes later, with a sprightly, "What's up?" Patrick joined me. He knew I had been meeting with the Provost to discuss retirement. I'm sure he knew what was up.

"Have a seat," I invited. I told him my request for retirement had been approved and I would be stepping down as dean at the end of the academic year. There was only a controlled smile in response. I was disappointed by his seemingly indifferent reaction, but in retrospect, there was probably little he could have said that would relieve any uncertainty he might have felt at the moment. An "I'm sorry" or "Congratulations" might have been nice, but verged on being strictly ceremonial. I'm sure his silence also masked questions of personal concern. Those questions would have to gestate.

I didn't need to worry about informing my former Associate Dean Father Matthew, who had also been appointed by me without tenure or union protection. It had been a year since he leap-frogged from the position of my associate dean to an administration position in the castle of Father Steve on Lone Mountain—no intermediate stops between. Unlike Mark Twain's leaping frogs of Calaveras County, Father Matthew could declare himself a winner after only one University jump: Associate Dean to Associate Vice President for Finance and Special Assistant to the Provost. He was safe on the Jesuit express as it sped its Jesuit passengers to ever-higher Jesuit university positions across the country. As my retirement negotiations had unfolded, he probably knew more about their status than I.

Departure of a dean always has an unsettling effect on office staff who serve at the dean's will and who often are among the first to pick up tidbits of information that suggest something out of the ordinary may be up.

I asked Catherine to personally notify staff that I would like to meet with them later that afternoon. I wanted to thank them for their assistance and offer any assurances that might be helpful and provide an opportunity for them to ask questions. We had worked too closely for too long for me to have them first learn of my resignation when I formally announced it to the full School community. More selfishly, a smaller meeting with staff would serve as a dress rehearsal for my meeting with the full School community. I would get a clue as to what comments play well and what don't. And, I suspected, following a dress rehearsal, I would be less nervous when I met with the full School community three days later.

I was simultaneously confident and nervous as I entered the faculty lounge to join the gathered professors and staff for the Special Meeting I had called for the School community. Most were already present when I entered the Lounge, almost on time, for my Special Meeting.

Gray Dante put his arm on my shoulder and smiled as I wove to the front of the horseshoed huddle of professors packed in the half-walled embankment of seats. His smile, seldom present since our lunch and subsequent duels over Job, and arm on shoulder said it all: he suspected he had outlasted another dean.

Folding chairs pulled into the horseshoe opening of the embankment seating were full; staff sat in small clusters of chairs at the rear entrance to the circumference. There was some relief knowing that at least I would be playing to a full house. The hum of small talk subsided when I reached the open end of the horseshoe. As I stood alone before the silent School community, the anxiety I had brought to the meeting faded. I was very much alone but I was very comfortable as I opened, "I felt it important to tell you personally that I will be stepping down as dean at the end of this academic year. It's not been an easy decision for me to reach. My years as dean have been rewarding and challenging."

With a smile, I threw in an aside, "I must admit, some days were better than others." There were a few sympathetic chuckles. "I also have to admit, there were far more good days than frustrating days. I have truly enjoyed being a dean of the School." There was some murmuring between professors, knowing nods from staff with whom I had met earlier, before I added, "And the personal pleasure and pride from the accomplishments of the School over those years would not have been possible without the help of all of you."

After perhaps an overly generous recognition of professors and staff contributions, I fell to the generic retiring officer malady of providing an over generous assessment of accomplishments I had witnessed during my tenure. I thanked everyone one more time before observing, "I'm sure you have some questions."

The silence that followed my brief soliloquy of departure, save for occasional subdued mutterings from professor to professor, was frighteningly similar to that which followed my presentation to office staff. It was finally broken by a question from Dante, "Will you stay on as a professor?"

He was curious whether there would be one more member in the School's dethroned deans' club—and whether the School would lose a professor slot. I assured him I wasn't seeking membership in the former deans' professor club and would be moving on. His opening question broke the wall of silence.

"Will there be an interim dean?"

"How will the University go about selecting a new dean?"

"Do you plan to stay at the University?"

Attendees were justifiably curious or concerned what my resignation might mean to them. Questions too personal to ask, and impossible to answer, rested just below the surface.

"Who will review my application for promotion and tenure?"

"Will my program be supported by a new dean?"

"What will be the priorities of a new dean?"

There was a lull in question-asking. It was time for closure. Everyone was polite but I was disappointed that few questions were wrapped with words of thanks for my service over the years. I felt let down rather than uplifted.

I thanked the professors and staff again for their help over the years. They stood and softly and politely applauded. A smattering of "thank yous" and "good lucks" floated in the room as they turned and left for their offices. The meeting was over.

A few professors held back as others filed silently from the lounge. Sister Rachel folded my hand in hers, "God speed. My prayers are with you. Thank you." Through rimless glasses, her almond brown eyes exuded warmth. Professor Fiametta of the dancing rings stood uncomfortably behind Sister, waiting to say a few words. She dropped a soft personal "thank you" on Sister's departure and perkily departed. Dante stood aside and waited for Sister Rachel and Fiametta to finish. His knowing wink as he drifted in front of me after Sister and Fiametta left, signaled that he had seen too many deans come and go to assign special importance to my departure.

Reformer Herb stood by himself in the back of the room. He waited to say anything until all the others had gone. He and I, along with a few staff chatting in a corner, were soon the only ones left in the lounge. He slowly ambled to the front and stood next to me. He had been silent for the past hour. I fully understood. He was still perceived an outsider, a special appointment of the dean, and Management, by most professors. I was glad he had waited.

"Paul, you've made a difference. Thanks." He turned and left the room alone. Those words meant a lot. Maybe I would be leaving some footprints behind. I had no way of knowing how long they would last before being filled in by time.

Thirty
Last Suppers

May is a month for ceremonies, celebrations, congratulations, and farewell dinners at universities across the country. May was all those things to me this year, but I was a guest at retirement dinners rather than the host, recipient of fond farewells rather than donor.

Retirement or farewell dinners for deans came in two models at the University: Ford for Labor, Lexus for Management. For me, this spring, the Ford retirement ride preceded the Lexus.

Damp fingers of Pacific fog streamed from between downtown buildings as Janet and I searched for a place to park our car close to the San Francisco Culinary Institute—venue selected by School professors for my retirement dinner. I swerved across Pine Street, adrenaline flowing, to lay claim to a suddenly discovered parking spot. Skill from years of alternate-side-of-the-street parking maneuvers in Greenwich Village still served me well. Janet and I bowed our heads as we left the car to escape the gutter-driven shrapnel driven by raw San Francisco spring wind. It was only a matter of minutes, but very long minutes, before we spotted a man wearing a chef-like apron, lit cigarette in hand, huddled in a sheltered building entryway. Above our aproned event harbinger, we made out the aged, soiled lettering: *San Francisco Culinary Institute.* We had arrived.

The Institute lobby was barren but warm. White block letters affixed to a black flannel events calendar, announced, *University of San Francisco Reception.* A white flannel arrow pointed to a lobby stairwell.

"Does this entryway remind you of anything?" I asked Janet as we descended the worn, rug-carpeted stairs that led in one direction only, to the basement, and answered my own question before she had a chance to reply, "There may be no Luana paneling but whoever designed the foyer in the School before I came to the University must have had a second job here."

Janet laughed, "There's something to be said for aesthetic closure but . . ." We both chuckled.

We successfully negotiated the gloomy stairwell that led to a windowless room, our farewell banquet hall for the evening. As we emerged from the stairwell, ever-gracious Sister Rachel, wrapped in silk floral finery rather than habit, drifted toward us in welcome. Small groups of professors were scattered behind her; a cluster of more boisterous professors stood by a make-shift bar. Steam rose from food trays strung out on white tablecloths at the rear of the room.

Our arrival was the signal for the evening's festivities to begin. Professors broke from their groups to share warm hugs, handshakes, and smiles. Conversation flowed. Groups broke down and reformed; individuals would leave to pluck favorites from the elaborate display of hors d'oeuvres, masterpieces of chefs-in-training, and return.

Janet and I inserted ourselves into small group conversations. We slipped from one cluster of professors to another. We clumsily co-opted conversations already underway as we dropped over-used niceties.

"I'm glad you're here."

"Thanks for your help."

"I'll miss the School."

"Quite an array of food."

I couldn't suppress the occasional but not entirely honest observation, "I can't think of a better place for a dean of a School of Education to have a retirement dinner than at the one in which the banquet is prepared by students in training."

I left Janet's side to say hello to professors who had joined the School in the past few years and were finding it difficult to connect with the dwindling cliques of divas. I made a special point to thank reformer Herb and his loyal assistant, keeper of Birdy, for joining us this evening. They, along with now-tenured Jane, product of 1960s' Berkeley and survivor of John II and Father Francis's inquisition, sat at a table outside the buffet flow.

I rejoined Janet who was absorbed as she listened to Professor Luke, the School's Uriah Heep of a scholar, recite the history of the School until seemingly out of nowhere, Sister Rachel was at our side and purred, "Aren't you and Janet eating?" We hadn't noticed that most professors and staff were now seated, their plates overflowing with specialties of our ascendant chefs gathered from the steaming trays at the rear of the room. Sister's command of a question provided a pretext for Janet and me to disentangle from the history recitation of suspendered Professor Luke. We begged his pardon and broke off to approach the steaming servers. Luke's tales of School history continued unabated as he latched on to courteous but now entrapped Sister Rachel. "Sister, do you remember . . .?"

There was still enough food on the buffet table to host a second or third reception. How many people had my planners expected will be here? I hoped the Institute had found a way to distribute the leftover food to the homeless huddled on downtown San Francisco sidewalks.

Sister Rachel was soon at our side again and directed us to a vacant pair of unoccupied seats not already taken by gorging professors. We were thankful for her intervention for we had almost talked ourselves out of seats. Conversational time-fillers were running low at our table when Sister shortly proceeded to the front of the room.

"Can I have your attention?" The conversation volume lowered a decibel or two. "Can I have your attention?" she repeated softly. The hum of the professors dimmed to a murmur. Sister's presence demanded attention, habit or no habit. Her smile radiated as she peered over bifocals; her eyes swept the gathering.

"Dean Warren, won't you join me?" I had barely finished eating—the price for late seating. Like most retirement dinner celebrations, the main event commences with attendees' swallowing their dinner's last bite. With a "here-we-go" roll of the eyes to Janet, I turned on my dean smile and weaved my way through too-close tables, self-assured and self-conscious, to join Sister.

"Dean, we'd like to express our thanks to you by sharing a poem a few of us have written for you." Sister's eyes sparkled. She looked up at me beatifically. I stood in her shadow, silent and uncomfortable.

"Thomasina, Grace, won't you join us."

Thomasina, professor and statistician of the many rings, who had long ago been silenced by the presence of Professor Emilia in the faculty confrontation of *researcher v. philosopher*, popped up from her seat and strutted like a sandpiper on the beach to join Sister. Professor Grace, a seasoned New York City transplant who had become more isolated and idiosyncratic since she had been awarded tenure, followed as she slowly wend her way to the front of the room. Perky, many-ringed, carefully made-up Thomasina and designer glassed, New York-tailored Grace standing next to stolid rose-flowered Sister made quite an impression.

I only remember the poem of forcibly rhymed couplets dropped by my improbable chorus of three that sought to convey an inventory of the virtues and vices of my deanship. With the delivery of a final couplet, there was a gentle clapping of hands, an isolated guffaw, and chortles of relief from the assemblage. I murmured, "I thank you. I thank you." I took a beat, and added, "I think." There were friendly laughs from the assembly and a more boisterous clapping of hands. We had all been together too long for there not to be a sense of camaraderie.

"You're not going to get off that easily." Sister pirouetted as Thomasina of the rings lifted a brown, construction paper–wrapped gift resting on a table behind her. Thomasina stepped forward, gift held in front, as one might hold a shield.

"Dean Warren, the faculty of the School wants you to have this reminder of your years here." She thrust the object toward me, and I clumsily accepted the large, flat package.

Thomasina proudly stepped back into the goodbye trio. She was pleased. I murmured an uncomfortable "thank you" and held the wrapped object in front of me, not sure of my next move. To open or not to open? I have never been sure of the protocol for receiving gifts in public settings.

"Paul, open it," Thomasina whispered, loud enough for everyone to hear.

"Open it," Dante's forceful voice erupted from somewhere in the back of the room.

"Oh, yes, open it," Sister Rachel echoed softly.

She was obviously pleased with what lurked beneath the brown parchment. I had no choice. As I carefully peeled the paper back, a handsome, burled wooden frame, clearly and carefully selected, was exposed. I extricated the frame from its paper pocket. It bordered a collection of impressively matted photographs, captions beneath:

"Retirement is never having . . .

To stay in the office on a glorious day

To walk down the hall to the dean's office

To put up with the dinky swimming pool in Koret

To comment on the sunny summer weather you left in Vermont . . ."

"Read them, Dean," Sister ordered with a smile. When Sister asks, the recipient obeys. I painfully read them.

Couplets completed, gift opened, captions read, Thomasina and Grace returned proudly to their seats. There were other gifts, wishes for well-being, and thanks for a job well done. But I only vividly recall the couplet reading of Sister's choir. It wasn't great theater but it was fun.

Surfeited with food and wine, gifts and best wishes, the evening's program for Janet and me rapidly wound down. Professors slowly prepared to leave, each at their own pace. Hugs, warm handshakes, and an occasional "stay in touch" were shared with us before they slowly folded into the stairwell to trudge up the steps to San Francisco springtime evening cold. Gifts and scattered wrapping on a tabletop, steam still rising from half-empty hot trays, and Sister with her warm smile in her floral dress at Janet and my side were all that remained of the evening's festivities.

Primed by salutations and farewells of the Culinary Institute farewell, only one more exit protocol awaited: the Management Farewell Dinner. Father President, his colleagues, and my fellow deans had it far easier than School faculty when it came time to plan a celebration of departure: far fewer people had to be invited, date selection was open-ended, and cost, within reason, wasn't a consideration. For we were all Management.

I accelerated my trusty old rag-top into the parking circle of *The Four Seasons* and downshifted as I pulled to a stop. For all its peppiness, my '87 Beamer suddenly seemed old in the queue of freshly waxed, new model luxury cars, vanities of the rich waiting for valet pick-up. I didn't care. The car was more than the ultimate driving machine for me; I had inherited it from my boyhood friend when he died more than a dozen years earlier.

The valet ambled over to open the door for Janet. The latch stuck briefly before he could get it open. The car's age was showing. Latch freed, Janet released, the valet carefully shut the door behind her. As I circled behind the car to join her, he delivered a too rehearsed, "Have a good evening."

Hand in hand, Janet and I entered the lobby of the hotel that was an architectural testimony to taste and affluence and self-consciously proceeded through the opulent corridor that led to the hotel lounge and restaurant. When we finally emerged from the many football-fields-long corridor into a glass-bordered pod, territorial wall to the hotel's restaurant,

I directed as much as asked the maître d'hôtel standing guard, "University of San Francisco Party." Janet, wearing a tailored suit and classily accessorized, me in my freshly dry-cleaned *Bonfire of the Vanities* suit, exuded an appropriate aura of privilege.

The suited maître d'hôtel turned to his equally well-dressed assistant and directed, "San Francisco Party."

"San Francisco Party," repeated the assistant. "Please follow me." Protocol for service must have called for three-word communications. Follow we did.

We were led to a private dining area reserved for the occasion, cordoned off from the larger room serving *Four Seasons'* patrons without corporate sponsor. The University's powerful had chosen to bid Janet and me farewell, safe from the glances of the well-heeled but still general public—or perhaps to protect *Four Seasons* patrons from us.

This was the kingdom of the accomplished and privileged, Lexus rather than Ford territory. Heavy, polished silver utensils rested on creased linen napkins placed with precision on a gracefully draped, carefully pressed tablecloth. Deep-red velvet upholstered chairs embraced the table. The sinking sun silhouetted the urban landscape through western windows. And Father President seated at the head of our table, back to the setting sun with a penumbra of light cast from behind, provided a sense of spiritual mystery.

Fellow officers, twelve men and a woman, wine glasses already filled, lined the length of the table as they sat waiting our arrival. Two chairs at the table's midpoint sat empty across from one another, no doubt, chosen to provide Janet and me maximum exposure to the group and the group maximum access to us. Father President anchored one end of the table, Wise Jim the other.

Wise Jim rose as we entered and, as if on command ,all players followed his lead. Janet and I shared warm handshakes with Jim, his hands placed over ours in welcome. With a flow of the arm, he gestured toward the empty chairs.

Before we had time to fully pull in our chairs, a waiter rose magically behind Janet and, in hushed voice, asked, "Would you care for something to drink?"

"I'll have water for now, thank you," Janet replied.

"Bottled or tap?"

"Tap, please."

"Tap?" repeated the waiter. His tone was credulous.

"Water from the faucet will be just fine." Janet looked up and smiled at him. She always chafed at San Francisco Perrier power. She had let our waiter off easy.

He circled the table and whispered over my shoulder, "And you, sir?

"I'll have a dry Manhattan on the rocks, Makers Mark, twist of lemon please."

Janet threw a questioning look from across the table on hearing my request. I'm sure she couldn't remember the last time I had ordered anything other than a glass of wine before dinner. But this evening was a time to celebrate transitions: from active to retired, from dean to *professor emeritus*, from west coast possibly to east coast—from wine to Manhattans. Small talk filled time until our drinks arrived. With the rapid delivery of our drinks and drinks now before all of us, Wise Jim raised his glass to propose a toast.

"Paul, I want to thank you for the irremediable good you have done for the School and the University. I wish you and Janet the best." There was a clinking of glasses, accompanied by a hearty "Here, here," from South African Saul. Opening toast delivered, we got to the business of drinking and talking.

The cacophony of talking and drinking academics was soon interrupted by the presentation of ornate oversize menus that sung of *Four*

Seasons' cornucopia of offerings. No prices were listed. No one was intimidated. We were here to celebrate and Father President was paying the bill.

With the downing of pre-prandials and arrival of appetizers selected from the Bill of Fare, we got down to the business of the evening: celebration of my departure, accompanied by traditional duels of oenological one-ups-man-ship between Deans Saul and Samuel to select a wine most appropriate for each course, a ritual that had been an integral part of all Dean Retreat dinners.

True to form, wine selection took center stage. Wine pairing to complement each course was accompanied by Saul and Samuel's review ritual: swirl of wine in crystal glass held up to the light to check body and color, nose dipped into glass to assay bouquet or perfume, sip taken and gargled to permit choice of adjectives to describe taste, and swallow and pause to ascertain finish. Once the wine passed Saul and Samuel's swirl, bouquet, taste, and finish test selections, and were deemed appropriate for each course, the wine was poured. Even Father Steve, a proletarian at heart, champion of the poor, enjoyed participation in Samuel and Saul's sport—and a glass of good wine.

In retirement dinner tradition, gentle jibes and fond memories punctuated the dining and wining, or more accurately, the wining and dining, until the staccato of silver knife on wine glass by Dean Samuel broke the flow of informal conversation. It was time for toasts—or roasts. Samuel had important words to share. Others would follow.

"It has been a privilege to work with you, Dean Warren. I didn't always understand what you were saying but you sure made it sound good."

A high-pitched guffaw followed by a "Yes, yes, you've got it," jumped from Saul's lips.

"My, my," toned Jerome, "aren't we something?" There was hearty laughter. Even I laughed. I wasn't sure Janet was as amused as I, but she hadn't sat through all those interminable deans' meetings.

Toast delivered, Samuel returned to examine the claret red of his wine through the glow of a table candle's flame. He had done his job. The floodgates for roasts and toasts, some presented with love, others to serve the toaster's ego, were now open. There was nothing for me to do but hunker down until the flow ran its course. I couldn't escape. I nodded appreciatively at the words of thanks. I laughed, not always comfortably, at pointed jests.

For the balance of the evening, Janet and I sat at the tipping point between humor and hurt, comfort and malaise. I wanted the toasts and testimonials to continue; they fed my ego. I wanted the jibes to end; they hurt as well as humored. I wanted to luxuriate in the opulence of the evening; I wanted to escape the embrace of *Four Seasons*, so antithetical to the social justice mission of the University and so distant from my childhood roots.

Sated by wine, words, and food, in that order, we sipped after-dinner cordials translucent in the amber of candlelight. The passage of time had transformed the cityscape from sun-backed silhouettes to an urban light show when Father President apologetically intruded, "I don't know about your schedule but I have an early morning meeting tomorrow."

I suspect he may have interrupted the flow of stories as much to avoid hearing more of the follies of his deans as to be fresh for the next morning's meeting. He rose from his chair; deans rose in response. Conversations ended as chairs were pushed back from the table and a chorus of thanks for the evening was extended to Father. I got a chance to share a solo heartfelt "thanks," he a "warm thanks" to me, before he and Wise Jim together left our luxurious sanctuary.

Once Father President and Provost Jim departed, evening festivities quickly wound down. Handshakes were shared, "good lucks" extended, farewells delivered, and we soon all scattered to the rest of our lives: colleague deans to family and career, me to family and retirement. Where had everyone gone so quickly? How had the camaraderie of the evening evaporated so suddenly?

The corridor back to the *Four Seasons* entrance seemed longer and quieter to Janet and me than when we had entered. We exchanged few words before we reached the *Four Seasons* entrance where our evening had begun. When my trusty Beamer rounded the bend and came into sight, a car jockey wearing hotel silks at the wheel, the dinner celebration already seemed ages ago.

It wasn't until days later, formal University farewells behind us, that Janet and I felt comfortable enough to go beyond the rehashing of retirement dinner happenings to share the emotional complexity of retirement: the sadness and the elation, the ambiguity and the certainty. The only thing we knew for certain was that my days as dean would officially be over at the end of the month. With the rituals of retirement behind us, all that remained for me to do before I left the School now was to remove trappings of my presence from the Dean's Office and leave the space sanitary for a dean who would preside once I left.

There was something relaxing about taking down personal photographs from office walls, locating surrogate parents for potted plants, removing books from shelves, and emptying desk drawers that had become depositories for quite a collection of odds n' ends. I luxuriated being alone in my office. I enjoyed the quiet as I pulled old calendars from my desk drawer, collected papers and reports from my files, and cleared my computer in preparation for departure. As I slowly riffed through saved emails, file folders, my personal log, and years of desk book calendars, I was surprised at how well they had captured the range of events that shaped my life in this Jesuit and Catholic University. I would have to return to them. I was also surprised how well my final University spring-cleaning had soothed the anxiety of departure.

Desk drawers were empty, save standard office supplies. My desktop was clean. Office shelves were bare, save a copy of the *University of San Francisco Trustees—University of San Francisco Faculty Association Collective Bargaining Agreement* conspicuously placed for a new dean, along with the University catalogue and the most recent copy of *Jesuit Magazine. School of Education Annual Reports* that I had written over the years of deanship rested on the coffee table. I would take my copy of *The Myth of Sisyphus* with me.

Photographs of travels as dean that had hung on my walls and those of Janet and my children that had rested on my desktop stood in a carton. All that waited for me to do now was to carry the cartons to my car and say goodbye to my staff. Spring-cleaning was over.

I would like to believe Wise Jim's observation that my years as dean resulted in irremediable good for the School and University. I only wish I was more certain. I am certain, however, that my mother would have forgiven my move to San Francisco and would have applauded the social justice stance of my last university home. I also suspect she would have been proud of me, even if I ended my career in a Jesuit and Catholic university—as Management.

finis

Epilogue

When Janet and I made the decision to retire in our Vermont home, we made a commitment to ourselves to return to the Bay Area for at least a month every winter. We had collected too many friends over our San Francisco years to permanently say goodbye. We also knew that the length and cold of Vermont winters demanded regular escapes to kinder climates.

Only weeks before our late winter return in the first year of retirement, I received a University of San Francisco newsletter that featured a story about Father President Steve's decision to hold annual University retreats for officers in El Salvador, Nicaragua, and Mexico rather than Bay Area locations. During my years in San Francisco, the Provost and deans had annually retreated to lodges, religious retreats, or upscale motels in the Vineyard hills or on the Pacific Coast—Inverness, Napa, Sonoma, Tiburon, Silomar, or Palo Alto—for extended discussions of mission, long-term planning, enrollment, or some other vital component of University life. Dinner complemented with vintage wines in a fine restaurant would be the final item on a day's agenda. Father Steve's change of location for annual meetings provided quite a sea change. I had to learn more about what led to his decision and made an appointment to meet with him during our late winter visit to San Francisco.

Father met me at the door to his office. His strong handshake, broad smile, dancing dark brown eyes, priest's collar over a comfortable charcoal-gray wool sweater, signaled all was under control at the University. There may have been a bit more gray in his hair, a few more lines on his chiseled face than when I saw him last, but there was no less enthusiasm.

"Have a seat," Father Steve gestured toward the couch and joined me, wingback chair across from mine. I shared progress on my writing agenda that had become an integral part of my Vermont life. He shared progress on University projects that had only been goal statements when I left the University. Talk flowed easily. Updates shared, I got to the reason I had asked for us to meet.

"Father, what prompted you to schedule University Management Annual Retreats in El Salvador, Nicaragua, and Mexico? It's quite a change from the Academic Officer Retreats in Napa and Sonoma in which I participated while I was dean." Obviously, this was not the first time someone had asked him the question.

"Let me give you some background before I get to your question." I was to appreciate for the first time the source of the passion that had marked many of Father's pronouncements while I was dean.

"It was serendipity that introduced me to Central America." I had often cited *serendipity* when explaining my professional decisions to friends or colleagues, but the term assumed new attributes on learning of Father's life experiences.

Father shared how he had come to learn Spanish rather than the more difficult German language to meet PhD study requirements and subsequently learned from a good friend that the best Spanish language tutor was to be found in a seminary in Bolivia. When on leaving his residence for an evening walk one night in Bolivia, he found himself alone in the silence of city streets, the bustle of daytime gone. But it was the silence of martial law, not of a city asleep. The silence was to be shortly broken by the sounds of lumbering government tanks assigned to carry and deposit bodies of slain citizens suspected as being disloyal to the government. Violence was a counterpoint to the silence.

Father was more than a student of the Spanish language, more than chaff tossed in the cyclone of social turmoil; he was a man in the final stages of making a commitment to God—and social justice. Violence on Bolivian streets swung the needle of his social justice compass toward the oppressed of South and Central America. Subsequent assignments to Salvador fixed the compass needle.

"I can still visualize government posters pasted on city walls that shouted, "Army and People Working Together for a New Salvador." Rebels who agitated for change were subject to military retribution. And like the rebels in Bolivia, they were laid out in city plazas."

In the midst of the horror spawned by dictatorships in El Salvador and Bolivia, the Church for Father represented a constant, vibrant force that contested the carnage carried out by these countries' dictatorships. Far more than the term *serendipity* had elevated the theme of social justice from abstraction to action for Father. There was no need to take an intuitive leap to understand what had prompted him to change the venue and expand University officer participation in the University Academic Retreat. His experiences may have been wrapped in his Catholic faith but it wasn't necessary to be Jesuit or Catholic to understand why he had chosen to expose his officers to the press of poverty and powerlessness. The concept of social justice, central to the University mission, cannot be fully internalized as an abstraction in the hills of Sonoma and Napa.

As I left Father's office, I remembered Father Jack rushing into my first meeting with assembled deans at the University, shattered by his recent experience in El Salvador, dismayed at America's support of that country's government. Father President's tales of Bolivia and El Salvador provided a bookend to Father Jack's expression of horror at that first Council of Deans meeting and a fitting closure for my years at the University.

Chronometric Dating in Archaeology

ADVANCES IN ARCHAEOLOGICAL AND MUSEUM SCIENCE

Series Editors:
Martin J. Aitken, *Oxford University*
Edward V. Sayre, *Smithsonian Institution*
and R. E. Taylor, *University of California, Riverside*

Volume 1 PHYTOLITH SYSTEMATICS: Emerging Issues
Edited by George Rapp, Jr. and Susan C. Mulholland

Volume 2 CHRONOMETRIC DATING IN ARCHAEOLOGY
Edited by R. E. Taylor and Martin J. Aitken

Chronometric Dating in Archaeology

Edited by

R. E. TAYLOR

University of California, Riverside
Riverside, California

and

MARTIN J. AITKEN

Oxford University
Oxford, England

Published in cooperation with the
Society for Archaeological Sciences

PLENUM PRESS • NEW YORK AND LONDON

Library of Congress Cataloging-in-Publication Data

Chronometric dating in archaeology / edited by R.E. Taylor and Martin J. Aitken.
p. cm. -- (Advances in archaeological and museum science ; v. 2)
Includes bibliographical references and index.
ISBN 0-306-45715-6
1. Archaeological dating. I. Taylor, R. E. (Royal Ervin), 1938- . II. Aitken, M. J. (Martin Jim) III. Series.
CC78.C46 1997
930.1'028'5--dc21
97-31098
CIP

ISBN 0-306-45715-6

A Division of Plenum Publishing Corporation
233 Spring Street, New York, N. Y. 10013

http://www.plenum.com

10 9 8 7 6 5 4 3 2 1

Printed in the United States of America

Consulting Editors

Jacqueline S. Olin
Smithsonian Institution
Washington, D.C.

Ernst Pernicka
Max Planck Institute
for Nuclear Physics
Heidelberg, Germany

John R. Prescott
University of Adelaide
Adelaide, Australia

Frank Preusser
Los Angeles, California

T. Douglas Price
University of Wisconsin, Madison
Madison, Wisconsin

François Schweizer
Laboratory of the Museum of
Art and History
Geneva, Switzerland

Julie K. Stein
University of Washington
Seattle, Washington

Henrik Tauber
National Museum of Denmark
Copenhagen, Denmark

Michael S. Tite
Oxford University
Oxford, England

Giorgio Torraca
University of Rome
Rome, Italy

Lambertus Van Zelst
Smithsonian Institution
Washington, D.C.

This volume is dedicated to

Annette Laming

editor of
La Découverte du Passé:
Progrès Récents et Techniques Nouvelles
en Préhistoire et en Archéologie
(Paris, 1952)

Contributors

Martin J. Aitken • Research Laboratory for Archaeology, Oxford University, OX1 3QJ, United Kingdom

Paul R. Bierman • Department of Geology, University of Vermont, Burlington, Vermont 05405, USA

Jeffrey S. Dean • Laboratory of Tree-ring Research, University of Arizona, Tucson, Arizona 85721, USA

Irving Friedman • Laboratory of Isotope Geology, United States Geological Survey, Denver, Colorado 80225, USA

Rainer Grün • Quaternary Dating Research Centre, Australian National University, Canberra, ACT #0200, Australia

P. E. Hare • Geophysical Laboratory, Carnegie Institution of Washington, Washington, DC, 20015, USA

Richard E. Hughes • Geochemical Research Laboratory, Portola Valley, California 94028, USA

Julie E. Kokis • Geophysical Laboratory, Carnegie Institution of Washington, Washington, DC, 20015, USA

Amanjit Sandhu • Department of Physics, Guru Nanak Dev University, Amritsar, India

Joan S. Schneider • Department of Anthropology, University of California, Riverside 92521, USA

Henry P. Schwarcz • School of Geography and Geology, McMaster University, Hamilton, Ontario L85 4M1, Canada

Philip Shane • Department of Geology, University of Auckland, Auckland, New Zealand

Robert S. Sternberg • Department of Geosciences, Franklin and Marshall College, Lancaster, Pennsylvania 17604, USA

Stephen Stokes • School of Geography, Oxford University, OX1 3QJ United Kingdom

R. E. Taylor • Radiocarbon Laboratory, Department of Anthropology, Institute of Geophysics and Planetary Physics, University of California, Riverside, California 95251, USA

Fred W. Trembour • Laboratory of Isotope Geology, United States Geological Survey, Denver, Colorado 80225, USA

David W. Von Endt • Conservation Analytical Laboratory, Smithsonian Institution, Washington, DC, 20015, USA

Robert C. Walter • Institute of Human Origins, Berkeley, California 94710, USA

John Westgate • Physical Sciences Division, University of Toronto, Scarborough, Ontario M1C 1A4, Canada

Series Foreword

This volume is the second in the Advances in Archaeological and Museum Science series sponsored by the Society for Archaeological Sciences (SAS). The purpose of this series is to provide summaries of advances in various topics in archaeometry, archaeological science, environmental archaeology, preservation technology, and museum conservation.

The SAS exists to encourage interdisciplinary collaboration between archaeologists and colleagues in the natural sciences. SAS members are drawn from many disciplinary fields. However, they all share a common belief that natural science techniques and methods constitute an essential component of archaeological field and laboratory studies.

Preface

From the vantage point of the last half-century—essentially the period since World War II—it is probably correct to conclude that, of all of the various areas encompassed within archaeological science or archaeometry, researchers dealing with new dating methods have probably enjoyed the most outstanding overall success. Archaeologists and other scientists working in the late 1990s, especially younger colleagues, may not realize the transformations in many accepted viewpoints that have resulted—the so-called "radiocarbon revolution" was only the first of these. In addition, major changes in archaeological research strategies have come about as a direct or indirect result of the development and increasing accuracy and precision of the various techniques and their applications to a whole range of archaeological questions. The ability to assign directly chronometric age to an increasing range of samples is a scientific accomplishment that should not be minimized.

It is the view of the editors that, because of the increasing complexity of many techniques, it is no longer possible for one author to encompass adequately the literature and current research direction of more than one or, at most, two techniques. In our view, the last volume for which that was possible was written by one of us (MJA). In the present volume, the author (or, in most cases, the authors) of each chapter were asked to provide a summary of progress in their respective technique over the last three decades—with an emphasis on a review of developments doing the last five years—and the status of current research. We were interested in providing archaeologists, specialists interested in techniques with which they do not directly work, and advanced undergraduates and postgraduate students in archaeology, with an authoritative review of the current status of the major Quaternary dating methods.

Both editors have noted in earlier, separate discussions that an important goal of assembling these volumes is to facilitate communication between those involved in basic and applied archaeological science studies—in this case, involving chronometric methods— and the archaeologist. Unfortunately, there is a problem in that archaeology, especially in the United States, is not a single discipline. In its institutional and conceptual development, archaeological studies have not evolved in the same manner as have, for example, physics or chemistry. There has not developed an agreement on a single model of what constitutes the basis of how archaeologists are to "understand" the phenomenon they study since they cannot even agree on what constitute the primary unit(s) of cultural analysis. In light of the increasing heterogeneity in conceptual frameworks of those engaged in professional archaeology, an important task of those involved in archaeological science is to initiate and institutionalize interactions with those archaeological colleagues for whom "archaeology is science or it is nothing" and to demonstrate that only with empirically based data can valid generalizations about what actually occurred in the past be accomplished. Essentially this is to answer the question of why humans exhibited the individual and collective behaviors reflected in the materials being examined by archaeologists.

The editors wish to thank very warmly the authors who have contributed to this volume as well as the reviewers of each of the chapters for their excellent comments and suggestions. We also wish to thank Chriss Jones for her invaluable assistance in the preparation of the text for submission to the publisher.

Finally, we should note that in several chapters the term "ka" appears. In such cases. 1ka = 1kvr = 1000 Years.

R. E. TAYLOR
Loma Linda, California

MARTIN J. AITKEN
The Ofslang, Islip, Oxfordshire

Contents

Chapter 1

Climatostratigraphy

MARTIN J. AITKEN AND STEPHEN STOKES

ABSTRACT

The initial framework for global Quaternary climate change and climatostratigraphy was that based on the advance and retreat of alpine glaciers. Subsequently, this was supplemented by observation of such climatic indicators as fossil pollen, varves and loess. In recent decades, knowledge of past climate has been revolutionised by measurement of the oxygen isotope ratios of fossil microfauna in cores extracted from sediment on the floor of the deep ocean and detailed analysis of physical properties of continuous loess sequences and polar ice cores. The oxygen isotopic variations observed in ocean cores define the major global warm-cold transitions which characterise the glacial and interglacial stages (the basic climatostratigraphic units). An absolute timescale for the climatic variations is derived from the Milankovitch astronomical theory of climate. Isotopic and other variations on higher resolution timescales have been obtained for the last glacial-interglacial cycle from the polar ice caps and some deep sea cores. It is increasingly being realised that the frequently rapid climatic shifts between glacial stadial and interstadial sub-stages are more pronounced than had previously been thought. There is growing indication that the climatic predictions from ice core and oceanic sources are manifested terrestrially by climatic indicators such as those mentioned above, thereby allowing linkage of Palaeolithic chronology with the timescales used. Climate changes during the Quaternary period exhibit global synchroneity on millennial and longer timescales. On multimillennial (> 10 ka) timescales, they are

---

MARTIN J. AITKEN • Research Laboratory for Archaeology, Oxford University, OX1 3QJ United Kingdom. **STEPHEN STOKES** • School of Geography, Oxford University, OX1 3QJ United Kingdom.

Chronometric Dating in Archaeology, edited by Taylor and Aitken.
Plenum Press, New York, 1997.

principally controlled by the solar radiation budget. On shorter (millennial and sub-millennial) timescales, the changes are likely to be modulated to a large extent by changing ocean circulation patterns and interactions between the oceans, the cryosphere and the atmosphere. Fine resolution analysis of ice core climatic proxies have demonstrated that late Quaternary climatic changes have occurred, on occasions, on timescales of relevance to human activities, sometimes as short as decades.

INTRODUCTION

Most of the techniques in this volume utilise a physical change occurring within the material of the sample which allows the determination of age which may then be used as a basis for stratigraphic or archaeological correlation. These physical "clocks" may be based on radioactive decay, on the build-up of some radiation-stimulated effect, or on chemical change. The dating is intrinsic to the sample and is dependent, essentially, only on laboratory measurements. A complimentary approach to archaeological chronology, particularly for the Paleolithic, established long before technological advance made the intrinsic methods possible, is the placement of sites within a climatically-determined framework, i.e. by climatostratigraphy. Initially, this was on the basis of such parameters as geomorphic units (e.g., moraines) flora, fauna, and soil conditions. An interlocking dimension was, and is, the archaeological record based on such parameters as hominid development and technology, particularly stone tools.

The basic climatostratigraphic units are glacials and interglacials: an *interglacial* being defined as a time when climate is sufficiently stable and benign to enable the development of deciduous forests similar to the present ones in northwestern Europe, and a *glacial* being all periods of the Quaternary which do not fit into the definition of an interglacial (Kukla and Cilek 1996). In the present chapter, a brief indication is given of the basis of three of the directly-observed climatic frameworks: pollen sequences, glacial varves and loess profiles.

In recent decades, as first proposed by Urey (1948), the climatically-related parameters have been extended to include isotopic ratios. Primarily, this has been the isotopic ratio of oxygen as measured in fossil microfauna taken from long cores extracted from the bed of the deep ocean (Emiliani 1955). This ratio is now accepted as an indicator of global ice volumes and therefore climate, and the successive warm and cool stages so indicated have been shown to correlate with climatic predictions (Hayes *et al.* 1976), first formalised by Milankovitch (1941), based on fluctuations of heat input (insolation) from the sun due to variations in the earth's orbital parameters. This correlation allows "astronomical dating" of the successive isotope stages and, increasingly, archaeological sites are being related to these stages, and hence dated with good accuracy on an absolute timescale (e.g., Wendorf *et al.* 1994).

Because of the slow sedimentation rate on the ocean floor, and sometimes because of bioturbation, there is a tendency for any short-term changes to be smoothed out so that in most cores changes persisting for less than a few thousand years are unlikely to be seen and the record is one of long-term changes (see, for example, Fig. 1.1). Isotopic and other records are obtainable with greater temporal resolution from long cores extracted from the polar ice-caps and these give evidence of rapid changes superimposed on the long-term changes indicated by the marine record. Rapid changes are evidenced also in some marine cores having high sedimentation rate and low bioturbation.

The extent to which these rapid changes were seen on land is a matter of continuing research, but there is growing evidence that this was the case, for example, from the climatic indications of long pollen sequences. This makes more complex the attribution of short-term sites to the marine isotope stages, particulary during glacial periods. After outlining the current (early 1997) state of marine core and ice core isotope chronostratigraphy, a final section of the chapter gives some examples of linkage between isotope-based climatic predictions and what is inferred from terrestrial palaeoenvironmental records. The rapidity of development in this field precludes the possibility of a definitive account. However, it is hoped that what is presented in this chapter will at any rate give readers familiarity with nomenclature which is likely to gain increasing archaeological currency in the years to come.

More detailed accounts of Quaternary climatic frameworks and climatostratigraphy are available in Aitken (1990), Corfield (1995), Dowdeswell and White (1995), Kukla and Click (1996), and Lowe and Walker (1997). We should note that here and elsewhere in this volume, 1 ka = 1 kyr = 1000 years. In this chapter, the convention is followed that an age quoted as "BP" (meaning *Before Present*) indicates an uncalibrated radiocarbon date. Otherwise, a calendar age should be presumed, this being either a calibrated radiocarbon date, or a date from another technique.

FRAMEWORKS BASED ON PROXY INDICATORS

The Ice Ages

Climatic frameworks originated in the nineteenth century following geological recognition that there had been several successive periods of European alpine glacier advance and retreat. In the Alps, the four periods of major advance, the "Ice Ages", were named *Günz*, *Mindel*, *Riss*, and *Würm*, the latter being the more recent. This Alpine framework was, and still is, widely used in Palaeolithic archaeology, including the non-alpine parts of Europe. In North

America, the acknowledged glacial periods were also four in number (*Nebraskan, Kansan, Illinoian*, and *Wisconsin*) and it was natural to hypothesise contemporaneity and a common cause, namely variation in the amount, and distribution, of solar radiant energy falling on the earth (*insolation*). However, as research on archaeological and other sites intensified complexity ensued. Warmish, short-lived, *interstadials* within glacial periods were recognised and with this increase in detail correlation between regions became less clear. One reason was that what was recognised as an interstadial in one region might show itself more strongly in another region and recognised there as an *interglacial* between two major glacial periods. Additional problems were the discontinuous nature of the record and the obliteration of earlier phases by later glaciations. Despite these problems, recent analysis of the climatic variations recorded in ocean core and loess records for the last 0.7 Ma (Kukla 1995) confirm the occurrence of four *supercycles* of climate which comprise more than a single glacial-interglacial cycle and culminate in a glacial of exceptional intensity, suggesting that the initial four fold alpine subdivisions were surprisingly accurate and still have some utility.

Because of difficulties in correlation and the general incompleteness of the sedimentary record, these land-based schemes are not satisfactory in understanding inter-regional human interaction and the wider issues with which Palaeolithic and later archaeology is concerned. Hence, the desirability of relating to a worldwide climatic framework—a global *climatostratigraphy*. In broad terms, this is provided by the marine record but, as mentioned above, the more rapid fluctuations revealed by pollen sequences, and now by ice-cores, complicate the task although, at the same time, giving the eventual possibility of a framework of higher resolution.

Pollen Sequences

Flowering trees and shrubs propagate themselves by means of pollen grains which transfer genetic material to female flowers to effect fertilzation. In the case of ferns and mosses, spores undertake a similar function. Both pollen and spores are produced in great abundance and are extremely small—few exceed 0.1 mm. Nevertheless, their degree of preservation is remarkable, particularly in acid soils and peat bogs. In general terms, dominance of tree pollen is indicative of warmth and the relative abundance of different species gives finer detail. Thus there tends to be a dominance of birch and pine during the initial and final phases of an interglacial with mixed oak forest [comprising oak (*Quercus*), elm (*Ulnus*), ash (*Fraxinus*) and hazel (*Corylus*)] following the initial phase in the temperate regions. However, different interglacials show different profiles, and to a limited degree, interglacials can be identified on this basis.

It was through intensive study of pollen and other botanical remains that there was early realization that the initial concept of four ice ages was too simple. Particularly for the last glaciation in Europe (the *Weichselian*, equivalent to the Würm in the Alpine chronology), short warm interstadials were identified and in the most frequently-used system of nomenclature the type sites used to label them are: successively *Amersfoort*, *Brörup* and *Odderade* for the Early-glacial; *Moerschoofd*, *Hengelo* and *Denekamp* for the Pleniglacial; *Bølling* and *Allerød* for the Late-glacial (Table 1.1). The short cool period (stadial) separating the Bølling and the Allerød is the *Older Dryas*, and following the Allerød, before commencement of the present interglacial (the Holocene), the *Younger Dryas* occurred. Prior to the Bølling there was the *Oldest Dryas*. Around the world, there is a multitude of other nomenclatures, but the names just given are widely used, though often with regional variants and indeed additions, e.g., the *Oerel* and *Glinde* interstadials for the Pleniglacial in northern Germany (Behre and van der Plicht 1992). In Europe, the last interglacial is known as the *Eem*, which is taken to be equivalent to the *Riss-Würm* interglacial in Alpine chronology. In North America, the last interglacial is known as the *Sangamonian*.

An early important role for pollen was in charting the way in which northerly latitudes emerged from the last glaciation. This emergence was described in terms of successive pollen *zones*, each having a particular pollen spectrum, and on the assumption of synchroneity between regions these zones formed a chronological framework. Absolute dating of the more northerly zones was obtained by reference to the Scandinavian glacial varve chronology (see below). The advent of radiocarbon dating allowed checking of the assumption of synchroneity, indicating it to be valid for more southerly zones only to a limited degree. At the same time, it reduced reliance on the pollen zone framework as far as archaeological dating was concerned. The main emphasis in pollen analysis is now on climatic reconstructions. One approach to this (see for example, Guiot *et al.* 1989; Pons *et al.* 1992) involves establishing quantitative relationships between selected taxa abundance and modern climatic conditions (e.g., precipitation, temperature, humidity), enabling past conditions to be derived from fossil pollen spectra using *transfer functions*.

Loess Profiles

The most complete and relatively detailed records of Pleistocene climates on land come from the sequences of loess with interbedded soils. Loess is a porous calcareous material composed of wind blown sediment (silt-sized 2–60 μm) partially cemented by a pedogenic process called loessification. Thick layers of loess extend from north-west Europe across northern Asia to China as well as occurring in the Americas and many other parts of the world. Climatic indication is provided by the (interglacial) palaeosol layers that are interbedded between the (glacial) loess layers and embedded fossils within the loess, the former being indicative of warmth and the latter of cold, windy, continental

Table 1.1. Selected Climatic and Climatostratigraphic Subdivisions of the Last Glacial-Interglacial Cycle[a,b]

Glacial-Interglacial cycle	Global climate	Marine oxygen isotope stage	Substage	Terrestrial climatostratigraphic units: N.W. Europe	British Isles	North America	European Interstadials	European Stadials	Age estimate
A	Interglacial	1	Recent	Holocene	Flandrian	Holocene			
B	Glacial	2	Late-glacial	Late Weichselian	Late Devensian	Late Wisconsinan		Younger Dryas	11-10 ka BP
							Allerød		11.8-11 ka BP
								Older Dryas	12-11.8 ka BP
							Bølling		13-12 ka BP
								Oldest Dryas	>13 ka BP
		3	Pleniglacial	Middle Weichselian	Middle Devensian	Middle Wisconsinan	Denekamp		32-28 ka
							Hengelo		39-36 ka
							Moerschoofd		46-44 ka
							Glinde		51-48 ka
							Oerel		58-54 ka
		4			Early Devensian	Eowisconsinan			
		5a	Early glacial	Early Weichselian			Odderade		84-74 ka
		5b							92-84 ka
		5c					Brörup/Amersfoort		105-92 ka
		5d							115-105 ka
	Interglacial	5e	Last-interglacial	Eemian	Ipswichian	Sangamonian			130-115 ka
C	Glacial	6	Penultimate glacial	Saalian	Wolstonian	Illinoian			190-130 ka

[a]Data compiled from Aitken (1990), Martinson *et al.* (1987), and Lowe and Walker (1997).

[b]A total of 24 numbered interstadial sub-stages are now recognised for the last glacial stage (see text for details).

climatic conditions. Hence in a long loess sequence, there is a record of successive climatic phases which, in places, appears as an uninterrupted Quaternary record. By extensive studies (e.g., Fink and Kukla 1977) in central Europe, the occurrence of a substantial number of interglacials during the last two million years was inferred giving early indication that the marine record (Fig. 1.3) was matched terrestrially, and could correspondingly be accurately correlated (Kukla and Cilek 1996). More recently, there has been intensive research in the thick loess deposits of China where the climatic history of the Quaternary is revealed in some detail on account of the high rates of deposition (An *et al.* 1991; Beer *et al.* 1993; Kukla *et al.* 1990). Because a remanent magnetization is acquired at deposition or shortly afterwards, magnetic reversals can be detected, notably the Brunhes-Matuyama transition at 780 ka, and hence some correlative dating control has been obtained.

Magnetic susceptibility is independent of the geomagnetic field at deposition and reflects the nature and amount of iron oxide (principally magnetite and maghemite) present within a sediment. It has been found to be highly useful for the characterization of loess and palaeosol units. In Alaska, the loess contains coarse magnetite derived from source rocks and the loess units therefore exhibit high magnetic susceptibilities compared to adjacent palaeosol. Conversely, for various reasons, the palaeosol layers in Chinese loess have a substantially higher magnetic susceptibility than the loess layers and measurement of this turns out to be a highly convenient index to correlate the loess sequences with marine records and therefore with global climates. More recent studies have also incorporated the analysis of loess grain size and cosmogenic ^{10}Be content as a means of characterization and correlation (e.g., Beer *et al.* 1993; Hovan *et al.* 1989).

Glacial and Other Varves

The summer melting of glaciers produces streams carrying a fine suspension of sand, silt, and clay. In lakes fed by this meltwater, the coarse particles settle first followed by finer material as the year goes on. The resulting annual layers (*varves*) are distinguishable to the eye in sections cut into the beds of dried-out lakes because of colour change as the sediment goes from coarse to fine. The thickness of a layer reflects the amount of melting, and abnormally hot summers giving rise to layers that may reach several tens of centimetres and cold ones giving layers that may be only a fraction of a millimetre. Hence, since the sequence of thin and thick layers is determined by climate, cross-dating is possible between different localities in the same climatic region. In a region where the early part of one exposure overlaps with the late part of an earlier one, and this is repeated a number of times, it is possible to build up a reference plot spanning thousands of years in the same way as for tree-ring chronology. Such a reference plot is "floating" unless it can be anchored by some dated event.

The most remarkable varve chronology is that of Scandinavia where climate amelioration at the end of the last glacial period caused the glaciers to retreat northwards across Sweden and Finland, leaving behind a series of glacial lakes which gradually dried up once their source of water supply had disappeared. The varve system observed in these, first by Baron de Geer around 1912, extend back to about 13 ka ago for varves in the southern tip of Sweden. This extended chronology, which provides absolute dating for pollen zones, is possible because the Scandinavian ice-sheet retreated in a simple and almost unidirectional manner. This in contrast to the complicated situation that was prevalent in North America during the retreat of the Laurentide ice sheet.

Annual varves also occur in some non-glacial lakes because of the annual overturning of the water column, seasonal variation in accumulation of organic detritus, sedimentation, or chemical precipitation. The Lake of Clouds, Minnesota, is a notable example, some 10,000 laminations being obtained in a 5-metre core. A similarly continuous and significant varve sequence has recently been described for central North America from Elk Lake, Minnesota (Bradbury and Dean 1991). Both these and the Scandinavian varves have been important in calibrating the radiocarbon timescale (see Chapter 3). In the case of the Scandinavian varves, direct radiocarbon dating of the varves themselves is not reliable because most of the organic matter is of secondary origin. Instead, the measurements are made on neighbouring peat bogs at pollen zone boundaries and time linkage is obtained through observation of the same zone boundaries in the varves.

Although the above are concerned with emergence from the last glaciation, there are other cases where much earlier varve chronologies, although floating, are important. One of these is at Bispingen in northern Germany where annually laminated diatomite deposits span the Eemian interglacial (Müller 1974), allowing its duration to be estimated as *circa* 11 ka as well as giving a timescale for the changing spectrum of pollen, and hence climate, as the interglacial progressed (Field *et al.* 1994).

MARINE AND ICE CORE PREDICTIONS

Oxygen-Isotope Ratio Climatic Proxy Indicator

There are three stable isotopes of oxygen, the principal one being ^{16}O, with ^{17}O and ^{18}O as minor ones. The latter is the more abundant of the two but even so its ratio with respect to ^{16}O is only in the range 0.0019–0.0021 in natural materials. Although almost similar in chemical behaviour, there are some processes which discriminate against the heavier isotopes and some which give preference to them, to a degree dependent on temperature. As a net result of such fractionation processes, the ratio of ^{18}O to ^{16}O in glaciers is slightly lower than in sea-water, i.e., the oxygen in the water of glaciers is isotopically "lighter." The consequence of this is that during glacial times, because of the greater amount of water locked up in glaciers, sea-water is isotopically "heavier." Shells formed in this water are heavier still because there is further fractionation during the formation of shell carbonate, lower temperature favouring incorporation of ^{18}O. However, in most regions, the dominant influence is glacier volume. Hence the expectation that the variations are the same worldwide, an expectation borne out in practice.

Variations in the ratio are expressed *per mil* (‰), a difference of 1 per mil corresponding to 0.1% (i.e., a change of about 0.000002 in the actual ratio). The value of the ratio for a sample is given as the difference from the value for a certain standard, e.g., the Pee Dee belemnite (PDB) in the case of shells, and standard mean ocean water (SMOW) in the case of precipitation. The difference is denoted by $\delta^{18}O$, sometimes abbreviated to δ, and it is also on the per mil scale. For shell formed at the most intense part of an ice age, the ratio ($^{18}O/^{16}O$) is a few parts per mil higher than the value at the peak of an interglacial. There are variations in amplitude between different regions on account of reinforcement by local fractionation effects, but in any case a high-precision mass spectrometer is necessary for measurement (Corfield 1995). Corals are an additional marine archive from which oxygen isotopes and other parameters relating to sea surface temperature may be measured.

Precipitation deposited as snow in ice cores exhibit hydrogen (see below) and oxygen isotopic variations which are controlled by air temperature and, conversely to the situation in sea water, the ratio is lower during cold periods than during warm ones; the overall change between full interglacial and full glacial conditions approaches 10 per mil. Measurements may also be made on air bubbles trapped within the ice; changes in the oxygen isotope ratio in air closely follow those in sea water.

Other Isotopes

The abundance of deuterium (D), the heavy isotope of hydrogen (^{2}H), relative to light hydrogen (^{1}H), is another isotope ratio that can be used as a climatic indicator, e.g., in ice (Jouzel *et al.* 1987, 1993). Likewise, stable isotopes of carbon ($^{13}C/^{12}C$) are also increasingly being employed as a proxy indicator of precipitated carbonates, e.g., ostracods in lake sediments (Holmes 1992) and cave speleothems (Winograd *et al.* 1988; Coplen *et al.* 1994; Lauritzen 1995).

Deep Ocean Cores

A record of past oxygen and carbon isotope ratio values is available from calcareous skeletons (commonly called shells) of marine organisms (usually foraminifera) in successive layers on the ocean floor, these being a mixture of clastic sediment and biogenic ooze. Samples are obtained by means of long coring tubes, of the order of 10 cm in diameter and up to 50 m in length. The deposition rate in the relevant regions is typically of the order of a few millimetres per century. The continuous sediment cores so obtained carry, in addition, a magnetic polarity record which allows correlation of the climatic variations with the magnetic polarity timescale (see Chapter 11). The magnetic record is carried by the clastic sediment because, as in loess, it acquires a weak but permanent magnetisation at deposition (or shortly afterwards, during consolidation), thus indicating the successive reversals of the earth's magnetic field.

One of the first records of marine oxygen isotopes was obtained by Emiliani (1955) and this showed variations initially interpreted as primarily reflecting the temperature of the water in which the shells had been formed. However, it was later argued that the influence of glacier volume was dominant and that the isotope variations could be considered as a palaeoglaciation record, which, by definition, would be worldwide. This core showed evidence of 13 warm and cold phases and these were numbered from the top down, with odd numbers corresponding to warm stages and limited global ice volumes and

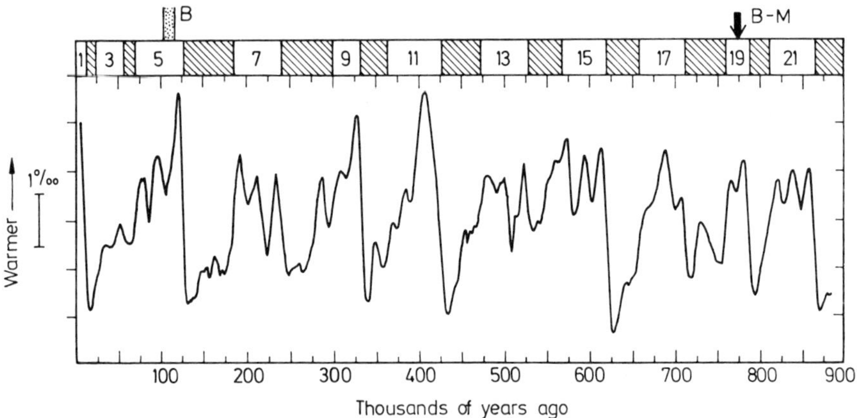

Figure 1.1. Oxygen isotope variation in microfaunal remains of deep-ocean sediment (redrawn, with additions, from Bassino *et al.* 1994). The vertical scale indicates the deviation (in parts per thousand, ‰) of the isotope ratio from a standard. Along the top, the numbers allocated by Emiliani (1955) to warm stages are given, with intervening (even-numbered) cold stages being shown shaded; the Brunhes-Matuyama magnetic transition is indicated by *B-M* and the Blake magnetic event by *B*. Using longer cores, many earlier stages than shown here have been identified. The timescale is astronomically-based; see Table 1.2 for details. Essentially the same pattern of variation is found in cores all around the world (see Lowe and Walker 1997), in agreement with the interpretation of the variations as primarily reflecting the amount of water locked up in the polar ice caps and in glaciers.

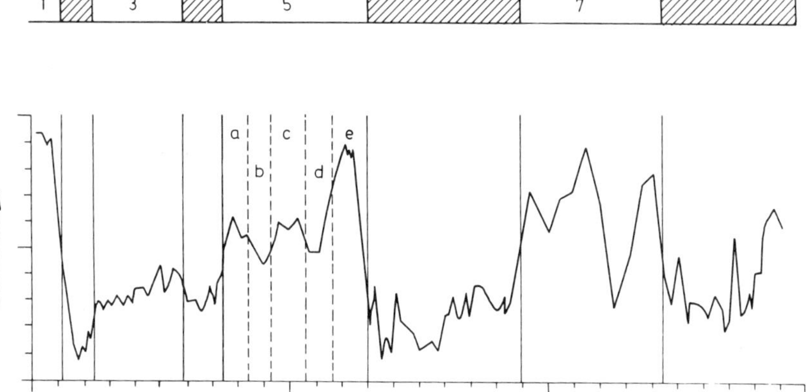

Figure 1.2. Oxygen isotope variation for the past 300 ka, with astronomically-based timescale (redrawn, with additions, from Martinson 1987). The vertical axis represents changes in the averaged isotope ratio found in benthic (bottom-dwelling) foraminifera from five locations in the oceans of the world: 5 divisions equals a change of one part per mil. Along the top, the numbers allocated by Emiliani (1955) to warm stages are given, with intervening (even-numbered) cold stages being shown shaded. The letters (a,c,e) refer to warm substages. There are intervening cool troughs, b and d. Rather than the whole of MIS 5, the last interglacial is now usually, but not always, taken to mean substage 5e, with the last glacial period beginning with substage 5d. Substage 5e has been identified with the Eemian interglacial of Europe (the Riss-Würm in Alpine terminology; Table 1.1). There is less unanimity in identifying the Sangamonian interglacial of North America with only substage 5e rather than the whole of MIS 5.

even numbers to cold stages with greater global ice volumes. They are now referred to as *marine isotope stages* (MIS).

Subsequently, for a somewhat longer core carrying evidence of 23 stages (Shackleton and Opdyke 1973, 1976) it was possible to provide a time-scale for the variations. Magnetic measurements indicated that only one major reversal of geomagnetic polarity had occurred in the time period covered by the core and this was during MIS 19. Through its recording in volcanic rocks which have been dated by potassium-argon, this reversal was placed at about 730 ka ago (now revised to 780 ka; see note in Table 1.2). The upper part of the core was dated by radiocarbon and the timescale for intervening stages was estimated on the assumption of constant sedimentation rate, an assumption confirmed as approximately valid by later chronological assessments. The basis is now astronomical as outlined below. Figs. 1.1 and 1.2 are examples of cores so dated. Global sea level regression were associated with the transitions from interglacial to glacial conditions which resulted in sea levels falling over 100 m below their present level. This causes a number of follow-on effects which include increased continentality of land masses and the potential development of land bridges connecting otherwise isolated geographical locations. Both of these have direct relevance to archaeology.

In addition to the oxygen isotope ratio, there is much other information extractable from the cores, e.g., variation in sea surface temperature (using abundance of surface dwelling foraminifera). There is also variation in the accumulation rate of aeolian dust which is indicative of the prevalence of strong winds as expected during cold periods, the abundance and geographical distribution of ice-rafted detritus which may be linked to catastrophic ice sheet destabilization events during glacial periods, surface temperature estimates based on algal organic geochemistry (e.g., Bard *et al.* 1997), and the presence of contourites which are indicative of strong ocean bottom currents.

Stages and Horizons (Substages)

The stage numbers allocated by Emiliani continue in use but have been developed so as to include substages. Commonly, this is by letters, e.g., the warm substages of MIS 5 are named 5a, 5c, and 5e, with the intervening cool troughs being named 5b, and 5d (Fig. 1.2 and Table 1.1). A decimal system has also been developed for the naming of *horizons* within the marine isotope stages so as to give greater flexibility in dealing with the complexities of the isotope curve (see Prell *et al.* 1986). For example, the peak of MIS 5e is labelled 5.5 with further subdivision into 5.51, 5.52, and 5.53. Alternatively, the subdivisions may be labelled 5e1, 5e2, 5e3, etc., retaining the convention that even numbers refer to cool troughs and odd to warm peaks. Additionally, boundaries between pronounced isotopic maxima (full glacials) and consecutive pronounced minima (peak interglacials) were called *Terminations* by Broecker and Van Donk (1970). These are numbered by roman numerals in order of increasing age.

Astronomical Dating of the Marine Isotope Stages

Speculation that the ice ages were triggered by variations in insolation culminated in the work of Milankovitch (1941) which gave detailed insolation curves for the past 600 ka, calculated for a latitude of 65°N, with an absolute timescale based on the known parameters of the earth's orbital motions. These parameters were: (i) the eccentricity of the orbit around the sun (varying with periodicites of 413 ka and 100 ka), (ii) the obliquity, or tilt, of the ecliptic (average periodicity about 41 ka), and (iii) the precession of the equinoxes (mean periodicity about 22 ka). The variations in these parameters are due to gravitational perturbations resulting from the changing configurations of the planets. The calculations of Milankovitch have subsequently been refined and extended further back in time (e.g., Berger and Loutre 1991).

The dated climatic framework provided by the Milankovitch predictions was used by Zeuner (1946) to develop chronologies throughout the world. However, when radiocarbon dating became available in the early 1950s, although initial application (to the last phase of the Wisconsinan glaciation) gave results in agreement with the Milankovitch time-scale, subsequent applications going further back in time—essentially beyond the age range for which radiocarbon was then reliable—gave a picture that was more complex than predicted. There was then general rejection of Milankovitch theory.

It was not until the mid-1960s that reinstatement began. This was triggered by the uranium-series dates obtained (Broecker *et al.* 1968; Mesolella *et al.* 1969) for raised coral beaches in Barbados and elsewhere indicative of high sea-levels and hence of minima in ice volume, as would be the situation during interglacials. The dates obtained correlated well with maxima in the insolation curves: at 125 ka ago, at 105 ka ago, and at 80 ka ago. At the same time, analyses of the growing body of deep-ocean climatic data were leading increasingly to speculation that there was correlation in timing with insolation variations. One aspect was that there were periodicities in the oxygen-isotope record that corresponded to the orbital periodicities (e.g., Hays *et al.* 1976; Imbrie and Imbrie 1980). A highly readable account of this reinstatement of the astronomical theory has been given by Imbrie and Imbrie (1986). These authors also trace developments since the earliest recognition of glacier advance and retreat.

With the correlation between isotope ratio variations and insolation variations firmly established, it became possible to date the former with an accuracy of a few thousand years on the basis of the latter, independently of radiometric dating. This was through the complex reiterative process of orbital tuning. The chronostratigraphy developed for the past 300 ka has been shown in Fig. 1.2 and a longer record reaching back to 900 ka in Fig. 1.1. Ages for stage boundaries back to MIS 22 are given in Table 1.2. A total of 116 named MIS stages are now formally recognised which span almost the last 3 million years (Ruddiman *et al.* 1989)

Isotopic and Other Variations in Ice Cores

A continuous high resolution climatic record is available in long cores, some more than 3 km in length and extending beyond the last glacial cycle, drilled from the crests of polar ice-caps. As the build-up of polar ice involves the accumulation of snow, trapped air bubbles and aerosolic components, e.g., dust, salt, and volcanic ash, ice cores are a powerful multiproxy archive of environmental change. The stable oxygen isotope ratio in ice reflects the ambient temperature at formation, with higher $\delta^{18}O$ values indicating higher temperatures. The long-term pattern of variation is similar to the marine pattern, but there is the possibility of seeing shorter-term (stadial and interstadial) fluctuations as the accretion rate is much greater and there is little opportunity for

Table 1.2. Marine Isotope Stages: Commencement Ages (in ka)[a,b]

Stage	Age	Stage	Age	Stage	Age
1	11	8	301	15	621
2	24	9	334	16	659
3	60	10	364	17	712 (689)
4	71 (74)	11	427	18	760 (726)
5	130	12	474	19	787 (736)
6	190	13	528	20	810 (763)
7	244	14	568	21	865 (790)

[a]Except for those given in parenthesis the ages are from Bassinot *et al.* (1994). For stages 1-16 the ages do not differ from the SPECMAP calibration of Imbrie *et al.* (1984) by more than 5 ka. For stages 17-21 the SPECMAP ages are given in parenthesis. The ages given by Martinson *et al.* (1987), which span stages 1-7, agree with those given above, except for stage 4, for which the age of Martinson *et al.* is given in parenthesis.

[b]As indicated in Fig. 1.1, the last major reversal of the geomagnetic field, the Brunhes-Matuyama transition, is recorded in the sediment of stage 19. The revised dating for this stage, first proposed by Shackleton *et al.* (1990), is consistent with subsequent potassium-argon determinations for lava in which the transition was recorded. Until recently the accepted ages were those given by Mankinen and Dalrymple (1979). However re-evaluations (e.g., Baksi *et al.* 1992; Cande and Kent 1992; Spell and McDougall 1992; Baksi 1993) indicate a slight lengthening of the timescale so that the Brunhes-Matuyama boundary is now placed at 0.78 Ma (rather 0.73 Ma), the Jaramillo event from 0.99 to1.05 Ma (rather than 0.90-0.97 Ma), and the Olduvai event from 1.78 to 2.02 Ma (rather than 1.67-1.87 Ma).

bioturbation or other disturbances to occur. In the upper part of cores, annual layers are discernible because of seasonal variation of dust and acidity, allowing dating by counting back to about 14.5 ka. Further down, estimates have to be made on the basis of models of glacier flow and ice movement or of past accretion rates. Confirmation of the validity of these estimates is given by the agreement of the ages obtained for the main climatic phases with those of the marine record (Bender *et al.* 1994). As their snow accumulation rates and proximity to ocean current systems are strongly contrasting, the ice core records from Greenland and Antarctica are discussed separately below.

Greenland

The two most recently obtained cores from the Greenland Ice Sheet are from Summit: GRIP and GISP-2, drilled 30 km apart. These reach down deep enough to encompass the last interglacial (MIS 5e: 130–115 ka) and even into the penultimate glacial. Both indicate rather rapid fluctuations of climate which must be related to dramatic changes in the arctic atmosphere (Fig. 1.3), which correlate between cores during the last glacial period (115–10 ka). These interstadials are referred to as *Dansgaard-Oeschger events* and given a number-

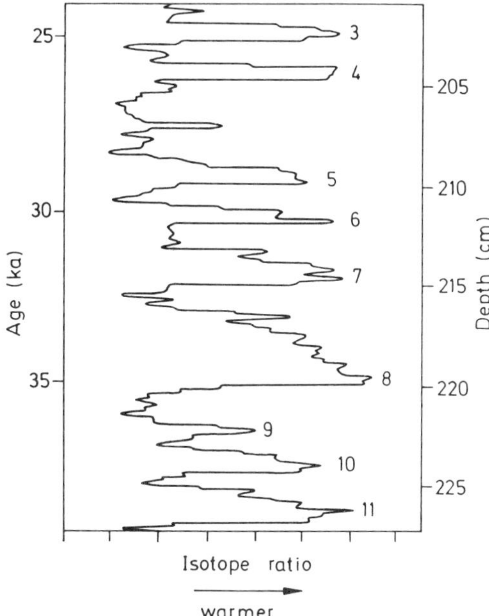

Figure 1.3. Part of the oxygen isotope record for ice from the continuous GRIP core drilled at Summit, Greenland (redrawn, with additions, from Dansgaard *et al.* 1993). One division of the isotope ratio scale corresponds to a change of one part per mil. The change in ratio between the coldest part of the last glaciation and the fairly steady level of the Holocene is about 7 parts per mil. The major warm peaks are termed *Dansgaard-Oeschger events* and represent interstadials (IS 3–11 being shown here). The pollen record also indicates warm periods within the last glacial period and from radiocarbon dating of European pollen sections there is indication of correlation with the warmer peaks of the ice core record. The strongest of the warm peaks shown above (IS 8) is taken to represent the Denekamp horizon.

ing system with the prefix *IS*. Their duration was only the order of a thousand years, with the onset and termination sometimes being only a matter of decades. The pattern of cooling and warming during an interstadial-glacial cycle is not symmetrical, instead cooling occurs gradually and the cycle is completed by rapid warming. A total of 24 interstadial intervals have been recognised, lasting in durating from 500 to 2000 years (Grootes *et al.* 1993; Dowdeswell and White 1995). Oxygen isotopic variations during this period are on the order of 4–6 per mil which implies rapid temperature shifts on the order of 7–8°C, with full glacial conditions some 10–13°C cooler than the Holocene.

The steadiness of climate indicated for the present interglacial—the Holocene, from about 10 ka ago to the present—is in marked contrast to the variability of climate indicated for the last glacial and earlier periods. The variability has been ascribed to *thermohaline circulation* changes in the North

Atlantic Ocean and associated reorganisations of the cryosphere and atmosphere (Broecker 1994a). During the last interglacial and beyond, there are also rapid fluctuations but these do not correlate between cores. Hence during the earlier period, the extent to which either core reflects climate rather than deformation of the layers is currently under discussion (e.g., Boulton 1994; Broecker 1994b; Taylor *et al.* 1994; Grootes *et al.* 1994; Dowdeswell and White 1995; Johnsen *et al.* 1995). The current consensus favours core deformation as the most likely cause of the observed last interglacial isotopic variability principally due to non-reproducibility of the observed patterns in adjacent ice core and the absence of evidence of last interglacial climatic variability in ocean core archives (Keigwin *et al.* 1994; McManus *et al.* 1994). As noted earlier, it should be mentioned that some independent evidence supporting greater Eemian variability is obtained on land from magnetic susceptibility variations in lacustrine sediments from France and Germany (Thouveny *et al.* 1994; Field *et al.* 1994), offshore via foraminifera-based reconstructions of bottom temperatures in the North Sea (Seidenkrantz *et al.* 1995) and polar water interfaces in the Norwegian Sea (Sejrup *et al.* 1995). Importantly, if such variability were to be established as real it would be necessary to seek the causes of such rapid (sub-Milankovitch) variations during interglacial climates and to exhibit caution in employing the relatively stable Holocene period as an analogue of past interglacials.

From the point of view of dating Palaeolithic cultures, the interest of these rapid glacial phase climatic variations is the suggestion (Dansgaard *et al.* 1993) that the more pronounced of the interstadials (Fig. 1.3) correlate with European pollen horizons. This gives possible additional age control for those horizons as well as showing that the climatic indications of the ice-cores are relevant to Europe.

Surface Temperature of the Sea

The rapid fluctuations during the last glacial period recorded in the arctic ice-cores are matched by global variations in mid and high latitude sea surface temperature and hence in air temperature. These fluctuations were initially deduced from the abundance, rather than the isotopic ratio, of a temperature-sensitive planktonic (i.e, surface dwelling) foraminifera in two cores from the North Atlantic around latitude 50–55° (Heinrich 1988; Bond *et al.* 1993) and are now recognised within other ocean basins via isotopic and other sediment parameters (e.g., Charles *et al.* 1997; Hueghen *et al.* 1996). These group into *Bond cycles.* In each cycle, there is a gradual decrease in amplitude of the variations as well as a decrease in the temperature of the base level. Near the end of each cycle (i.e., at the coldest part), the nature of the ocean-floor detritus indicates occurrence of a *Heinrich event,* ascribed to a massive discharge of icebergs into the North Atlantic (Heinrich 1988; Broecker *et al.* 1992). Two leading theories have emerged to explain the observed sub-Milankovitch climatic excursions: one proposes catastrophic collapse of large Northern Hemisphere ice sheets caused by internal feedbacks and basal instability, the so-called *binge-purge* cycles (MacAyeal 1993), while the other argues that the global synchroneity of the rapid shifts requires an atmospheric mechanism, probably relating to a water vapour feedback process (e.g., Lowell *et al.* 1995). Whatever the cause and whatever the details, these observations reinforce the pollen indications just mentioned that the rapid climatic fluctuations in the Arctic are seen also further to the south. Altogether six events are seen in the cores with approximate ages of 16.5 ka for *H1*, 23 ka for *H2*, 29 ka for *H3*, 37 ka for *H4*, 50 ka for *H5*, and 66 ka for *H6*; there is also evidence of iceberg discharge during the Younger Dryas cold snap at 12 ka and hence this is sometimes referred to as *H0*.

Antarctica

The time span of the two cores from Greenland is also covered by cores which are longer in age range from Vostok (Jouzel *et al.* 1987, 1993). Although the climatic fluctuations indicated are less pronounced, perhaps because of the slower deposition rate, perhaps because of remoteness from the North Atlantic region, warmth was indicated during the last glaciation whenever the interstadials of Greenland lasted more than 2 ka (Bender *et al.* 1994). On the other hand there was no indication during MIS 5e of climatic instability.

All three cores suggest (Dansgaard *et al.* 1993) that the last interglacial lasted somewhat longer than indicated by the marine record, nearly 20 ka rather than 10 ka, beginning about 133 ka ago rather than about 125 ka. This is also indicated by oxygen isotope measurements on calcite from Devil's Hole, Nevada (Winograd *et al.* 1992; Imbrie *et al.* 1993). The fact that this terrestrial calcite also shows the same pattern as the marine record is further support for the relevance of the latter for land-based archaeology. The earlier onset of the interglacial according to both this calcite and the ice-cores has been attributed to delay in melting of the glaciers, the latter being the event influencing the marine record (Dansgaard *et al.* 1993; Jouzel *et al.* 1993).

Methane

Measurements of air bubbles trapped in the ice of the GRIP core reveal marked increases in the methane content that are synchronous with the oxygen isotope interstadials, excepting those of short duration (Chappellaz *et al.* 1993). There are also similar indications at Vostok (Jouzel *et al.* 1993) though less definitive on account of the greater time delay between ice formation and air entrapment. Of the several possible causes for these methane increases, the favoured one is enhanced emission from tropical wetlands (Chappellaz *et al.* 1990; Street-Perrott 1993, 1994) indicating the relevance of the ice core interstadials to low-latitudes. Additionally, Blunier *et al.* (1995) recently documented systematic changes in methane content during the Holocene section of the GRIP ice core. While small in comparison to the total changes observed between glacial-interglacial or glacial-interstadial transitions, these variations contrast markedly to the distinct stability of the Holocene oxygen isotope record from ice cores and may relate to some of the Holocene palaeoecological changes which have previously been described (Lowe and Walker 1997).

Dust

Among other information retrievable from ice cores—and, as mentioned earlier, also from marine cores—are indications that high winds were associated with cold periods, evidenced by the high rate of dust deposition. In ice cores, a rapid primary measure of dust concentration is provided by electrical conductivity. In the upper part of cores seasonal *grey scale* variations allow visual identification of annual layers. Aeolian dust is additionally found in large

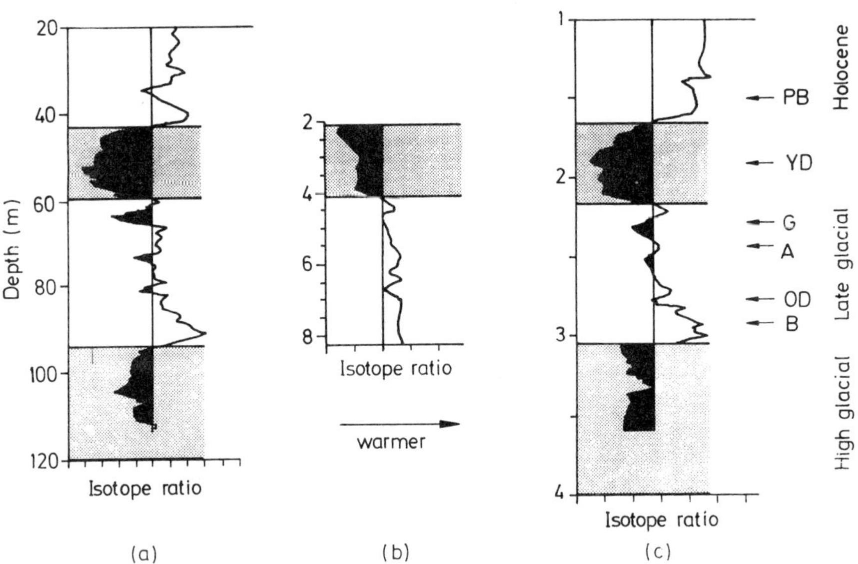

Figure 1.4. Comparison (adapted from Kaiser 1993) with that in ice from the Greenland ice core, Dye 3, shown at (a), of the oxygen isotope ratio found in mollusc shells at Dättnau (b) and in lake marl at Gerzensee (c), both in Switzerland; the respective publications are (a) Siegenthaler *et al.* (1984), (b) Kaiser and Eicher (1987), and (c) Eicher (1979). For all ratio scales, 1 division corresponds to 1 part per mil. All depth scales are in metres. The events indicated are: *B* = Bölling, *OD* = Older Dryas, *A* = Alleröd, *G* = Gersensee deviation, *YD* = Younger Dryas, *PB* = Preboreal. The Younger Dryas lasted about 1.3 ka and terminated close to 11.5 ka ago, there being agreement between ice core layer counting and calibrated radiocarbon dating (see Alley *et al.* 1993).

quantities in ocean cores collected from tropical oceans and is a useful indicator of continental aridity (see below).

Continental Isotope Measurements

Indications of the direct global relevance of the marine and ice core data may be provided by oxygen isotope measurements on sequences of mollusc and of some other materials, the ratio being a measure of air temperature (Kaiser and Eicher 1987). Fig. 1.4 gives two examples of this. Continental measurements have also been reported from Nevada at Devil's Hole where stable isotopes of carbon ($^{13}C/^{12}C$) were also measured (Coplen *et al.* 1994).

MANIFESTATIONS OF MARINE AND ICE CORE PREDICTIONS

The methane variations to which reference has just been made are an indication, intrinsic to the cores, that the terrestrial biosphere is responding to the climatic variations inferred from the isotopic variations. Likewise, the dust content variations take us out of the realm of subtle nuclear effects into the real world of wind-dominated cold periods, confirming the interpretation of those effects in a way that can be assimilated by any observer. Of course, glacier advance and retreat, as well as sea-level changes, had already done this on the longer timescale of the marine isotope stages.

In respect of methane, as noted, the favoured hypothesis is that the gas originated from tropical wetlands (Street-Perrott 1993, 1994). This suggests that the climate variations are on a global scale. Hence, the absence of manifestation in a given bioclimatic system is likely to be due to a too-slow response of that system rather than regional absence of variations. Despite this, for archaeological dating the question at issue is which systems do in fact show variations which correlate, the reason being to some extent irrelevant. In the following paragraphs some of the published instances of correlation are outlined.

Loess

As mentioned earlier, magnetic susceptibility is a convenient proxy indicator of climatic variation in loess deposits and extensive studies of Chinese, Czech and other loess deposits using this parameter indicate the same pattern of variation as do the marine cores (Kukla 1987). Workers have additionally used grain size and mineral abundance data to correlate variations in loess profiles with significant climatic changes (Rutter and Ding 1993; Porter and An 1995). Furthermore, there is good matching to astronomical prediction in a similar way as for marine cores, for loess in both China (Kukla 1990) and further to the north in Tadjikistan (Forster and Heller 1994; Shackleton *et al.* 1995).

Direct demonstration of correlation between periods of loess deposition and marine cold stages has been made by measurement of the aeolian component of an ocean core downwind from China (Hovan *et al.* 1989). The aeolian component acts as intermediary because it is, of course, much enhanced during the windy periods of loess deposition. Another linkage of continental climate to marine cores is through magnetic studies of the core itself (e.g., Robinson 1986).

Pollen

Similar direct linkage is obtained from marine cores in which, because of proximity to land, there is sufficient pollen to allow tying in the terrestrial sequences (e.g., Turon 1984). A difficulty is that close to land the marine stages are not so clearly exhibited as in the deep ocean. On the other hand, there is increasing evidence that the pattern of climatic variation indicated by pollen sequences matches that of the marine cores, and, in some cases, that of the Greenland ice cores. One of the early examples of matching to the marine core variations was from a peat bog, La Grande Pile, in north-eastern France (Woillard 1978; Woillard and Mook 1982; Aitken 1990). This sequence also gives indication of some of the Dansgaard-Oeschger events of the ice cores. Fig. 1.5 shows an example from another French peat bog further to the south. In northern Germany there is a long sequence at Oerel (Behre and van der Plicht 1992) with the pattern of warm periods corresponding to the marine record back to MIS 5e. Radiocarbon-dated levels back to 60 ka BP show good agreement with the minor peaks of the marine record of Fig. 1.2 and, as mentioned earlier, correspondence with the warmer of the Dansgaard-Oeschger peaks of the GRIP ice core (Fig. 1.3) with these European interstadials has been proposed (Dansgaard *et al.* 1993). As confirmation of this correlation proceeds, a valuable link will be developed between pollen sequences and the ice-core timescale, the latter now being linked to the astronomically-based timescale of the marine isotope chronostratigraphy (Sowers *et al.* 1993; Bender *et al.* 1994). Indication of sharp changes is also given by the long sequences at Ioanina and Tenaghi Philippon in Greece (Tzedakis 1993).

In North America, a long sequence from Lake Tulane, Florida, spanning 50–10 ka ago, indicates large changes in vegetation that appear to have been coeval with Heinrich events (Grimm *et al. 1993*). This is consistent with the observation that in the North Atlantic cores mentioned earlier each Heinrich event is followed by a prominent warming, the first of a new package of Dansgaard-Oeschger events. Earlier than this, there is a sequence from Clear Lake in California reaching into MIS 5e (Adam *et al.* 1981). As pointed out by Keigwin *et al.* (1994), there are indications of sharp changes throughout MIS 5 (though not markedly within 5e) but no Heinrich events have, so far, been ascribed to this period.

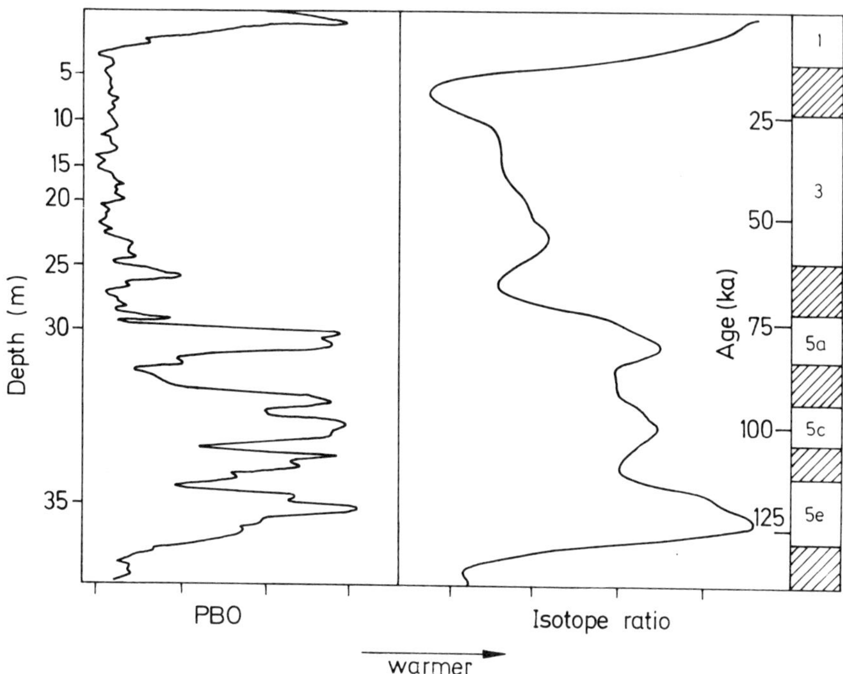

Figure 1.5. The left-hand curve (redrawn, with additions, from Guiot *et al.* 1989) is derived from analysis of the pollen found in a peat bog at Les Echets, central France. The right-hand curve is the SPECMAP version (Imbrie *et al.* 1984) of the marine oxygen isotope variation, with astronomically-based timescale and marine isotope stages indicated. Each scale division corresponds to a change in ratio of one part per thousand. The pollen record is expressed in terms of the *palaeobioclimatic operator (PBO)*, a more subtle indicator of temperate conditions than the formerly-used percentage of tree pollen. The term *palaeobioclimate (PBC)* is also used (e.g., Pons *et al.* 1992). Each division corresponds to a temperature change of about 4°C. Radiocarbon dating of the peat extended only to 30 ka. Earlier ages have been assigned on the basis of matching to the isotope variations and this accounts for the non-linearity in the depth scale.

The most successful correlation of ice core records and AMS radiocarbon dated terrestrial sequences was recently described by Lowe *et al.* (1995). They used coleopteran and pollen data from well dated late glacial (15,000–12,000 BP) sequences to link thermal changes in summer temperatures in the United Kingdom to reconstructed snow accumulation rates in the GISP-2 ice core. They estimate an overall shift (cooling) of about 10°C during the period spanning the Allerod through Younger Dryas which was closely matched by a 50% reduction in snow accumulaton rates over Greenland. This importantly implies a high degree of synchroneity between atmospheric circulation changes over Greenland and parts of northwestern Europe and thus that the ice core record is capturing climatic events at high resolution globally, beyond the polar regions.

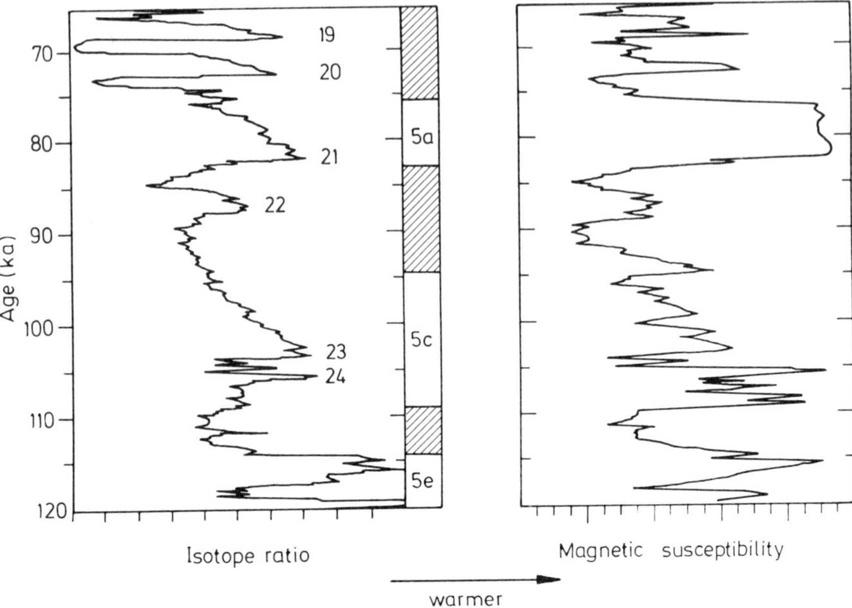

Figure 1.6. Part of the magnetic susceptibility record from Lac du Bouchet, France, compared with oxygen isotope ratio values of ice from the GRIP core, Greenland (redrawn, with additions, from Thouveny *et al.* 1994). Numerals on the isotope record are *IS* numbers of Dansgaard-Oeschger events (Dansgaard *et al* 1993). Each division of the isotope ratio scale corresponds to 1 part per mil; marine isotope stages are also shown. For the magnetic susceptibility scale, 1 division corresponds to 5.10^9 m^3 kg^{-1}. Contrary to the situation in loess, low values of susceptibility are indicative of warmth. The record shown is averaged over 12 parallel cores. The timescale is that of the GRIP core and slight adjustments (not more than 5 ka) to the radiocarbon- and pollen horizon-based timescale have been made by the authors in order to obtain a good match between the two records. On the basis of the above, together with lithological and pollen data, the authors remark on the support given to the hypothesis of climate variability during the Eemian interglacial (*MIS 5e*) suggested by the ice core data.

Magnetic Susceptibility

The role of this parameter in loess studies has been mentioned earlier. It has also been found to be relevant in a maar lake deposit in central France from which a long pollen sequence had been obtained. Fig. 1.6 shows the remarkable correspondence between susceptibility variations and the GRIP ice core record.

The Eemian Interglacial

It was mentioned earlier that discordance between the deeper sections of the two nearby Greenland ice-cores, GRIP and GISP 2, led to doubt about the reality of the climatic fluctuations indicated for MIS 5e (the Eemian interglacial) and that this instability was not shown in two carefully-examined North Atlantic cores. However, the good match between the magnetic susceptibility and ice core records just mentioned (Thouveny *et al.* 1994) does indeed extend into the Eemian thus giving support to the possibility of climatic instability during that interglacial. Another pollen sequence of the Eemian is that from lake sediment at Bispingen in northwest Germany where annual laminations in the sediment give a timescale, albeit floating (Müller 1974). Climate reconstruction from this (Field *et al.* 1994) leads to the conclusion that there was potentially greater instability in the Eemian than during the Holocene. An initially warm period of about 3 ka being followed by cooling and a series of colder episodes. There are other European pollen sequences also showing large shifts during the Eemian (Tzedakis *et al.* 1994). At Vostok, the ice cores indicate an initial warm period followed by a slightly cooler period (Bender *et al.* 1994; Jouzel 1994). The details of this debate are yet to be resolved, its pertinence to ongoing studies of the development of anatomically modern humans at around this time is, however, unquestionable.

Low Latitude Environmental Change

While much of the discussion presented has focussed either on high latitude or marine evidence of environmental change, it is becoming increasing apparent that low latitude localities are potentially rich sources of paleoenvirnmental information (e.g., Wendorf *et al.* 1994; Bar Yosef and Kra 1994). Such locations have been significant pathways for hominid dispersal and places where profound human adaptions have taken place (Sherratt 1996). These low latitude environments did not experience glacial conditions during cold phases at higher latitudes. The climatic transitions at these latitudes being related more to changes in moisture balance than temperature (de Menocal *et al.* 1993). The main sources of palaeoclimatic evidence in these settings are records of past aeolian activity (e.g., Stokes *et al.* 1997), palaeolake data (e.g., Gasse *et al.* 1990) and analyses of terrestrial (aeolian dust) sedimentary components from within marine cores (e.g., de Menocal *et al.* 1993). It is widely recognised that the period of the last glacial was characterised on-land by cold, dry and windy conditions, and that the transition into the Holocene period was accompanied by widespread increases in moisture, at least for the low latitude regions of the northern hemisphere (Lowe and Walker 1997; Sarnthein 1978; Williams *et al.* 1992). One of the most contentious contemporary debates relates to the degree of cooling of tropical sea surface temperatures (SSTs) during glacial periods and its impacts on tropical and extratropical climate. The long-standing view that tropical SSTs have varied little (CLIMAP 1981) has recently been challenged, based on coral geothermometry (Beck *et al.* 1997), records of alpine glacier snowlines (Broecker and Denton 1989), terrestrial pollen assemblages and rare gas analyses from glacial-age tropical groundwaters (Stute *et al.* 1995), which collectively indicate a cooling of about 4–6°C.

Influences on moisture balance in these low latitude areas include the direct effect of changing monsoon intensity caused by variations in the approximately 22 ka precessional cycle, and the effects of changing rates of evaporation in adjacent tropical oceans, in part related to sea surface temperatures which are linked to ocean-cryosphere interactions at higher latitudes and which are more closely related to the eccentricity (about 100 ka) and obliquity (about 41 ka) cycles. It has also been noted that dramatic changes in low latitude moisture may occur over shorter (sub-Milankovitch) timescales (Street-Perrott and Perrott 1990).

Some Late-Glacial Manifestations

It is during emergence from the last glacial period that various sequences provide optimum opportunity for obtaining evidence about the extent to which detailed climatic indications from the polar ice caps are relevant to continental archaeology (as illustrated in Fig. 1.4). In particular (see Broecker 1994; Peteet *et al.* 1993), there are widespread manifestations of the short, cold Younger Dryas event which preceded the present interglacial. The termination of the Younger Dryas which heralded the onset of the interglacial, as observed within ice core (and terrestrial) records, appears to have occurred in less than a human lifetime in terms of oxygen isotope evidence, in less than a generation (20 years) from dust content and deuterium measurements, and in only a few years from the shift in snow accumulation rates.

CONCLUSION

Stratigraphic analysis of sedimentary sequences is essential for correlation, dating, and interpretation of landscape and the environmental changes which manifest themselves within it. During the Quaternary period the repeated pattern of glacial through interglacial climatic fluctuation has resulted in contrasting morphological, biological, lithological and isotopic signatures which act as archives which we may use to interpret past changes. Large scale climate changes occurred effectively globally and synchronously during the Quaternary period, being the result of the changing distribution of solar insolation caused by variations in the earths orbit. While the manifestation of these climate changes varied spatially, their temporal equivalence provides a remarkable framework around which to develop climatostratigraphic schemes for the Quaternary period. Few periods of earth history have experienced such profound climatic excursions on millennial and shorter timescales and these changes may in themselves have strongly influenced hominid evolutionary and behavioural patterns (e.g., Calvin 1991; Sherratt 1996).

We live in exciting times during which there has been an explosion in the scope of both the environmental archives to which we have access, and the techniques by which the climatic proxies may be measured. The most complete proxy records of climatic change are derived from marine cores and loess sequences, the former having been used to confirm the astronomical theory of climate change first predicted by Melutin Milankovitch, and to construct the most complete and versatile Quaternary climatostratigraphy based on oxygen isotopic variations in deep sea marine organisms. These general patterns have been confirmed by correlation to loess sequences, ice cores and a range of terrestrial environmental archives. Comparison of different types of palaeoclimatic record from ice sheets and ice caps, peat bogs, lake and ocean sediments, loess deposits, speleothems and tree rings from different parts of the world provides a mosaic of local responses to global climate change and therefore a detailed picture of such changes as well as a basis for climatostratigraphic correlation. Timescales tuned against astronomical variations probably represent the most precise method yet developed of determining the date of events in the Quaternary.

The comparatively straightforward picture indicated by the marine cores, of a succession of warm (interglacial) and cool (glacial) stages, dated astronomically, has now been complicated by the rapid oscillations of climate indicated by the higher-resolution ice cores, at any rate during the last glacial period. Indication of rapid changes is also evident in some pollen sequences and there are other indications of special relevance to Palaeolithic chronology. There is increasing indication that the latter can be linked to the astronomical timescale. Palaeoclimatic research is in a stage of rapid development and this chapter should be regarded as an *aperçu* of the situation as it was at the start of 1997. Nevertheless, the aspects discussed are likely to remain relevant to Quaternary dating for some years to come.

REFERENCES

Adam D.P., Sims, J.D. and Throckmorton, C.K. 1981 130,000 year continuous pollen record from Clear Lake County. *Geology* 9: 373–377.

Aitken, M.J. 1990 *Science-based dating in archaeology* . Longman, London and New York.

Alley, R.B., Meese, D.A., Shuman, C.A., Gow, A.J., Taylor, K.C., Grootes, P.M., White, J.W.C., Ram, M., Waddington, E.D., Mayewski, P.A. and Zielinski, G.A. 1993 An abrupt increase in Greenland snow at the end of the Younger Dryas event. *Nature* 362: 527–529.

An, Z.S., Kukla, G.J., Porter, S.C., Xiao, J. 1991 Magnetic susceptibility evidence of monsoon variation on the Loess Plateau of Central China during the last 130,000 years. *Quaternary Research* 8: 29–36.

Baksi, A.K. 1993 A new geomagnetic polarity time scale for 0–17 Ma. *Geophysical Research Letters* 20 (15): 1607–1610.

Baksi, A.K., Hsu, V., McWilliams, M.O. and Farrer, E. 1992 $^{40}Ar/^{39}Ar$ dating of the Brunhes-Matuyama geomagnetic field reversal. *Science* 256: 356–357.

Bard, E., Rostek, F. and Songzogni, C. 1997 Interhemispheric synchrony of the last deglaciation inferred from alkenone palaeothermometry. *Nature* 385: 707–710.

Bar-Yosef, O. and Kra, R.S. (eds.) 1994 *Late Quaternary chronology and palaeoclimates of the Eastern Mediterranean*. Tucson, Radiocarbon.

Bassino, F.C., Labeyrie, L.D., Vincent, E., Quidelleur, X., Shackleton, N.J. and Lancelot, Y. 1994 The astronomical theory of climate and the age of the Brunhes-Matuyama magnetic reversal. *Earth and Planetary Science Letters* 126: 91–108.

Beck, U.W., Récy, J., Taylor, F., Edwards, R.L. and Cabioch, G. 1997 Abrupt changes in early Holocene tropical sea surface temperature derived from coral records. *Nature* 385: 705–707.

Beer, J., Shen, C.D., Heller, F., Liu, T.S., Bonani, G., Dittrich, B., Suter, M. and Kubik, P.W. 1993 ^{10}Be and magnetic susceptibility in Chinese loess. *Geophysical Research Letters* 20: 57–60.

Behre, K.-E. and van der Plicht, J. 1992 Towards an absolute chronology for the last glacial period in Europe: radiocarbon dates from Oerel, northern Germany. *Journal of Vegetational History and Archaeobotany* 1: 111–117.

Bender, M., Sowers, T., Dickson, M.-L., Orchardo, J., Grootes, P., Mayewski, P.A. and Meese, D.A. 1994 Climate correlations between Greenland and Antarctica during the past 100,000 years. *Nature* 372: 663–666.

Berger, A. and Loutre, M.F. 1991 Insolation values for the climate of the last 10 million years. *Quaternary Science Reviews* 10: 297–317.

Blunier, T., Chapaellaz, J., Schwander, J., Stauffer, B. and Raynaud, D. 1995 Variations in atmospheric methane concentrations during the Holocene epoch. *Nature* 374: 46–49.

Bond, G., Broecker, W., Johnsen, S.J., McManus, J., Labeyrie, L., Jouzel, J. and Bonani, B. 1993 Correlations between climate records from North Atlantic sediments and Greenland ice. *Nature* 365: 143–147.

Boulton, G.S. 1993 Two cores are better than one. *Nature* 366: 507–508.

Bradbury, J.P. and Dean, W.E. 1991 Holocene limnology, vegetation and climatic history of Elk Lake, Minnesota. *Geological Society of America, Special Paper No. 224*.

Broecker, W.S. 1994a Massive iceberg discharges as triggers for global climate change. *Nature* 372: 421–424.

Broecker, W.S. 1994b An unstable superconveyor. *Nature* 367: 414–415.

Broecker, W.S. and Van Donk, J. 1970 Insolation changes, ice volumes, and the O-18 record in deep-sea cores. *Reviews in Geophysics and Space Physics* 8: 169–188.

Broecker, W.S. and Denton, G.H. 1989 The role of ocean-atmosphere reorganisations in glacial cycles. *Geochemica et Cosmochimica Acta* 53: 2465–2501.

Broecker, W.S., Bond, G., Klas, M., Clark, E. and McManus, J. 1992 Origin of the northern Atlantic's Heinrich events. *Climate Dynamics* 6: 265.

Broecker, W.S., Thurber, D.L., Goddard, J., Ku, T.-L., Mathews, R.K. and Mesolella, K.J. 1968 Milankovitch hypothesis supported by precise dating of coral reefs and deep-sea sediments. *Science* 159: 297–300.

Calvin, W.H. 1991 *The ascent of mind: Ice age climates and the evolution of intelligence*. Bantam Books, New York.

Cande, S.C. and Kent, D.V. 1992 A new geomagnetic polarity timescale for the late Cretaceous and Cenozoic. *Journal of Geophysical Research* B97: 13917–13951.

Chappellaz, J., Barnola, J.M., Raynaud, D., Korotkevich, Y.S. and Lorius, C. 1990 Ice-core record of atmospheric methane over the past 160,000 years. *Nature* 345: 127–131.

Chappellaz, J., Blunier, T., Raynaud, D., Barnola, J.M., Schwander, J. and Stauffer, B. 1993 Synchronous changes in atmospheric CH_4 and Greenland climate between 40 and 8 kyr BP. *Nature* 366: 443–445.

Charles, C.D, Lynch-Stieglitz, J., Ninnemann, U.S. and Fairbanks, R.G. 1996 Climatic connections between the hemispheres revealed by deep sea sediment core/ice core correlations. *Earth and Planetary Science Letters* 142: 19–27.

Coplen, T.B., Winograd, I.J., Landwehr, J.M. and Riggs, A.C. 1993 500,000-year stable carbon isotope record from Devil's Hole, Nevada. *Science* 263: 361–365.

Corfield, R.M. 1995 An introduction to the techniques, limitations and landmarks of carbonate oxygen isotope palaeothermometry. *In* Bosence, D.W.J and Allison, P.A., eds., *Marine Palaeoenvironmental Analysis from Fossils*. Geological Society Special Publication No. 83: 27–42.

Dansgaard, W., Johnsen, S.J., Clausen, H.B., Dahl-Jensen, D., Gundesrup, N.S., Hammer, C.U., Hvidberg, C.S., Steffersen, J.P., Sveinbjrnsdottir, A.E., Jouzel, J. and Bond, G. 1993 Evidence for general instability of past climate from a 250-kyr ice-core record. *Nature* 364: 218–220.

de Menocal, P.B., Ruddiman, W.F. and Pokras, E.M. 1993 Influences of high- and low-latitude forcing on african terrestrial climate: Pleistocene aeolian record from equatorial Atlantic Ocean drilling program, site 663. *Palaeoceanography* 8: 209–242.

Dowdeswell, J.A. and White, J.W.C. 1995 Greenland ice core records and rapid climate change. *Philosophical Transactions of the Royal Society of London* A32: 359–371.

Eicher, U. 1979 Pollen- und Sauerstoffisotopenananysen an sptglazialen Profilen von Gerzensee, Faulenseemoos und vom Regenmoos ob Boltigen. *Mitt. N.G. Bern* 37: 65–80.

Emiliani, C. 1955 Pleistocene temperatures. *Journal of .Geology* 63: 538–578.

Field, M.H., Huntley, B. and Mller, H. 1994 Eemian climate fluctuations observed in a European pollen record. *Nature* 371: 779–783.

Fink, J. and Kukla, G.J. 1977 Pleistocene climates in central Europe: at least 17 interglacials after the Olduvai event. *Quaternary Research* 7: 363–371.

Forster, Th. and Heller, F. 1994 Loess deposits from the Tajik depression (Central Asia): Magnetic properties and paleoclimate. *Earth and Planetary Science Letters* 128: 501–512.

Gasse, F., Tehet, R., Durand, A., Gilbert, E. and Fontes, J.-C. 1990 The arid-humid transition in the Sahara during the last deglaciation. *Nature* 346: 141–146.

Grimm, E.C., Jacobson, G.L., Watts, A.W., Hansen, B.C.S. and Maasch, K.A. 1993 A 50,000-year record of climate oscillations from Florida: Temporal correlation with the Heinrich events. *Science* 261: 198–200.

Grootes, P.M., Stuiver, M., White, J.W.C., Johnsen, S. and Jouzel, J. 1993 Comparison of oxygen isotope records from the GISP2 and GRIP Greenland ice cores. *Nature* 366: 552–554.

Guiot, J., Pons, A., de Beaulieu, J.L. and Reille, M. 1989 A 140,000-year continental climate reconstruction from two European pollen records. *Nature* 338: 309–313.

Hays, J.D. Imbrie, J., and Shackleton, N.J 1976 Variations in the earth's orbit: pacemaker of the ice ages. *Science* 194: 1121–1132.

Heinrich, H. 1988. Origin and consequences of cyclic ice-rafting in the Northeast Atlantic Ocean during the past 130,000 years. *Quaternary Research* 29: 143–152.

Heller, F. and Evans, M.E. 1995 Loess Magnetism. *Reviews of Geophysics* 33: 211–240.

Holmes, J.A. 1992 Nonmarine ostracods as Quaternary palaeoenvironmental indicators. *Progress in Physical Geography* 16: 405–431.

Hovan, S.A., Rea, D.K., Pisias, N.G and Shackleton, N.J. 1989 A direct link between the China loess and marine $\delta^{18}O$ records: aeolian flux to the north Pacific. *Nature* 340: 296–298.

Hughen, K.A., Overpeck, J.T., Peterson, L.C. and Trumbore, S. 1996 Rapid climate changes in the tropical Atlantic during the last deglaciation. *Nature* 380: 51–54.

Imbrie J.A. and Imbrie, J.K. 1980 Modelling the climatic response to orbital variations. *Science* 207: 943–953.

Imbrie J.A. and Imbrie, K.P 1986 *Ice Ages*. Cambridge, Harvard University Press.

Imbrie J.A., Mix, A.C. and Martinson, D.G. 1993 Milankovitch theory viewed from Devils Hole. *Nature* 363: 531–533.

Imbrie J.A., Hays, J.D., Martinson, D.G., McIntyre, A., Mix, A.C., Morley, J.J., Pisias, N.G., Prell, W.L. and Shackleton, N.J. 1994 The orbital theory of Pleistocene climate: support from a revised chronology of the marine $\delta^{18}O$ record. *In* Berger, A., Imbrie, J., Hays, J., Kukla, G., and Saltzman, B., eds., *Milankovitch and Climate, part I*: 269–305, Amsterdam, Plenum, Reidel, and Dordecht.

Johnsen, S.J., Clausen, H.B., Dansgaard, W., Gundestrup, N.S., Hammer, C.U. and Tauber, H. 1995 The Eem stable isotope record along the GRIP ice core and its interpretation. *Quaternary Research* 43: 117–124.

Jouzel, J., Lorius, C., Petit, J.R., Genthon, C., Barkov, N.I., Kotlyakov, V.M. and Petrov, V.M. 1987 Vostok ice core: a continuous isotope temperature record over the last climatic cycle 160,000 -years. *Nature* 329: 403–408.

Jouzel, J., Barkov, N.I., Barnola, J.M., Bender, M., Chappellaz, J., Genthon, C., Kotlyakov, V.M., Lipenkov, V., Lorius, C., Petit, J.R., Raynaud, D., Raisbeck, G., Ritz, C., Sowers, T., Stievenard, M., Yiou, F. and Yiou, P. 1993 Extending the Vostok ice-core record of palaeoclimate to the penultimate glacial period. *Nature* 364: 407–412.

Kaiser, K.F. 1993 *Beitrge zur Klimageschichte vom spten Hochglazial bis ins frhe Holozn rekonstruiert mit Jahrringen und Molluskenschalen aus verschiedenen Vereisungsgebieten*. Winterthur, Zeigler Druck- and Verlags-AG.

Kaiser, K.F. and Eicher, U. 1987 Fossil pollen, molluscs, and stable isotopes in the Dttnau valley, Switzerland. *Boreas* 16: 293–303.

Kukla, G. 1987 Loess stratigraphy in central China. *Quaternary Science Reviews* 6: 191–219.

Kukla, G. 1995 Supercycles, superterminations and the classical Pleistocene subdivisions. In *Abstracts*, Terra Nostra, Schriften der Alfred-Wegener-Stiftung, International Union for Quaternary Research, XIV International Congress: 149.

Kukla, G. and Cilek, V. 1996 Plio-Pleistocene megacycles: record of climate and tectonics. *Palaeogeography, Palaeoclimatology, Palaeoecology* 120: 171–194.

Kukla, G., An, Z.S., Melice, J.L., Gavin, J. and Xiao, J.L. 1990 Magnetic susceptibility record of Chinese loess. *Transactions of the Royal Society of Edinburgh* 81: 263–288.

Lauritzen, S.-E. 1995 High-resolution paleotemperature proxy record for the last interglacial based on Norwegian speleothems. *Quaternary Research* 43: 133–146.

Lowe, J.J. and Walker, M.J.C. 1997 *Reconstructing Quaternary Environments*. 2nd Edition. London, Longmans.

Lowe, J.J., Coope, G.R., Sheldrick, C., Harkness, D.D. and Walker, M.J.C. 1995 Direct comparison of UK temperatures and Greenland snow accumulation rates, 15000–12000 yr ago. *Journal of Quaternary Science* 10: 175–180.

Lowell, T.V., Heusser, C.J., Andersen, B.G., Moreno, P.I., Hauser, A., Heusser, L.E., Schluchter, C., Marchant, D.R., Denton, G.H. 1995 Interhemispheric correlation of late Pleistocene glacial events. *Science* 269: 1541–1549.

MacAyeal, D.R. 1993 Binge/purge oscillations of the Laurentide Ice Sheet as a cause of the North Atlantics Heinrich Events. *Palaeoceanography* 8: 775–784.

Maher, B.A. & Thompson, R. 1992 Paleoclimatic significance of the mineral magnetic record of the Chinese loess and paleosols. *Quaternary Research* 37: 155–170.

Mankinin, E.A. and Dalrymple, G.P. 1979 Revised geomagnetic polarity timescale for the interval 0–5 m.y. B.P. *Journal of Geophysical Research* 84(B2): 615–626.

Martinson, D.G., Pisias, N.G., Hays, J.D., Imbrie, J., Moore, T.C. and Shackleton, N.J. 1987 Age dating and the orbital theory of the Ice Ages: development of a high-resolution 0 to 300,000-year chronostratigraphy. *Quaternary Research* 27: 1–29.

Mesolella, K.J., Mathews, R.K., Broecker, W.S. and Thurber, D.L. 1969 The astronomical theory of climate change: Barbados data. *Journal of Geology* 77: 250–274.

Milankovitch, M.M. 1941 *Canon of insolation and the Ice-age problem*. Kniglich Serbische Akadamie, Beograd. English translation by the Israel Program for Scientific translations, published for the US Department of Commerce and the National Science Foundation, Washington, D.C. 1969.

Müller, H. 1974 Pollenanalytische Untersuchungen und Jahresschichtenzlung an der eemzeitlichen Kieselgur von Bispingen/Luhe. *Geol. Jahrbuch* A21: 161–177.

Peteet D. 1993 Global Younger Dryas? *EOS* 74: 587–589.

Pons, A., Guiot, J., de Beaulieu, J.L. and Reille, M. 1992 Recent contributions to the climatology of the last glacial-interglacial cycle based on French pollen sequencies. *Quaternary Science Reviews* 11: 439–448.

Porter, S.C. and An., -Z. 1995 Correlation between climatic events in the North Atlantic and China during the last Glaciation. *Nature* 375: 305–307.

Prell, W.L., Imbrie, J., Martinson, D.G., Morley, J.J., Pisias, N.G. Shackleton, N.J. and Streeter, H.F. 1986 Graphic correlation of oxygen isotope stratigraphy and application to the Late Quaternary. *Paleoceanography* 1: 137–162.

Robinson, S.G. 1986 The late Pleistocene palaeolclimatic record of North Atlantic deep-sea sediments revealed by mineral-magnetic measurements. *Physics of the Earth and Planetary Interiors* 42: 22–47.

Ruddiman, W.F., Raymo, M.E., Martinson, D.G., Clement, B.M. and Backman, J. 1989 Pleistocene evolution: Northern hemisphere ice sheets and North Atlantic Ocean. *Palaeoeanography* 4: 353–412.

Rutter, N. and Ding, Z. 1993 Paleoclimates and monsoon variations interpreted from micromorphogenic features of the Baoji palaeosols, China. *Quaternary Science Reviews* 12: 853–862.

Seidenkrantz, M.-S., Kristensen, P. and Knudsen, K.L. 1995 Marine evidence for climatic instability during the last interglacial in shelf records from Northwest Europe. *Journal of Quaternary Science* 10: 77–82.

Sejrup, H.P., Haflidason, H., Kristensen, D.K. and Johnsen, S.J. 1995 Last Interglacial and Holocene climate development in the Norwegian Sea region: ocean front movements and ice core data. *Journal of Quaternary Science* 10: 385–390.

Shackleton, N.J. and Opdyke, N.D. 1973 Oxygen isotope and palaeomagnetic stratigraphy of equatorial Pacific core V28–238: temperatures and ice volumes on a 10^3 and 10^6 year scale. *Quaternary Research* 3: 39–55.

Shackleton, N.J. and Opdyke, N.D. 1976 Oxygen-isotope and palaeomagnetic stratigraphy of equatorial Pacific core V28–239: Late Pliocene to latest Pleistocene. *In* Cline, R.M. and Hays, J.D., eds., *Investigation of Late Quaternary Paleooceanography and Paleoclimatology*. Memoir 145, Geological Society of America, Boulder, Colorado: 449–464.

Shackleton, N.J., Berger, A. and Peltier, W.R. 1990 An alternative astronomical calibration of the lower Pleistocene timescale based on ODP Site 677. *Transactions of the Royal Society of Edinburgh: Earth Sciences* 81: 251–261.

Shackleton, N.J., An,-Z., Dodonov, A.E., Gavin, J., Kukla, G.J., Ranov, V.A. and Zhou, L.P. 1995 Accumulation rate of loess in Tadjikistan and China; relationship with global ice volume cycles. *In* Derbyshire, E. ed., *Wind blown sediments in the Quaternary record. Quaternary Proceedings* 4: 1–6.

Sherratt, A. 1996 Plate tectonics and imaginary prehistory. *In* Harris, D.J. ed., *The origins and spread of agriculture and pastoralism in Eurasia*. Baton Racon, UCL Press: 130–140.

Siegenthaler, U., Eicher, U. and Oeschger, H. 1984 Lake sediments as continental $\delta^{18}O$ records from the Glacial/Postglacial transition. *Annals of Glaciology* 5: 149–152.

Sowers, T., Bender, N., Labeyrie, L., Martinson, D., Jouzel, J., Raynaud, R., Pichon, J.J. and Korotkevich, Y.S 1993 A 135,000-year Vostok-Specmap common temporal framework. *Paleoceanography* 8: 737–766.

Spell, T.L. and McDougall, I. 1992 Revisions to the age of the Brunhes-Matuyama boundary and the Pleistocene geomagnetic polarity timescale. *Geophysical Research Letters* 19: 1181–1184.

Stokes, S., Haynes, G., Thomas, D.S.G., Horrocks, J.L., Higginson, M. and Malifa, M. 1997 Punctuated aridity in southern Africa during the last glacial cycle: The chronology of linear dune construction in the northeastern Kalahari. *Palaeoclimatology, Palaeogeography. Palaeoecology*, in press.

Street-Perrott, F.A. 1993 Ancient tropical methane. *Nature* 366: 411–412.

Street-Perrott, F.A. 1994 Palaeo-perspectives: Changes in terrestrial ecosystems. *Ambio* 23(1): 37–44.

Street-Perrott, F.A. and Perrott, R.A. 1990 Abrupt climate change in the tropics: an oceanic feedback mechnism. *Nature* 343: 607–612.

Stute, M, Forster, M., Frischkorn, H., Serejo, A., Clark, J.F., Schlosser, P., Broecker, W.S. and Bonani, G. 1995 Cooling of tropical brazil (5°C) duing the Last Glacial Maximum. *Science* 269: 379–383.

Taylor, K.C., Hammer, C.U., Alley, R.B., Clausen, H.B., Dahl-Jensen, D., Gow, A.J., Gundestrup, N.S., Kipfstuhl, J., Moore, J.C. and Waddington, E.D. 1993 Electrical conductivity measurements from the GISP2 and GRIP Greenland ice cores. *Nature* 366: 549–552.

Thouveny, N., de Beaulieu, J.-L., Bonifay, E., Creer, K.M., Guiot, J., Icole, M., Johnsen, S., Jouzel, J., Reille, M., Williams, T. and Williamson, D. 1994 Climate variations in Europe over the past 140 kyr deduced from rock magnetism. *Nature* 371: 503–506.

Turon, J.-L. 1984 Direct land/sea correlations in the last interglacial complex. *Nature* 309: 673–676.

Tzedakis, P.C. 1993 Long-term tree populations in northwest Greece through multiple Quaternary climatic cycles. *Nature* 364: 437–440.

Tzedakis, P.C., Bennett, K.D. and Magri, D. 1994 Climate and the pollen record. *Nature* 370: 513.

Urey, H.C. 1948 Oxygen isotopes in nature and in the laboratory. *Science* 108: 489–496.

Wendorf, F., Schild, R., Close, A.E., Schwarcz, H.P., Miller, G.H., Grun, R., Bluszcz, Stokes, S., Morawska, M., Huxtable, J., Lundberg, J., Hill., C.L. and McKinney, C. 1994 A chronology for the Middle and Late Pleistocene wet episodes in the Eastern Sahara. *In* Bar-Yosef, O. and Kra, R.S., eds., *Late Quaternary chronology and palaeoclimates of the Eastern Mediterranean*. Tucson, Radiocarbon: 147–168.

Williams, M.A.J., Dunkerley, D.L., DeDeckker, P., Kershaw, A.P. and Stokes, T. 1992 *Quaternary Environments*. New York, Edward Arnold.

Winograd, I.J., Coplen, T.B., Landwehr, J.M., Riggs, A.C., Ludwig, K.R., Szabo, B.J., Kolesar, P.T. and Revesz, K.M. 1992 Continuous 500,000-year climate record from vein calcite in Devil's Hole, Nevada. *Science* 258: 255–260.

Zeuner, F. 1946 *Dating the Past* (1st ed.). Methuen, London.

Chapter 2

Dendrochronology

JEFFREY S. DEAN

ABSTRACT

Dendrochronology, the science that uses tree rings for dating past events and reconstructing past environmental conditions, has undergone a period of explosive growth in the last three decades. From a discipline of limited topical and geographic scope, dendrochronology has been transformed into a global phenomenon relevant to a broad range of subjects. Firmly grounded in the principle of crossdating—using aspects of ring morphology to identify contemporaneous rings in different trees—dendrochronology provides absolute dates accurate to the calendar year and qualitative and quantitative reconstructions of environmental variations on seasonal to century scales. Archaeological applications of dendrochronology fall into three categories: chronological, behavioral, and environmental. Chronological analysis involves the dating of both concrete and abstract units of archaeological analysis. Archaeological tree-ring collections provide a broad spectrum of information on past human behavior including the treatment of trees as a natural resource and wood as a raw material, sources of timbers, season of wood procurement, and numerous specific wood use practices. Archaeologically-relevant environmental information derives from site species assemblages, geologic dating, and the dendroclimatic analysis of archaeological tree-ring sequences. Further expansion of the geographic compass and topical relevance of dendrochronology can be expected as scholars from around the globe pursue the ramifications of this technique.

JEFFREY S. DEAN • Laboratory of Tree-ring Research, University of Arizona, Tucson, Arizona 85721, USA.

Chronometric Dating in Archaeology, edited by Taylor and Aitken.
Plenum Press, New York, 1997.

INTRODUCTION

Thirty years ago, in Brothwell and Higgs' *Science in Archaeology*, Bryant Bannister (1963) summarized the state of dendrochronology poised on the threshold of an era of unprecedented growth and expansion. Since then, the field has been transformed from a somewhat parochial discipline focused on archaeological dating and rudimentary climatic analysis of limited geographic scope to a global phenomenon applicable to an astonishing range of research topics. In 1963, a handful of dendrochronological operations existed in the United States and Europe. Today, more than 100 tree-ring programs cover all areas of the globe. The magnitude of this transformation is exemplified by the contrast between the First International Dendroclimatic Workshop in 1974, which was attended by 30 scholars from nine European and North American countries, and the 1994 International Conference on Tree Rings, Environment, and Humanity, which involved 332 participants from 35 countries (Dean *et al.* 1996). Bannister's article, therefore, provides an excellent benchmark for assessing the discipline's progress during the last three decades.

DENDROCHRONOLOGY

Bannister's (1963: 161) definition of dendrochronology—"the method of employing tree-rings as a measurement of time . . . and . . . the process of inferring past environmental conditions that existed when the rings were being formed . . ."—is as apt today as then. It captures the two principal components of dendrochronology, the dating of past events and the reconstruction of past environmental conditions. The range of phenomena subsumed under these categories, however, has expanded immensely since 1963. Where dating once was restricted primarily to archaeological contexts, it now applies to a broad spectrum of human and natural events including construction episodes, tree modification, volcanic eruptions, earthquakes, alluvial deposition and erosion, floods, forest fires, arboreal insect infestations, plant community establishment and dieback, and radioisotopic fluctuations. Once restricted to climate, dendrochronological reconstruction now encompasses many additional environmental factors, such as streamflow, flood frequency and intensity, plant community composition and distribution, wildfire frequency and intensity, alluvial hydrology, and glacier advances and retreats.

HISTORICAL BACKGROUND

Although knowledge of the growth layers in trees originated in antiquity, the first recorded use of tree rings in a dendrochronological sense occurred in 1737 when Duhamel and Buffon used a prominent frost damaged ring as a marker of the year 1709 in northern Europe. Alexander C. Twining in Connecticut in 1827 (Studhalter 1955) and Charles Babbage in England in 1838 (Heizer 1956) suggested that sequences of wide and narrow rings could be used to date past events and reconstruct climate, although neither of them pursued these insights. Later in the nineteenth century, Jacob Kuechler in Texas (Stallings 1937), J.C. Kapteyn in Germany and the Netherlands (Schulman 1937), and O. Shvedov in Russia (Eckstein and Wrobel 1983) independently used matched tree-ring sequences for dating natural events and making inferences about climate. It remained, however, for Andrew Ellicott Douglass to develop his own recognition of ring-width correspondences among different trees into the science of dendrochronology (Webb 1983).

Around the turn of the century, Douglass, an astronomer at the Lowell Observatory in Flagstaff, Arizona, was frustrated in his efforts to relate the earth's climate to sunspot activity by the lack of meteorological data long enough to reveal cycles comparable to the 22-year sunspot cycle. In 1904, he initiated a study of rings in local ponderosa pine trees as potential climatic records long enough to be related to the sunspot cycle. He discovered that different trees exhibited identical patterns of ring-width variability and realized that these commonalities indicated external climatic control of tree growth over a wide area. By 1914, he had used the correspondences in ring width to construct a 500-year composite chronology of the variability common to the pines of the area and had established a positive correlation between ring width and the precipitation of the preceding winter (Douglass 1914).

Stimulated by the interest of archaeologists, Douglass devoted much of the next 15 years to building a tree-ring chronology long enough to date wood samples from the prehistoric sites that dot the Southwestern landscape. In 1929, the Whipple Ruin at Show Low, Arizona, yielded a fragment of charred wood whose rings bridged the gap between the dated living tree sequence and a 585-year "floating" chronology composed of samples from prehistoric archaeological sites (Douglass 1929; Haury 1962). This achievement allowed Douglass to assign calendar dates to these sites, the first independent dating of archaeological sites in the world.

Douglass' success inspired the application of dendrochronology in other regions including the North American Arctic (Giddings 1941) and Great Plains (Weakly 1940), Scandinavia (Høeg 1944; Schulman 1944), and southern Germany (Huber 1941). World War II terminated this nascent expansion, and momentum was not regained until long after the end of hostilities. Beginning around 1960, dendrochronology experienced a renaissance that continues to accelerate as new applications of the method are developed and it is expanded into new regions. Driven primarily by interests in archaeological dating, climate reconstruction, and calibration of the radiocarbon time scale, this explosive growth began in northern Europe and expanded around the world. Today, validated tree-ring chronologies have been developed everywhere but in tropical Africa, and research is being pursued wherever conditions permit. The range of topics and methods encompassed by modern dendrochronology is exemplified by the proceedings of the 1994 international conference in Tucson (Dean *et al.* 1996).

CONCEPTS AND PRINCIPLES

The concepts and principles that underlie dendrochronology (Baillie 1982, 1995; Bannister 1963; Dean 1986; Eckstein *et al.* 1984; Fritts 1976; Glock 1937; Schweingruber 1988) are well known, and only salient features and new developments are discussed here.

The layers of woody growth that sheathe a tree's trunk beneath the bark appear in cross section as a series of concentric "rings" around the pith at the center. A ring is composed of a light-colored inner band (earlywood) and a dark outer band (latewood) whose abrupt termination marks the outer boundary of the ring (Fig. 2.1). Occasionally, bands of latewood within the earlywood form "false" or "double" rings, which are distinguished from true rings by indefinite outer boundaries. In the trees used in dendrochronology, the progression of rings from pith to circumference establishes an unalterable temporal order, and the production of but one ring per year provides the incremental regularity necessary to establish a fixed time scale.

More than 180 tree and shrub species (Grissino-Mayer 1995) possess the attributes necessary for successful tree-ring analysis: visible and unambiguous ring definition, the production of a set number of rings per unit of time (one ring per year), a substantial proportion of radial growth controlled by one or a small number of external environmental factors (usually climate), and the existence of morphological features (e.g., width, density) that allow the environmental "signal" to be extracted from ring sequences.

Two types of ring series, which represent end points on a continuum of variation, are recognized (Fig. 2.2). *Complacent* series display little between-ring variation and are produced when the factors that regulate growth vary little from year to year. *Sensitive* series are characterized by high between-ring variability that results from annual fluctuations in the environmental factors that limit growth. Sensitive series are the fundamental data source of dendrochronology. Both complacent and sensitive ring series exhibit a characteristic *age trend* in which individual rings become progressively smaller from the pith to the circumference independently of between-ring variability.

Crossdating, the matching of patterns of ring variation among trees, is the one immutable principle of tree-ring science (Fig. 2.2). Any analysis that does not employ rigorous, replicable crossdating is not dendrochronological in nature; counting rings does not afford the comparative validation necessary to produce absolutely dated ring sequences. Crossdating is defined as the "exist-

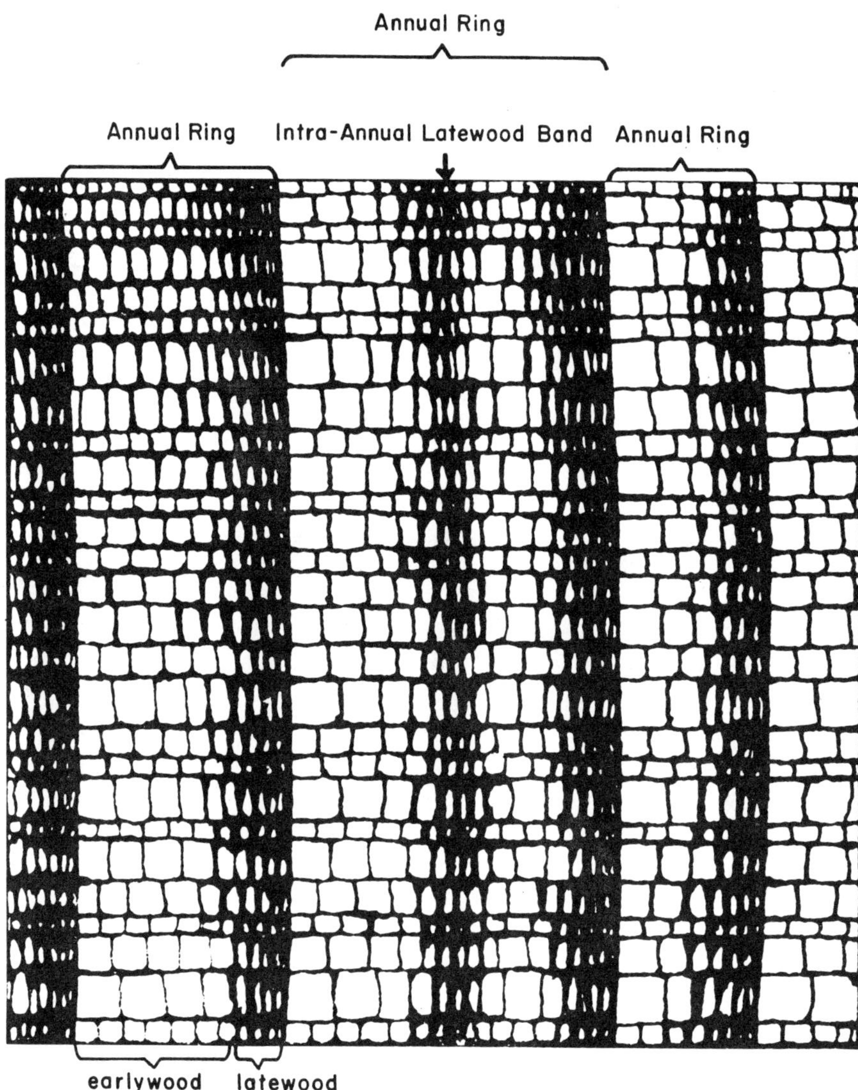

Figure 2.1. Transverse section of coniferous ring series showing dendrochronologically important features of ring morphology including cell structure, annual rings, earlywood and latewood, and intra-annular growth bands (false rings).

ence of characteristics in tree-ring structure that permit the identification in many different trees of rings that were formed contemporaneously with one another" (Dean 1986: 133–134). Although the first recorded instance of crossdating, that of Duhamel and Buffon in 1737, involved the intertree

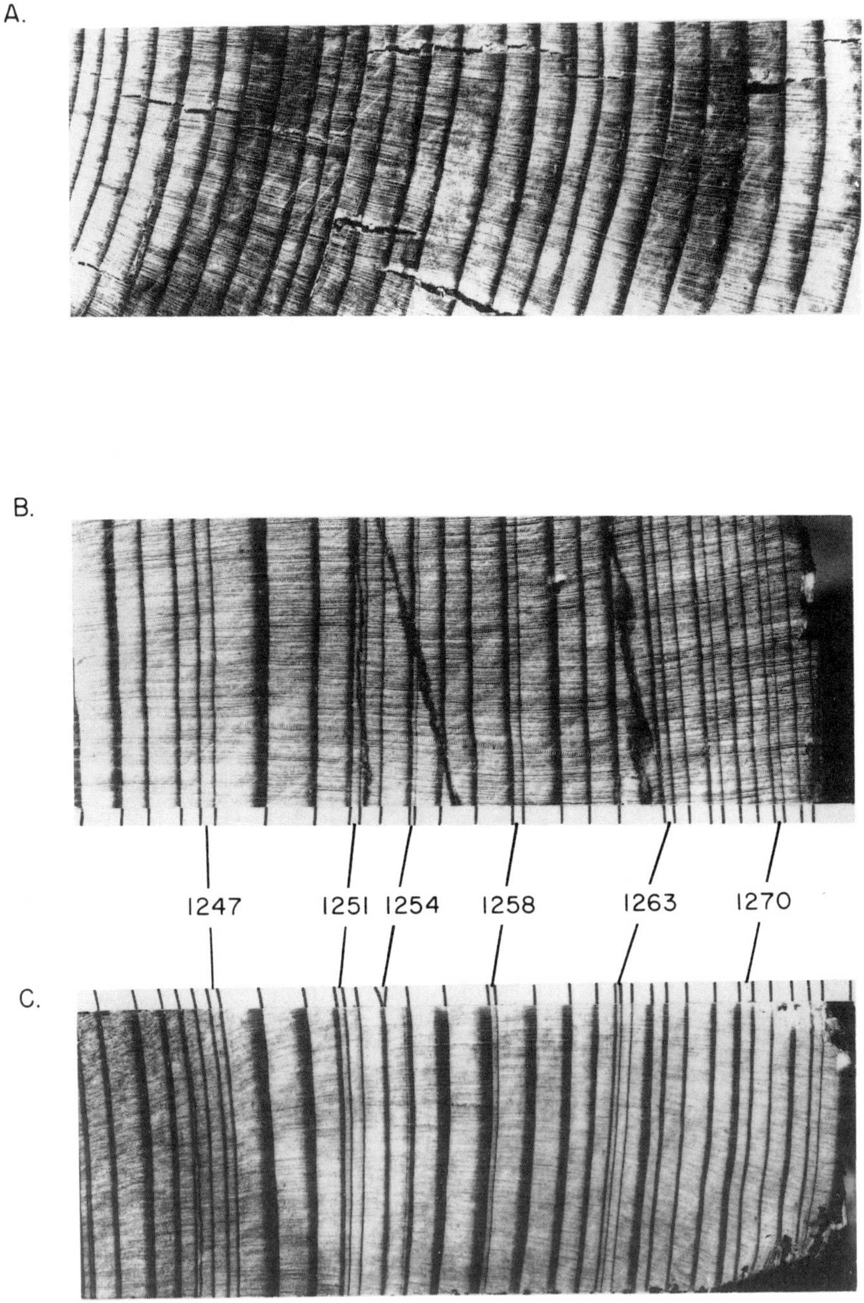

A.

B.

1247 1251 1254 1258 1263 1270

C.

Figure 2.2. Complacent (A) and sensitive (B and C) ring series illustrating crossdating between sensitive series.

matching of frost damaged rings, the most commonly used indicators are covariation in ring widths or densities among different trees. Although other phenomena can be used for limited crossdating, only width and density covary consistently enough over large enough areas to support regional scale dendrochronological research. The fact that ring widths and densities crossdate over large areas specifies a spatial scale of external control that can only be climatic in nature, a condition that underlies most environmental reconstruction based on tree rings.

Ring-width crossdating is expressed primarily in the narrow rings, which reflect external conditions that limit tree growth over wide areas, rather than in larger rings, which are more affected by local factors or the physiological capacities of individual trees. The climatic variables that control radial growth vary considerably depending on large scale climatic patterns (Fritts 1976). Precipitation is the principle limiting factor in arid regions, temperature is the major limiting factor in cold habitats, and combinations of these and other variables control growth in intermediate climate regimes. As a result, the climatic signal in tree rings is weaker and crossdating is more difficult in intermediate environments than in those where radial growth is governed by a single strong factor. Ring density exhibits climatically controlled variation that is independent of ring-width variability and can be used for crossdating even when ring-widths are uselessly complacent.

Strict implementation of crossdating is necessary for three reasons. First, crossdating assigns exact calendar dates to all the rings in a sequence when the date of only one ring is known. Second, a ring series of unknown age can be dated by finding the unique place at which it crossdates with a sequence of known date. When such a match is achieved, each ring in the previously undated sample is assigned to the year in which it was grown. Third, crossdating is the only certain means of detecting the absence of rings from a sequence or the presence of "false" rings, which render ring counts too low or too high, respectively. Ring absence occurs when external stresses limit growth to such a small part of the tree that any sample from the tree is unlikely to contain that ring (Glock 1937: 43–51). False rings are caused by conditions that stimulate the production of one or more additional bands of earlywood cells after latewood cells have begun to form but before the tree stops growing for the year (Glock *et al.* 1960). Careful crossdating against a dated sequence indicates points on a sample at which expected small rings do not occur (locally absent rings) or points at which extra rings (false rings) appear. Thus, crossdating establishes the actual number of true rings in a sample as well as specifies the exact calendar date of each of those rings.

The second basic principal of dendrochronology, *chronology building* is the process of constructing long, absolutely dated ring sequences from many individual crossdated ring series (Fig. 2.3). Chronology building produces composite ring sequences that are longer than any of their individual compo-

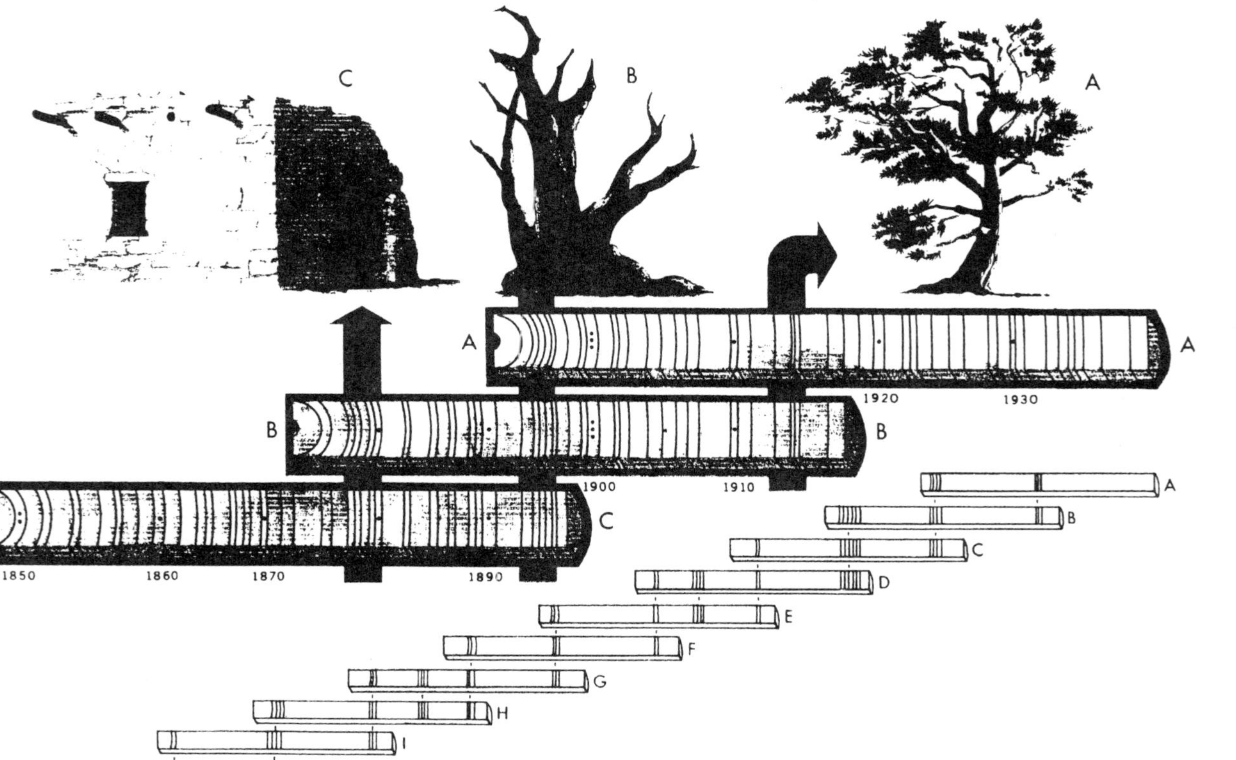

Figure 2.3. Chronology building: the construction of a composite tree-ring chronology from progressively older crossdated ring sequences representing, from youngest to oldest, living trees, dead tree remnants, and ancient human structures.

nents. Furthermore, combining ring records enhances the variability common to many trees and reduces variability due to individual tree or local habitat factors. Composite tree-ring chronologies serve as standards for dating samples of unknown age and as bases for reconstructing past environmental variability.

Tree-ring chronologies are anchored in time by samples from living trees, the year of sampling providing a date for the latest ring in the sequence. Chronologies are extended beyond the range of living trees by crossdating in ring series from progressively older deadwood, archaeological, or geologic samples (Figure 2.3). Long chronologies usually are constructed in pieces as "floating" segments (ring sequences that do not overlap with others) are linked to each other or to the dated, living-tree segments.

The area subsumed by a particular tree-ring chronology varies as a function of the geographic compass of the factors that regulate tree growth. The general Southwestern chronology extends from western California to central New Mexico and from central Utah to northern Mexico. The bald-cypress chronology in the southeastern United States covers the area from the Mississippi River to the Atlantic Ocean and from North Carolina to northern Florida. The western European sequence extends from Northern Ireland to the Carpathian Mountains (Pilcher *et al.* 1984) and may eventually be linked with the eastern Mediterranean chronology south of the Alps (Kuniholm 1995; Kuniholm *et al.* 1996). More localized crossdating exists in other areas including temperate North America, southern South America, the British Isles, northern and eastern Europe, the Mediterranean Basin, southern Africa, temperate and tropical Asia, Australia, Tasmania, and New Zealand.

TECHNIQUES

Although the basic concepts and principles of dendrochronology have remained constant since the inception of the discipline, the *methods* used to analyze rings and ring series, document crossdating, build chronologies, and extract environmental information have changed dramatically. Once the data categories (e.g., ring width, ring density, fire scars, frost rings) have been chosen, technical development furthers five general objectives: data capture (measurement), data equalization (standardization), data comparison (crossdating), data consolidation (chronology building), and environmental reconstruction.

Data Categories

A major change since 1963 has been the development of an attribute of ring morphology other than width as a basis for tree-ring analysis. Faced with complacent ring-width series, researchers in France turned to ring density as a potential source of crossdatable variability (Polge 1963). The discoveries that density variations existed in trees with uniform ring widths and that these variations could be matched from tree to tree opened an avenue of dendrochronological inquiry that is now routinely used throughout the world. Similar advances have been made in recognizing and characterizing other aspects of ring morphology (e.g., fire, flood, frost, and insect damage) that can be matched among different trees. Usually, these attributes supplement ring width and density correspondences that actually validate the crossdating.

Data Capture

Both qualitative and quantitative methods are used to record ring-width variations and crossdate ring series. Whatever technique is used for dating, quantitative measurements are the ultimate record of ring-width variability. Measurements capture the full range of variation and can be statistically manipulated and evaluated. Several different devices that measure ring widths to the nearest 0.01 mm and store the data on computer disks currently are in use. Density data are more difficult to acquire. Radiodensitometry (Parker 1971; Schweingruber 1988: 58–73), which uses densitometers to analyze X-radiographs of ring sequences, places severe restrictions on sample collection and preparation and is cumbersome, expensive, and of limited applicability to samples with small rings and to charcoal. Recent advances in sample collection and preparation methods and in X-ray and densitometric technology have simplified the process, but it still remains a costly procedure of restricted applicability. Currently, image analysis technology is being used to develop automated electronic "work stations" that extract both width and density data from wood samples or CRT images and perform routine data analyses (Schweingruber 1988: 55; Sheppard and Graumlich 1996).

Standardization

Accurate dating and environmental reconstruction rest on maximizing the variability common to the trees of a region (signal) by eliminating as much of the noncommon variability (noise) as possible. This objective is achieved in two ways. First, averaging data from at least two cores from each of at least ten trees reduces within—and between—tree variability at a growth site. Second, various standardization (normalization) procedures are used to remove idiosyncratic variability from individual ring series and reduce between-sample differences.

Standardization minimizes variability that is unique to individual trees and growth sites. Variability of this sort results from individual trees' physiological capabilities, local site conditions that modulate climatic influences, changes in site conditions, and a host of specific traumatic events that affect individual trees. These factors can cause growth surges, suppressions, or other anomalies that obscure the environmental signal. The individual tree attributes that most commonly must be removed are the age trend from large to small rings, which is not related to climate, and between-tree differences in mean ring width, which must be adjusted to prevent the variability in samples with large rings from swamping that in samples with small rings.

Ring-width standardization methods have changed considerably since 1963 when techniques developed by Douglass and his colleagues still prevailed. These techniques involved manually fitting a trend line to the plotted ring widths and calculating the percentage departure of each ring from the trend line to produce a sequence of ring-width *indices* with a mean ≈1.0 and a unique standard deviation (Bannister 1963; Schulman 1956: 29–30). This procedure removes the growth trend and other low frequency variations, emphasizes between-ring variability, and converts all sequences to the same scale. The advent of computers and statistical advances after 1960 allowed the laborious standardization process to be automated (Cook and Holmes 1986; Graybill 1979, 1982), which in turn permitted the rapid processing of many samples. Standardization programs mathematically fit trend lines of appropriate forms to the ring-width series and calculate the indices. Because these techniques minimize potentially important low frequency variations, much attention has been devoted to developing methods that preserve this range of variability. While polynomial curves proved somewhat unsatisfactory (Blasing *et al.* 1983), spline functions (Blasing *et al.* 1983; Cook and Peters 1981; Sheppard 1993), Box-Jenkins modeling (Biondi and Swetnam 1987), and other time series techniques preserve a broad spectrum of climate-related tree-ring variability. Continuing efforts to retain long term variability include the search for new curve-fitting and data consolidation methods (Sheppard 1993) and the use of ring widths from long series with little trend. Density series are standardized in much the same way (Schweingruber 1988: 85–87).

Crossdating

Two basic approaches to crossdating exist, visual-graphical and statistical. The first involves the visual comparison of wood samples themselves or of graphical representations of ring variability. The second involves computing mathematical measures of crossdating between quantified ring series data that usually are expressed in terms of probability distributions.

In regions characterized by width-sensitive ring series, visual-graphical methods commonly are used to establish crossdating, which subsequently can be quantified through measuring and statistical comparison. Most archaeological and geological tree-ring dating in North America is done visually or with *skeleton plots*. Skeleton plotting (Bannister 1963: 167; Dean 1986: 142; Glock 1937; Stokes and Smiley 1968) is a subjective, graphical means of quickly recording, at a standard scale, aspects of ring-width variability relevant to crossdating, that is, the sequence and relative sizes of small rings. A representative subset of samples is measured for chronology building and dendroclimatic reconstruction. Alternatively, crossdating can be established by visually comparing plotted ring widths or indices.

In regions characterized by more complacent tree growth, statistical techniques are used to establish crossdating. The first quantitative crossdating technique was developed in the 1930s by Huber (Huber *et al.* 1949) in southern Germany. This method involves a statistic, W (the "gleichläufigkeitswert" or coefficient of parallel variation), that is based on the percentage of cases in which the ring widths in paired series increase or decrease together. In the United States, Gladwin (1940) developed a technique based on the percentage of cases in which rings in matched samples exceed or fall below the mean together as a quantitative alternative to the "Douglass Method" (skeleton plotting). Gladwin's method, however, does not specify probabilities for putative matches, and it has been rejected as a crossdating technique.

As might be expected, the use of computers led to the development of several crossdating programs to supplement the visual and graphical procedures. Programs SNCHR (Eckstein and Bauch 1969) and CATRAS (Aniol 1983) employ versions of Huber's W statistic. Pearsonian correlation forms the basis of several crossdating programs. The most commonly used of these is CROS (Baillie 1982: 82–85, 1995: 20–21; Baillie and Pilcher 1973; Pilcher and Baillie 1987), which uses a modification of Student's *t* to evaluate the probability of each of a series of correlation coefficients for successive matches between a dated chronology and a sequence of unknown age moved forward in one year increments. Usually, only one match point produces a significant *t* value, thereby dating the unknown sample. CATRAS (Aniol 1983), which employs *t* evaluations of correlations as well as the W statistic, also is widely used. COFECHA (Holmes 1986), a program for checking and verifying crossdating, also can be used to date samples of unknown age. Matches indicated by these (and other) statistical techniques cannot be uncritically accepted but must be checked and validated against the wood itself (Baillie 1982: 85; Schweingruber 1988: 78).

The chief weakness of all computer crossdating programs is their inability to deal effectively with measurement sequences that have missing values, caused by the absence of rings from the samples, or extra values, caused by the measurement of false rings. Either condition destroys the synchroneity between master chronology and undated sample that is necessary to produce significant correlation coefficients. COFECHA attempts to circumvent this problem by calculating coefficients for overlaps of short chronology segments incremented in both directions, but it still misses matches when many values are absent from the unknown samples. For this reason, statistical dating techniques are seldom used in regions, such as western North America, where ring absence is common.

Density crossdating is established by both visual comparison of plotted values and statistical techniques similar to those used on ring widths.

Chronology Building

Composite tree-ring chronologies are constructed subjectively or mathematically. The visual averaging of skeleton plots is adequate for building chronologies designed purely for dating samples of unknown age. Statistical analyses, however, require quantitative chronologies, which are produced by averaging ring widths, indices, or density values for each year over a number of samples to produce sequences of mean values. Although a fairly straightforward process, considerable attention has been given to preserving in the final chronology important statistical attributes and the full range of climatic information (Cook *et al.* 1995; Cook and Holmes 1986; Sheppard 1993).

Environmental Reconstruction

No aspect of dendrochronology has undergone a greater transformation since 1963 than the derivation of environmental information from tree-ring data (Fritts 1976). Before 1960, dendroclimatic analysis consisted of the laborious construction of climate sensitive ring-width chronologies, the occasional use of correlation to document relationships between ring widths and various climatic parameters, and the inference of relative climatic variability from the ring sequences. This approach is epitomized by Edmund Schulman's (1956) monumental book *Dendroclimatic Changes in Semiarid America*, which is the culmination of years of painstaking work by this dedicated scholar and many colleagues.

In the 1960s, the development of computers capable of handling complex mathematical manipulations and huge quantities of tree-ring and meteorological data revolutionized dendroclimatology and fostered two types of environmental reconstruction. *Qualitative* reconstructions (Dean and Robinson 1977; Fritts 1965; Jacoby *et al.* 1996; Lara and Villalba 1993), which estimate relative variations in climate from tree-ring data, carry on the tradition of Douglass and Schulman. *Quantitative* reconstructions use mathematical relationships between environment and ring attributes to retrodict variability in specific environmental parameters in appropriate units of measurement, such as inches or millimeters of precipitation (D'Arrigo and Jacoby 1991; Fritts 1977; Hughes *et al.* 1994; Rose *et al.* 1981; Stahle and Cleaveland 1992), degrees (Briffa *et al.* 1990; Fritts 1977; Graumlich 1993; Shiyatov *et al.* 1996) or degree days (Jacoby *et al.* 1985) of temperature, millibars of atmospheric pressure (Fritts 1971; Hirschboeck *et al.* 1996), various measures of streamflow (Cleaveland and Stahle 1989; Graybill 1989; Stockton 1975), drought indices (Cook *et al.* 1996; Meko *et al.* 1980; Rose 1994; Stockton and Meko 1975; Van West 1994), and others. Response and transfer functions, regression analysis, autoregressive modeling, spectral analysis, and numerical modeling (Fritts *et al.* 1991) are used to calibrate ring and climatic variability, verify these relationships, and reconstruct annual and seasonal values of specific climatic parameters. In addition, dendroclimatology illuminates large and small scale temporal (Dean 1988; Jacoby *et al.* 1985) and spatial (Dean and Robinson 1977; Fritts 1965, 1971, 1991; Fritts and Shao 1992) patterns in climate including phenomena such as the Medieval Warm Period (Graybill and Shiyatov 1992; Hughes and Diaz 1994), the Little Ice Age (Briffa *et al.* 1990; Jacoby *et al.* 1985), El Niño-Southern Oscillation (ENSO) (D'Arrigo and Jacoby 1991; Lough and Fritts 1985; Swetnam and Betancourt 1990; Woodhouse 1993), and Global Climate Change (Jacoby and D'Arrigo 1995). Many of these reconstructions are invaluable to archaeology in their contribution to better understanding cultural ecology, sociocultural evolution, and human adaptive behavior (Dean 1988; Plog *et al.* 1988).

A major development since 1963 has been the investigation of measures of climatic variability other than ring width. Density attributes have been used to reconstruct a variety of climatic variables (Briffa *et al.* 1990; Cleaveland 1986). Where widths generally reflect precipitation of a twelve-month period prior to and including the current growing season (Fritts 1976), density is more sensitive to rainfall and temperature of the growing season itself (Cleaveland 1986; Parker and Henoch 1971), and the two phenomena can be used together to apprehend a broader spectrum of climatic variability. Recently, between-ring variability in isotopic content has been used to reconstruct past climatic fluctuations (Leavitt 1994; Lipp *et al.* 1996; Switsur *et al.* 1996).

In addition to qualitative and quantitative reconstructions, tree-ring evidence has been used to identify and date individual extreme or episodic events that could have impacted human groups. Among these occurrences are droughts (Van West 1994), floods (McCord 1996), hurricanes (Reams and Van Deusen 1996), and killing frosts (Stahle 1990).

ARCHAEOLOGICAL TREE-RING ANALYSIS

Dendrochronology provides three different kinds of information germane to archaeology: chronological, behavioral, and environmental (Dean 1986, 1996a). *Chronological* analysis uses tree rings to date archaeological phenomena ranging from concrete entities (e.g., pithouses, pueblos, cabins, churches, ships) to conceptual units (e.g., phases, periods, artifact types, design styles). A tree-ring date is an absolute calendric placement of the outermost ring on a sample achieved by crossdating the sample's ring series with a dated master chronology. These dates are accurate to the year and have no associated statistical error. Under ideal circumstances, the outermost-ring date specifies the year in which the tree was felled for use by the inhabitants of the site. Within the limits established by archaeological dating theory, the date can be applied to the feature with which the sample is associated. The accurate dating of features also dates associated time-sensitive materials, such as ceramics, that can then be used for the temporal placement of sites that lack tree-ring dates. In this fashion, dendrochronology can become the foundation for detailed local and regional archaeological chronologies, such as those in the American Southwest where tree-ring dated ceramic types and styles specify intervals as short as 25 years (Breternitz 1966).

Another chronological application of dendrochronology is as a standard for rectifying other chronometric systems characterized by less accuracy, precision, and resolution. Dendrochronology has been instrumental in calibrating the radiocarbon time scale (Taylor 1987) and archaeomagnetic curves (Sternberg and McGuire 1990). These comparisons enhance the chronometric attributes of the other dating systems and improve understanding of the dates and how to apply them to archaeological phenomena.

Analyzing archaeological tree-ring materials as collections of artifacts produces information on a wide range of past human *behavior* including treatment of trees as a natural resource, use of wood as a raw material, seasonal timing of tree felling, sources of wood, tools and techniques of tree felling and wood modification, differential use of species, use of dead wood, reuse of timbers salvaged from older structures, stockpiling, structure remodeling and repair, and others.

Dendrochronology produces three types of *environmental* information: that provided by comparing past species assemblages with modern plant communities, that yielded by tree-ring analysis of geological samples, and that derived from dendroclimatic analysis of tree-ring chronologies.

APPLICATIONS

The explosive growth of dendrochronology over the last thirty years significantly expanded existing applications of the method and generated numerous new applications, many of them only dimly imaginable in 1963. These applications encompass a wide range of subjects including paleoenvironment, climatic reconstruction, climate modeling, global change, alluvial geology and hydrology, volcanology, glaciology, oceanography, botany, forestry, ecology, chronometry, history, art history, anthropology, archaeology, and others. Rather than attempt to summarize all these developments here, I present a sample of applications pertinent to archaeology as it is most broadly conceived, the attempt to understand past and present human behavior and the processes of sociocultural stability, change, and evolution.

Chronological Applications

In 1963, active archaeological tree-ring dating was confined to the U.S. Southwest and Great Plains, western Europe, and Russia, having lapsed in

Alaska. The subsequent global expansion of dendrochronology has enormous archaeological potential, which has been partially realized in western North America, Europe, Siberia, and the eastern Mediterranean where systematic archaeological tree-ring dating has become routine.

An important consequence of the expansion has been the construction of extremely long (>1000 years) tree-ring chronologies of great potential for archaeological dating. The bristlecone pine sequence from the North American Great Basin reaches 8,700 years into the past with earlier floating segments that may eventually extend it beyond 10,000 years (Ferguson *et al.* 1985). The 7,272-year western European sequence (Pilcher *et al.* 1984) has been extended into the 10,000-year range (Becker 1993). The eastern Mediterranean chronology, which at present consists of a dated series and several floating segments, has the potential to reach beyond 7,000 BC (Kuniholm 1995). Southwestern chronologies extend back to 322 BC with floating segments that may allow further extension. In Europe, archaeological or subfossil tree-ring chronologies, some discontinuous, with segments longer than 1,000 years have been constructed in the eastern midlands of England (Laxton and Litton 1988), the Netherlands (Jansma 1996), France (Girardclos *et al.* 1996; Lambert *et al.* 1996), and Poland (Krąpiec 1996). Long living-tree chronologies include a 3,622-year alerce sequence from Chile (Lara and Villalba 1993), a 3,220-year sequoia sequence from California (Brown *et al.* 1994), several multimillennial bristlecone pine series from the Great Basin, a 1,600-year baldcypress sequence from the southeastern U.S. (Stahle *et al.* 1988), a 1,555-year Scots pine sequence from Fennoscandia (Briffa *et al.* 1990), a 1,210-year Huon pine sequence from Tasmania (Cook *et al.* 1992), and 1000+-year sequences from Morocco, the Polar Urals (Graybill and Shiyatov 1992), and various areas in Europe.

A principal global application of tree-ring chronology building has been the calibration of the radiocarbon time scale, which involves the evaluation of radiocarbon determinations from absolutely dated wood samples. Initially, this effort focused on giant sequoias from California, but it soon progressed to the older bristlecone pines, which eventually produced a series of calibrations extending beyond 6,000 BC (Damon *et al.* 1974; Klein *et al.* 1982; Suess 1970). This research demonstrated that radiocarbon dating systematically underestimates the true ages of materials older than 2000 years and that ^{14}C dates must be corrected. Increasing the ages of radiocarbon-dated European sites relative to the fixed Egyptian calendric chronology had implications for Old World prehistory (Renfrew 1973) that caused some archaeologists to question the global validity of the bristlecone pine calibration. The desire to independently test this calibration was an important stimulus to the development of the western European tree-ring chronology. When the radiocarbon analysis of dated European samples (Pearson *et al.* 1986; Stuiver and Kra 1986; Stuiver *et al.* 1993) confirmed the bristlecone calibration, efforts turned to lengthening both chronologies to extend the calibration further back in time. On a smaller geographic scale, burned clay samples from tree-ring dated archaeological contexts are used to calibrate archaeomagnetic dating systems. This approach has allowed the construction and refinement of the Southwestern archaeomagnetic curve, which traces the movement of the virtual geomagnetic pole during the last millennium (Sternberg and McGuire 1990). The dendrochronological calibration of radiocarbon and archaeomagnetic dating techniques provides more accurate and precise independent dates for archaeological contexts that lack datable tree-ring materials.

Direct chronological contributions to archaeology fall into two categories: theory and practice. Dendrochronology has been instrumental in refining archaeological dating theory both in general and as it applies to specific dating techniques. Because dendrochronology lacks the internal variability (chronometric noise) inherent in other dating systems, the consideration of tree-ring dating elucidates external sources of uncertainty and error. Except for pioneering efforts by Haury (1934, 1935) and Smiley (1955, 1961), most contributions to dating theory postdate 1963. Bannister (1962, 1963) codified possible associations between dated materials and archaeological phenomena, delineated different types of potential error inherent in dating situations, and specified the conditions for successful archaeological tree-ring dating. Dean (1969) clarified the special attributes of tree-ring dates and the assumptions that underlie archaeological tree-ring dating. Baillie elucidated the temporal limits that tree-ring dates place on associated archaeological materials (Baillie 1982) and examined recurring problems in the application of archaeological tree-ring dates (Baillie 1995: 57–68). Dean (1978) elaborated the attributes of tree-ring dating into a consideration of assumptions, principles, and procedures for conceptualizing and evaluating independent dates and assessing the impact of past human behavior on dating. Ahlstrom (1985) developed a scheme for characterizing and comparing chronometric systems and dates and clarified the most powerful tool in evaluating independent dates, clustering.

Practical archaeological dating applications involve time scales ranging from seasons to millennia and spatial scales ranging from individual structures to regions. Many innovative studies of individual sites and the implications of the results for issues including social structure and organization, processes and rates of site establishment, growth, decline, and abandonment, internal and external relationships, and the identification and timing of specific events have been accomplished since 1963. Outstanding examples include chronological studies of the inhabited pueblos of Walpi (Ahlstrom *et al.* 1991) and Acoma (Robinson 1990), 13th-century cliff dwellings in northeastern Arizona (Dean 1969), the 9th century Duckfoot Site in southern Colorado (Lightfoot 1992), Neolithic lake dwellings in Germany (Billamboz 1996) and Switzerland (Tercier *et al.* 1996), Neolithic wooden trackways in England (Hillam *et al.* 1990; Morgan *et al.* 1987), Viking burial ships in southern Norway (Bonde and Christensen 1993), the settlement of Haithabu in Schleswig-Hollstein (Eckstein 1978), the medieval city of Novgorod southeast of St. Petersburg (Kolchin 1967), the Hanseatic town of Lübeck (Wrobel 1994) and Trier Cathedral (Hollstein 1980) in Germany, and the Tudor warship the *Mary Rose* (Bridge and Dobbs 1996).

Multisite studies illuminate the temporal and spatial patterning of settlement and interrelationships among contemporaneous communities. Examples include Bannister's (1965) analysis of 9th-12th century towns in Chaco Canyon, Harrill and Breternitz's (1976) comparison of site construction episodes in Johnson Canyon in southeastern Colorado, Towner's (1992) work on historical Navajo settlement and intergroup relations in northwestern New Mexico, Schlanger *et al.*'s (1993) study of prehistoric regional settlement dynamics in the Four Corners area of the Southwest, and Hurni and Orcel's (1996) and Tercier *et al.*'s (1996) analyses of the spatial patterning of dates from, respectively, medieval buildings and Neolithic sites in Switzerland.

Akin to the dating of individual sites is the dating of particular wooden artifacts including utensils, containers, furniture, statues, figurines, and the backing panels of paintings. In the Old World (Baillie 1995: 45–56; Baillie *et al.* 1985; Eckstein *et al.* 1986; Lavier and Lambert 1996), tree-ring dating not only places particular art objects in time but helps evaluate the status of pieces of questionable authenticity. In the New World, artifact dating has involved objects ranging from Eskimo wooden masks, containers, and tools (Giddings 1941) to historic religious paintings from New Mexico (Wroth 1982).

Behavioral Applications

Following Robinson's (1967) lead, the use of tree-ring sample collections to infer various aspects of past human behavior has proliferated. Wood procurement activities are revealed by various attributes of archaeological tree-ring samples. The abundance of fir and spruce beams in Chaco Canyon sites documents the prehistoric long-distance (>50 km) transport of thousands of timbers from surrounding mountains (Betancourt *et al.* 1986). In northern Europe, geographic affinities indicated by the strength of crossdating between archaeological ring series and various local master chronologies show that timber was imported from the eastern Baltic region and Belgium into, respectively, Hanseatic cities in northern Europe (Bonde *et al.* 1994) and the medieval Dutch town of 's-Hertogenbosch (Jansma 1992) and specify eastern Baltic sources for art-historical timbers in England and Flanders (Baillie *et al.* 1985).

Four tree-cutting seasons are indicated by diagnostic combinations of dates and complete and incomplete terminal—the last ring grown by a tree before death—rings (Dean and Warren 1983: 229–230). A suite of incomplete terminal rings dated to a single year indicates cutting during the summer growing season; a set of complete terminal rings dated to the same year specifies cutting during the winter between growing seasons; a mix of complete and incomplete terminal rings dated to the same year indicates felling in the late summer or early fall when some trees had ceased growth (complete) and others had not (incomplete); complete terminal rings dated to one year and incomplete terminal rings dated to the following year specify tree cutting in the spring when some trees had started to grow (incomplete) and some had not (complete). In the northern Southwest, terminal ring data indicate (1) a general shift from spring to fall wood procurement after AD 800 (Robinson 1967: 73–88), (2) autumn tree cutting at Betatakin and year-round felling at Kiet Siel (Dean 1969), (3) spring wood procurement at Chetro Ketl (Dean and Warren 1983: 229–230), and (4) summer and fall wood procurement at, respectively, Navajo summer and winter sheep corrals (Russell and Dean 1985). These results illuminate several aspects of human behavior: (1) a shift of wood procurement away from the spring planting season as agriculture became more important, (2) tighter social integration at Betatakin than at Kiet Siel, (3) a scale of social organization at Chetro Ketl that allowed major wood procurement activities during the planting season, and (4) confirmation of the Navajo biseasonal herding pattern. In Europe, incomplete terminal rings confirm that the famous Oseberg ship burial in southern Norway occurred in the summer of AD 834 (Bonde and Christensen 1993).

Modification traces on archaeological tree-ring samples provide data on the tools and techniques used in tree felling, debarking, limb removal, length reduction, and shaping. Tool marks allowed Wrobel (1994) to develop chronologies for wood working techniques, carpenters' marks, and ornamental styles in Hanseatic Lübeck, Germany. Dates from modified beams from northeastern Arizona place the replacement of girdling and burning by stone-ax cutting at about AD 600 (Robinson 1967: 27–42), a technological change that allowed important architectural developments. Similarly, the shift from groundstone to metal woodworking implements after the arrival of European colonists in the Southwest is evident in metal-tool marks on post-AD 1600 beams from pueblos and Navajo sites. Archaeological tree-ring collections specify prehistoric Southwestern bark removal practices ranging from retention in the Kayenta region (Dean 1969) to careful debarking with stone tools in Chaco Canyon (Dean and Warren 1983: 228–229) to allowing cambium-eating beetle larvae to loosen the bark at Mesa Verde (Graham 1965). Shaping of timbers is evident in the removal of the taper to produce cylindrical beams at Casas Grandes, Chihuahua, in the 14th century (Scott 1966: 35–37), in the squaring of timbers by Spanish builders after AD 1600 in the U.S. Southwest (Douglass 1929: 738), and in the manufacture of specialized structural elements for the *Mary Rose* in 16th-century England (Bridge and Dobbs 1996).

Differential use of species is indicated by the distribution of species among functional contexts. In the Southwest, for example, decay- and insect-resistant juniper was preferred for posts and other elements that came in contact with the ground, while other species more commonly were used as roof timbers.

Date distributions from individual contexts provide information on several different wood use practices. Stockpiling is evident when large numbers of logs cut in a particular year can be shown not to have been used until some years later as at Betatakin (Dean 1969: 77) and Chetro Ketl (Dean and Warren 1983). Early dates often indicate the reuse of elements salvaged from older, abandoned structures. Physical attributes of the timbers often confirm this inference as in Room 6 at Betatakin where older beams had been cut to fit other rooms, were more heavily weathered than freshly cut timbers, and were broken off rather than ax cut (Dean 1969: 65). Similar date distributions, combined with beam attributes diagnostic of natural tree death (extreme weathering, spiral grain, presence of the root crown, and diminished growth toward the end of the ring series) indicate the use of wooden elements from long dead trees. Deadwood commonly was used for fuel, for split-log "shakes" (Dean 1969: 144), in Navajo corrals (Russell and Dean 1985), and in Eskimo sites where driftwood was the primary source of timber (Giddings 1941). Finally, late dates may indicate the repair of an existing building, an inference that can be confirmed by evidence for later acquisition of the timbers, such as differential weathering or smoke blackening, or for attendant architectural modifications. For example, the contrasts between 1230s dates from smoke blackened timbers and 1930s dates from unsmoked logs identify modern repair of a prehistoric kiva at Spruce Tree House on Mesa Verde.

Finally, tree-ring data provide information on human use of living trees. Dated stone ax cut limb stubs on old living trees reveal that the 13th century AD occupants of Mesa Verde bent young Douglas-fir trees parallel the ground and then harvested the limbs that grew vertically from the horizontal trunks (Nichols and Smith 1965). The removal of bark from living trees by humans often leaves scars that illuminate the purpose, date, and seasonal timing of this activity. Numerous partially peeled trees testify to the use of the inner bark of ponderosa pine trees as a "starvation" food by Native Americans in western North America over the last few centuries (Martorano 1988; Swetnam 1984). Other bark removal activities, such as securing raw material for artifacts and blazing trails or surveys, also have been dendrochronologically identified and dated.

Environmental Information

If the preferential selection of species by the occupants of a site can be characterized or discounted, similarities in or differences between the species in the site and the modern plant community can indicate persistence or change in the local environment since the site was occupied. Numerous aspen beams in Kiet Siel, a cliff dwelling in an area presently devoid of such trees, specify a major environmental shift since the site was occupied at the end of the 13th century AD (Dean 1969: 148). In contrast, identical prehistoric and modern species assemblages show that such a transformation did not occur at Betatakin, only four miles away in the same canyon system (Dean 1969: 81).

Human impact on local or regional environments also can be inferred from archaeological tree-ring collections. Changing species dominance through time at Kiet Siel reveals a steady deforestation of the locality as increasingly less accessible species were procured for construction beams between AD 1250 and 1286 (Dean 1969: 148). Increasing use of spruce and fir beams after A.D. 1030 in Chaco Canyon indicates regional resource depletion that eventually required the importation of logs from high elevation forests 75 kilometers from the canyon (Betancourt *et al.* 1986). Similarly, dendrochronological sourcing studies indicate that the depletion of local wood supplies led to the medieval importation of timber into the southern Baltic region (Bonde *et al.* 1994), the Netherlands (Jansma 1992), and England (Baillie *et al.* 1985).

Geological dendrochronology also elucidates behaviorally relevant environmental variability. Perhaps the most well known geologic study is the placement of an eruption of Sunset Crater in northern Arizona at AD 1064 by dating prehistoric structures containing Sunset ash (Breternitz 1967) and tree-growth effects of the ashfall in wood from nearby archaeological sites (Smiley 1958). On a larger scale, inferred growth responses to the global cooling caused by the ejection of large quantities of dust into the atmosphere have been used to identify possible eruptions (Baillie 1995: 73–121). Frost-damaged bristlecone pine rings in the Great Basin (La Marche and Hirschboeck 1984) and tree-growth anomalies in Ireland (Baillie 1989a, 1989b, 1994) and Anatolia (Kuniholm *et al.* 1996) have been used in combination with other paleoenvironmental indicators and historical records to refine the dating of major known eruptions (such as those attributed to Santorini around 1628 BC, Hekla 3 around 1159 BC, and an unknown source around AD 536) and to suggest the existence of previously undocumented eruptions (Baillie 1996). Tree-ring evidence also has been used to identify earthquakes (Jacoby *et al.* 1992) and landscape alterations (Heikkinen 1994) that may have impacted human groups. Equally significant is the construction of high resolution alluvial chronologies through the tree-ring dating of living and dead trees buried in floodplain sediments on the Colorado Plateau (Dean 1988; Karlstrom 1988) and elsewhere (Alestalo 1971; Becker 1975; Shroder 1980). The Colorado Plateau sequences allow the reconstruction of alluvial depositional and hydrologic conditions and processes that directly affected agriculture productivity and the survival of human populations in the region (Plog *et al.* 1988).

Archaeologically important environmental information also resides in the ring width and density variation that allows the dendroclimatic reconstruction of past environmental variability (Fritts 1976). A network of 25 climate sensitive chronologies was used for qualitative reconstructions that measure relative variability in climate from AD 680 to 1989 at each of the stations and across the Southwest (Dean and Funkhouser 1995; Dean and Robinson 1977). Combining dendroclimatic retrodictions with reconstructions of other environmental phenomena reveals the temporal and spatial patterning in a broad spectrum of environmental variability (Baillie 1996: 135–148; Dean *et al.* 1985; Diaz *et al.* 1989). These reconstructions are rich sources of hypotheses about human adaptive behavior to be tested against archaeological data on local (Dean *et al.* 1978) and regional (Plog *et al.* 1988) scales of analysis.

Quantitative dendroclimatic reconstructions at local (Lebo 1991; Rose 1994; Rose *et al.* 1981; Van West 1994) and regional (Briffa *et al.* 1990; Fritts and Shao 1992) scales illuminate past climatic variations that affected human populations. Annual crop production reconstructions in the Southwest (Burns 1983; Van West 1994; Van West and Altschul 1994) measure the effects of climatic variability on cultural production and storage systems. Dendrohydrologic reconstructions of annual and seasonal streamflow in the Salt River (Graybill 1989) reveal low and high flows that would have impacted prehistoric Hohokam irrigation agriculture through, respectively, deficient water supplies or the flooding of canal systems (Nials *et al.* 1989).

The burgeoning field of dendroecology uses tree-ring data to elucidate phenomena such as changes in the composition and distribution of plant communities, air pollution, and CO_2 enrichment of the atmosphere. An aspect of dendroecology particularly relevant to human behavior is the use of dated fire scars in trees to reconstruct the frequency, intensity, and extent of past forest fires. These efforts have produced detailed fire histories for numerous areas in western North America, the most impressive of which is a 3,000-year record for Sequoia National Park, California (Swetnam 1993). Obviously, the rate and intensity of natural wildfires is potentially important to human populations, and in many areas humans set fires to prepare fields, control undergrowth, or enhance natural productivity. Equally interesting are human behavioral impacts on natural fire regimes. Reduced fire frequencies resulting from both grazing (Savage and Swetnam 1990) and fire suppression (Dieterich 1980) are visible in dendroecological fire histories.

FUTURE PROSPECTS

Based on the growing level of interest in dendrochronology around the world, it is safe to predict that the discipline will continue to expand its geographic scope and its relevance to an even broader spectrum of scientific enquiry. An easily projectable trend is the construction of ring chronologies in areas hitherto unexplored or thought to be unsuitable for tree-ring studies. Paramount among the former are vast areas of Asia where studies in China, Siberia, and the Tibetan uplands are beginning to tap a huge dendrochronological potential. The latter include the South American and southeast Asian tropics and wet areas of Australia, New Zealand, and Tasmania where, against all expectations, crossdatable ring records have been discovered. These developments have enormous archaeological potential in terms of both site dating and climatic reconstruction, particularly in China, Siberia, the Near East, northern Africa, South America, and the Arctic. In addition to the chronological and environmental improvements occasioned by this expansion will be the development of new behavioral applications, which are limited only by the archaeologists' imagination and skill.

A number of future developments can be predicted for the practice of dendrochronology. The ongoing search for additional relevant attributes of ring morphology is likely to establish the dendrochronological potential of several density measures, density and width characteristics of earlywood and latewood, cell size and wall thickness, pore size in deciduous species, and others (Evans *et al.* 1996; Tardif 1996). Refined sample collection and preparation methods along with advances in radiography and densitometry will make the analysis of density variables simpler, more efficient, and less costly. Image analysis, which captures both width and density data from samples or CRT images, underlies the development of integrated work stations capable of capturing, storing, and analyzing a broad spectrum of tree-ring data.

Expectable developments in the analysis of tree-ring data include the refinement of curve fitting procedures and data equalization techniques to remove nonclimate related variability while preserving the full spectrum of frequency and amplitude attributes of tree-growth response to climatic and other exogenous factors. Similarly, improved collection, preparation, and extractive procedures will advance analysis of the contents of rings, such as radioactive and stable isotopes and trace elements. These developments undoubtedly will improve the resolution of the dendrochronological calibration of the radiocarbon time scale through the use of smaller, more temporally discrete samples (Stuiver 1993). At the same time, automated crossdating routines are continually being perfected, and they may eventually be able to deal with missing and false rings.

Important developments can be expected in dendroclimatic reconstruction, one of the most active components of tree-ring science due to its relevance to climate modeling and large scale natural and anthropogenic climate processes such as ENSO, atmospheric CO_2 enrichment, and global change. The use of very large tree-ring data arrays of continental or even hemispherical extent (Briffa *et al.* 1996; Cook *et al.* 1996; Meko *et al.* 1993) will illuminate extremely large scale climatic variations (Fritts 1991; Hirschboeck *et al.* 1996), while tightly focused studies will elucidate fine-grained, locality-level variability in various climatic parameters. New mathematical techniques of maximizing and characterizing the climate signal in tree rings and of producing climatic reconstructions that preserve the full range of variability in past climate are being developed, tested, and applied (Van Deusen and Reams 1996). Mechanistic models of climatic effects on the formation, growth, and maturation of individual cells and rings will clarify climate-growth relationships and allow better dendroclimatic retrodictions (Fritts *et al.* 1991). Improved reconstructions resulting from these efforts will, of course, enhance understanding of culture-environment interactions on spatial scales ranging from localities to regions and temporal scales ranging from seasons to millennia.

A clear trend in dendrochronology that undoubtedly will persist is the increasing global interaction and cooperation among practitioners of the science. Growth in the geographic scale of dendrochronological investigation will stimulate concomitant growth in the sharing of data and techniques among scientists from the regions involved. A manifestation of this trend is the International Tree-Ring Data Base (ITRDB), a cooperative effort to pool dendrochronological data, chronologies, reconstructions, references, and analysis programs and make them available to interested parties. These data can be accessed through the World Data Center for Paleoclimatology at the National Oceanic and Atmospheric Administration's National Geophysical Data Center in Boulder, Colorado. A further indication of this cooperative effort is the ITRDB Forum for Dendrochronologists, an e-mail network that facilitates the rapid dissemination of information among workers and allows important issues to be raised and debated in a timely fashion. This interaction has pinpointed and resolved numerous problems and differences in tree-ring practice, exposed the strengths and weaknesses of different approaches and methods, and fostered attempts at systematizing and standardizing the principles and procedures of dendrochronology. Enhanced cooperation, the sharing of data, methods, and results, and lively debate of pertinent issues will strengthen dendrochronology's stature as a science of growing relevance to a host of concerns that face humankind today.

The bright future of the discipline, however, should not be allowed to obscure some problems that will become increasingly vexatious as the method is expanded. Several archaeologically relevant problems must be seriously addressed (Dean 1996a). First is the necessity to develop acceptable procedures for evaluating dates that are challenged on historical, archaeological, geological, or other grounds. Such challenges would involve only a tiny fraction of the dates derived and would entail the statistical and visual inspection of quantified ring attribute data *and* of the actual samples or of representations of the samples such as photographs. Since dating and verification require access to the samples, the second problem is providing for the preservation and curation of wood and charcoal samples. In addition to maintaining samples for inspection, such collections are valuable research resources for a gamut of not always foreseeable studies. Third, a standard nomenclature is necessary to characterize and compare tree-ring dates so that they can be related to the archaeological or other contexts with which they are associated. Fourth, a real need exists to develop criteria for characterizing and ranking date clusters, the most powerful indicators of the dating of past events. Fifth is the need for formal principles for identifying anomalous dates, that is, dates that do not apply to the archaeological materials with which they are associated. Finally, since past human behavior toward trees and wood is the foremost cause of dating anomalies, it is necessary to develop general and specific models of human wood use behavior (Dean 1996b).

CONCLUSION

Although problems exist, they are being seriously addressed by the world dendrochronological community, and progress can be expected on all fronts. The carefully controlled expansion of tree-ring science into all areas of the globe, its application to an ever broader range of past and present phenomena, and its unparalleled utility as a source of baseline data for measuring current environmental excursions and predicting future variations endow dendrochronology with a bright future. In all likelihood, the next thirty years will produce changes and progress equal to those accomplished since Bannister's landmark paper of 1963.

REFERENCES

Ahlstrom, R.V.N. 1985 *The Interpretation of Archaeological Tree-Ring Dates*. Ph.D. dissertation, University of Arizona, Tucson.

Ahlstrom, R.V.N., Dean, J.S. and Robinson, W.J. 1991 Evaluating tree-ring interpretations of Walpi Pueblo, Arizona. *American Antiquity* 56: 628–644.

Alestalo, J. 1971 Dendrochronological interpretation of geomorphic processes. *Fennia* 1: 1–140.

Aniol, R.W. 1983 Tree-Ring analysis using CATRAS. *Dendrochronologia* 1: 45–53.

Baillie, M.G.L. 1982 *Tree-Ring Dating and Archaeology*. Chicago, Illinois, University of Chicago Press.

_____1989a Do Irish bog oaks date the Shang Dynasty? *Current Archaeology* 10: 310–313.

_____1989b Hekla 3: how big was it? *Endeavor* 13(2): 78–81.

_____1994 Dendrochronology raises questions about the nature of the AD 536 dust-veil event. *The Holocene* 4: 212–217.

_____1995 *A Slice Through Time: Dendrochronology and Prehistoric Dating*. London, England, B.T. Batsford, Ltd.

_____1996 Extreme environmental events and the linking of the tree-ring and ice-core records. *In* Dean, J.S., Meko, D.M. and Swetnam, T.W., eds., *Tree Rings, Environment and Humanity: Proceedings of the International Conference, Tucson, Arizona, 17–21 May 1994*. Tucson, Arizona, Radiocarbon: 703–711.

Baillie, M.G.L., Hillam, J., Briffa, K.R. and Brown, D.M. 1985 Re-dating the English art-historical tree-ring chronologies. *Nature* 315: 317–319.

Baillie, M.G.L. and Pilcher, J.R. 1973 A simple crossdating program for tree-ring research. *Tree-Ring Bulletin* 33: 7–14.

Bannister, B. 1962 The interpretation of tree-ring dates. *American Antiquity* 27: 508–514.

_____1963 Dendrochronology. *In* Brothwell, D. and Higgs E., eds., *Science in Archaeology*. New York, New York, Basic Books: 161–176.

_____1965 Tree-ring dating of the archaeological sites in the Chaco Canyon region, New Mexico. *Southwestern Monuments Association Technical Series* 6(2). Globe, Arizona, Southwestern Monuments Association: 117–206.

Becker, B. 1975 Dendrochronological observations on the postglacial river aggradation in the southern part of central Europe. *Biuletyn Geologiczny* 9: 127–136.

_____1993 An 11,000-year German oak and pine dendrochronology for radiocarbon calibration. *Radiocarbon* 35: 201–213.

Betancourt, J.L., Dean, J.S. and Hull, H.M. 1986 Prehistoric long-distance transport of construction beams, Chaco Canyon, New Mexico. *American Antiquity* 51: 370–375.

Billamboz, A. 1996 Tree rings and pile dwellings in southwestern Germany: following in the footsteps of Bruno Huber. *In* Dean, J.S., Meko, D.M. and Swetnam, T.W., eds., *Tree Rings, Environment and Humanity: Proceedings of the International Conference, Tucson, Arizona, 17–21 May 1994*. Tucson, Arizona, Radiocarbon: 471–483.

Biondi, F. and Swetnam, T.W. 1987 Box-Jenkins models of forest interior tree-ring chronologies. *Tree-Ring Bulletin* 47: 71–96.

Blasing, T.J., Duvick, D.N. and Cook, E.R. 1983 Filtering the effects of competition from ring-width series. *Tree-Ring Bulletin* 43: 19–30.

Bonde, N. and Christensen, A.E. 1993 Dendrochronological dating of the Viking age ship burials at Oseberg, Gokstad, and Thune, Norway. *Antiquity* 67: 575–583.

Bonde, N., Tyers, I. and Wazny, T. 1994 From where does the timber originate? dendrochronological evidence of timber trade in northern Europe, 14th to 17th century. Poster presented at the International Conference on Tree Rings, Environment, and Humanity: Relationships and Processes, Tucson, Arizona, 17–21 May 1994.

Breternitz, D.A. 1966 An appraisal of tree-ring dated pottery in the Southwest. *Anthropological Papers of The University of Arizona* 10. Tucson, Arizona, University of Arizona Press.

_____1967 Eruptions of Sunset Crater: dating and effects. *Plateau* 40: 72–76.

Bridge, M.C. and C. Dobbs. 1996 Tree-ring studies on the Tudor warship *Mary Rose*. *In* Dean, J.S., Meko, D.M. and Swetnam, T.W., eds., *Tree Rings, Environment and Humanity: Proceedings of the International Conference, Tucson, Arizona, 17–21 May 1994*. Tucson, Arizona, Radiocarbon: 491–496.

Briffa, K.R., Bartholin, T.S., Eckstein, D., Jones, P.D., Karlén, W., Schweingruber, F.H. and Zetterberg, P. 1990 A 1,400-year tree-ring record of summer temperatures in Fennoscandia. *Nature* 346: 434–439.

Briffa, K.R., Jones, P.D., Schweingruber, F.H., Shiyatov, S.G. and Vaganov, E.A. 1996 Development of a north Eurasian chronology network: rationale and preliminary results of comparative ring-width and densitometric analyses in northern Russia. *In* Dean, J.S., Meko, D.M. and Swetnam, T.W., eds., *Tree Rings, Environment and Humanity: Proceedings of the International Conference, Tucson, Arizona, 17–21 May 1994*. Tucson, Arizona, Radiocarbon: 25–41.

Brown, P.M., Hughes, M.K., Baisan, C.H., Swetnam, T.H. and Caprio, A.C. 1994 Giant sequoia ring-width chronologies from the central Sierra Nevada, California. *Tree-Ring Bulletin* 52: 1–14.

Burns, B.T. 1983 *Simulated Anasazi Storage Behavior Using Crop Yields Reconstructed from Tree Rings: A.D. 652–1968*. Ph.D. dissertation, University of Arizona, Tucson.

Cleaveland, M.K. 1986 Climatic response of densitometric properties in semiarid site tree rings. *Tree-Ring Bulletin* 46: 13–29.

Cleaveland, M.K. and Stahle, D.H. 1989 Tree ring analysis of surplus and deficit runoff in the White River, Arkansas. *Water Resources Research* 25: 1391–1401.

Cook, E., Bird, T., Peterson, M., Barbetti, M., Buckley, B., D'Arrigo, R. and Francey, R. 1992 Climatic change over the last millennium in Tasmania reconstructed from tree-rings. *The Holocene* 2: 205–217.

Cook, E., Briffa, K.R., Meko, D.M., Graybill, D.A. and Funkhouser G. 1995 The 'segment length curse' in long tree-ring chronology development for paleoclimatic studies. *The Holocene* 5: 229–237.

Cook, E. and Holmes, R.L. 1986 Users manual for program ARSTAN. *In* Holmes, R.L., Adams, R.K. and Fritts, H.C., Tree-ring chronologies of western North America: California, eastern Oregon and northern Great Basin with procedures used in the chronology development work including users manuals for computer programs COFECHA and ARSTAN. *Chronology Series VI*. Tucson, Arizona, Laboratory of Tree-Ring Research, The University of Arizona: 50–65.

Cook, E.R., Meko, D.M., Stahle, D.H. and Cleaveland, M.K. 1996 Tree-ring reconstructions of past drought across the coterminous United States: tests of a regression method and calibration/verification results. *In* Dean, J.S., Meko, D.M. and Swetnam, T.W., eds., *Tree Rings, Environment and Humanity: Proceedings of the International Conference, Tucson, Arizona, 17–21 May 1994*. Tucson, Arizona, Radiocarbon: 155–169.

Cook, E.R. and Peters, K. 1981 The smoothing spline: a new approach to standardizing forest interior tree-ring width series for dendroclimatic studies. *Tree-Ring Bulletin* 41: 45–53.

Damon, P.E., Ferguson, C.W. and Long, A. 1974 Dendrochronologic calibration of the radiocarbon time scale. *American Antiquity* 39: 350–366.

D'Arrigo, R. and Jacoby, G.C. 1991 A 1000-year record of winter precipitation from northwestern New Mexico, USA: a reconstruction from tree-rings and its relation to El Niño and the Southern Oscillation. *The Holocene* 1: 95–101.

Dean, J.S. 1969 Chronological analysis of Tsegi phase sites in northeastern Arizona. *Papers of the Laboratory of Tree-Ring Research* 3. Tucson, Arizona, The University of Arizona Press.

_____1978 Independent dating in archaeological analysis. *In* Schiffer, M.B., ed., *Advances in Archaeological Method and Theory* 1. New York, New York, Academic Press: 223–255.

_____1986 Dendrochronology. *In* Zimmerman, M.R. and Angel, J.L., eds., *Dating and Age Determination of Biological Materials*. London, England, Croom Helm: 126–165.

_____1988 Dendrochronology and paleoenvironmental reconstruction on the Colorado Plateaus. *In* Gumerman, G.J., ed., *The Anasazi in a Changing Environment*. Cambridge, England, Cambridge University Press: 119–167.

_____1996a Dendrochronology and the study of human behavior. *In* Dean. J.S., Meko, D.M. and Swetnam, T.W., eds., *Tree Rings, Environment, and Humanity: Proceedings of the International Conference, Tucson, Arizona, 17–21 May 1994*. Tucson, Arizona, Radiocarbon: 461–469.

_____1996b Behavioral sources of error in archaeological tree-ring dating: Navajo and Pueblo wood use. *In* Dean, J.S., Meko, D.M. and Swetnam, T.W., eds., *Tree Rings, Environment and Humanity: Proceedings of the International Conference, Tucson, Arizona, 17–21 May 1994*. Tucson, Arizona, Radiocarbon: 497–503.

Dean, J.S., Euler, R.C., Gumerman, G.J., Plog, F., Hevly, R.H. and Karlstrom, T.N.V. 1985 Human behavior, demography, and paleoenvironment on the Colorado Plateaus. *American Antiquity* 50: 537–554.

Dean, J.S. and Funkhouser, G.S. 1995 Dendroclimatic reconstructions for the southern Colorado Plateau. *In* Waugh, W.J., ed., *Climate Change in the Four Corners and Adjacent Regions: Implications for Environmental Restoration and Land-Use Planning*. Grand Junction, Colorado, US Department of Energy, Grand Junction Projects Office: 85–104.

Dean, J.S., Lindsay, A.J., Jr. and Robinson, W.J. 1978 Prehistoric settlement in Long House Valley, northeastern Arizona. *In* Euler, R.C. and Gumerman, G.J., eds., *Investigations of the Southwestern Anthropological Research Group: An Experiment in Archaeological Cooperation: Proceedings of the 1976 Conference*. Flagstaff, Arizona, Museum of Northern Arizona: 25–44.

Dean, J.S., Meko, D.M. and Swetnam, T.W., eds, 1996. *Tree Rings, Environment and Humanity: Proceedings of the International Conference, Tucson, Arizona, 17–21 May 1994*. Tucson, Arizona, Radiocarbon.

Dean, J.S. and Robinson, W.J. 1977 *Dendroclimatic Variability in the American Southwest, A.D. 680 to 1970*. Springfield, Virginia, U.S. Department of Commerce National Technical Information Service: PB-266 340.

Dean, J.S. and Warren, R.L. 1983 Dendrochronology. *In* Lekson, S.H., ed, The architecture and dendrochronology of Chetro Ketl, Chaco Canyon, New Mexico. *Reports of the Chaco Center* 6. Albuquerque, New Mexico, Division of Cultural Research, U.S. National Park Service: 105–240.

Diaz, H.F., Andrews, J.T. and Short, S.K. 1989 Climate variations in northern North America (6000 BP to present) reconstructed from pollen and tree-ring data. *Arctic and Alpine Research* 21: 45–59.

Dieterich, J.H. 1980 Chimney Spring forest fire history. *Research Paper RM-220*. Fort Collins, Colorado, USDA Forest Service Rocky Mountain Forest and Range Experiment Station.

Douglass, A.E. 1914 A method of estimating rainfall by the growth of trees. *In* Huntington, E., ed., The climatic factor as illustrated in arid America. *Carnegie Institution of Washington Publication* 192. Lancaster, Pennsylvania, Carnegie Institution of Washington: 101–121.

_____1929 The secret of the Southwest solved by talkative tree rings. *National Geographic Magazine* 56: 736–770.

Eckstein, D. 1978 Dendrochronological dating of the medieval settlement of Haithabu (Hedeby). *In* Fletcher, J., ed, Dendrochronology in Europe. *British Archaeological Reports, International Series* 51: 267–274.

Eckstein, D., Baillie, M.G.L. and Egger, H. 1984 *Handbook for Archaeologists No. 2: Dendrochronological Dating*. Strasbourg, France, European Science Foundation.

Eckstein, D. and Bauch, J. 1969 Beitrag zur Rationalisizierung eines dendrochronologischen Verfahrens und zur Analyse seiner Aussagesicherheit. *Forstwissenschaftliches Centralblatt 88, Jahrgang* 4: 230–250.

Eckstein, D., Wazny, T., Bauch, J. and Klein, P. 1986 New evidence for the dendrochronological dating of Netherlandish paintings. *Nature* 320: 465–466.

Eckstein, D. and Wrobel, S. 1983 Dendrochronologie in Europa. *Dendrochronologia* 1: 9–20.

Evans, R., Downs, J. and Murphy, J. 1996 Application of new wood characterization technology to dendrochronology and dendroclimatology. *In* Dean, J.S., Meko, D.M. and Swetnam, T.W., eds, *Tree Rings, Environment and Humanity: Proceedings of the International Conference, Tucson, Arizona, 17–21 May 1994*. Tucson, Arizona, Radiocarbon: 743–749.

Ferguson, C.W., Lawn, B. and Michael, H.N. 1985 Prospects for the extension of the bristlecone pine chronology: radiocarbon analysis of H-84–1. *Meteoritics* 20(2): 415–421.

Fritts, H.C. 1965 Tree-ring evidence for climatic changes in western North America. *Monthly Weather Review* 93: 421–443.

_____1971 Dendroclimatology and dendroecology. *Quaternary Research* 1: 419–449.

_____1976 *Tree Rings and Climate*. London, England, Academic Press.

_____1977 *Tree Rings: A Record of Climate Past*. Washington, D.C., U.S. Department of Commerce, National Oceanic and Atmospheric Administration, Environmental Data Service.

_____1991 *Reconstructing Large-Scale Climatic Patterns from Tree-Ring Data: A Diagnostic Analysis*. Tucson, Arizona, The University of Arizona Press.

Fritts, H.C. and Shao, X.M. 1992 Mapping climate using tree-rings from western North America. *In* Bradley, R.S. and Jones, P.D., eds, *Climate Since A.D. 1500*. London, England, Routledge: 269–295.

Fritts, H.C., Vaganov, E.A., Sviderskaya, I.V. and Shashkin, A.V. 1991 Climatic variation and tree-ring structure in conifers: empirical and mechanistic models of tree-ring width, number of cells, cell size, cell-wall thickness and wood density. *Climate Research* 1: 97–116.

Giddings, J.L., Jr. 1941 Dendrochronology in northern Alaska. *University of Alaska Publication* IV, *University of Arizona Bulletin* 12(4), *Laboratory of Tree-Ring Research Bulletin* 1. Tucson, Arizona, The University of Arizona Press.

Girardclos, O., Lambert, G. and Lavier, C. 1996 Oak tree-ring series from France between 4000 B.C. and 800 B.C. *In* Dean, J.S., Meko, D.M. and Swetnam, T.W., eds., *Tree Rings, Environment and Humanity: Proceedings of the International Conference, Tucson, Arizona, 17–21 May 1994*. Tucson, Arizona, Radiocarbon: 751–768.

Gladwin, H.S. 1940 Tree-ring analysis methods of correlation. *Medallion Papers* 28. Globe, Arizona, Gila Pueblo.

Glock, W.S. 1937 Principles and methods of tree-ring analysis. *Carnegie Institution of Washington Publication* 486. Washington, D.C., Carnegie Institution.

Glock, W.S., Studhalter, R.A. and Agerter, S.R. 1960 Classification and multiplicity of growth layers in the branches of trees at the extreme lower forest border. *Smithsonian Miscellaneous Collections* 140 (1). Washington, D.C., Smithsonian Institution.

Graham, S.A. 1965 Entomology: an aid in archaeological studies. In Osborne, D., assembler, Contributions of the Wetherill Mesa Archeological Project. *Memoirs of the Society for American Archaeology* 19: 167–174.

Graumlich, L.J. 1993 A 1000-year record of temperature and precipitation in the Sierra Nevada. *Quaternary Research* 39: 249–255.

Graybill, D.A. 1979 Revised computer programs for tree-ring research. *Tree-Ring Bulletin* 39: 77–82.

_____1982 Chronology development and analysis. *In* Hughes, M.K., Kelly, P.M., Pilcher, J.R. and La Marche, V.C., eds., *Climate from Tree Rings*. Cambridge, England, Cambridge University Press: 21–28.

_____1989 The reconstruction of prehistoric Salt River streamflow. *In* Graybill, D.A., Gregory, D.A., Nials, F.L., Fish, S.H., Gasser, R.E., Miksicek, C.H. and Szuter, C.R., The 1982–1984 excavations at Las Colinas: environment and subsistence. *Cultural Resource Management Division Archaeological Series* 162(5). Tucson, Arizona, Arizona State Museum: 25–38.

Graybill, D.A. and Shiyatov, S.G. 1992 Dendroclimatic evidence from the northern Soviet Union. *In* Bradley. R.S. and Jones, P.D., eds., *Climate Since A.D. 1500*. London, England, Routledge: 393–414.

Grissino-Mayer, H.D. 1995 An updated list of species used in tree-ring research. *Tree-Ring Bulletin* 53: 17–43.

Harrill, B.G. and Breternitz, C.D. 1976 Chronology and cultural activity in Johnson Canyon cliff dwellings: interpretations from tree-ring data. *Journal of Field Archaeology* 3: 375–390.

Haury, E.W. 1934 The Canyon Creek Ruin and the cliff dwellings of the Sierra Ancha. *Medallion Papers* 14. Globe, Arizona, Gila Pueblo.

_____1935 Tree rings - the archaeologist's time-piece. *American Antiquity* 1: 98–108.

_____1962 HH-39: recollections of a dramatic moment in Southwestern archaeology. *Tree-Ring Bulletin* 24(3–4): 11–14.

Heikkinen, O. 1994 Using dendrochronology for the dating of land surfaces. *In* Beck, C., ed., *Dating in Exposed and Surface Contexts*. Albuquerque, New Mexico, University of New Mexico Press: 213–235.

Heizer, R.F. 1956 The first dendrochronologist. *American Antiquity* 22: 186–188.

Hillam, J., Groves, C.M., Brown, D.M., Baillie, M.G.L., Coles, J.M. and Coles, B.J. 1990 Dendrochronology of the English Neolithic. *Antiquity* 64: 210–220.

Hirschboeck, K.K., Ni, F., Wood, M.L. and Woodhouse, C.A. 1996 Synoptic dendroclimatology: overview and outlook. *In* Dean, J.S., Meko, D.M. and Swetnam, T.W., eds., *Tree Rings, Environment and Humanity: Proceedings of the International Conference, Tucson, Arizona, 17–21 May 1994*. Tucson, Arizona, Radiocarbon: 205–223.

Høeg, O.A. 1944 Dendrokronologi. *Viking: Norsk Arkeologisk Selskaps Tidskrift*: 231–282.

Hollstein, E. 1980 Mitteleuropäische Eichenchronologie: Trierer dendrochronologische Forschungen zur Archäologie und Kunstgeschichte. *Trierer Grabungen und Forschungen* 11. Mainz am Rhein, Germany, Verlag Philipp von Zabern.

Holmes, R.L. 1986 Quality control of crossdating and measuring: a users manual for program COFECHA. *In* Holmes, R.H., Adams, R.K. and Fritts, H.C., Tree-ring chronologies of western North America: California, eastern Oregon and northern Great Basin with procedures used in the chronology development work including users manuals for computer programs ARSTAN and COFECHA. *Chronology Series VI.* Tucson, Arizona, Laboratory of Tree-Ring Research, The University of Arizona: 41–49.

Huber, B. 1941 Aufbau einer Mitteleuropäischen Jahrringschronologie. *Mitteilungen des Hermann Göring Akademie* 1: 110–125.

Huber, B., von Jazewitsch, W., John, A. and Wellenhofer, W. 1949 Jahrringchronologie der Spessarteichen. *Forstwissenschaftlisches Centralblatt* 68: 706–715.

Hughes, M.K. and Diaz, H.F., eds. 1994 *The Medieval Warm Period.* Dordrecht, the Netherlands, Kluwer Academic Publishers.

Hughes, M.K., Wu, X., Shao, X. and Garfin, G.M. 1994 A preliminary reconstruction of rainfall in north-central China since A.D. 1600 from tree-ring density and width. *Quaternary Research* 42: 88–99.

Hurni, J.-P. and Orcel, C. 1996 Dendrochronological results on buildings in Switzerland: geographical aspects. *In* Dean, J.S., Meko, D.M. and Swetnam, T.W., eds., *Tree Rings, Environment and Humanity: Proceedings of the International Conference, Tucson, Arizona, 17–21 May 1994.* Tucson, Arizona, Radiocarbon: 533–542.

Jacoby, G.C., Jr., Cook, E.R. and Ulan, L.D. 1985 Reconstructed summer degree days in central Alaska and northwestern Canada since 1524. *Quaternary Research* 23: 18–26.

Jacoby, G.C. and D'Arrigo, R.D. 1995 Indicators of climatic and biospheric change: evidence from tree rings. *In* Woodwell, G.M. and Mackenzie, F.T., eds., *Biotic Feedbacks in the Global Climatic System: Will the Warming Feed the Warming?* Oxford, England, Oxford University Press: 108–118.

Jacoby, G.C., D'Arrigo, R.D. and Davaajamts, T. 1996 Mongolian tree rings and 20th-century warmth. *Science* 273: 771–773.

Jacoby, G.C., Williams, P.L. and Buckley, B.M. 1992 Tree ring correlation between prehistoric landslides and abrupt tectonic events in Seattle, Washington. *Science* 258: 1621–1623.

Jansma, E. 1992 Dendrochronological methods to determine the origin of oak timber: a case study on wood from 's-Hertogenbosch. *Helinium* 32: 195–214.

_____1996 An 1100-year tree-ring chronology of oak for the Dutch coastal region (2258–1141 B.C.). *In* Dean, J.S., Meko, D.M. and Swetnam, T.W., eds, *Tree Rings, Environment and Humanity: Proceedings of the International Conference, Tucson, Arizona, 17–21 May 1994.* Tucson, Arizona, Radiocarbon: 769–778.

Karlstrom, T.N.V. 1988 Alluvial chronology and hydrologic change of Black Mesa and nearby regions. *In* Gumerman, G.J., ed., *The Anasazi in a Changing Environment.* Cambridge, England, Cambridge University Press: 45–91.

Klein, J., Lerman, J.C., Damon, P.E. and Ralph, E.K. 1982 Calibration of radiocarbon dates: tables based on the consensus data of the Workshop on Calibrating the Radiocarbon Time Scale. *Radiocarbon* 24:103–150.

Kolchin, B.A. 1967 Dendrochronology. *In* Thompson, M.W., compiler, *Novgorod the Great: Excavations at the Medieval City by A.V. Artsikhovsky and B.A. Kolchin.* New York, New York, Frederick A. Praeger: 23–34.

Krąpiec, M. 1996 Subfossil oak chronology (474 B.C.-A.D. 1529) from southern Poland. *In* Dean, J.S., Meko, D.M. and Swetnam, T.W., eds., *Tree Rings, Environment and Humanity: Proceedings of the International Conference, Tucson, Arizona, 17–21 May 1994.* Tucson, Arizona, Radiocarbon: 813–819.

Kuniholm, P.I. 1995 *Aegean Dendrochronology Project December 1995 Progress Report.* Ithaca, New York, The Malcolm and Carolyn Wiener Laboratory for Aegean and Near Eastern Dendrochronology, Cornell University.

Kuniholm, P.I., Kromer, B., Manning, S.W., Newton, M., Latini, C.E. and Bruce, M.J. 1996 Anatolian tree rings and the absolute chronology of the eastern Mediterranean, 2220–718 B.C. *Nature* 381: 780–783.

La Marche, V.C., Jr. and Hirschboeck, K.K. 1984 Frost rings in trees as records of major volcanic eruptions. *Nature* 307: 121–126.

Lambert, G.-N., Bernard, V., Doucerain, C., Girardclos, O., Lavier, C., Szepertisky, B. and Trenard, Y. 1996 French regional oak chronologies spanning more than 1000 years. *In* Dean, J.S., Meko, D.M. and Swetnam, T.W., eds., *Tree Rings, Environment and Humanity: Proceedings of the International Conference, Tucson, Arizona, 17–21 May 1994*. Tucson, Arizona, Radiocarbon: 821–832.

Lara, A. and Villalba, R. 1993 A 3620-year temperature record from *Fitzroya cuppressoides* tree rings in South America. *Science* 260: 1104–1106.

Lavier, C. and Lambert, G. 1996 Dendrochronology and works of art. *In* Dean, J.S., Meko, D.M. and Swetnam, T.W., eds., *Tree Rings, Environment and Humanity: Proceedings of the International Conference, Tucson, Arizona, 17–21 May 1994*. Tucson, Arizona, Radiocarbon: 543–556.

Laxton, R.R. and Litton, C.D. 1988 An East Midlands master tree-ring chronology and its use for dating vernacular buildings. *University of Nottingham Department of Classical and Archaeological Studies (Archaeology Section) Monograph Series III*. Nottingham, England.

Leavitt, S.W. 1994 Major wet interval in White Mountains Medieval Warm Period evidenced by $\delta^{13}C$ of bristlecone pine tree rings. *Climatic Change* 26: 299–307.

Lebo, C.J. 1991 *Anasazi Harvests: Agroclimate, Harvest Variability, and Agricultural Strategies on Prehistoric Black Mesa, Northeastern Arizona*. Ph.D. dissertation, Indiana University, Bloomington.

Lightfoot, R.R. 1992 Architecture and tree-ring dating at the Duckfoot Site in southwestern Colorado. *Kiva* 57: 213–236.

Lipp, J., Trimborn, P., Graf, W., Edwards, T. and Becker, B. 1996 Climate signals in a ^{2}H and ^{13}C chronology (1882–1989) from tree rings of spruce (*Picea abies* L.), Schussbach Forest, Germany. *In* Dean, J.S., Meko, D.M. and Swetnam, T.W., eds., *Tree Rings, Environment and Humanity: Proceedings of the International Conference, Tucson, Arizona, 17–21 May 1994*. Tucson, Arizona, Radiocarbon: 603–610.

Lough, J.M. and Fritts, H.C. 1985 The Southern Oscillation and tree rings: 1600–1961. *Journal of Climate and Applied Meteorology* 24: 952–966.

Martorano, M.A. 1988 Culturally peeled trees and Ute Indians in Colorado. *In* Nickens, P.R., ed., Archaeology of the eastern Ute: a symposium. *Colorado Council of Professional Archaeologists Occasional Papers* 1: 5–21.

McCord, V.A.S. 1996 Fluvial process dendrogeomorphology: reconstruction of flood events from the southwestern United States using flood-scarred trees. *In* Dean, J.S., Meko, D.M. and Swetnam, T.W., eds., *Tree Rings, Environment and Humanity: Proceedings of the International Conference, Tucson, Arizona, 17–21 May 1994*. Tucson, Arizona, Radiocarbon: 689–699.

Meko, D.M., Cook, E.R., Stahle, D.W., Stockton, C.W. and Hughes, M.K. 1993 Spatial patterns of tree-growth anomalies in the United States and southeastern Canada. *Journal of Climate* 6: 1773–1786.

Meko, D.M., Stockton, C.W. and Boggess, W.R. 1980 A tree-ring reconstruction of drought in southern California. *Water Resources Bulletin* 16: 594–600.

Morgan, R.A, Litton, C.D. and Salisbury, C.R. 1987 Trackways and tree trunks-dating Neolithic oaks in the British Isles. *Tree-Ring Bulletin* 47: 61–68.

Nials, F.L., Gregory, D.A. and Graybill, D.A. 1989 Salt River streamflow and human irrigation systems. *In* Graybill, D.A., Gregory, D.A., Nials, F.L., Fish, S.H., Gasser, R.E., Miksicek, C.H. and Szuter, C.R., The 1982–1984 excavations at Las Colinas: environment and subsistence. *Cultural Resource Management Division Archaeological Series* 162(5). Tucson, Arizona, Arizona State Museum: 59–76.

Nichols, R.F. and Smith, D.G. 1965 Evidence of prehistoric cultivation of Douglas-fir trees at Mesa Verde. *In* Osborne, D., assembler, Contributions of the Wetherill Mesa Archeological Project. *Memoirs of the Society for American Archaeology* 19: 57–64.

Parker, M.L. 1971 Dendrochronological techniques used by the Geological Survey of Canada. *Geological Survey of Canada Paper 71–25*. Ottawa.

Parker, M.L. and Henoch, E.S. 1971 The use of Englemann spruce latewood density for dendrochronological purposes. *Canadian Journal of Forest Research* 1: 90–98.

Pearson, G.W., Pilcher, J.R., Baillie, M.G.L., Corbett, D.M. and Qua, F. 1986 High precision ^{14}C measurements of Irish oaks to show the natural ^{14}C variations from A.D. 1840 to 5210 B.C. *In* Stuiver, M. and Kra, R., eds., Proceedings of the Twelfth International Radiocarbon Conference, June 24–28, 1985, Trondheim, Norway. *Radiocarbon* 28(2B): 911–934.

Pilcher, J.R. and Baillie, M.G.L. 1987 The Belfast CROS program—some observations. *In* Ward, R.G.W., ed, Applications of tree-ring studies: current research in dendrochronology and related subjects. *British Archaeological Reports, International Series* 333: 157–163.

Pilcher, J.R., Baillie, M.G.L., Schmidt, B. and Becker, B. 1984 A 7,272-year tree-ring chronology for western Europe. *Nature* 312: 150–152.

Plog, F., Gumerman, G.J., Euler, R.C., Dean, J.S., Hevly, R.H. and Karlstrom, T.N.V. 1988. *In* Gumerman, G.J., ed., *The Anasazi in a Changing Environment*. Cambridge, England, Cambridge University Press: 230–276.

Polge, H. 1963 L'analyse densitométrique de clichés radiographiques. *Annales de l'Ecole Nationale des Eaux et Forets et la Station Recherches et Expériences* 20: 531–581.

Reams, G.A. and Van Deusen, P.C. 1996 Detection of a hurricane signal in baldcypress tree-ring chronologies. *In* Dean, J.S., Meko, D.M. and Swetnam, T.W., eds., *Tree Rings, Environment and Humanity: Proceedings of the International Conference, Tucson, Arizona, 17–21 May 1994*. Tucson, Arizona, Radiocarbon: 265–271.

Renfrew, C. 1973 *Before Civilization: The Radiocarbon Revolution and Prehistoric Europe*. New York, New York, Alfred A. Knopf.

Robinson, W.J. 1967 *Tree-Ring Materials as a Basis for Cultural Interpretations*. Ph.D. dissertation, The University of Arizona, Tucson.

____1990 Tree-ring studies of the Pueblo of Acoma. *Historical Archaeology* 24: 99–106.

Rose, M.R. 1994 Long term drought reconstructions for the Lake Roosevelt region. *In* Ciolek-Torrello, R. and Welch, J.R., eds., The Roosevelt Rural Sites Study, Vol 3: changing land use in the Tonto Basin. *Statistical Research Technical Series* 28. Tucson, Arizona, Statistical Research, Inc.: 311–359.

Rose, M.R., Dean, J.S. and Robinson, W.J. 1981 The past climate of Arroyo Hondo, New Mexico, reconstructed from tree rings. *Arroyo Hondo Archaeological Series* 4. Santa Fe, New Mexico, School of American Research Press.

Russell, S.C. and Dean, J.S. 1985 The sheep and goat corral: a key structure in Navajo site analysis. *The Kiva* 51: 3–18.

Savage, M. and Swetnam, T.W. 1990 Early 19th-century fire decline following sheep pasturing in a Navajo ponderosa pine forest. *Ecology* 71: 2374–2378.

Schlanger, S., Lipe, W.D. and Robinson, W.J. 1993 An atlas of occupation and abandonment across the northern Southwest. Poster presented at the 58th Annual Meeting of the Society for American Archaeology, 14–18 April, St. Louis, Missouri.

Schulman, E. 1937 Some early papers on tree rings II: J.C. Kapteyn. *Tree-Ring Bulletin* 3: 28–29.

_____1944 Tree-ring work in Scandinavia. *Tree-Ring Bulletin* 11(1): 2–6.

_____1956 *Dendroclimatic Changes in Semiarid America*. Tucson, Arizona, The University of Arizona Press.

Schweingruber, F.H. 1988 *Tree Rings: Basics and Applications of Dendrochronology*. Dordrecht, Netherlands, D. Reidel Publishing Company.

Scott, S.D. 1966 Dendrochronology in Mexico. *Papers of the Laboratory of Tree-Ring Research* 2. Tucson, Arizona, The University of Arizona Press.

Sheppard, P.R. 1993 Identifying low-frequency tree-ring variation. *Tree-Ring Bulletin* 51: 29–38.

Sheppard, P.S. and Graumlich, L.J. 1996 A reflected-light video imaging system for tree-ring analysis of conifers. *In* Dean, J.S., Meko, D.M. and Swetnam, T.W., eds, *Tree Rings,*

Environment and Humanity: Proceedings of the International Conference, Tucson, Arizona, 17–21 May 1994. Tucson, Arizona, Radiocarbon: 879–889.

Shiyatov, S.G., Mazepa, V.S., Vaganov, E.A. and Schweingruber F.H. 1996 Summer temperature variations reconstructed by tree-ring data at the polar timberline in Siberia. *In* Dean, J.S., Meko, D.M. and Swetnam, T.W., eds., *Tree Rings, Environment and Humanity: Proceedings of the International Conference, Tucson, Arizona, 17–21 May 1994*. Tucson, Arizona, Radiocarbon: 61–70.

Shroder, J.F., Jr. 1980 Dendrogeomorphology: review and new techniques of tree-ring dating. *Progress in Physical Geography* 4: 161–188.

Smiley, T.L. 1955 The geochronological approach. *In* Smiley, T.L., ed., Geochronology: with special reference to the southwestern United States. *University of Arizona Bulletin Series* 26(2) *Physical Science Bulletin* 2. Tucson, Arizona, The University of Arizona Press: 15–28.

_____1958 The geology and dating of Sunset Crater, Flagstaff, Arizona. *In* Anderson, R.Y. and Harshbarger, J.W., eds., *Guidebook of the Black Mesa Basin, Northeastern Arizona*. Socorro, New Mexico, New Mexico Geological Society, Ninth Field Conference: 186–190.

_____1961 General aspects of dating in the field of archaeology. *Asian Perspectives* 5: 181–187.

Stahle, D.W. 1990 *The Tree-Ring Record of False Spring in the Southcentral USA*. Ph.D. dissertation, Arizona State University, Tempe.

Stahle, D.W. and Cleaveland, M.K. 1992 Reconstruction and analysis of spring rainfall over the southeastern U.S. for the past 1000 years. *Bulletin of the American Meteorological Society* 73: 1947–1961.

Stahle, D.W., Cleaveland, M.K. and Hehr, J.G. 1988 North Carolina climate changes reconstructed from tree rings: A.D. 372–1985. *Science* 240: 1517–1519.

Stallings, W.S. 1937 Some early papers on tree rings I: J. Kuechler. *Tree-Ring Bulletin* 3: 27–28.

Sternberg, R.S. and McGuire, R.H. 1990 Archaeomagnetic secular variation in the American Southwest, A.D. 700–1450. *In* Eighmy, J.L. and Sternberg, R.S., eds., *Archaeomagnetic Dating*. Tucson, Arizona, The University of Arizona Press: 199–225.

Stockton, C.W. 1975 Long-term streamflow records reconstructed from tree rings. *Papers of the Laboratory of Tree-Ring Research* 5. Tucson, Arizona, The University of Arizona Press.

Stockton, C.W. and Meko, D.M. 1975 A long-term history of drought occurrence in western United States as inferred from tree rings. *Weatherwise* 20: 245–249.

Stokes, M.A. and Smiley, T.L. 1968 *An Introduction to Tree-Ring Dating*. Chicago, University of Chicago Press.

Studhalter, R.A. 1955 Tree growth: I. some historical chapters. *The Botanical Review* 21: 1–72.

Stuiver, M. 1993 A note on single-year calibration of the radiocarbon time scale, A.D. 1510–1954. *In* Stuiver, M., Long, A. and Kra R.S., eds., Calibration 1993. *Radiocarbon* 35(1):67–72.

Stuiver, M. and Kra, R.S., eds, 1986 Proceedings of the Twelfth International Radiocarbon Conference - Trondheim, Norway. *Radiocarbon* 28(2B): Calibration Issue: 805–1030.

Stuiver, M., Long, A. and Kra, R.S., eds, 1993 Calibration 1993. *Radiocarbon* 35(1): 1–244.

Suess, H. 1970 Bristlecone-pine calibration of the radiocarbon time-scale 5200 B.C. to the present. *In* Olsson, I.U., ed., *Radiocarbon Variations and Absolute Chronology: Proceedings of the Twelfth Nobel Symposium*. Stockholm, Sweden, Almqvist and Wiksell: 303–309.

Swetnam, T.W. 1984 Peeled ponderosa pine trees: a record of inner bark utilization by Native Americans. *Journal of Ethnobiology* 4(2): 177–190.

_____1993 Fire history and climate change in giant sequoia groves. *Science* 262: 885–889.

Swetnam, T.W. and Betancourt, J.L. 1990 Fire - Southern Oscillation relations in the southwestern United States. *Science* 249: 1017–1020.

Switsur, V.R., Waterhouse, J.S., Field, E.M. and Carter, A.H.C. 1996 Climatic signals from stable isotopes in oak tree rings from East Anglia, Great Britain. *In* Dean, J.S., Meko, D.M. and Swetnam, T.W., eds., *Tree Rings, Environment and Humanity: Proceedings of the International Conference, Tucson, Arizona, 17–21 May 1994*. Tucson, Arizona, Radiocarbon: 637–645.

Tardif, J. 1996 Earlywood, latewood and total ring width of a ring-porous species (*Fraxinus nigra* Marsh.) in relation to climatic and hydrologic factors. *In* Dean, J.S., Meko, D.M. and Swetnam, T.W., eds., *Tree Rings, Environment and Humanity: Proceedings of the International Conference, Tucson, Arizona, 17–21 May 1994*. Tucson, Arizona, Radiocarbon: 315–324.

Taylor, R.E. 1987 *Radiocarbon Dating: An Archaeological Perspective*. Orlando, Florida, Academic Press.

Tercier, J., Orcel, A. and Orcel, C. 1996 Dendrochronological study of prehistoric archaeological sites in Switzerland. *In* Dean, J.S., Meko, D.M. and Swetnam, T.W., eds., *Tree Rings, Environment and Humanity: Proceedings of the International Conference, Tucson, Arizona, 17–21 May 1994*. Tucson, Arizona, Radiocarbon: 567–582.

Towner, R.H. 1992 Dating the Dinetah pueblitos: the tree-ring data. *In* Jacobson, L.A. and Piper, J.-E., eds., Interpreting the past: research with public participation. *Cultural Resource Series* 10. Santa Fe, New Mexico, USDI Bureau of Land Management: 55–71.

Van Deusen, P.C. and Reams, G.A. 1996 Bayesian procedures for reconstructing past climate. *In* Dean, J.S., Meko, D.M. and Swetnam, T.W., eds., *Tree Rings, Environment and Humanity: Proceedings of the International Conference, Tucson, Arizona, 17–21 May 1994*. Tucson, Arizona, Radiocarbon: 335–339.

Van West, C.R. 1994 Modeling prehistoric agricultural productivity in southwestern Colorado: a GIS approach. *Reports of Investigations* 67. Pullman, Washington, Department of Anthropology, Washington State University, Cortez, Colorado, Crow Canyon Archaeological Center.

Van West, C.R. and Altschul, J.H. 1994 Agricultural productivity and carrying capacity in the Tonto Basin. *In* Ciolek-Torrello, R. and Welch, J.R., eds., The Roosevelt Rural Sites Study, Vol 3: changing land use in the Tonto Basin. *Statistical Research Technical Series* 28. Tucson, Arizona, Statistical Research, Inc.: 361–435.

Weakly, H.E. 1940 Tree-rings as a record of precipitation in western Nebraska. *Tree-Ring Bulletin* 6: 18–19.

Webb, G.E. 1983 *Tree Rings and Telescopes: The Scientific Career of A.E. Douglass*. Tucson, Arizona, The University of Arizona Press.

Woodhouse, C.A. 1993 Tree-growth response to ENSO events in the central Colorado Front Range. *Physical Geography* 14: 417–435.

Wrobel, S. 1994 Timber supply for the Hanseatic town of Lübeck, North Germany. Paper presented at the International Conference on Tree Rings, Environment, and Humanity: Relationships and Processes, Tucson, Arizona, 17–21 May 1994.

Wroth, W. 1982 *Christian Images in Hispanic New Mexico: The Taylor Museum Collection of* Santos. Colorado Springs, Colorado, The Taylor Museum of the Colorado Springs Fine Art Center.

Chapter 3

Radiocarbon Dating

R. E. Taylor

ABSTRACT

This chapter reviews the basic elements of the radiocarbon (^{14}C) dating method and summarizes three generations of ^{14}C studies in archaeology. It considers in greater detail several major advances in ^{14}C research including the extension of the calibration of the ^{14}C time scale into the late Pleistocene, further detailed characterization of Holocene short-term perturbations (de Vries effects), and the development of accelerator mass spectrometry.

INTRODUCTION

Radiocarbon (^{14}C) dating, now in its fifth decade of general use, continues to be the most widely employed method of inferring chronometric age for late Pleistocene and Holocene age materials. An international conference held in 1990 and resulting volume, *Radiocarbon After Four Decades: An Interdisciplinary Perspective* (Taylor *et al.* 1992) summarized the major contributions that ^{14}C had made as a dating and biological and environmental tracer isotope over its first 40 years. The overall influence of the ^{14}C method is eloquently reflected in a statement nominating Willard F. Libby (1908–1980) for the 1960 Nobel Prize in chemistry: "Seldom has a single discovery in chemistry [^{14}C dating] had such an impact on the thinking in so many fields of human endeavor" (Nobel Foundation 1964).

R. E. TAYLOR • Radiocarbon Laboratory, Department of Anthropology, Institute of Geophysics and Planetary Physics, University of California, Riverside, California 92521 USA.

Chronometric Dating in Archaeology, edited by Taylor and Aitken.
Plenum Press, New York, 1997.

The influence of ^{14}C dating in archaeology was quickly recognized. Glyn Daniel equated the discovery of the ^{14}C method in the 20th century with the discovery of the antiquity of the human species in the 19th century (Daniel 1967:266). Grahame Clark (1970:38) pointed to ^{14}C dating as making a *world* prehistory possible by contributing the first world-wide chronometric time scale that transcended local, regional and continental boundaries. Lewis Binford expressed the view that the development of ^{14}C-based chronologies was responsible for refocusing the attention of archaeologists beginning in the early 1960s from "chronology building" to "theory building" (Gittens 1984: 238).

RADIOCARBON DATING MODEL

The natural production of ^{14}C is a secondary effect of cosmic-ray bombardment in the upper atmosphere (Fig. 3.1). Following production, it is rapidly oxidized—on a time scale from several hours to, at most, several days—to form $^{14}CO_2$. In this form, ^{14}C is distributed throughout the earth's atmosphere by stratospheric winds, becoming reasonably well-mixed by the time a ^{14}C-tagged CO_2 molecule reaches the planetary surface. Most ^{14}C—about 85%—is absorbed in the oceans, while about 1% becomes part of the terrestrial biosphere, primarily by means of the photosynthetic process and the distribution of carbon compounds through the chemically-complex pathways of the carbon cycle. Metabolic processes in living organisms maintain the ^{14}C content such biological systems in approximate equilibrium with atmospheric ^{14}C concentrations, i.e., while ^{14}C decays in living tissue, it is replaced through the ingestion of plant or animal tissue. Once metabolic processes cease, as at the death of an animal or plant, the amount of ^{14}C begins to decrease by radioactive decay—in the case of ^{14}C, by beta decay—at a rate measured by the ^{14}C half-life (Taylor 1987).

The *radiocarbon age* of a sample is based on a measurement of its residual ^{14}C content. For a ^{14}C age to be equivalent to its actual or calendar age at a reasonable level of precision, a set of primary assumptions needs to be satisfied. These assumptions are that: (1) the concentration of ^{14}C in each carbon reservoir has remained essentially constant over the ^{14}C time scale, (2) complete and rapid mixing of ^{14}C occurs throughout the various carbon reservoirs on a worldwide basis, (3) carbon isotope ratios in samples have not been altered except by ^{14}C decay since the death of an organism, (4) the half-life of ^{14}C is accurately known, and, (5) natural levels of ^{14}C can be measured to appropriate levels of accuracy and precision. Much of the history of the ^{14}C dating method, as it interfaces with archaeological applications, is composed, in large measure, of two types of efforts: first, the documentation of the stratigraphic or geomorphological relationship between a sample on which a ^{14}C age estimate is obtained and the archaeological object, feature or geological context for which

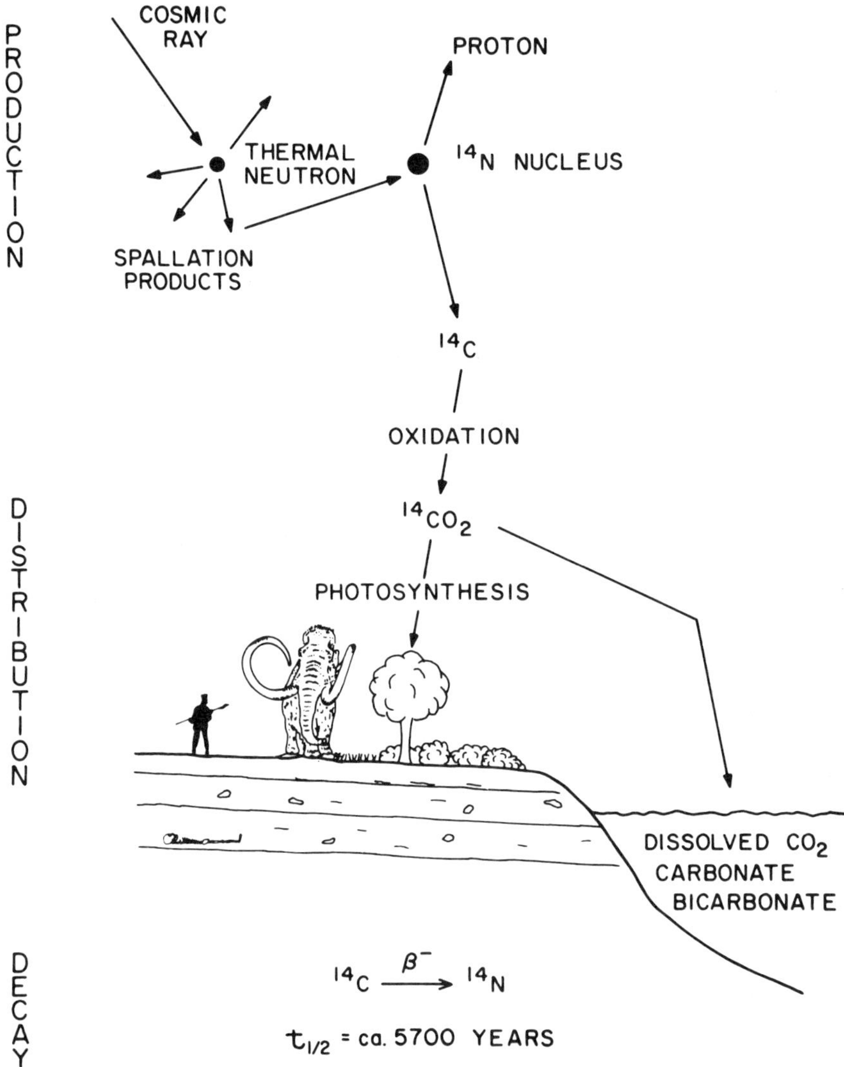

Figure 3.1. Radiocarbon dating model: production, distribution, and decay of ^{14}C. Taken from Taylor (1990: 500).

an age determination is desired and second, investigations designed to examine and compensate for the effects of violations of the primary assumptions as applied to specific sample types or portions of the carbon reservoirs.

Radiocarbon age estimates are generally expressed in terms of a set of characteristic parameters that define a *conventional radiocarbon age*. These parameters, introduced in the mid-1970s by Stuiver and Polach (1977) and now widely employed, include (1) the use of 5568 (±30) years as the defined ^{14}C half-life (8033 yr mean life) even though the actual half-life value is probably closer to 5730 (±40) years; (2) the direct or indirect use of one of the United States National Institute of Standards and Technology (formerly U.S. National Bureau of Standards [NBS])-distributed oxalic acid preparations as a contemporary or modern reference standard to define a "zero" ^{14}C age; (3) the use of A.D. 1950 as the zero point from which to count ^{14}C time; (4) to account for fractionation effects, a normalization of ^{14}C in all samples to a common $^{13}C/^{12}C$ ($\delta^{13}C$) value of −25.0‰, and (5), an assumption that ^{14}C in all reservoirs has remained constant over the ^{14}C time scale. In addition, each ^{14}C determination is expected to be accompanied by an expression that provides an estimate of the *experimental* or *analytical uncertainty*. Since statistical constraints associated with the measurement of ^{14}C concentrations in samples is usually the dominant component of the analytical uncertainty, this value is informally referred to as the "statistical error." This "±" term is suffixed to all appropriately documented ^{14}C age estimates and is typically expressed as ± *one standard deviation* ($\pm 1\sigma$).

For samples from some carbon reservoirs, conventional contemporary standards may not define a zero ^{14}C age. A *reservoir corrected radiocarbon age* can sometimes be calculated by documenting the apparent age exhibited in control samples and correcting for the observed deviation. Reservoir effects are most often observed in samples from fresh water lakes and marine environments. A *calibrated radiocarbon age* takes into consideration the fact that ^{14}C activity in living organisms has not remained constant over the ^{14}C time scale because of changes in ^{14}C production rates or parameters of the carbon cycle. The study of the various factors responsible for the variability in ^{14}C production rates and changes in the world-wide distribution of ^{14}C in various carbon reservoirs over the Holocene has occupied the attention of a number of researchers for more than two decades. The various issues raised by the nature of the variability over time in the ^{14}C time scale—with the documentation of this variability now extended into the late Pleistocene—will be discussed in greater detail in the next two sections.

In the current nomenclature of the journal *Radiocarbon*, "^{14}C years BP" is expressed only as "BP" with the "^{14}C years" implied (e.g. 2510±50 BP). Calibrated ages are expressed with only the "cal" designation attached (e.g., cal AD 1520, 3720 cal BC) with the "years" implied. As M. Stuiver has previously noted (M. Stuiver, personal communication), calibrated years are, within counting errors, *solar years*. If one wishes to use a strictly-defined terminology, calibrated years are not calendar years, since the length of a calendar year varies from calendar system to calendar system. The journal *American Antiquity* adopted the nomenclature of *Radiocarbon* except for punctuation (B.P. rather than BP). In the early 1970s, the journal *Antiquity* adopted a nomenclature which distinguished conventional (uncalibrated) and calibrated ^{14}C values whereby "bp" and "ad/bc" are employed to designate conventional ^{14}C values while "BP" and "AD/BC" are used to designate calibrated ^{14}C values (Daniel 1972).

The ^{14}C time scale now extends from about 300 years to between 40,000 and 60,000 years. The limitations on the young end of the ^{14}C time scale are a consequence of three factors: first, recent significant variability in ^{14}C production rates associated with modulations in ^{14}C production, primarily due to rapid changes in solar magnetic intensity in the 17th century; second, the effect of the combustion of large quantities of fossil fuels beginning in the late 19th century (*Suess* or *industrial effect*); and, third, the production of artificial ^{14}C ("bomb" ^{14}C) as a result of the detonation of nuclear and thermonuclear devices in the atmosphere particularly during the period between 1955 and 1963 (*atomic bomb*, *nuclear* or *Libby effect*). As a result of the complex interplay of these factors, it is not currently possible, except under very special circumstances, to assign unambiguous ages to materials living less than 300 years by the use of the ^{14}C method. One exception is the period of rapid increase in ^{14}C activity produced by the testing of nuclear and thermonuclear weapons in the atmosphere. "Bomb" ^{14}C increased dramatically beginning in the late 1950s, peaking in 1963 almost at double pre-bomb contemporary ^{14}C reference level (Levin *et al.* 1992). An international agreement in 1963 halted atmospheric nuclear testing by most nations. This allowed ^{14}C to begin the process of reestablishing a new atmospheric ^{14}C equilibrium. Because of the rapid change of ^{14}C in such a short period, it is possible to assign an "age" with a 95% confidence interval of ±3–5 years for materials growing in 1963–64 and two possible ages on materials growing during the period of rapid rise and slower decay.

The maximum ^{14}C ages that can be inferred depend on characteristics of different laboratory instrumentation and experimental configurations—e.g., counter size, length of counting, background values—and, to some degree, the amount of sample available for analysis. Employing relatively large sample sizes, typically not available from archaeological contexts, a few laboratories have the capability to obtain finite ages up to about 70,000 years. With isotopic enrichment—again using relatively large (> 15 grams of carbon) amounts of sample material—ages up to 75,000 years have been reported on a small number of samples (Grootes *et al.* 1975; Stuiver *et al.* 1978; Erlenkeuser 1979). There are efforts now underway to exploit accelerator mass spectrometry (AMS) technology to extend the ^{14}C time scale out to as much as 90,000 years using sample weights of less than a gram of carbon. The status of that effort will be briefly noted in the section discussing AMS technology.

FIRST AND SECOND GENERATION RADIOCARBON STUDIES

Over its four-decade history, the development of ^{14}C dating can be divided into three phases distinguished partly by the type of detection technology employed and, in part, on understandings concerning the relationship between radiocarbon and "real" or calendric time. The first generation of archaeological ^{14}C applications, the "First Radiocarbon Revolution"—at least for archaeology—(Renfrew 1973: 48–68), began with the appearance of the first ^{14}C "date list" (Arnold and Libby 1950; 1951). Second generation studies began with the appreciation of the need to calibrate ^{14}C data. The result was the "Second Radiocarbon Revolution" (Renfrew 1973). The "Third Radiocarbon Revolution" in ^{14}C studies was ushered in by the advent of accelerator mass spectrometry in the late 1970s (Muller 1977; Linick *et al.* 1989).

First Generation (1950–1970)

The first suite of archaeologically-relevant ^{14}C dates produced by Libby and his co-workers during the first decade of ^{14}C studies revised views concerning the antiquity of agriculture and sedentary village societies in Southwestern Asia documenting their appearance in the 7th-9th millennium B.C. in this region as well as in several areas of Western Europe and Mesoamerica several millennia later. This initial corpus of ^{14}C data contained age estimates at variance with long-held views of some archaeologists—particularly of the older generation of archaeologists in central and eastern Europe (e.g., Neustupny 1970). As a result, some archaeologists initially questioned the overall validity of the ^{14}C method—at least for some periods and in some regions. However, the rapidly mounting evidence of the general correctness of the ^{14}C model in broad outline changed discussions within the professional archaeological community from a question of validity to questions of the accuracy of ^{14}C values from specific archaeological or geological contexts, geochemical environments or sample types (e.g., Broecker and Kulp 1956). Since the late 1950s, objections to the *overall* accuracy of the method have been based almost exclusively on quasi-theological grounds most often—but not exclusively (e.g., Cremo and Thompson 1993:764–794)—expressed within a European and American Protestant fundamentalist, young-earth, "creationist" framework (e.g., Brown 1983, 1986; Aardsma 1991).

Second Generation (1970–1980)

The first empirical test of the validity of the assumption of an equilibrium between ^{14}C production and decay was the analysis of the ^{14}C activity of a suite of assumed known-age samples ranging in age from about 1400 to 4600 years. The results of these measurements were presented as the first "Curve of Knowns" (Arnold and Libby 1949). The reasonable agreement of the measured ^{14}C values with the expected values to about ±10% supported the initial assumption of constant ^{14}C concentration in living organisms over the recent past. Increases in measurement precision resulting from developments in counting technology began to identify apparent discrepancies between some third-millennium BC (mostly Egyptian) "known-age" and ^{14}C-derived ages of samples. This stimulated interest in a more systematic investigation of apparent anomalies (Libby 1963).

In the early 1960s, data began to appear which confirmed the suggestion of the pioneering Dutch researcher, Hessel de Vries, that "radiocarbon years" and solar years should not be assumed to be equivalent values (de Vries 1958). For the next 30 years, the pursuit of a more accurate and detailed understanding of the character of the various components of what came to be known as *secular variation* phenomena in natural ^{14}C concentrations would occupy the attention of an increasing number of researchers. The implications of the ^{14}C deviations in geophysical, solar physics, atmospheric chemistry, climatological, as well as in historical and archaeological studies quickly became apparent.

In this context, secular variation refers to any systematic variability in the ^{14}C time spectrum other than that caused by ^{14}C decay. Throughout the 1960s, using primarily dendrochronologically [tree-ring]-dated wood to provide known-age controls, ^{14}C secular variation perturbations were documented further and further back into middle and early Holocene (Willis *et al.* 1960; Stuiver and Suess 1966). By the end of the decade, ^{14}C/tree-ring data reached back about 7,000 years (Suess 1970; Ralph *et al.* 1973). The data appeared, at least to some investigators, to exhibit two types of periodicity: a *major trend*, with what initially appeared to be a "sine wave" characteristic, and a series of medium- and short-term, higher frequency components of various durations and apparent periodicities. These short-term variations have been informally referred to variously as "wriggles," "wiggles," "kinks", "windings," or "warps." Since the mid-1960s, they have come to be more formally known as *de Vries effects*.

The principal documentation of the various types of variations in the ^{14}C time scale was initially derived from ^{14}C determinations carried out, most typically, on dendrochronologically-dated wood including samples obtained from the giant California sequoia (*Sequoia gigantea*), the European oak (*Quercus* sp.) and, for the oldest portions of the time series, from the bristlecone pine (*Pinus longaeva* [originally known as *Pinus aristata*]). Using this dendrochronological/^{14}C data base, by the early 1970s the amount of correction required to bring middle and late Holocene ^{14}C values into approximate alignment with solar time varied from a minimum of about -250 years in the middle of the first millennium AD, to a maximum of about +800 years in the fifth millennium BC Figure 3.2 is one representation of the degree of deviation of ^{14}C time from solar time as documented by tree-ring data (Klein *et al.* 1982).

In the early 1970s, Renfrew (1973) pointed to the role of calibration as the basis of the "Second Radiocarbon Revolution:" a reevaluation of traditional views of the timing of the introduction of important innovations in prehistoric Europe. For example, calibrated ^{14}C age estimates played a major role in revisions in traditional understandings of the factors involved in the origins of

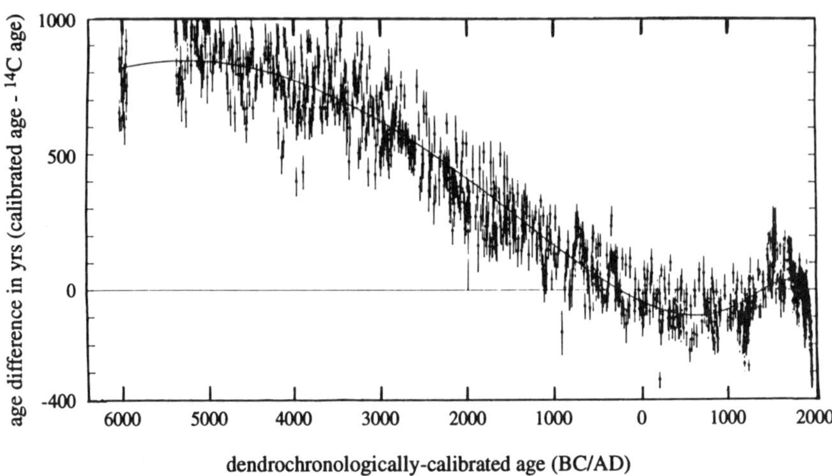

Figure 3.2. Characterization of Middle and Late Holocene deviations of ^{14}C from dendrochronological-based ages: 0–8000 years. Taken from Figure 2.8 in Taylor (1987) based on Figure 1 in Klein *et al.* (1982).

several important archaeological features of "European barbarism"—the megalithic chamber tombs, European metallurgy, and Stonehenge in England. Since the 1930s, the generally accepted view saw the first two developments as having their ultimate origins in the Near East while Stonehenge reflected the inspiration of Mycenaean Greece. According to this perspective, European advances in areas such as monumental architecture and metallurgy were initiated or stimulated by diffusion of knowledge initially from Egypt and southern Mesopotamia through the eastern Mediterranean and Aegean and hence to southeastern, east central and then western Europe. Renfrew insisted that diffusionist views were seriously undermined by the calibrated ^{14}C values which appeared to place the megalithic tomb structures earlier than the Egyptian pyramids and copper metallurgy in the Balkans earlier than in Greece. Also, he noted that Stonehenge appeared to have been essentially completed before Mycenean civilization in Greece began.

In place of diffusionist explanations for these cultural innovations, Renfrew, and those influenced by him, emphasized local factors such as increasing population pressures, trade and exchange systems, as well as the manner in which social organization interrelated with developing indigenous economies and technologies (Renfrew 1973: 248). Atkinson (1975: 174) characterized the impact of both conventional and calibrated ^{14}C data on British prehistory as "radical . . . therapy" for the "progressive disease of 'invasionism'".

Because calibrated ^{14}C data are often cited and highlighted in many current discussions concerning ^{14}C values, the next section will include a brief review of recent developments in calibration studies.

THIRD GENERATION STUDIES: RECENT DEVELOPMENTS

Several recent technical and methodological advances have provided contexts for a series of significant applications of the ^{14}C method in archaeological studies. These include the extension of the calibrated ^{14}C time scale into the late Pleistocene, a more detailed characterization of Holocene short-term perturbations (de Vries effects), and the development of accelerator mass spectrometry (AMS) technology. The extension of the calibration of the ^{14}C time scale beyond that provided with tree ring data was accomplished by the use of AMS-based ^{14}C and U-series measurements on marine coral samples.

Extending the Calibration of the ^{14}C Time Scale

Comparisons of ^{14}C and dendrochronological data based on Irish and German oaks, Douglas fir, sequoia and bristlecone pine now document about 9,800 years of dendrochronological time with 20-yr [bidecadal] time-ring segments (Stuiver, Long, and Kra 1993). The ^{14}C measurements comprising these data sets are characterized as "high-precision," referring to carefully measured counting uncertainties typically at the $\pm 1\sigma$ level of < 20 years ($\pm 2.5‰$) for the ^{14}C values used to provide the calibration data. The validity of the stated uncertainties has been extensively examined by detailed interlaboratory comparisons by a number of the laboratories producing the calibration data (Scott, Long and Kra 1990).

The dendrochronologically-based calibration record has been provisionally extended to 11,390 cal BP with the interlinking of the German oak and pine dendrochronological sequences (Kromer and Becker 1993; Becker 1993). The earlier component of the calibration data base is provisional because it currently includes what apparently is a relatively short (i.e., several decades) but still "floating" tree-ring segment of uncertain length. Future revisions in the overlap correlations are possible. Thus, for the period from 9840 to 11,440 cal BP—in radiocarbon time back to about 10,050 BP—calibrated values are not, as yet, confidently and precisely fixed in time. For the pre-10,050 BP late Pleistocene period, paired uranium/thorium ($^{234}U/^{230}Th$) and ^{14}C samples from cores drilled into coral formations provide the data on which a late Pleistocene ^{14}C calibration curve has been extended to 21,950 cal BP (as expressed in ^{14}C time to 18,400 BP) in 50 year increments. A half-life based offset is built into most ^{14}C time/calibrated time comparisons since conventionally expressed ^{14}C values are calculated on the "Libby" half-life of 5568±30 years which is about 3% below the most likely ^{14}C half-life value.

With the extension of the ^{14}C calibration framework using the uranium-series data on corals (Bard *et al.* 1993a, 1993b; Edwards *et al.* 1993), it now appears that the "sine-wave"-like characterization of the Holocene ^{14}C calibration curve was an artifact of the limited time frame documented by the original

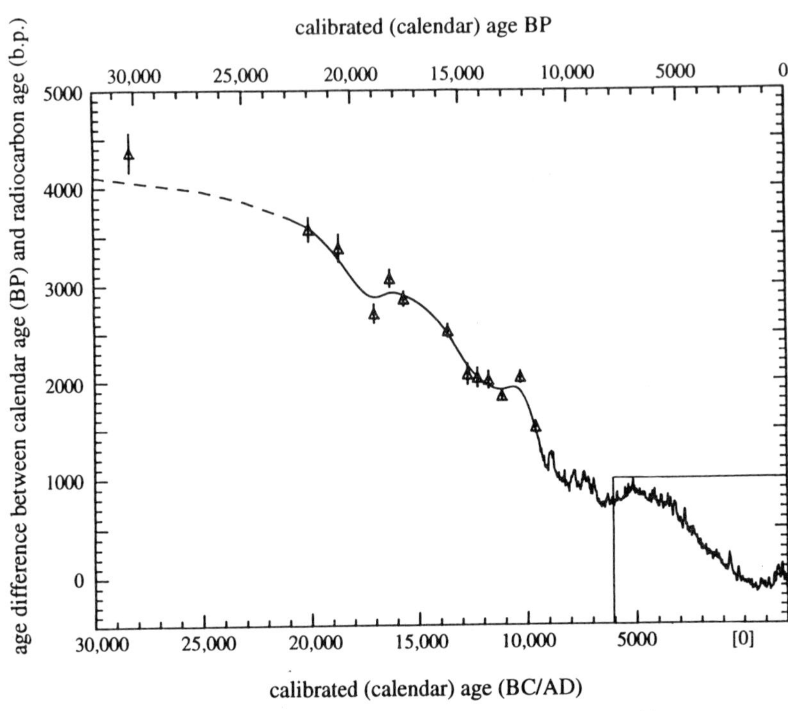

Figure 3.3. Characterization of Late Pleistocene and Holocene deviation of ^{14}C from dendrochronological- and uranium-series-based ages: 0 to 30,000 years. Taken from Figure 2 in Taylor *et al.* (1996), based on Figure 1 in Stuiver and Braziunas (1993).

tree-ring/^{14}C data. Figure 3.3 represents a plot of the off-set between ^{14}C and assumed "true" ages for the last 30,000 years based on the current combined dendrochronological/^{14}C and coral uranium-series/^{14}C data (Taylor *et al.* 1996). The rectangle in the right hand corner of Figure 3.3 represents that portion of the time scale represented in Figure 3.2. Based on the expanded calibration data, it now appears that the long-term secular variation ^{14}C anomaly over about the last 30,000 years can be characterized as representing a slow-decay function on which has been superimposed middle- and short-term perturbations.

Age estimates obtained from ^{14}C and other Quaternary dating methods applied to samples obtained from associated stratigraphic contexts are, to some degree, inconsistent with regard to indications of the magnitude of the ^{14}C age offsets for the period before 25,000 years. For example, comparisons between ^{14}C values (adjusted by 3% to take into consideration the most likely ^{14}C half-life) and thermoluminescence age estimates on materials from hearths at Lake Mungo, Australia suggest deviations in the range of between 3,500 and 5,000 years between 27,000 and 31,000 years (Bell 1991). Studies of variations in the intensity of the earth's dipole magnetic field, a major cause of the long-term ^{14}C secular variation trend, as well as comparisons of precisely determined ^{14}C and associated $^{40}Ar/^{39}Ar$ values from volcanic deposits suggested somewhat less age offsets for this period. However, the geomagnetic data suggest an increasing ^{14}C/solar time offset in the range of 1,500 to 2,700 years between 25,000 and 40,000 years but predicts there will be good agreement between ^{14}C and solar time at about 45,000–50,000 years (Mazaud *et al.* 1992; Southon *et al.* 1995).

In most cases, bidecadal-based ^{14}C/tree-ring data provide the most appropriate basis for the calibration of most of the terrestrial samples—e.g., wood and charcoal—routinely recovered from archaeological sites. Such a data base "averages out" the high-frequency fine structure in the ^{14}C time spectrum. For the ideal "match" with bidecadal-based calibration data, the same 20-year segment used for calibration should be matched in the wood or charcoal sample used for the determination of ^{14}C age. Also, the sample should contain an equal amount of carbon from each year within the 20-year time span. While this ideal situation rarely occurs, for most species of wood, a range of 10–30 years of wood growth would probably encompass the vast majority of wood and charcoal samples recovered from most archaeological sites on which decay-counting ^{14}C determinations are made.

For samples formed during intervals of a decade or less, a decadal-or sub-decadal calibration data base, which reflects more precisely the fine structure of ^{14}C variability, is potentially a more appropriate choice as the calibration data base. Situations where this would be particularly advisable would be those with samples with very short (i.e., a few months to a few weeks) annual growth periods such as some cereal grains, and for microsamples of wood/charcoal (< 10 mg of carbon) using AMS-based measurements. Under these conditions, it would be likely for plant tissue to represent less than 10-year growth increments. For those samples composed of material spanning *more* than 30 years, it would be more accurate to calibrate with the equivalent of a moving average of the calibration values in order to take into consideration the time span represented in the sample.

For non-terrestrial, aquatic samples, e.g., shells from oceans, estuaries or lakes, and a small number of terrestrial samples, calibration is a more complex process involving considerations that extend beyond the calibration data base. These extended considerations derive from the possibility that some samples may not have been formed in isotopic equilibrium with atmospheric CO_2, as are the tree-rings which form the primary calibration data base. In most coastal marine environments, this is primarily due to the effect of oceanic "upwelling" in which water from the deeper parts of the ocean is periodically brought to the surface and mixed with surface ocean water. As a result, the ^{14}C concentration in the carbonates of the surface waters is depressed and the marine shells drawing on these carbonates exhibit apparent ^{14}C ages. In such cases, before a calibration operation can be performed, it is first necessary to determine a ^{14}C reservoir effect or apparent age offset for the specific region from which the sample is derived (Stuiver and Braziunas 1993).

Such reservoir age offsets can also occur for terrestrial samples growing in special environments. Documented examples include situations where plants gain a significant percentage of their carbon from CO_2 dissolved in fresh water springs or small lakes (e.g., Long and Miller 1981:192; Kaufman 1980) and plants growing adjacent to active volcanic gas vents (Saupe *et al.* 1980; Bruns *et al.* 1980). Other possible reservoir effects may be associated with terrestrial materials growing in arid regions adjacent to large bodies of water with depleted ^{14}C activities and consistent wind patterns (e.g., the Salton Sea in southern California or the Dead Sea in Palestine) or desert coastal areas adjacent to marine zones exhibiting significant upwelling and winds constantly blowing landward. Whether the "long" and "short" ^{14}C time scales that Rowe (1965) suggested are present in the suite of ^{14}C values from some Peruvian archaeological sites reflect such localized terrestrial reservoir condition or can be explained by other means is still unclear.

Detailing Holocene de Vries Effects

A fuller rendering of the entire Holocene ^{14}C time scale permits researchers to review more precisely the timing and characteristics of the de Vries "wiggles" over the last ten millennia. Figure 3.4 plots the series of defined Holocene "time warps" reflecting the time ranges of the de Vries effect perturbations in the calibration curve (Taylor *et al.* 1996: Fig. 3A and 3B). Figure 3.4A represents 0 to 5000 BP and Figure 3.4B represents the 5000 to 10,000 BP period in ^{14}C years. The inherent uncertainties and fluctuations in the calibration curve cause discrete cal ages to broaden into ranges, even when, as in Figures 3.4A and 3.4B, the ^{14}C ages are plotted with a hypothetical zero variance. Thus, ^{14}C age determinations deriving from time periods with larger calibration range values will be inherently less precise. For example, on the average, calibrated age values for the 8000–10,000 BP period are inherently much less precise than those in the 0–2500 BP period.

In Figure 3.4A and 3.4B, 12 major and 5 intermediate de Vries effect perturbations are identified. Major de Vries effects have been defined as warps exceeding 250 cal years; intermediate de Vries effects warps exhibit ranges in excess of 140 cal yrs, and minor de Vries effects are those with ranges of less than 140 cal yr. The 17 major and intermediate de Vries perturbations have been assigned roman numeral and letter combinations. Roman numerals identify the ^{14}C millennium, i.e., I = 0 to 1000 BP, II = 1000 to 2000 BP, while lower case letters identify the perturbation in chronological order within each ^{14}C millennial period. Table 3.1 illustrates the effect of calibration assuming a ±40 yr 1σ standard deviation and using a ±2σ calibrated range for a series of

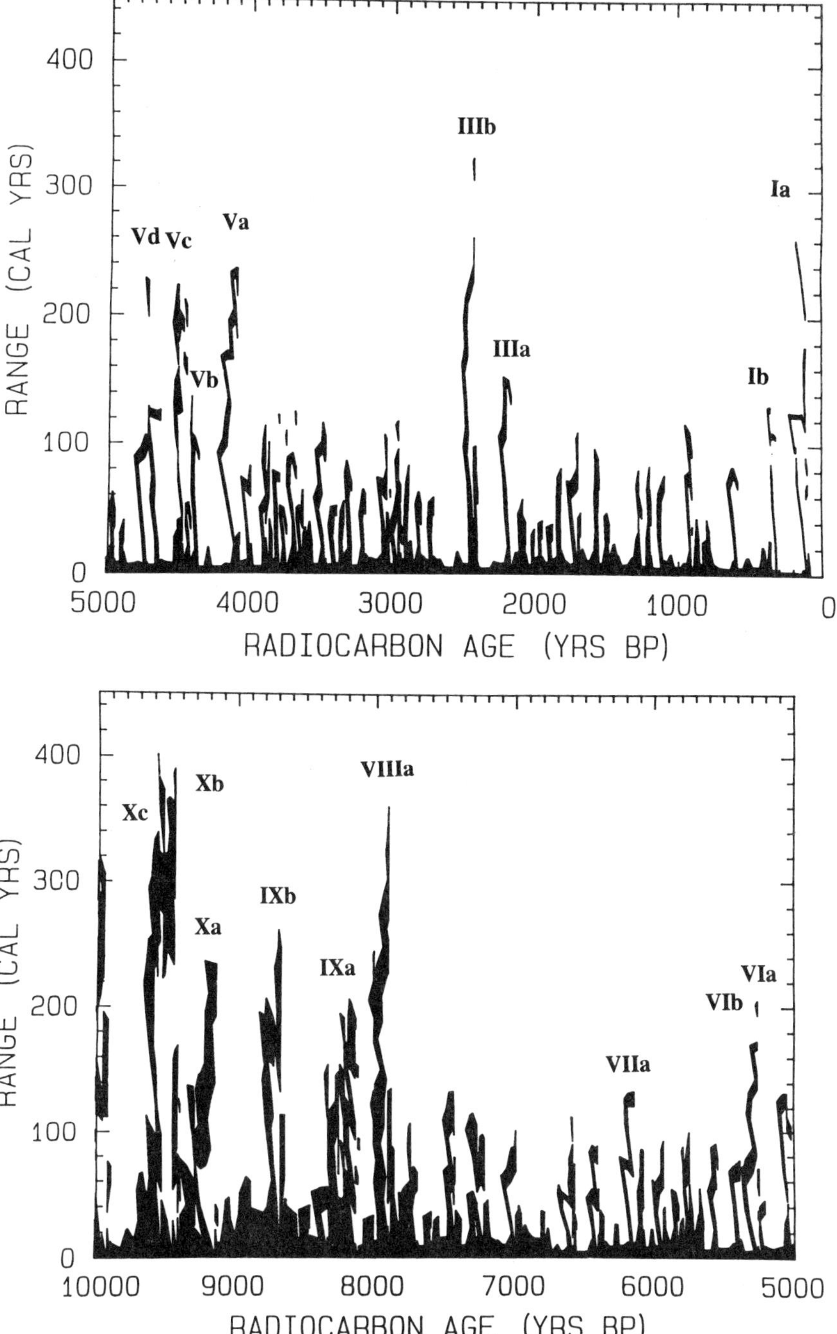

Figure 3.4. Holocene ^{14}C ranges in cal yr obtained from the calibration of conventional ^{14}C ages from Taylor *et al.* (1996) based on data from Stuiver and Reimer (1993:Figs 3A-3D). Figure 3.4A represents 0–5000 BP and Figure 3.4B represents 5000–10,000 BP. Ranges produced for an ideal hypothetical case with zero ^{14}C sample standard deviation. The youngest cal age obtained for each ^{14}C was set at zero. The sample was assumed to have been formed during a 20-yr or shorter interval.

Table 3.1. Characteristics and Effects of Major and Intermediate Holocene and Terminal Pleistocene de Vries Effects on Selected ^{14}C Values[a]

Perturbation Designation[a]	Conventional ^{14}C age (approx. mid point; ^{14}C BP)	$\pm 2\sigma$ Calibrated age range (cal BP)	$\pm 2\sigma$ Calibrated age range (cal AD/BC)	Length of Range Interval
Ia	150	0 - 285	AD 1665-1955	285
Ib	350	300-500	AD 1450-1650	200
II		[all spans less than 140 years]		
IIIa	2220	2120-2335	170-385 BC	215
IIIb	2470	2355-2730	405-780 BC	375
IV		[all spans less than 140 years]		
Va	4150	4530-4830	2580-2880 BC	300
Vb	4400	4860-5050	2910-3105 BC	350
		5190-5210	3245-3265 BC	
Vc	4500	4985-5300	3035-3350 BC	315
Vd	4730	5320-5585	3370-3635 BC	265
VIa	5070	5725-5915	3775-3965 BC	190
VIb	5300	5940-6190	3990-4240 BC	250
VIIa	6180	6925-7175	4980-5230 BC	250
VIIIa	7940	8555-8960	6605-7010 BC	405
IXa	8180	8985-9250	7035-7305 BC	265
IXb	8750	9535-9885	7585-7940 BC	350
Xa	9240	10040-10355	8090-8405 BC	315
Xb	9600	10950-10475	8525-9000 BC	475
Xc	10100	11090-11185	9140-9235 BC	975
		11195-12065	9250-10115 BC	

[a] Taken from Taylor *et al.* 1985: Table 2.
[b] Other designations of major perturbations: Ia = "Maunder" (Eddy 1976), II = "Spörer" (Eddy 1976); IIIb = "Hallstattzeit" (Damon and Jirikowic 1992).

hypothetical samples. In each case, the hypothetical conventional ^{14}C age was located at the midpoint of each of the 17 major and intermediate de Vries ^{14}C time warps.

Accelerator Mass Spectrometry

From the initiation of ^{14}C studies until the late 1970s, the basis of inferring ^{14}C concentrations and, therefore the ^{14}C age of samples, employed exclusively *decay counting* technology. In decay counting, isotopic concentrations are measured by counting decay events in an ionization or scintillation detector and comparing the count rate observed in an unknown-age sample to that exhibited by appropriate standards under a common set of experimental conditions. For ^{14}C, this involves counting beta particles, i.e., negatively charged electrons emitted from the ^{14}C nucleus. In decay counting a relatively small fraction of the ^{14}C atoms present in a carbon sample are actually measured during the course of measurement. While there are approximately 5.9×10^{10} atoms of ^{14}C in 1 gram of modern "pre-bomb" carbon, on the average, over a l-minute period, less than 15 of these atoms will decay and be available for detection. In large part, it was this consideration that gave impetus to efforts to develop *direct* or *ion counting* technology using a form of mass spectrometry.

Mass spectrometers take advantage of the differences in mass of different isotopes to detect and measure their relative concentrations. The process of measurement requires that the sample atoms be ionized by stripping off or adding to the electrons on the outer "shells" of the atoms. The atom, now in the form of an ion, can then be influenced by magnetic fields while in motion. This property permits ions to be accelerated in a vacuum. When such acceleration occurs, the trajectories of these particles can be deflected when they are passed through a magnetic field of appropriate strength. The degree of deflection in such a magnetic field can be used to measure the relative concentration of isotopes of different masses.

As early as 1970, Oeschger and his co-workers noted the great increase in sensitivity that could be obtained with ion counting for ^{14}C applications using mass spectrometric methods, especially if combined with isotopic enrichment (Oeschger *et al.* 1970: 487–488). Unfortunately, throughout the 1970s, experiments using a conventional, low-energy (several thousand electron volt acceleration) mass spectrometer were frustrated because of the extremely low natural ^{14}C concentrations ($^{14}C/^{12}C$=ca. 10^{-12}) and because ^{14}N and stable molecular ions with similar charge-to-mass ratios as ^{14}C, e.g., ^{13}CH or $^{12}CH_2$—could not be sufficiently eliminated from the mass spectra. Because of this, relatively high backgrounds could not be suppressed sufficiently for natural ^{14}C measurements (Anbar 1978; Wilson 1979).

In the late 1970s, this problem was overcome by accelerating sample atoms, in the form of ions, to much higher energies (several million electron volt acceleration) in particle accelerators. Initially, the term high energy mass spectrometry (HEMS) was employed to describe this technology. Currently, the term *accelerator mass spectrometry* (AMS) is typically used, focusing on the linkage of particle accelerator and mass spectrometry technologies.

Two types of AMS systems have been employed for direct or ion counting ^{14}C measurements: cyclotrons and tandem accelerators. The basic concept behind the cyclotron-based AMS approach was briefly explored during experiments conducted just before World War II by the late Nobel laureate Luis Alvarez, using the 60-inch Berkeley cyclotron (Alvarez 1981). This approach was employed in the late 1970s by UC Berkeley physicist Richard Muller (Muller 1977). In cyclotrons, high energies are imparted to particles by accelerating ions through two semi-circular high-voltage electrodes within a magnetic field. An alternating accelerating voltage is applied between the electrodes and repetitive acceleration continues until the particles reach a sufficient energy to move to the edge of the magnet, where a beam can be extracted.

An important characteristic of the cyclotron is that magnetic separation of different ions takes place simultaneously with acceleration; i.e., the process of acceleration in the cyclotron itself acts as a charge-to-mass ratio filter. For example, when the cyclotron frequency is tuned to accelerate ^{14}C, ideally the only other ion present would be ^{14}N. Other ions with the wrong charge-to-mass ratio should quickly drop out of phase and are lost from the ion beam. One means of removing most of the ^{14}N from the beam is to use a range-separation method. This method takes advantage of the fact that the distance traveled by ^{14}N in a solid or gas is about 30% less than that of ^{14}C. A gas cell or metal foil placed in the beam line is used to discriminate against ^{14}N. The ^{14}C ions are detected by an ionization chamber and a solid-state device to obtain the total energy and energy loss of the particles respectively (Mast and Muller 1980). An alternate approach accelerated negative ions to take advantage of the fact that ^{14}N either does not form negative ions or, if formed, they have very short lives (Bertsche 1989).

The first published AMS-based ^{14}C determination on an archaeologically-related sample was obtained using the 88-inch (224-cm) cyclotron at the University of California Lawrence Berkeley Laboratory [LBL] (Muller *et al.* 1978). Throughout the 1980s, research was undertaken in Muller's LBL group in an attempt to develop the potential capabilities of a cyclotron-based system to obtain AMS ^{14}C measurements focused on the development of a smaller, relatively low energy (40-keV) "cyclotrino" using an external ion source. Unfortunately, their studies identified several major difficulties which frustrated the use of such a technology for routine work in ^{14}C dating (Welch *et al.* 1984; Bertsche *et al.* 1987; Bertsche 1989). However, another laboratory has reported more encouraging results (Chen *et al.* 1995).

The second type of AMS system employs an electrostatic tandem accelerator. Typically, TAMS (tandem accelerator mass spectrometry) is used to refer to this type of AMS system. "Tandem" here refers to the fact that particle acceleration in electrostatic systems is accomplished in a two-step "pull-push" process. For example, negative ions can be accelerated to a positive terminal ("pull") and then "stripped," i.e., electrons removed from the outer shells, to produce a positive ion which is then accelerated away from the terminal ("push"). In 1977, two groups of physicists simultaneously published suggestions of how a tandem accelerator could be employed to measure ^{14}C and other cosmogenic isotopes at natural concentrations using milligram amounts of sample (Nelson *et al.* 1977; Bennett *et al.* 1977; 1978). This approach proved to be a practical AMS technology for a whole range of rare, cosmogenic isotopes including ^{14}C, and, to date, almost all routine AMS ^{14}C determinations have employed a TAMS-based approach.

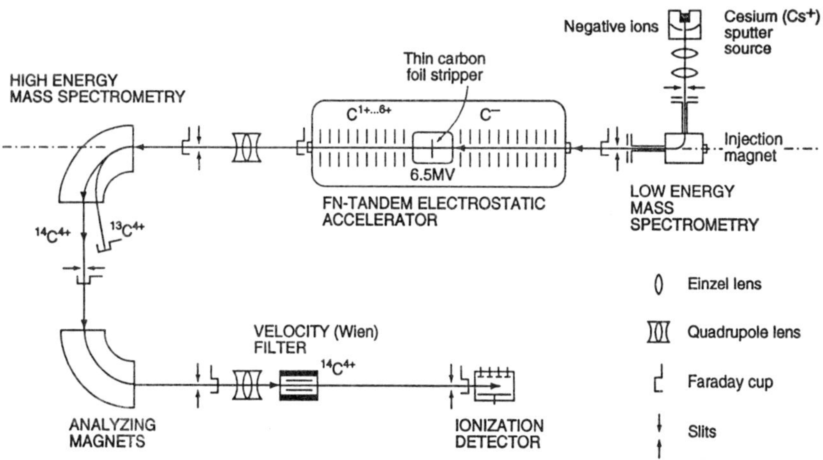

Figure 3.5. Schematic of major elements of a TAMS-type AMS system at the University of California Lawrence Livermore National Laboratory (LLNL). Figure prepared with the generous assistance of Dr. John R. Southon, LLNL.

The great advantage of TAMS instruments is a feature already noted: ^{14}N does not form negative ions or does not form negative ions that live long enough to pass through the accelerator to the detector. In addition, the "stripping" that takes place in a tandem accelerator system ensures that no molecules survive in their transit through the accelerator. This process removes most of the sources of the background experienced in the initial conventional mass spectrometry experiments with ^{14}C.

Figure 3.5 is a simplified schematic representation of a TAMS-type AMS system. Typically, an ion source produces ions by cesium bombardment of the surface of a target. In most AMS laboratories operating currently, the target consists of catalytically-condensed graphitic carbon which has been prepared from CO_2 obtained from the combustion or acidification of a sample (Vogel *et al.* 1984; 1987). The ions produced by cesium bombardment are accelerated and passed through an analyzing magnet at the low energy end of the accelerator. This first magnet operates both as a conventional mass spectrometer and as an injection magnet directing the ions into the accelerator as C^-.

As previously noted, the accelerator functions not only to accelerate the negative ions to several million electron volts, but also, in the "stripping process", dissociates all molecular species. On exiting the accelerator the carbon beam is in the C^{4+} charge state. In the system illustrated in Figure 3.5, the ^{13}C beam current is measured following the first high energy analyzing magnet. After analyses in a second magnet, the ^{14}C is measured in an ionization chamber and solid-state detector. Measurements are obtained as ratios of

$^{13}C/^{12}C$ and/or $^{14}C/^{13}C$ and known standards are used for normalization. Technical features of the various types of AMS systems have been discussed in a number of review papers (e.g., Gove 1992).

Three advantages of AMS technology in the measurement of ^{14}C were anticipated as a result of the greatly enhanced detection efficiency. First, major reductions in sample sizes would be possible—from gram amounts of carbon to milligram amounts and, with additional efforts, to the level of less than 100 micrograms. Second, major reductions in counting times would be possible. Reductions from several days for conventional systems and even weeks and months with micro- and mini-counting systems (e.g., Harbottle *et al.* 1979; Sayre *et al.* 1981; Otlet *et al.* 1983) could be achieved with several minutes of counting for AMS systems to achieve ±1% counting statistics. Finally, it was anticipated that significant increases in the applicable dating time frame—from the currently routine 40,000/50,000 years out to as much as 100,000 years (Muller 1977).

The first two of the three originally-anticipated benefits of AMS technology—major reductions in sample size and counting times—have been fully realized over the last decade (Taylor *et al.* 1984; Hedges and Gowlett 1986; Taylor 1991). For both sample sizes and counting times, order-of-magnitude reductions have been made possible on a routine basis. However, the projected third advance has not, as yet, occurred due to the inability, at present, to exclude microcontamination of samples primarily with modern carbon introduced during sample preparation. The source of a significant portion of this contamination results from the current requirement in most laboratories that samples must be converted to graphitic carbon for use in the ion source of an AMS system. Parts per million of modern carbon contamination translates into background levels which generally limit the maximum ages that can be resolved to between 40,000 and 50,000 years. One laboratory has developed a CO_2 gas source but reports similar background values (Bronk and Hedges 1987).

The nature of the problem is illustrated by experiments by the University of Washington AMS group. An AMS ^{14}C measurement of 69,030±1,700 BP was obtained on a specially prepared sample of geological graphite. However, graphite prepared from CO_2 obtained from a sample of marble, which, like geologic graphite, should exhibit no ^{14}C activity due to its great geologic age, yielded an apparent age of 47,960±670 BP (Schmidt *et al.* 1987). A study carried out jointly by the University of California/Lawrence Livermore National Laboratory AMS Laboratory and the UC Riverside ^{14}C Laboratory obtained an average apparent age of 64,460±3200 BP on samples of geologic graphite and an average (N=19) apparent age of 52,140±439 BP on duplicate 1 mg samples of catalytically-reduced graphitic carbon prepared from carefully-pretreated wood of reportedly Pliocene age (Kirner *et al.* 1995; 1996). The lowest Pliocene wood blank value achieved to date by the LLNL/UCR laboratory is 60,540±620 BP (Kirner *et al.* 1997).

Table 3.2. Comparison of Decay and AMS-based Direct/Ion Counting for ^{14}C Analysis[a]

<table>
<tr><th colspan="2">RADIOCARBON MEASUREMENT</th></tr>
<tr><th>Decay Counting[b]</th><th>Direct/Ion Counting</th></tr>
<tr><td colspan="2">Physical and chemical pretreatment:
Isolation of in situ/indigenous fraction of sample</td></tr>
<tr><td colspan="2">Preparation: conversion of sample to form required by method of measurement</td></tr>
<tr><td>Measurement: gas or liquid in ionization detection instrument</td><td>Measurement: Produce ions from sample

Accelerate ions

Separate ^{14}C from all other isotopes and molecules</td></tr>
<tr><td colspan="2">Count ^{14}C decay events/ions</td></tr>
<tr><td colspan="2">Infer ^{14}C concentration by comparison with standards</td></tr>
</table>

[a] Adapted from Table 9 in Taylor 1994.
[b] Gas counting using carbon dioxide (CO_2), methane (CH_4), acetylene (C_2H_2) and rarely, ethane (C_2H_2) or liquid scintillation counting employing benzene (C_6H_6).

The development of AMS technology has provided the technical means by which very low organic carbon content sample types, such as organic extracts from bone and ceramics, along with microsample materials such as single seeds, can now be routinely dated by ^{14}C. It should be emphasized that AMS-based ^{14}C age determinations are not necessarily more—or less—accurate than decay counting. AMS technology provides the technical means to obtain suites of ^{14}C measurements on samples containing milligram amounts of carbon and, with additional efforts, samples containing as little as less than 100 micrograms of carbon (Kirner *et al.* 1995). The much higher efficiency of AMS systems translates into higher counting rates for samples and therefore, *potentially*, on some samples, under some circumstances, greater counting precision. Table 3.2 identifies differences in the procedures to obtain ^{14}C determinations employing decay as opposed to direct counting. It is important to note that whether decay or direct counting is used to infer age, there is a fundamental requirement: that physical and chemical pretreatment be employed to isolate an uncontaminated *in-situ* or indigenous carbon-containing fraction.

CASE STUDY: ARCHAEOLOGICAL APPLICATIONS OF AMS TECHNOLOGY

Over the last decade, the expanding utilization of AMS-based ^{14}C analysis has continued to open up new and expanded areas of research where ^{14}C data have yielded important new understandings that would have not been possible or practical with decay counting. In archaeology, there have been a variety of issues and topics which have been significantly impacted by the new capability to obtain ^{14}C measurements on milligram amounts of sample.

Table 3.3. AMS ^{14}C Dating of the Shroud of Turin[a]

Laboratory	Known age Egyptian linen AMS ^{14}C age (yrs. BP)	Shroud AMS ^{14}C (yrs. BP)
	2,010±80 110 BC-AD 75	
Arizona AMS	1,838±47 2,041±43 1,960±55 1,983±37 2,137±46	591±30 690±35 606±41 701±33
	Mean=1,995±46	Mean= 646±31
Oxford AMS	1,955±70 1,975±55 1,990±50	795±65 730±45 745±55
	Mean=1,980±35	Mean= 750±30
Zurich AMS	1,984±50 1,886±48 1,954±50	733±61 722±56 635±57 639±45 679±51
	Mean= 1,940±30	Mean= 676±24
Combined	Mean ^{14}C age = 1,964±20	Mean ^{14}C age = 689±16
	Calibrated age = 10 BC-AD 80[b]	Calibrated age = AD 1260-1390[b]

[a] Based on data from Damon *et al.* 1989.

[b] 95% confidence interval.

Some AMS-based ^{14}C values have been obtained in situations where larger amounts of sample were available. However, those having responsibility for an unique archaeological or historic object would consent to the removal of only a small portion of the larger sample. Such was the case with the AMS ^{14}C dating of the Shroud of Turin. This 4.3 by 1 meter rectangular-shaped linen cloth housed in the Cathedral of St. John the Baptist in Turin, Italy has been characterized, since 1353 when its existence is first documented, as the "True Burial Sheet of Christ." Table 3.3 presents the results of an analysis by three AMS laboratories of a known-age Egyptian linen approximately 2,000 years old and the Shroud. The calibrated ^{14}C age indicates that the flax from which the linen was fabricated was most probably growing sometime during the later part of the 13th or in the 14th century, exactly the period during which the shroud first appeared (Damon *et al.* 1989).

An excellent illustration of the ability of AMS technology to obtain ^{14}C measurements on microsamples is illustrated by a study of maize specimens excavated from two rockshelters in the Tehuacan Valley, Mexico. Samples of *Zea mays* from these sites had been regarded as the earliest example of cultivated maize in the New World. In the early 1970s, their age had been determined on the basis of conventional ^{14}C determinations obtained on charcoal assumed to be stratigraphically associated with the maize samples in the Tehuacan Valley sites. Table 3.4 compares the ^{14}C values previously obtained on associated charcoal with the AMS ^{14}C values obtained directly on the maize samples. In contrast to the 5350 to 7000 BP values on the charcoal, the range in ^{14}C values directly obtained on maize is 1560 to 4700 BP for the samples from San Marcos Cave and 450 to 4090 BP for the specimens from Coxcatlan Cave (Long *et al.* 1989). The significantly later occurrence of maize at Tehuacan raises questions concerning assumptions about where the center(s) of maize domestication in Mesoamerica may have been.

A further example of usefulness of AMS technology in ^{14}C studies is the use of such data as part of efforts to address one of most acrimonious debates in New World archaeology—the nature and timing of the peopling of the Western Hemisphere. Historically, this debate has centered on two issues: the scientific validity of data offered as evidence for human presence and the accuracy of the age estimates associated with these data (Dillehay and Meltzer 1991).

A number of discussions have centered on questions concerning the validity of purported Paleoindian materials with assigned ages purportedly in excess of the well-documented Clovis period occupation of North America (Haynes 1992). Of the more than 100 sites in North America that have been reported to contain evidence of "pre-Clovis" occupation, only a relatively small number currently remain under active consideration. Of these remaining alleged pre-Clovis sites in North (Payen 1982) or South (Lynch 1990; Meltzer 1994) America, either the cultural nature of the material or the adequacy of

Table 3.4. Comparison of ^{14}C Determination on Samples of Charcoal and Maize from Tehuacan Valley, Mexico

Decay counting on associated charcoal[a]		AMS on maize specimens[b]	
^{14}C age BP (range)	calibrated AD/BC (range)	^{14}C age BP	calibrated range AD/BC
		San Marcos Cave	
5350-7000	4150-5800 BC	1560±45	AD 440-620
		4150±50	2880-2660 BC
		4600±60	3380-3360 BC
		4680±50	3500-3380 BC
		4700±60	3500-3380 BC
		4700±110	3640-3360 BC
		Coxcatlan Cave	
		450±40	AD 1400-1460
		1860±45	AD 80- 220
		1900±60	AD 20- 220
		3740±60	2280-2040 BC
		4040±100	2580-2500 BC
		4090±50	2870-2580 BC

[a] Taken from Johnson and Willis 1970 and Johnson and MacNeish 1972.
[b] Taken from Long *et al.* 1989.

the geochronological data associated with the remains—or both—have been, and continues to be, questioned.

It is generally accepted that debates concerning the validity of dating frameworks associated with Paleoindian materials—and particularly purported pre-Clovis materials—were substantively transformed with the introduction of the ^{14}C method. For almost all archaeologists, the ^{14}C method has acquired the status of the final arbiter of the accuracy of chronological inferences for materials associated with actual or apparent Paleoindian contexts. There is, however, the recognition that the validity of ^{14}C-inferred ages can depend on the type of sample material being dated. One of these problematical sample types is bone.

There are numerous examples in the history of ^{14}C applications in archaeology of misassociation of a ^{14}C-dated sample with the item or context for which a date had been sought. When ^{14}C age determinations are obtained directly on a bone sample clearly identified on widely-accepted morphological criteria as being genus *Homo*, any question of human involvement or instrumentality is, by definition, rendered moot. One is thus able to evaluate the validity of a ^{14}C-based age determination on physiochemical grounds alone. This highlights one of the great advantages of AMS technology for ^{14}C analysis—the ability to obtain a ^{14}C value directly on a specific fraction of a target organic, in this case mammalian bone, and more specifically in this discussion, human bone.

From the very inception of ^{14}C studies, bone acquired a reputation as an unreliable sample type. Rather quickly, a major problem was recognized. Early bone ^{14}C determinations had most often been carried out employing the whole-bone matrix which is composed largely of inorganic constituents. Inorganic carbonates can be derived either from the apatite structure in the bone itself or from secondary, diagenetic carbonates which had been transported into the bone matrix from groundwater and soil constituents by chemical exchange and/or through dissolution and reprecipitation processes. Therefore, the ^{14}C contained in a total inorganic carbonate fraction may reflect the environmental source(s) of the carbonates contained in the soils to which the bone has been exposed and the degree of isotopic exchange between the bone and ground water carbonates rather than the age of the bone sample itself. Radiocarbon measurements on a carbonate component of bone can be older, younger, or of essentially the same age as an organic fraction from the same bone.

In contrast to the carbonate fraction, bone contains a relatively stable organic product, the protein collagen, representing between 60–70% of the organics in fresh, fat-free bone. Collagen in modern bone can be distinguished by several types of biogeochemical "fingerprints" including characteristic amounts of nitrogen, a distinctive nitrogen/carbon ratio, and a pattern in the relative concentration of the approximately 20 amino acids which make up mammalian collagen.

By the early 1960s, collagen—in some cases characterized as gelatin—became the target of much of the chemical pretreatment of bone for ^{14}C analysis. Initially, most often "collagen" was the label given to an acid insoluble product isolated by a treatment of the bone with dilute acid, which destroyed the carbonates, leaving, it was assumed, the collagen fraction. In some cases, this product was heated at a constant temperature and pH to form gelatin. An early application of this approach to the ^{14}C dating of human bone was that of the Galley Hill skeleton in England. When discovered in the 19th century, the Galley HIll skeleton was thought to be Pleistocene in age. However, bone fluorine values suggested that it was a post-Pleistocene burial that had intruded into Pleistocene sediments. The ^{14}C age of the acid-insoluble fraction ("collagen") of a humerus of this skeleton yielded a date of 3310±150 BP (Barker and Mackey 1961: 41).

The ability of AMS technology to permit ^{14}C values to be measured routinely using milligram amounts of carbon provided the technical capability to undertake a direct examination of a series of human skeletons from North American sites that, on various grounds, had been declared to date to a period before 11,000–12,000 BP; i.e., these human skeletons were alleged to be pre-Clovis in age. AMS technology permitted a detailed analysis of the validity of ^{14}C age estimates on a range of extracts from bone including individual amino acids and other highly specific organic constituents contained in bone. Table 3.5 is a summary of ^{14}C values obtained on various organic fractions extracted from human skeletal samples and, in one case, an artifact fabricated from a

Table 3.5. Revisions in Age Estimates on Human Bone (Except Old Crow) from North America Sites of Purported Pleistocene Age Based on AMS ^{14}C Determinations and Related Data[k]

Skeleton(s)/ artifact	[A] Original estimate Basis	Age	[B] Revised estimate ^{14}C Age	Laboratories
Sunnyvale	AAR U-series	70,000 8300/9000	3600-4850 6300[a]	UCR/Arizona AMS UCSD(Scripps)/ Oxford AMS
Haverty [Angeles Mesa]	AAR	>50,000	4050-5350[d] 5200[d] 7900-10,500[d] 2730-4630[e] 4600-13,500[f] 5250[e] 15,900[f]	UCR GX (Geochron) UCLA UCR/LLNL-CAMS AMS UCR/LLNL-CAMS AMS DSIR, New Zealand AMS DSIR, New Zealand AMS
Del Mar	AAR U-series	41,000-48,000 11,000/11,300	4900[a] 4830 1150-5060[a]	UCSD(Scripps)/ Oxford AMS Arizona AMS Arizona AMS
Los Angeles [Baldwin Hills]	^{14}C AAR	>23,000[a] 26,000	3560	UCR/Arizona AMS
Taber	geologic	22,000-60,000	3550	Chalk River AMS
Yuha	^{14}C AAR U-series	22,000[b] 23,000 19,000	1650-3850	Arizona AMS
Old Crow[c]	^{14}C	23,000	1350	Simon Frazer/ McMaster AMS
Laguna	^{14}C	7100[g] 17,150[h] >14,800[i]	5100[a]	UCSD(Scripps)/ Oxford AMS
Natchez	geologic	"Pleistocene"	5580	Arizona AMS
Anzick	Clovis	10,000-11,000	8610-10,680[i]	Arizona AMS
Tepexpan	geologic	"Pleistocene"	920-1980[j]	Arizona AMS
Calaveras	geologic	"Pliocene"	740	UCR/Arizona AMS

[a] Amino acid fraction. [b] Diagenetic carbonate. [c] Artifact fabricated from bone. [d] Acid insoluble raction, decay counting. [e] collagen (gelatin) fraction. [f] Osteocalcin fraction. [g] skull, "first run" (Berger 1992). [h] Skull, "second run" (Berger 1992). [i] long-bone. [j] multiple analysis of different fractions (Stafford *et al.* 1991). [k] References for all values except Calaveras are cited in the caption for Table 25.5 in Taylor 1992. Yuha U-series value listed in Taylor (1992) has been corrected. Calaveras data from Taylor *et al.* 1992.

non-human bone from North America sites, all of which had been assigned a pre-Clovis age. The basis of the initial age assignment of these samples included other Quaternary dating methods such as amino acid racemization and uranium-series and, in a small number of cases, prior ^{14}C determinations.

The AMS-based ^{14}C values on these human skeletal samples indicate that, with two exceptions, all are younger than 11,000 BP. These data are the basis of the conclusion that all currently-known, ^{14}C-dated human skeletons from the Western Hemisphere are of Clovis age or younger. The only exceptions are two ^{14}C values obtained in connection with experiments to determine the validity of ^{14}C determinations on a non-collagen component of bone, osteocalcin (Ajie *et al.* 1992). These two values are interpreted to represent fractions which have been contaminated in the process of being chemically extracted since a significant corpus of ^{14}C dates, along with other evidence, points to the age of the Haverty (Angeles Mesa) skeletons as being in the range of 4000 to 5000 years BP (Brooks *et al.* 1991).

The experimental osteocalcin ^{14}C determinations reflect current efforts to deal with the problem of bones containing only trace amounts of residual collagen. The assumption that an acid insoluble fraction is primarily composed of intact collagen would be a reasonable inference for relatively young bone or bone from environments where diagenetic effects would be less severe, i.e., very cold and/or very arid climates; but such an assumption would not be necessarily valid for bone subject to elevated temperatures and high humidity environments and/or for Pleistocene-age bone.

The collagen contained in *post mortem* bones deposited in temperate and tropical environments would be expected to undergo diagenetic chemical reactions which degrades them into their constituent peptides and amino acids which can then be removed from the bone matrix by ground-water action. In this process, the bone loses its collagen-like amino acid pattern biochemical "fingerprint" while, at the same time, the total amount of residual organics—primarily derived from the collagen—in the bone may be significantly reduced to the point where it is extremely difficult, if not impossible, to distinguish trace amounts of collagen-derived products from exogenous contamination in the form of various organic compounds such as soil bacteria and humic or fulvic acids.

An example of the capabilities of AMS technology is provided by Stafford and his collaborators (Stafford *et al.* 1987; 1990; 1991) who examined the range of ^{14}C ages exhibited in different chemical fractions of collagen-profile and non-collagen-profile bones. Using a relatively well-preserved bone—i.e., a bone exhibiting a collagen-like amino acid profile—associated with a wood sample dated at 11,490±450 BP, these researchers obtained ^{14}C measurements on a wide spectrum of organic fractions prepared by a variety of chemical separation methods. These fractions ranged from untreated gelatin, HCl-insoluble residues with and without gelatinization, ion exchange purified com-

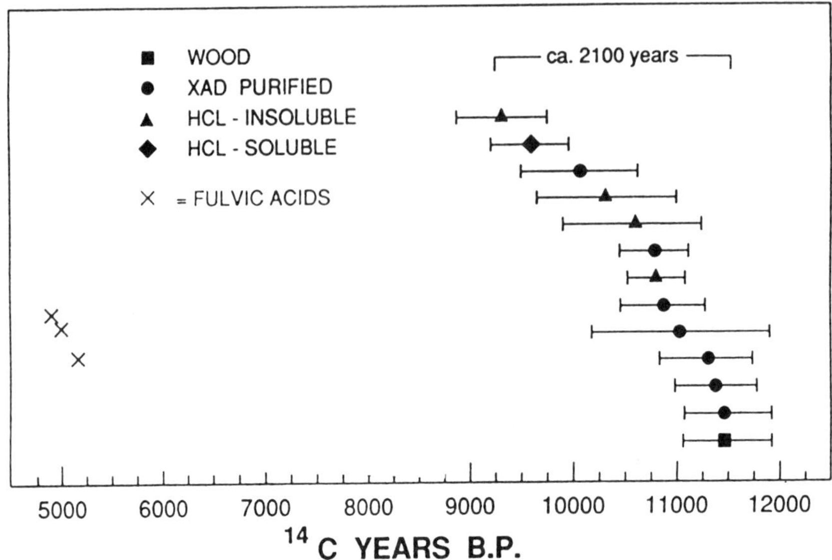

Figure 3.6. Distribution of AMS-based ^{14}C values on wood and various organic extracts from mammoth bone. Data taken from Stafford *et al.* (1987).

ponents, individual and combined amino acids, and humic/fulvic acids. As illustrated in Figure 3.6, nine fractions yielded ^{14}C ages within two sigma of the wood value, whereas five fractions exhibited still younger ages. With the exception of one organic fraction which was prepared using a solvent extraction technique and humic acids, the youngest organic fraction was about 2000 (±500) years younger than the actual age of the bone. The principal contaminant in the bone was identified as humic compounds with ages of about 5000 BP.

AMS ^{14}C measurements were also obtained on a comparable series of fractions (25 analyses on 14 different chemical fractions) from another mammoth bone exhibiting a non-collagen amino acid composition pattern. The actual age of the mammoth was inferred to be approximately 11,000 BP on several lines of evidence. The ^{14}C age of individual amino acids extracted from this mammoth ranged from about 3000 to 4500 BP. The youngest ^{14}C value (2270±360 BP) was obtained on a combined aliquot containing four amino acids: aspartic acid, glutamic acid, serine and threonine. Extracted fulvic acid yielded ages ranging from about 7200 to 8800 BP. The oldest ^{14}C value obtained (12,280±110 BP) was obtained on a fraction described as "nonhydrolyzable organic matter (humins)."

There now appears to be a general consensus among investigators concerning the reliability of bone ^{14}C values: that where appropriate biochemical purification procedures are employed, accurate ^{14}C age estimates can be obtained on bones retaining significant amounts of intact collagen. However, bones seriously depleted in protein (mostly collagen) content (< 5% of the original amount) can yield seriously anomalous ^{14}C values. Various studies have examined other organic components in bone that might resist the effects of contamination. Initial experiments with osteocalcin, a non-collagen protein, has been previously noted. Experiments that examined the ^{14}C ages exhibited by the characteristic amino acid of osteocalcin, gamma-carboxylglutamic acid (Gla), indicated that, in some cases, the isotopic integrity of Gla can be compromised (Burky 1996).

CONCLUSION

The impact of ^{14}C dating on the conduct of archaeological research has been, in some aspects, clear and explicit and in others, subtle. In addition to providing a common chronometric time scale for the entire late Quaternary, an important contribution of the ^{14}C method for archaeology is that the technique provides a means of deriving relatively precise chronometric relationships completely independent of any assumptions about cultural processes and totally unrelated to any type of manipulation of artifact data. It has also been suggested that ^{14}C dating led to a noticeable improvement in archaeological field methods (Johnson 1965: 764) and was, at least in part, responsible for the increasing attention given to statistical approaches in the evaluation of archaeological data (Thomas 1978:323).

Radiocarbon data provide the foundation on which most of the prehistoric archaeological time scales in most areas of the world for the last 40,000 years are, directly or indirectly, constructed. While currently not often stressed, the influence of ^{14}C data continue to be profound and pervasive.

ACKNOWLEDGMENTS

The UCR Radiocarbon Laboratory is supported by the National Science Foundation (Archaeology/Archaeometry Program), the Accelerator Mass Spectrometry Laboratory, University of California, Lawrence Livermore National Laboratory and the Gabrielle O. Vierra Memorial Fund with additional resources provided by the Intramural Research Fund and Dean of the College of Humanities, Arts, and Social Sciences, University of California, Riverside. The comments of Joan Schneider on an earlier draft of this chapter are very much appreciated as are the very helpful suggestions of Sylvia Broadbent and Austin Long. This is contribution 95-06 of the Institute of Geophysics and Planetary Physics, University of California, Riverside.

REFERENCES

Aardsma, G.E. 1991 *Radiocarbon and the Genesis Flood*. El Cajon (California), Institute for Creation Research.

Ajie, H.O., Kaplan, I.R., Hauschka, P.V., Kirner, D., Slota, P.J., Jr., and Taylor, R.E. 1992 Radiocarbon dating of bone osteocalcin: isolating and characterizing a non-collagen protein. *Radiocarbon* 34: 296–305.

Alvarez, W. 1981 The early days of accelerator mass spectrometry. *In* Henning, W., Kutschera, W., Smither, R.K. and Yntema, J.L. eds., *Symposium on Accelerator Mass Spectrometry*. Argonne, Argonne National Laboratory: 1–15.

Anbar, M. 1978 The limitations of mass spectrometric radiocarbon dating using CN^- ions. In Gove, H.E. ed., *Proceedings of the First Conference on Radiocarbon Dating with Accelerators*, Gove, H.E. ed., Rochester, University of Rochester: 152–155.

Arnold, J.R. and Libby, W.F. 1949 Age determinations by radiocarbon content. Checks with samples of known age. *Science* 110: 678–680.

Arnold, J.R. and W.F. Libby 1950 *Radiocarbon dates (September 1, 1950)*. Chicago, University of Chicago, Institute for Nuclear Studies.

Arnold, J.R. and W.F. Libby 1951 Radiocarbon dates. *Science* 113: 111–120.

Atkinson, R.J.C. 1975 British prehistory and the radiocarbon revolution. *Antiquity* 49: 173–177.

Bard, E., Arnold, M., Fairbanks, R.G., and Hamelin, B. 1993a ^{230}Th-^{234}U and ^{14}C ages obtained by mass spectrometry on corals. *Radiocarbon* 35: 191–199.

Bard, E., Stuiver, M. and Shackleton N.J. 1993b How accurate are our chronologies of the past? *In* Eddy, J.A. and Oeschger, H. eds., *Global Changes in the Perspective of the Past*. New York, John Wiley and Sons.

Barker, H. and Mackey, J. 1961 British Museum natural radiocarbon measurements III. *Radiocarbon* 3: 39–45.

Becker, B. 1993 An 11,000-year German oak and pine dendrochronology for radiocarbon calibration. *Radiocarbon* 35: 210–213.

Bennett, C.L., Beukens, R.P., Clover, M.R., Gove, H.E., Liebert, R.B., Litherland, A.E., Purser, K.H. and Sondheim W.E. 1977 Radiocarbon dating using accelerators: Negative ions provide the key. *Science* 198: 508–509.

Bennett, C. L., Beukens, R.P., Clover, M.R., Elmore, D., Gove, H.E., Kilius, L., Litherland, A.E. and Purser, K.H. 1978 Radiocarbon dating with electrostatic accelerators: Dating of milligram samples. *Science* 201: 345–347.

Berger, R. 1992 Libby's UCLA Radiocarbon Laboratory: Contributions to archaeology. *In* Taylor, R.E., Long, A., Kra, R.S., eds., *Radiocarbon After Four Decades An Interdisciplinary Perspective*. New York, Springer-Verlag: 421–434.

Bertsche, K. J., Friedman, P.G., Morris, D.E., Muller, R.A. and Welch, J.J. 1987 Status of the Berkeley small cyclotron AMS project. *Nuclear Instruments and Methods* B29: 105–109.

Bertsche, K.J. 1989 A small low energy cyclotron for radioisotope measurements. Ph.D. dissertation, University of California, Berkeley.

Broecker, W.S. and Kulp J.L. 1956 The radiocarbon method of age determination. *American Antiquity* 22:1–11.

Bronk, C.R. and Hedges, R.E.M. 1987 A gas ion source for radiocarbon dating. *Nuclear Instruments and Methods* B29: 45–49.

Brooks, S., Brooks, R.H., Kennedy, G.E., Austin, J., Firby, J.R., Payen, L.A., Prior, C. A., Slota, P.J., Jr., and Taylor, R. E. The Haverty Human Skeletons: Morphologial, Depositional and Geochronological Characteristics. *Journal of California and Great Basin Anthropology* 12: 60–83.

Brown, R.H. 1983 The interpretation of carbon-14 age data. *In* Coffin, H.G. with Brown, R.H.,eds., *Origin by design*. Washington, D.C., Review and Herald Publishing Association: 309–329.

Brown, R.H. 1986 ^{14}C depth profiles as indicators of trends in climate and $^{14}C/^{12}C$ ratios. *Radiocarbon* 28: 350–357.

Bruns, M., Levin, I., Munnish, K.O., Hubberten, H.W. and Fillipakis, S. 1980 Regional sources of volcanic carbon dioxide and their influence on ^{14}C content of present-day plant material. *Radiocarbon* 22: 532–536.

Burky, R.R. 1996 Radiocarbon dating archaeologically significant bone using gamma-carboxyglutamic acid (Gla) and alpha-carboxyglycine (aminomalonate). Ph.D. disseration, University of Califronia, Riverside.

Chen, M., Li, D., Xu, S., Chen, G., Shen, L., Lu, X., Zhang, W., Zhang, Y., Zhong, Z, Zhang, Y. 1995 Breakthrough of the mini-cyclotron mass spectrometer for ^{14}C analysis. *Radiocarbon* 37: 675–682.

Clark, G. 1970 *Aspects of prehistory*. Berkeley, University of California Press.

Cremo, M.A. and Thompson, R.L. 1993 *Forbidden archeology, The hidden history of the human race*. San Diego (California), Bhaktivedanta Institute.

Damon, P.E., Donahue, D.J., Gord, B.H., Hatheway, A.L. Jull, A.J.T., Linick, T.W., Sercelo, P.J., Toolin, L.J., Bronk, C.R., Hall, E.T., Hedges, R.E.M., Housley, R., Law, I.A., Perry, C., Bonani, G., Trumbore, S., Wolfli, W., Ambers, J.C., Bowman, S.G.E., Leese, M.N. and Tite, M.S. 1989 Radiocarbon dating the shroud of Turin. *Nature* 337: 611–615.

Damon, P. E. and J. I. Jirikowic 1992 Solar forcing of global climate change? *In* Taylor, R.E., Long, A., and Kra, R. eds., *Radiocarbon after four decades: An Interdisciplinary Perspective*. New York, Springer-Verlag: 177–179.

Daniel, G. 1967 *The origins and growth of archaeology*. New York, Crowell.

Daniel, G. 1972 Editorial. *Antiquity* 46:265.

Dillehay, T.D. and Meltzer, D.J., eds. 1991 *The First Americans: Search and Research*. Baca Raton: CRC Press.

Eddy, J. 1976 The Maunder minimum. *Science* 192: 1189–1202.

Edwards, R.L. 1993 A large drop in atmospheric $^{14}C/^{12}C$ and reduced melting in the Younger Dryas, documented with ^{230}Th ages of corals. *Science* 260: 962–968.

Erlenkeuser, H. 1979 A thermal diffusion plan for radiocarbon isotope enrichment from natural samples. *In* Berger, R. and Suess, H.E., eds., *Radiocarbon dating*. Berkeley, University of California Press: 216–237.

Gittins, G.O. 1984 *Radiocarbon chronometry and archaeological thought*. Ph.D. disseration, University of California, Los Angeles.

Gove, H.E. 1992 The history of AMS, its advantages over decay counting: Applications and Prospects. *In* Taylor, R.E., Long, A., Kra, R.S., eds., *Radiocarbon After Four Decades An Interdisciplinary Perspective*. New York, Springer-Verlag: 214–229.

Grootes, P.M., Mook, W.G., Vogel, J.C., de Vries, A.E., Haring, A. and Kismaker, J. 1975 Enrichment of radiocarbon for dating samples up to 75,000 years. *Zeitschrift füer Naturforschung* 30A: 1–14.

Harbottle, G., Sayre, E.V. and Stoenner, R.W. 1979 Carbon 14 dating of small samples by proportional counting. *Science* 206: 683–685.

Hedges, R.E.M. and Gowlett, J.A.J. 1986 Radiocarbon dating by accelerator mass spectrometry. *Scientific American* 254: 100–107.

Johnson, F., 1965 The impact of radiocarbon ating upon archaeology. *In* Chatters, R.M. and Olson, E.A., eds., *Proceedings of the Sixth International Conference radiocarbon and Tritium Dating*. Springfield (Virginia): Clearinghouse for Federal Science and Technical Information: 762–780.

Johnson, F. and MacNeish, R.S. 1972 Chronology of the Tehuacan Valley. *In* Byers, D.S., ed., *Prehistory of the Techuacan Valley*, vol. 4, Austin, University of Texas Press.

Johnson, F. and Willis, E.H. 1970 Reconciliation of radiocarbon and sideral years in Meso-American chronology. *In* Olsson, I.U., ed., *Radiocarbon variations and absolute chronology*. Stockholm, Almqvist & Wiksell: 93–104.

Kaufman, T.S. 1980 Early prehistory of the Clear Lake area, Lake County, California. Ph.D. dissertation, University of California, Los Angeles.

Kirner, D., Taylor, R.E. and Southon, J.R. 1995 Reduction in backgrounds of microsamples for AMS ^{14}C dating. *Radiocarbon* 37: 697–704.

Kirner, D., Southon, J.R., Hare, P.E. and Taylor, R.E. 1996 Acclerator mass spectrometry radiocarbon measurement of submilligram samples. *In* Orna, M. V., ed., *Archaeological Chemistry Organic, Inorganic, and Biochemical Analysis*. Washington, D.C., American Chemical Society: 434–442.

Kirner, D., Burky, R., Taylor, R.E., and Southon, J.R. 1997 Radiocarbon dating organic residues at the microgram level. *Nuclear Instruments and Methods in Physics Research*, in press.

Klein, J., Lerman, J.C., Damon, P.E. and Ralph, E.K. 1982 Calibration of radiocarbon dates: Tables based on the consensus data of the owrkshop on calibrating the radiocarbon time scale. *Radiocarbon* 24: 103–150.

Kromer, B. and Becker, B. 1993 German Oak and pine ^{14}C calibration, 7200–9439 BC. *Radiocarbon* 35: 125–135.

Levin, I., Bosinger, R., Bonani, G., Francey, R.J., Kromer, B., Munnich, K.O., Suter, M., Trivett, N.B.A. and Wolfli, W. 1992 Radiocarbon in atmopsheric carbon dioxide and methane: Gloval Distribution and Trends. *In* Taylor, R.E., Long, A., and Kra, R., eds., *Radiocarbon after four decades: An Interdisciplinary Perspective*. New York, Springer-Verlag: 503–518.

Libby, W.F. 1963 Accuracy of radiocarbon dates. *Antiquity* 37: 7–12.

Linick, T.W., Damon, P.E., Donahue, D.J. and Jull, A.J.T. 1989 Accelerator mass spectrometry: The new revolution in radiocarbon dating. *Quaternary International* 1: 1–6.

Long, A., Benz, B.F., Donahue, D.J., Jull, A.J.T., and Toolin, L.J. 1989 First direct AMS dates on early Maize from Tehuacán, Mexico. *Radiocarbon* 31: 1035–1040.

Long, A and Miller, A.B. 1981 Arizona radiocarbon dates X. *Radiocarbon* 23: 191–217.

Lynch, T.F. 1990 Glacial-age man in South America: A critical review *American Antiquity* 55: 12–36.

Mast, T.S. and Muller, R.A. 1980 Radioisotope detection and dating with accelerators. *Nuclear Science Applications* 1: 7–32.

Mazaud, A., Laj, C., Bard, E., Arnold, M. and Tric, E. 1992 A geomagnetic calibration of the radiocarbon time-scale. *In* Bard, E. and Broecker, W.S., eds., *The Last Deglaciation: Absolute and Radiocarbon Chronologies*. Berlin: Springer-Verlag: 163–169.

Meltzer, D.J., Adovasio, J.M. and Dillehay, T.D. 1994 On a Pleistocene human occupation at Pedra Furada, Brazil. *Antiquity* 68: 695–714.

Muller, R.A. 1977 Radioisotope dating with a cyclotron. *Science* 196: 489–494.

Muller, R.A. 1979 Radioisotope dating with accelerators. *Physics Today* 32(2): 23–30.

Muller, R.A., Stephenson, E.J. and Mast, T.S. 1978 Radioisotope dating with an accelerator: A blind measurement. *Science* 201: 347–348.

Nelson, D.E., Korteling, R.G. and Scott, W.R. 1977 Carbon-14: Direct detection at natural concentrations. *Science* 198: 507–508.

Neustupny, E. 1970 The accuracy of radiocarbon dating. *In* Olsson, I. U., ed., *Radiocarbon variations and absolute chronology*. Stockholm, Almqvist & Wiksell: 22–34.

Nobel Foundation 1964 *Nobel Lectures, Chemistry 1942–1962*. Amsterdam, Elsevier.

Oeschger, H., Houtermans, J., Loosli, H., and Wahlen, M. 1970 The constancy of cosmic radidation from isotope studies in meteorities and on the earth. *In* Olsson, I.U. ed., *Radiocarbon variations and absolute chronology*. Stockholm, Almqvist & Wiksell: 471–496.

Otlet, R.L., Huxtable, G., Evans, G.V., Humphreys, D.G., Short, T.D. and Conchie, S.J. 1983 Development and operation of the Harwell small counter facility for the measurement of ^{14}C in very small samples. *Radiocarbon* 25: 565–575.

Payen, L.A. 1982 The pre-Clovis of North America: Temporal and artifactual evidence. Ph.D. dissertation, University of California, Riverside.

Ralph, E.K., Michael, H.N. and Han, M.C. 1973 Radiocarbon dates and reality. *MASCA Newsletter* 9: 1–20.

Rowe, J.H. 1965 An interpretation of radiocarbon measurements on archaeological samples from Peru. *In* Chatters, R.M. and Olson, E.A. eds., *Proceedings of the Sixth International Conference Radiocarbon and Tritium*. Springfield (Virignia), Clearinghouse for Federal Scientific and Technical Information: 187–198.

Renfrew, C. 1973 *Before civilization: the radiocarbon revolution and prehistoric Europe*. New York: Alfred A. Knopf.

Saupe, F., Strappa, O., Coppens, R., Guillet, B., and Jaegy, R. 1980 A possible source of error in ^{14}C dates: Volcanic emanations (examples from the Monte Amiata District, Provinces of Gorsseto and Sienna, Italy) *Radiocarbon* 22: 525–531.

Sayre, E.V., Harbottle, G., Stoenner, R.W., Otlet, R.L. and Evans, G.V. 1981 The use of the small gas proportional counters for the carbon 14 measurement of very small samples. *IAEA Proceedings on Methods of Low Level Counting and Spectrometry* Vienna, International Atomic Energy Agency: 393.

Schmidt, F.H., Balsley, D.R. and Leach, D.D. 1987 Early expectations of AMS: Greater ages and tiny fraction. One failure?-One success. *In* Gove, H.E., A.E. Litherland, A.E. and Elmore, D. eds., *Accelerator Mass Spectrometry*. Amsterdam, North-Holland Physics Publishing: 97–99.

Scott, E.M., Long, A., and Kra, R., eds. 1990 Proceedings of the International Workshop on Intercomparison of Radiocarbon Laboratories. *Radiocarbon* 32: 253–397.

Southon, J.R., Deino, A.L, Orsi, G., Terrasi, R., and Campajola, L. 1995 Calibration of the radiocarbon time scale at 37Ka BP. *Abstract of Papers*, 209th American Chemical Society National Meeting, Part 2, p. 10.

Stafford, T.W. Jr, Jull, A.J.T., Brendel, K., Duhamel, R.C. and Donahue, D. 1987 Study of bone radiocarbon dating accuracy at the University of Arizona NSF accelerator facility for radioisotope analysis. *Radiocarbon* 29: 24–44.

Stafford, T.W., Hare, P.E., Currie, L., Jull, A.J.T. and Donahue, D.J. 1990 Accuracy of North American human skeleton ages. *Quaternary Research* 34: 111–120.

Stafford, T.W., Hare, P.E., Currie, L., Jull, A.J.T. and Donahue, D.J. 1991 Accelerator radiocarbon dating at the molecular level. *Journal of Archaeological Science* 18: 35–72.

Stuiver, M. and Braziunas, T.G. 1993 Modeling atmospheric ^{14}C influences and ^{14}C ages of marine samples to 10,000 BC. *Radiocarbon* 35: 137–189.

Stuiver, M. and Reimer, P.J. 1993 Extended ^{14}C data base and revised CALIB 3.0 ^{14}C age calibration program. *Radiocarbon* 35: 215–230.

Stuiver, M., Heusser, C.H. and Yang, I.C. 1978 North American galcial history extended to 75,000 years ago. *Science* 200: 16–21.

Stuiver, M., Long, A. and Kra, R.S., eds. Calibration 1993 *Radiocarbon* 35: 1–244.

Stuiver, M. and Polach, H.A. 1977 Discussion: Repoorting of ^{14}C data. *Radiocarbon* 19: 355–363.

Stuiver, M. and Suess, H.E. 1966 On the relationship between radiocarbon dates and true sample ages. *Radiocarbon* 8: 534–540.

Suess, H.E. 1970 Bristlecone-pine calibration of radiocarbon time 5200 B.C. to present. *In* Olsson, I.U., ed., *Radiocarbon variations and absolute chronology*. Stockholm, Almqvist & Wiksell: 303–312.

Taylor, R.E. 1987 *Radiocarbon dating An archaeological perspective*. San Diego, Academic Press.

_____ 1990 Radiocarbon dating. *Encyclopedia of Physical Science and Technology*, 1990 Yearbook. New York, Academic Press: 499–504.

_____ 1991 Radioisotope dating by accelerator mass spectrometry: archaeological and paleoanthropological perspectives. *In* Göksu, H.Y., Oberhofer, M., Regulloi, D., eds., *Scientific Dating Methods*. Dordrecht (Netherlands), Kluwer Academic Publishers: 37–54.

_____ 1992 Radiocarbon dating of bone: To collagen and beyond. *In* Taylor, R.E., Long, A., and Kra, R. eds., *Radiocarbon after four decades: An Interdisciplinary Perspective*. New York, Springer-Verlag: 375–402.

_____ 1994 Radiocarbon dating of bone using accelerator mass spectrometry: Current discussions and future directions. *In* Bonnichsen, R. and Steele, D.G. eds., *Method and Theory for Investigating the Peopling of the Americas*. Corvallis, Center for the Study of the First Americans, Oregon State University: 27–44.

Taylor, R.E., Long, A., and Kra, R. eds. 1992 *Radiocarbon After Four Decades: An Interdisciplinary Perspective*. New York, Springer-Verlag.

Taylor, R.E., Donahue, D.J., Zabel, T.H., Damon, P.E. and Jull, A.T.J. 1984 Radiocarbon dating by particle accelerators: An archaeological perspective. *In* Lambert, J.B. ed., *Archaeological Chemistry III*. Washington, D.C., American Chemical Society: 333–356.

Taylor, R.E., Payen, L.A. and Slota, P.J., Jr. 1992 The age of the Calaveras Skull: Dating the "Piltdown Man" of the New World. *American Antiquity* 57: 269–275.

Taylor, R.E., Haynes, C. V., Jr. and Stuiver, M 1996 Clovis and Folsom age estimates: stratigraphic context and radiocarbon calibration. *Antiquity* 70: 515-525.

Taylor, R.E., Stuiver, M., and Reimer, P.J. 1996 Development and extension of the calibration of the radiocarbon time scale: Archaeological applications. *Quaternary Science Reviews (Quaternary Geochronology)* 15: 655–668.

Thomas, D.H. 1978 The awful truth about statistics in archaeology. *American Antiquity* 43: 231–244.

Vries, H. de 1958 Variations in concentration of radiocarbon with time and location on earth. *Proceedings, Nederlandsche Akademie van Wetenschappen*, Series B61: 1.

Vogel, J.S., Southon, J.R., Nelson, D.E. and Brown, T.A. 1984 Performance of catalytically condensed carbon for use in accelerator mass spectrometry. *Nuclear Instruments and Methods in Physics Research* B52: 301–305.

Vogel, J.S., Nelson, D.E. and Southon, J.R. 1987 ^{14}C background levels in an accelerator mass spectrometry system. *Radiocarbon* 29: 323–333.

Welch, J.J., Bertsche, K.J., Firedman, P.G., Morris, D.E., Muller, R.A. and Tans, P.P. 1984 A 40 keV cyclotron for radioisotope dating *Nuclear Instruments and Methods in Physics Research* B5: 230–232.

Willis, E.H., Tauber, H. and Munnich, K.O. 1960 Variations in the atmospheric radiocarbon concentration over the past 1300 years. *Radiocarbon* 2: 1–4.

Wilson, H.W. 1979 Possibility of measurement of ^{14}C by mass spectrometer techniques. *In* Berger, R. and H. E. Suess, eds., *Radiocarbon Dating*. Berkeley, University of California Press: 238–245.

Chapter 4

Potassium-Argon/Argon-Argon Dating Methods

Robert C. Walter

ABSTRACT

During the latter half of this century anthropological surveys in East Africa have made significant contributions to understanding how the human species has evolved. In the past two decades, particularly, discoveries of our fossil ancestors have been made in unprecedented numbers and diversity. Detailed studies of these fossils provide new insights into human evolution, such as the origin of locomotion and cultural activity, and the evolution of the brain, among many other complex features that have come to define humanity. Even during the time this manuscript was written, new hominid discoveries in Ethiopia and Kenya were announced that trace our earliest ancestors further back into the Pliocene. The ages assigned to these fossils have been obtained through radiometric dating of volcanic rocks interbedded with the fossiliferous sediments. Such numerical calibrations are crucial to understanding rates and timing of evolutionary change.

K-Ar dating has played a key role in unraveling the temporal patterns of hominid evolution as far back as the first significant discovery of East African australopithecines at Olduvai Gorge in 1959. It was in large part due to the desire to understand the age of the Olduvai hominid remains that pioneering attempts were made to date geologically young materials using the K-Ar

ROBERT C. WALTER • Institute of Human Origins, Berkeley, California 94710, USA.

Chronometric Dating in Archaeology, edited by Taylor and Aitken.
Plenum Press, New York, 1997.

method. Yet even this seminal K-Ar dating study was plagued by the seemingly insurmountable problem of contamination. The principal materials for dating East Africa hominid sites are volcanic ashes, yet many of these ashes are not deposited as primary air fall *tephras* (Greek for ash). Rather, most are reworked by stream action and are redeposited into the sedimentary environment. In the process of reworking, these ashes can pick up pre-existing detrital grains that, by definition, are older than the juvenile ash. If during K-Ar analyses these detrital grains are not recognized and eliminated then they can cause the measured ages to be systematically too old.

Recent advances in K-Ar geochronology, specifically the $^{40}Ar/^{39}Ar$ variant of the K-Ar method, have helped to establish a precise and accurate temporal framework for hominid evolution in East Africa. Single-crystal laser-fusion $^{40}Ar/^{39}Ar$ dating has been a major factor in this success. This grain-discrete method now permits precise and accurate ages to be measured on single grains and, thus, contaminating grains can be eliminated. The laser-fusion $^{40}Ar/^{39}Ar$ technique has had a profound impact on geochronology by enabling reliable ages to be obtained where none were possible before.

INTRODUCTION

The basis for K-Ar dating can trace its origins to von Weiszäcker (1937) who proposed that ^{40}Ar was generated from ^{40}K by radioactive decay and that old potassium-bearing minerals should, therefore, contain measurable quantities of radiogenic ^{40}Ar. Aldrich and Nier (1948) confirmed von Weiszäcker's predictions by observing ^{40}Ar concentrations (actually $^{40}Ar/^{36}Ar$ ratios) in four minerals that were significantly greater than atmospheric values (von Weiszäcker 1937; Aldrich and Nier 1948). By the mid 1950s, K-Ar dating experiments were performed on many different materials (Shaeffer and Zäringer, 1966) but the development of ultra-high vacuum mass spectrometers by Reynolds (1956) paved the way for making precise K-Ar measurements on geologically young samples. When the K-Ar method was first applied to young volcanic rocks it was largely in response to the need for calibrating hominid evolution (Evernden *et al.* 1957; Leakey *et al.* 1961; Evernden and Curtis 1965). Since then, K-Ar geochronology has played an increasingly important role in calibrating geological and biological events throughout Earth's history, from the Precambrian to the late Quaternary. As a consequence, this radiometric method is one of the most widely used of all geochronological techniques. The purpose of this discussion is to address the conditions and problems encountered in dating geologically young deposits by the K-Ar and $^{40}Ar/^{39}Ar$ methods, and to help the users of these data to understand the geological and experimental factors that can contribute to or diminish analytical success.

The Radiometric Method

In one of its most useful forms, radiometric dating relies on the accumulation of a daughter isotope over time in a closed system due to the radioactive decay of a parent isotope. The U-Th-Pb, Rb-Sr, Sm-Nd, and K-Ar methods are examples of these so-called *accumulation clocks*. These methods are in contradistinction to the radiocarbon (^{14}C) method, which is a *decay clock* based on the activity or quantity of ^{14}C remaining after a period of time.

Accumulation clocks can be used to determine the age of ancient materials, such as the age of the earth, moon, and meteorites, because the number of daughter atoms increases with time. In general, the older the sample, the easier the measurement. The corollary to this is that accumulation clocks have an age limit below which the number of radiogenic daughter isotopes is too small to measure accurately, and therefore are generally not very useful for determining the age of geologically young deposits. The exact opposite is true for the radiocarbon decay clock, where the older the sample the less ^{14}C there is to measure, yielding an older age limit beyond which ^{14}C measurements are impractical.

The radioactive decay process is independent of external factors, such as temperature, pressure, and chemical environment. It is a statistical process in which, simply put, the number of parent atoms, P, that disintegrate over time, t, is proportional to the number of parent atoms times a constant, λ:

$$-dP/dt = P\lambda \tag{1}$$

the minus sign is required because the number of atoms decreases with time. The decay constant, λ, is a proportionality constant that is characteristic of each specific radioactive nuclide. Establishing the differential and integrating Equation 1 yields:

$$-\int dP/P = \lambda \int dt \tag{2}$$

and

$$-\ln P = \lambda t + c \tag{3}$$

where c is the constant of integration. Defining P_o as the number of parent atoms at $t = 0$, then $c = -\ln P_o$. Substituting for c yields:

$$-\ln P = \lambda t - \ln P_o \tag{4}$$

Solving for P gives the *fundamental relationship for radioactive decay*:

$$P_t = P_0 e^{-\lambda t} \tag{5}$$

which states that the number of parent atoms, P_t, remaining after a certain period of time, t, and with a specific decay constant, λ, is an exponential function of the number of parent atoms, P_0, present at t=0. This equation was first deduced empirically by Rutherford and Soddy in 1902 from their experiments on the decay of ^{220}Rn (Dalrymple 1991).

In order for Equation 5 to be useful for radiometric dating there must be a way to determine the original amount of the parent, P_0. This is done by summing the number of parent atoms remaining, P_t, and the number of daughter atoms accumulated, D_t, over time, which from mass balance considerations must be equal to the number of original parent atoms, P_0, provided that closed system conditions were maintained:

$$P_0 = P_t + D_t \tag{6}$$

Substituting for P_0 in Equation 5 yields:

$$P_t = (P_t + D_t)e^{-\lambda t} \tag{7}$$

Solving for D_t expresses how the number of daughter atoms grows through time:

$$D_t = P_t(e^{\lambda t} - 1) \tag{8}$$

Solving Equation 8 for t yields the *fundamental age equation for isotope geochronology*:

$$t = 1/\lambda \ln(D_t/P_t + 1) \tag{9}$$

For simple accumulation clocks the age of a rock or mineral can be determined if the amount of the parent and daughter isotopes can be accurately determined. If the sample contained none of the daughter isotope at the time of formation, then the age of the sample can expressed by Equation 9. In most systems, however, an unknown amount of *initial daughter* can be present in the sample, which precludes the use of the simple accumulation clock presented in Equation 9. If the sample retained some amount of the daughter isotope when it formed, D_0, then this quantity must be subtracted from the total measured amount for the equation to produce the correct age. Though seemingly an insurmountable problem, correcting for initial daughter isotope contents can be resolved empirically through the application of isochron and other methods (Dalrymple 1991). In general, the initial daughter problem does not apply to the K-Ar method, as explained below.

THE K-Ar METHOD

Principles

Potassium (K) is a common rock-forming element. It has the electronic configuration of the noble gas argon (Ar), plus a single valence electron, and it has three natural isotopes; ^{39}K (93.258%), ^{40}K (0.012%), and ^{41}K (6.730%)(Dalrymple and Lanphere, 1969; Steiger and Jäger 1977). Argon has three natural isotopes as well; ^{36}Ar, ^{38}Ar and ^{40}Ar. The first two are stable (neither radioactive nor produced by radioactivity), whereas ^{40}Ar is produced by the radioactive decay of ^{40}K. Actually, only about 10.5% of ^{40}K decays to ^{40}Ar; the rest decays to the common isotope of calcium, ^{40}Ca. In the K-Ar decay scheme the ^{40}K nucleus converts to ^{40}Ar by capturing an orbital electron and transforming a proton to a neutron. The atomic mass (Z = number of protons + neutrons) of the nucleus remains the same (Z = 40) but the number of protons, the atomic number (N), is reduced by one (N = 18). One obvious outcome of this process is that the abundance of ^{40}Ar in the earth and atmosphere increases through time. In fact, von Weiszäcker (1937) predicted that K underwent such a decay scheme partly on the fact that the abundance of argon in the atmosphere was far greater than expected. The present-day atmosphere, for example, contains nearly 1% Ar, of which 99.60% is ^{40}Ar; ^{38}Ar and ^{36}Ar comprise only 0.063% and 0.337%, respectively. The ^{40}Ar/^{36}Ar ratio in the modern atmosphere is 295.5 (Nier 1950).

The K-Ar method of dating is one of the most commonly used accumulation clocks because it has an effective age range from less than 100,000 years to the age of the universe, and it is the only decay scheme that can be used with little or no concern for the presence of the initial daughter isotope, ^{40}Ar, in the sample. This is because Ar, an inert gas, readily diffuses out of the system when heated. Therefore, the principal materials used for K-Ar dating are igneous and metamorphic rocks because they formed from magmas or were transformed by heat (metamorphosed) sometime after formation. The reader is referred to Dalrymple and Lanphere (1969) for a thorough account of the common rocks and minerals used in the K-Ar method.

Volcanic rocks provide the simplest model to explain K-Ar systematics. Imagine a magma chamber beneath a large central volcano. Such magma systems generally have temperatures in excess of 800°C, depending on composition, depth and volatile content, and they can be long-lived, often exceeding tens to hundreds of thousands of years before erupting (Halliday et al. 1989; van den Bogaard 1995). The element K is a major component of most volcanic rocks, comprising up to several weight percent of the bulk magma composition. Although ^{40}K continually decays to ^{40}Ar, even in the magma system, the temperature is so high that the ^{40}Ar gas readily diffuses out of the magma. After erupting, the magma cools quickly to ambient surface temperatures, essentially freezing the molten liquid to form either rocks or pyroclastic materials depending on the mode of eruption. At this point there is expected to be no initial radiogenic (daughter) ^{40}Ar in the system. Any subsequently produced ^{40}Ar will accumulate as the system cools below the closure temperature for the retention of Ar (generally between 500°C and 150°C). The ^{40}Ar atom is large enough that it is physically trapped within chilled, solid crystal lattices and glass networks, where it can remain indefinitely at ambient surface temperatures. In volcanic systems, *time zero* (t = 0) is the moment of eruption, which is analogous to resetting a stopwatch: the subsequent accumulation of ^{40}Ar in the rock records the time elapsed since eruption.

Many radioactive nuclei decay by the emission of electrons from the unstable parent nucleus, called β-decay. The radioactive decay of ^{40}K is unusual in that it occurs by two schemes, by electron capture to ^{40}Ar ($\lambda_\varepsilon = 0.581 \times 10^{-10}$ yr^{-1}) and by β-decay to ^{40}Ca ($\lambda_\beta = 4.962 \times 10^{-10} yr^{-1}$). This dual scheme is referred to as a *branching decay*. Roughly 90% of the total decay of ^{40}K is by β-decay to ^{40}Ca. The half-life of the total decay ($\lambda_\varepsilon + \lambda_\beta$) of ^{40}K is 1.250×10^9yr. It follows that the fraction of ^{40}K atoms that decay to ^{40}Ar is $(\lambda_\varepsilon/\lambda)^{40}K$, where $\lambda = \lambda_\varepsilon + \lambda_\beta$. In the K-Ar dating method the growth of ^{40}Ar over time is expressed as follows:

$$^{40}Ar^* = \lambda_\varepsilon/\lambda[^{40}K(e^{\lambda t} - 1)] \qquad (10)$$

where $^{40}Ar^*$ is *radiogenic argon*. Compare the form of this equation with Equation 8. Solving Equation (10) for t yields the fundamental K-Ar age equation, which the reader is encouraged to compare with Equation (9):

$$t = 1/\lambda \ln[(^{40}Ar^*/^{40}K)(\lambda/\lambda_\varepsilon) + 1] \qquad (11)$$

where t is the calculated age; l is the total decay constant ($5.543 \times 10^{-10} yr^{-1}$), the proportion of ^{40}K atoms that decay per unit time; $\lambda_\varepsilon/\lambda = 0.1048$ is the fraction of ^{40}K decays yielding radiogenic ^{40}Ar, and $^{40}Ar^*$ and ^{40}K are the amounts of radiogenic daughter and parent isotopes in the sample at the present time. The constants are those recommended by the IUGS Subcommission on Geochronology (Steiger and Jäger 1977), based on physical measurements of ^{40}K and its decay. It is evident from Equation 11 that to determine a K-Ar age the amounts of $^{40}Ar^*$ and ^{40}K must be measured. Several excellent books cover the background of the K-Ar method in more detail (Dalrymple and Lanphere 1969; York and Farquhar 1972; Faure 1986).

Procedures

In *conventional K-Ar dating*, the sample is split into two aliquots; one split is used to measure potassium and the other to determine argon. Potassium is usually measured by flame photometry or atomic absorption. Argon gas, which is liberated by melting the sample in a high vacuum extraction system, usually by radio-frequency induction or resistance heating, is measured by mass spectrometry and the Ar isotopic abundances are obtained by isotope dilution (Dalrymple and Lanphere 1969). Generally milligrams to grams of material are fused in a single experiment, depending on age and K content, which can be equivalent to hundreds to thousands of mineral grains.

Assumptions

The primary assumption is that the two aliquots are homogeneous, and each is representative of the K and Ar composition of the bulk rock. If, however, a rock is highly heterogeneous, as are some porphyritic lavas and ignimbrites, the two aliquots might not be chemically equivalent, causing a *decoupling* of ^{40}K and ^{40}Ar from one split to the other. In this case the K-Ar result is generally useless as a measure of geological "age" since formation. Therefore, to facilitate sample homogeneity, the best materials for K-Ar dating are fine-grained lavas and obsidians (homogenous glasses), or pure mineral separates.

A K-Ar age is a function of the accumulation of ^{40}Ar over time. Another crucial assumption is that there is no initial radiogenic ^{40}Ar in the sample at the time of formation, that all ^{40}Ar in the sample is attributed to the *in situ* radioactive decay of ^{40}K (except for that which can be ascribed to atmospheric ^{40}Ar contamination, see below), a condition met by most volcanic rocks. It is further assumed that ^{40}Ar and ^{40}K can be accurately measured.

There are several other equally significant conditions that must be met if the K-Ar method is to yield valid dates: (1) The rock or mineral must remain a "closed system" with respect to K and Ar throughout its history. A closed system is one in which matter neither enters or leaves. A system may be of any size, from a single grain to the size of the universe, but for radiometric dating, the system, usually a rock or mineral grain, need only be closed to the parent and daughter isotopes. Weathering, alteration, and thermal overprinting, by leaching or enriching the rock in K, or by diffusion of Ar out of the rock after its formation, are examples of open system behavior that can dramatically change the sample from its true K-Ar age; (2) Atmospheric argon contamination should be small and appropriate corrections can be made. Since the modern atmosphere is 1% argon, of which 99.6% is ^{40}Ar, it is important to eliminate the atmospheric ^{40}Ar contaminant from the sample; (3) The isotopic composition of K is assumed to be the same for all samples and unchanged except for that change which can be accounted for by radioactive decay of ^{40}K; and (4) It is assumed that the decay constants (λ_ε and λ_β) are accurately known.

Limitations

In practice, the limiting factors in dating geologically young samples by the K-Ar method are twofold. First, severe problems can arise in attempting to measure small volumes of $^{40}Ar^*$ produced by young and/or K-poor samples. The reason is simple; the older the sample, the more $^{40}Ar^*$ there is to measure, and the easier the measurement becomes. The corollary of this is that the younger the sample, the less $^{40}Ar^*$ there is to measure, and the more difficult the measurement becomes.

Second, errors in detecting small amounts of gas are magnified if the sample contains significant amounts of atmospheric argon contamination. Atmospheric argon is present to some degree in all volcanic rocks primarily due to absorption of atmospheric gases into the magma before and during eruption, and secondarily from adsorption onto rock surfaces during even incipient hydration and alteration. This atmospheric gas is enriched in ^{40}Ar, which is analytically indistinguishable from radiogenic $^{40}Ar^*$. However, since the present-day atmospheric abundance ratio of $^{40}Ar/^{36}Ar$ is well known ($^{40}Ar/^{36}Ar_{atmos} = 295.5$), then the desired radiogenic component is merely the difference between the measured $^{40}Ar/^{36}Ar$ value and 295.5:

$$^{40}Ar^* = {}^{40}Ar \text{ measured} - 295.5\ {}^{36}Ar \tag{12}$$

An additional limitation is imposed on rocks that have been physically contaminated. This is particularly true for pyroclastic rocks that can pick up vent-wall fragments during eruption, or detrital minerals during secondary redeposition (Fig. 4.1). Such contamination may not be volumetrically significant in older rocks, but will cause significant errors in Quaternary samples (Curtis, 1966).

THE $^{40}Ar/^{39}Ar$ METHOD

Principles, Assumptions, and Procedures

The $^{40}Ar/^{39}Ar$ method is based on the same fundamental principles and assumptions as the conventional K-Ar method. The main difference is the way in which K is measured. In this method K and Ar are measured virtually simultaneously on the same sample split. Prior to analysis the sample is irradiated with high-energy neutrons at a nuclear reactor. This process converts ^{39}K (a stable isotope of K) in the sample to ^{39}Ar, an isotope that does not occur in nature and is only produced in nuclear reactors according to the following relationship:

$$^{39}Ar = {}^{39}K\ \Delta T \int \varphi(\varepsilon)\ \sigma(\varepsilon)\ d\varepsilon \tag{13}$$

where ^{39}K is the number of atoms of the target isotope, ΔT is the duration of the irradiation, and $\varphi(\varepsilon)$ is the neutron fluence density at energy ε and $\sigma(\varepsilon)$ is the capture cross section for ^{39}K at energy ε, and the integration is carried out

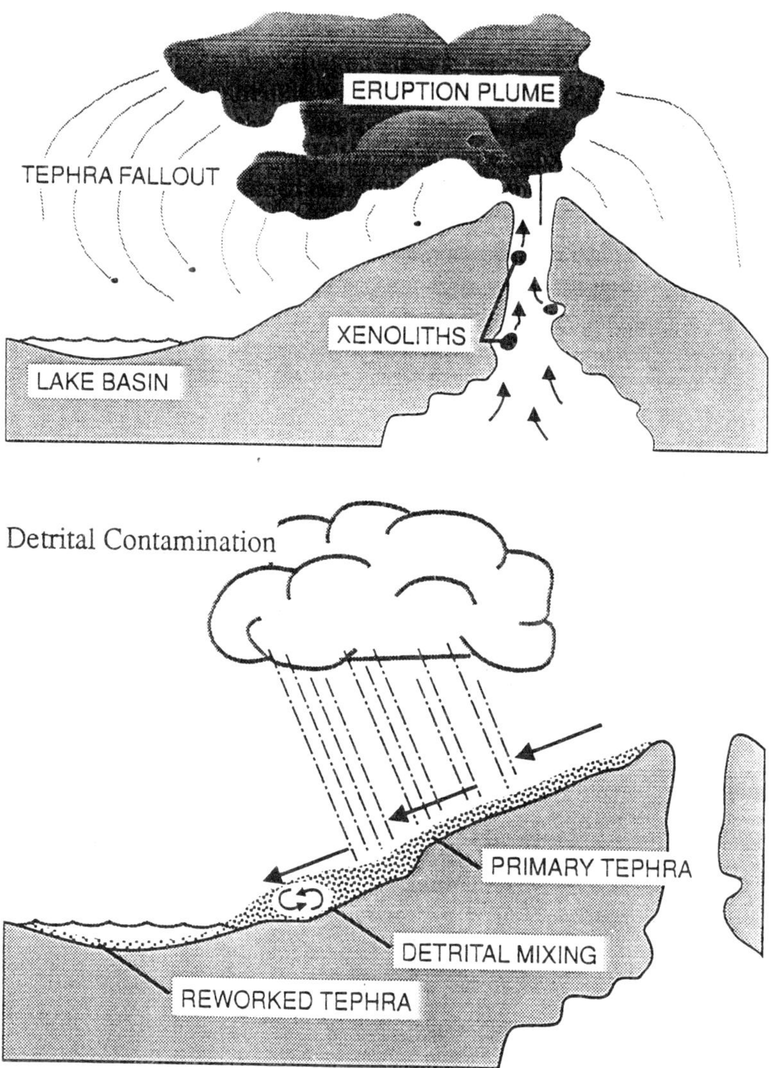

Figure 4.1. Illustration of the processes by which older grains can become incorporated in a tephra deposit. The upper figure shows a cross section of a composite volcano that is erupting explosively. Here, the force of the eruption is shown to rip clasts of country rock (*xenoliths*=strange or foreign rock) from the vent, which become part of the primary tephra fallout. Xenoliths obviously predated the eruption, and—depending on the their age and abundance—can cause measured radiometric ages to be systematically too old. The lower figure illustrates that an unconsolidated volcanic ash can be reworked into the sedimentary environment by storm and river action. During the reworking processes, the primary tephra can pick up older detrital grains from the preexisting surface. Detrital mixing is the most common source of contamination and systematic error in tephras used to calibrate hominid evolution in East Africa.

over the entire energy spectrum of the neutrons (Mitchell 1968). The basis for the $^{40}Ar/^{39}Ar$ dating method was laid down by Merrihue (1965) and Merrihue and Turner (1966).

The irradiated sample is heated in a high vacuum extraction system, usually by radio-frequency induction or resistance heating, liberating the three natural isotopes of Ar plus the new artificially produced ^{39}Ar isotope. The ^{39}Ar concentration becomes a proxy measurement for the concentration of K. All argon isotopes are measured by mass spectrometry, and the $^{40}Ar^*/^{39}Ar$ ratio now replaces the $^{40}Ar^*/^{40}K$ ratio in Equation 11. The $^{40}Ar/^{39}Ar$ age is calculated by comparing the measured $^{40}Ar^*/^{39}Ar$ ratio of the sample to the $^{40}Ar^*/^{39}Ar$ ratio of a standard of known age that is irradiated along with the unknown as a neutron dosimeter (Merrihue 1965; Merrihue and Turner 1966; Dalrymple and Lanphere 1971). Combining Equations 10 and 13 yield the following relationships:

$$^{40}Ar^*/^{39}Ar_K = \lambda_\varepsilon/\lambda\ (^{40}K/^{39}K)\ (1/\Delta T)\ e^{\lambda t} - 1/\int\varphi(\varepsilon)\sigma(\varepsilon)d\varepsilon \qquad (14a)$$

and

$$^{40}Ar^*/^{39}Ar_K = (e^{\lambda t} - 1)/J \qquad (14b)$$

where $^{39}Ar_K$ signifies the production of this isotope from ^{39}K, and J, which represents the constants ($\lambda_\varepsilon/\lambda$ and $^{40}K/^{39}K$) and irradiation parameters (ΔT, φ, and σ), is empirically determined by irradiating a rock or mineral standard of known age (t_s) together with the sample in question. The neutron fluence (φ) and the capture cross section (σ) are difficult parameters to determine uniquely because the energy spectrum of the incident neutrons and the capture cross sections of ^{39}K for neutrons of varying energies are not well known. However, by measuring the ^{40}Ar and ^{39}Ar isotopes of the irradiated standard, φ and σ become implicit to the standard, and J becomes:

$$J = (e^{\lambda ts} - 1)/(^{40}Ar^*/^{39}Ar_K)_s \qquad (15)$$

where the subscript s refers to the standard. The $^{40}Ar/^{39}Ar$ age equation, then, reduces to:

$$t = 1/\lambda\ \ln\{(^{40}Ar^*/^{39}Ar_K)_u J + 1\} \qquad (16a)$$

The subscript u is for the unknown sample.

Unfortunately, there are several unwanted reactions that produce interfering isotopes during irradiation (Mitchell 1968; Berger and York 1970; Brereton 1970). Specifically, ^{39}Ar and ^{36}Ar are produced from fast neutron reactions with Ca, and ^{40}Ar is produced from slow neutron reactions with ^{40}K during neutron bombardment in the reactor. Since ^{36}Ar is crucial in determining the atmospheric argon correction, the extent of this interference must be known if reliable atmospheric corrections and $^{40}Ar/^{39}Ar$ ages are to be achieved. Clearly, young, Ca-rich samples, such as basalt, plagioclase and hornblende, could yield erroneous ages if the appropriate Ca corrections are not applied. These corrections are made by irradiating pure calcium and potassium salts, measuring the Ar isotopes produced, and applying the corrections to the unknown as follows:

$$^{40}Ar^{*}/^{39}Ar_{K} = (1-f_1)(^{40}Ar/^{39}Ar)_m - 295.5(1-f_2)(^{36}Ar/^{39}Ar)_m - (^{40}Ar/^{39}Ar)_K \quad (16b)$$

where:

$$f_1 = 1/|1-(^{37}Ar/^{39}Ar)_{Ca}\,(^{39}Ar/^{37}Ar)_m| \quad (16c)$$

$$f_2 = f_1|1-(^{36}Ar/^{39}Ar)_{Ca}(^{39}Ar/^{36}Ar)_m| \quad (16d)$$

The subscript m signifies the measured quantity, and Ca and K refer to the calcium and potassium-derived isotopes, respectively (Hall and York 1984).

Advantages

The $^{40}Ar/^{39}Ar$ method has several advantages over the conventional K-Ar technique, including: (1) ages are based entirely on measurements of Ar isotopic ratios in a single sample, and do not require a separate measurement of K content; (2) smaller samples can be dated; (3) precision and accuracy are improved because points 1 and 2 eliminate problems of sample heterogeneity and because ratios, not amounts, are measured; and (4) the sample can be heated to progressively higher temperatures and the Ar released from each step can be collected, measured, and an age calculated. If the sample has remained a closed system with respect to K and Ar, then the age of each temperature step should be equivalent to each other within analytical uncertainty. If this is not the case, then one or more of the fundamental assumptions has not been met. Such incremental heating data provide a self-checking mechanism and can provide valid ages for samples that have not been closed systems (Dalrymple and Lanphere 1971).

The Laser Revolution

A laser was first applied to $^{40}Ar/^{39}Ar$ dating by Megrue (1973), who used the short burst of energy from a pulsed laser to fuse tiny fragments (sub milligram in size) of rock in order to determine the spatial distribution of $^{40}Ar/^{39}Ar$ ages within lunar breccias. York *et al.* (1981) demonstrated that a continuous laser held several distinct advantages over the pulsed laser system, such as permitting step heating for the acquisition of age spectra, and providing rapid and complete fusion of a variety of mineral grains. Following irradiation, the samples are loaded into an ultra-high vacuum extraction line and fused by the laser beam through a vacuum window (Megrue 1973; York *et al.* 1981). The argon gas that is released during fusion is purified and analyzed by mass spectrometry, and an age is calculated after the appropriate corrections are applied. A useful by-product of the laser-fusion method is a cleaner system. The Ar background of the system is dramatically reduced because such small amounts of material are fused and only the material itself is heated.

Early experiments with the laser were done on lunar and Precambrian terrestrial materials, because the great age of these rocks made the $^{40}Ar/^{39}Ar$ age determination relatively straightforward despite small sample size. The limitation of the laser-fusion method, however, is the detection limit of small amounts of ^{40}Ar and ^{36}Ar in very young and, now, very small samples. Primarily an instrumentation problem, this limitation was overcome in the past decade by the development of sensitive, low-background mass spectrometers. For example, the pioneering work at the University of Toronto was accomplished on a 25 year old AEI MS-10 mass spectrometer, showing that step-heating analyses could be made on single grains of Precambrian biotite by sequentially increasing the wattage of the continuous laser (York *et al.* 1981). After the acquisition of a new, sensitive mass spectrometer, the Toronto group quickly advanced the applicability of the laser method to much younger ages. By 1986, single grain ages of 35.4±0.6 Ma were achieved on microtektites from the marine record, which helped to calibrate the Eocene-Oligocene boundary (Glass *et al.* 1986). By 1987 the Toronto group was routinely dating single grains of 500 ka old sanidines from volcanic ashes in France and Germany (LoBello *et al.* 1987; van den Bogaard *et al.* 1987).

Perhaps even more important than demonstrating that the single-crystal laser-fusion ages could be measured on Quaternary minerals, LoBello *et al.* (1987) and Bogaard *et al.* (1987) showed that the method provides meaningful eruption ages even for volcanic rocks that have been severely contaminated by older grains, because ages were obtained on individual mineral grains. The grain-discrete laser-fusion method is essential for dating samples that consist of mixed ages, and/or when large amounts of samples are unavailable. Not only can ages be measured from single mineral grains, but Ca/K ratios can be discerned via measured $^{37}Ar/^{39}Ar$ ratios. Such geochemical information is useful in helping to identify multiple age populations (Walter *et al.* 1991).

PRECISION AND ACCURACY

Precision is the measure of analytical uncertainty, and it is caused by pure *random* fluctuations in data acquisition (Bevington 1969). Very low concentrations, such as the rare ^{36}Ar isotope, and $^{40}Ar^*$ of very young and K-poor samples, are very difficult to measure, and contribute the largest sources of random error in K-Ar and $^{40}Ar/^{39}Ar$ dating of young samples.

For example, for Quaternary samples the difference between $^{40}Ar/^{36}Ar$ in the sample and the atmospheric $^{40}Ar/^{36}Ar$ value of 295.5 can be vanishingly small. Since ^{36}Ar concentrations are also typically very small, the error in its measurement is the dominant source of error in the calculated age. Thus, a sample with 95% atmospheric argon contamination (typical for Quaternary basalts, plagioclase, and hornblende) with ^{36}Ar measured with a precision of 0.5% will have an approximate age error of 10% (Hall and York 1984).

Methods of calculating analytical error have been described in detail by Dalrymple and Lanphere (1969) for the K-Ar method and by Berger and York (1970), and Dalrymple and Lanphere (1971) for the $^{40}Ar/^{39}Ar$ method. Dalrymple and Duffield (1988) illustrate that yet another advantage of the laser-fusion technique is that because of its speed and ease of analysis precision is improved simply by increasing the number of replicate analyses. In their laser-fusion study of sanidine from Oligocene rhyolite flows, the standard error of the mean of 6 grains per sample yielded uncertainties of about 0.5% (1σ) and that increasing the number of analyzed grains by a factor of four improved the precision to 0.2% or less (Dalrymple and Duffield 1988).

Accuracy is controlled by *systematic* errors that cause the measurement to deviate in a consistent manner from the true response (Bevington 1969). In the generic K-Ar system, alteration and contamination are the largest sources of systematic errors from natural causes, whereas poor calibration procedures and erroneous constants can lead to systematic errors in the laboratory. Most laboratory errors can be assessed and minimized by analyzing well-known international standards, with the assumption that the standard ages themselves are accurately known. Systematic errors from contamination can be overcome by application of the grain-discrete laser-fusion method (LoBello *et al.* 1987), whereas step-heating, by the laser or by more traditional heating methods, can be used to overcome some problems caused by alteration or metamorphism (McDougall and Harrison 1988).

APPLICATIONS TO HOMINID EVOLUTION

Several examples have been chosen that illustrate how K-Ar and $^{40}Ar/^{39}Ar$ dating have helped to calibrate hominid evolution. This is not a comprehensive survey, but one that illustrates a variety of applications with particular emphasis on the East African hominid record. Not all cases directly involve human evolution, but they are mentioned because they provide interesting insights that are potentially useful for anthropological and archaeological studies.

Olduvai Gorge: Early K-Ar Dating & Recent Laser $^{40}Ar/^{39}Ar$ Revisions

K-Ar Dating and the Pleistocene

A pioneering application of K-Ar dating was brought about by the discovery of hominid fossils and artifacts at Olduvai Gorge, Tanzania. In the late 1950s, Jack Evernden, a geophysicist at the University of California at Berkeley, visited Olduvai Gorge and collected samples, principally tephras, for K-Ar dating from the lowest artifact-bearing deposits in Bed I. The discovery of the hominid fossil, "Zinjanthropus" (*Australopithecus boisei*), from lower Bed I in 1959 made this seminal K-Ar study even more timely. Seven tephra deposits from the hominid-bearing portion of Bed I were initially dated, with ages ranging from 1.89 to 1.57 Ma, demonstrating for the first time the great antiquity of the hominid remains from Olduvai (Evernden *et al.* 1957; Evernden and Curtis 1965).

The discovery of Zinjanthropus coincided with the advent of ultra-high vacuum mass spectrometers for K-Ar dating, such as those developed by John Reynolds, a physicist also at Berkeley (Reynolds 1956). Using this new technology, Evernden analyzed the volcanic rocks from Olduvai, in part, to test the K-Ar method on Pleistocene materials (Evernden *et al.* 1957). It should be borne in mind that even by the early 1960s the age of the Pleistocene was still in question, and that the *old* K-Ar ages from Olduvai were met with skepticism. Such skepticism was expressed by von Koenigswald *et al.* (1961), who stated that "As the lower part of Bed I is said to have an age of 1.75 Myr *(in reference to Leakey et al. 1961)*, the whole Pleistocene Period would have lasted well over 2.00 Myr. This is more than double of what we, cautiously and with good reasons, have estimated". Straus and Hunt (1962) echoed von Koenigswald in their general conclusion that "Having considered the many unanswered sedimentological and paleontological questions which make Olduvai a difficult test case, we prefer . . . to be cautious until more dates for the lower Pleistocene are available". Ultimately, with more dates, these concerns were alleviated, providing anthropologists and geologists alike with the first hard evidence for an "old" Pleistocene, more than doubling its time span, and for the age of associated hominid and archaeological remains (Leakey *et al.* 1961; von Koenigswald *et al.* 1961; Curtis and Evernden 1962; Leakey *et al.* 1962; Straus and Hunt 1962). In addition, this groundbreaking K-Ar study provided calibration points for defining the Olduvai Geomagnetic Event (Grommé and Hay 1963; Grommé and Hay 1967; Brock and Hay 1976), the first magnetostratigraphic study of fossiliferous terrestrial sediments, paving the way for numerical and paleomagnetic calibration of faunal sequences worldwide.

Despite these dramatic successes, the vast majority of the K-Ar dates from Olduvai Gorge were considered unreliable (Evernden and Curtis 1965). The criteria used for *accepting* an age at Olduvai were: (1) if several samples from the same tephra at different localities produced the same age; and (2) if the sample was shown to be a primary volcanic deposit with no contaminating mineral grains. The criteria for *rejecting* an age were: (1) if the tephra showed any visible signs of being reworked and thus subject to admixture of detrital grains; and (2) if different concentrations of mineral separates from the same tephra yielded markedly different ages. The consistency of K-Ar ages with stratigraphy also influenced the evaluation of each analysis. Using these criteria, of 41 ages obtained on tephras from Bed I, only 15 were considered valid (Evernden and Curtis 1965). Even the 15 "valid" dates showed considerable scatter and were difficult to interpret in terms of stratigraphy (Hay 1992), and upon further study it was shown that only a fraction of the 15 dates accepted as valid were ultimately considered reliable. The difficulty in selecting a valid K-Ar age was aptly expressed by R.L. Hay, who noted, "The implication is that accurate K-Ar dating depends to a considerable extent of the ability to select a small number of reliable dates from a much larger number of unreliable ones" (Hay 1992).

Laser-Fusion Method Resolves Anomalies

Recent laser-fusion $^{40}Ar/^{39}Ar$ studies based on analyses of single crystals marked a great improvement over the conventional K-Ar dating of Bed I (Walter *et al.* 1991; Hay 1992; Walter *et al.* 1992b). Ages on all the marker tuffs fall in the correct stratigraphic order, spanning from 2.02 to 1.75 Ma. Tephra yielding two or more ages were identified by the single-crystal laser-fusion method, thus accounting for some and perhaps most of the variability in the earlier K-Ar dates. For example, Tuff 1A is a reworked tephra exposed west of the Fifth Fault above the Naabi Ignimbrite at Olduvai Gorge (Hay 1976). Seven of the ten feldspar grains analyzed by the single-crystal laser-fusion $^{40}Ar/^{39}Ar$ method yielded ages ranging from 340 to 740 Ma, no doubt derived from nearby outcrops of the Pan-African crystalline basement. Two of the remaining three grains yielded concordant ages of 1.98±0.02 Ma, which is in excellent agreement with its stratigraphic age above and below well-dated tephras (Walter *et al.* 1991; Walter *et al.* 1992b). A bulk fusion K-Ar or $^{40}Ar/^{39}Ar$ analyses of these feldspars would yield an erroneous age in excess of 300 Ma.

One of the most illuminating aspects of the laser-fusion study at Olduvai Gorge was the discovery of contaminating grains in primary pyroclastic deposits, such as the Naabi Ignimbrite and pumice clasts from Tuff IE, indicating that simply identifying a unit as a primary volcanic rock is not enough to validate a bulk fusion K-Ar or $^{40}Ar/^{39}Ar$ age. It is only through a population study of single-grain ages that primary eruptive ages can be determined with certainty.

Berekhat Ram and Disturbed $^{40}Ar/^{39}Ar$ Age Spectra

A useful illustration of the application of $^{40}Ar/^{39}Ar$ age spectra is given by the work of Feraud *et al.* (1983) at Berekhat Ram, a small crater lake in

Pleistocene basalts of the Golan Heights in Israel. In the northwest quadrant of the crater two basalt flows are interbedded with 2 meters of reddish-brown paleosols that contain Acheulian handaxes. The upper lava yields concordant K-Ar and $^{40}Ar/^{39}Ar$ ages of about 230 ka, providing a minimum age for the artifacts (Feraud *et al.* 1983).

The lower flow, however, yields discordant K-Ar and $^{40}Ar/^{39}Ar$ ages, as well as a disturbed release spectrum, with ages increasing from 205 to 780 ka (Fig. 4.2), suggesting that the lower lava was not a "closed" K-Ar system. The

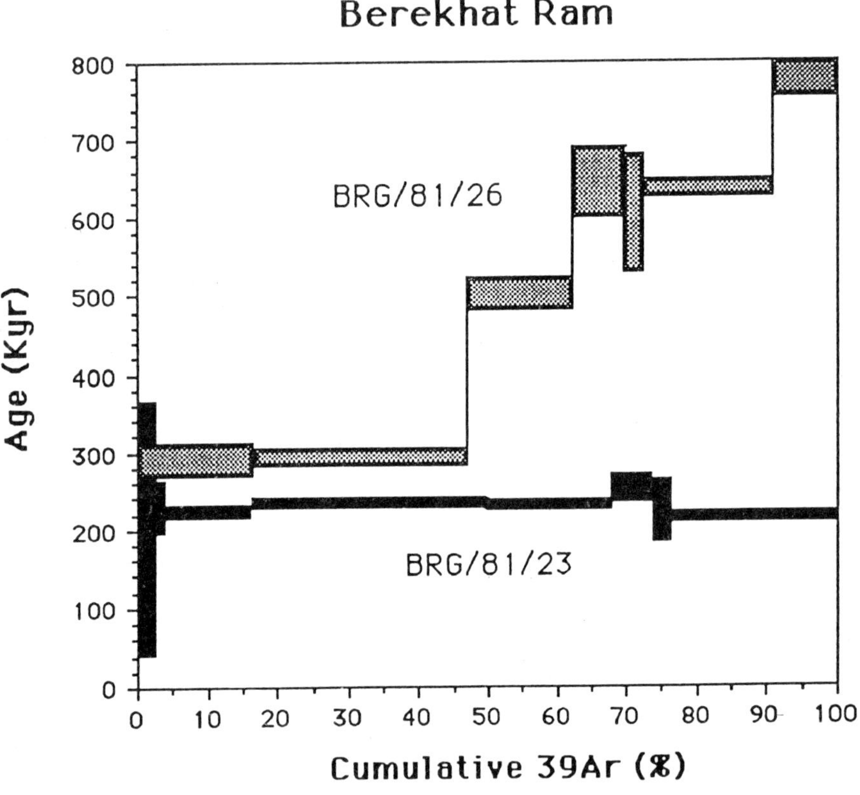

Figure 4.2. $^{40}Ar/^{39}Ar$ age spectra from Berekhat Ram upper (BRG/81/23) and lower (BRG/81/26) basalt flows. Length of bars indicate percent ^{39}Ar released. Width of bars represent ±1 sigma errors. Each bar represents an $^{40}Ar/^{39}Ar$ analysis at a specific temperature increment, from lowest at the left to highest (fusion) at the right. If the sample is undisturbed, that is, if it behaved as a closed system with respect to K and Ar, then the age measured at each temperature increment will be the same, within analytical uncertainty, as it is with BRG/81/23. Such ideal behavior implies that the measured age is the true formation age of the sample. If the sample has been disturbed, however, then the release spectra will be discordant, as it is for BRG/81/26. In this case, no meaningful formation age can be determined. Data and figure from Feraud *et al.* (1983).

integrated $^{40}Ar/^{39}Ar$ age of 470 ± 8 ka is in good agreement with the conventional K-Ar age of 510±32 ka. However, the disturbed pattern indicates the lava probably formed somewhere between 290 and 800 ka (Feraud et al. 1983). The spectrum exhibits two poorly defined age plateaus, at roughly 290 ka and 640 ka, and it is not possible to give a single, satisfactory interpretation. The most likely explanation for this pattern is either argon loss at low temperatures due to alteration or thermal overprinting, or the presence of excess argon in the flow. There is no independent support for either hypothesis. Nevertheless, the important point to be gleaned is that its K-Ar age of 510±32 ka is unreliable. Without contrasting $^{40}Ar/^{39}Ar$ spectra (Fig. 4.2) there would be no analytical reason to question the validity of the conventional K-Ar age of the lower basalt.

Young Lavas with Excess ^{40}Ar and the Initial Daughter Problem

During the Pleistocene Nome River glaciation of northwestern Alaska, glaciers covered an area ten times more extensive than any later glacial interval. The Nome river glaciation was initially believed to be about 800 ka old based on conventional K-Ar ages on basaltic lavas that overlie Nome River drift at Minnie Creek, in the central Seward Peninsula (Kauffman and Hopkins 1985). Based on these results the Nome River glaciation was assigned to the early Pleistocene (Kauffman and Hopkins 1986). Subsequent analysis by the laser-fusion $^{40}Ar/^{39}Ar$ method, on milligram-size subsamples of the Minnie Creek basalt, indicated the presence of extraneous ^{40}Ar that rendered the conventional K-Ar ages on larger bulk samples of the same flow too old (Kauffman *et al.* 1991). The younger age for the Nome River glaciation is supported by a new K-Ar age of 564±64 ka on the Lava Creek basalt flow that stratigraphically predates the Minnie Creek basalt.

Laser-fusion $^{40}Ar/^{39}Ar$ analyses on 14 milligram-size subsamples of the Minnie Creek basalt produced a wide variation in ages, yielding an apparent mean age of 600±340 ka.. Evaluating these data further using an age-frequency plot (Fig. 4.3) revealed that 2 of the 14 analyses produced ages greater that 1 million years. This bimodal age distribution was interpreted to mean that the analyses were composed of 2 isotopically distinct phases: a primary population of 12 subsamples that represent the true age of the Minnie Creek basalt (0.467±0.049 Ma), and the 2 older contaminated subsamples (1.31±0.16 Ma).

An isochron plot of this data set provides additional evidence supporting the notion that the basalt is contaminated. Isochron diagrams are constructed from $^{40}Ar/^{39}Ar$ data plotted as either $^{40}Ar/^{36}Ar$ versus $^{40}Ar/^{39}Ar$ or $^{36}Ar/^{40}Ar$ versus $^{39}Ar/^{40}Ar$: such plots will yield a straight line provided that all data in the set represent portions of the same rock that formed at the same time with the same initial $^{40}Ar/^{36}Ar$ ratio. Such plots permit an evaluation of whether the data conform to ideal behavior or whether systematic errors occur, such as the presence of excess ^{40}Ar (York 1969; McDougall and Harrison 1988). An

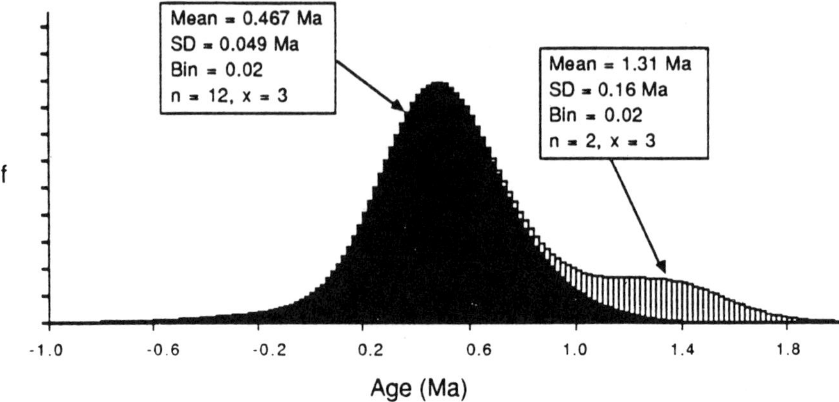

Figure 4.3. An age-probability graph of fourteen mini-bulk analyses of the late Pleistocene Minnie Creek basalt. The plot, based on a Gaussian probability distribution function, is a powerful way to graphically depict a suite of $^{40}Ar/^{39}Ar$ results from a single sample. If all the subsamples analyzed are the same age, then the data would yield a single bell-shaped curve, where the peak of the curve is equivalent to the mean age and the tails of the curve represent purely random analytical error If, however, the sample is contaminated by grains significantly older than the primary age, then multiple curves will be displayed. In the case of the Minnie Creek basalt, the histogram yields two curves, one with an mean age of 1.31±0.16 Ma (n=2), whereas the other yeilds a mean age of 0.47±0.05 Ma (n=12). The horizontal scale is in millions of years. and the vertical scale is relative probability. Bin is the bin width (Ma) used to construct the plot, and X is a scaling factor (Deino and Potts, 1992).

"inverse" isochron plot, so-named when ^{40}Ar is in the denominator, of all 14 laser-fusion analyses was constructed using the least-squares regression technique for correlated errors (York 1969). In this plot, the Y-intercept is equal to the initial $^{40}Ar/^{36}Ar$ ratio and the x-intercept is a function of the sample's age as defined by the fitted line. Although the initial $^{40}Ar/^{36}Ar$ ratio is not significantly different from the atmospheric, the mean square of weighted deviates (MSWD) is greater than expected from pure random errors alone, suggesting that the fit is poor and that nonrandom errors are associated with the data. The MSWD is a reduced χ^2 statistic ($\chi^2/n-2$), which by definition equals 1 if the observed population meets the expected distribution (Bevington 1969). A second isochron was constructed excluding the 2 analyses that produced the anomalously old dates yielding a MSWD of 1, defining an age of 466±55 ka, and an initial $^{40}Ar/^{36}Ar$ ratio of 296±4 (Fig. 4.4). This age compares favorably with the minimum age observed in the age-frequency plot (Fig. 4.3).

These results demonstrate that extraneous ^{40}Ar enrichments can occur even in basaltic lava flows that erupted at temperatures exceeding 1000°C, contrary to one of the primary assumptions in the K-Ar method. In the case of the Minnie Creek basalt, the excess ^{40}Ar observed in 2 of 14 rock fragments

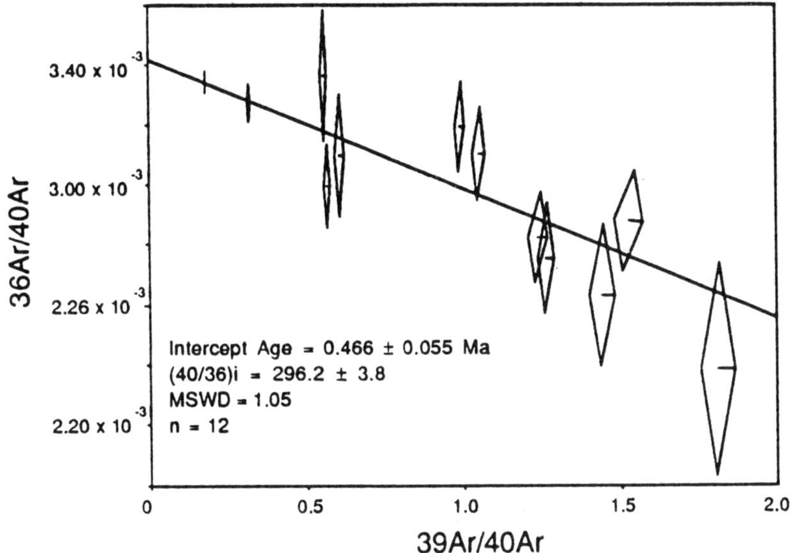

Figure 4.4. Inverse $^{40}Ar/^{39}Ar$ correlation diagram showing the X-intercept age (0.47±0.05 Ma) and the Y-intercept value for the initial $^{40}Ar/^{36}Ar$ ratio (296.2±0.8) for the Minnie Creek basalt. This so-called isochron diagram (*isochron*=Gr. same age) can be used to test how well these data conform to ideal $^{40}Ar/^{39}Ar$ behavior. It is a fundamental assumption that all phases of a rock regardless of K content begin at t=0 with the same initial $^{40}Ar/^{36}Ar$ value. The amount of $^{40}Ar^*$ that accumulates is a function of K content and time. If these assumptions are met, then all data points will fall on or statistically near a straight line constructed through the points using a least-squares, linear regression technique (York 1969). For example, this plot shows that the mean square of weighted deviates (MSWD) is one, which indicates that the scatter about the line is solely from random error, suggesting that the Gaussian model used in Fig 4.3 is appropriate. The MSWD is a reduced Chi-squared statistic (c^2/n-2), which by definition is one if the observed population meets the expected distribution.

indicates that the contamination is a discrete phase that is inhomogeneously dispersed in the lava, as if xenocrysts of basement material were incorporated into the lava during eruption and were incompletely degassed before the lava itself cooled below the blocking temperature for the retention of argon. It seems that the laser-fusion $^{40}Ar/^{39}Ar$ method was able to measure the dispersion of ages in rock fragments small enough to reveal this isotopic heterogeneity.

A similar case was made for young basaltic lavas from the Auckland volcanic field of New Zealand (McDougall *et al.* 1969), where excess ^{40}Ar was assumed because conventional K-Ar ages on large bulk samples were significantly older than expected from stratigraphic and ^{14}C considerations. The ubiquitous occurrence of xenolithic quartz and pyroxene aggregates in the Auckland lavas suggested that the excess ^{40}Ar was from contamination of the magmas by older country rock, probably the underlying Mesozoic graywackes and argillites (McDougall *et al.* 1969). In a ^{40}Ar/^{39}Ar step heating analysis of one of the same samples analyzed by McDougall *et al.* (1969), Hall and York (1984) established the presence of excess ^{40}Ar in the Auckland lavas by observing an ^{40}Ar* enrichment throughout the spectrum, but particularly at the high temperature, low K portion of the release spectrum. This pattern is most readily explained by the high temperature release of excess ^{40}Ar from Mesozoic pyroxene xenocrysts, as first suggested by McDougall *et al.* (1969).

Hominid Evolution, Time Scale Calibrations, and Laser-Fusion

Koobi Fora Formation

In the vicinity of Lake Turkana, Kenya, there occurs a thick sequence of Plio-Pleistocene lacustrine, fluvial and deltaic sediments named the Koobi Fora Formation that contain abundant remains of vertebrate fossils, including hominids, and stone tools. Interbedded rhyolitic tephras facilitate stratigraphic mapping, correlation and dating. Some of the tephras contain pumice clasts, from which anorthoclase phenocrysts were separated for K-Ar and ^{40}Ar/^{39}Ar analysis. Seven tuffs were dated (McDougall 1985), ranging from 4.1 to 0.74 Ma, yielding concordant ages on multiple samples from each tephra. The results are stratigraphically consistent, and their ^{40}Ar/^{39}Ar age spectra are nearly flat, indicating that the feldspars remained a closed system with respect to K and Ar isotopes since eruption. The radiometric ages established by this study helped to place the abundant hominid remains from Koobi Fora into a precise temporal framework (Feibel *et al.* 1989). The Turkana Basin is the longest and most comprehensively dated hominid sequence in the world, based on these and subsequent studies (Brown *et al.* 1985; McDougall, 1985; McDougall *et al.* 1985; Feibel *et al.* 1989; McDougall *et al.* 1992a; Leakey *et al.* 1995).

The radiometric dating story at Koobi Fora has not always been so tidy. It has, on occasion, been the source of heated controversy, as was the case for the KBS Tuff (Hay 1980). The KBS Tuff, a water lain, pumice-bearing volcanic ash, is a prominent stratigraphic marker in the middle of the Koobi Fora Formation. In 1969, primitive stone artifacts were discovered in the tuff itself (Isaac *et al.* 1971). Feldspars from this tuff were dated by both the conventional K-Ar total fusion method and the newly developed ^{40}Ar/^{39}Ar step-heating method (Fitch and Miller 1970). The conventional K-Ar method produced an age of 2.37±0.01 Ma, whereas an age of 2.61±0.26 Ma was assigned to the tuff based on the ^{40}Ar/^{39}Ar age spectrum. The younger conventional K-Ar age was believed to be erroneous due to argon loss caused by regional hydrothermal alteration. Extraneous argon contamination via detrital minerals, which could account for the older age, was not considered to be a serious problem.

By 1972, numerous hominids were found stratigraphically below the KBS Tuff, including individuals attributed to *Australopithecus* and *Homo*

(Leakey 1973). The age of the KBS was critical for determining when the divergence between these two hominid groups occurred. Doubt about the 2.61 Ma age for the KBS began to surface as faunal correlations suggested that an age of 2.0 Ma would be more compatible with evidence from other East African sites (Cooke and Maglio 1972; White and Harris 1977). The controversy was compounded by new K-Ar dates of 1.60 Ma for the KBS Tuff from one locality and 1.82 Ma from another (Curtis *et al.* 1975). The 1.6 Ma age was later found to be too young due to a K measurement error (Drake *et al.* 1980). This confusion was further complicated by a fission track study that yielded an age of 2.44±0.08 Ma on zircons from the tuff (Hurford *et al.* 1976). Fitch *et al.* (1976) recalculated their original $^{40}Ar/^{39}Ar$ step-heating data and revised their age to 2.42 Ma.

In the meantime, paleomagnetic data strongly supported the view that the KBS Tuff was in the Olduvai Event and could be no older than about 1.8 Ma (Hillhouse *et al.* 1977). Furthermore, glass shards and feldspar grains from the KBS Tuff were found to be chemically similar to the ~1.8 Ma old Tuff H2 of the Shungura Formation north of Lake Turkana (Cerling *et al.* 1979). The most comprehensive and conclusive study of the KBS Tuff was provided by McDougall *et al.* (1980) and Gleadow (1980) who used careful K-Ar and fission track analyses to suggest ages of 1.89±0.01 Ma and 1.87±0.04 Ma, respectively (Gleadow 1980; McDougall *et al.* 1980). These studies showed that the 2.4–2.6 Ma age (Fitch and Miller 1970; Fitch *et al.* 1976) for the KBS Tuff is too old, perhaps due to detrital contamination (Gleadow 1980), which could be avoided with assiduous sample preparation. Likewise, the slightly younger K-Ar ages of ~1.8 Ma suggested by Curtis *et al.* (1975) were incorrect, most likely due to incomplete fusion of the feldspars during argon analysis. Subsequent $^{40}Ar/^{39}Ar$ analyses yielded a concordant age of 1.88±0.02 Ma, resolving the earlier conflict between K-Ar and $^{40}Ar/^{39}Ar$ measurements on the KBS Tuff (McDougall 1981). Furthermore, McDougall (1981) suggested that unrecognized, systematic, analytical errors may explain the erroneously old $^{40}Ar/^{39}Ar$ results.

In addition to providing calibration points for hominid evolution, the radiometric ages were used in conjunction with paleomagnetic measurements to construct a detailed magnetostratigraphic framework for the Koobi Fora Formation (Hillhouse *et al.* 1986). Feibel *et al.* (1989) noted that although the tephra ages from Koobi Fora were internally consistent, they were apparently at variance with the estimated boundary ages for the geomagnetic polarity time scale (GPTS) (McDougall and Chamaluan 1966; Mankinen and Dalrymple 1979), exceeding the boundary ages by about 100,000 years. At first, this discrepancy was thought to be due to a time lag between tephra eruption and redeposition in the sedimentary record (Feibel *et al.* 1989), but in due time it was recognized that the radiometric ages for Koobi Fora actually provided data to revise and recalibrate the GPTS (McDougall *et al.* 1992a; McDougall *et al.* 1992b).

The notion that the GPTS needed to be revised was first proposed by Johnson (1982) and elaborated by Shackelton *et al.* (1990) based on marine-astronomical calibrations using oxygen isotopes as proxy indicators of climatic fluctuations due to variations in the earth's orbit. The initial purpose of this type of study was to evaluate the orbital theory of the Pleistocene ice ages and to develop a high resolution time scale for the past 780 ka (Johnson 1982; Imbrie *et al.* 1984). Such orbitally tuned data have now been used to calibrate an "astronomical" polarity time scale (APTS) for the past 3 to 4 Ma (Shackleton *et al.* 1990; Hilgen, 1991), indicating that the ages for the radiometrically based GPTS were consistently too young by 5 to 7%. Similar age discrepancies were subsequently noted radiometrically for the Olduvai Subchron (Walter *et al.* 1991) and for the Brunhes/Matuyama boundary (Baksi *et al.* 1992). The most likely explanation for the consistent underestimation of the widely used K-Ar based GPTS is due to loss of small but significant amounts of $^{40}Ar^{*}$ from basalts—until now the most commonly used material for GPTS calibration—most likely from glassy, poorly crystallized, or altered phases, despite careful choice of samples (McDougall *et al.* 1992a).

Hadar Formation

The Hadar Formation of Ethiopia is one of the most prolific early hominid sites in the world. Initial surveys in the early 1970s recovered more than 240 hominid specimens including the partial skeleton nicknamed "Lucy" and the fossil assemblage of 13 hominid individuals called the "First Family". All of these specimens are attributed to *Australopithecus afarensis* (Johanson *et al.* 1978). Accurate age estimates for the Hadar hominid fossils, however, were elusive for many years. Initial dating attempts were hampered by either a scarcity of datable components in the tephras or by detrital contamination (Walter 1981; Walter and Aronson 1982) Unlike at Koobi Fora, none of the Hadar tephra contain pumice clasts from which primary feldspar could be extracted, prohibiting the selection of obvious primary phases. Attempts to date the altered Kadada Moumou basalt by bulk K-Ar and $^{40}Ar/^{39}Ar$ methods proved difficult because of an apparent loss of ^{40}Ar during alteration, coupled with variable amounts of excess ^{40}Ar (Aronson *et al.* 1977; Walter and Aronson 1982; Renne *et al.* 1993; Walter and Aronson 1993).

The apparent K-Ar age of 3.6 Ma for this basalt was challenged when a chemical correlation was proposed between the Sidi Hakoma Tuff at Hadar and the Tulu Bor Tuff at east Turkana (Brown and Cerling 1982). The Sidi Hakoma Tuff defines the base of the Sidi Hakoma Member of the Hadar Formation, and is stratigraphically below the basalt. The Tulu Bor Tuff is a widespread marker bed in the Turkana basin of northern Kenya and southern Ethiopia, where its age is well constrained within the Gauss normal chron (Brown *et al.* 1978), between 3.15 and 3.4 Ma (using boundary ages for the GPTS known at that time). By inference, the Sidi Hakoma Tuff, and the Kadada Moumou basalt, could be no older that 3.4 Ma. Subsequently, a tephra layer was found in DSDP cores from the Gulf of Aden that matched the glass chemistry of the Sidi Hakoma and Tulu Bor Tuffs (Sarna-Wojcicki *et al.* 1985), suggesting an age of about 3.2 Ma for the tephra layer. Additional dating studies at Turkana refined the age estimate of the Tulu Bor Tuff to 3.36±0.02 Ma, based on stratigraphic scaling between units of known age (Feibel *et al.* 1989). However, the Tulu Bor Tuff itself has never been directly or reliably dated by any radiometric technique.

In 1990, after a 14-year hiatus in field activity, the Hadar Formation was resampled for dating. The renewed sampling strategy was guided by recent technological improvements in $^{40}Ar/^{39}Ar$ analyses that achieved a breakthrough in dating young, small samples using a laser beam to melt the material (York *et al.* 1981; LoBello *et al.* 1987; van den Bogaard *et al.* 1987). This technique provided the first reliable radiometric ages for important tephrostratigraphic markers at Hadar, including the Sidi Hakoma Tuff, the Triple Tuff, and the Kada Hadar Tuff (Walter and Aronson 1993; Walter 1994).

Alkali feldspars are extremely rare in the Sidi Hakoma Tuff. In 1977, just six small grains (ca. 0.2 mm in diameter) were recovered from roughly 50 kg of tephra. Some grains had glass rims, suggesting that they were comagmatic with the primary tephra. Being insufficient by far for conventional K-Ar dating, in 1984 the six grains were consumed in a failed attempt to date them using the new laser-fusion $^{40}Ar/^{39}Ar$ dating system then being developed at the University of Toronto, prior to the advent of the latest generation of sensitive mass spectrometers. After resampling this tephra in 1990, 20 feldspar grains (0.4 to 0.2 mm in width) were recovered from approximately 200 kg of tephra. Four single grain and four multiple grain dates were obtained, using a laser to fuse the grains and a sensitive, low blank mass spectrometer, yielding an age of 3.40±0.03 Ma (Walter and Aronson 1993). This result established a firm age for the lower Hadar Formation, providing the first direct radiometric age estimate for the oldest *A. afarensis* fossils at Hadar.

The Kada Hadar Tuff is a widespread marker that defines the base of the Kada Hadar Member, the youngest member of the Hadar Formation. Lucy and the First Family occur a few meters above and below this tephra, respectively. Previous attempts to date the Kada Hadar Tuff yielded K-Ar dates of 4.1 to 4.6 Ma on bulk fusions of K-feldspars (Aronson *et al.* 1980). Fission track dates on zircon indicated significant amounts of Miocene contamination in Hadar tephras, including the Kada Hadar Tuff (Aronson *et al.* 1980; Walter 1981). New single-crystal laser-fusion $^{40}Ar/^{39}Ar$ analyses (Walter 1994) yielded mean dates of 3.17±0.03, 3.18±0.02, and 3.19±0.01 Ma for three subsamples of the tephra, where 10 individual grain ages were pooled for each subsample. Of the thirty grains measured, four produced Miocene ages ranging from 8 to 24 Ma, explaining the anomalously old dates obtained by the conventional K-Ar method. Pooling the remaining 26 grains yielded a mean age of 3.18±0.01 Ma.

Lucy, recovered from a small sand channel 2–3 m above this tuff, is now precisely dated to just less than 3.18 Ma, probably within the standard error of the mean.

Early work at Hadar and elsewhere showed morphological stasis in *A. afarensis* (Johanson and White 1979), but temporal controls were inadequate. We are now in a position to accurately measure rates of faunal change at Hadar, and to suggest that *A. afarensis* existed, virtually unchanged for at least 500 ka (Kimbel *et al.* 1994). The tempo of hominid evolution at Hadar is now well established solely because the laser-fusion $^{40}Ar/^{39}Ar$ method was able to date individual mineral grains.

In addition to calibrating hominid evolution at Hadar, these ages provided supportive evidence that the boundary ages for the Kaena and Mammoth subchrons of the GPTS needed to be increased (Walter *et al.* 1992a; Renne *et al.* 1993; Walter and Aronson 1993; Walter 1994) similar to the conclusion drawn by McDougall *et al.* (1992). It seems that high-precision ages on K-feldspars from rhyolitic tephra in long sedimentary sequences is an excellent way to calibrate magnetostratigraphic events.

Recent Discoveries

In addition to the examples presented above, the laser-fusion $^{40}Ar/^{39}Ar$ method has been applied to: (1) dating the earliest evidence of Acheulian artifacts to 1.4 Ma at the site of Konso-Gardula in Ethiopia (Asfaw *et al.* 1992); (2) the oldest *Australopithecus afarensis* fossils dated to between 3.4±0.04 Ma and 3.89 ± 0.02 Ma, from Maka, Ethiopia (Hall *et al.* 1984; White *et al.* 1993); (3) calibrating a new hominid genus, *Ardipithecus ramidus*, dated to around 4.4 Ma, from Aramis, Ethiopia (White *et al.* 1994; WoldeGabriel *et al.* 1994; White *et al.* 1995) and (4) calibrating a new 4.0 Ma old species, *Australopithecus anamensis*, from Kenya that appears to be a direct ancestor of *Australopithecus afarensis* (Leakey *et al.* 1995). In each case, the ability to detect and eliminate detrital contamination by dating single grains has been the only way that reliable dates could have been obtained. Without the single-crystal laser-fusion $^{40}Ar/^{39}Ar$ method, hominid evolution in East Africa would not be as precisely calibrated as it is today.

CONCLUSION

The K-Ar method is one of the most commonly used of all radiometric techniques mainly because of its versatility and its applicability to such a wide range of ages. Over the past thirty years, the $^{40}Ar/^{39}Ar$ technique, an elegant variation of the conventional K-Ar method, has become a major force in K-Ar geochronology because: (1) ages are based entirely on the measurement of Ar isotopes in a single sample, and do not require a separate measurement of K:

(2) smaller samples can be dated; (3) by circumventing errors due to sample heterogeneity, precision and accuracy are improved; and (4) age spectra can be obtained by incrementally heating the sample, providing a means to evaluate whether the fundamental assumption of closed system behavior has been met. The advent of the laser-fusion $^{40}Ar/^{39}Ar$ technique over the past 20 years permits precise ages to be obtained on very small samples, even the size of single mineral grains or smaller.

The $^{40}Ar/^{39}Ar$ laser-microprobe has revolutionized K-Ar dating because it can be used on problematic samples, such as contaminated samples or those that have insufficient material, which could not have been dated by traditional bulk fusion methods. The grain-discrete ability of the laser-fusion method has provided new insights into K-Ar systematics that can now be applied to a variety of igneous (Pringle *et al.* 1991; Pringle *et al.* 1992), metamorphic (Hames and Hodges 1993), impact (Izett *et al.* 1991), and even sedimentary rocks (Smith *et al.* 1993). An excellent example of its effectiveness is seen in how well it has been employed to calibrate the hominid record in East Africa, where detrital contamination of tephra has long plagued earlier attempts to accurately date these ashes by bulk-fusion K-Ar and $^{40}Ar/^{39}Ar$ means.

The laser-fusion $^{40}Ar/^{39}Ar$ method will continue to be an invaluable research tool for some time to come. Currently, the method is being used to date the late Quaternary (Deino *et al.* 1994; Hu *et al.* 1994; van den Bogaard 1995; Chen *et al.* 1996), with the aim of providing precise single-grain ages on samples that overlap in time with the ^{14}C method. If this can be achieved, then $^{40}Ar/^{39}Ar$ dating will be used as a means to check and possibly even calibrate ^{14}C ages, particularly those at the older end of the radiocarbon spectrum where the correction for the variation in cosmogenic production of ^{14}C through time may not be well defined. The future of K-Ar dating lies in its versatility. It will be intriguing to see where, how, and in what form the next generation of this method will be applied.

ACKNOWLEDGMENTS

I extend my sincere appreciation to Professor R. E. Taylor for inviting me to contribute a chapter to this volume. His encouragement and forbearance are gratefully acknowledged. I wish to thank Donald Johanson, Eric Meikle, and an anonymous reviewer for critically reading the manuscript, and for providing helpful suggestions. I am indebted to a number of individuals (teachers, advisors, friends, students, and colleagues) who have helped to formulate my knowledge of K-Ar and $^{40}Ar/^{39}Ar$ systematics and tephrochronology: Jim Aronson, Derek York, John Westgate, Stan Mertzman, Bill Hart, Giday WoldeGabriel, Bill Hackett, Chris Hall, Paul van den Bogaard, Norm Evensen, Pat Smith, Yanshao Chen, Paul Manega, and Richard Hay, to name but a few. If, however, this chapter suffers from any errors, they are mine alone. I am extremely grateful for the financial support of the Institute of Human Origins, the National Science Foundation, and the National Geographic Society for providing the research platform from which this manuscript was written. I extend my thanks to the Ethiopian Ministry of Culture and Information and the Ethiopian Institute of Geological Surveys for their continued support of our research at Hadar. I also thank my colleagues at the Institute of Human Origin and with the Hadar Research Project for the many shared experiences that have helped to shape my appreciation for the complexities of human evolution. Finally, I dedicate this work to my wife, Gail, for her patience and wisdom.

REFERENCES

Aldrich, L.T., and Nier, A.O. 1948 Argon 40 in potassium minerals. *Physical Review.* 74: 876–877.

Aronson, J.L., Schmitt, T.J., Walter, R.C., Taieb, M., Tiercelin, J.-J., Johanson, D.C., Naeser, C.W., and Nairn, A.E.M. 1977 New geochronologic and paleomagnetic data for the hominid-bearing Hadar Formation of Ethiopia. *Nature* 267: 323–327.

Aronson, J.L., Walter, R.C., Taieb, M., and Naeser, C.W. 1980 New Geochronological Information for the Hadar Formation and the adjacent Central Afar, Ethiopia. *In* Leakey, R.E., and Ogot, B.A., eds., *Proceedings of the 8th Pan African Congress of Prehistory and Quaternary Studies, Nairobi 5 to 10 September 1977*. Nairobi, The International Louis Leakey Memorial Institute for African Prehistory: 47–52.

Asfaw, B., Beyne, Y., Suwa, G., Walter, R.C., White, T.D., WoldeGabriel, G., and Yemane, T. 1992 Konso-Gardula: the earliest Acheulian. *Nature* 360: 732–735.

Baksi, A.K., Hsu, V., McWilliams, M.O., and Farrar, E. 1992 ^{40}Ar/^{39}Ar Dating of the Brunhes-Matuyama Geomagnetic Field Reversal. *Science* 256: 256–257.

Berger, G.W., and York, D. 1970 Precision of the ^{40}Ar/^{39}Ar dating technique. *Earth Planetary Science Letters* 9: 39–44.

Bevington, P.R. 1969 *Data Reduction and Error Analysis for the Physical Sciences.* New York, McGraw-Hill, Inc.

Brereton, N.T. 1970 Corrections for interfering isotopes in the ^{40}Ar/^{39}Ar dating method. *Earth and Planetary Science Letters* 8: 427–433.

Brock, A., and Hay, R.L. 1976 The Olduvai Event at Olduvai Gorge. *Earth and Planetary Science Letters* 29: 126–130.

Brown, F.H., and Cerling, T.E. 1982 Stratigraphical significance of the Tulu Bor Tuff of the Koobi Fora Formation. *Nature* 299: 212–215.

Brown, F.H., McDougall, I., Davies, T., and Maier, R. 1985 An integrated Plio-Pleistocene chronology of the Turkana Basin. *In* Delson, E., ed., *Paleoanthropology: The Hard Evidence*. New York, Alan R. Liss: 82–90.

Brown, F.H., Shuey, R.T., and Croes, M.K. 1978 Magnetostratigraphy of the Shungura and Usno Formations, southwestern Ethiopia: new data and comprehensive reanalysis. *Geophysical Journal of the Royal Astromomical Society* 54: 519–538.

Cerling, T.E., Brown, F.H., Cerling, B.W., Curtis, G.H., and Drake, R.E. 1979 Preliminary correlations between the Koobi Fora and Shungura Formations, East Africa. *Nature* 79: 118–121.

Chen, Y., Smith, P.E., Evensen, N.M., and York, D. 1996 The edge of time: dating young volcanic ash layers with the ^{40}Ar-^{39}Ar laser probe. *Science* 274: 1176–1178.

Cooke, H.B.S., and Maglio, V.J. 1972 Plio-Pleistocene stratigraphy in East Africa in relation to proboscidean and suid evolution *In* Bishop, W.W. and Miller, J.A., ed., *Calibration of Hominoid Evolution* Edinburgh, Scottish Academic Press, Ltd.: 303–329.

Curtis, G.H. 1966 The problem of contamination in obtaining accurate dates of young geologic rocks. *In* Shaeffer, O.A., and Zäringer, J., eds., *Potassium argon dating*. New York, Springer-Verlag: 151–162.

Curtis, G.H., Drake, R.E., Cerling, T.E., and Hampel, J. 1975 Age of KBS tuff in Koobi Fora Formation, East Rudolf, Kenya. *Nature* 258: 395–398.

Curtis, G.H., and Evernden, J.F. 1962 Age of basalt underlying Bed I, Olduvai. *Nature* 194: 610–612.

Dalrymple, G.B. 1991 *The Age of the Earth*. Stanford, Stanford University Press.

Dalrymple, G.B., and Duffield, W.A. 1988 High precision $^{40}Ar/^{39}Ar$ dating of Oligocene rhyolites from the Mogollon-Datil volcanic field using a continuous laser system. *Geophyscial Research Letters* 15: 463–466.

Dalrymple, G.B., and Lanphere, M.A. 1969 *Potassium-Argon Dating*. San Francisco, W.H. Freeman.

Dalrymple, G.B., and Lanphere, M.A. 1971 $^{40}Ar/^{39}Ar$ technique of K-Ar dating: a comparison with the conventional technique *Earth and Planetary Science Letters* 12: 300–308.

Deino, A.L., Curtis, G.H., Southon, J., Terrasi, F., and Campajola, L. 1994 ^{14}C and $^{40}Ar/^{39}Ar$ dating of the Campanian Ignimbrite, Phelgrean Fields, Italy, Dalrymple, G.B., Lanphere, M.A., and Turrin, B. ICOG-8 Abstract. Circular 1107 32. Berkeley, U.S. Geological Survey:

Drake, R.E., Curtis, G.H., Cerling, T.E., Cerling, B.W., and Hampel, J. 1980 KBS Tuff dating and geochronology of tuffaceous sediments in the Koobi Fora and Shungura Formations, East Africa. *Nature* 283: 368–372.

Evernden, J.A., and Curtis, G.H. 1965 The potassium-argon dating of late Cenozoic rocks in East Africa and Italy. *Current Anthropology*. 6: 343–364.

Evernden, J.F., Curtis, G.H., and Kistler, R.W. 1957 Potassium-argon dating of Pleistocene volcanics. *Quaternaria* 5: 348–385.

Faure, G. 1986 *Principles of isotope geology*. New York, John Wiley & Sons.

Feibel, C.S., Brown, F.H., and McDougall, I. 1989 Stratigraphic Context of Fossil Hominids From the Omo Group Deposits: Northern Turkana Basin, Kenya and Ethiopia. *American Journal of Physical Anthropology* 78: 595–622.

Feraud, G., York, D., Hall, C.M., Goren, N., and Schwarcz, H.P. 1983 $^{40}Ar/^{39}Ar$ age limit for an Acheulian site in Israel. *Nature* 304: 263–265.

Fitch, F.J., Hooker, P.J., and Miller, J.A. 1976 $^{40}Ar/^{39}Ar$ dating of the KBS tuff in Koobi Fora Formation, East Rudolf, Kenya. *Nature* 263: 740–744.

Fitch, F.J., and Miller, J.A. 1970 Radioisotopic age determinations of Lake Rudolf artefact site. *Nature* 226: 226–228.

Glass, B.P., Hall, C.H., and York, D. 1986 $^{40}Ar/^{39}Ar$ Laser-Probe Dating of North American Tektite Fragments from Barbados and the Age of the Eocene-Oligocene Boundary. *Chemical Geology (Isotope Geoscience)* 59: 181–186.

Gleadow, A.J.W. 1980 Fission track age of the KBS tuff and associated hominid remains in northern Kenya. *Nature* 284: 225–230.

Grommé, C.S., and Hay, R.L. 1963 Magnetization of basalt in Bed I, Olduvai Gorge. *Nature* 200: 560–561.

Grommé, C.S., and Hay, R.L. 1967 Geomagnetic polarity epochs: New data from Olduvai Gorge. *Earth and Planetary Science Letters* 2: 111–115.

Hall, C.M., Walter, R.C., Westgate, J.A., and York, D. 1984 Geochronology, stratigraphy and geochemistry of Cindery Tuff in the Pliocene hominid-bearing sediments of the Middle Awash, Ethiopia. *Nature* 308: 26–31.

Hall, C.M., and York, D. 1984 The applicability of $^{40}Ar/^{39}Ar$ dating to young volcanics. *In* Mahaney, W.C., eds., *Quaternary dating methods*. New York, Elsevier: 67–74.

Halliday, A.N., Mahood, G.A., Holden, P., Metz, J.M., Dempster, T.J., and Davidson, J.P. 1989 Evidence for long residence times of rhyolitic magma in the Long Valley magmatic system:

the isotopic record in the precaldera lavas of Glass Mountain. *Earth and Planetary Science Letters* 94: 272–290.

Hames, W.E., and Hodges, K.V. 1993 Laser $^{40}Ar/^{39}Ar$ evaluation of slow cooling and episodic loss of ^{40}Ar from a sample of polymetamorphic muscovite. *Science* 261: 1721–1723.

Hay, R.L. 1976 *Geology of the Olduvai Gorge: A Study of Sedimentation in a Semiarid Basin*. Berkeley, University of California Press.

Hay, R.L. 1980 The KBS controversy may be ended. *Nature* 284: 401.

Hay, R.L. 1992 Potassium-argon dating of Bed I, Olduvai Gorge, 1961–1972. *Quaternary International* 13/14: 31–36.

Hilgen, F.J. 1991 Astronomical calibration of Gauss to Matuyama sapropels in the Mediterranean and implications for the Geomagnetic Polarity Timescale. *Earth and Planetary Science Letters* 104: 226–244.

Hillhouse, J.W., Cerling, T.E., and Brown, F.H. 1986 Magnetostratigraphy of the Koobi Fora Formation, Lake Turkana, Kenya. *Journal of Geophysical Research* 91: 11581–11595.

Hillhouse, J.W., Ndombi, J.W.M., Cox, A., and Brock, A. 1977 Additional results on paleomagnetic stratigraphy of the Koobi Fora Formation, east of Lake Turkana (Lake Rudolf), Kenya. *Nature* 265: 411–415.

Hu, Q., Smith, P.E., Evensen, N., and York, D. 1994 Lasing in the Holocene: extending the $^{40}Ar/^{39}Ar$ laser probe method into the carbon-14 range. *Earth and Plalnetary Science Letters* 123: 331–336.

Hurford, A.J., Gleadow, A.J.W., and Naeser, C.W. 1976 Fission-track dating of pumice from the KBS tuff, East Rudolf, Kenya. *Nature* 263: 738–744.

Imbrie, J., Hays, J.D., Martinson, D.G., McIntyre, A., Mix, A.C., Morley, J.J., Pisias, N.G., Prell, W.L., and Shackleton, N.J. 1984 *The orbital theory of Pleistocene Climate: Support from a revised chronology of the marine d18O record Milankovitch and Climate*. Hingham, (Massachusettes), D. Reidel: 269–305.

Isaac, G.L., Leakey, R.E.F., and Behrensmeyer, A.K. 1971 Archaeological traces of early hominid activities, east of Lake Rudolf, Kenya. *Science* 173: 1129–1134.

Izett, G.A., Dalrymple, G.B., and Snee, L.W. 1991 $^{40}Ar/^{39}Ar$ Age of Cretaceous-Tertiary boundary tektites from Haiti. *Science* 252: 1539–1542.

Johanson, D.C., and White, T.D. 1979 A systematic assessment of early African hominids. *Science* 202: 321–330.

Johanson, D.C., White, T.D., and Coppens, Y. 1978 A new species of the genus Australopithecus (Primates: Hominidae) from the Pliocene of eastern Africa. *Kirtlandia* 28: 1–14.

Johnson, R.G. 1982 Brunhes-Matuyama magnetic reversal dated at 790,000 yr B.P. by marine-astronomical correlations. *Quaternary Research* 17: 135–147.

Kauffman, D.S., and Hopkins, D.M. 1985 Late Cenozoic radiometric dates, Seward and Baldwin Peninsulas and adjacent continental shelf, Alaska. *U.S. Geological Survey Open-File Report* 85–374.

Kauffman, D.S., and Hopkins, D.M. 1986 Glacial history of the Seward Peninsula. *In* Hamilton, T., Reed, K., and Thorson, R., eds., *Glaciation in Alaska: The Geologic Record*. Anchorage, Alaska, Alaska Geological Survey: 51–77.

Kauffman, D.S., Walter, R.C., Brigham-Grette, J., and Hopkins, D.M. 1991 Middle Pleistocene age of the Nome River glaciation, northwestern Alaska. *Quaterary Research* 36: 277–293.

Kimbel, W.H., Johanson, D.C., and Rak, Y. 1994 The first skull and other new discoveries of *Australopithecus afarensis* at Hadar, Ethiopia. *Nature* 368: 449–451.

Leakey, L.S.B., Evernden, J.A., and Curtis, G.H. 1962 Age of Basalt underlying Bed I, Olduvai. *Nature* 194: 1–7.

Leakey, L.S.B., Evernden, J.F., and Curtis, G.H. 1961 Age of Bed I, Olduvai Gorge, Tanganyika. *Nature* 191: 478–479.

Leakey, M.G., Feibel, C.S., McDougall, I., and Walker, A. 1995 New four-million-year-old hominid species from Kanapoi and Allia Bay, Kenya. *Nature* 376: 565–51.

Leakey, R.E.F. 1973 Further evidence of lower Pleistocene hominids from East Rudolf, North Kenya, 1972. *Nature* 242: 170–173.

LoBello, P., Féraud, G., Hall, C.M., York, D., Lavina, P., and Bernat, M. 1987 $^{40}Ar/^{39}Ar$ step-heating and laser fusion dating of a Quaternary pumice from Neschers, Massif Central, France: The defeat of xenocrystic contamination. *Chemical Geology (Isotope Geoscience)* 66: 61–71.

Mankinen, E.A., and Dalrymple, G.B. 1979 Revised geomagnetic polarity time scale for the interval 0–5 m.y. B.P. *Journal of Geophysical Research* 84: 615–626.

McDougall, I. 1981 $^{40}Ar/^{39}Ar$ age spectra from the KBS Tuff, Koobi Fora Formation. *Nature* 294: 120–124.

McDougall, I. 1985 K-Ar and $^{40}Ar/^{39}Ar$ dating of the hominid-bearing Pliocene-Pleistocene sequence at Koobi Fora, Lake Turkana, northern Kenya. *Geological Society of American Bulletin* 96: 159–175.

McDougall, I., Brown, F.H., Cerling, T.E., and Hillhouse, J.W. 1992a A reappraisal of the geomagnetic polarity time scale to 4 Ma using data from the Turkana Basin, East Africa. *Geophysical Research Letters* 19: 2349–2352.

McDougall, I., Brown, F.H., Cerling, T.E., and Hillhouse, J.W. 1992b A reappraisal of the geomagnetic polarity time scale to 4 Ma using data from the Turkana Basin, East Africa. *Eos* 73: 629.

McDougall, I., and Chamaluan, F.H. 1966 Geomagnetic polarity scale of time. *Nature* 212: 1415–1418.

McDougall, I., Davies, T., Maier, R., and Rudowski, R. 1985 Age of the Okote Tuff Complex at Koobi Fora, Kenya. *Nature* 316: 792–794.

McDougall, I., and Harrison, T.M. 1988 *Geochronology and Thermochronology by the* $^{40}Ar/^{39}Ar$ Method. New York, Oxford University Press.

McDougall, I., Maier, R., Southerland-Hawkes, P., and Gleadow, A.J.W. 1980 K-Ar age estimate for the KBS tuff, East Turkana, Kenya. *Nature* 284: 230–234.

McDougall, I., Polach, H.A., and Stipp, J.J. 1969 Excess radiogenic argon in young subaerial basalts from the Auckland volcanic field, New Zealand. *Geochemica et Cosmochimica Acta* 33: 1485–1520.

Megrue, G.H. 1973 Spatial distribution of $^{40}Ar/^{39}Ar$ ages in lunar breccia 14301. *Journal of Geophysical Research* 78: 3216–3221.

Merrihue, C.M. 1965 Trace-element determinations and potassium-argon dating by mass spectroscopy of neutron-irradiated samples. *Transactions of the American Geophysical Union* 46: 125.

Merrihue, C.M., and Turner, G. 1966 Potassium-argon dating by activation with fast neutrons. *Journal of Geophysical Research* 71: 2852–2857.

Mitchell, J.G. 1968 The argon-^{40}/argon-^{39} method for potassium-argon age determination. *Geochimica et Cosmochimica Acta* 32: 781–790.

Nier, A.O. 1950 A redetermination of the relative abundances of the isotopes of carbon, nitrogen, oxygen, argon, and potassium. *Physical Review* 77: 789–793.

Pringle, M.S., McWilliams, M., Houghton, B.F., Lanphere, M.A., and Wilson, C.N.J. 1992 $^{40}Ar/^{39}Ar$ dating of Quaternary feldspar: Examples from the Taupo Volcanic Zone, New Zealand. *Geology* 20: 531–534.

Pringle, M.S., Staudigel, H., and Gee, J. 1991 Jasper Seamount: Seven million years of volcanism. *Geology* 19: 364–368.

Renne, P.R., Walter, R.C., Verosub, K.L., Sweitzer, M., and Aronson, J.L. 1993 New data from the Hadar Formation (Ethiopia) support orbitally tuned time scale to 3.3 Ma. *Geophysical Research Letters* 20: 1067–1070.

Reynolds, J. 1956 High sensitivity mass spectrometer for noble gas analysis. *Review of Scientific Instruments* 27: 928–934.

Sarna-Wojcicki, A.M., Meyer, C.E., Roth, P.H., and Brown, F.H. 1985 Ages of tuff beds at East African early hominid sites and sediments in the Gulf of Aden. *Nature* 313: 306–308.

Shackleton, N.J., Berger, A., and Peltier, W.R. 1990 An alternative astronomical calibration of the lower Pleistocene timescale based on ODP Site 667. *Transactions of the Royal Society of Edinburgh* 81: 251–261.

Shaeffer, O.A., and Zäringer, J. 1966 *Potassium argon dating*. New York Springer-Verlag.

Smith, P.E., Evensen, N.M., and York, D. 1993 First successful ^{40}Ar-^{39}Ar dating of glauconies: Argon recoil in single grains of cryptocrystalline material. *Geology* 21: 41–44.

Steiger, R.H., and Jäger, E. 1977 Subcommission on Geochronology: Convention on the use of decay constants in geochronology and cosmochronology. *Earth and Planetary Science Letters* 36: 359–362.

Straus, W.L., and Hunt, C.B. 1962 Age of Zinjanthropus. *Science*, 136: 293–295.

van den Bogaard, P. 1995 ^{40}Ar/^{39}Ar ages of sanidine phenocrysts from the Laacher See Tephra (12,900 yr BP): Chronostratigraphic and petrological significance. *Earth and Planetary Science Letters* 133: 163–174.

van den Bogaard, P., Hall, C.M., Schminke, H.-U., and York, D. 1987 ^{40}Ar/^{39}Ar Laser Dating of Single Grains: Ages of Quaternary Tephra from the East Eifel Volcanic Field, FRG. *Geophysical Research Letters* 14: 1211–1214.

von Koenigswald, G.H.R., Gentner, W., and Lippolt, H.J. 1961 Age of the basalt flow at Olduvai, East Africa. *Nature* 192: 720–721.

von Weiszäcker, C.F. 1937 Über die Möglichkeit eines dualen—Zerfalls Kalium. *Physik Zeitschrift* 38: 623–624.

Walter, R.C. 1981 The Volcanic History of the Hadar Early Man Site and the Surrounding Afar Region of Ethiopia. Ph.D. disseration, Case Western Reserve University.

_____ 1994 Age of Lucy and the First Family: Laser ^{40}Ar/^{39}Ar Dating of the Denen Dora Member of the Hadar Formation. *Geology* 22: 6–10.

Walter, R.C., and Aronson, J.L. 1982 Revisions of K/Ar ages for the Hadar hominid site, Ethiopia. *Nature* 296: 122–127.

Walter, R.C., and Aronson, J.L. 1993 Age and source of the Sidi Hakoma Tuff, Hadar Formation, Ethiopia. *Journal of Human Evolution* 25: 229–240.

Walter, R.C., Deino, A., Renne, P., and Tauxe, L. 1992a Refining the Plio-Pleistocene GPTS using laser-fusion ^{40}Ar/^{39}Ar tephrochronology: case studies from the East African Rift. *Eos* 73: 629.

Walter, R.C., Manega, P.C., and Hay, R.L. 1992b Tephrochronology of Bed I, Olduvai gorge: An Application of Laser-fusion ^{40}Ar/^{39}Ar Dating to Calibrating Biological and Climatic Change. *Quaternary International* 13/14: 37–46.

Walter, R.C., Manega, P.C., Hay, R.L., Drake, R.E., and Curtis, G.H. 1991 Laser-fusion ^{40}Ar/^{39}Ar dating of Bed I, Olduvai Gorge, Tanzania. *Nature* 354: 145–149.

White, T.D., and Harris, J.M. 1977 Suid evolution and correlation of African hominid localities. *Science* 198: 13–21.

White, T.D., Suwa, G., and Asfaw, B. 1994 *Australopithecus ramidus*, a new species of early hominid from Aramis, Ethiopia. *Nature* 371: 306–312.

White, T.D., Suwa, G., and Asfaw, B. 1995 *Nature* 375: 88.

White, T.D., Suwa, G., Hart, W.K., Walter, R.C., WoldeGabriel, G., de Heinzelin, J., Clark, J.D., Asfaw, B., and Vrba, E. 1993 New discoveries of *Australopithecus* at Maka in Ethiopia. *Nature* 366: 261–265.

WoldeGabriel, G., White, T.D., Suwa, G., Renne, P., de Heinzelin, J., Hart, W.K., and Heiken, G. 1994 Ecological and temporal placement of early Pliocene hominids at Aramis, Ethiopia. *Nature* 371: 330–333.

York, D. 1969 Least squares fitting of a straight line with correlated errors. *Earth and Planetary Science Letters* 5: 320–324.

York, D., and Farquhar, R.M. 1972 *The Earth's Age and Geochronology*. Oxford, Pergamon Press.

York, D., Hall, C.M., Yanese, Y., and Hanes, J.A. 1981 ^{40}Ar/^{39}Ar dating of terrestrial minerals with a continuous laser. *Geophysical Research Letters* 8: 1136–1138.

Chapter 5

Fission-Track Dating

JOHN WESTGATE, AMANJIT SANDHU, AND PHILIP SHANE

ABSTRACT

Fission tracks are zones of intense damage formed by the passage of fission fragments through a solid. Given that the spontaneous fission of ^{238}U occurs at a known rate, the age of a mineral or glass can be calculated from the amount of uranium and number of spontaneous fission tracks it contains. Zircon and glass are the most suitable materials for dating archaeological samples and Quaternary deposits by the fission-track method. Zircon has been considered as the most desirable phase because of its high uranium content and superior track retention properties. However, the recent development of correction procedures for partial track fading in hydrated volcanic glass shards has considerably improved the status of glass in this respect.

Accurate and precise age estimates can be obtained on glass by use of the isothermal plateau fission-track (ITPFT) dating method. Correction for partial track fading is achieved by heating the natural sample and its irradiated aliquot for 30 days at 150°C. This grain-specific technique is particularly suited to the dating of fine-grained, distal tephra beds and will greatly facilitate development of detailed chronologies of tephra-bearing sedimentary sequences located far from volcanic centres.

Glass-ITPFT dating in conjunction with tephrochronological and magnetostratigraphic techniques together provide a formidable toolkit with which

JOHN WESTGATE • Physical Sciences Division, University of Toronto, Scarborough, Ontario M1C 1A4, Canada. **AMANJIT SANDHU** • Department of Physics, Guru Nanak Dev University, Amritsar, India. **PHILIP SHANE** • Department of Geology, University of Auckland, Auckland, New Zealand.

Chronometric Dating in Archaeology, edited by Taylor and Aitken.
Plenum Press, New York, 1997.

to tackle late Cenozoic stratigraphic problems. This point is illustrated by reference to studies in Alaska, Ethiopia and the Indian subcontinent.

INTRODUCTION

Quaternary and archaeological events can be accurately and precisely dated by fission-track methods provided the relevant deposits are of appropriate composition and origin. Zircon and glass are the most suitable materials for dating Quaternary deposits by the fission-track method so that the most desirable deposits are those of igneous origin, especially silicic volcanics, because they typically contain zircon and high-silica glass. Silicic volcanic ash (tephra) deposits are the most useful in this respect because not only can they be reliably dated by several isotopic methods but their widespread distribution and common distinctiveness means that they can serve as excellent stratigraphic markers linking the stratigraphy of isolated sites, sometimes over distances exceeding 1000 km.

An impediment to the successful use of tephra beds for Quaternary and archaeological stratigraphic studies has been the common presence of detrital, foreign grains, caused, for the most part, by post-depositional reworking. This is especially true of the fine-grained, thin distal beds. This problem has been overcome by the development of grain-specific methods of characterization and dating. The external detector zircon fission-track method and the isothermal plateau fission-track (ITPFT) dating method (Westgate 1989; Sandhu *et al.* 1993) are grain-specific techniques in that the track data is accumulated by examination of individual grains so that any foreign material that is encountered in the counting process can be readily ignored.

The purpose of this discussion is to outline the basic principles of the fission-track dating method with special reference to the external detector zircon method and the ITPFT technique, to show the suitability of these two methods for dating events in the time window of interest to archaeologists, and to illustrate their application to the Quaternary Sciences and Archaeology by reference to three case studies: (1) Toba tephra on the Indian subcontinent and its archaeological significance, (2) dating distal tephra beds associated with hominid-bearing sediments in Ethiopia, and (3) temporal calibration of the late Cenozoic loess record in central Alaska. Reviews on fission-track dating include Westgate and Naeser (1985, 1995), Naeser and Naeser (1988), Walter (1989), Aitken (1990), Wagner and Van den haute (1992) and Dumitru (in press).

FISSION-TRACK DATING

A fission track is a zone of intense damage formed by the passage of a heavily-ionizing fission particle through an insulating solid. A narrow region containing a high concentration of positive ions is left in its wake and these positive ions repulse each other into interstitial positions, and, at the same time, a series of vacancies are formed (Fleischer *et al.* 1975). This damaged zone persists in the solid after the fission fragment has come to rest and is called a latent track. Its length is variable, depending upon the charge and energy of the particle and the properties of the detector. ^{238}U fission events form latent tracks several nm (nanometers) wide and 10 to 20 μm long. These latent tracks can only be observed with a transmission electron microscope unless enlarged with a suitable chemical etchant. Etching takes place by rapid dissolution of the disordered region of the track core which exists in a state of higher free energy than the undamaged bulk material.

Fission-track dating is based on the spontaneous fission of ^{238}U, a naturally-occurring isotope of uranium. Fission fragments from the spontaneous break-up of ^{238}U are capable of registering chemically etchable tracks in many minerals and glasses. This circumstance combined with the common occurrence of uranium in trace amounts in many geological materials opens up the possibility of a widely usable dating method for rocks (Price and Walker 1962).

The spontaneous fission of ^{238}U follows the law of radioactive decay. In principle, the fission-track dating method is similar to other isotopic dating methods based on the decay of a natural radioactive parent to a stable daughter atom. However, in fission-track dating, it is the spontaneous fission tracks instead of daughter isotopes that are measured as a product of the decay of ^{238}U. Simply put, given that the spontaneous fission of ^{238}U occurs at a known rate, the age of a mineral or glass can be calculated from the amount of uranium and number of spontaneous fission tracks it contains. Fission-track ages are conventionally calculated using the following equation (Price and Walker 1963):

$$t = (1/\lambda_D)\{\ln[1+(\lambda_D/\lambda_F)(\rho_s/\rho_i)\, gI\sigma\phi]\} \qquad (1)$$

where, t = age in years; λ_D = total decay constant for ^{238}U (1.551×10^{-10} yr^{-1}; (Jaffey *et al.* 1971); λ_F = decay constant for spontaneous fission of ^{238}U (7.03×10^{-17} yr^{-1}; Roberts *et al.* 1968); σ = cross-section for thermal neutron-induced fission of ^{235}U (580×10^{-24} cm^2; Hanna *et al.* 1969); I = isotopic ratio $^{235}U/^{238}U$ (7.252×10^{-3}); ϕ = thermal neutron fluence (neutrons/cm^2); g = geometry factor (equals 1 for the glass-IPTFT method; 0.5 for zircon external detector method); ρ_s = spontaneous areal track density from ^{238}U (tracks/cm^2); and, ρ_i = induced areal track density from ^{235}U (tracks/cm^2).

By entering the values of the various parameters into equation (1), we obtain:

$$t = 6.45 \times 10^9 \{\ln [1 + 9.28 \times 10^{-18} (\rho_s/\rho_i)\, \phi]\} \qquad (2)$$

which is the numerical age equation of the fission-track method for glass. A fission-track age is calculated by determining the spontaneous areal track density from ^{238}U, the neutron-induced areal track density from ^{235}U, and the thermal neutron fluence, which, in turn, is determined from standard glass dosimeters of known uranium content (e.g., NBS glass SRM962: 37.38 ± 0.08 ppm U) that are included along with the samples in the irradiation can.

As has been noted by others (Hurford and Green 1982, 1983; Naeser and Naeser 1988; Wagner and Van den haute 1992; Dumitru, in press), the values of λ_F, σ, and ϕ in age equation (1) have proven difficult to determine. In our studies, which involve irradiation at McMaster Nuclear Reactor Centre, Hamilton, Ontario, we have found that the calibration factor we use to determine ϕ, when combined with the value of λ_F given by Roberts *et al.* (1968) and σ given by Hanna *et al.* (1969), gives fission-track ages that are concordant with K–Ar and $^{40}Ar/^{39}Ar$ age estimates. Evaluation of the accuracy of the neutron fluence determination (ϕ) for each irradiation is done by incorporation of two age standards: the Moldavite tektite glass and the Borchers ash from Meade County, Kansas, equivalent to the Huckleberry Ridge ash of Yellowstone National Park, Wyoming, U.S.A.

A more formal approach to the problem of uncertainty of λ_F, σ, and ϕ has been proposed by Hurford and Green (1982, 1983) through use of a zeta calibration factor in age equation (1), namely,

$$t = (1/\lambda_D)\{\ln [1 + \lambda_D(\rho_s/\rho_i)\, g\, \zeta\, \rho_d]\} \tag{3}$$

where ρ_d = areal density of fission tracks in the detector covering the glass dosimeter, and ζ = the calibration factor for a given glass dosimeter, evaluated from standards of known age.

Rearranging (3) for a standard of known age (t_{std}):

$$\zeta = [e^{\lambda_D t_{std}} - 1] / [\lambda_D g \rho_s (\rho_s / \rho_i)_{std}] \tag{4}$$

This value of ζ can then be used in equation (3) to determine the age of an unknown sample.

Zircon, sphene, apatite and glass are suitable materials for dating archaeological samples and Quaternary deposits by the fission-track method. However, zircon and glass are by far the most commonly used phases.

FADING OF FISSION TRACKS

When detectors with unetched (latent) damage trails are held at high temperatures for a sufficient period of time, it is found that the disordered structure, caused by the passage of a fission fragment, becomes restored, presumably by a diffusion mechanism. A number of geological parameters are capable of influencing the stability of latent nuclear tracks in solids (Fleischer *et al.* 1964; 1965) but temperature is by far the most important parameter affecting track stability.

As latent damage trails are progressively heated, they gradually shorten. For internally distributed tracks, the observed areal track density at a surface depends on the etchable length of the tracks and so this length reduction is accompanied by an areal track density reduction. In deriving the age equation (1), it was assumed that the spontaneous and induced fission tracks had the same etchable range and etching efficiency. If, however, the range of spontaneous fission tracks has been lowered by heating, then the calculated age will be younger than the true age. Glasses and apatites typically suffer from partial fading of their fission tracks. Over a time scale of a few million years, tracks in apatite are erased at temperatures of ~100°C (Dumitru, in press) and partial fading of tracks in glasses takes place at ambient surface temperatures (Naeser *et al.* 1980). This fading effect must be allowed for if a meaningful fission-track age is to be obtained. On the other hand, tracks in zircon and sphene are stable to temperatures of ~300°C, assuming heating times of a few million years (Dumitru, in press) so that in most cases a correction for partial track fading is not necessary.

Fission-track ages lowered by thermal fading can be corrected by the track size measurement method (Storzer and Wagner 1969) and the isochronal or step-heating plateau method (Storzer and Poupeau 1973). The track size correction method involves measuring the length (or diameter) distribution of spontaneous tracks in the natural sample and comparing it to the length (or diameter) distribution of neutron-induced fission tracks produced in irradiated aliquots of the same sample. If the mean spontaneous track length (or diameter) is smaller than that of the induced fission tracks then partial fading must have affected the spontaneous tracks in the natural sample producing a corresponding reduction in its areal track density. A correction for the lowered track density is made by reference to a calibration curve (Fig. 5.1) which shows the correlation between areal track density and track size for that sample, the points defining this curve being derived from a series of heating experiments on the irradiated aliquots (Arias *et al.* 1981).

A modified version of the size correction method has recently been developed by Sandhu and Westgate (1995). Apparent ages of natural glasses are corrected for partial track fading by using a 1:1 relationship between track diameter reduction and areal track density reduction—an approach supported by experimental data. Given that the sample has been adequately etched, the corrected areal density of spontaneous tracks (ρ_{SC}) is given by:

$$\rho_{SC} = (\rho_s)\ (D_i\ /\ D_s) \qquad (5)$$

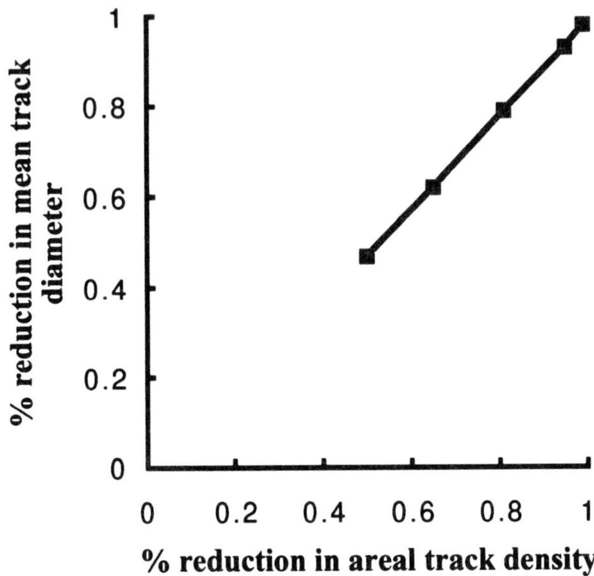

Figure 5.1. Calibration line for the Moldavite tektite glass showing relationship between % reduction in mean track diameter and % reduction in areal track density with progressively prolonged heating times at 250°C (see Sandhu and Westgate 1995). Correction for partial track fading can be made by measuring the mean diameter of spontaneous tracks in the natural sample (one that has not been subjected to any laboratory heating) and comparing it to that of its induced tracks. This gives a point on the Y-axis. The calibration line gives the corresponding % reduction in areal track density which then allows the corrected spontaneous track density to be determined once the spontaneous track density in the natural sample has been measured.

where ρ_s is the measured spontaneous areal track density and D_i and D_s are the mean diameter of induced and spontaneous fission tracks, respectively.

The step-heating plateau correction method takes advantage of the higher thermal stability of partially faded spontaneous tracks. The fission-track age of a sample is proportional to the ratio of spontaneous areal track density in the natural sample to the induced areal track density in the irradiated aliquot. If partial track fading has occurred, this ratio will be too low. However, when pairs of the natural sample and its irradiated aliquot are heated together for a given time at progressively higher temperatures, this ratio value increases until a plateau level is reached (Fig. 5.2). The ratio value at this plateau level is used to give an age corrected for partial track loss (Storzer and Poupeau 1973; Wagner 1979).

Another correction method is the isothermal plateau technique (Burchart *et al.* 1975). This method is similar to the step-heating plateau technique except that it involves heating the sample at constant temperature for progressively longer times. A modified version of the plateau technique, involving only one

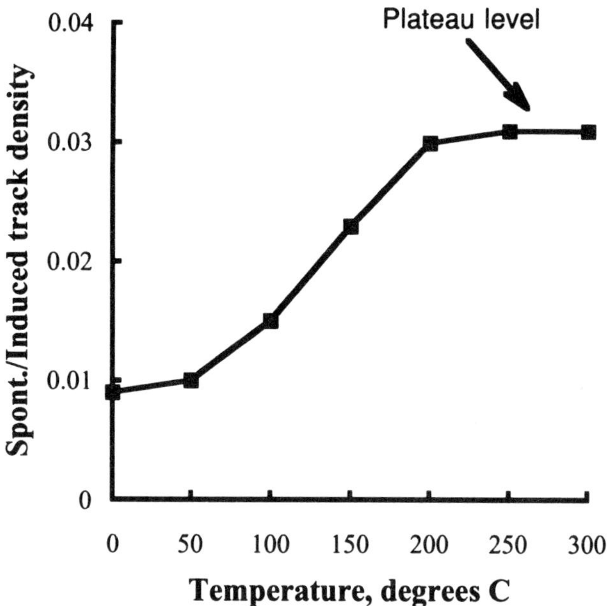

Figure 5.2. Hypothetical example showing the increase in the spontanous to induced track density (ρ_s/ρ_i) with progressive heating of pairs of the natural sample and its irradiated aliquot. Each data point is defined by a ρ_s and ρ_i measurement after heating at a particular temperature for a time interval that is the same for all heating steps. The plateau level defines the value of ρ_s/ρ_i used to give an age corrected for partial track fading. The mean track diameters, D_s and D_i, are equal at the plateau position.

heating step, has been recently developed (Westgate 1988, 1989). This technique has been successfully applied to hydrated glass shards from silicic tephra beds and it has been shown that a single heat treatment of 150°C for 30 days is sufficient to correct fully for partial track fading. The plateau is recognized by a coincidence in the size distributions of the spontaneous and induced tracks and by a ratio of mean spontaneous track diameter to mean induced track diameter equal to unity (Fig. 5.3) (Miller and Wagner 1981; Westgate 1989; Sandhu *et al.* 1992; Sandhu *et al.* 1993). The latter correction procedure is the one used in the ITPFT method.

ISOTHERMAL PLATEAU FISSION-TRACK DATING METHOD APPLIED TO VOLCANIC GLASS SHARDS

We have applied the ITPFT method to volcanic glass shards from silicic tephra beds, allowing us to follow the procedures of the population-subtraction method (Naeser 1967), which can be used for material of uniform uranium

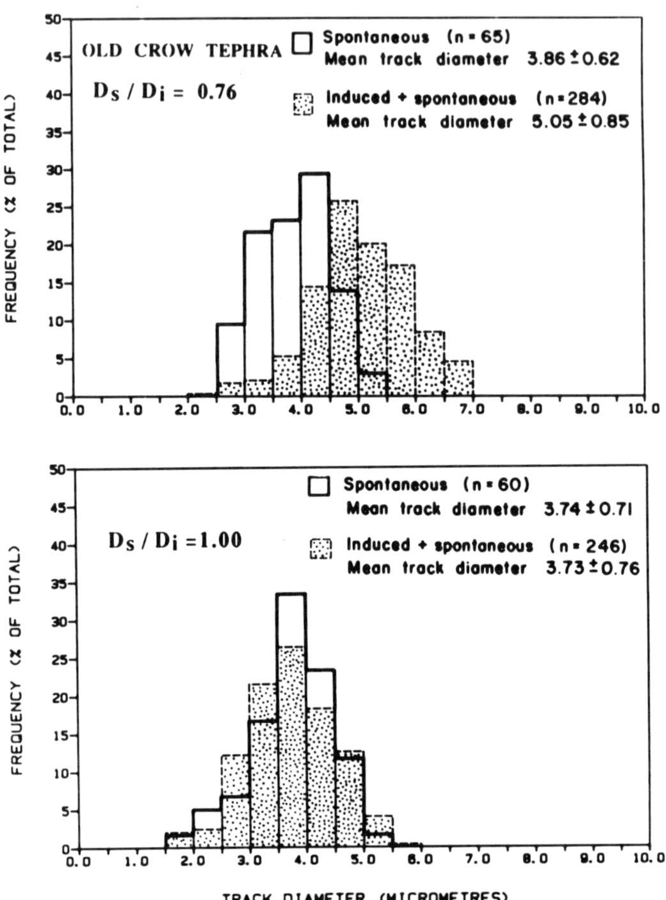

Figure 5.3. Size distribution of fission-track diameters in Old Crow tephra. Top, glass shards that have been exposed only to ambient temperatures. Bottom, glass shards heated at 150°C for 30 days. n=number of measurements, made at about 4000x magnification, using an interactive, semi-automatic image-analysis system. Coincidence of the two size distributions in the lower diagram indicates that the sample has been corrected for partial track fading but the low mean track diameter shows that it is underetched (see text).

content. Therefore, samples of glass shards must be evaluated for uranium homogeneity prior to dating. This is done by determining the major-element composition of a number of single glass shards in the sample, using an electron microprobe. If the analyses cluster tightly (Fig. 5.4), it is assumed that the uranium content of the glass is uniform, permitting the sample to be dated. Direct assessment of uranium homogeneity on a grain to grain basis is now possible by laser ablation ICP-MS (Pearce *et al.* 1994; Westgate *et al.* 1995).

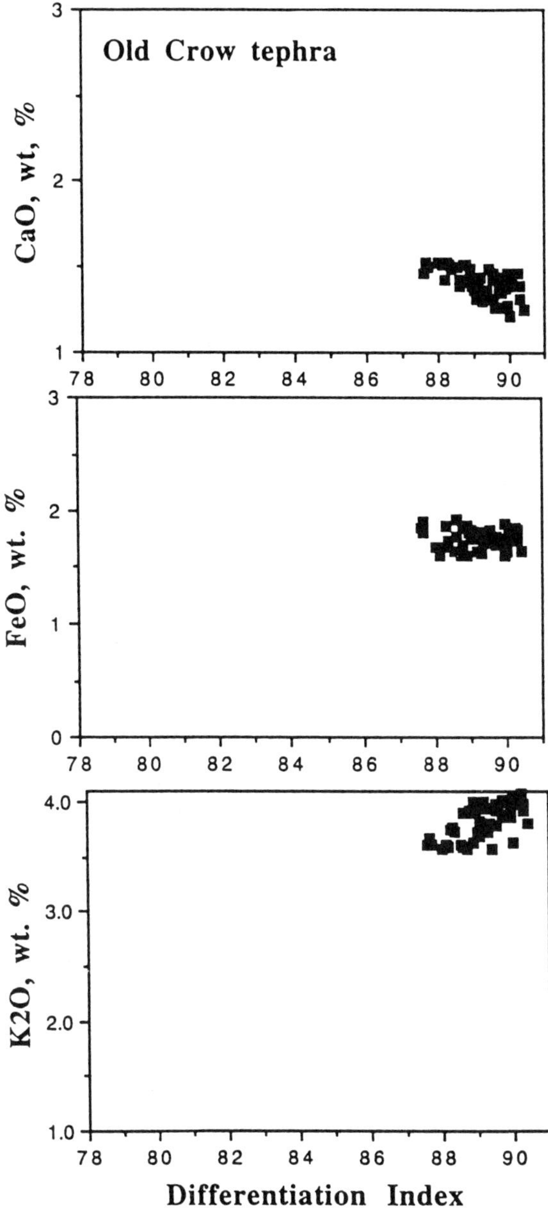

Figure 5.4. Narrow range in major-element composition of glass shards in Old Crow tephra as determined by electron microprobe analyses (EMA). Total iron expressed as FeO.

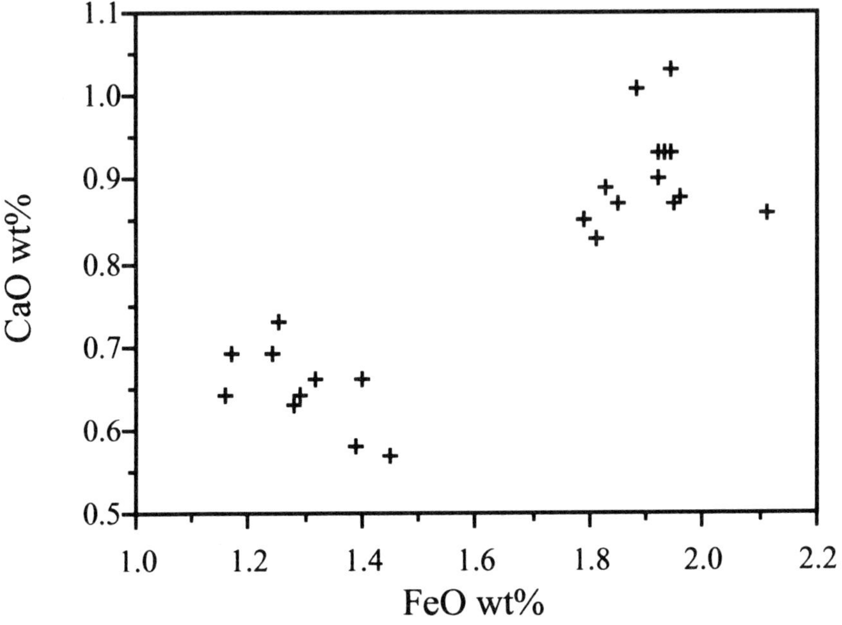

Figure 5.5. Individual glass shard compositions determined by EMA for a tephra bed consisting of two different glass populations. This example is from the early Pleistocene, fluvial Mangatarata Formation in New Zealand (Shane 1991). Fluvial processes have reworked and mixed different eruptive products and deposited them as a single tephra emplacement unit. Total iron expressed as FeO.

Samples that show multiple compositional clusters (Fig. 5.5) due to magma mixing or post-depositional reworking cannot be dated by the ITPFT method, although a single cluster could be isolated and dated.

The glass separate is divided into two aliquots, both being regarded as representative of the "population" of glass shards in the sample. The first aliquot (the natural sample) is reserved for measurement of the areal density of the spontaneous fission tracks and the second aliquot is irradiated. Both aliquots are then heated at 150°C for 30 days to correct for partial track fading in the glass shards, as mentioned earlier. Our experience is that all tephra beds can be corrected fully for partial track fading by this heat treatment. However, we have shown that some volcanic glasses are fully corrected within 15 days at 150°C (see Ester Ash Bed in Table 1; Sandhu *et al.* 1993) and we are presently investigating the compositional control on the thermal stability of fission tracks in natural glasses.

It has been shown that track fading can occur in hydrated glass shards at ambient surface temperatures over geologic time (Naeser *et al.* 1980) so that the 30 days at 150°C correction is done on a routine basis. A low temperature long time combination ensures minimal structural damage to the glass with no deleterious effects on its etching characteristics. Naeser *et al.* (1980) found that when hydrated glass shards are exposed to temperatures greater than 200°C they become badly fractured, making it difficult to count the tracks. Furthermore, these fractures increase the surface area of the glass available for chemical attack during etching thereby reducing the glass surface area available for counting tracks. Some fine-grained, distal tephra beds could be rendered undatable by the IPTFT method because of this condition.

The irradiated and natural samples are then mounted in epoxy, ground, polished and etched. Details of the laboratory procedures are given in Sandhu *et al.* (1993). Glass shards in the irradiated aliquot will contain both spontaneous and induced fission tracks so that the quantity ρ_i can be obtained by subtracting the value of ρ_s, determined in the natural sample. Revelation and observation of spontaneous and induced tracks are done under identical conditions. Etching is critical. Under-etching can result in age estimates that are too young (Westgate 1989) whereas over-etching can cause tracks to extend beyond the length of the damaged zone, producing bowl-shaped structures that can be confused with etch pits derived from irregularities of the surface produced by polishing. Etching conditions should be such as to give an average track diameter in the range of 6 to 8 μm; a mean size in the higher part of this range is preferable (Sandhu and Westgate 1995).

The counting of fission tracks in hydrated glass shards is done at 500x magnification. If the shards are large and blocky, the areal track density can be determined with an eyepiece graticule but if the shards are thin-walled or moderately pumiceous, the point-counting method must be used. The track count increases much more rapidly with the point-counting method becaus the surface area of glass that can be included in the analysis is greater, allow more precise age estimates to be made. In practice, the latter method ent noting the number of fission tracks in each field of view and whether or no the center point is on glass or epoxy (Sandhu *et al.* 1993). A good estimation of the areal fission-track density is obtained when the ratio of tracks to points on glass has stabilized (Fig. 5.6).

The accuracy of the thermal neutron fluence determination is monitored by two internal standards: the Moldavite tektite with an $^{40}Ar/^{39}Ar$ age of 15.21±0.15 Ma (Staudacher *et al.* 1982) and the Borchers Ash, correlated to the Huckleberry Ridge Tuff, which has a K-Ar age of 2.02±0.08 Ma (Naeser and Naeser 1988).

Glass-ITPFT age estimates of some Quaternary tephra beds are given in Table 5.1. All samples have suffered from partial track fading. These ages are accurate because they compare very well with age estimates on co-existing mineral phases, as determined by K-Ar, $^{40}Ar/^{39}Ar$, zircon external detector fission-track and thermoluminescence methods. For example, Old Crow tephra, widespread in Alaska and the Yukon, has a thermoluminescence (TL)

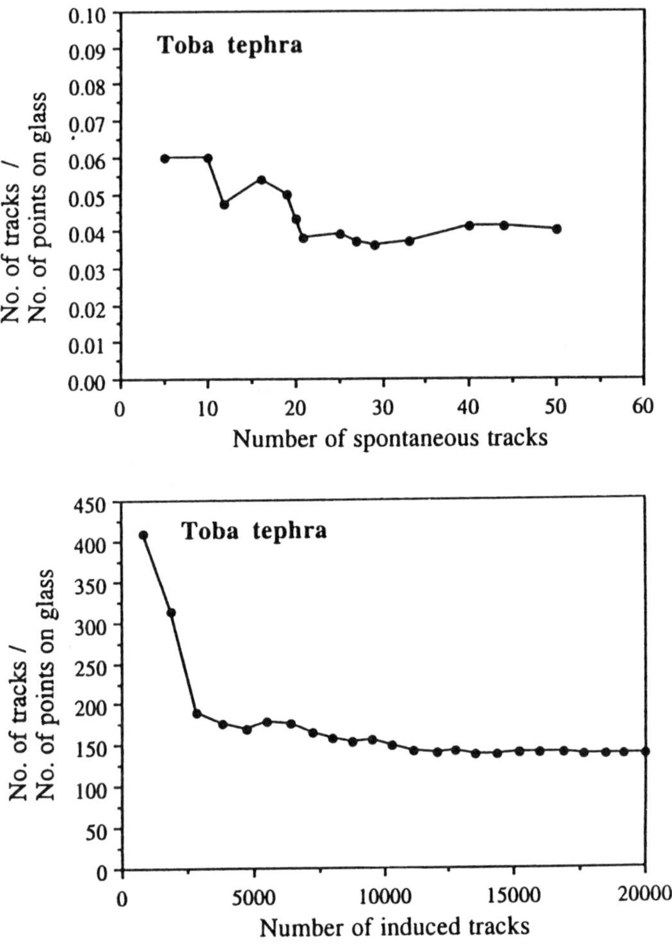

Figure 5.6. Variation of track density ratio with number of tracks counted in spontaneous sample and induced sample, using a point-counting technique. A good estimation of areal fission-track density is obtained when ratio value has stabilized.

age between 110±32 and 140±30 ka (Berger *et al.* 1992). Sanidine phenocrysts from the Toba tephra in Indonesia yield a mean $^{40}Ar/^{39}Ar$ age of 73±4 ka (Chesner *et al.* 1991). The Ester Ash Bed has a weighted mean ITPFT age of 0.81±0.07 Ma, based on 8 determinations (Westgate *et al.* 1990). The age is compatible with its reversed magnetic polarity and stratigraphic position just above the Jaramillo Subchron (0.99–1.07 Ma; Valet and Meynadier 1993). Basalt flows above the Fort Selkirk tephra in the central Yukon have whole-rock K-Ar ages of 1.35±0.08 and 1.47±0.11 Ma and an underlying flow has a whole-rock K-Ar age of 1.60±0.08 Ma (Westgate 1989). The Borchers Ash

Table 5.1. Glass ITPFT Age Estimates of Some Quaternary Tephra Beds (Uncorrected Ages Also Given)[a]

Sample name	Days heated at 150°C	Etching conditions HF: (%)	Temp.: (°C)	Time (s)	Spontaneous track density ($x10^2$ t/cm^2)	Induced track density ($x10^4$ t/cm^2)	Neutron fluence ($x10^{15}$ n/cm^2)	D_s/D_i	Age±1σ (Ma)	References
Toba tephra (UT778)	30	26	21.0	145	0.79(50)	26.8(19976)	3.84(14021)	1.07	0.07±0.01	Chesner *et al.* (1991)
Old Crow tephra (UT613)	0	24	20.5	65	1.47(61)	11.25(7000)	1.88(6871)	0.83	0.15±0.02	Westgate *et al.* (1990)
	30	24	23.0	82	0.85(36)	6.62(3748)	1.88(6871)	1.00	0.15±0.02	
Mamaku Ignimbrite (UT1168)	0	25	25.0	90	1.81(57)	19.1(14048)	3.55(16798)	0.86	0.20±0.03	Shane *et al.* (1994)
	30	25	25.0	160	1.59(106)	14.7(11492)	3.55(16798)	1.00	0.23±0.02	
Rockland tephra (RPT(L)15)	30	26	23.6	140	5.60(32)	24.60(10336)	3.45(53493)	0.98	0.47±0.08	Alloway *et al.*(1992)
Ester Ash Bed (UA743)	0	25	21.5	60	3.95(41)	14.55(3244)	3.96(12363)	0.83	0.64±0.10	Westgate *et al.*(1990)
	15	25	22.0	60	3.36(18)	9.59(1902)	3.94(7317)	1.04	0.83±0.20	
	30	25	23.0	50	3.07(21)	9.25(4355)	3.96(12363)	0.98	0.79±0.17	
Lake Tapps tephra (UT462)	0	24	23.0	55	6.53(68)	12.20(5340)	2.02(5720)	0.76	0.65±0.08	Westgate *et al.* (1987)
	30	24	23.0	105	5.08(104)	5.43(2482)	1.89(6871)	0.95	1.06±0.11	
Fort Selkirk tephra (UT82)	0	24	23.0	55	6.33(120)	12.05(7877)	3.79(16842)	0.81	1.19±0.11	Westgate (1989)
	30	24	23.0	105	5.29(32)	8.38(1382)	3.79(16842)	1.09	1.43±0.26	
Pakihikura tephra (BP-303)	0	26	20.0	100	7.11(50)	12.40(3189)	3.42(32050)	0.77	1.17±0.17	Alloway *et al.*(1993)
	15	26	22.0	115	6.81(104)	9.36(3718)	3.42(32050)	0.95	1.49±0.15	
	30	26	22.0	135	5.11(123)	6.41(2804)	3.42(32050)	0.98	1.63±0.15	
Borchers Ash (UA598)	0	26	23.0	55	22.83(301)	28.58(4550)	2.42(9617)	0.78	1.16±0.07	Westgate (1989)
	30	26	23.5	120	20.59(164)	12.46(5924)	2.07(14935)	1.01	2.04±0.16	

[a]Thermal neutron fluence is determined from calibrated muscovite detector covering glass dosimeter (NBS SRM 962:37.38±0.08 ppm) placed at top and bottom of irradiated can. Samples are irradiated at McMaster Nuclear Reactor Centre, McMaster University, Hamilton, Ontario, Canada. Results on the internal standard (Moldavite tektite glass) compare well with the $^{40}Ar/^{39}Ar$ plateau age of 15.21±0.15 Ma (Staudacher et al.,1982); the weighted mean fission-track age as determined at the University of Toronto is 15.1±0.3 Ma based on eight determinations. Number of tracks counted is indicated in parentheses and error (±1σ) is calculated by combining the Poisson errors in the spontaneous and induced track counts and on the counts in the detector covering the dosimeter. D_s is mean spontaneous track diameter and D_i is mean induced track diameter. See text for information on age estimates of these tephra beds using other methods.

in southern Kansas is correlated to the Huckleberry Ridge Tuff, which has been dated by the K-Ar method at 2.02±0.08 Ma (Naeser and Naeser 1988). The weighted mean age of three zircon fission-track age estimates from Lake Tapps tephra is 0.88±0.11 Ma, slightly younger than the glass-ITPFT age (Westgate *et al.* 1987). The recently discovered proximal equivalent at Mt. Baker, Washington has an $^{40}Ar/^{39}Ar$ age of 1.15 Ma, very close to the ITPFT age estimate for Lake Tapps tephra (Hildreth and Lanphere 1994; Hildreth, personal communication 1995). The Rockland tephra in California has a TL age of 0.49±0.11 Ma (Berger 1991) and a tephra bed immediately beneath a correlative of the Pakihikura tephra from the Oroua River, North Island, New Zealand, has an $^{40}Ar/^{39}Ar$ age of 1.54±0.12 Ma (R.C. Walter, personal communication 1992).

The uncertainty of a particular age estimate can be lowered by increasing the number of tracks counted, especially the spontaneous tracks, as well as by dating the sample several times, preferably by different persons, and then using the standard weighting by inverse variance. In this way, the precision of age estimates for Quaternary tephra beds can be reduced to less than 5% (Westgate *et al.* 1990; Alloway *et al.* 1993; Shane *et al.* 1994). The data presented in Table 5.1 show that the ITPFT dating method can be successfully applied to volcanic glass shards, giving accurate and precise age estimates for Quaternary tephra beds. Moreover, this grain-discrete method is ideally suited to the dating of distal tephra beds, which are typically thin, discontinuous, fine-grained, and contaminated by detrital material. It will greatly facilitate the development of detailed chronologies of tephra-bearing sedimentary sequences located far from volcanic centres (Westgate *et al.* 1990).

Unfortunately, not all tephra beds can be dated by the ITPFT method. Some are simply too fine-grained, others are too pumiceous. In both cases, insufficient glass surface area is exposed to count an adequate number of tracks. Preferred shard morphologies are those with low vesicularity and blocky or platy forms (Fig. 5.7). About 0.25 g of glass shards in the 0.25 to 0.13 mm size fraction is required in order to attempt an age determination on a distal tephra bed. Of course, more proximal tephra beds with larger glass shards and thicker bubble-walls are much easier to date because of the large surface area of glass available for counting fission tracks. The areal density of fission tracks in glass shards is determined by the uranium content, age, and extent of partial track fading. The combined effect of these factors must be such as to produce enough tracks to give a statistically meaningful age. Glass shards in rhyolitic to dacitic tephra beds have uranium contents typically in the range of 2–4 ppm, sufficient for good Quaternary age estimates. However, the uranium content in glass of andesitic and basaltic tephra is commonly less than 1 ppm, making such deposits of Quaternary age difficult if not impossible to date by the ITPFT method. The same is true of tephra beds younger than ~50,000 years unless their glass shards have exceptionally high uranium values.

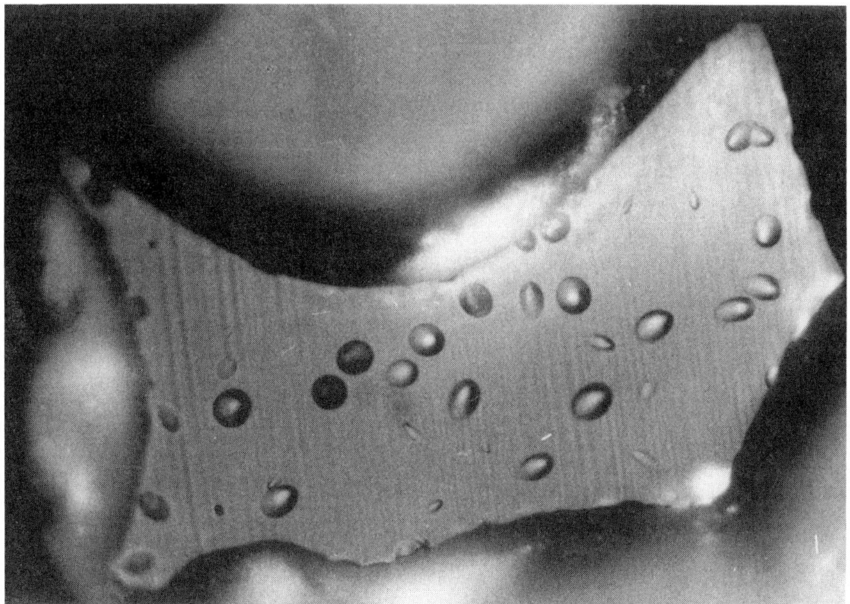

Figure 5.7. Fission tracks in a glass shard from the 74 ka Toba tephra bed. The larger tracks are in the range of 6–8 μm in diameter.

EXTERNAL DETECTOR FISSION-TRACK DATING METHOD APPLIED TO ZIRCONS

Zircon grains cannot be dated by the population method because of the heterogeneous distribution of uranium both within a grain and from grain to grain in a particular sample. Instead, the external detector method must be used. Given the relatively high uranium content (300 to > 1000 ppm) of zircon, this method allows the age of a single crystal to be determined—a property of great value in that it permits discrimination of contaminant grains in tephra beds. The relatively high thermal stability of fission tracks in zircon is another advantage in that it is seldom necessary to correct for partial track fading in zircons from Quaternary deposits, although it is possible that the fission-track clock of zircons in Quaternary deposits has been reset, for example, by fire (Naeser and Naeser 1988). On the other hand, a limitation is that zircon grains < 75 μm are too small to be dated by the fission-track method. Hence, the geochronology of some distal tephra sequences cannot be tackled by zircon fission-track dating.

The external detector method involves the mounting of zircon grains in a Teflon wafer, grinding and polishing the grains to expose an internal surface, and then etching in molten KOH–NaOH at about 225°C (Gleadow *et al.* 1976) to reveal the spontaneous fission tracks on the polished surface. The polished and etched grain mount is covered with a cleavage sheet of low uranium mica—the external detector—and irradiated with an appropriate dose of thermal neutrons. Fission fragments of ^{235}U near the polished surface traverse the zircon-mica interface to produce induced fission tracks in the mica. The irradiated mica is then removed from the grain mount and etched in HF acid to reveal the induced fission tracks.

A fission-track age determination requires matching an individual zircon grain (which gives ρ_s) with its corresponding induced-track print on the external detector (which gives ρ_i). In this way the age of each zircon grain can be calculated. The grain-to-print matching process is greatly facilitated by use of a computer-automated microscope scanning and digitizing tablet system (Dumitru 1993).

A comparison of age estimates on co-existing phases in a number of late Cenozoic tephra beds is shown in Table 5.2. Zircons have been dated by the

Table 5.2. Age Determinations on Co-existing Phases of Some Widespread Late Cenozoic Tephra Beds

Tephra bed	Phase date			References[a]
	zircon EDFT Age±1σ (Ma)	glass ITPFT Age±1σ(Ma)	feldspar $^{40}Ar/^{39}Ar$ or K-Ar Age±1σ (Ma)	
Lake Tapps tephra (Washington, U.S.A.)	0.84±0.21 0.87±0.27	1.06±0.11	1.15±0.01	Naeser and Naeser 1988 Westgate *et al.* 1987 Hildreth and Lanphere 1994
Rangitawa tephra (New Zealand)	0.34±0.03	0.34±0.03	0.33±0.02	Kohn *et al.* 1992 Alloway *et al.* 1993 Pringle *et al.* 1992
Fort Selkirk tephra (Yukon, Canada)	0.94±0.20	1.48±0.19	1.35±0.08[b] (Min.) 1.60±0.08[b] (Max.)	Naeser *et al.* 1982 Westgate 1989 Westgate 1989
Borchers ash bed (Kansas, U.S.A.)	1.90±0.10	2.04±0.16	2.02±0.08[b]	Naeser *et al.* 1973 Westgate 1989 Naeser and Naeser 1988
Cindery Tuff (Ethiopia)	3.93±0.28	3.70±0.14	3.85±0.08	Hall *et al.* 1984 Westgate 1989 White *et al.* 1993
Bishop Tuff (California, U.S.A.)	0.74±0.03	0.72±0.05	0.760±0.001	Izett and Naeser 1976 Westgate 1989 Bogaard and Schirnick 1995

[a]References cited for each tephra bed refer to columns 2, 3, and 4, respectively. EDFT = external detector fission-track method. ITPFT = isothermal plateau fission-track method.
[b]Indicates age estimates based on the K-Ar method.

external detector fission-track method, glass shards by the ITPFT method, and feldspars by the $^{40}Ar/^{39}Ar$ or K-Ar method. These age estimates are in excellent agreement at the one sigma level with the exception of the Fort Selkirk tephra, whose zircon age estimate is young compared to the glass and feldspar ages—a result most likely of under-etching.

TOBA TEPHRA (c. 74 ka) ON THE INDIAN SUBCONTINENT AND ITS ARCHAEOLOGICAL SIGNIFICANCE

A widespread tephra layer in Asia consisting predominantly of glass and containing detrital contaminants provides a good example of the combined approach of ITPFT and geochemical techniques in dating and identifying distal tephra layers.

The eruption of the Youngest Toba Tuff at the Toba caldera in northern Sumatr, about 74 ka produced a widespread tephra layer (Fig. 5.8) found in the Indian Ocean (Rose and Chesner 1987). Oxygen isotope stratigraphies from deep sea cores place the eruption at the stage 5a/4 boundary (Rampino and Self 1993), a period of rapid change from interglacial to glacial conditions. Tephra layers found with terrestrial faunas and cultural artifacts onshore, in Malaysia (Stauffer 1973) and the Indian subcontinent (Korisettar *et al.* 1989; Acharyya and Basu 1993) have been attributed to the Toba caldera due to their rhyolitic composition. However, eruptions of the Toba caldera have been frequent (Dehn *et al.* 1991), and without precise isotopic ages and geochemical characterisation of the glasses in the distal tephras, correlation to a particular eruption could not previously be confirmed (Shane *et al.* 1995).

An ash found in Malaysia, near Serdang, Selanger (Fig. 5.8), occurs in lacustrine sediments and overlies Acheulean tool artifacts. A zircon fission-track age of 30±4.5 ka was determined for the tephra (Nishimura and Stauffer 1981), in accord with ^{14}C ages for material beneath it (Stauffer 1973). However, two ITPFT ages on glass from the tephra give an older weighted mean age of 68±7 ka (Chesner *et al.* 1991). This is in accord with K-Ar data from sanidine (74±3 ka, Ninkovich *et al.* 1978) and $^{40}Ar/^{39}Ar$ single crystal laser fusion ages (73±4 ka, Chesner *et al.* 1991) for the ignimbrite phase of the Youngest Toba Tuff on Sumatra. As large Pleistocene eruptions in the last ca. 30–40 ka are not known from the Toba caldera (Dehn *et al.* 1991; Chesner *et al.* 1991), it would appear that the zircon and ^{14}C ages for the Malaysia tephra are in error. The identity of the tephra, on the basis of its ITPFT age, is the Youngest Toba Tuff. Thus, the underlying Acheulean tools are older than 74 ka.

Many localities of rhyolitic tephra associated with Acheulean and Paleolithic artifacts have been reported in the Indian subcontinent (Williams and Royce 1982; Korisettar *et al.* 1989; Acharyya and Basu 1993). These localities are up to 3500 km from Malaysia and the Toba caldera (Fig. 5.8). Korisettar *et*

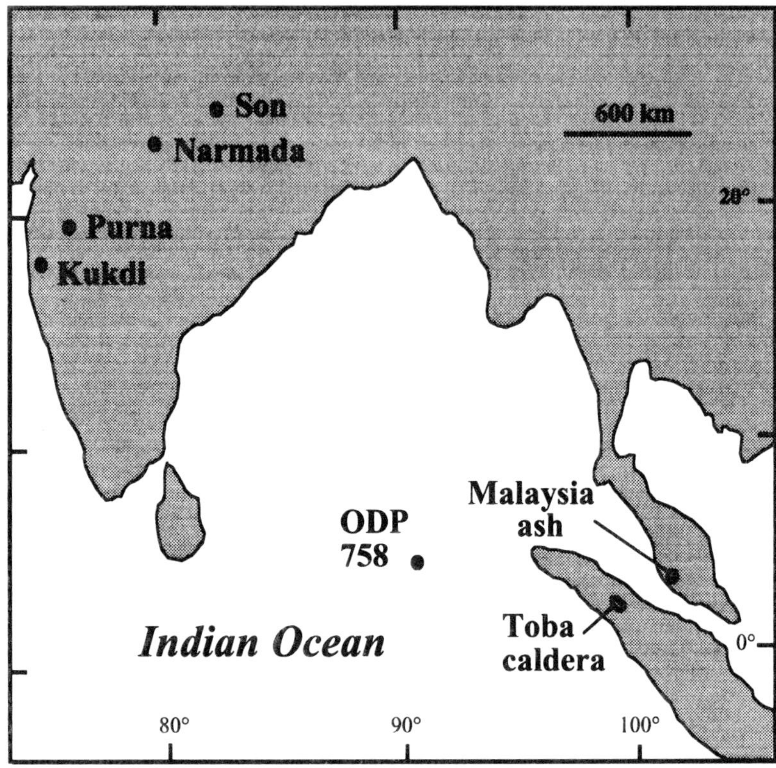

Figure 5.8. Localities of distal tephra layers at archaeological sites in India, Malaysia and Ocean Drilling Project (ODP) 758 hole in the Indian Ocean, correlated to the Youngest Toba Tuff at the Toba caldera in Sumatra.

al. (1989) determined a K-Ar age of 1.4 Ma for a bulk tephra sample from the Kukdi River, Maharashtra in western India. Another distal ash locality occurs in the nearby Purna valley. Our attempt to determine an ITPFT age was hindered by the scarcity of spontaneous tracks and the small size of the shards. To identify the tephra at the distal Indian localities we obtained major-element data on individual glass shards by electron microprobe analysis (EMA) and trace-element data on small (ca. 200 mg), pure glass separates by instrumental neutron activation analysis (INAA). The major element composition of the tephra at Kukdi River and other Indian localities match closely with that of the Malaysia tephra and layer A of Dehn *et al.* (1991) in ODP hole 758 in the Indian Ocean (Fig. 5.9), correlatives of the Youngest Toba Tuff. Furthermore, glasses from ODP 758 correlated with older Toba eruptives by means of isotope stratigraphy, including the Middle Toba (ca. 500 ka) and Oldest Toba (ca. 850 ka) Tuffs, are chemically distinguishable from tephra we have analysed from

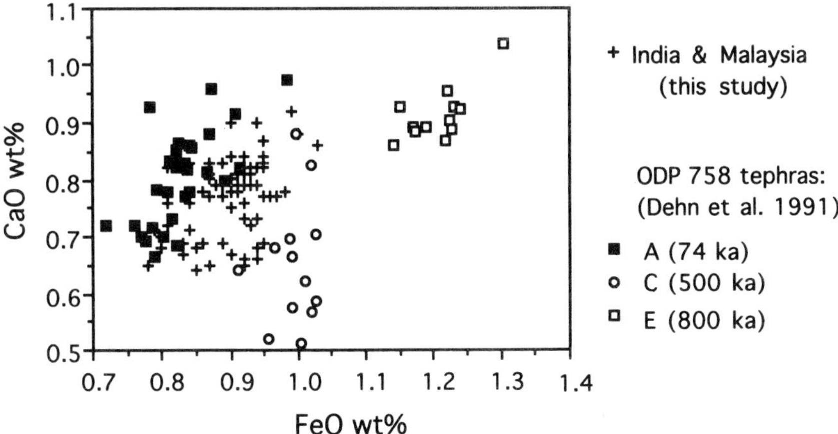

Figure 5.9. Electron microprobe analyses (EMA) of individual glass shards from tephra beds in India and Malaysia compared to those from Quaternary tephra layers in ODP 758 hole.

Indian localities and Malaysia (Fig. 5.9). Glass rare-earth-element (REE) data, which is highly sensitive to particular crystallisation and eruption conditions, clearly demonstrates the similarity between tephra layers in Malaysia and India (Fig. 5.10). Early Acheulean tools found above and below the tephra are contained in alluvial gravels exposed by the Kukdi River and are likely to be reworked (Shane *et al.* 1995). This is confirmed by the correlation of the tephra bed to the Youngest Toba Tuff (ca. 74 ka).

We also examined tephra samples from the Narmada and Son valley basins in central and north India (Fig. 5.8). In the Narmada valley, tephra is exposed laterally up to 20–30 km in fluvial sediments of the Jhalon Formation along with Mid-Paleolithic and Upper Paleolithic tools and mammalian faunas (Acharyya and Basu 1993). Sediments beneath the formation contain Acheulean tools and a specimen of *Homo*. In the Son valley, tephra occurs in the Baghor Formation with mammalian fossils and Mid-Paleolithic tools (Acharyya and Basu 1993). Williams and Royce (1982) estimated an age of ca. 18 ka for this part of the Baghor Formation. Previous attempts to characterise chemically the tephra layers using bulk ash samples show great variation (e.g., Acharyya and Basu 1993) and do not allow confident correlation to a particular Toba eruption. Our major element and rare-earth element (REE) data indicate these tephra beds are correlatives of layer A in ODP 758 and thus Youngest Toba Tuff (74 ka) (Figs. 5.9 and 5.10) and are dissimilar to other Pleistocene Toba tephra layers. The Youngest Toba tephra provides a temporal control point of 74 ka to the sequences, indicating that these sequences are older than previously expected. In the Son valley, the tephra gives a minimum age for the older Middle Paleolithic tool industries of the

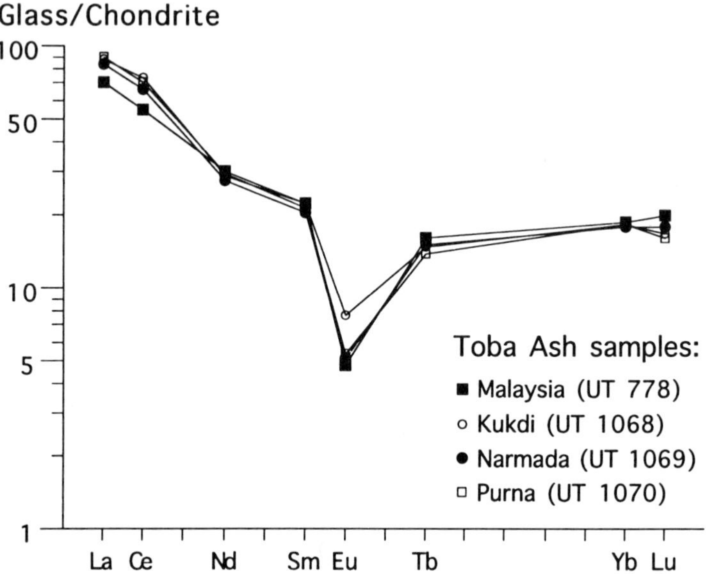

Figure 5.10. Chrondrite normalized rare-earth-element (REE) composition of pure glass separates from tephra beds in India and Malaysia, determined by instrumental neutron activation analysis, following the method of Barnes and Gorton (1984).

Patpara Formation (M. Williams, personal communication 1994). The presence of the tephra also allows precise correlation between widespread localities. These archaeological sites are probably contemporaneous with climatic cooling at the oxygen isotope stage boundary 5a/4.

We suspect previous attempts to date these distal tephra layers and characterise them chemically were hindered by diagenetic alteration, variations in phenocryst contents and the presence of detrital contaminants, all of which may be encountered in bulk samples. By the use of grain-specific methods for fission-track dating and chemical analyses on pure glass, we can confirm the identity of the Youngest Toba Tuff at archaeological sites widespread in Asia. The tephra bed provides an age for artifact sites and demonstrates some artifact assemblages are reworked (Shane *et al.* 1995).

ITPFT AGES OF DISTAL TEPHRA BEDS ASSOCIATED WITH PLIOCENE HOMINID-BEARING SEDIMENTS IN ETHIOPIA

The Middle Awash region of the western Afar, Ethiopia (Fig. 5.11) contains a Plio-Pleistocene sedimentary record that is rich in vertebrate fossils,

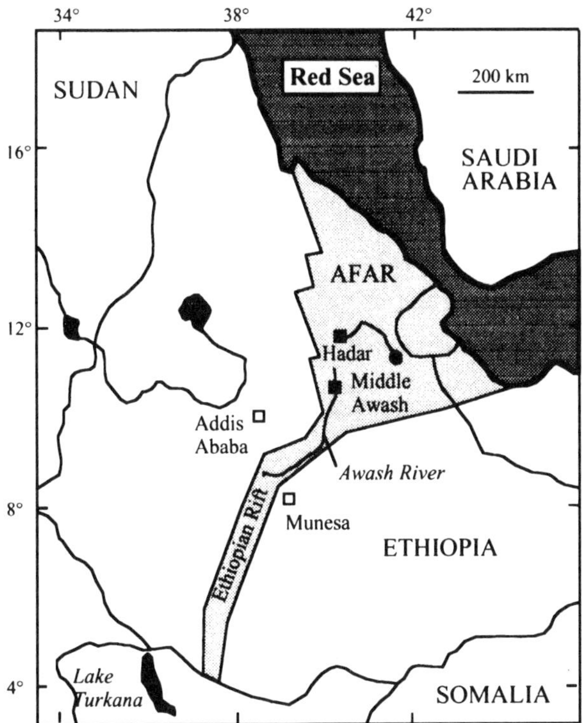

Figure 5.11. Map of Ethiopia showing the Afar and Main Ethiopian Rifts and the location of the Middle Awash and Hadar regions (modified after Walter and Aronson 1993).

including hominids, and Acheulean archaeological occurrences. Numerous distal tephra beds occur in these deposits and application of tephrochronological techniques supported by single-grain laser fusion $^{40}Ar/^{39}Ar$ ages on feldspar phenocrysts has resulted in the development of a secure stratigraphic framework (Walter and Aronson 1993; White *et al.* 1993; Walter 1994; Asfaw *et al.* 1992). The major elements of the tephrostratigraphy and location of hominid fossils and Acheulean gravels are shown in Fig. 5.12. The $^{40}Ar/^{39}Ar$ age estimates for some of the more extensive tephra beds are also indicated on this diagram.

The glass-ITPFT ages for the tephra beds shown in Fig. 5.12 are presented in Table 5.3. Although the uncertainty associated with the ITPFT ages is much greater than that of the $^{40}Ar/^{39}Ar$ ages, there is a close correspondence of the mean ages. A correlative of the Moiti Tuff is dated by $^{40}Ar/^{39}Ar$ at 3.89±0.02 Ma (White *et al.* 1993); the glass-ITPFT age of an occurrence in the Omo Gorge is 3.89±0.25 Ma. The weighted mean age of 21 $^{40}Ar/^{39}Ar$ dates on plagioclases from the Cindery Tuff is 3.85±0.08 Ma, which compares with a glass-ITPFT age of 3.70±0.14 Ma. Eight anorthoclase

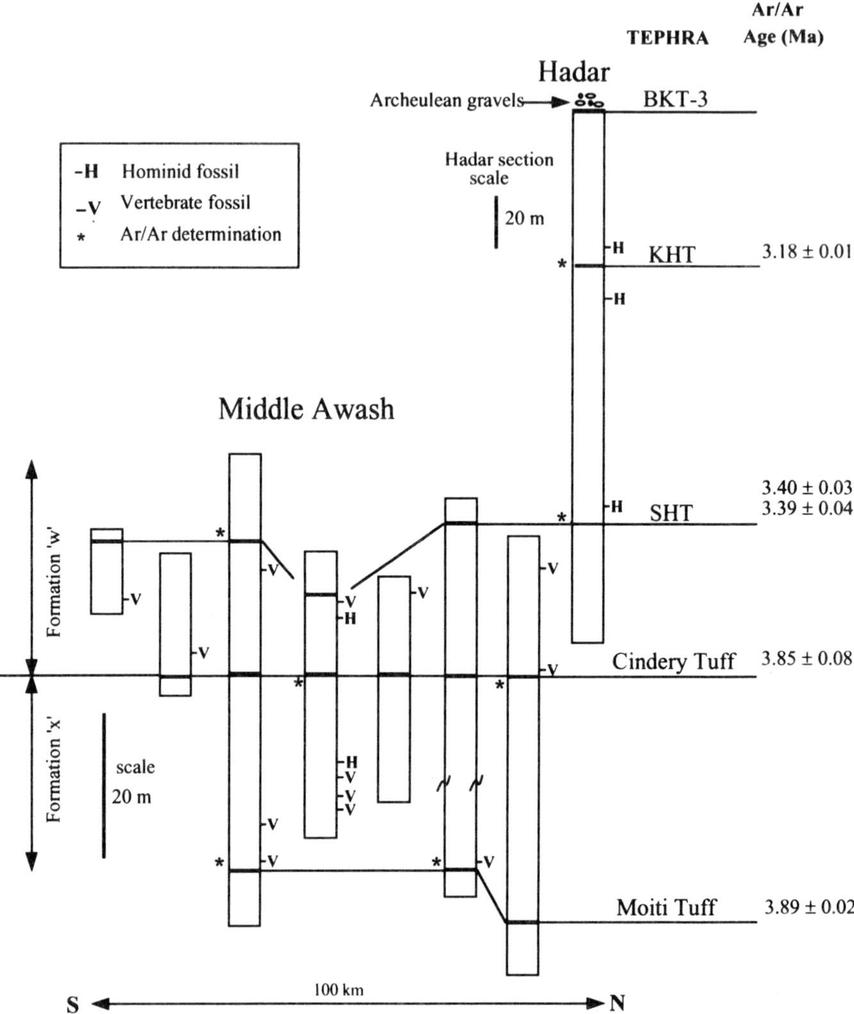

Figure 5.12. Stratigraphic position of tephra beds (mentioned in text) in Pliocene deposits of the Middle Awash and Hadar regions of Ethiopia. Ar/Ar age data, hominid fossil and vertebrate fossil localities are shown. Note difference in scale between the Middle Awash and Hadar sites (modified after White *et al.* 1993; Walter and Aronson 1993).

grains from a correlative of the Sidi Hakoma Tuff (SHT) in the central part of the Middle Awash area yield a mean $^{40}Ar/^{39}Ar$ date of 3.39±0.04 Ma (White *et al.* 1993); the glass-ITPFT age of an occurrence near Hadar is 3.53±0.37 Ma. Sanidines from the Kada Hadar Tuff (KHT) in the Hadar area give a mean $^{40}Ar/^{39}Ar$ age of 3.18±0.01 Ma (Walter 1994), which is older than the glass-

Table 5.3. Glass ITPFT Age Estimates of Some Ethiopian Tephra Beds[a]

Sample name	Days heated at 150°C	Etching conditions HF : Temp.: Time (%)	(°C)	(s)	Spontaneous track density ($x10^2$ t/cm^2)	Induced track density ($x10^4$ t/cm^2)	Neutron fluence ($x10^{15}$ n/cm^2)	D_s/D_i	Age±1σ (Ma)	References
BKT-3	0	25	26.0	60	11.62(147)	15.88(5750)	3.91(70573)	0.75	1.71±0.14[b]	Walter and Aronson (1993)
(Hadar)	30	26	20.0	70	9.81(105)	9.33(5265)	3.26(27836)	1.02	2.05±0.20	
(UT 1021)										
KHT(Hadar)	0	26	23.5	70	3.80(46)	18.21(9122)	3.24(27836)	0.47	0.40±0.06	Walter (1994)
(UT 1020)	15	26	20.0	90	6.11(50)	4.47(2304)	3.24(27836)	0.98	2.65±0.38	
SHT(Hadar)	0	25	23.0	70	12.84(168)	14.43(5987)	3.51(53493)	0.55	1.87±0.15	Walter and Aronson (1993)
(UT 1019)	30	26	25.0	145	10.01(98)	5.96(1820)	3.51(53493)	1.01	3.53±0.37	
Cindery Tuff	0	24	23.8	55	22.74(284)	11.31(7891)	2.03(14935)	0.74	2.44±0.15	Hall et al. (1984)
(UT859)	30	24	23.0	105	17.76(880)	5.83(4880)	2.03(14935)	1.02	3.70±0.14	White *et al.* (1993)
Moiti Tuff	0	25	25.0	80	18.03(269)	27.60(25795)	3.89(70573)	0.59	1.52±0.09	White *et al.* (1993)
(UT 1022)	30	26	25.0	135	13.62(265)	8.15(4388)	3.89(70573)	0.99	3.89±0.25	

[a]Methodological details are given in Table 1.
[b]Correction for partial track fading in BKT-3 by the track size method gives an age of 2.28±0.20 Ma (Sandhu and Westgate 1995).

ITPFT age of 2.65±0.38 Ma, although the difference is not significant at the 2σ level due to the relatively large error associated with the latter date. We were unable to date the sample that was heated for 30 days at 150°C. The etch rate of fission tracks is decreased by heat treatment requiring longer etch times to produce tracks in the range of 6–8 μm. Because the glass shards in this sample were relatively small, the long etch time resulted in removal of most of the glass. The 15-day heat treatment has probably not fully corrected for the significant amount of track fading that has affected this sample (Table 5.3). The BKT-3 tephra in the Hadar area occurs just below Acheulean gravels and has a glass-ITPFT age of 2.05±0.20 Ma; its age as estimated by the track-size correction technique is 2.28±0.20 Ma. Hart *et al.* (1992) give a zircon fission-track age of 2.3 Ma.

It can be seen, therefore, that application of the glass-ITPFT dating method to distal tephra beds in the Middle Awash region can play a useful role in attempts to decipher the hominid fossil record. Independent age estimates on two different, co-existing phases in a tephra bed (e.g. glass and feldspar) give more confidence in the accuracy and reliability of the age determination. Attempts to date glass shards from tephra beds (e.g. SHT and KHT) by the K-Ar and $^{40}Ar/^{39}Ar$ methods have given spuriously old apparent ages (Walter 1994). This is thought to be the consequence of glass preferentially losing K compared to Ar during alteration (Cerling *et al.* 1985). On the other hand, our ITPFT data show that glass shards, at least for the units we have dated (Table 5.3), act as a closed system with respect to uranium.

AGE OF THE LATE CENOZOIC LOESS RECORD IN INTERIOR ALASKA

Loess deposits in the Fairbanks area of interior Alaska (Fig. 5.13) are thick and fossiliferous. In places, the sequence is more than 50 m thick (Péwé 1955). Investigations have suffered from poor chronological controls, and, prior to the 1980s, the general belief was that the entire loess record was young. For example, using sedimentological and palaeontological criteria, Péwé (1975a) assigned the oldest unit, the Gold Hill Loess (Fig. 5.14), to a single glaciation, the Illinoian (penultimate).

The presence of thin, discontinuous tephra beds in the loess has long been known, and their chronological potential has been fully recognized (Péwé 1975a, 1975b). However, little attention has been given to them in the past because of their assumed young age, common dearth of crystals, fine grain size, and typical presence of detrital grains, reworked into the tephra following initial deposition. Bulk methods of analysis are inappropriate for such tephra deposits and their stratigraphic value could not be fully realized until the development of grain-specific methods. More than 30 distinct, distal tephra

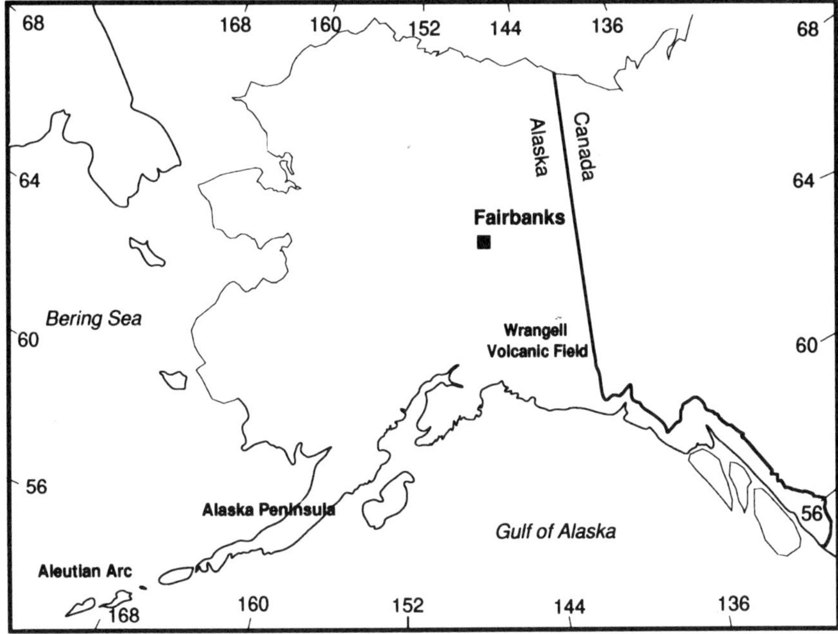

Figure 5.13. Map of Alaska showing location of the Fairbanks area, the Alaska Peninsula-Aleutian arc region, and the Wrangell Volcanic Field.

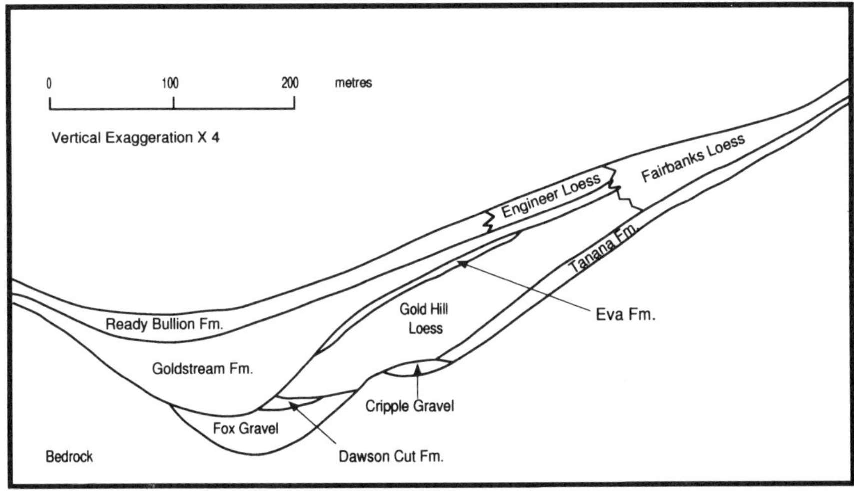

Figure 5.14. Schematic composite cross section of a valley near Fairbanks, Alaska, illustrating stratigraphic relations of late Cenozoic deposits (modified after Péwé 1975a).

beds have now been recognized in the Gold Hill Loess (GHL). Twenty beds have been characterized in detail and 5 have been dated by the ITPFT method (Westgate *et al.* 1990). They are derived from volcanoes in the Alaska Peninsula - Aleutian arc region and the Wrangell Volcanic Field (Fig. 5.13), their respective source area being readily determined on the basis of their petrographic and geochemical attributes (Preece *et al.* 1992). These tephrochronological studies in combination with magnetostratigraphic data have permitted the first insight

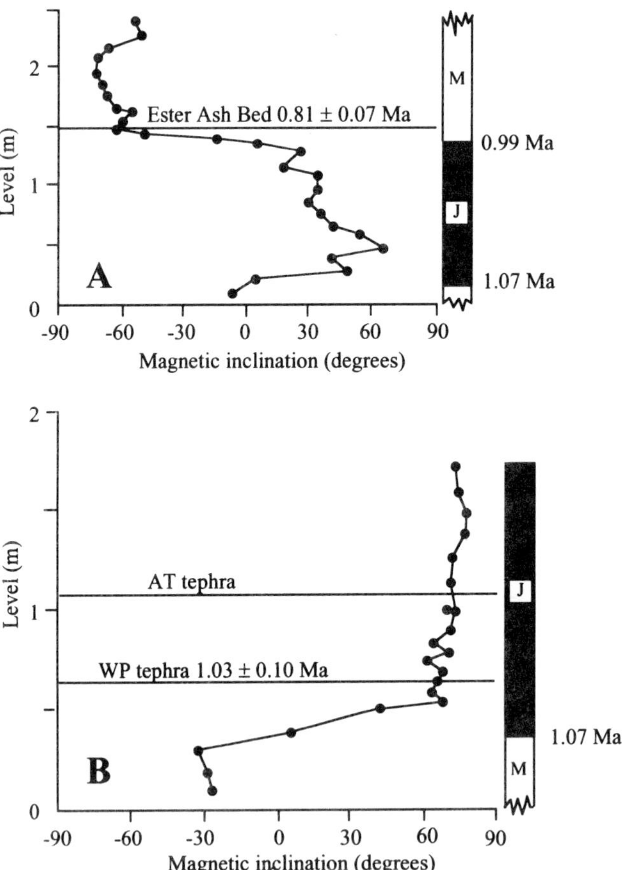

Figure 5.15. A: Magnetic inclination changes in basal Gold Hill Loess, which contains Ester Ash Bed, at Ester Island, 4 km west of Fairbanks. Data smoothed by using three-point running mean. All samples AF demagnetized at 600 Oe. B: Magnetic inclination changes in loess containing the AT and WP tephra beds at site a few hundred metres east of A. Data smoothed using a three-point running mean. All samples AF demagnetized at 100 Oe. M=Matuyama Reversed Chron; J=Jaramillo Normal Subchron.

into the chronology of the entire loess sequence in the Fairbanks region of Alaska. The results have revealed a long history of loess deposition that began in the late Pliocene. The GHL, formerly thought to be related to one glaciation, the Illinoian, actually spans a period of time greater than two million years and has major unconformities within it.

Tephrochronological details on the GHL provide a measure of the reliability of the latter statement. Old Crow tephra is situated in the uppermost part of the GHL, a few metres below the interglacial Eva Forest Bed (Fig. 5.14) and has been discovered at several localities in the Fairbanks region. Its weighted mean age and uncertainty based on 6 deteminations is 0.14±0.01 Ma. The Ester Ash Bed (EAB) (Péwé 1975b) at Ester Island, about 4 km west of Fairbanks, has a weighted mean ITPFT age of 0.81±0.07 Ma based on 8 determinations (Westgate *et al.* 1990). It has reversed magnetic polarity and was deposited very soon after a well-defined normal polarity event, interpreted to represent the Jaramillo Subchron (Fig. 5.15A). A few hundred metres to the east, the loess contains two different tephra beds: a thin, discontinuous rhyolitic unit, called WP tephra, and, one metre above it, a thin andesitic bed, called AT tephra (Fig. 5.15B). Two age determinations on WP tephra give a mean age of 1.03±0.10 Ma. Both tephra beds have a normal magnetic polarity, interpreted to represent the Jaramillo Subchron and the WP bed lies close to the base of this subchron. The age data on EAB, AT, and WP units are in good agreement with age estimates for the top and bottom of the Jaramillo Subchron, namely, 0.99 and 1.07 Ma, respectively (Fig. 5.15).

AT tephra has also been discovered in the 30 m loess exposure at Gold Hill, located immediately to the west of Fairbanks (Fig. 5.16). Its position within the Jaramillo Subchron is confirmed by the presence of the overlying, reversed SP tephra, dated at 0.86±0.06 Ma. The short normal-polarity event recorded in loess 2 m lower in the sequence is interpreted as the Cobb Mountain Subchron, dated at 1.19 Ma (Valet and Meynadier 1993).

PA tephra is the oldest known tephra in the GHL and is located 15 m above the base of the loess (Fig. 5.16). It has a reversed magnetic polarity and a weighted mean ITPFT age based on 2 determinations of 2.01±0.14 Ma, placing it in the lower part of the Matuyama Chron. Given these constraints, together with the earlier magnetostratigraphic studies of Westgate *et al.* (1990), the basal 12 m of the GHL is interpreted as representing the upper part of the Gauss Chron, suggesting that the loess record at Fairbanks began about 3 million years ago.

CONCLUSION

In sum, it can be seen that tephrochronological and magnetostratigraphic techniques in conjunction with glass-ITPFT dating together make-up a formi-

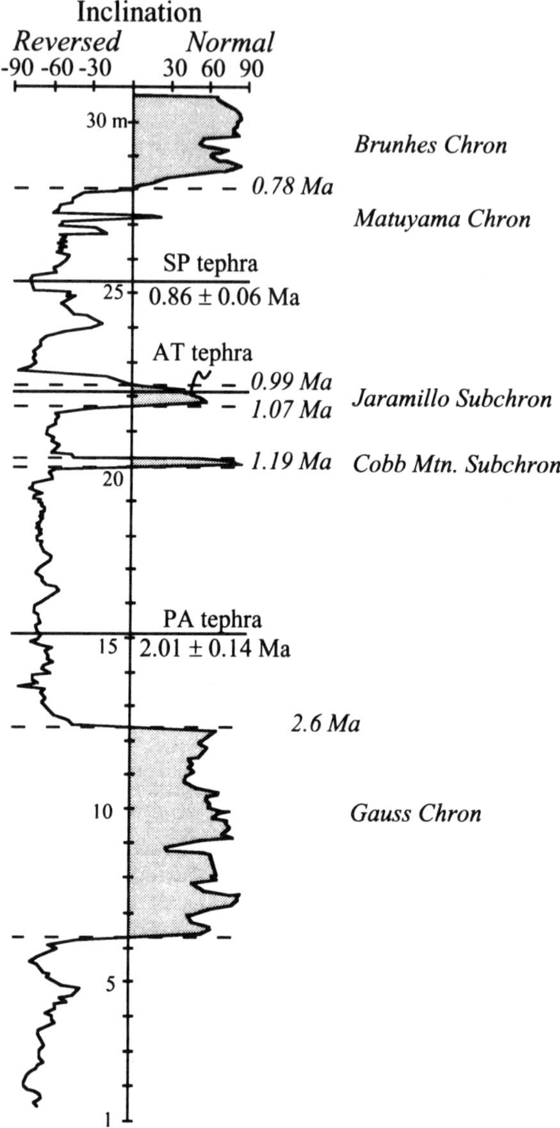

Figure 5.16. Magnetostratigraphy of the Gold Hill Loess at eastern end of Gold Hill locality, Fairbanks, Alaska. Oriented samples collected at 10 cm intervals, two per level; inclination curve smoothed by using three-point running average. All samples demagnetized with an AF system. Positive inclinations correspond to samples with a normal magnetic polarity (shaded areas) and negative inclinations correspond to a reversed magnetic polarity. Vertical axis is metres above the basal contact of the GHL with the underlying Cripple Gravels. Dashed horizontal lines are polarity reversal boundaries which we correlate to known polarity chrons and subchrons. Solid bold lines represent tephra horizons some of which have been dated by the ITPFT method. The age of the lowermost polarity transition is uncertain because of poor chronological control in this part of the loess sequence (see text).

dable toolkit with which to tackle stratigraphic problems. In particular, their use permits the development of high-resolution late Cenozoic stratigraphic frameworks—an essential prerequisite towards the solution of many problems in the Quaternary Sciences and Archaeology.

ACKNOWLEDGMENTS

This research was made possible by funds from the Natural Sciences and Engineering Research Council of Canada, the National Science Foundation, Washington, D.C., and the American Chemical Society through the Petroleum Research Fund. We thank Martin Williams, Ravi Korisettar, Giday Wolde-Gabriel, and Jim Aronson for tephra samples and information related to them. Bob Walter kindly provided information on some unpublished $^{40}Ar/^{39}Ar$ dates and Becky Stemper did most of the palaeomagnetic determinations.

REFERENCES

Acharyya, S.K. and Basu, P.K. 1993 Toba ash on the Indian subcontinent and its implications for correlation of Late Pleistocene alluvium. *Quaternary Research* 40: 10–19.

Aitken, M.J. 1990 *Science-based dating in Archaeology*. London, Longman.

Alloway, B.V., Pillans, B.J., Sandhu, A.S. and Westgate, J.A. 1993 Revision of the marine chronology in the Wanganui Basin, New Zealand, based on the isothermal plateau fission-track dating of tephra horizons. *Sedimentary Geology* 82: 299–310.

Alloway, B.V., Westgate, J.A., Sandhu, A.S. and Bright, R.C. 1992 Isothermal plateau fission-track age and revised distribution of the widespread Mid-Pleistocene Rockland tephra in west-central United States. *Geophysical Research Letters* 19: 567–572.

Arias, C., Bigazzi, G. and Bonadonna, F.P. 1981 Size corrections and plateau age in glass shards. *Nuclear Tracks* 5: 129–136.

Asfaw, B., Beyene, Y., Suwa, G., Walter, R.C., White, T.D., WoldeGabriel, G. and Yemane, T. 1992 The earliest Acheulean from Konso-Gardula. *Nature* 360: 732–735.

Barnes, S. and Gorton, M.P. 1984 Trace element analysis by neutron activation with a low flux reactor (Slowpoke-II): results for international reference rocks. *Geostandards Newsletter* 8: 177–23.

Berger, G.W. 1991 The use of glass for dating volcanic ash by thermoluminescence. *Journal of Geophysical Research* 96: 19705–19719.

Berger, G.W., Pillans, B.J. and Palmer, A.S. 1992 Dating loess up to 800 ka by thermoluminescence. *Geology* 20: 403–406.

Bogaard, P. van den and Schirnick, C. 1995 $^{40}Ar/^{39}Ar$ laser probe ages of Bishop Tuff quartz phenocrysts substantiate long-lived silicic magma chamber at Long Valley, Unites States. *Geology* 23: 759–762.

Burchart, J., Dakowski, M. and Galazka, J. 1975 A technique to determine extremely high fission track densities. *Bull. Acad. Polon. Sci., Sér. Sci Terre* 23: 1–7.

Cerling, T.C., Brown, F.H. and Bowman, J.R. 1985 Low temperature alteration of volcanic glass: hydration, Na, K, ^{18}O, and Ar mobility. *Chemical Geology* 52: 281–293.

Chesner, C.A., Rose, W.I., Deino, A., Drake, R. and Westgate, J. A. 1991 Eruptive history of Earth's largest Quaternary caldera (Toba, Indonesia) clarified. *Geology* 19: 200–203.

Dehn, J., Farrel J.W. and Schminke, H.-U. 1991 Neogene tephrochronology from site 758 on Ninety east Ridge: Indonesian arc volcanism of the past 5 Ma. *Proceedings of the Ocean Drilling Program, Scientific Results* 121: 273–295.

Dumitru, T.A. 1993 A new computer-automated microscope stage system for fission track analysis. *Nuclear Tracks and Radiation Measurements* 21: 575–580.

Dumitru, T.A. in press Fission-track geochronology. *In* Noller, J.S., ed. *Quaternary geochronology: applications of age-estimation methods in Quaternary geology and paleoseismology*. Boulder, Geological Society of America.

Fleischer, R.L., Price, P.B. and Walker, R.M. 1965 Effects of temperature, pressure and ionization on the formation and stability of fission tracks in minerals and glasses. *Journal of Geophysical Research* 70: 1497–1502.

Fleischer, R.L., Price, P.B. and Walker, R.M. 1975 *Nuclear Tracks in Solids: Principles and Applications*. Berkeley, University of California Press.

Fleischer, R.L., Price, P.B., Symes, E.M. and Miller, D.S. 1964 Fission track ages and track annealing behaviour of some micas. *Science* 143: 349–351.

Gleadow, A.J.W., Hurford, A.J. and Quaife, R.D. 1976 Fission track dating of zircon: improved etching techniques. *Earth and Planetary Science Letters* 33: 273–276.

Hall, C.M., Walter, R.C., Westgate, J.A. and York, D. 1984 Geochronology, stratigraphy and geochemistry of Cindery Tuff in Pliocene hominid-bearing sediments of the Middle Awash, Ethiopia. *Nature* 308: 26–31.

Hanna, G.C., Westcott, C.H., Lemmel, H.D., Leonard, B.R., Story, J.S. and Attree, P.M. 1969 Revision of values for the 2200 m/s neutron constants for four fissile nuclides. *Atomic Energy Review* 7(4): 3–92.

Hart, W.K., Walter, R.C. and WoldeGabriel, G. 1992 Tephra sources and correlation in Ethiopia: application of elemental and neodymium isotope data. *Quaternary International* 13/14: 77–86.

Hildreth, W. and Lanphere, M .A. 1994 Geochronology of Kulshan Caldera and Mt. Baker, North Cascades, Washington [U.S.A.]. *Eos* 75: 751.

Hurford, A.J. and Green, P.F. 1982 A users' guide to fission track dating calibration. *Earth and Planetary Science Letters* 59: 343–354.

Hurford, A.J. and Green, P.F. 1983 The zeta calibration of fission-track dating. *Isotope Geoscience* 1: 285–317.

Izett, G.A. and Naeser, C.W. 1976 Age of the Bishop Tuff of eastern California as determined by the fission-track method. *Geology* 2: 587–590.

Jaffey, A.H., Flynn, K.F., Glendenin, L.E., Bentley, W.C. and Essling, A.M. 1971 Precision measurements of half-lives and specific activities of ^{235}U and ^{238}U. *Physical Review* C4: 1889–1906.

Kohn, B.P., Pillans, B. and McGlone, M.S. 1992 Zircon fission track age for middle Pleistocene Rangitawa Tephra, New Zealand: stratigraphic and paleoclimatic significance. *Palaeogeography, Palaeoclimatology, Palaeoecology* 95: 73–94.

Korisettar, R., Venkatesan, T.R., Misra, S., Rajaguru, S.N., Somayajulu, B.L.K., Tandon, S.K., Gogte, V.D., Ganjoo, R.K. and Kale, V.S. 1989 Discovery of a tephra bed in the Quaternary alluvial sediments of Pune district (Maharashtra), Peninsular India. *Current Science* 58: 564–567.

Miller, D.S. and Wagner, G.A. 1981 Fission-track ages applied to obsidian artifacts from South America using the plateau-annealing and the track-size age-correction techniques. *Nuclear Tracks* 5: 147–155.

Naeser, C.W. 1967 The use of apatite and sphene for fission track age determinations. *Geological Society of America Bulletin* 78: 1523–1526.

Naeser, C.W. and Naeser, N.D. 1988 Fission-track dating of Quaternary events. *Geological Society of America, Special Paper* 227: 1–11.

Naeser, C.W., Izett, G.A. and Obradovich, J.D. 1980 Fission-track and K-Ar ages of natural glasses. *U.S. Geological Survey Bulletin* 1489: 1–31.

Naeser, C.W., Izett, G.A. and Wilcox, R.E. 1973 Zircon fission-track ages of Pearlette family ash beds in Meade County, Kansas. *Geology* 1: 187–189.

Naeser, N.D., Westgate, J.A., Hughes, O.L. and Péwé, T.L. 1982 Fission-track ages of late Cenozoic distal tephra beds in the Yukon Territory and Alaska. *Canadian Journal of Earth Sciences* 19: 2167–2178.

Ninkovich, D., Shackleton, N.J., Obradovich, J.D. and Izett, G. 1978 K-Ar age of the late Pleistocene eruption of Toba, north Sumatra. *Nature* 276: 574–577.

Nishimura, S. and Stauffer, P.H. 1981: Fission-track dating of zircons from the Serdang volcanic ash, Peninsular Malaysia. *Warta Geologi* 7: 39–41.

Pearce, N.J.G., Westgate, J.A. and Perkins, W.T. 1994 Trace element analysis of single glass shards in volcanic deposits by laser ablation ICP-MS: applications to tephrochronology. *Geological Society of America, Program with Abstracts* 26: A483.

Péwé, T.L. 1955 Origin of the upland silt near Fairbanks, Alaska. *Geological Society of America Bulletin* 66: 699–724.

_____ 1975a Quaternary geology of Alaska. *U.S. Geological Survey Professional Paper* 835: 1–145.

_____ 1975b Quaternary stratigraphic nomenclature in central Alaska. *U.S. Geological Survey Professional Paper* 862: 1–32.

Preece, S.J., Westgate, J.A., and Gorton, M.P., 1992. Compositional variation and provenance of late Cenozoic distal tephra beds, Fairbanks area, Alaska; *Quaternary International* 13/14: 97–101.

Price, P.B. and Walker, R.M. 1962 Chemical etching of charged particle tracks. *Journal of Applied Physics* 33: 3407–3412.

_____ 1963 Fossil tracks of charged particles in mica and the age of minerals. *Journal of Geophysical Research* 68: 4847–4862.

Pringle, M.S., McWilliams, M., Houghton, B.F., Lanphere, M.A. and Wilson, C.J.N. 1992 $^{40}Ar/^{39}Ar$ dating of Quaternary feldspar: Examples from the Taupo Volcanic Zone, New Zealand. *Geology* 20: 531–534.

Rampino, M.R. and Self, S. 1993 Climate-volcanism feedback and the Toba eruption of ~74,000 years ago. *Quaternary Research* 40: 269–280.

Roberts, J.H., Gold, R. and Armani, R.J. 1968 Spontaneous fission decay-constant of ^{238}U. *Physical Review* 174: 1482–1484.

Rose, W.I. and Chesner, C.A. 1987 Dispersal of ash in the great Toba eruption. *Geology* 15: 913–917.

Sandhu, A.S. and Westgate, J.A. 1995 The correlation between reduction in fission-track diameter and areal track density in volcanic glass shards and its application in dating tephra beds. *Earth and Planetary Science Letters* 131: 289–299.

Sandhu, A.S., Westgate, J.A. and Alloway, B.V. 1993 Optimizing the isothermal plateau fission-track dating method for volcanic glass shards. *Nuclear Tracks and Radiation Measurements* 21: 479–488.

Sandhu, A.S., Westgate, J.A. and Stemper, B.A. 1992 Isothermal plateau correction for partial fading fission tracks in hydrated glass shards. *Quaternary International* 13/14: 121–125.

Shane, P. 1991 Remobilised silicic tuffs in middle Pleistocene fluvial sediments, southern North Island, New Zealand. *New Zealand Journal of Geology and Geophysics* 34: 489–499.

Shane, P., Black, T. and Westgate, J.A. 1994 Isothermal plateau fission-track age for a paleomagnetic excursion in the Mamaku Ignimbrite, New Zealand, and implications for late Quaternary stratigraphy. *Geophysical Research Letters* 21: 1695–1698.

Shane, P., Westgate, J.A., Williams, M., and Korisettar, R., 1995. New geochemical evidence for the Youngest Toba Tuff in India. *Quaternary Research* 44: 200–204.

Staudacher, T.H., Jessberger, E.K., Dominik, B., Kirsten, T. and Schaeffer, O.A. 1982 ^{40}Ar-^{39}Ar ages of rocks and glasses from the Nördlinger Ries Crater and the temperature history of impact breccias. *Journal Geophysics* 51: 1–11.

Stauffer, P.H. 1973 Late Pleistocene age indicated for volcanic ash in west Malaysia. *Geological Society of Malaysia Newsletter* 40: 1–4.

Storzer, D. and Poupeau, G. 1973 Ages-plateaux de minéraux et verres par la méthode des traces de fission. *C.R. Acad. Sci. Paris Sér* D 276: 137–139.

Storzer, D. and Wagner, G.A. 1969 Correction of thermally lowered fission track ages of tektites. *Earth and Planetary Science Letters* 5: 463–468.

Valet, J-P. and Meynadier, L. 1993 Geomagnetic field intensity and reversals during the past four million years. *Nature* 366: 234–238.

Wagner, G.A. 1979 Correction and interpretation of fission track ages. *In* Jäger, E. and Hunziker, J.C., eds., *Lectures in isotope geology*. Berlin, Springer Verlag: 170–177.

Wagner, G.A. and Van den haute, P. 1992 *Fission-track dating*. Stuttgart, Ferdinand Enke Verlag.

Walter, R.C. 1989 Application and limitation of fission-track geochronology to Quaternary tephras. *Quaternary International* 1: 35–46.

Walter, R.C. 1994 Age of Lucy and the First Family: single-crystal $^{40}Ar/^{39}Ar$ dating of the Denen Dora and lower Kada Hadar members of the Hadar Formation, Ethiopia. *Geology* 22: 6–10.

Walter, R.C. and Aronson, J.L. 1993 Age and source of the Sidi Hakoma Tuff, Hadar Formation, Ethiopia. *Journal of Human Evolution* 25: 229–240.

Westgate, J.A. 1988 Isothermal plateau fission track age of the late Pleistocene Old Crow tephra, Alaska. *Geophysical Research Letters* 15: 376–379.

Westgate, J.A. 1989 Isothermal plateau fission-track ages of hydrated glass shards from silicic tephra beds. *Earth and Planetary Science Letters* 95: 226–234.

Westgate, J.A. and Naeser, N.D. 1985 Dating methods of Pleistocene deposits and their problems: Tephrochronology and fission-track dating. *Geoscience Canada, Reprint Series* 2: 31–38.

Westgate, J.A. and Naeser, N.D. 1995 Dating methods of Pleistocene deposits and their problems: Tephrochronology and fission-track dating. *Geoscience Canada, 2nd edition*: 15–28.

Westgate, J.A., Pearce, N.J.G. and Perkins, W.T. 1995 Analysis of single shards in tephra deposits by ultra-violet laser ablation ICP-MS. *Goldschmidt Conference, Program with Abstracts*, Pennsylvania State University, State College, PA: 96.

Westgate, J.A., Stemper, B.A. and Péwé, T.L. 1990 A 3 m.y. record of Pliocene-Pleistocene loess in interior Alaska. *Geology* 18: 858–861.

Westgate, J.A., Easterbrook, D.J., Naeser, N.D. and Carson, R.J. 1987 Lake Tapps tephra: an early Pleistocene stratigraphic marker in the Puget Lowland, Washington. *Quaternary Research* 28: 340–355.

White, T.D., Suwa, G., Hart, W.K., Walter, R.C., WoldeGabriel, G., Heinzelin, J. de, Clark, J.D., Asfaw, B. and Vrba, E. 1993 New discoveries of *Australopithecus* at Maka in Ethiopia. *Nature* 366: 261–264.

Williams, M.A.J. and Royce, K. 1982 Quaternary geology of Middle Son Valley, North Central India: implications for prehistoric archaeology. *Palaeogeography, Palaeoclimatology and Palaeoecology* 38: 139–162.

Chapter 6

Uranium Series Dating

HENRY P. SCHWARCZ

ABSTRACT

Uranium decays through a number of radioactive daughter isotopes, some of which have half-lives comparable to the time scale of prehistoric archaeology. The growth of these isotopes in naturally occurring materials at archaeological sites can be used to determine the age of sites. The growth of ^{230}Th from its parent, ^{234}U, can be used over a time range from a few hundred to half a million years. Calcite precipitated from running or dripping water in springs and caves, as well as marls and soil-deposited calcretes may be spatio-temporally associated with archaeological materials; they can be dated by $^{230}Th/^{234}U$ and $^{234}U/^{238}U$ measurements with a precision of ±5–10% of the age (by alpha counting) or ±1% (by mass spectrometry). Bones, teeth, mollusk and egg shells, are also datable but present problems due to migration of parent U in and out of the samples during their burial history.

INTRODUCTION

Uranium series (U-series) dating is one of the methods of choice for determination of the age of prehistoric sites older than the range of radiocarbon (ca. 40,000 years). It is applicable to a wide variety of materials found in archaeological and anthropological contexts. The potential range of the method is from a few hundred to approximately 500,000 years ago, covering much of

HENRY P. SCHWARCZ • School of Geography and Geology, McMaster University, Hamilton, Ontario L85 4M1 Canada.

Chronometric Dating in Archaeology, edited by Taylor and Aitken.
Plenum Press, New York, 1997.

the range of interest to archaeologists. Improvements in the technique over the past few years have greatly increased the precision of the method, and opened up the possibility of dating smaller samples, a revolution comparable to that which occurred with the introduction of accelerator mass spectrometry to radiocarbon dating.

This chapter will present a brief introduction to the theory of U-series dating, describe the materials that can be dated and the limitations of the method, and conclude with two examples of its application to prehistoric archaeological sites. Readers interested in more detailed and technically complete treatment of these topics should refer to the treatise on uranium series dating edited by Ivanovich and Harmon (1992). In particular, a chapter in that book by Schwarcz and Blackwell (1992) deals with applications to archaeology.

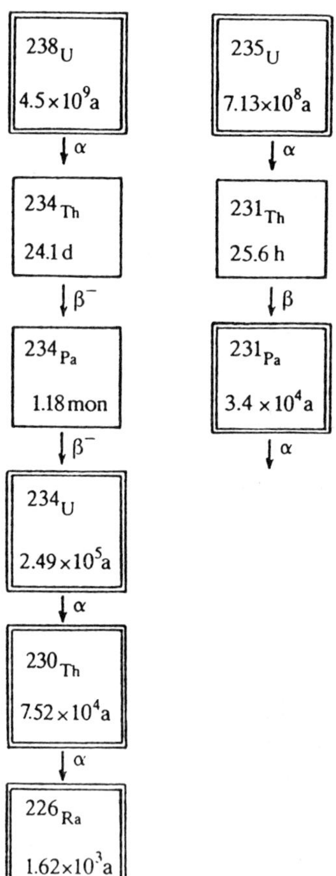

Figure 6.1. The initial part of the decay series for uranium-238 and uranium-235, showing the isotopes used for dating of Quaternary deposits. Natural uranium contains both of these parent isotopes in the ratio $^{235}U/^{238}U=7.25\times10^{-3}$.

A further update is given by Schwarcz (1992, 1993). A more general summary of U-series dating of Quaternary deposits is to be found in Schwarcz (1989).

U-series dating is based on the radioactive decay of isotopes which are themselves the decay products ("daughters") of one of the two naturally occurring isotopes of the element uranium (Fig. 6.1). The name U-series thus refers to the fact that each of these daughters is a member of a decay-chain or series, beginning with either uranium-238 (^{238}U) or uranium-235 (^{235}U). Each series ends with a stable isotope of lead (lead-206 and -207, respectively). The decay of U isotopes to stable isotopes of lead is also the basis of a radioactive dating method but, because of the slow rate of growth of lead from its parent uranium, this method is not applicable on the time scale of human evolution. On the other hand, the lifetimes of several of the radioactive daughters of U (Fig. 6.1) are comparable to the archaeological time scale, and are therefore well suited to the dating of events in prehistory.

The history of U-series dating has been recently reviewed by Schwarcz (1989). The fact that uranium decays through a chain-like series of daughters was recognized since the early days of the study of radioactivity and, in the late 1930's it was first appreciated that the growth or decay of the shorter-lived members of the chain in natural materials could provide information about times of formation or deposition. The earliest applications were in the dating of marine deposits, first of sediments from the deep sea, and later of reef-forming corals. The first suggestion of its application in archaeology was by Cherdyntsev (1971) who attempted to date bones and cave-deposited calcite found in archaeological associations He already drew attention to some of the hazards of the method. Since then it has been used with increasing frequency as archaeologists recognized its applicability to sites which they were studying, and sought out isotopic geochemists with the necessary expertise (Schwarcz 1980).

THE BACKGROUND OF U-SERIES DATING

Figure 6.1 shows that, as uranium decays, it produces a series of daughter isotopes of various elements, each daughter being itself radioactive. Isotopes are of course, simply different species of a chemical element. The isotopes of an element are chemically indistinguishable, but differ from one another in respect to their nuclear properties (just as the isotope ^{14}C behaves chemically like ordinary carbon and can therefore be assimilated by plants and animals). Considering for example the decay of ^{238}U, we note that, with the exception of the first decay step, the daughters of this U isotope are chemically different from one another. That is, we have daughters which are isotopes of different chemical elements: thorium, protactinium, radium, radon, and even uranium. This is because the radioactive breakdown of the nucleus of an atom leads to the formation of a new nucleus which almost always has a different atomic number than the parent atom. We shall see that this chemical transformation from parent to daughter is critical to the feasibility of U-series dating.

In general, the rules for the use of radioisotopes in dating are as follows. First, the time range over which the isotope can be used to date must be no more than 6 to 10 times its half-life, and not much less than a tenth of a half-life. We recollect that the *half life* of a radioisotope is the time needed for the decay of half the number of atoms in a batch of the isotope. For example, if we start with a million atoms of the daughter isotope thorium-230 (^{230}Th), after 75,200 years, 500,000 atoms will remain.

The second rule of radioactive dating is that the starting conditions for the sample must be known. For example, if we are using the simple decay of an isotope (like ^{14}C) to measure elapsed time, we must know how much of the isotope was present in the sample when it was deposited. But we can also use the *growth* of an isotope to determine the age, as long as there is present in the sample a parent which is decaying to produce it. This is typically the way in which we use the uranium series to tell ages. Then, according to the second rule, we must be sure that none of the isotope in question was present in our sample at $t = 0$. Alternatively, if some of the parent was present at $t = 0$, we must be able to know how much, so we can correct for it when we calculate the age from the growth of the isotope. We refer to samples which do not comply with this rule as contaminated or, more simply, "dirty", while compliant samples are described as "clean".

Finally, the third rule is that any changes in the amount of the isotope must have been as a result of radioactive decay, and not due to some intrusion or leakage of the isotope into or out of the sample as it lay buried in the site. This is a particularly bothersome problem in archaeology because hominid dwelling-places are typically located in sites where movement of water and contaminating substances has gone on continuously before, during and after the occupation of the site. We speak of samples which perfectly satisfy this rule as behaving as "closed systems". Imperfect samples may have behaved as "open systems", that is ones in which there has been movement of radioisotopes into and out of the sample through time. Perfect, clean, closed-system samples are difficult to obtain, and we must often make do with imperfect samples in order to provide any useful information about the age of a site.

Radioactive dating is generally based on the measurement of the number of atoms (or the decay rate) of some radioisotope. The rate of decay of a radioisotope does not depend at all on the chemical or physical conditions in which it is stored. The decay rate is, on the other hand, governed by some simple rules of physics. As is true for all radioisotopes, the rate of decay of the daughter isotopes of U are determined by the half life and by the number of atoms of the isotope that are present, according to the following equation:

$$\text{Decay rate} = [0.693/(\text{half-life})] \times (\text{no. of atoms}) \tag{1}$$

This equation leads to the result that the rate of decay of each isotope changes with time, precisely because the number of atoms are changing (which is what the equation shows). One consequence of this is that there is a continuous decrease in the amount of change per unit time of both the decay rate and the number of atoms. That is, with the passage of time, it gets harder to tell what time the clock is reading, because samples older than a certain age all appear identical, and give identical, "infinite" ages. In effect, the radioactive clock comes to a stop. For U-series dating, this state occurs when the radioactivity of the daughter isotopes rises to equal that of their parent; this is quite the opposite of the situation in radiocarbon dating where the limit is defined by the point at which the activity of ^{14}C drops to zero.

Let us imagine that at the time of occupation of a site, a material of some sort is formed containing some uranium. For example a stalagmite might be formed by water dripping into a cave being occupied by early hominids. The uranium enters the stalagmite because it has been carried in solution in the dripping water; but ^{230}Th, the eventual daughter of ^{238}U will not be deposited in the stalagmite. This is true because thorium is much less soluble in water than is uranium. Any thorium which was present in the source region of the uranium, was left behind as the uranium was carried off in solution. This absence of the daughter isotope sets up an isotopic imbalance which nature proceeds to correct: the uranium trapped in the stalagmite begins to grow a new crop of daughter thorium-230. For technical reasons too complicated to explain here, the rate of growth of the thorium is determined by the half-life of the ^{230}Th.

At this point it useful to explain an important law of radioactive decay that applies to radioactive series such as the uranium series. Let us measure the amount of each radioisotope in the series in units of number of radioactive disintegrations per minute per unit weight of (e.g., gram) of material. We call this the *activity* of the isotope in a sample. Then, the law states that after a long time has passed, the activity of all the daughters becomes equal to that of the initial parent. This state of equality is called secular equilibrium. If a sample is formed in a non-equilibrium state, it will gradually return to equilibrium. So, if we return to our hypothetical stalagmite in a cave, we see that it was formed out of equilibrium, because the activity of ^{230}Th was much less than that of its parent, and indeed was initially zero. As time passes the activity of the ^{230}Th gradually rises, and reaches a maximum value equal to that of the ^{238}U in the stalagmite. This picture is made slightly more complicated if we look back at the decay scheme of ^{238}U and note that the first daughter of the decay of the parent ^{238}U is in fact another isotope of uranium, ^{234}U, with a half-life of 248,000 years. In most cases, however, this isotope of uranium is not chemically separated from its parent, even as the uranium is carried in solution; this is because both are isotopes of the same chemical element and behave similarly. In some cases, however, a small degree of separation can occur, so that the

$^{234}U/^{238}U$ activity ratio deviates slightly from unity, and therefore also becomes a (not very sensitive) U-series clock.

The growth into equilibrium of the ^{230}Th can be shown on a graph of the ratio of the activity of ^{230}Th to that of ^{234}U (Fig. 6.2). We see that this ratio rises from an initial value of zero, at t = 0, and gradually approaches a value of 1.0, never quite reaching it. Now, if we collect the sample today, at time = T years after deposition, the activity ratio $r_{04} = {}^{230}Th/^{234}U$ will have risen to some value $r_{04}(T)$. If we measure that ratio, it will give us an estimate of the time of deposition of the stalagmite and, thus, the time of occupation of the site. More importantly, since ^{230}Th is actually a daughter of ^{234}U, we must take into account the deviation of the $^{234}U/^{238}U$ ratio from unity when calculating the age (see caption of Fig. 6.2).

From Fig. 6.2. we can see that the maximum age that can be determined by $^{230}Th/^{234}U$ dating is defined by the point at which the ratio is indistinguishable from the equilibrium value of 1.0 (or a slightly higher value where $^{234}U/^{238}U >> 1$). The actual limit depends on the analytical methods used, to be discussed later.

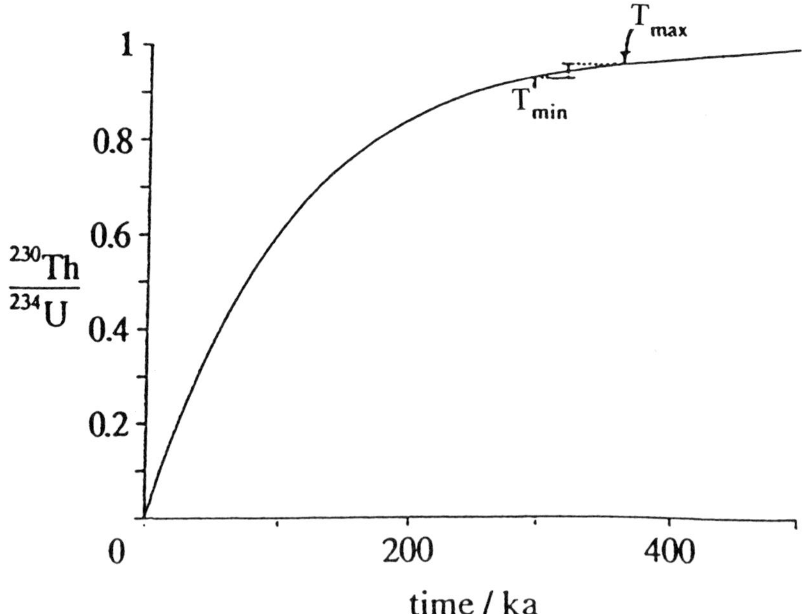

Figure 6.2. Graph of the ratio of the activity of thorium-230 to the activity of uranium-234 ($^{230}Th/^{234}U$) versus time. The age of a sample with a particular $^{230}Th/^{234}U$ ratio can be determined from this graph, if the $^{234}U/^{238}U$ ratio of the sample is equal to unity (1.0). For samples with higher or lower $^{234}U/^{238}U$ ratios, other curves similar to this are used.

Although there are other moderately long-lived isotopes in the two U-series decay schemes, the only one that has any practical utility is protactinium-231 (^{231}Pa), with a half-life of 34,300 years. The abundance of its parent ^{235}U is always in a fixed ratio to that of ^{238}U, namely less than 1 per cent of it. Therefore, the abundance of ^{231}Pa is always much lower than that of ^{230}Th and is much harder to determine with accuracy. Where total U concentration is high, we can sometimes use the ^{231}Pa/^{235}U ratio as an addition test of the age of a sample. The age limit for ^{231}Pa/^{235}U dating is about 300 ka.

What if the initial concentration of ^{230}Th was *not* zero at t = 0? This can sometimes happen, because the sample was contaminated with some solid material containing thorium: "dirt". Then we must make some corrections in the data when we calculate the age to take this into account; the best approach is to use the method of isochrons, to be explained later.

In the example we have described, it was possible to determine the age from the present-day ^{230}Th/^{234}U because U is relatively soluble in water whereas thorium is insoluble. This is true for any natural waters, e.g., lakes, spring- or cave-seepages, or seawater. Therefore any place where materials are being deposited from natural waters sets up the conditions needed for U-series dating. In addition, many biological materials such as shells, bones or teeth, trap uranium in their structures soon after death of the organism, and can also act as U-series clocks. When such organic materials are analysed today, they may contain substantial concentrations of U, even though the living organism was essentially U-free. The question then arises: when was the U taken up by the material? In the case of coral, it is known that U is actually incorporated into the limy skeleton of the coral animal while it is alive. For all other fossil materials, we must make some assumption about the history of U uptake. We will return to this topic when we discuss the problems associated with such materials. In only one case, namely for tooth enamel, an independent test of U-uptake history is possible by cross checking against the electron spin resonance (ESR) response of the enamel (Grün *et al.* 1988a).

Many chemically precipitated materials are found today to have ^{234}U/^{238}U ratios greater than unity. Therefore the initial ratio at the time of deposition must have been higher yet and has decayed to the present day value with a half life of 248 ka. In principle it is possible to determine their age from the present-day ^{234}U/^{238}U ratio *if* we know the initial ratio. U in seawater today has a ^{234}U/^{238}U ratio of 1.14. Pleistocene marine carbonates (corals, molluscs) probably had this ratio at the time of their deposition, and could be dated to a limit of about 800 ka, using mass spectrometry. Also, travertines deposited from water emerging from large, stable aquifers, are likely to have had constant ^{234}U/^{238}U ratios equal to that in the water. In general, the past history of the initial ^{234}U/^{238}U ratio of a travertine or speleothem can be calculated from its ^{230}Th/^{234}U age and the present day ^{234}U/^{238}U ratio. If the ratio appears to have remained constant up to 350 ka, it may be safe to calculate the age of older deposits from their ^{234}U/^{238}U ratios.

In conclusion, U-series dating is the measurement of the degree of departure from secular equilibrium of a daughter/parent pair in the decay scheme of either ^{238}U or ^{235}U. For the most part, when discussing applications to archaeology, this can be identified with measurement of the $^{230}Th/^{234}U$ and $^{234}U/^{238}U$ ratios, and calculation of ages from them.

DATABLE MATERIALS

If we apply the rules as stated above, we can see what materials are potentially datable by U-series. Basically they must be formed at $t = 0$ with zero content of ^{230}Th and must have behaved ever afterwards as chemically closed systems. As we shall see, many of the materials that have actually been dated from sites do not strictly adhere to these constraints. Later, we shall discuss the selection of samples and their use in dating of archaeological events.

Carbonates

Calcium carbonate ($CaCO_3$) in the form of calcite or, rarely, aragonite, is commonly found deposited in close association with archaeological materials. This can be either as a result of purely chemical action, as in the growth of a stalagmite, or as a biological product: mollusk shells, egg shells, etc. In each case, the material is a possible target for U-series dating. We shall first consider chemically precipitated calcite, and then turn to biological deposits.

Speleothem

This is a generic term for stalagmites, stalactites, flowstones, and other calcite "decorations" of caves. Typically these form from waters dripping into caves; the water has passed through a soil zone where it picked up some U and also became saturated in carbonic acid. The latter allowed it to dissolve some limestone bedrock and, as the water passes into the cave, the water gives off carbon dioxide, becomes less acid and causes calcite to deposit, entrapping U. All speleothems are potentially U-series datable, but some may also contain large amounts of detritus that was carried into the cave suspended in wind or water. The detritus also contains isotopes of thorium (including ^{230}Th), and the freshly deposited speleothem will therefore have a non-zero $^{230}Th/^{234}U$ ratio.

Spring-Deposits

Where springs emerge as seepages from carbonate aquifers, they can build up deposits of calcite in the form of sheets and mounds of *travertine.*

As these deposits are later excavated either naturally through stream erosion, or artificially by limestone quarrying, archaeological layers interstratified with the travertine layers are often revealed. Travertine can be dated by U-series; where detritus is present, various strategies for correction of the data must be applied.

Marl

Calcite-charged spring waters can locally accumulate in pools, ponds or small lakes, where the calcite can precipitate as a fine-grained form of limestone. Typically the deposition is assisted by the action of unicellular algae (*Chara*). Such limestone deposits can also form in desertic regions as a result of evaporation of salt-charged waters. Here other minerals beside calcite may be initially present, although later dissolution in the ground may remove all but the calcite deposits. Prehistoric sites may be present along the shores of such lakes, but the deposits are rarely well-enough exposed (or excavated) to reveal these features.

Caliche, Calcrete

In subarid regions, the downward passage of water from infrequent rains can be highly charged with lime, and leads to the formation of intra-soil carbonate deposits of substantial thickness. Surficial sites in arid regions are commonly associated with such calcrete/caliche deposits.

Molluscan Shells

Many species of mollusks build shells of calcite or aragonite: snails, bivalves, limpets, etc. Bivalves live in marine and fresh waters, while snails live also on the land. Aragonitic shells are particularly useful because the aragonite is intrinsically unstable and its survival shows that the shell has not been remineralized by the action of ground water. Unfortunately, many mollusks, both aragonitic and calcitic, have been found to give anomalous U-series dates, for reasons which are not well understood.

Ratite Egg Shells

Ratites are large, flightless birds including the ostrich and the emu. Ratite shells are constructed of calcite, are quite robust, and survive in many archaeological sites, especially in arid or semi-arid terrains. Like mollusk shells, any U found in them must have been taken up post-mortem, since living shells have none.

Bones and Teeth

Vertebrate skeletons are made of a composite of the mineral apatite (calcium hydroxy-phosphate) and protein (principally collagen). The U content of buried fossil bones typically ranges from a few parts per million (ppm) of U to several hundred ppm; essentially all this U has been taken up during burial. U-series dating of bones has led to highly problematic data, going back to the original work of Cherdyntsev (1971). He concluded that they were not useful for dating, but many researchers have continued the quest, using a variety of strategies to avoid the pitfalls engendered by diagenesis and open-system behavior.

Teeth, and especially tooth enamel, seem to behave somewhat better than bones, as judged from recent results by McKinney (1992; 1993) and by McDermott *et al.* (1993). In some sites it appears that U is taken up soon after burial, and that the teeth remain closed systems thereafter. However, we shall see that data from other sites are contradictory.

Iron and Manganese Hydroxides

In some arid or subarid regions soils are strongly reddened by accumulations of ferric oxides or hydroxides, with admixed manganese oxides. Short *et al.* (1989) have shown that these materials also trap substantial amounts of U from soil water seeping through them, although they may also contain significant amounts of thorium isotopes. In lime-poor regions where no other chemically precipitated materials are available, these ferriferous deposits may be interesting targets for U series dating, but the data from them should be treated with caution.

Peat, Wood

Organic matter buried near the surface can extract U out of soil water that is circulating past it. This is largely because organic matter acts as a reducing agent, lowering the oxidation state of the U from +6 to +4. Whereas U^{+6} is soluble in ground water, U^{+4} is not. Therefore, there is a tendency for the U^{+4} to become immobilized and concentrated in peaty layers or within masses of fossil wood. These materials may behave as quasi-closed systems as the flow of water through them is cut off by later overlying deposits of clayey sediments. A few attempts have been made to date such material, but so far with not much success (Vogel and Kronfeld 1980).

Other Materials

While these constitute the main materials that can be dated by U-series, one should be alert to other materials encountered in archaeological sites which are possibly datable. Any materials which appear to have been formed synchronously with the deposit have the potential to be dated, but either they must have formed by precipitation from water, or else their U content must have been acquired from water flowing through them. One exception is volcanic ash, which can be dated by U-series though not with great accuracy (Condomines *et al.* 1988).

TECHNIQUES OF ANALYSIS

This chapter is not intended to present extensive details of analytical methods; for these, see relevant chapters Ivanovich and Harmon (1992). Here we shall simply outline the procedures needed to obtain a date, and the various options available for analysis of the U-series isotopes. In principle the goal is always the same: to determine the activities (or concentrations) of daughter and parent pairs, isotopes of Th, U or Pa, and from their ratios to determine the age.

Most of the techniques require that the elements thorium and uranium (and possibly protactinium) be separated from each other and from the material in which they occurred. The analysis begins, therefore, with the dissolution of the sample in acid, followed by chemical separations of U and Th, typically by use of ion exchange chromatography. The purified U and Th must then be isotopically analysed, since the chemical separation does not separate isotopes from one another (e.g., ^{234}U from ^{238}U). Isotopic analysis of the separated elements can be done either by alpha particle spectrometry or by mass spectrometry.

Alpha Spectrometry

Most of the isotopes of U and Th decay by the emission of an energetic helium nucleus, called an alpha (α) particle. Each isotope emits α-particles of specific energies. We can determine the relative concentrations of the various isotopes of U and Th by determining the rate of emission of these characteristic alphas in a counting system which tallies them in separate "bins" depending on their energy, and allows us to determine the number of alphas emitted by each isotope. To get the age, we need to know the absolute ratio of ^{230}Th to ^{234}U, but the number of alphas actually recorded from the various Th and U isotopes depends on the efficiency of the counter and also, importantly, on the degree of success of the preceding chemical extraction in extracting all the Th and U from the sample; the latter is referred to as the yield and can range anywhere from zero to 100%. Therefore, to correct for this variable yield, we add to the sample (before the Th and U are chemically separated) a *tracer*, a mixture of artificial isotopes of Th and U in a known proportion. The apparent proportions of these isotopes in the final counts can thus be used to determine the true $^{230}Th/^{234}U$ ratio in the sample. The upper age limit attainable by α-spectrometry is about 350 ka, and the precision of the dates is generally between 5 and 10%.

Mass Spectrometry

In the last few years, a new and more sensitive method for measurement of the isotopes has been developed: thermal ionization mass spectrometry [TIMS](Edwards *et al.* 1987). In α-counting the precision of the date is determined by the number of counts that has been recorded. To obtain a date of useful accuracy we must wait for a long enough time (usually several days) to accumulate an adequate number of counts. In mass spectrometry, atoms of each isotope are accelerated through a magnetic field that sorts them according to mass, and they are then counted directly (rather than waiting for them to decay). This is analogous to AMS dating of ^{14}C atoms. The counting procedure takes less than one hour. In addition TIMS allows us to count smaller numbers of atoms than could be detected by α-counting. As a result, the minimum sample size needed is reduced, and the precision of age determinations is increased to about 1%. Both the upper and lower age limits of TIMS dating are also broader than for α counting, from a few hundred to about 500,000 years. TIMS dating of corals from submerged reefs on Barbados has been used to calibrate the ^{14}C chronology beyond the range of dendrochronology (Bard *et al.* 1990).

Gamma Spectrometry

Both of the methods just described require separation of purified U and Th from the samples, because of the short penetrating range of the α-particles or, in the case of TIMS, because of the need to introduce only purified materials into the mass spectrometer. A third method of isotopic measurement exists: counting of gamma rays which are emitted by isotopes of Th, U and their daughters. Since gamma rays are more penetrating, than α particles, they can be measured as they are emitted from bulk samples, without need for chemical separation. This allows us to do non-destructive analyses of archaeological materials, such as hominid skeletal remains, although some correction must be made for the effect of the shape of the object on the absorbtion and counting of the weaker gamma rays (Yokoyama and Nguyen 1980). The precision of this method is not very high (±10% or worse).

Isochron Dating

A common problem in the dating of samples from archaeological sites is the presence of contaminant, "common" thorium, usually admixed with detrital contaminants in the sample. The presence of contaminant thorium is normally revealed by the presence, in either the alpha-, gamma, or mass-spectrum, of a peak for the isotope ^{232}Th. This is a primordial isotope of thorium (half-life = 14 billion years) and is not the daughter of any other isotope. We note that modern detritus contains both ^{232}Th and ^{230}Th, at approximately equal activities (^{230}Th/^{232}Th = 1 to 1.5). Therefore we might expect that whatever activity of ^{232}Th we find in a sample today was initially matched by an approximately equal activity of common ^{230}Th. Today, some of that initial activity has decayed away, but we still must correct for however much of it remains. Various schemes for doing this have been proposed. but the best procedure is to analyse different subsamples of the same contaminated deposit (e.g., a speleothem or travertine). We can assume that the deposit consists of a mixture of pure, uncontaminated calcite of a certain age, together with varying amounts of a single contaminant. It can shown mathematically that, if the isotope ratios ^{230}Th/^{232}Th and ^{234}U/^{232}Th plot on a straight line, then the slope of that line gives the ^{230}Th/^{234}U ratio of the uncontaminated calcite that had been mixed with varying proportions of the contaminant. The line is called an isochron. A similar plot of ^{238}U/^{232}Th vs ^{234}U/^{232}Th is used to obtain the ^{234}U/^{238}U ratio, which is also needed to obtain the U-series age. Different techniques have been proposed for chemical analysis of the samples for construction of isochrons (Luo and Ku 1990; Bischoff and Fitzpatrick 1990; Schwarcz and Latham 1989), and these papers should be consulted for details. Generally, where the ^{230}Th/^{232}Th ratio of a sample is greater than 20, we believe that no correction for contaminant thorium is necessary. The presence of detrital residue on dissolution of the sample is usually, but not always, associated with low ^{230}Th/^{232}Th ratios.

Selection of samples and their possible use in U-series dating depends on the quality of the samples. Briefly, the following should be considered:

U-Content

The precision of an alpha spectrometric date increases with the number of α particles that have been counted. To obtain an acceptable precision in a reasonable time, we therefore require that the sample should contain at least 10 micrograms of U. The size of the sample must be adjusted according to its concentration of U. Typically, speleothems contain 0.05 to 2 ppm U, with a median around 0.3 ppm. Therefore samples typically range in weight from a few grams to 200 grams. The low U content of many speleothems limits the possible precision of α spectrometric dates. The sample requirement of TIMS is about 10 times lower, and we can therefore either analyse smaller samples, or use samples with lower U content. Carbonates with U $<<$ 0.01 ppm U are difficult to analyse by any technique.

Detritus Content

The samples should be as "clean" as possible. If the bulk sample contains significant detrital contamination, it may be possible to isolate sub-samples which are relatively cleaner. The isochron method requires the use of subsamples of varying detrital content, but will not work at all if the detritus contains any significant amount of limestone fragments, since these will be chemically indistinguishable from the carbonate being dated. There is no routine procedure to check for the presence of limestone contaminant, but this material should be recognizable to a geologist studying a thin section of the material.

Diagenetic Features

Like any dating method, U-series dating requires that the sample be pristine, and not recrystallized or replaced by secondary minerals. This can best be tested by microscopic examination; simply testing by X-ray diffraction is not sufficient, since even aragonite can occur as a replacement or pore-filling mineral (Bar-Matthews *et al.* 1993). Recrystallization of calcite and other minerals can occur when the material is exposed to ground water in the sub-soil. If a calcitic material is recrystallized, we generally expect that it will lose the crop of ^{230}Th and other daughters that has grown from the uranium originally contained in the calcite. Therefore, the clock will be reset to close to zero.

APPLICATION TO ARCHAEOLOGY: ANTE-, SYN-, AND POST-QUEM DEPOSITION

U-series dating allows us to determine the age of formation of some material which is spatio-temporally associated with an archaeological site. We should now consider how each type of datable material can be thus associated, and how the U-series dates can contribute to the chronology of a site.

Speleothems

Calcite deposition in caves occurs as a result of the dripping of water from the roof or walls of the cave. The resulting deposits can serve as U-series "clocks" in various ways, depending on their spatial arrangement with respect to the cave deposits (Fig. 6.3). We assume here that the cave is partially or wholly filled with stratified sediments which contain archaeological materials. It is possible for stratiform sheets of calcite to enclose the archaeological layers in sandwich-like fashion (Fig. 6.3a). Then the ages of the calcite sheets serve to bracket the age of the deposit. An even closer estimate of the age of a layer can be found where a layer of calcite can be stratigraphically correlated with the archaeological layer (Fig. 6.3b). Alternatively, fine stalactites ("soda straws") which grow quickly on the roof of the cave and fall to the floor, can provide a coeval precipitate. Hollow openings in the deposit, such as bone-marrow cavities, can be infilled with calcite. This provides an *ante quem* date for the deposit. Finally, there may be calcite deposits in a cave which are not obviously related to the archaeological layers at all but which are clean, tempting targets for U-series dating. Dating of such deposits can be very misleading and it might be better not to date them at all rather than to risk mystification and error-mongering.

Whereas speleothems formed deep inside caves can be quite free of detrital contamination, those from the mouths of caves are commonly highly contaminated by wind-blown or stream-deposited detritus. One should care-

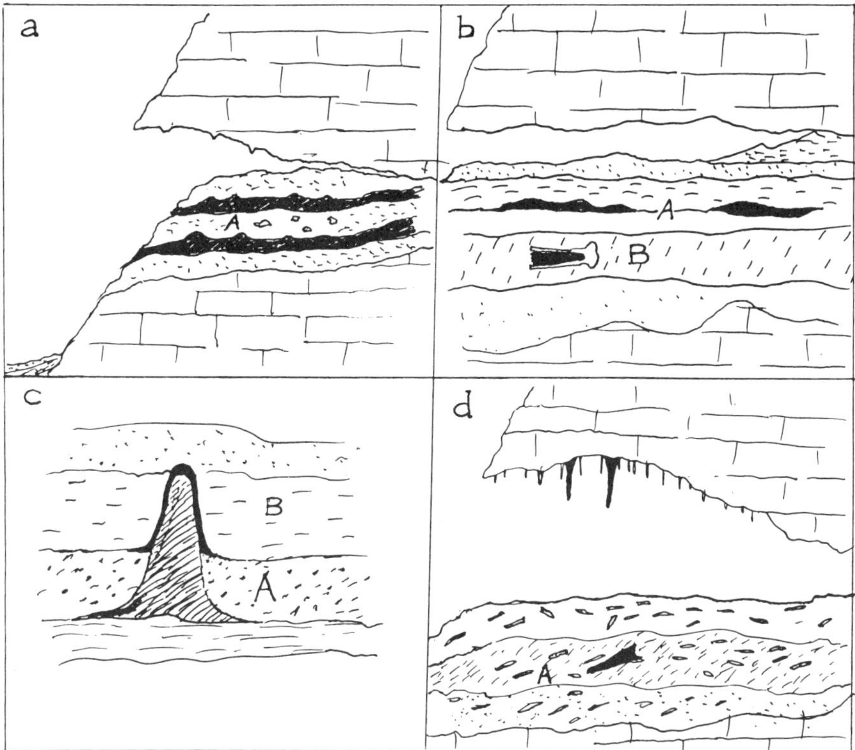

Figure 6.3. Possible modes of occurrence of speleothems in archaeological sites. a) sandwich of archaeological layer A between two flowstone layers; b) flowstone that was formed at same time as archaeological layer A; and calcite filling marrow-cavities in bones, giving an *ante quem* date for layer B; c) stalagmite growing out of a series of layers: shaded part gives date for layer A; black part for layer B; d) small stalactites ("soda straws") fallen into a layer give a date for the layer; tip of larger stalactite gives a *post quem* date for layer A.

fully select the least contaminated portions of deposits for dating. For example, the axes of stalagmites are commonly kept quite clean compared to the flanks, because the dripping of water on the growing tip of the stalagmite washes off detritus.

Travertine, Marl, Calcrete

Erosion or quarrying of spring-deposited travertines sometimes reveals archaeological deposits, typically interstratified between successive carbonate layers whose ages bracket the time of occupation. In many travertines one can see a primary, highly porous framework formed by precipitation of calcite around plant stems and fronds, which later filled in with calcite deposits, as lime-saturated water continued to percolate through the deposit. However, even in largely porous deposits one can easily find restricted zones of dense, non-porous precipitates (Grün *et al.* 1988b); a practiced eye may be needed to spot them. Contamination with detritus is common in travertine; detritus free layers should be selected for analysis, if possible.

Marls and calcretes, being surficial deposits, are prone to contamination. They can, however, be used as stratiform markers of *ante-* or *post-quem* deposition. Rarely, archaeological materials are actually found embedded in such materials.

Shells

Both mollusk shells and ratite egg shells tend to be relatively "clean" materials in the sense that they have high $^{230}Th/^{232}Th$ ratios. However, comparisons of $^{230}Th/^{234}U$ and ^{14}C ages of mollusk shells by Kaufmann *et al.* (1971) showed that many mollusk samples gave erroneous ages. Most commonly the $^{230}Th/^{234}U$ ages were too young, suggesting that U had been absorbed by the shell long after deposition, in an open-system fashion. Nevertheless, the abundance of mollusk shells at some sites and the absence of alternative (or better) datable material continues to lure archaeologists and geochemists into analysing these materials (e.g., Stearns, 1984). Such dates should be treated with caution, and the precision of the analysis should not be taken as a measure of its accuracy. Coral appears to be the exception to this rule, perhaps because it takes up U from seawater as it grows. Coral is unfortunately rarely found in archaeological sites.

Bones, Teeth

In principle these materials are ideal *syn-quem* indicators. However, as with mollusks, several studies have shown that U-series dates on even well-preserved bone can be younger or older than the most probable age of an associated deposit. We attribute these discrepancies to open system behavior, and to late uptake (or possibly loss) of U by the bone. Tooth enamel at least offers the possibility to check the U uptake model by a comparison of ESR and U-series ages of the same sample (Grün *et al.* 1988b; McDermott *et al.* 1993). Two possible models are usually considered as limiting cases: Early uptake (EU) in which U is absorbed soon after deposition; and linear uptake (LU) in which the present day U content is assumed to have been absorbed by the tooth at a constant rate since deposition. The validity of the EU model is demonstrated by concordance between ^{230}Th/^{234}U ages and EU-model ESR ages. If continuous (e.g., linear) uptake has occurred, the U-series age will be less than the ESR EU age. Only a few samples have been so far studied for this effect. McDermott et al. showed that the EU model adequately described most but not all teeth from Israeli cave sites dating from 40 to 200 ka. On the other hand, Schwarcz and Grün (1993) showed that teeth from the Hoxne, UK deposit must have taken up U continuously. McKinney (1993) showed profiles of U concentration in tooth enamel: some showed high U content near the surface of the tooth suggestive of early uptake, while others exhibited shallow internal gradients in U, bespeaking gradual uptake.

CASE STUDIES

I shall conclude with brief reviews of some classic applications of U-series dating to archaeological sites. I will limit this to one example of each type of deposit: speleothem in a cave site; spring deposited travertine; and an isochron in a contaminated carbonate deposit.

Speleothem: La Chaise de Vouthon, France (Blackwell et al. 1983)

At this site in the Charente District, there occur three adjacent caves two of which (Abris Bourgeois-Delaunay and Suard) contain thick sequences of detrital sediments rich in Middle Paleolithic artefacts, as well as numerous Neanderthal skeletal fragments. Four distinct flowstone horizons occur within the this detrital sequence (Fig. 6.4) which have been dated by α-spectrometry. The lowermost flowstone, in Abri Suard, underlies an Acheulian industry, and is dated at 245 $^{+42}/_{-28}$ ka. Two superimposed but discrete flowstones in Bourgeois-Delaunay date at 151 and 117 ka, respectively. The older layer immediately overlies the mandible of a juvenile Neanderthal. This flowstone complex was buried by detrital sediments containing Mousterian artefacts, which were in turn capped by a flowstone and stalagmites dating between 100 and 71 ka. The dates of the Mousterian deposits are therefore tightly constrained by the ages of the under- and over-lying speleothems. A flowstone of similar age range occurs in Suard, showing that speleothem

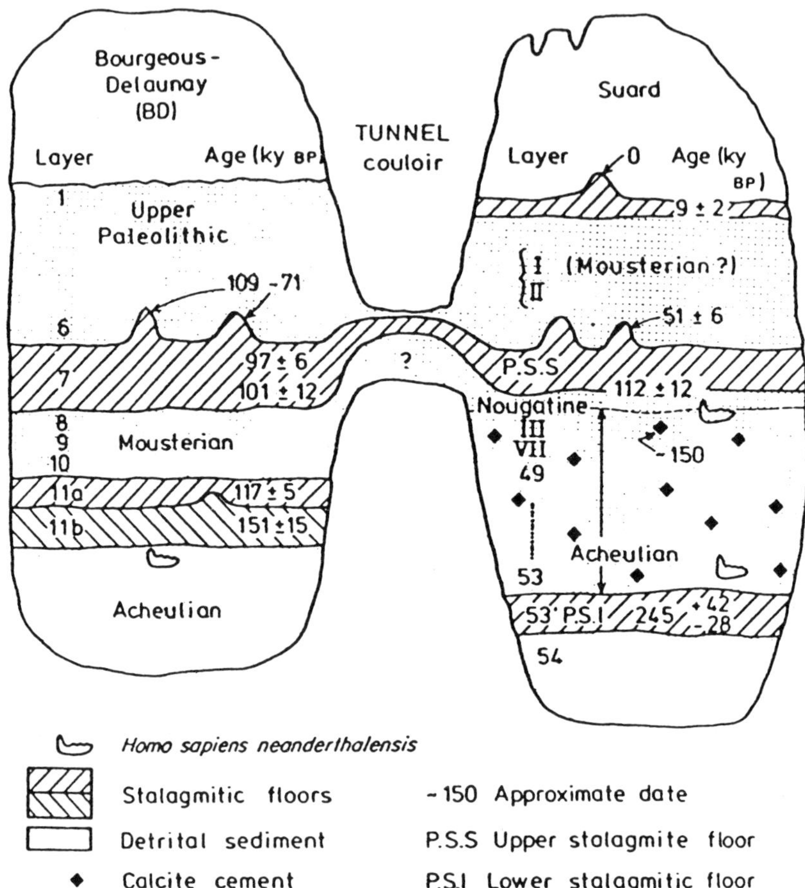

Figure 6.4. Schematic cross section of the caves of La Chaise de Vouthon, showing dated speleothem layers (from Blackwell *et al.* 1983).

deposition was synchronized to some extent between the two cave chambers, which are connected by a narrow, flowstone-lined tunnel. Stalagmites grew upwards from these younger flowstones and were later engulfed in detrital sediment. While the flowstones were being deposited, we presume the caves were unoccupied, as no artefacts are embedded directly in them. Presumably the caves were too wet to be habitable at these times. These wetter periods may have coincided with periods of generally higher precipitation in the region. All but one (bed 11b) correlate with periods of the relatively warmer climates of isotope stages 7, 5e, 5c and 5a. Such apparent correlation between growth of speleothem and climate is encountered at many sites (e.g., in the Negev Desert: Schwarcz et al. 1980).

Table 6.1. Examples of U-Series Dates from Cave Sites

Site	Reference
Grotte du Prince, Liguria, Italy	Shen 1986
Pech de l'Aze, Dordogne, France	Schwarcz and Blackwell 1983
Abri Vaufrey, Dordogne, France	Blackwell and Schwarcz 1990
Pontnewydd, Wales, UK	Schwarcz 1983
Coygan, Wales, UK	Aldhouse-Green *et al.* 1994
Abric Romani, Spain	Bischoff *et al.* 1988
Zuttiyeh, Israel	Schwarcz *et al.* 1980
Sclayn, Belgium	Gewelt *et al.* 1992
Grotta Guattari, Italy	Schwarcz *et al* 1991a
Grotta San Agostino, Italy	Schwarcz *et al* 1991b
Klasies River Mouth, South Africa	Deacon *et al.* 1986

Some other archaeological sites in caves which have been dated by U-series analysis of speleothem are listed in Table 6.1.

Travertine: Ehringsdorf, Germany (Blackwell and Schwarcz 1986)

At Ehringsdorf, near Weimar, a travertine sequence contains archaeological deposits and remains of Neanderthal hominids. The sequence has been divided into a Lower Travertine (LT; 7 - 10 m), and intervening paleosol called "Pariser" (0.5–1.5 m), and the overlying Upper Travertine (UT; c. 2 m), capped by covering sediments that display periglacial features. Prior to U-series dating, it was believed that the entire sequence represented the last interglacial (stage 5e). Early attempts to date the deposits were inconclusive (Cherdyntsev *et al.* 1975; Brunnacker *et al.* 1983). In our study, we found that the LT had a uniform U content of about 0.37 ppm, and a uniform $^{234}U/^{238}U$ ratio of 1.42±0.22, significantly lower than that for the UT. Most samples from the LT gave finite ages, averaging to 226±28 ka. A few samples gave apparently infinite ages. An isochron plot of these data gave a $^{230}Th/^{234}U$ ratio of 0.920, corresponding to an age of 230 ka; the apparently infinite-age samples also plotted on the isochron. We concluded that the LT was deposited during the interglacial of isotope stage 7. The UT gave generally poor results, and a poorly defined age of 110±47 ka, which is consistent with deposition during stage 5. These age estimates are considered to be consistent with the faunal evidence, such as the difference in morphology between taxonomically identical species of vertebrates found in the LT and UT.

The nearby Bilzingsleben site, also interstratified with travertines, was studied later (Schwarcz *et al.* 1988), and found to date from an earlier interglacial, beyond the 350 ka limit of α-spectrometric U-series dating. ESR ages

Table 6.2. U-Series Dates on Sites Associated with Travertine and Marl

Site	Reference
Travertine	
Banyolas, Spain*	Julia and Bischoff 1991
Nahal Zin, Israel	Schwarcz *et al.* 1980
Tata, Hungary*	Schwarcz and Skoflek 1982
Vértesszölös, Hungary*	Schwarcz and Latham 1984
El Kwom, Syria	Hennig and Hours 1982
Bad Cannstatt, Germany	Grün *et al.* 1982
Marl	
Southern Egypt*	Szabo *et al.* 1989
Bir Tarfawi*	Schwarcz and Morawska 1993

* Isochron method used

on the site suggested an age of about 400 ka. Other archaeological sites associated with travertines and marls are listed in Table 6.2.

Isochron Date: El Castillo, Spain (Bischoff et al. 1992)

The cave of El Castillo lies near Santander in northern Spain. An 18 m thick sequence of detrital fill in the outer part of the cave contains one of the most complete and extensive records of Paleolithic culture in Western Europe. A laminar speleothem occurs near the base of the exposed section, more or less at the boundary between the Acheulian and Mousterian industries. The speleothem is described as "ranging from marl to agglomerate of chalky dripstone grit, oolites and spheroidal 'cave pearls'" (K. Butzer 1981, cited in Bischoff *et al.* 1992). Bischoff *et al.* subjected six samples of well-crystallized oolitic flowstone to U-series dating. The U content was generally quite low (0.13 ± 0.04 ppm). The uncorrected $^{230}Th/^{234}U$ ages scattered widely ranged from 108 to 152 ka. However, the $^{230}Th/^{232}Th$ ratio of all the samples was below 5, indicating that there was significant contamination with common ^{230}Th. Therefore, the isochron method was used to obtain a better estimate of the age: 89±11 ka. The actual detrital content of the samples was surprisingly low (c. 1%). Given the low $^{230}Th/^{232}Th$ values, this suggests that some of the common Th was introduced as a solution or suspension of ultrafine particles, rather than as visible detrital grains. This study shows the importance of using the isochron method. This method requires the analysis of several samples to obtain a single date, but in most cases one would be obliged to analyse several replicate samples in any case, to confirm the age. Most of the sites described in Table 6.2 were analysed using the isochron method.

CONCLUSION

The U-series methods allow us to determine date materials found at archaeological sites whose ages range from a few hundred years (possible using TIMS on high-uranium samples) up to about 500 ka; the oldest dates are also accessible only by use of TIMS. The optimal materials for dating are clean, well-crystallized deposits of calcium carbonate such as stalagmites, flowstones or travertines. Contaminated samples can generally be dated using the isochron method, except where the detritus contains significant amounts of limestone clasts. Less reliability can be attributed to dating of biogenic materials such as mollusk or egg shells, bones, and teeth. TIMS analyses of tooth enamel, however, show great promise if they are coupled with ESR measurements, since the combination of the two methods allows us to determine the U uptake history of the sample. If early uptake is indicated, then the highly precise TIMS U-series date should be considered to be the best estimate of the age of the sample.

As with all methods of chronometric dating, it is important to collect the best possible samples for analysis. For this reason it is desirable to have the site visited by the scientists doing the dating; even experienced archaeologists have difficulty identifying the optimal samples, or appreciating how much material of a given type may be needed for analysis. Repeated visits to a site after an initial attempt at dating may be very useful, especially when the samples are found to have a surprisingly high content of detritus, or low content of U. Although U-series dates do not have to be calibrated like ^{14}C dates, systematic errors can occur during U-series analyses for a variety of reasons such as miscalibration of the U-Th tracer, isotopic fractionation during mass spectrometry of Th, or "hidden" contamination with ^{230}Th (not coupled to ^{232}Th). These effects may only show up when U-series ages are compared with other chronometric dates (^{40}Ar/^{39}Ar, TL, ESR).

ACKNOWLEDGMENTS

The research summarized in this chapter was supported by grants to HPS by the National Science Foundation (DBS-9210469), and by the Natural Sciences and Engineering Research Council (Canada) and the Social Sciences and Humanities Research Council (Canada).

REFERENCES

Aldhouse-Green, S., Scott, K., Bevins, R., Grün, R., Housley, R., Rae, Angela, Redknap, M. and Schwarcz, H.P. 1994 *Coygan Cave, a Mousterian Site and Hyaena Den: A Report on the University of Cambridge Excavations*. Wales, National Museum of Wales.

Bar-Matthews, M., Wasserburg, G.J., and Chen, J.H. 1993 Diagenesis of fossil coral skeletons: correlations between trace elements, textures and U-234/U238. *Geochimica et Cosochimca Acta* 57: 257–276

Bard, E., Hamelin, B., Fairbanks, R.G. and Zindler, A. 1990 Calibration of the ^{14}C timescale over the past 30,000 years using mass spectrometric U-Th ages from Barbados corals. *Nature* 345: 405–410.

Bischoff, J.L., and Fitzpatrick, J.A. 1990 U-series dating of impure carbonates: An isochron technique using total sample dissolution. *Geochimica et Cosochimca Acta* 55: 543–554.

Bischoff, J.L., Garcia, J.F., and Straus, L.G. 1992 Uranium-series dating at El Castillo Cave (Cantabria, Spain): The "Acheulian"/"Mousterian" question. *Journal of Archaeological Science* 19: 49–62

Bischoff, J.L., Julia, R., and Mora, R. 1988 Uranium-series dating of the Mousterian occupation at Abric Romani, Spain. *Nature* 332:68–70

Blackwell, B., and Schwarcz, H. P. 1986 Absolute age of the Lower Travertine at Ehringsdorf DDR. *Quaternary Research* 25: 215–222.

Blackwell, B. and Schwarcz, H.P. 1990 Uranium series dating of travertines from Abri Vaufrey. *In* Rigaud, J. P., ed., *Memoire de la Societé Préhistorique Française* 19: 365–379.

Blackwell, B., Schwarcz, H.P. and Debenath, A. 1983 Absolute dating of hominids and Paleolithic artifacts of the cave of La Chaise-de-Vouthon (Charente), France. *Journal of Archaeological Science* 10: 493–513.

Brunnacker, K., Jäger, K.D. Hennig, G.J., Preuss, J., and Grün, R. 1983 Radiometrische Untersuchungen zur Datierung mitteleuropäischer Travertin-vorkommen. *Ethographisch-Archäologische Zeitschrift* 24: 217–266.

Butzer, K. 1981 Cave sediments, Upper Pleistocene stratigraphy and Mousterian facies in Cantabrian Spain. *Advances in Old World Archaeology* 5: 201–252.

Cherdyntsev, V.V. 1971 *Uranium-234*. Jerusalem, Israel Program for Scientific Translation.

Cherdyntsev, V.V., Senina, Y. and Kuz'mina, Ye.A. (1975) Die Alterbestimmung der Travertin von Weimar-Ehringsdorf. *Abhandlungen des Zentralen Geologischen Instituts* 23: 7–14.

Condomines, M., Hemond, C. and Allègre, C.J. 1988 U-Th-Ra radioactive disequilibria and magmatic processes. *Earth and Planetary Sciences Letters* 90: 243–262.

Deacon, H., Gelijnse, V., Thackeray, A., Thackeray, J., Tusenius, M., and Vogel, J. 1986 Late Pleistocene cave deposits in the southern Cape: current research at Klasies River, South Africa. *Palaeoecology Africa* 17: 31–7

Edwards, L., Chen, J.H. and Wasserburg, G.J. 1986 ^{238}U-^{234}U-^{230}Th-^{232}Th systematics and the precise measurement of time over the past 500,000 years. *Earth and Planetary Sciences Letters* 81: 175–192.

Gewelt , M., Schwarcz, H.P. and Szabo, B.J. 1992 Datations $^{230}Th/^{234}U$ et ^{14}C de concrétions stalagmitiques. *In* Otte, M., ed. *Recherches aux Grottes de Sclayn. I. Le Contexte*. Etudes et Recherches Archaeologie de l'Universit de Liege 27: 159–172. Liege, l'Universit de Liege.

Grün R., Brunnacker K., and Hennig G.J 1982 Th230/U234 -daten mittel-und jungpleistozaner travertine im Raum Stuttgart. *Jber. Mitt. Oberrrhein. Geol. Ver., N. F.* 64: 201–211.

Grün, R., Schwarcz, H. P. and Chadam, J. 1988a ESR dating of tooth enamel: Coupled correction for U-uptake and U-series disequilibrium. *Nuclear Tracks and Radiation Measurement* 14: 237–241.

Grün, R., Schwarcz, H. P., Ford, D. C., and Hentsch, B. 1988b ESR dating of spring-deposited travertines. *Quaternary Science Reviews* 7: 429–432.

Ivanovich, M. and Harmon, R.S. eds. 1992 *Uranium Series Disequilibrium: Application to Environment Problems in the Earth Sciences*, 2nd ed., Oxford, Oxford University Press.

Ivanovich, M., Latham, A. and Ku, T.-L. 1992 Uranium-series disequilibrium applications in geochronology. *In* Ivanovich, M. and Harmon, R.S., eds., *Uranium Series Disequilibrium: Application to Environment Problems in the Earth Sciences*, 2nd ed., Oxford, Oxford University Press: 62–94.

Hennig, G. and Hours, F. 1982 Dates pour le passage entre l'Acheuleen et le Paleolithique Moyen a El Kwom (Syrie). *Paleorient* 8: 81–83.

Julia, R. and Bischoff, J.L. 1991 Radiometric dating of Quaternary deposits and the hominid mandible of Lake Banyolas, Spain. *Journal of Archaeological Science* 18: 707–722.

Kaufman, A., Broecker, W.S., Ku, T.L. and Thurber, D.L. 1971 The status of U-series methods of mollusk dating. *Geochimica Cosmochimica Acta* 35: 1155–1189.

Luo, S. and Ku, T.-L. 1990 U-series isochron dating: A generalized method employing total-sample dissolution. *Geochimica et Cosmochimica Acta* 55: 555–564.

McDermott F., Grun R., Stringer, C.B. and Hawkesworth, C.J. 1993 Mass-spectrometric U-series dates for Israeli Neanderthal/early modern hominid sites. *Nature* 363: 252–255.

McKinney, C. R. 1992 *The determination of the reliability of uranium series dating of enamel, dentine, and bone*. Ph.D. dissertation, Southern Methodist University.

McKinney, C.R. 1993 Bir Tarfawi: a stratigraphic test of uranium-series dating of tooth enamel. *In* Wendorf, F., Close, A. and Schild, H., eds., *Egypt During the Last Interglacial*. New York, Plenum: 218–223

Schwarcz, H. P. 1980 Absolute age determination of archaeological sites by uranium series dating of travertine. *Archaeometry* 22: 3–25.

_____ 1983 Uranium-series dating and stable-isotope analyses of calcite deposits from Pontnewydd Cave. *In* Green, H. S., ed., *Studies of Pontnewydd Cave, Wales*. National Museum of Wales: 88–97.

_____ 1989 Uranium series dating of quaternary deposits. *Quaternary International* 1: 7–17.

_____ 1992 Uranium series dating and the origin of modern man. *Philosophical Transactions of the Royal Society of London* B337: 131–137.

_____ 1993 Uranium series dating and the origin of modern man. *In* Aitken, M., Stringer, C.B. and Mellars, P.A., eds., *The Origin of Modern Humans and the Impact of Chronometric Dating*. Princeton, University of Princeton Press: 12–26.

Schwarcz, H.P., Bietti, A., Buhay, W.M., Stiner, M., Grün, R. and Segre, E. 1991a On the reexamination of Grotta Guattari: Uranium series and ESR dates. *Current Anthropology* 32: 313–316.

Schwarcz, H. P. and Blackwell, B. 1983 $^{230}Th/^{234}U$ age of a Mousterian site in France. *Nature* 301: 236–237.

Schwarcz, H.P. and Blackwell, B. 1992 Archaeometry. Ch. 11 *In* Ivanovich, M. and Harmon, R.S. eds., *Uranium Series Disequilibrium: Application to Environment Problems in the Earth Sciences*, 2nd ed., Oxford, Oxford University Press: 513–552.

Schwarcz, H.P., Buhay, W., Grün, R., Stiner, M., Kuhn, S. and Miller, G.H. 1991b Absolute dating of sites in coastal Lazio. *Quaternaria Nova* 1: 51–67.

Schwarcz, H. P., Goldberg, P. and Blackwell, B. 1980 Uranium series dating of archaeological sites in Israel. *Israel Journal of Earth Sciences* 29: 157–165.

Schwarcz, H. P. and Grün, R. 1993 Electron spin resonance (ESR) dating of the Lower Industry. *In* Singer, R., Wymer, J. J. and Gladfelter, B. G., eds., *The Lower Paleolithic Site at Hoxne, England*. Chicago, University of Chicago Press: 207–217.

Schwarcz, H. P., Grün, R., Mania, D., Brunnacker, K., and Latham, A. G. 1988 The Bilzingsleben archaeological site: new dating evidence. *Archaeometry* 30: 5–17.

Schwarcz, H.P. and Latham, A.F. 1984 Uranium series age determinations of travertines from the site of Vertesszollos, Hungary. *Journal of Archaeological Science* 11: 327–336.

Schwarcz, H.P. and Latham, A.G. 1989 Dirty Calcites, 1. Uranium series dating of contaminated calcites using leachates alone. *Isotope Geoscience* 80: 35–43.

Schwarcz, H.P. and Morawska, L. 1993 Uranium-series dating of carbonates from Bir Tarfawi and Bir Sahara East. *In* Wendorf, F., Schild, R. and Close, A., eds. *Egypt During the Last Interglacial*. New York, Pleunum: 205–217.

Schwarcz, H.P. and Skoflek, I. 1982 New dates for the Tata, Hungary Paleolithic site. *Nature* 295: 590–591.

Shen, G. 1986 U-series dating from the Prince Cave, northern Italy. *Archaeometry* 28: 179–184.

Short, S.A., Lowson, R.T., Ellis, J. and Price, D.M. 1989 Thorium-uranium disequilibrium dating of Late Quaternary ferruginous concretions and rinds. *Geochimica et Cosmochimica Acta* 53: 1379–1389.

Stearns, C.E. 1984 Uranium-series dating and the history of sea level. *In* Mahaney, W.C., ed., *Quaternary Dating Methods*. Amsterdam, Elsevier: 53–66.

Szabo, B.J., McHugh, W.P., Schaber, G.G., Haynes, C.V.Jr., and Breed, C.S. 1989 Uranium-series dated authigenic carbonates and Acheulian sites in southern Egypt. *Science* 243:1053–1056

Vogel J.C., and Kronfeld J. 1980 A new method for dating peat. *South African Journal of Science* 76: 557–558.

Yokoyama Y., and Nguyen H.-V. 1980 Direct and non-destructive dating of marine sediments, manganese nodules, and corals by high resolution gamma-ray spectrometry. *In* Saruhashi, K., ed., *Isotope Marine Chemistry*. Tokyo, Uchida-Rokaku: 235–265.

Chapter 7

Luminescence Dating

MARTIN J. AITKEN

ABSTRACT

The basic principles are explained in terms of thermoluminescence dating of pottery, with particular regard for the interests of archaeologists. Extensions of luminescence dating to other fired materials such as burnt flint, and to stalagmitic calcite and unburnt sediment are then outlined, including optical dating of the latter. Final sections deal with limitations in age range, accuracy and error limits.

INTRODUCTION

The techniques of luminescence dating are applicable to such materials as pottery (and other forms of baked clay), burnt stone, burnt flint, volcanic products, stalagmitic calcite, and windblown/waterborne sediment. There are two branches: *thermoluminescence dating* (TL) and *optical dating* (OD), the latter being primarily used for sediment. With the former the dating signal consists of the luminescence emitted when, in the laboratory, an extract from the sample is heated. Various minerals emit thermoluminescence suitable for dating, principally quartz, feldspar, and calcite, but there are others also, such as zircon and volcanic glass. With optical dating, the signal is obtained by exposure to a beam of blue/green light or of infrared radiation. *Optically-stimulated luminescence* (OSL) is commonly used as an umbrella term that includes both types of stimulation as well as the use of other wavelengths. *Photon-stimulated luminescence* (PSL) and *Photoluminescence* (PL) are also used.

MARTIN J. AITKEN • Research Laboratory for Archaeology, Oxford University, OX1 3QJ United Kingdom.

Chronometric Dating in Archaeology, edited by Taylor and Aitken.
Plenum Press, New York, 1997.

This chapter begins with an outline of the four major aspects of luminescence dating, namely: (1) TL dating of pottery (including a general introduction to TL); (2) Thermoluminescence dating of non-pottery materials, principally burnt flint (plus other materials that have been heated) and stalagmitic calcite, allowing extension in range beyond the limit of radiocarbon; (3) TL dating of sediment; and, (4) Optical dating of sediment. These are followed by discussion more or less common to all four: (5) Limitations in age range and, (6) Accuracy, involving error limits and conventions of data citation.

The sequence of the first four sections more or less follows historical development and it is appropriate to retain it here because the technology developed for pottery was the starting point for that of other applications. The text is oriented primarily to the archaeologist reliant on luminescence dates wishing to have some understanding of the method rather than the laboratory practitioner or researcher. The former will find additional useful information in the publications by Aitken (1990, 1991); Duller (1996); Feathers (1997a) and Roberts (1997). The latter are referred to Aitken (1985, 1998); Berger (1988); and Fleming (1979) and to McKeever (1985) in respect of the basic physics. To some extent, references to publications given in those texts have been omitted from the present chapter.

OUTLINE OF TL DATING; APPLICATION TO POTTERY

If a small ground-up portion of ancient pottery is heated rapidly to 500°C, there is a weak emission of light, measurable by means of a sufficiently sensitive photomultiplier. This thermoluminescence, emitted from around 250°C onwards, is in addition to the red-hot glow (or incandescence, also referred to as "black body") emitted when any substance is sufficiently hot and, unlike this latter, the thermoluminescence is only emitted during the first heating of a sample. It comes from mineral grains in the pottery, principally quartz and feldspar, and it results from the cumulative effect of prolonged exposure to the weak flux of nuclear radiation emitted by radioactivity in the pottery and in the surrounding burial soil. There is also a contribution, usually small, from cosmic radiation. The sources of radioactivity are ^{40}K, ^{87}Rb, thorium, and uranium at concentrations of a few parts per million; the flux is constant over millions of years.

The latent thermoluminescence acquired by the minerals during geological times is "drained" when the raw clay is fired by the potter, thereby setting the "thermoluminescence clock" to zero. From cooling onwards, the latent thermoluminescence begins to accumulate afresh, and when measured, it is indicative of the years that have elapsed since firing. The amount of thermoluminescence also depends on the energy absorbed from the radiation flux and the sensitivity of the minerals in acquiring thermoluminescence.

The rate of absorption of energy is referred to as the dose-rate or annual dose, and is calculated from radioactive analysis of pottery and soil, or measured directly. The sensitivity is measured by exposing portions of the self-same sample to radiation from a calibrated radioisotope source. Then, in principle, the basic equation by which the age, in calendar years, is evaluated is:

$$Age = \frac{(thermoluminescence)}{(dose-rate) \times (sensitivity)} \tag{1}$$

In practice there are many complications and several dozen measured quantities rather than three are involved in the evaluation. Also, for accurate results, it is necessary to make measurements on only particular groups of grains (selected according to size/mineral type). One reason for complications is that the nuclear radiation consists of alpha and beta particles from the sample itself, gamma radiation from the soil, and cosmic radiation. All four have different penetrating power and additionally the sensitivity to alpha particles is substantially less than to the other two types of radiation.

Because of the way in which the measurements are made, it is convenient to utilise the concept of *paleodose* (P)—the dose of nuclear radiation (from laboratory radioisotope sources) needed in order for artificially-induced luminescence to be equal to the "as-found" or "natural" thermoluminescence. The age equation then simplifies to:

$$Age = \frac{(paleodose)}{(dose-rate)} \tag{2}$$

Alternative names used for paleodose are: *equivalent dose* (ED), *past radiation dose*, *dose-equivalent* (D_e), *total dose* (TD), *accrued dose*, *accumulated dose*, *archaeological dose* (the three latter being denoted by AD). The unit of dose is the gray (Gy); formerly the rad was used (100 rad = 1 gray).

The above outline is also applicable to other sample types except that, for some, the zeroing agency is different. It is heat also in the cases of burnt flint (through accidentally falling into the fire, or through deliberate heat treatment), volcanic products and other burnt materials. For unburnt sediment, the "zeroing" occurs through exposure to light during deposition but, depending on circumstances, it is not always complete. For stalagmitic calcite, the latent thermoluminescence is effectively zero at crystal formation.

The latent thermoluminescence is carried in the form of "trapped electrons." These are electrons which have been displaced by nuclear radiation from their usual locations in the crystal structure of the mineral concerned and held, metastably, at trapping sites in that structure. Elevation of temperature causes release of trapped electrons and those of them that find luminescence centres give rise to thermoluminescence. In some minerals (e.g., quartz, feldspar and zircon), light can also cause release.

Because of dependence on trapped electrons, luminescence dating is often referred to as a branch of *Trapped Electron Dating* (TED), the other branch being *Electron Spin Resonance* (ESR). A preferred term is *Trapped Charge Dating* (TCD) because the luminescence can equally well be produced by positive charges ("holes")—but it is simpler in discussion to use "electrons."

Development

Although the phenomenon of thermoluminescence had been studied since the seventeenth century, it was not until the 1960s that development for dating began. Initially, this was in application to archaeological pottery, mineral grains being present through having been added as temper. Subsequently, it has been extended to types of sample that enable it to reach back well beyond the limit of radiocarbon. Burnt flint in particular is useful in this context, reaching to several hundred thousand years. During the late 1980s, the potential of unburnt sediment was increasingly explored. Although of primary importance for Quaternary studies, this application is also important for archaeology mainly, but not entirely, in the Palaeolithic.

Because of its lesser precision than radiocarbon, the impact of thermoluminescence more recently has not been so great. Nevertheless, the technique does have the strong advantage in dating pottery in that it is directly linking to archaeological chronology and uncertainties of association are avoided. Also, from the late 1960s onwards, the technique has had a dominant role in testing the authenticity of art ceramics, the poor precision then being of less importance since it is usually a matter of deciding between an age of less than a hundred years and one of upwards of several hundred.

The Radiation Flux

In typical pottery, alpha, beta, and gamma radiation contribute roughly equal amounts of TL. There is also a contribution from cosmic rays, usually minor except at sites of high altitude. The different characteristics of these radiations complicate assessment of dose-rate as well as the procedures required for preparation of portions for measurement. In the first place, for a given amount of absorbed energy alpha radiation is much less effective in inducing TL than beta and gamma radiation. Secondly the ranges are very different: alpha 0.03 mm; beta 3 mm; gamma 0.3 m (Fig. 7.1). Furthermore, in pottery, there is considerable heterogeneity in the levels of radioactivity of its constituents. Quartz grains have a very much lower radioactivity than the clay matrix in which they are embedded, and potassium feldspar grains have a higher radioactivity.

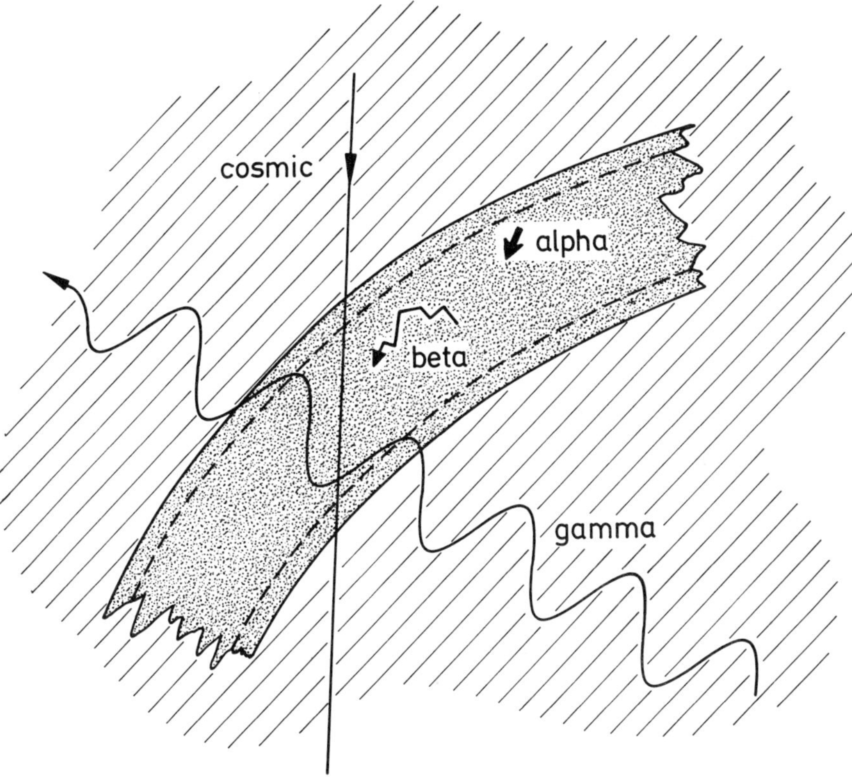

Figure 7.1. Illustration of the different ranges of the components of the radiation flux giving rise to TL. Because of their very short range, the alpha particle contribution to the TL of a grain is from thorium and uranium impurities carried within the fragment. On the other hand the gamma ray contribution is almost entirely from the surrounding burial soil because of the greater penetrating power of this type of radiation (in reality the path of a gamma ray is irregular due to being scattered; there is also degradation into secondary gamma rays and electrons). Beta particles are intermediate, having a penetration depth in pottery of a few millimetres, but as long as the 2mm surface layer is sawn off and discarded, the beta contribution is effectively of internal origin. For "typical" pottery and soil, the relative contributions to fine grains are: alpha, 45%; beta, 30%; gamma, 21%; cosmic 3%. The relative contributions from the three principal radioactive impurities are: potassium, 21%; thorium, 37%; uranium, 39%. However there are wide variations in these typical values, with potassium and the beta component often being much stronger (from Aitken 1990).

The long range of gamma radiation means that the contribution of that radiation is determined by the radioactivity of the burial soil. The short range of alpha radiation means that radiation penetrates only the outer skin of a sand-sized quartz grain (say, 0.1 mm diameter and upwards—a "coarse" grain in TL parlance) and the average alpha dose to the grain is much less than that to a silt-sized grain (e.g., one of diameter 0.01 mm or less—a "fine grain" in

TL parlance). The high level of potassium in a sand-sized grain of potassium feldspar means that its level of beta dose-rate is substantially enhanced and, for a grain of a millimetre or more, this contribution is advantageously dominant because dependence on the gamma dose from the soil is then weaker. The dose due to beta particles from rubidium is also important.

The contributions from thorium and uranium are provided by series of "daughter" radioisotopes which derive from the "parents." Ideally, these are in radioactive equilibrium, meaning that each daughter of a series has the same rate of radioactive decay. If soil conditions are such that there is preferential leaching of the parent or of one of the daughters, then disequilibrium ensues and evaluation of dose-rate is not straightforward.

Sample Collection

Because part of the radiation dose-rate is provided by gamma rays from the burial soil (or other surroundings) within about 0.3 metres of the sample, in general it is only possible to obtain an accurate date when samples are extracted in the course of excavation, or when the section from which they were obtained is still available. An exception is when there are plentiful zircon grains in the sample (but few laboratories are equipped for use of this mineral) or when it is feasible to employ the *isochron technique* (see under Burnt Flint). Also, in testing authenticity, the accuracy attainable without knowledge of the gamma ray component is usually adequate.

Close collaboration between archaeologist and laboratory scientist is essential and ideally, the latter is on-site at the time the samples are extracted, or at any rate has visited the site. There are a number of ways in which the gamma ray component may be assessed. Which of these is employed is dependent on sample type, laboratory facilities and feasibility of on-site measurements of radioactivity. The latter can be made by means of a portable gamma ray spectrometer of which the measurement head is inserted at least 0.3 metres into the section by means of an auger hole. The head (between 30 and 70 mm in diameter according to the instrument and model) is positioned in as similar a situation as possible to the sample location. Alternatively, the measurement is by means of a highly sensitive thermoluminescence phosphor contained in a small capsule (about 30 mm long by 10 mm diameter) which is likewise buried to a depth of 0.3 metres. Whereas the spectrometer measurement can be completed in an hour or less, the capsule needs to be left in position for several months—ideally for a year. When on-site measurements are not feasible, the assessment can be made through radioactive analysis, in the laboratory, of a sample of the burial soil. Particularly in this case, it is important that the soil is uniform (in terms of radioactivity) to a distance of 0.3 metres from the sample (Fig. 7.2). Obviously, this means that the sample needs to be at a depth of at least 0.3 metres. Of course, it is also important that it has been covered to

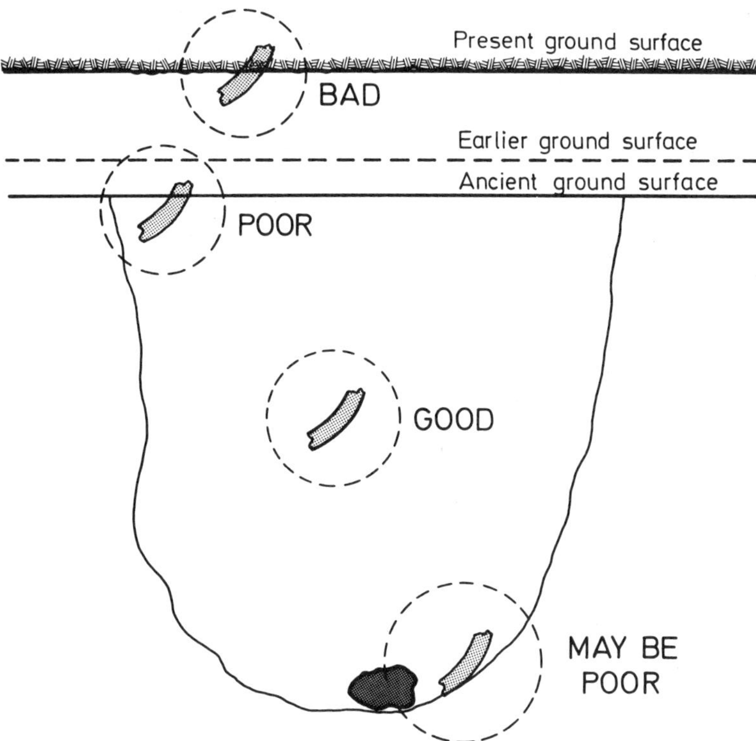

Figure 7.2. Good and bad situations for TL samples. Gamma rays reach the sample from a distance of up to about 0.3 metres; hence for a reliable assessment of the gamma contribution to the TL to be made from laboratory analysis of the soil the sample should be in a uniform surround of soil, such as may obtain in the middle of a pit or ditch. The situation for the sample at the bottom will be poor if the subsoil, or the lump of rock, has an appreciably different level of radioactivity to that of the filling. Likewise a sample at the top will be poor unless subsequent soil accretion took place rapidly.

at least that depth for the major part (say, two-thirds) of its burial time. On the other hand, Dunnell and Feathers (1994) have pointed out advantages in the use of surficial samples and have reported relevant results.

The uncertainties inherent in heterogeneous surroundings are alleviated if on-site measurements are made with either a gamma spectrometer or by burial of a capsule. However, it is necessary to be able to place the detecting head of the spectrometer or the capsule in a position that replicates that from which the sample was removed.

Another quantity that enters into the date calculation is an estimate of the average water content over the whole burial period. Various approaches are employed by different laboratories. Sites which have always been dry are advantageous. Knowledge of average water content is required, for both sample and soil, because the water absorbs part of the radiation that would otherwise reach the mineral grains. Further discussion is given under dose-rate determination.

Between six and twelve pottery fragments are required from each archaeological level. As far as possible, the size should be about 10 mm in thickness by 30 mm across. Undue exposure to daylight during collection should be avoided and the samples should be stored and transported in opaque containers. Most laboratories make a estimate of the "as found" water content and for this purpose the samples should be tied up tightly in a plastic bag immediately after extraction from the ground, together with any adhering soil. For an evaluation of radioactivity, samples of soil-types and rocks that were within 0.3 metres of the samples should be similarly tightly bagged. However, for these, exposure to daylight does not matter.

Sample Preparation for Measurement

The first step after removal of any adhering soil is to remove the outside 2-mm layer using a diamond wheel. This must be done in dim red light and likewise in all subsequent operations. Discard of this outer layer eliminates material in which the beta dose-rate is poorly defined, being transitional between sample and soil, and at the same time, avoids utilisation of material in which reduction of the thermoluminescence through "bleaching" by light may have taken place. However, it is nevertheless prudent to avoid undue exposure of samples to light after extraction and, in the case of unconsolidated sediment, special precautions must be taken to avoid the slightest exposure whatsoever.

The separation process, into one or more of various grain size ranges, starts with crushing. This is usually by gently squeezing in a vice, care being taken to avoid degradation in the size of the grains—it is important that the size fractions obtained represent the situation in the pottery. Suspension in acetone allows deposition of polymineral fine grains (2 to 8 μm) onto aluminium or stainless steel discs, usually 10 mm in diameter. Alternatively, mineralogical techniques (e.g., separation according to density by means of heavy liquids) are used to obtain coarse-grain (upwards of 100 μm) portions usually either of quartz or of potassium feldspar. These too are carried on discs for measurement. This separation is essential in order that a valid assessment of the effective dose-rate can be made. As noted earlier, whereas quartz is low in radioactive impurity content, potassium feldspar is intrinsically radioactive due to its potassium content. Also, for dosimetry considerations, it is necessary to etch off, with hydrofluoric acid, the surface of coarse grains in order to be left with a core into which there has been no penetration of alpha particles. Otherwise, the grains carry an ill-defined contribution of this component.

Measurement of Paleodose

The dating signal is a *glow-curve* (Fig. 7.3). This is a plot of thermoluminescence versus temperature and it is obtained by placing a prepared portion of the sample on an electrically-heated plate which is rapidly raised to 500°C, usually at a rate of around 10°C per second. To avoid the emission of parasitic ("spurious") luminescence, the heating must be done in an oven flushed with high purity nitrogen or other inert gas. Colour filters are placed in front of the photomultiplier to avoid the signal being swamped by red-hot glow. Additional filters may also be used to discriminate against portions of the wavelength spectrum specific to minerals. The paleodose is determined by comparing the "natural" glow-curve with a glow-curves obtained from portions to which known doses of artificial radiation have been administered. The simplest approach (Fig. 7.4) is by measuring the natural TL from portions and comparing the average with artificial TL from the same portions after exposure to various known dosages of radiation from a radioisotope source. However, this *regeneration method* usually gives only a rough indication of the paleodose because of the tendency for the TL sensitivity to be changed by the heating suffered during measurement of the natural TL. Unless special procedures are employed to check that no sensitivity change occurs or, if present, to make a

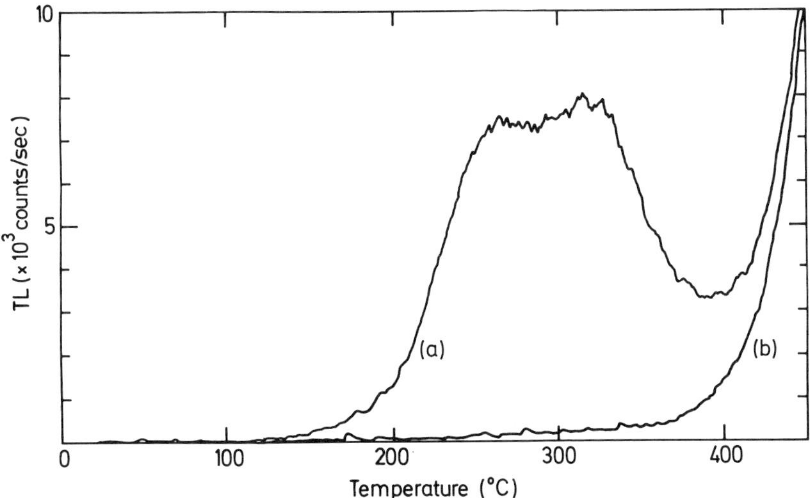

Figure 7.3. Thermoluminescence glow-curve observed from a small sample taken from a terracotta statue (measurement by D. Stoneham). Curve (a) shows the light emission observed during the first heating , and curve (b) the light observed during a second heating. The latter is the red-hot glow that occurs whenever a sample is heated, but during the first heating there is additionally the substantial emission of TL (From Aitken 1985).

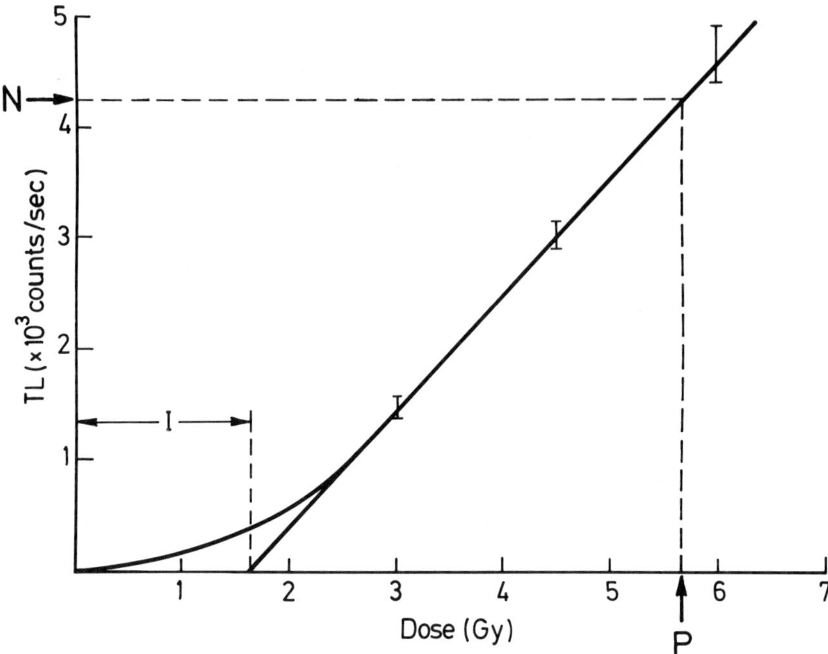

Figure 7.4. The regeneration method of evaluating paleodose, P (From Aitken 1985). The average value, N, for the natural TL observed from several portions is compared with the TL observed from the same portions after exposure to various doses of artificial radiation. In the latter, the natural TL has of course been eliminated by the heating inherent in the first measurement. The drawback of this method is that the TL sensitivity is liable to change during the heating. If there is an increase in sensitivity, the value of P will be erroneously low, if there is a decrease it will be erroneously high. The intercept, I, is used as a correction in the additive dose method (see Fig. 7.5).

correction, the possibility of such change necessitates the use of the *additive dose method* (Fig. 7.5), alternatively called the *extrapolation method.*

A disadvantage with the additive method is that the form of the growth curve below the level of the natural TL has to be established by further measurements, particularly for low dose levels. This is because, although the growth of TL above the level of the natural may be at a uniform rate (so that the growth is linear with dose), the initial growth is liable to be *supralinear* (Fig. 7.5). For higher dose levels, *sublinearity* may be encountered (Fig. 7.6). Another complication with the additive method is that there is liable to be portion-to-portion variation in TL sensitivity. This is particularly so when using a coarse grain technique, even if the portions have been assiduously made equal by weighing. Some form of portion-to-portion *normalization* is necessary.

By constructing growth curves based on TL levels at successive temperatures of the glow-curves, say every 10°C, a plot of paleodose versus temperature

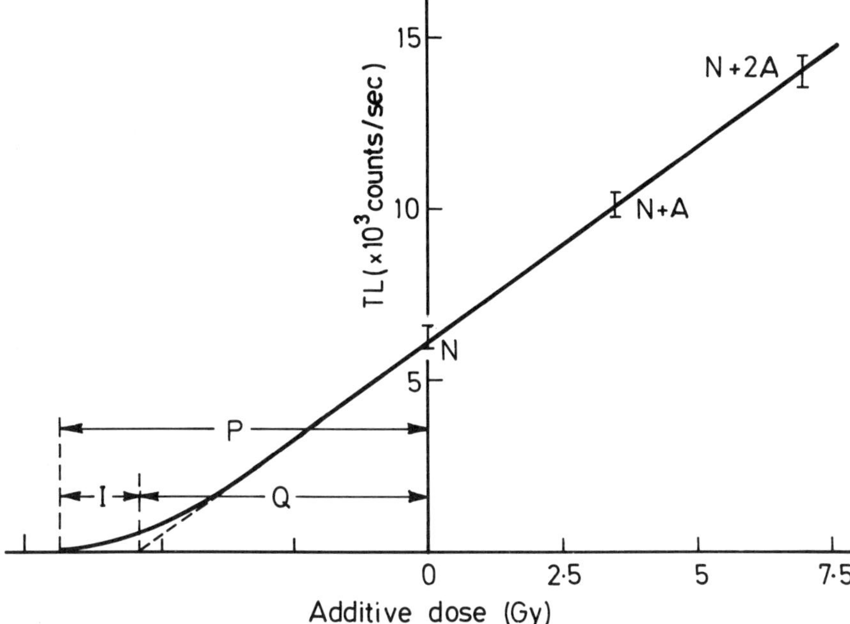

Figure 7.5. The additive (or extrapolation) method. Separate portions are used to measure the natural TL, N, and the "natural + artificial" levels. The paleodose, P, is usually greater than the value Q obtained by linear extrapolation. This is because of initial supralinearity of response. After evaluation of the supralinearity intercept, I, the paleodose is obtained as P = Q + I. In the literature, both P and Q may be referred to as Equivalent Dose, ED. Assessment of I is obtained by means of a regenerative growth curve (see Fig. 7.4). The validity of the supralinearity correction so obtained rests on the assumption that although the sensitivity of the portions may have been changed the form of the growth curve has not. From tests on samples of known age, it appears that this assumption is valid (From Aitken 1985).

can be obtained (Fig. 7.7). For a dating to be valid, the paleodose should rise to a steady level somewhat above 300°C. Samples that do not pass this *plateau test* are rejected.

The rationale of the test is as follows: Within a given mineral, there are traps of different depths. It is only traps deep enough to have an electron retention lifetime of over a million years or more—as required for a sample that is a hundred thousand years old—that are useful for dating. These deep traps do not release their captive electrons until the temperature rises to around 300°C or more. The deeper the trap, the higher the temperature needed for release. Luminescence observed below 300°C is liable to be associated with traps from which there has been leakage of electrons during burial. Such leakage will not have had time to occur in the case of the artificially-induced signal and hence the ratio of the "natural" signal to the latter will be lower than

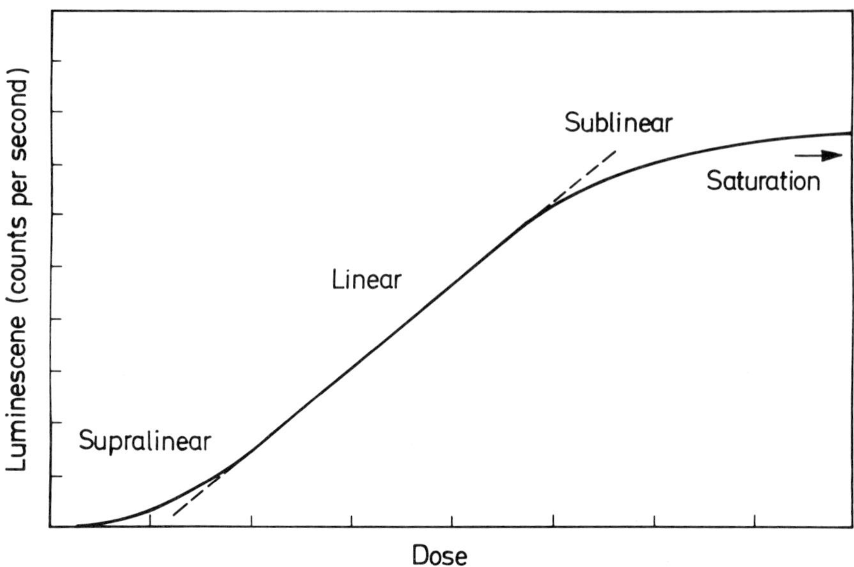

Figure 7.6. Various features of the growth curve. The curve becomes sublinear because of the onset of saturation (as all available traps become full). Sublinearity is frequently encountered in Palaeolithic application and evaluation of paleodose then requires curve fitting. See Curve Fitting in the section on the TL dating of sediment.

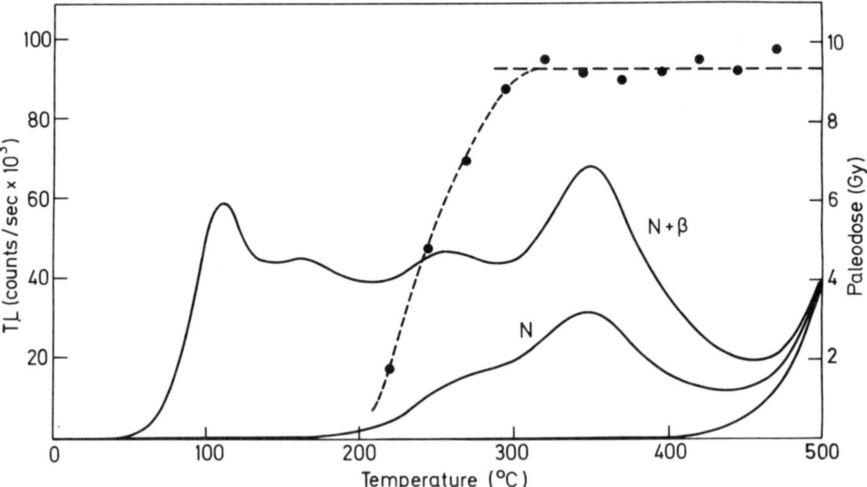

Figure 7.7. The plateau test. Curve N is the "natural" glow-curve from one portion of the sample and curve N+β is the "natural+artificial" glow-curve obtained from another portion to which a dose of radiation has been administered from an artificial radioisotope source. The thermal signal ("red-hot glow") is also shown. Above about 300°C (depending on mineral type), the TL is associated with traps deep enough to retain electrons stably over archaeological times but below 300°C the traps are too shallow and there has been leakage (curve N). A value for the paleodose, P, can be obtained (as in Fig. 7.5) for each temperature segment of the glow-curve and only if these level off into a plateau (as shown), is the sample acceptable (From Aitken 1985).

in the region of stability. Once the temperature is high enough, the ratio, and hence the paleodose also, reach a steady value. Unfortunately, this does not rule out the possibility that there has been anomalous fading. This malign phenomenon is liable to occur with feldspars (and hence also with polymineral fine grains, since the signal is usually dominated by feldspar luminescence) and is discussed later under Limitations in age ranges.

Pre-Dose Dating

Instead of being based on the size of the natural TL, this technique utilizes the change of TL sensitivity—the degree of sensitization—in the 110°C glow-curve peak in quartz, which has remarkable properties. It is a powerful technique for the last one or two millennia, particularly for very recent pottery, even of only a few decades in age. Hence, it has a strong role in testing the authenticity of art ceramics and also in retrospective dosimetry of nuclear explosions and accidents.

Because of its short lifetime (about an hour), the 110°C peak is not present in the natural glow-curve of a sample. However, exposure of a portion to a small test-dose allows measurement of its initial sensitivity. If the sample is now heated to between 500° and 600°C, this thermal activation causes a strong increase in the subsequent response to the test-dose. The increase is proportional to the total dose that the pottery has received since it was last fired, i.e., to the paleodose. By observing the increase in sensitivity resulting from a known dose delivered by a radioactive source, the paleodose can be evaluated.

Dose-Rate Determination

Various techniques are employed: alpha counting, beta counting, gamma spectrometry, neutron activation analysis, X-ray fluorescence analysis, flame photometry and thermoluminescence dosimetry. Which of these is used is determined by the facilities available in the laboratory concerned, but it is advantageous to obtain dose-rate evaluations based on two or more approaches. Disagreement gives a warning that some interfering factor is involved. One such possibility is significant escape during burial of radon (a radioactive gas forming part of the uranium decay chain) during burial. Another is geochemical leaching—so that the level of radioactivity to-day is different to that in the past. High resolution gamma spectrometry is advantageous in giving assessment of these possibilities, as also is the on-site advice of a soil geochemist.

Water Content

As mentioned earlier, the effective dose-rate is influenced by the past water content of soil and sample. If the effect is ignored, there may be appreciable underestimation of the age. Uncertainty about water content is a common limitation in the accuracy with which the dose-rate may be determined—typically ±5% at the 68% level of confidence. Of course, this does not apply in regions which have been arid throughout the burial period.

There are two approaches to estimation of the correction factor. The simplest is to measure the as-found water content (of pottery and soil) and assume that this has been the same throughout the burial period. The extent to which that assumption may be valid is a matter for discussion with soil scientists and palaeoclimatologists. Such discussion is also required for the second approach. In this, the saturation content (porosity) is measured and then an estimate is made of fractional uptake averaged over the burial period. Obviously, low porosity is at a premium with either approach. Whereas typical pottery has a porosity of around 10%, that of soil may be as high as 40%. Uncertainty in the average fractional uptake will then make a strong contribution to the error limits that can be given for the age. This is particularly serious if the dose-rate contribution from the soil is predominant—as may be the case with burnt flint, calcite, and sediment but unlikely with pottery.

Cosmic Radiation

As its name implies, cosmic radiation arrives from outer space. The "soft" component is absorbed in the top half-metre of sediment, and so it is normally the "hard" component that is relevant. This is more highly penetrating than gamma radiation and from a metre downwards, the attenuation in sedimentary deposit is by only about 14% per meter. The cosmic dose-rate at a depth of a meter is about 0.18 gray per ka. This is strictly for sites at sea-level around latitude 50° but the value at other latitudes is within 7% and there is not much increase until the altitude exceeds a kilometre (Prescott and Hutton 1988).

It should be noted that it is the soft component that is modulated by the magnetic fields of earth and sun, with consequent distortion of the radiocarbon timescale. As discussed by Prescott and Hutton (1994), luminescence dating (and ESR dating) are practically immune.

A Worked Example

As an example of how a TL age is determined, measurements are quoted now for one of the samples, kindly supplied by Professor Graham Webster, used in the early testing of the method. This was from a small Romano-British camp known to have been in use from AD 50–60 on the basis of coin evidence and other archaeological considerations.

The fragment weighed about 5 g and from it 60 mg of etched quartz grains were obtained. Paleodose evaluation was by means of the additive dose method (Fig. 7.5). The average value of Q was 5.3 gray and that of I was 0.4 gray. The plateau was good, with the paleodose within ±5% of the average (5.7 gray) over the glow-curve region above 320°C. After allowance for the water content of 15%, the effective dose-rate from beta, gamma and cosmic radiation was evaluated as 2.87 gray per ka, there being no contribution from alpha particles because of the etching off of the surface layer of the grains. Hence the quartz-based TL age for the fragment was (5.7/0.00287) = 1990 years. Because of error limits, the value would be rounded off to 2000 years.

In the fine-grain measurements on the fragment, a value of 9.6 gray was obtained for the paleodose, the higher value resulting from the fact that the alpha particle contribution is "seen" by fine-grains because their size is smaller than the particle range. With inclusion of the alpha contribution, the effective dose-rate, after allowance for the water content, was 5.1 gray per ka. Hence the fine-grain age obtained was (9.6/0.0051) = 1880 years or 1900 after rounding off. Within the expected error limits of around ±100 years on each age, this is concordant with the quartz-based age. Evidently, for this sample, any *anomalous fading* of the feldspar TL in the fine-grains was unimportant, as indeed was suggested by a two-month storage test (see under Limitations and age ranges).

THERMOLUMINESCENCE DATING OF OTHER HEATED MATERIALS

Burnt flint

With any burnt flint, the crucial question is whether the degree of heating was sufficient to set all previously acquired thermoluminescence to zero. Depending on the duration of heating a temperature at least in the range 300–400°C is required. A stringent check on sufficiency of heating, the plateau test mentioned earlier, is intrinsic to the measurement procedure and there is no point in considering ancillary techniques for this, which in any case are usually less reliable. It seems that visual appearance is not always a reliable guide to degree of heating, and the policy should be to collect too many rather than too few. Upwards of half a dozen satisfactory samples are desirable though some dating indication can be obtained by one or two if necessary. Flints should be transferred to a black bag as soon as excavated, any exposure to direct sunlight being avoided.

Even more so than with pottery, it is important to saw off and discard the outer 2 mm on commencement of processing, all operations of course being in subdued red light. The shape and size need to be such that after sawing a core remains which is at least 5 mm thick and 30 mm across. Unfortunately, the bigger the flint the longer must have been the duration of heating in order to reach the necessary temperature. The requirement for removal of a 2 mm layer is accentuated for flint because it is translucent and, if there has been exposure to light since excavation, the TL of the surface layer is liable to have been reduced by "bleaching," thereby yielding an age which is erroneously too recent. Also, because flint is sometimes much weaker in radioactivity than its burial soil it is essential to avoid the layer in which the beta dose-rate is intermediate between sample and soil. The core remaining after sawing is crushed in a vice or in a hydraulic press and from the resulting grains, after washing in dilute hydrochloric or acetic acid, the desired size fractions are separated: typically coarse grains of around 100 μm and fine grains in the range 1–8 μm. The grains are deposited on small stainless steel discs as for pottery. Unlike the situation with quartz grains in pottery, the fine-grain paleodose and the coarse-grain paleodose should be the same.

The upper limit on the age that can be reached is set by the onset of saturation and this varies from type to type. Depending on the level of radioactivity of the site, the age limit is likely to be in the range 100–500 ka. The stability of the TL signal appears to be adequate for this. In any case, the plateau test gives a check for each sample being dated. At the other end of the time-scale, the limit is set by the intensity of the TL. Flints burnt more recently than several thousand years ago are liable to have TL that is too weak for reliable measurement.

Among applications, an important one has been to flints associated with skeletons found in cave sites in the Levant, Western Asia (Aitken and Valladas 1993; Mercier and Valladas 1994). This has established the presence there of anatomically modern humans at around 100 ka ago, a result adding weight to the view that these hominids developed in parallel with Neanderthals rather than being descendants as had been accepted formerly. Dating of the Palaeolithic levels at Tabun Cave (Mercier *et al.* 1994) reaches back to around 300 ka for the lowest, indicating a much longer chronology than had been inferred from other data (Fig. 7.8).

The Isochron Technique

Use of this is sometimes feasible and it is particularly advantageous in the case of flint. It allows evaluation of average paleodose for a group of coeval samples even though the external dose-rate (from gamma and cosmic radiation) is unknown. However it requires firstly that there is evidence (from buried capsules, or otherwise) that this was the same for all members of the group and secondly that the members of the group have strong differences in internal radioactivity (Fig. 7.9). One might question the advantage if, in fact, the external dose-rate is known well enough to establish that it is the same for all members. However it obviates the uncertainty due to possible differences between present water content and the water content averaged over the burial period as is relevant and likewise in respect of geochemical leaching of radioactivity. Flint itself, being impermeable, is immune to these influences.

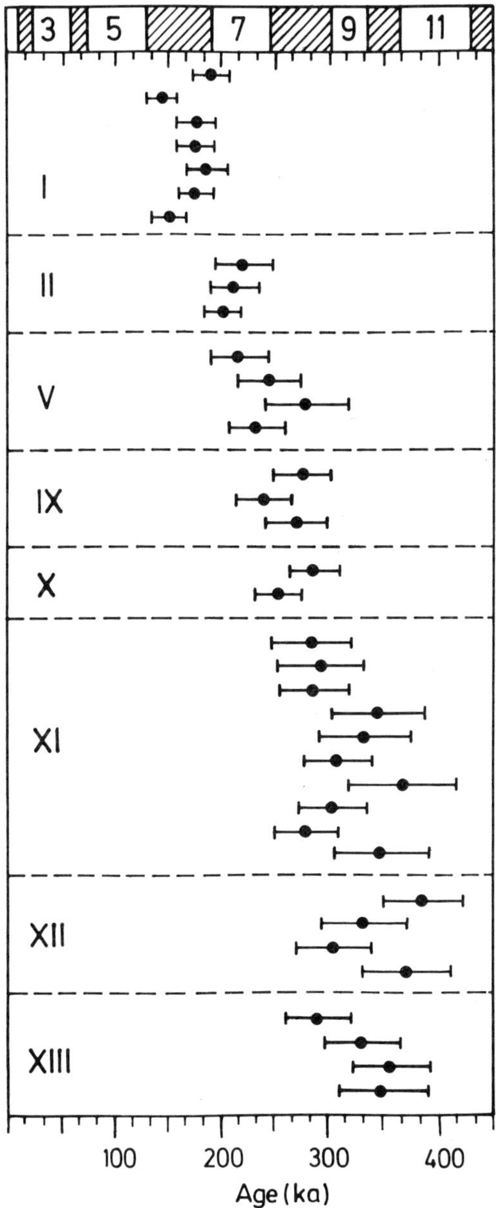

Figure 7.8. TL ages for individual flints from Tabun Cave, Israel (Mercier *et al.* 1994). Oxygen isotope stages are shown at the top. The Roman numerals indicate the Units (Jelenek 1982) from which the flints were obtained. Isochron analysis of the data for Unit XI yielded an age of 287 (±20) ka in good agreement with the 306 (±33) ka value obtained by averaging the ages of all 10 flints from the unit, thus giving strong support to the external dose-rate values used. These TL ages are substantially older than other proposed chronologies including those based on recent ESR and uranium-series determinations (Grun *et al.* 1991; McDermott *et al.* 1993).

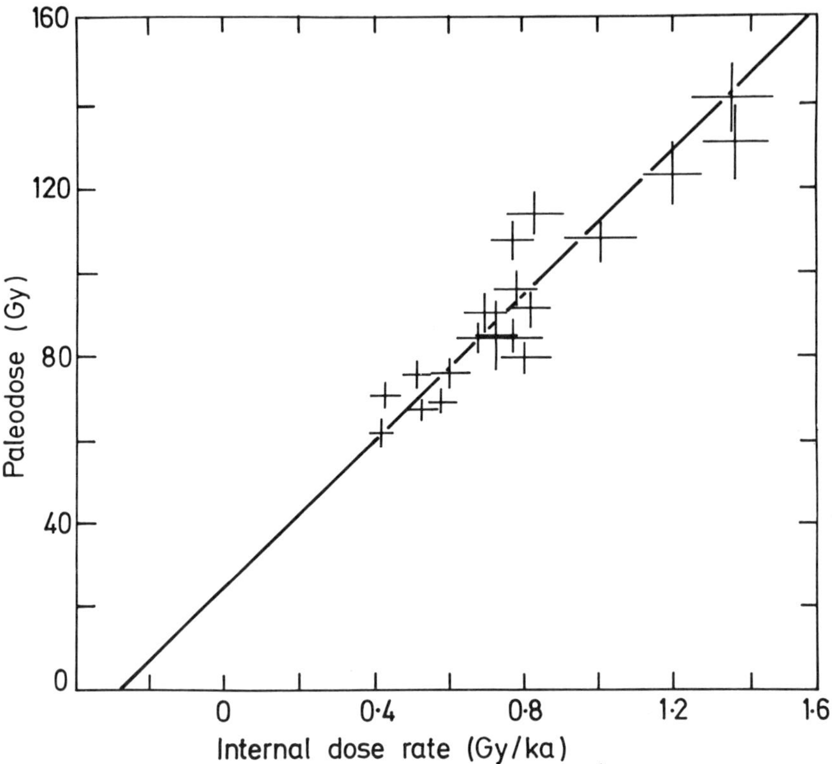

Figure 7.9. Isochron plot (from Aitken and Valladas 1993) of paleodose values for flints from Qafzeh Cave, Israel, in which skeletons of anatomically modern humans had been found (Valladas *et al.* 1988). Circumstances were such that it was valid to assume that the external (gamma+cosmic) dose-rate was the same for all flints and confirmation of this is given by the good linear fit to the data points. The slope of the line indicates an age of 88 (±9) ka. This agrees with the conventionally-obtained age of 93 (±5) ka.

Other Burnt Materials

The use of "pot-boilers" in pre-pottery cultures, either stones or balls of clay, provide material that can be conveniently dated by TL. The heated rocks of vitrified forts are similarly important, particularly as the date obtained is for the specific event of destruction by enemy action. Large mineral grains are more likely in stones/rocks than in pottery and the advantage of using large grains of potassium feldspar, in which the dose-rate is dominated by potassium within the grains, has been demonstrated by Mejdahl (1983).

Although slag is of prime importance in archaeometallurgy, successful dating has not yet been achieved. This is also true for glass from ancient windows and vessels.

Volcanic Products

Lava is difficult to date because of the tendency of feldspars to exhibit anomalous fading. However, by using the 600°C region of the glow-curve Guerin and Valladas (1980) have successfully dated extracted grains of plagioclase feldspar. These authors suggest that the useful dating range is 3–300 ka. An encouraging development is the use of the far-red component of the luminescence from sanidine feldspars. Unlike the blue component, the far-red appears to be immune to anomalous fading (Zink and Visocekas 1997).

Quartz, which does not show fading, is not present in most lavas but has been used for dating other volcanic products often employing the indirect method of sampling soil or rock over which molten lava has flowed (Pilleyre *et al.* 1992). Also, quartz pebbles trapped in lava may be used (Valladas amd Gillot 1978). Dating of airborne volcanic ash samples in the age range 0.5–400 ka has been achieved using the glass component (Berger 1992).

THERMOLUMINESCENCE DATING OF STALAGMITIC CALCITE

Because the latent TL is effectively zero at crystal formation, unburnt calcite can be dated by TL (and also by ESR). Clean calcite is preferable and this can be used to date speleothems in Palaeolithic caves (in limestone regions). An important point in measurement is to interpose the correct colour filter in front of the photomultiplier so as to reject TL from specks of limestone, carrying geological TL, which are presumed to have been incorporated in the calcite during its formation (Debenham *et al.* 1982).

The age range for calcite is roughly 5–500 ka, the latter limit being imposed by restricted signal stability. A difficulty with old samples is interference by recrystalization due to resetting of the TL clock. This also upsets the other techniques for dating calcite—uranium-series and ESR, though with the latter a signal indicative of recrystallization may sometimes be apparent.

In the usual situation in a cave, there is considerable difficulty in making reliable evaluation of the gamma dose both with TL and with ESR. This arises from non-uniformity of radioactivity within a cave. A secure circumstance in this respect is when a fragment of calcite is well buried in sediment. Even so, uranium-series should be regarded as the preferred technique for this type of sample.

Biogenic samples such as shell, bone, and teeth are not suitable for TL dating because there is decomposition when the sample is heated. Optical dating is a possibility to be investigated. Dating of tooth enamel is a powerful ESR application.

THERMOLUMINESCENCE DATING OF UNBURNT SEDIMENT

While grains of sediment are being carried by wind or water, and while lying on the surface after deposition, they are exposed to daylight/sunlight. With sufficiently long exposure, the latent TL acquired previously is reduced to a low residual level. As further sediment is deposited, the light is cut off and the latent TL builds up again in the same way as pottery after firing. Hence as long as a valid estimate of the residual, if non-zero, can be made the event of deposition can be dated. The technique is particularly useful for Palaeolithic sites that have been buried in loess or sand dunes for in such contexts the exposure to light will have been sufficiently prolonged for the residual to be negligible. In contexts in which the exposure may have been shorter, the residual has to evaluated by special laboratory techniques, as is also the case for waterborne sediment because of absorption of by water of the most effective part of the sunlight/daylight spectrum (the short wavelength region). Comprehensive techniques have been developed for this but, apart from the effort involved, there is a consequent increase in the uncertainty limits appropriate to the date obtained. There is then strong advantage in using the optical dating technique which is discussed shortly.

The mineral grains concerned are the same as with pottery, namely quartz and feldspars. Because of relevance to Palaeolithic sites, long range limitations are of increased relevance—signal saturation in the case of quartz and signal instability in the case of feldspars. With respect to quartz, one may note the impressive validification in this application back to somewhat beyond half-a-million years (Huntley *et al.* 1993a, 1994). This was using the particularly favourable circumstance of a series of low radioactivity sand dunes in Australia for which good confirmatory age estimates could be made using the oxygen-isotope chronostratigraphy (see Chapter 1).

Quartz has also been used impressively in dating the time of first human arrival on the Australian continent (Roberts *et al.* 1990). Quartz grains were extracted from sand on sites located on sand aprons at the foot of the Arnhem Land plateau and some dozen or more dates obtained at various depths. There was satisfactory agreement with calibrated radiocarbon ages obtained for the upper layers and a satisfactorily low age for a near surface sample—indicating that there had been adequate bleaching at deposition. At one of the sites (Fig. 7.10), two TL samples were associated with the lowest occupation level yielding stone artefacts and, from the dates obtained, the authors suggest that human arrival in northern Australia occurred between 50 and 60 ka ago, somewhat earlier than previous indications obtained using the radiocarbon technique (which is, of course, at its limit around 40 ka). Subsequently, optical dating has been used in this context (Roberts *et al.* 1994) and at one site, the lowest artifact-bearing level is bracketed between optical ages of 60.3 (±6.7) and 53.4 (±5.4) ka. Higher in the section, there is good agreement between

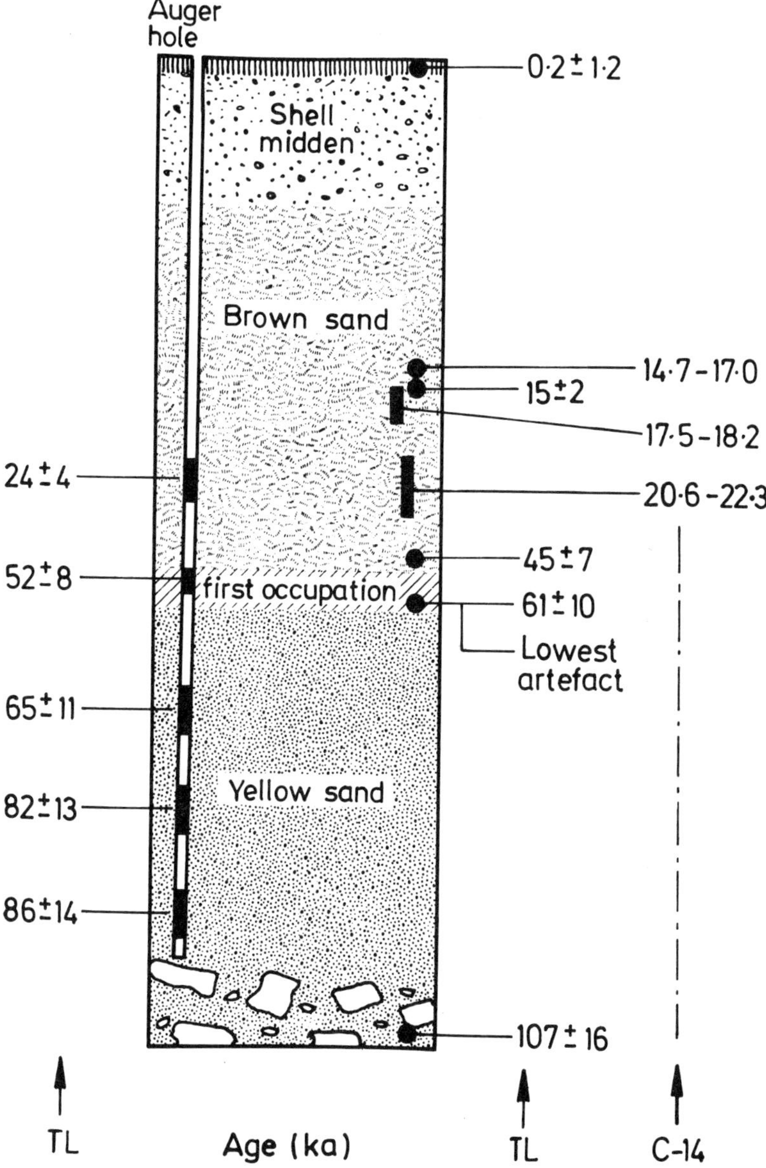

Figure 7.10. TL (quartz) and calibrated radiocarbon ages obtained for Malakunanja II, northern Australia (redrawn from Roberts *et al.* 1990). The first set of TL ages was obtained from sand at various depths in a 4-metre-long auger hole and the second set from deep into the section exposed during excavation. Error limits are at the 68% level of confidence for TL ages and at the 95% level for radiocarbon ages (which are calibrated). The authors suggest that human arrival in northern Australia occurred between 50 and 60 ka ago. This was subsequently confirmed by optical dating on another site (Roberts *et al.* 1994).

optical ages and calibrated radiocarbon values, as also is the case at another Australian site (David *et al.* 1997). Somewhat earlier TL dates for human arrival have been reported for artifact-bearing sand from a rock-shelter (Fullagar *et al.* 1996) but there is the possibility that the samples dated were contaminated with grains of decomposed bedrock. The latter would not have been set to zero at the time of occupation, having been hidden from sunlight for millions of years (Bahn 1996).

The Residual at Deposition

For well-bleached depositional circumstances, it is often the case, as above, that dating of a near-surface sample at the site gives indication of negligible residual. This can be assumed to be the case for the ancient samples as long as there is evidence that the depositional mode had been the same. Confirmation of negligible residual, or of evaluation in the case of poorly-bleached depositional circumstances, can be obtained by one of the following techniques.

In the *partial bleach method*—being method (c) of Wintle and Huntley (1980)—a second growth-curve is obtained using portions which have been subjected, after dosing, to mild bleaching (Fig. 7.11). The difference between the two represents the TL contribution from "easy-to-bleach traps," i.e., those traps most likely to have been emptied in poorly-bleached depositional circumstances. Hence, it does not matter if the bleaching at deposition was incomplete as long as it was more complete than that effected by the mild laboratory bleach.

With feldspar, it is advantageous to match the wavelength spectrum of the bleaching light to that of daylight, or to a spectrum appropriately modified in the case of sediment deposited under water. In the case of quartz, the efficacy of the method can be substantially enhanced by subtraction of the TL observed when detection is restricted to blue-green and longer wavelengths (Franklin and Hornyak 1990; Prescott and Fox 1990; Prescott and Mojarrabi 1993). This removes the now well-known rapidly bleaching peak (RBP), often referred to as the 325°C peak, the associated traps for which provide the signal in optical dating (see later). Hence, subtraction of the restricted growth-curve from the unrestricted growth-curve yields the growth-curve appropriate to the RBP. Further enhancement of the method is obtained by interposing colour filters in front of the photomultiplier so that only ultraviolet emission is detected. This discriminates against unwanted TL in favour of the RBP.

In the *regeneration method*, the paleodose is evaluated by comparing the natural TL with the regenerated growth curve obtained by measuring the TL from portions that have been bleached to a degree replicating that at deposition and then given various doses of artificial irradiation. It has to be checked that there is no change of TL sensitivity due to bleaching. For samples from well-bleached depositional contexts, a strong laboratory bleach is given and the method is then referred to as the *total bleach method*.

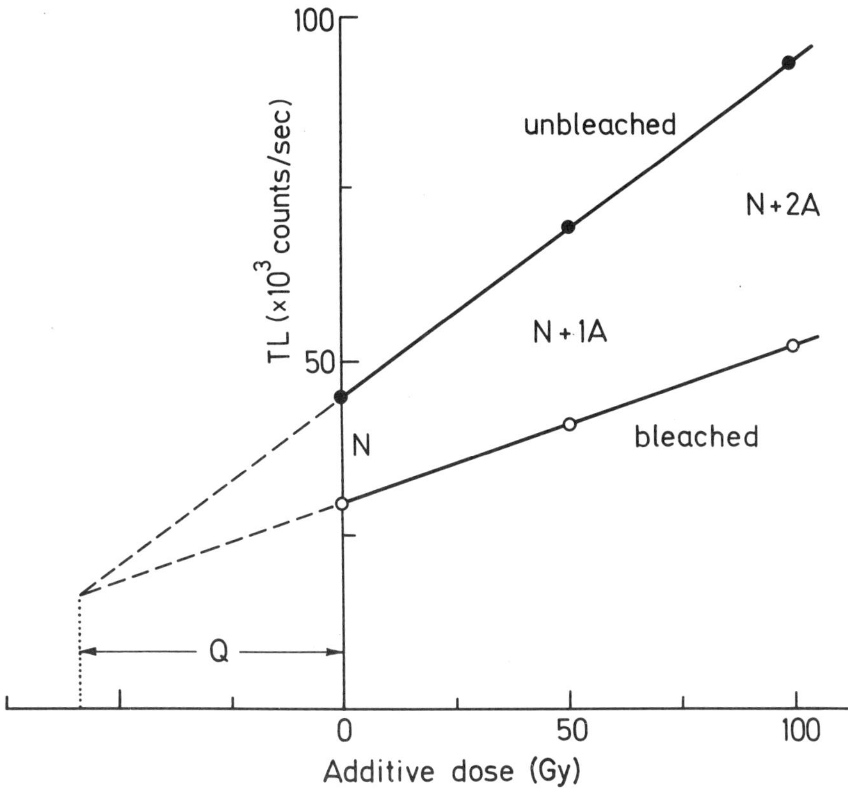

Figure 7.11. Partial bleach method for sediment that was poorly bleached at deposition. The unbleached line is obtained following the same procedure as in Fig.7.5. For the bleached line, portions are exposed to daylight or artificial illumination before measurement. The equivalent dose, Q, is that carried by traps not emptied by this bleaching but which are emptied by the bleaching at deposition, as long as the former is milder than the latter. If the reverse is the case, then the laboratory bleach will be able to reach components of the natural TL that were acquired prior to deposition—hence causing the paleodose obtained to be an overestimate. This circumstance is termed "overbleaching" (From Aitken 1990).

For other contexts, a modification developed by Mejdahl (1988) is used. This is based on the fact that different regions of the glow-curve exhibit different degrees of bleachability so that, when bleaching is incomplete, the residual is not the same for all parts of the glow-curve. Consequently, if the regeneration method is repeated using a number of different laboratory bleaching times, it will be found that it is only for one of these times that a good TL plateau is obtained. It is this bleaching time that best simulates what the sediment experienced at deposition and hence the associated residual levels represent the levels that pertained after the depositional bleaching. Subtraction of these allows evaluation of the paleodose.

Curve Fitting

In Fig. 7.5, except for the low-dose supralinearity region, the growth of signal with dose is shown as linear. Particularly with quartz, for high doses the growth becomes sublinear (Fig. 7.6) due to the gradual onset of saturation and a region is reached where there appears to be no further growth (i.e., all traps are full). For higher doses, slow linear growth may occur, probably due to the creation of new traps. Once the dose levels used take the sample beyond the first linear region, it is important to use the correct mathematical function in fitting the data points. Although an exponential curve or an exponential plus linear combination may often be correct, this is not always the case and a better procedure is to use the form of regenerated growth curve as a guide, making allowance for the possibility of sensitivity change. This has been done in various ways, of which the most recently put forward is the *Australian slide method* (Prescott *et al.* 1993). These remarks are applicable also to other materials, particularly flint, and to other techniques, particularly optical dating.

OPTICAL DATING OF UNBURNT SEDIMENT

Outline and Development

Using TL, the residual at deposition is due to electrons stored in traps that are hard to bleach but which nevertheless yield a signal when the sample is stimulated for measurement by heat. However, if light is used for stimulation, only electrons stored in traps which are easy to bleach contribute to the signal and hence the residual is very much smaller. This greatly reduces the effort needed for estimation of the level of the residual and allows extension to poorly-bleached circumstances such as waterborne sediment (e.g., alluvium and colluvium). Quartz, feldspar, and zircon are responsive to stimulation by light. The technique can also be used for pottery though any advantage over TL is then methodological rather than inherent.

There is one important disadvantage in the use of optical dating: there is no intrinsic indication of signal stability as is given by the glow-curve in the case of TL. Instead, it is necessary to apply mild heating (the pre-heat) before measurement so as to empty traps having inadequate lifetimes of signal retention, i.e., to empty traps that would give rise to TL at a lower temperature than the plateau region. Typically, a pre-heat at 220°C for 5 minutes is used with quartz and 160°C for 5 hours with feldspar. Otherwise the dating procedures are similar to those of TL. Of course, since there is total reliance on easy-to-bleach traps, very stringent precautions need to be taken in respect of light exposure during sample extraction and laboratory processing.

Although the dominant application is to Quaternary sediments of geological significance, the technique also has an important role in respect of sediment on archaeological sites, not only for windblown deposits but also for alluvium and colluvium such as might fill a pit or ditch. A remarkable extension is to the mud of wasp nests associated with rock art (Roberts *et al* 1997). Among reports, which have spanned the age range 1 to 300 ka, are those of Smith *et al.* (1990); Aitken and Xie (1992); Stokes (1993); Roberts *et al.* (1994); Huntley and Clague (1996); Lang and Wagner (1996); Rees-Jones and Tite (1997), and Feathers (1997b, 1997c).

Light Sources for Stimulation

Green light from a laser was used in initial development of the technique and this remains the best source for stimulation of quartz. However, other less expensive sources are now in common use: a xenon or a quartz-halogen lamp restricted in spectral range by means of colour filters and diodes that emit green light. Detection by the photomultiplier of the emitted luminescence is restricted to the near-ultraviolet (also by colour filters) as this gives good rejection of the stimulating light as well as, in the case of quartz, isolating the emission associated with the trap that is most easily bleachable—the trap responsible for the rapidly-bleaching (RBP) peak referred to above.

Although the above light sources may also be used in the case of feldspars (and polymineral fine grains), it is advantageous, as well as being very much cheaper, to use an array of infrared diodes emitting in the region of 850–900 nm. The use of infrared for stimulation allows a much wider wavelength range for detection (only emission at shorter wavelengths than the stimulating wavelengths are useful for dating). This gives a bigger signal as well as the possibility, when using polymineral grains, of some discrimination in favour of the light from potassium feldspars as against sodic feldspars (or vice versa) by means of colour filters. The abbreviation VsSL is used for luminescence stimulated by visible light, and IRSL for infrared-stimulated luminescence. Some authors restrict the meaning of OSL to luminescence stimulated by visible wavelengths only, but it is more usual to use it to include IRSL as well, as mentioned earlier.

Paleodose; Shine Plateau

The signal can be obtained either as a *short-shine* or as a *shine-down curve* (Fig. 7.12). For the former, the sample is exposed to the stimulating light for a duration too short to cause serious depletion of the trapped charge. For the latter, a longer exposure is employed and growth curves (vs. dose) can be

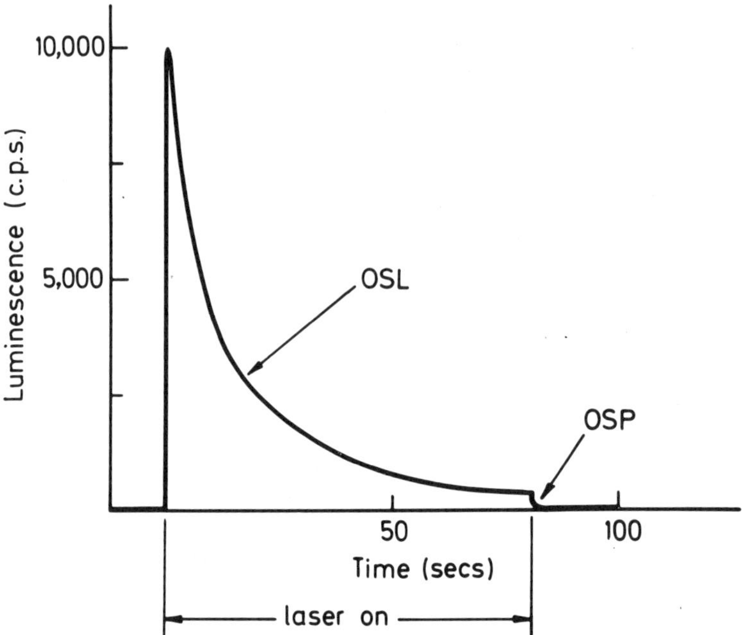

Figure 7.12. Example of a shine-down curve, obtained by exposure to a laser beam. The signal decreases with continued exposure because the number of trapped electrons is rapidly depleted (i.e., the sample is "bleached"). If the laser beam is shut off before depletion is complete, there is a weak phosphorescence (OSP) which disappears after a few seconds. (From Aitken 1990).

constructed for each interval of exposure. In this way a plot of paleodose versus shine time is obtained and for many samples there is a shine plateau, i.e., the paleodose remains constant throughout the shine-down. For sediment that was not well bleached at deposition, the paleodose is liable to be higher at the end of the shine than at the beginning. This is attributed to "hard-to-bleach" traps that were not fully bleached at deposition. On the other hand, there is also the possibility that a rising paleodose is due to complexities ("non-first-order kinetics") in the detrapping/luminescence process. In such cases, it is important to base evaluation of paleodose on the total light output rather than a restricted segment of the shine-down (unless short-shines are used).

Grain-to-Grain Variation in Residual; Single Aliquot and Single Grain Dating

With the optical dating technique, the residual at deposition is negligible in sediments for which, with TL, it was substantial. As application is made to younger and younger contexts which are poorly bleached, it becomes significant. The question then arises as to whether all the grains were equally bleached to a non-zero level or whether some grains were well bleached and others barely at all. In some contexts investigated, the latter has been found to be the case (e.g., Lamothe *et al.* 1994; Lamothe and Auclair 1997). This *single grain dating* is an extension of the *single aliquot technique* (Duller 1991, 1995; Murray *et al.* 1997) which avoids time-consuming normalization between aliquots. When, in a sample, there is the possibility that the sample is a mixture of well-zeroed and non-zeroed grains, as in the Australian rock-shelter mentioned above, then grain-by-grain dating is essential.

Optical Dating of Pottery

Because determination of paleodose by optical dating lends itself to automation, and because of potentially better precision, the application of the technique to pottery is being explored and so far results are encouraging (Mejdahl and Bøtter-Jensen 1994, 1997).

LIMITATIONS IN AGE RANGE

It is convenient to discuss these with reference to the three most commonly used modes of sample presentation.

Coarse-Grains of Quartz

The great advantage of quartz is that it is not afflicted by *anomalous fading* (see below). Its limitation in age range is due to *saturation*—when all the traps become full. This occurs at a lesser dose for quartz than for feldspar. The age at which it occurs is dependent both on the characteristics of the quartz concerned and on the radioactivity of the site. With TL, it has been demonstrated that quartz can give reliable ages at least back to 800 ka using samples from a sequence of stranded beach dunes of low radioactivity in South Australia (Huntley *et al.* 1993a, 1994). The same is to be expected with optical dating (on sites of low radioactivity) and optical ages of 120 ka have now been obtained from a dune of this sequence (Huntley *et al.* 1996); this dune is associated with the highest sea level of the last interglacial period (Marine Isotope Stage 5e) which occurred at 130–115 ka ago. In an archaeological context, one may note the optical age of 130 ka (Stokes 1993) for sediment from the lowest lake at Bir Tafawi (Egypt), consistent with mass-spectrometric uranium-series dating of ostrich eggshell and electron spin resonance dating of tooth enamel. At the other end of the timescale, there is agreement of optical dates with calibrated radiocarbon dates (e.g., Stokes and Gaylord 1993).

Whereas luminescence is observed from the majority of feldspars when exposed to infrared wavelengths in the region of 850 nm, this is not the case for quartz. This leads to a convenient purity test for quartz aliquots, though, of course, the absence of a signal does not rule out the presence of the few feldspar types only weakly stimulated by infrared.

Coarse Grains of Potassium Feldspar

The advantages of feldspars in general are that they are brighter and that there is no effective limitation arising from saturation. However, there is the severe disadvantage, at present, of uncertainty about the possibility of age underestimation due to anomalous fading. This is irrespective of whether stimulation is by heat (as in TL), by visible light or by infrared.

Anomalous fading refers to leakage of electrons from traps other than by the usual thermally-stimulated route via the conduction band. It is exhibited by deep traps as well as by shallow ones, and hence it can affect all regions of the TL glow curve, including the emission at temperatures above 350°C where good stability is the expectation.

There are various conclusions among practitioners as to whether or not adequate measures can be taken to avoid this malign phenomenon, whether in TL or optical dating. This probably reflects a wide variety of feldspar types and of characteristics for a given type. In work on the TL of zircon grains, it was concluded by Templer (1985) that as long as a pre-heat of 3 days at 100°C was employed before measurement, age underestimation could be avoided and some practitioners have found this pre-heat also to be efficacious with feldspar samples, whether in TL or optical dating. On the other hand, OSL laboratory studies of mineral specimens led Spooner (1994) to the conclusion that there was risk of age underestimation irrespective of pre-heat.

Use of blue-pass filters for detection has been found to be advantageous, although not in all cases (e.g., Lamothe and Auclair 1997). With the TL from several samples of sanidine feldspars for which the blue emission shows severe anomalous fading, Zink and Visocekas (1997) have demonstrated that the far-red emission (at around 700 nm) does not.

Polymineral Fine Grains (Feldspar Dominated)

In TL dating of polymineral fine grains from European loess (and to some extent from Chinese loess), it has common for practitioners to report what appears to be a "100 ka barrier," first noted by Debenham (1985). As that age is approached, the degree of underestimation rapidly increased, the degree of underestimation for Upper Palaeolithic samples being only slight. There is contrary evidence as to whether or not the situation for European loess can be alleviated by use of more stringent pre-heats (Zöller and Wagner 1990; Frechen

1992; Frechen *et al.* 1992). In the case of loess from Alaska and New Zealand, Berger *et al.* (1994) have reported correct TL age evaluations back to 800 ka ago. For a review of this topic see Berger (1994).

The barrier for European loess appears to be present also in optical dating irrespective of whether green light or infrared stimulation is used (Spooner and Questiaux, 1989). That weathering may be an important factor in the fading of fine grains is suggested by the acceptable optical ages obtained for microinclusions (probably of feldspar) in quartz grains, using infrared stimulation, back to 400 ka ago (Huntley *et al.* 1993b). These are for the stranded beach dunes of South Australia of which one was mentioned earlier. The view that such microinclusions benefit from the shielding given by the quartz matrix has also been put forward by Rendell and Wood (1994).

ACCURACY, ERROR LIMITS, CITATION

Although neither optical nor TL dating can approach the precision of radiocarbon, quoted error limits usually being in the range ±5 to ±10% of the age, there are nevertheless two strong advantages. First, the ages obtained are directly in calendar years, there being no intervention of calibration as with radiocarbon. This is of particular value for sites beyond the range for which radiocarbon calibration is available. Indeed it may be noted that one of the first indications of radiocarbon age underestimation by several thousand years in the region of 30 ka ago was given by TL dating of burnt quartz grains from the Lake Mungo fireplaces in Australia (Bell 1991; see also, Huxtable and Aitken 1977). There is also strong advantage, particularly using the pre-dose technique, in using luminescence to date pottery of the last few hundred years. During this period, there are wide error limits in the calendar dates derived with radiocarbon because of the flatness of the calibration curve in those centuries.

The appreciable error limits in TL and optical ages arise partly from uncertainty in paleodose evaluation and partly from uncertainties in dose-rate. Although it is to be hoped that the former will continue to be reduced, the latter is more obdurate, first because of the difficulty (on all but very arid sites) of estimating the average water content over the burial period, and secondly, because of the possibility that there has been geochemical leaching so that the radioactive evaluation made to-day does not necessarily represent what has gone before. On these accounts, it is optimistic to expect the error limits on TL and optical ages to be reduced to below ±5% except in special cases. This is the case also with the companion technique of electron spin resonance so important in dating tooth enamel. Additionally, for the latter, uncertainty of the uranium uptake history often leads to substantial ambiguity in the age obtained.

Whether in TL or optical dating, the evaluation of error limits is a complex task because of the many measured quantities that are involved in calculation of an age. Most laboratories use a system based on Aitken and Alldred (1972; see also Aitken 1985: 241–251). In this system, distinction is made between random and systematic uncertainties. The former include measurement errors and other errors likely to be different from sample to sample in the same level of a site. The latter arise from influences that would affect all samples from a given level, such as wetness uncertainties. Also included are the effect of uncertainties in the strength of the radioactive sources used in paleodose evaluation and in the counting facilities used for dose-rate evaluation. The error limits quoted are at the 68% level of confidence, i.e., one standard deviation.

As an example of the full citation on this system, we quote the date obtained for context e of site 143 of the Oxford laboratory: 1070 BC. (±110, ±220, OxTL 143e). The first error limit, ±110 years, is standard error on the mean value as derived from the scatter of the individual dates for the 7 individual samples from level e, for which the weighted average date is 1070 BC. The second error limit, ±220 years, is the overall predicted error taking into account all quantifiable sources of uncertainty. Unfortunately, it is not usually possible to quantify the uncertainty arising from such effects as anomalous fading and geochemical leaching. It is now usual to quote only the second error limit in the citation and to give further details in the accompanying report. Dates quoted without reference to proper publication should, of course, be treated with strict reserve.

It should be stressed that thermoluminescence gives ages directly in calendar years and it is not appropriate to quote as "so many years BP." This is because "BP" has the strict meaning of an uncalibrated radiocarbon age. For luminescence ages "so many years ago" is appropriate except that for Neolithic and later sites it is usual to quote as "BC" or "AD" as the case may be.

CONCLUSION

Although initially developed for pottery dating, luminescence currently has its greatest impact in the Palaeolithic (and Quaternary studies in general), particularly in application to burnt flint and unburnt sediment. However its important role in dating pottery of the last few centuries should not be overlooked, nor that of testing the authenticity of art ceramics of any period.

The span of time encompassed by the various luminescence techniques is remarkable: from a few decades to approaching a million years. Extension beyond the range of calibrated radiocarbon dating is particularly to be noted, and also that luminescence ages are not distorted by intensity fluctuations in cosmic radiation.

REFERENCES

Aitken, M.J. 1985 *Thermoluminescence Dating*. London: Academic Press.

Aitken, M. J. 1990 *Science-based Dating in Archaeology*. London: Longman.

Aitken, M.J. 1991. Sediment and optical dating. *In* Güksu, Y., Oberhofer, M. and Regulla, D., eds., *Scientific Dating Methods*. Kluwer Academic Publishers, Dordrecht, Boston & London: 141–154.

Aitken, M.J. 1998 *Optical Dating*. Oxford, Oxford University Press.

Aitken, M.J. and Alldred, J.C. 1972 The assessment of error limits in thermoluminescence dating. *Archaeometry* 14: 257–267.

Aitken, M.J. and Valladas, H. 1993 Luminescence dating relevant to human origins. *In* Aitken, M.J., Stringer, C.B. and Mellars, P.A.. eds., *The Origin of Modern Humans and the Impact of Chronometric Dating*. Princeton, Princeton University Press: 27–39.

Aitken, M.J. and Xie, J. 1992 Optical dating using infrared diodes: young samples. *Quaternary Science Reviews* 11: 147–152.

Bahn, P.G. 1996 Further back down under. *Nature* 383: 577–578.

Balescu, S. and Lamothe, M. 1992 The blue emission of K-feldspar coarse grains and its potential for overcoming TL age underestimation. *Quaternary Science Reviews* 11: 45–51.

Bell, W.T. 1991 Thermoluminescence dates for the Lake Mungo aboriginal fireplaces and the implictions for radiocarbon dating. *Archaeometry* 33: 43–50.

Berger, G.W. 1988 Dating Quaternary events by luminescence. *Geological Society of America Special Paper* 227: 13–50.

Berger, G.W. 1992 Dating of volcanic ash by use of thermoluminescence. *Geology* 20: 11–14.

Berger, G.W. 1994 Thermoluminescence dating of sediments older than 100 ka. *Quaternary Science Reviews* 13: 445–455.

Berger, G.W., Pillans, B.J. and Palmer, A.S. 1994 Dating of loess from New Zealand and Alaska. *Quaternary Science Reviews* 13: 309–333.

David, B., Roberts, R., Tuniz, C., Jones, R., and Head, J. 1997 New optical and radiocarbon dates from Ngarrabullgan Cave, a Pleistocene archaeological site in Australia: Implications for the comparability of time clocks and for the human colonization of Australia. *Antiquity* 71:183–188.

Debenham, N.C. 1985 Use of UV emissions in TL dating of sediments. *Nuclear Tracks & Radiation Measurements* 10: 717–724.

Debenham, N.C., Driver, H.S.T. and Walton, A.J. 1982 Anomalies in the dating of young calcites. *PACT* 6: 555–562.

Duller, G.A.T. 1991 Equivalent dose determination using single aliquots. *Nuclear Tracks & Radiation Measurements* 18: 371–378.

Duller, G.A.T. 1995 Luminescence dating using single aliquot: methods and applications. *Radiation Measurements* 24: 217–226.

Duller, G.A.T. 1996 Recent developments in luminescence dating of Quaternary sediments. *Progress in Physical Geography* 20: 133–151.

Dunnell, R.C. and Feathers, J.K. 1994 Thermoluminescence dating of surficial archaeological material. *In* Beck, C., ed., *Dating in Exposed and Surface Contexts*. Albuquerque, University of New Mexico Press.

Fleming, S.J 1970 Thermoluminescence dating: refinement of the quartz inclusion method. *Archaeometry* 12: 133–147.

Fleming, S.J. 1979 *Thermoluminescene Techniques in Archaeology*. Oxford, Clarendon.

Franklin, A.D. and Hornyak, W.F. 1990 Isolation of the rapidly bleaching peak in quartz TL glow curves. *Ancient TL* 8: 29–31.

Frechen, M. 1992 Systematic thermoluminescence dating of two loess profiles from the Middle Rhine area. *Quaternary Science Reviews* 11: 93–101.

Frechen, M., Bruckner, M. and Radke, U. 1992 A comparison of different TL techniques on loess samples from Rheindahlen (F.R.G.). *Quaternary Science Reviews* 11: 109–113.

Feathers, J.K. 1997a Application of luminescence dating in American archaeology. *Journal of Archaeological Method and Theory* 4:1–66.

Feathers, J.K. 1997b Luminescence dating of sediment samples from White Paintings Rockshelter, Botswana. *Quaternary Geochronology* 16: 321–331.

Feathers, J.K. 1997c Luminescence dating of Archaic mounds in Southeastern U.S. *Quaternary Geochronology* 16: 333–340.

Fullagar, R.L.K., Price, D.M., and Head, L.M. 1996 Early human occupation of northern Australia: archaeology and thermoluminescence dating of Jinmium rock-shelter, Northern Territory. *Antiquity* 70: 751–773.

Grün, R., Stringer, C.B. and Schwarcz, H.P. 1991 ESR dating of teeth from Garrod's Tabun cave collection. *Journal of Human Evolution* 20: 231–248.

Grün, G. and Valladas, G. 1980 Thermoluminescence dating of volcanic plagioclases. *Nature* 286: 697–699.

Huntley, D.J. and Clague, J.J. 1996 Optical dating of tsunami-laid sands. *Quaternary Research* 46: 127–140.

Huntley, D.J., Hutton, J.T. and Prescott, J.R. 1993a The stranded beach-dune sequence of south-east Australia: a test of thermoluminescence dating, 0–800 ka. *Quaternary Science Reviews* 12: 1–20.

Huntley, D.J., Hutton, J.T. and Prescott, J.R. 1993b Optical dating using inclusions within quartz grains. *Geology* 21: 1087–1090.

Huntley, D.J., Hutton, J.T. and Prescott, J.R. 1994 Further thermoluminescence dates from the dune sequence in the south-east of South Australia. *Quaternary Science Reviews* 13: 201–207.

Huntley, D. J., Short, M. A., and Dunphy K. 1996 Deep traps in quartz and their use for optical dating. *Canadian Journal of Physics* 74: 81–91.

Huxtable, J. and Aitken, M.J. 1977 Thermoluminescent dating of Lake Mungo geomagnetic polarity excursion. *Nature* 265: 40–41.

Jelenek, A. 1982 The Tabun Cave and Palaeolithic Man in the Levant. *Science* 216: 1369–1375.

Lamothe, M. and Auclair, M. 1997 Assessing the datability of young sediments by IRSL using an intrinsic laboratory protocol. *Radiation Measurements* 27:107–117.

Lang, A. and Wagner, G. A. 1996 Infrared stimulated luminescence dating of archaeosediments. *Archaeometry* 38: 129–141.

McDermott, F., Grün, R., Stringer, C.B. and Hawkesworth, C.J. 1993 Mass-spectrometric U-series dates for Israeli Neanderthal/early modern hominid sites. *Nature* 363: 252–255.

McKeever, S.W.S. 1985 *Thermoluminescence of Solids*. Cambridge, Cambridge University Press.

Mejdahl, V. 1983 Feldspar inclusion dating of ceramics and burnt stones. *PACT* 9: 351–364.

Mejdahl, V. 1988 The plateau method for dating partially bleached sediments by thermoluminescence. *Quaternary Science Reviews* 7: 347–348.

Mejdahl, V. and Bøtter-Jensen, L. 1994 Luminescence dating of archaeological materials using a new technique based on single aliquot measurements. *Quaternary Geochronology* 13: 551–554.

Mejdahl, V. and Bøtter-Jensen, L. 1997 Experience with the SARA OSL method. *Radiation Measurements* 27:291–294.

Mercier, N. and Valladas, H. 1994 Thermoluminescence dates for the Paleolithic Levant. *In* Bar-Yosef and R.S. Kra, eds., *Late Quaternary Chronology and Paleoclimate of the Eastern Mediterranean*. Tucson, Radiocarbon: 13–20.

Mercier, N., Valladas, H., Valladas, G., Jelenek, A., Meignen, L., Joron, J-L. and Reyss, J-L. 1994 TL dates of burnt flints from Jelenek's excavations at Tabun and their implications. *Journal of Archaeological Science* 22: 495–509.

Murray, A.S., Roberts, R.G. and Wintle, A.G. 1997 Equivalent dose measurements using a single aliquot of quartz. *Radiation Measurements* 27: 171–184.

Pilleyre, Th., Montret, M., Fain, J., Miallier, D. and Sanzelle, S. 1992 Attempts at dating ancient volcanoes using the red TL of quartz. *Quaternary Science Reviews* 11: 13–17.

Prescott, J.R. and Fox, P.J. 1990 Dating quartz sediments using the 325°C TL peak: new spectral data. *Ancient TL* 8: 32–34.

Prescott, J.R. and Hutton, J.T. 1994 Cosmic ray contributions to dose rates for luminescence and ESR dating: large depths and long-term variations. *Radiation Measurements* 23: 497–500.

Prescott, J.R. and Mojarrabi, B. 1993 Selective bleach: an improved partial bleach technique for finding equivalent doses in TL dating of quartz sediments. *Ancient TL* 11: 27–30

Prescott, J.R., Huntley, D.J. and Hutton, J.T. 1993 Estimation of equivalent dose in thermoluminescence dating-the Australian slide method. *Ancient TL* 11: 1–5.

Rees-Jones, J. and Tite, M.S. 1997 Optical dating results for British archaeological sediments. *Archaeometry* 39: 177–188.

Rendell, H.M. and Wood, R.A. 1994 Quartz sample pretreatments for TL/OSL dating: studies of TL emission spectra. *Radiation Measurements* 23: 575–580.

Roberts, R.G. 1997 Luminescence dating in archaeology: From origins to optical. *Radiation Measurements*, in press.

Roberts, R.G., Jones, R. and Smith, M.A. 1990 Thermoluminescence dating of a 50,000-year-old human occupation site in northern Australia. *Nature* 345: 153–156.

Roberts, R.G., Jones, R., Spooner, N.A., Head, M.J., Murray, A.S. and Smith, M.A. 1994 The human colonisation of Australia: optical dates of 53,000 and 60,000 years bracket human arrival at Deaf Adder Gorge, Northern Territory. *Quaternary Geochronology* 13: 575–584.

Roberts, R.G., Walsh, G., Murray, A., Alley, O., Jones, R., Morwood, M., Tuniz,C, Macphail, M., Bowdery, D., and Naumann, I. 1997 Luminescence dating of rock art and past environments using mud-wasp nests in northern Australia. *Nature* 387: 696–699.

Smith, B.W., Rhodes, E.J., Stokes, S., Spooner, N.A. and Aitken, M.J. 1990 Optical dating of sediments: initial quartz results from Oxford. *Archaeometry* 32: 19–31.

Spooner, N.A. 1994 The anomalous fading of infrared-stimulated luminescence from feldspars. *Radiation Measurements* 23: 625–632.

Spooner, N.A. and Questiaux, D.G. 1989 Optical dating-Achenheim beyond the Eemian using green and infrared stimulation. *In Long and Short Range Limits in Luminescence Dating. RLAHA Occasional Publication* no. 9: 97–103.

Stokes, S. 1993 Optical dating of sediment samples from Bir Tafawi and Bir Sahara: an initial report. *In* Wendorf, F., Close, A.E. and Schilde, S C., eds., *The Middle Palaeolithic in the Egyptian Sahara During the Last Interglacial*. Dallas, Southern Methodist University Press.

Stokes, S. 1994 The timing of OSL sensitivity changes in a natural quartz. *Radiation Measurements* 23: 601–606.

Stokes, S. and Gaylord, D.R. 1993 Optical dating of Holocene dune sands in the Ferris dune field, Wyoming. *Quaternary Research* 39: 274–281.

Templer, R.H. 1985 The removal of anomalous fading in zircons. *Nuclear Tracks and Radiation Measurements* 10: 531–537.

Valladas, G. and Gillot, P.Y. 1978 Dating of the Olby lava flow using heated quartz pebbles. *PACT* 2: 141–150.

Valladas, H., Reyss, J.L., Joron, J.L., Valladas, G., Bar-Yosef, O. and Vandermeersch, B. 1988 Thermoluminescence dating of Mousterian 'Proto-Cro-Magnon' remains from Israel and the origin of modern man. *Nature* 331: 614–616.

Wintle, A.G. and Huntley, D.J. 1980 Thermoluminescence dating of ocean sediments. *Canadian Journal of Earth Sciences* 17: 348–360.

Zimmerman, D.W. 1967 Thermoluminescence from fine grains from pottery. *Archaeometry* 10: 26–28.

Zink, A.J.C. and Visocekas, D. 1997 Datability of sanidine feldspars using the near infrared TL emission. *Radiation Measurements* 27: 251–261.

Zöller, L. and Wagner, G.A. 1990 Thermoluminescence dating of loess: recent developments. *Quaternary International* 7/8: 119–128.

Chapter **8**

Electron Spin Resonance Dating

RAINER GRÜN

ABSTRACT

Electron spin resonance (ESR) dating was introduced into archaeology about 20 years ago. Although the method is still in a rapid phase of development, it has demonstrated its value by providing new chronological evidence about the evolution of modern humans. ESR dating in archaeology has been applied to tooth enamel, speleothems, spring deposited travertines, shells and burnt flint. These applications are described in detail and examples are given to illustrate the contribution of ESR dating to the establishment of archaeological chronologies.

INTRODUCTION

Electron spin resonance dating was introduced into earth sciences when Ikeya (1975) dated a speleothem from Akiyoshi Cave, Japan. Since then, ESR dating has been applied to a wide range of materials in archaeology, geology, and geography. The method allows minerals which have been newly formed to be dated, such as carbonates (e.g. speleothems, mollusc shells, corals) or tooth enamel, as well as materials which have been heated in the past such

RAINER GRÜN • Quaternary Dating Research Centre, Australian National University, Canberra ACT 0200 Australia.

Chronometric Dating in Archaeology, edited by Taylor and Aitken.
Plenum Press, New York, 1997.

as volcanic minerals and flint. A summary of applications and a comprehensive description of the dating procedures have been given by Grün (1989a, 1989b) and Ikeya (1993).

In archaeology, ESR dating of tooth enamel and carbonates such as speleothems, spring deposited travertines and shells are of particular interest and these applications will be described in detail. Other materials that have been studied in archaeological contexts are burnt flint, and quartz extracted from ceramics. ESR dating of burnt flint has been developed in recent years with promising results (Porat *et al.* 1994). Maurer (1980) has demonstrated that, in principle, it is possible to use ESR for age assessments of quartz extracted from ceramics. However, the method is several orders of magnitude less sensitive than thermoluminescence and therefore this ESR dating approach has not been further pursued.

BASIC PRINCIPLES OF ESR DATING

Electron spin resonance (henceforth ESR), also called electron paramagnetic resonance (EPR), may be grouped together with thermoluminescence (TL) and optically stimulated luminescence (OSL) as trapped charge dating methods. Figure 8.1 shows the basic principle of these methods: radioactive rays knock negatively charged electrons off atoms in the ground state (valence band). The electrons are transferred to a higher energy state, the so-called conduction band, and a positively charged holes remain near the valence band. After a short time of diffusion, most electrons recombine with these holes and the mineral is unchanged. However, all natural minerals contain imperfections, such as lattice defects or interstitial atoms, which can trap electrons when they fall back from the conduction band. The trapped electrons form specific paramagnetic centres which can be measured by ESR spectrometry by giving rise to characteristic ESR lines (Figure 8.2). The ESR measurement does not affect the trapped electron population. The nature of the paramagnetic centres is usually well known.

The intensity of the ESR line is proportional to the number of trapped electrons and the number of trapped electrons in turn results from three parameters: (i) the strength of the radioactivity (dose rate), (ii) the number of traps (sensitivity), and (iii), the duration of radiation exposure (age).

Trapped electrons may be released by two processes: heating and light exposure. At sufficiently high temperatures which are related to the depth of a trap (activation energy, E_a), or on exposure to a light source where the photon energy corresponds to E_a, the electrons are released. Some may recombine with holes that are luminescence centres, resulting in the emission of light. These processes are called thermoluminescence and optically stimulated luminescence and are the basis for the respective dating methods (for further details see Chapter 7, Luminescence Dating).

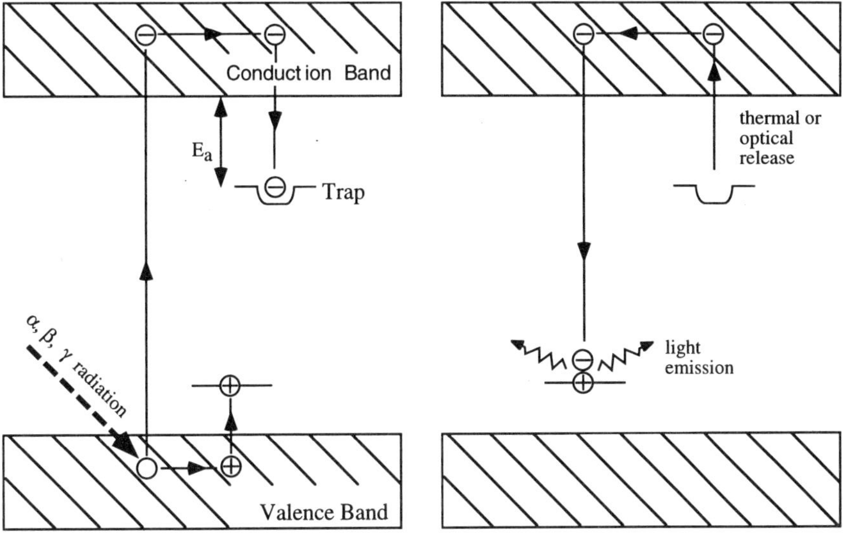

Figure 8.1. Trapping of electrons: the basis for ESR and TL/OSL dating. An insulating mineral has two energy levels which electrons may occupy. The lower energy level (valence band) is separated from the higher energy level (conduction band) by a so-called forbidden zone. When a mineral is formed or reset, all electrons are in the ground state. Ionising radiation (left) ejects negatively charged electrons from atoms. The electrons are transferred to the conduction band and positively charged holes are left behind near the valence band. After a short time of diffusion most of the electrons recombine with the holes. Some electrons can be trapped by defects (electron traps) in the crystal lattice. These electrons can be directly measured by electron spin resonance spectrometry (see Fig. 8.2). The ESR measurement does not affect the population of trapped electrons. E_a=activation energy or trap depth. Subsequent heating or light exposure (right) releases the electrons and light emission can be observed (thermoluminescence).

In order to obtain reliable dating results, an ESR signal should have the following properties: (i) a zeroing effect deletes all previously stored ESR intensity in the sample at the event to be dated, (ii) the signal intensity increases steadily with radiation dose, (iii) the signals must have a stability which is at least one order of magnitude higher than the age of the sample, (iv) the number of traps is constant or changes in a predictable manner; recrystallisation, crystal growth or phase transitions must not have occurred, (v) the signals should not show fading, and (vi) the ESR signal is not influenced by sample preparation (grinding, exposure to laboratory light).

The two major limitations of ESR dating are: (i) saturation: when all traps are filled any additional radiation cannot result in a further increase in the number of trapped electrons, and (ii) thermal stability: electrons have only a limited probability of staying in the traps. After a certain period of time, the so-called thermal mean life, T, 63% of the original population of trapped electrons will have left the traps and recombined with holes. Only

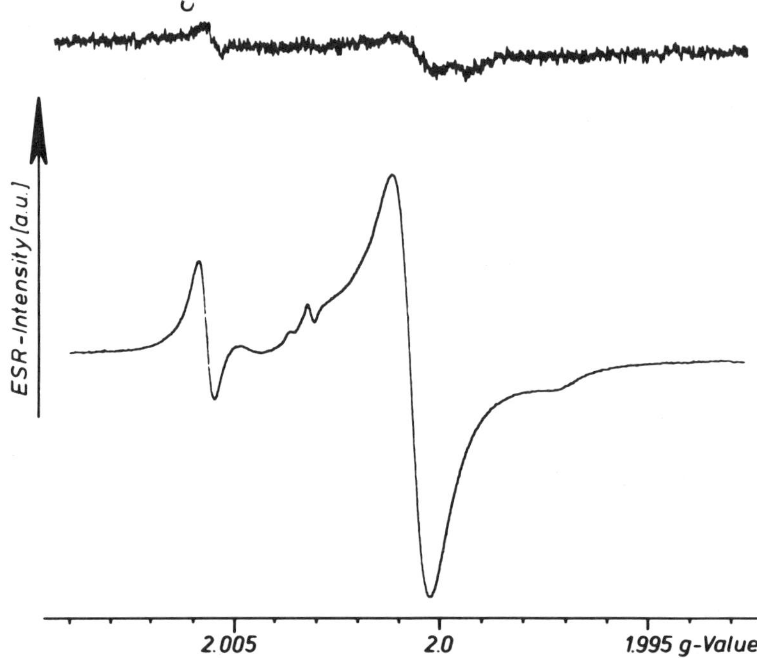

Figure 8.2. ESR signals of a young speleothem sample (upper) and an old one (lower). The upper spectrum is amplified relative to the lower by a factor of ten. The ESR signal intensity is a measure of the number of trapped electrons. The different ESR signals are due to separate, characteristic paramagnetic centres. It can immediately be seen that the intensity of the ESR lines is a measure of age.

if the mean life is at least ten times larger than the age of the sample, the effect of recombination or fading can be neglected. Because the thermal mean life is dependent on the nature of the paramagnetic centre, there is no general upper dating limit for ESR dating and each case has to be evaluated individually.

ESR age estimates are derived from the following formula:

$$\text{Age} = \text{Accumulated dose } (D_E) \ / \ \text{Dose rate } (\dot{D}) \qquad (1)$$

The measurement of the accumulated dose, D_E, which is the radioactive dose the sample has received since it was formed, is the actual ESR part of the dating procedure. This value is determined by the additive dose method (see below). The dose rate, $\dot{D}$, is derived from the chemical analysis of the radioactive elements (U, Th, and K; other elements are usually negligible) in the sample and its surroundings. The isotopic concentrations are converted into dose rates by published tables (e.g., Nambi and Aitken 1986). The determination of all radioactive sources influencing the sample is rather complex and has to be carefully evaluated.

ESR MEASUREMENT

Measurements are made with an ESR spectrometer. These instruments are found in nearly all chemistry departments of universities. Figure 8.3 shows the block-diagram of an ESR spectrometer. The sample is placed into a microwave cavity which is located in a strong external magnetic field. A paramagnetic centre (i.e., the trapped electron) has a magnetic moment which is oriented parallel to the magnetic field. In resonance, the magnetic moment is flipped into the opposite direction by microwave energy which is conducted to the sample from a microwave generator. The amount of absorbed microwave energy is directly proportional to the number of paramagnetic centres, and, in the end, to the age of the sample.

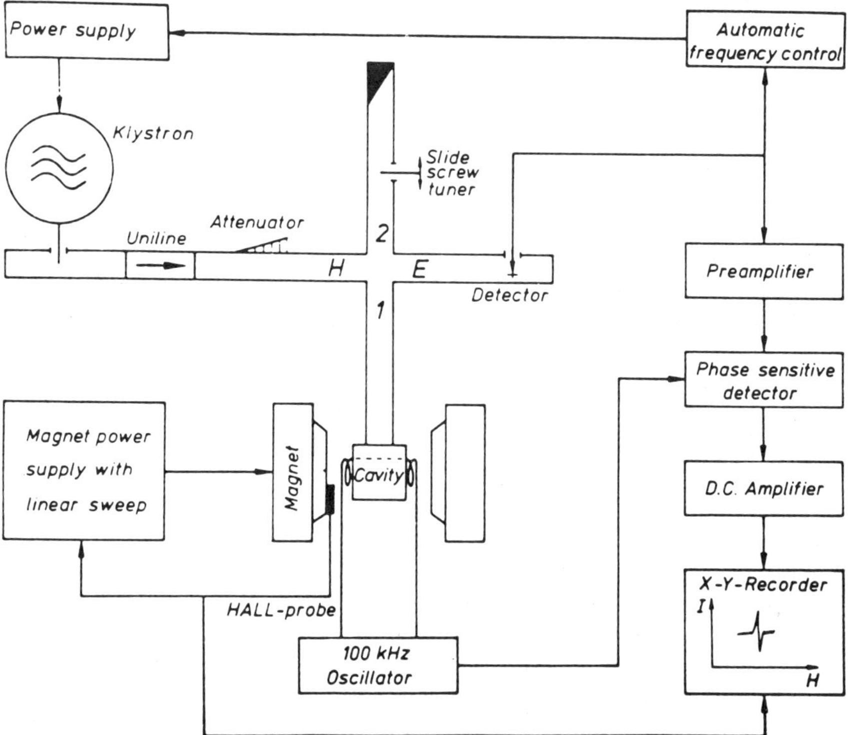

Figure 8.3. Block diagram of an ESR spectrometer. The sample is measured in the cavity which is located in a strong magnetic field. The magnetic field can be linearly changed. In resonance, microwave energy is absorbed by the sample giving rise to an ESR line as shown in Fig. 8.2.

The ESR spectrometer records the microwave absorption with respect to the magnetic field, resulting in characteristic ESR spectra. The intensity, I, of the ESR signal is always shown as the first derivative.

In order to become independent of specific equipment configurations, the position of an ESR line in a spectrum is described by the g-value, which is proportional to the ratio of microwave frequency over magnetic field strength (see X-axis in Figure 8.2). The g-value is characteristic for a given paramagnetic centre and is usually near the value of 2 (which corresponds approximately to the value for free electrons).

DETERMINATION OF THE ACCUMULATED DOSE, D_E

For the determination of D_E (equal to palaeodose in the Chapter 7, "Luminescence Dating"), the ESR response to radioactive irradiation must be known and mathematically expressed. For this purpose, aliquots of the sample are irradiated with a gamma source (e.g., ^{60}Co). Many hospitals and chemistry departments have such gamma sources for a variety of applications (e.g., sterilisation or cancer treatment). During radiation an amount of energy is transferred to the sample, measured in units of Grays (Gy).

In the laboratory a portion of the sample to be dated (between 400 and 1000 mg) is separated from the bulk and some surface layers are removed (about 50 μm are necessary to erase the volume that was irradiated by external alpha rays; about 2 mm will eliminate the volume that was irradiated by external alpha and beta rays). The removal of surface layers simplifies the dose rate calculations. The sample is ground and sieved for homogenisation and about ten equal quantities (aliquots) are weighed out; about 30 mg for enamel and 150 mg for carbonates and flint. The aliquots are irradiated by a calibrated gamma source. After a period of time following the irradiation (about 2 weeks) the sample is measured with an ESR spectrometer.

Figure 8.4 shows the relationship between the age of the sample and the D_E value. At the time of formation, the ESR intensity is supposed to be zero (this assumption may not be correct for some materials such as calcretes or spring deposited travertines; see Grün 1989a, 1989b). Natural radiation produces trapped electrons and the ESR intensity grows steadily with time until the sample is collected (left side of Figure 8.4). The directly measured ESR intensity of the sample is called natural intensity. The artificial gamma irradiation of the aliquots enhances the ESR intensity and by plotting the measured intensity values versus the known gamma doses, a so-called dose response curve is obtained (right side of Figure 8.4). The data points can now be used for extrapolation to zero ESR intensity which yields the D_E value on the intersection with the X-axis.

Although this extrapolation seems rather straight forward, there have recently been intense discussions about the correct procedures for D_E determi-

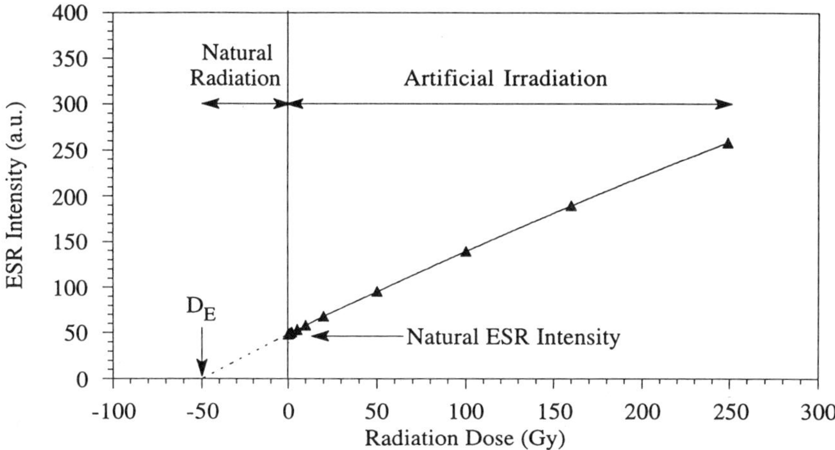

Figure 8.4. At the event to be dated, the sample has no ESR intensity. Trapped electrons are created by natural radiation and their number is dependent on the product of time and dose rate (= dose). When the sample is collected and measured, the ESR signal intensity is equivalent to the number of trapped electrons. Defined laboratory irradiation creates increased ESR signals. The plot of ESR intensity vs laboratory dose is called the "dose response curve." The D_E value results from fitting the data points of the dose response with an exponential function and extrapolation to zero ESR intensity.

nation and the assessment of the errors involved. Detailed simulations of dose response curves (Grün and Brumby 1994) have demonstrated that the data points are best fitted when using a single saturating exponential function for fitting, weights that are inversely proportional to the square of the measured ESR intensity and analytical expression for error calculation (Brumby 1992).

The random error in the D_E estimation that arises from the scatter of the data points around the fitted line lies in the range of 2 to 7% and the systematic error, due to source calibration, lies in the range of 2 to 5%.

DETERMINATION OF THE DOSE RATE, $\dot{D}$

The strength of the radioactive flux which irradiates the sample is determined by the concentration of radioactive elements in the tooth and its surroundings plus a component from cosmic rays. In ESR studies, only the U and Th decay chains and the ^{40}K-decay are of relevance (a minor contribution comes from ^{87}Rb in the sediment). There are three types of ionising radiation which are emitted from the radioactive elements (the ranges are given for a material with a density of about 2.5 g/cm^3): (i) alpha particles which have only a very short range of about 20 µm because of their large size. Alpha particles are not as efficient as beta and gamma rays in producing ESR intensity, therefore

Table 8.1. Dose Rates for U and Th Decay Chains and K

	Dose rate in μGy/a (micrograys/year)		
Concentration	$\dot{D}_\alpha$	$\dot{D}_\beta$	$\dot{D}_\gamma$
1 ppm $^{238}U + ^{235}U$	2781	147	114
1 ppm ^{232}Th	738	29	52
1 % K	814	242	

an alpha efficiency, or k value, (which is usually in the range of 0.05 to 0.3) has to be determined (see Aitken 1985, 1990), (ii) beta particles (electrons) which have a range of about 2 mm. and, (iii) gamma rays which have a range of about 30 cm. The concentrations of radioactive elements in the sample and its surrounding are usually very different. Therefore, it is necessary to determine the *internal dose rate* separately from the *external dose rate*.

Additionally, the effect of cosmic rays has to be considered. The cosmic dose rate is dependent on the geographic latitude, the altitude and the thickness of the covering sediments. The cosmic dose rate is about 300 μGy/a at sealevel and decreases with depth below ground (see Prescott and Stephan 1982, Prescott and Hutton 1988). Table 8.1 lists the dose rates for the U and Th decay chains and K.

For example, if a sample contains 2 ppm U, 3 ppm Th and 4% K, an α-efficiency of 0.1 is assumed or measured, the total internal dose rate is generated by alpha and beta particles:

$$
\begin{aligned}
\dot{D}_{internal} &= k\dot{D}_\alpha \dot{D}_\beta \\
&= (2 \times 0.1 \times 2781 + 3 \times 0.1 \times 738) + (2 \times 147 + 3 \times 29 + 4 \times 814)\ \mu Gy/a \\
&= 4415\ \mu Gy/a. \qquad (2)
\end{aligned}
$$

If an *external γ-dose rate* of 1300 μGy/a was measured and a *cosmic dose rate* of 150 μGy/a was calculated from the depth of the sample below surface, the total dose rate is:

$$
\begin{aligned}
\dot{D}_{total} &= \dot{D}_{internal} + \dot{D}_{external} \\
&= 4415 + 1300 + 150\ \mu Gy/a. \\
&= 5865\ \mu Gy/a. \qquad (3)
\end{aligned}
$$

Dose rate calculations become more complicated when disequilibria in the U-decay chains or attenuation factors have to be considered (for details see Grün 1989a, 1989b). If samples are thin (<5 mm), it is not possible to remove the volume that was reached by external beta particles. In this case the external beta dose rate has to be considered (see section on tooth enamel and mollusc shells).

Typical errors in the estimation of the total dose rate are in the range of 4 to 7%. The overall analytical error of ESR age estimations is in the range of 5 to 10%.

ESR DATING OF TOOTH ENAMEL

Many important archaeological sites cannot be dated because they are beyond the radiocarbon dating range and lack material suitable for dating techniques such U-series or K/Ar. Bones and teeth occur in most archaeological sites and are commonly coeval with other remains. Bones are probably not datable with ESR (Grün and Schwarcz 1987, see also below), whereas ESR dating of tooth enamel may provide valuable chronological information for many sites.

Determination of D_E in Tooth Enamel

Tooth enamel consists of more than 96% of the mineral hydroxyapatite (Driessens 1980), which is in contact with the more organically rich dentine and cementum (see Figure 8.6a-c). Figure 8.5 shows two ESR spectra of tooth enamel. The radiation sensitive signals at g=2.0018 and the signal at g=1.9976 are associated with a CO_2^- radical in hydroxyapatite (Callens *et al.* 1987). In

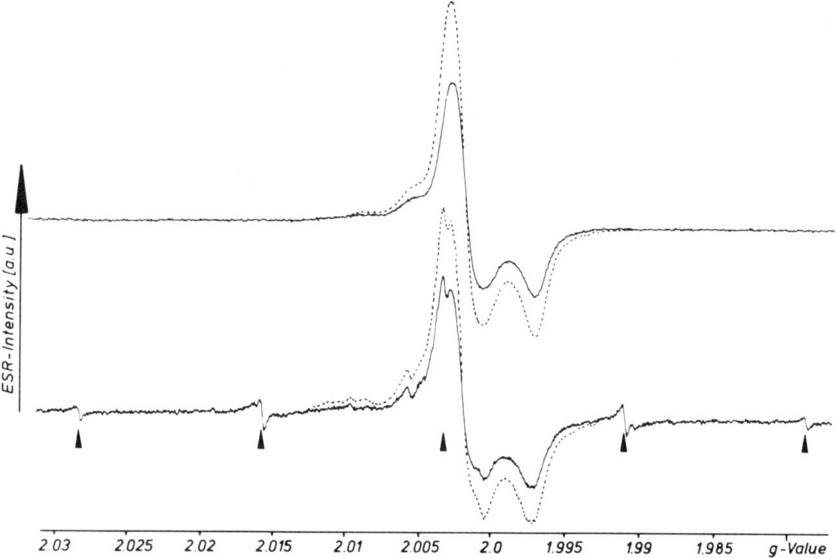

Figure 8.5. ESR spectra of tooth enamel. Solid line: natural sample; dotted line: irradiated sample. The upper spectrum displays non-interfered ESR signals whilst the lower spectrum shows various interferences by organic signals. The marked quintet has been attributed to alanine or dimethyl radicals.

many cases lines from organic radicals interfere with the dating signal (Figure 8.5, lower spectrum). These organic interferences can be suppressed using specific measurement conditions (a modulation amplitude of 0.5 mTpp; Grün *et al.* 1987). The ESR signal of recent teeth is below the sensitivity of an ESR spectrometer and in practical terms zero. Errors in the D_E estimation are typically in the 2 to 5% range.

Determination of $\dot{D}$ in Tooth Enamel

External Dose Rate

Material in contact with enamel (sediment, dentine or cementum) irradiates the sample with alpha, beta, and gamma rays, which are emitted from naturally occurring radioactive elements (U, Th, and K). Figure 8.6 shows possible configurations for the enamel layer. The removal of the outer 50 μm of the sample eliminates all the externally alpha irradiated volume (Figure 8.6G). Since the enamel layer is rather thin, it is normally not possible to remove the outer 2 mm which received external beta radiation. The externally

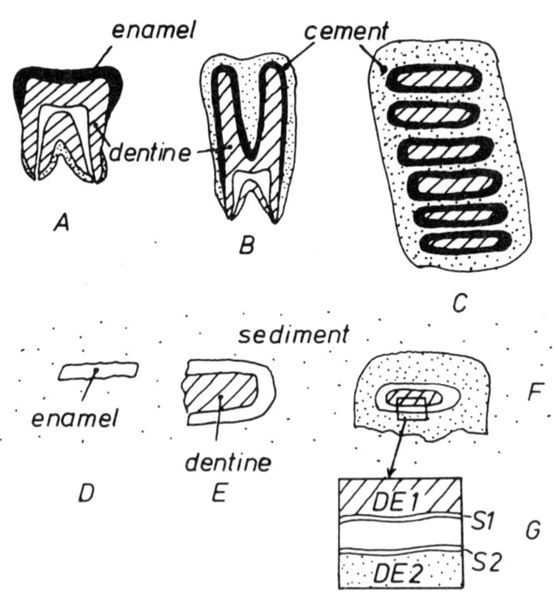

Figure 8.6. Structure of mammalian teeth: (A) human tooth with low crown; (B) high crowned tooth (e.g. horse, bovid); (C) elephant tooth. (D-F) possible environments of tooth enamel; (G) S1 and S2 are 50–200 μm thick enamel layers that are removed to eliminate the effect of the external alpha-dose. DE1 and DE2 denote the organic rich dentine/cement layers.

derived beta dose rate decreases with depth and therefore attenuation factors have to be considered (see Grün 1986).

The external beta dose rate has to be calculated separately from the external gamma dose rate because the beta dose rate is generated from the dentine or sediment immediately attached to the enamel layer, whereas the gamma dose rate originates from all sediment that is within a radius of about 30 cm around the sample. The beta dose rate from the sediment is derived from the chemical analysis of U, Th, and K (in cases of Figure 8.6D,E). The beta dose rate of the dentine (Figure 8.6E,F) originates from its U concentration (dentine is virtually free of Th and K). The dose rate for dentine is affected by U-disequilibrium and U-accumulation (see below).

The gamma dose rate can normally not be deduced from laboratory analyses but has to be measured *in situ* with a portable, calibrated gamma spectrometer or with TL dosimeters. This also has the advantage that the present-day water content is directly included. The gamma dose rate from dentine is negligible.

Water absorbs some β and γ rays and its presence in the surrounding sediment has to be considered in the calculation of the beta and gamma dose rate (Bowman 1976, Aitken and Xie 1990). Dentine may contain up to 25% water.

Internal Dose Rate

This parameter is mainly generated by alpha and beta rays emitted from elements of the uranium decay chains. An alpha efficiency of 0.15±0.02 has repeatedly been measured (Grün 1985, DeCanniere *et al.* 1986, Katzenberger pers. comm.) and this value is normally used for all samples. However, Chen *et al.* (1994) measured a higher α-efficiency of 0.227±0.013 for Chinese samples. Most enamel pieces are rather thin, therefore the internal beta dose rate is not 100% absorbed and a self-absorption factor has to be calculated (Grün 1986). Quaternary samples display disequilibrium in the U-decay chain which is actually the basis for U-series dating. This is also the case for the uranium in enamel and dentine. U-series disequilibrium affects the average dose rates and have to be taken into account mathematically.

Early and Linear U-Uptake

Teeth and bones show postdepositional U-uptake and this effect further complicates the dose rate determination of tooth enamel. The process of uranium uptake cannot normally be determined exactly. Dentine usually accumulates much more U than enamel (by a factor of 10 to 100). For teeth, two models have been suggested (Ikeya 1982): (i) U-accumulation shortly after burial of the tooth (early U-uptake, EU), (ii) continuous U-accumulation (linear U-uptake, LU).

Figure 8.7 shows the influence of the measured U-concentration on the ESR model ages. As long as the U-concentrations in the components of a tooth are low (<2 ppm in dentine) the discrepancy between EU and LU ages is less than 10%. However, with increasing U-concentrations this intrinsic uncertainty increases very rapidly. In the extreme, the LU model age is twice the EU age estimate. New developments in ESR and U-series dating have shown a strategy to overcome this problem (see below).

There are numerous sites where the EU model age seems closer to independent age estimates and some U-series studies seem to support this model (McKinney 1991). In other cases, the linear model seems to yield more accurate age estimates (for a compilation see Grün and Stringer 1991). If there are no specific indications to justify a particular U-uptake model, age estimates

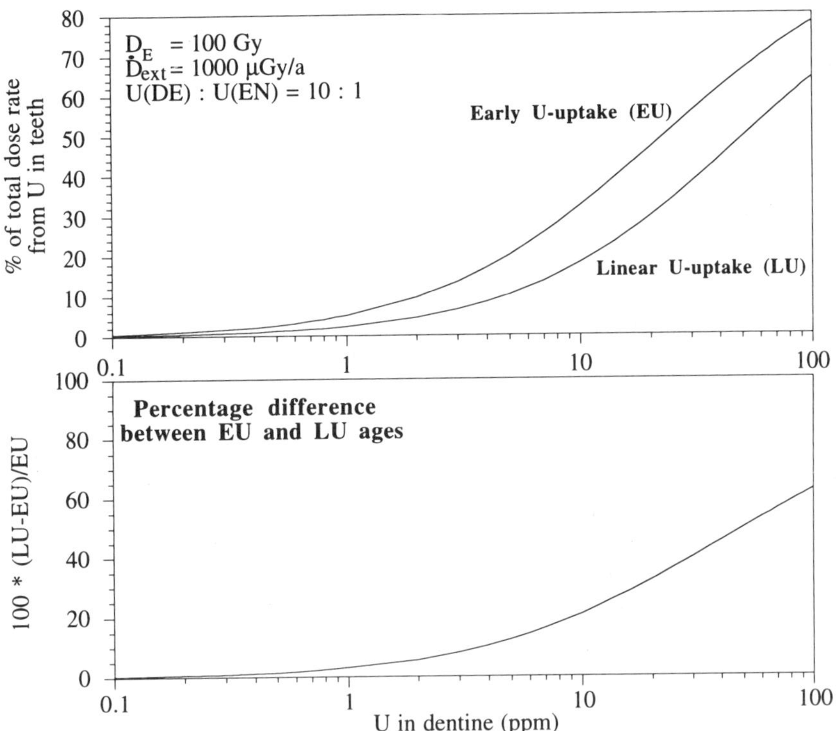

Figure 8.7. Effect of U-accumulation on the calculation of ESR age estimates. The calculated dose rate of enamel and dentine is critically dependent on the U-uptake model. The upper plot illustrates that the EU dose rate contribution to the total dose rate is always larger than the LU dose rate contribution. With increasing U-concentrations in teeth, the part of the total dose rate that originates from this uranium increases and therefore dose rate calculations become increasingly dependent on the U-uptake model. This causes an increasing difference between the early U-uptake (EU) and linear U-uptake (LU) ages (base). At high U-concentrations the LU age is twice the EU age.

for both models ought to be given. The most probable age of the sample is somewhere between the two estimates. Most teeth older than the last interglaciation which is widely accompanied by a more pluvial climate have accumulated considerable amounts of uranium and therefore most ESR age estimates of such teeth are associated with large uncertainties (> 25%). It is *important to note that the EU age estimate is the minimum possible age.* An overall precision of less than 7% can be obtained for teeth with low U-concentrations (see e.g., Grün *et al.* 1990).

A good example of the relative quality of ESR age estimates is given by the investigation of Pech de l'Aze II (Grün *et al.* 1991a, see Figure 8.8 and 8.9). In the upper part of the sediment package the U-concentrations are relatively low and the discrepancies between the EU and LU uptake are very small. Together with sedimentological and palaeontological evidence it becomes possible to establish a tight chronology for these layers. The scatter of the age results for repeated measurements and the scatter of the age results for teeth from a given geological unit are small, especially when disregarding those teeth with higher U-concentrations. Below layer 4, all teeth have considerably higher U-concentrations resulting in a large discrepancy between EU and LU age estimates. There is clearly a hiatus between the deposition of layer 4 and layer 5 which corresponds to the last interglacial, with a warmer and probably more pluvial climate. This may explain why during this time, water (carrying uranium) was mobilised and the teeth of the lower levels accumulated uranium.

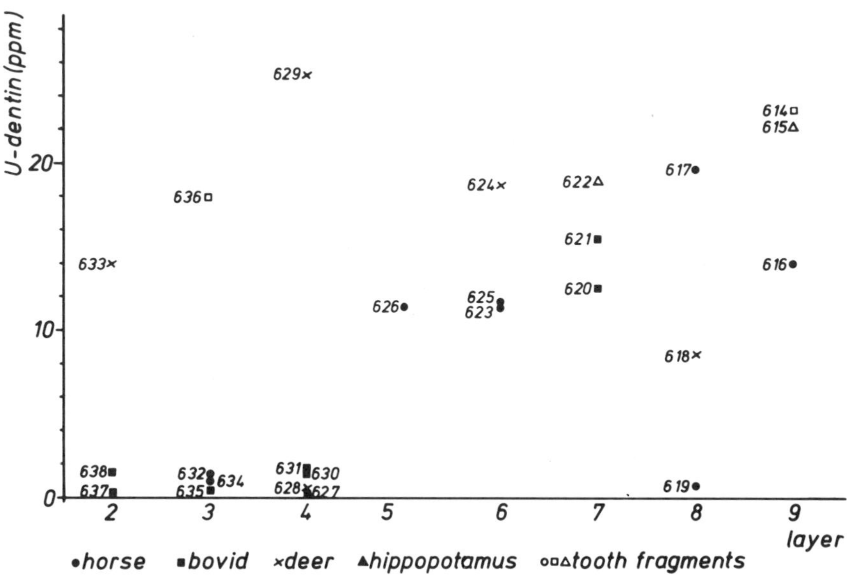

Figure 8.8. Uranium concentrations in dentine of teeth from Pech de l'Azé II (see Fig. 8.9).

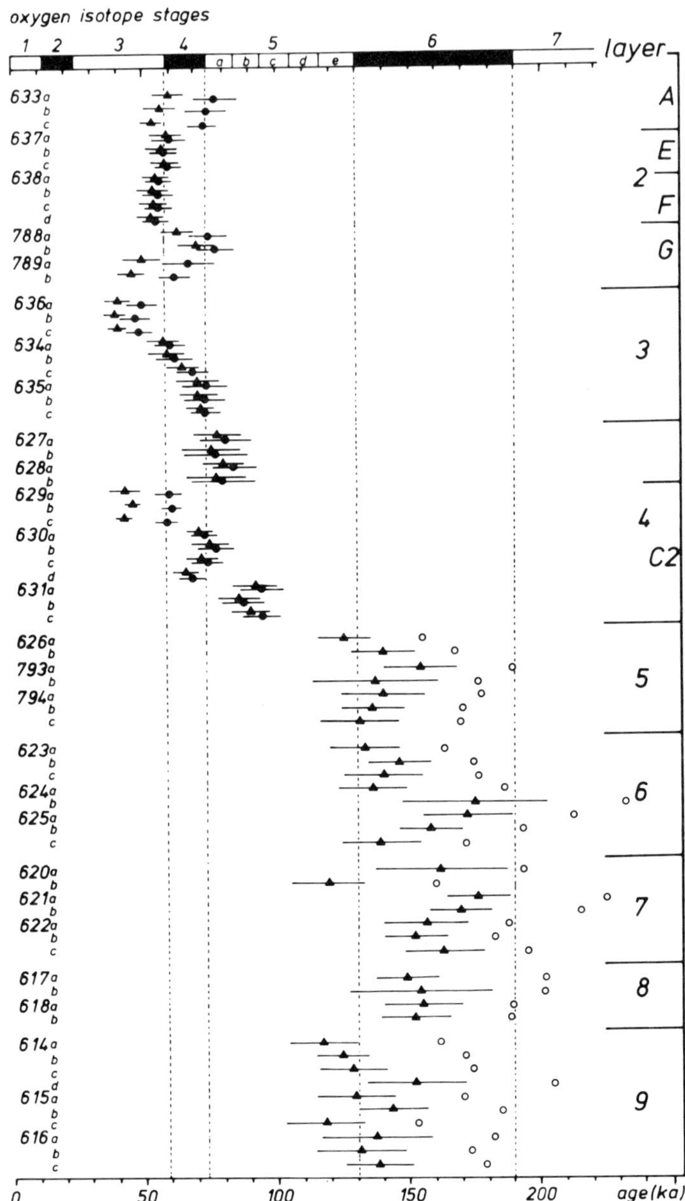

Figure 8.9. ESR age estimates of teeth from Pech de l'Aze II. Triangles: mean EU ages with errors, closed circles: mean LU ages with errors, open circles: mean LU age estimates. In layers 2 to 4, the U-concentration in the teeth is very small and there is little difference between EU and LU age estimates. For teeth with higher U-concentrations, sometimes EU age estimates show a better internal consistency with the rest of the data set (e.g. 633, 788), for other samples (e.g. 636, 629) the LU age estimates give a better consistency. The hiatus between layers 4 and 5 seems to correspond to the last interglacial period (oxygen isotope stage 5) which seems to have caused the increased U-concentrations in the teeth of the lower layers 5 to 9.

For the upper levels, it is not possible to postulate a general U-uptake model. Most larger teeth have low U-concentrations and therefore the EU and LU age estimates do not differ to a great extent. These teeth should give the most reliable results. For the teeth with higher U-concentrations, sometimes the EU uptake results seem to yield a better internal consistency (e.g., 633, 788) whilst in other cases the LU results seem more appropriate (636, 629). Without further evidence one can only assume that the ESR ages calculated with the EU and LU models more or less bracket the true age.

The ESR results for layers 5 to 9 would indicate without further information a deposition somewhere between 100 and 250 ka (representing a time range corresponding to oxygen isotope stages 5 to 7, Martinson *et al.* 1987). If it was known that the sediments relate to a glacial period, an assignment to stage 6 is possible. If the sediments were of interglacial character (they are not!) the ESR results would not allow the distinction between the last and the penultimate interglaciation (stages 5 and 7). However, the combination of faunal, sedimentological and archaeological evidence and ESR data results in a clear assignment of layers 5 to 9 to the penultimate glaciation (stage 6).

Isochrone Dating

Blackwell and Schwarcz (1993) have developed an isochrone technique enabling the determination of ESR ages without knowledge of the external dose rate. This is of particular advantage when ESR samples originate from museum collections and it is not possible to measure the γ-dose rate at the original locality. Figure 8.10 shows the principles: the method only works if the sub-samples have varying U-concentrations, resulting in a range of different combined enamel/dentine dose rates. Several D_E values are determined for a single tooth and are plotted versus the combined enamel and dentine dose rates for the two U-uptake models. A linear fit can be applied to the two data sets. In an ideal case, the two extrapolations will intersect the Y-axis at one point which corresponds to the total external dose (sediment β and γ-dose rates and cosmic dose rate). The slopes of the two lines give the EU and LU ESR age estimates for the sample.

This method has been applied in a test on samples from Bau de l'Aubesier (Blackwell and Schwarcz 1993) yielding a reasonable agreement between the isochrone ESR age estimates and independent U-series results.

The isochrone method actually has the advantage that ESR ages can be determined on teeth being completely independent of the U-uptake mode: as shown above, in an ideal case the linear fits of the EU and LU data intersect the dose axis at the same point. If the total external dose rates can be measured, the age of the sample can simply be derived by dividing the external dose by the external dose rates. However, tests to validate the latter procedure have so far been inconclusive.

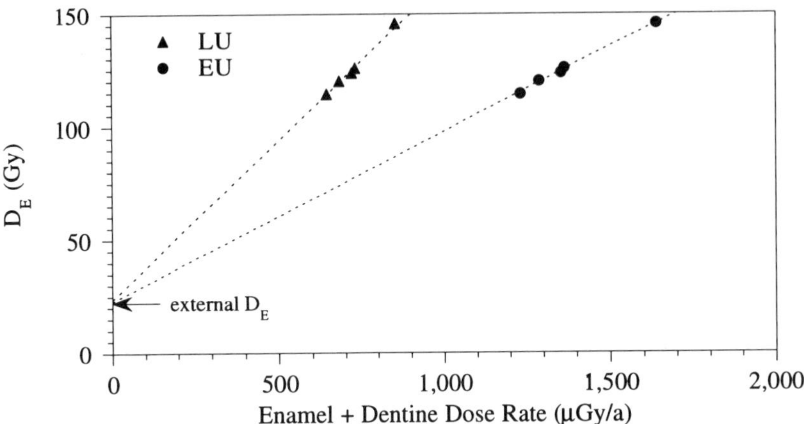

Figure 8.10. Isochrone dating (data from Blackwell and Schwarcz 1993). The dose rate which is dependent on the uranium in the teeth (dentine and enamel) is calculated for the early (EU) and linear (LU) uranium uptake models and plotted versus the measured D_E values. When these dose rates vary significantly, a linear extrapolation can be carried out and, in an ideal case, both lines intersect the Y-axis in one point. The intersection is the external dose. The slopes of the two lines can be used for calculating EU and LU age estimates without considering the external dose at all. This is of advantage when the ESR samples originate from museum collection and no *in situ* measurements can be carried out. On the other hand, if precise external dose rate values can be determined, ESR ages can be calculated which are independent of the uranium uptake by dividing the external dose by the external dose rate.

Combined ESR U-Series Dating

Grün *et al.* (1988a) proposed a one-parameter equation to describe uranium accumulation in tooth enamel (the model does not account for uranium leaching):

$$U(t) = U_m\ (t/T)^{p+1} \tag{4}$$

where U(t) = U-concentration at time t; U_m= measured U concentration; T = age and p = diffusion parameter.

The time dependency of U-uptake for some given p-values are illustrated in Figure 8.11(top). It can be seen that a p-value of p=-1 corresponds to a closed system (equal to the EU model), p=0 represents a linear uptake and higher values a supralinear U-accumulation. The measured $^{230}Th/^{234}U$ and $^{234}U/^{238}U$ ratios are used to establish the relationship between the p-value and a corresponding U-series age. Figure 8.11(middle) shows that a nearly linear relationship exists between the two parameters and hence the dose a sample has received at any given time can be calculated by considering the p/t relationship. The projection of the measured dose value of the enamel on this function

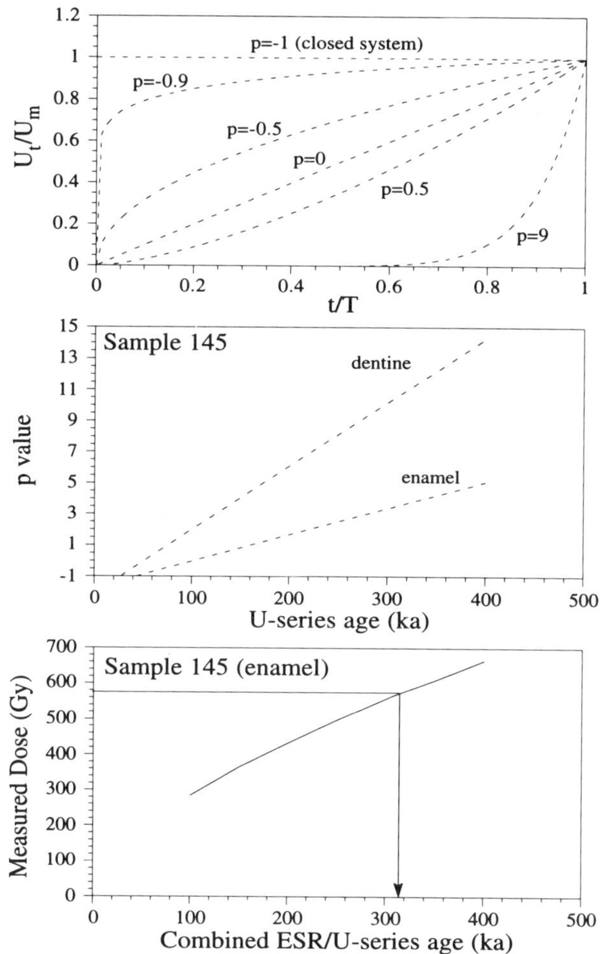

Figure 8.11. (upper): Uranium accumulation for selected p-values. A closed system (= EU model) is represented by a p-value of −1. The LU model corresponds to a p-value of 0. (middle): Relationship between p-values and U-series age for measured $^{234}U/^{238}U$ and $^{230}Th/^{234}U$ ratios for sample 145 (Hoxne). The relationship between p-value and U-series age is nearly linear (i.e. doubling the p-value results in nearly twice the U-series age). (lower): Plot of the dose that a piece of enamel has received based on the p/t relationship shown in the middle diagram.

(Figure 8.11, base) results in the combined ESR U-series age. The associated p-values follow from Figure 8.11(middle).

Until recently, only one experimental study has been published (Grün *et al.* 1988a). This reflects the fact that U-concentrations in enamel are usually very low and alpha spectrometry results have very large uncertainties, which results in large uncertainties in the modelling. New advances in U-series dating using mass spectrometers (Edwards *et al.* 1987a, 1987b) allow the measurement of U-series ratios with great accuracy on relatively small samples with low U concentrations. A new mass spectrometric study by McDermott *et al.* (1993) on Israeli palaeoanthropological sites is discussed below.

Why Is It Not Possible to Date Bones by ESR?

Although this application of ESR dating was reviewed by Grün and Schwarcz (1987), their conclusion that bones are not datable with ESR has not been widely recognised. Their views result from the following well known observations: (i) bones usually absorb more uranium than teeth and (ii) the mineral phase in bones is only somewhere in the region of 40–60% (enamel ca. 96%). Bones also contain a large proportion of an amorphous phase with a very similar chemical composition to hydroxyapatite. Along with the alteration of the organic constituents in bone during fossilisation, the mineralogic compounds change and conversion of the amorphous phase into hydroxyapatite is observed (Newesely 1989) as well as growth of the crystal size of hydroxyapatite (Hassan *et al.* 1977) even under subaerial conditions (Tuross *et al.* 1989). Formation of the new mineral phase (with new defects = traps) with time must generally lead to an age under-estimation regardless of the U-uptake model applied. This was demonstrated by Grün and Schwarcz (1987) who compared dating results of tooth enamel and dentine (which is similar to bone). Any ESR dating result on bone has to be regarded as the absolute age minimum. However, this may sometimes present valuable chronological information (see discussion on the age of the Petralona cranium).

Oduwole and Sales (1991) have suggested an alternative ESR procedure for dating bones: they observed that the ESR signal begins to fade immediately after irradiation. In older bones this fading component becomes smaller relative to the total signal and therefore this effect was suggested as a dating technique. The fading has been attributed to collagen, proteins or surface interactions of small sized hydroxyapatite crystals (Ostrowski *et al.* 1974). If the fading is controlled by the latter process, it actually shows the crystallinity of the hydroxyapatite component in the bone. The crystallinity is indeed age dependent, but is also influenced by many other processes (see previous paragraph).

Dating Range

The upper dating range of the ESR technique is mainly controlled by thermal stability of the paramagnetic centres. Trapped electrons only have a limited probability of staying in the traps. After some time, which is temperature dependent, the electrons leave the traps and recombine with holes. The thermal stability describes the mean life (T) of a trapped electron at the defect site. The influence of detrapping on age is negligible only if the mean life is approximately ten times higher than the age of the sample.

Preliminary annealing experiments by Schwarcz (1985) suggested a mean life in the range of 10 to 100 Ma. Apart from a very large scattering, an investigation of teeth from Sterkfontein (Schwarcz *et al.* 1994) showed no particular trend of underestimation in an age range of 1.6 to 2.4 Ma, which corresponds more or less to the expected age (Grine 1988). Therefore, the thermal stability seems sufficient for dating middle and late Pleistocene samples.

The lower dating range is determined by the sensitivity of the ESR spectrometer. It is easily possible to detect a signal that is generated by 1 Gy. This may correspond to a few thousand years in a low dose rate environment or a few tens of years in a high dose rate environment.

Case Study: The ESR Dating Results from the Levant

It has been known for many years that modern humans evolved from or replaced Neanderthals in Europe at sometime in the range of 35,000 to 40,000 years. This Eurocentric picture was then transposed to other areas and it was therefore thought that Neanderthal sites in the Levant, such as Kebara and Tabun were somewhat older than 45,000 years and that the sites where early modern humans were found, Qafzeh and Skhul, were somewhat younger. The following ESR dating studies of the hominid bearing sites in the Levant illustrate the potential of ESR dating of tooth enamel in archaeology and palaeoanthropology.

Kebara

The first thermoluminescence dating study in the Levant was carried out on the Neanderthal site of Kebara (Valladas *et al.* 1987). The age of about 60,000 years (60±4 ka) was taken as a confirmation that TL dating of burnt flint may be used as a reliable dating method. Later, an ESR dating study (Schwarcz *et al.* 1989) yielded age estimates of 60±6 ka (EU) and LU age estimates of 64±6 ka. Both the EU and LU results fall well within range of the TL results.

Qafzeh

The site of Qafzeh contained remains of at least 20 hominids which are generally regarded as early modern humans. The publication of TL age estimates of 92±5 ka carried out on 20 burnt flint samples from layers XVII to XXIII (Valladas *et al.* 1988) caused a serious disturbance in palaeoanthropological circles. Although some workers had already suggested earlier (Bar-Yosef and Vandermeersch 1981) that the site may be as old as 100,000 years, others rejected the dates because it was felt that the dates could not be verified independently and could be inaccurate, were still experimental, or would not stand the test of time (see citations in Grün and Stringer 1991). A subsequent ESR dating study (Schwarcz *et al.* 1988b) yielded EU and LU age estimates of 100±10 ka and 120±8 ka, respectively (on 19 sub-samples, the complete data set is shown in Figure 8.12).

Skhul

After the publication of the Qafzeh age estimates, the question arose about the age of Skhul, another site where early modern humans had been found. A first ESR study on multiple subsamples of two teeth yielded EU ages of 81±15 ka and LU ages of 110±12 years (Stringer *et al.* 1989). These results seemed to confirm the antiquity of the site. However, further ESR studies (McDermott *et al.* 1993) showed a larger scattering of the results on individual teeth, some of which being as young as 46±5 ka. On the one hand, the age spread can be interpreted that there were two faunal stages within layer B, on the other, this could be used to question the antiquity of the site. A judgement is difficult as the provenance of the samples within the site is ambiguous. Recent TL results yielded ages of 119±18 ka for layer B (Mercier *et al.* 1993).

Tabun

The archaeological layers of Tabun contain a long record of Palaeolithic industries and have been used as a reference sequence for the Levant. The chronology of the Tabun layers has therefore major implications for the archaeology in the Near East. According to Jelinek (1982a,b), the whole sequence (layers E to B) was deposited between 100 to 40 ka. A revision by Bar-Yosef (1989) resulted in the proclamation of a long hiatus between layers D and C so that layers E to D were deposited between 150 to 100 ka.

The ESR results on the Neanderthal site of Tabun have been extensively used to demonstrate the limited value of ESR dating (Bowdler and Cavalli-Sforza 1992). The study was carried out on the Garrod's collection stored in the British Museum (Grün *et al.* 1991b). The stratigraphy derived from the ESR results is considerably older than anything previously proposed (see Figure 8.13) and has, if correct, several implications: (i) Neanderthals and modern humans have occupied the same geographical area for considerable time spans (which does not mean that they lived there side by side at the same time), (ii) the archaeological sequence of Tabun, which has served as a reference for the types of industries in the Levant, is considerably older than previously assumed, and (iii), the ESR results are in contradiction to chronologies based on microfaunal evidence. A TL study on burnt flint has provided a chronology for Tabun that is even older than the ESR results (Mercier 1992).

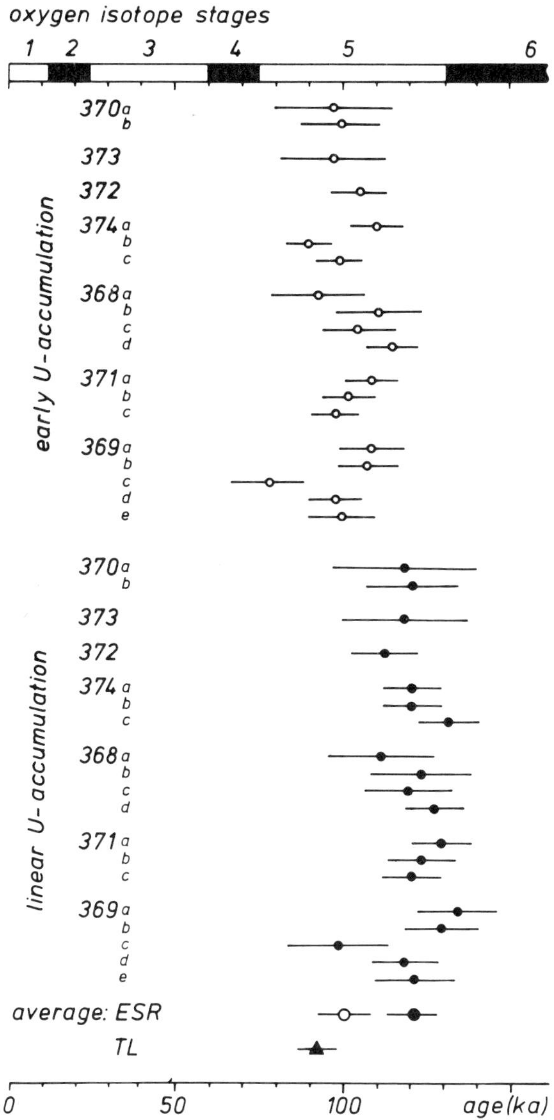

Figure 8.12. ESR age results on teeth from Qafzeh. Open circles: mean EU ages with errors; closed circles: mean LU ages with errors. Triangle: TL results from Valladas *et al.* (1988).

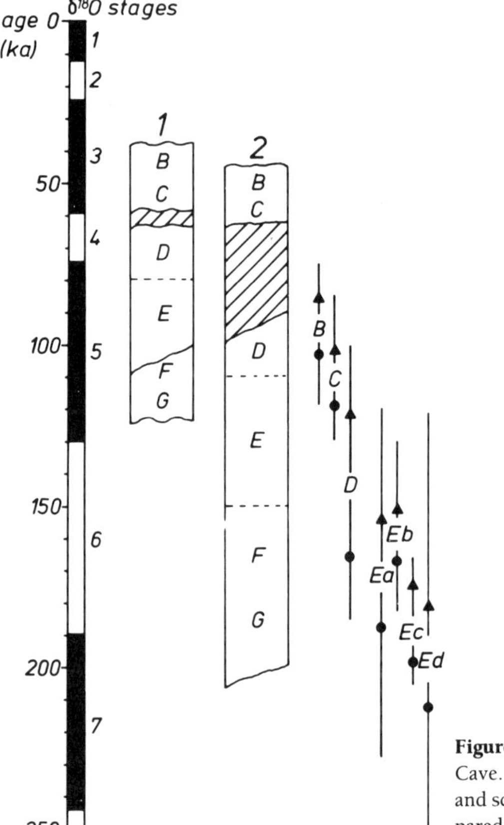

Figure 8.13. Three chronologies for Tabun Cave. Scheme 1 after Jelinek (1982a, 1982b) and scheme 2 after Bar-Yosef (1989) are compared with the averaged ESR results (Grün *et al.* 1991b).

Combined U-Series/ESR Dating of Skhul, Qafzeh and Tabun

Because of the unsatisfactory situation of not being able to assess the mode of U-uptake, a combined U-series and ESR dating study was carried out (McDermott *et al.* 1993). Figure 8.14 shows the U-series results compared to the EU-ESR results. Apart from a few samples from Skhul, there is a very good agreement between these two data sets. Analysis of uranium uptake (Grün and McDermott 1994: see Figure 8.15) shows that most samples (12 of 15) are closer to EU than LU uptake, five of which represent closed systems. Only one sample is closer to LU and another one shows a supralinear U-uptake. The analytical results of the last sample seems to show U-leaching. Closed system results are also supported by the better agreement between the TL and EU-ESR results at Qafzeh and Kebara. Therefore only the EU-ESR estimates will be further discussed.

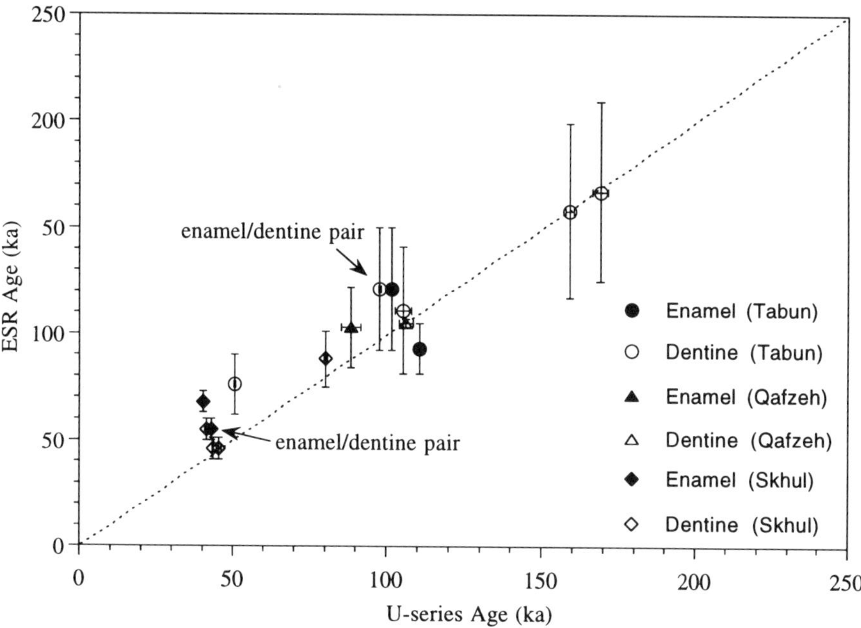

Figure 8.14. Plot of U-series and EU ESR age results for several palaeoanthropological sites in Israel. The error bars of the U-series results are usually within the size of the marker.

Comparison of the ESR Chronology with Other Chronological Evidence

Lithic industries of the Mousterian in the Levant show progressive changes in the ratio of width to thickness of un-retouched flakes within the sequence of Tabun (Jelinek 1982a,b). This master chronology has been used to correlate the lithic industries and chronologies of other sites in the Levant. Mousterian industry of type Tabun B is found in the hominid bearing layers of Kebara and possibly Skhul, Tabun C is found at Qafzeh. The Tabun type C and B have been regarded as late Mousterian with ages of about 55 to 40 ka and 80 to 65 ka for Tabun D (see Figure 8.13).

Microfaunal evidence (Tchernov 1988) suggest that the relative sequence of the above mentioned sites are: Tabun E (about 120 to 100ka), Qafzeh layers XXIV-XIV (100 to 80 ka), Tabun D (80–70 ka), Tabun C/B (55 to 40 ka) contemporaneous with Kebara layers XII to VII. The microfaunal analysis led to the revisions of the Tabun chronology shown in Figure 8.13 (scheme 2).

The ESR age estimates (EU) of the sites in question are: *Tabun*: layer E_a (154±34 ka); layer D (122±20 ka); layer C (102±17 ka); layer B (86±11 ka); *Qafzeh* (100±10 ka); *Skhul* (81±15 ka: Stringer *et al.* (1989) and 46±5 to 93±6 ka: McDermott *et al.* (1993)) and *Kebara* (60±6 ka).

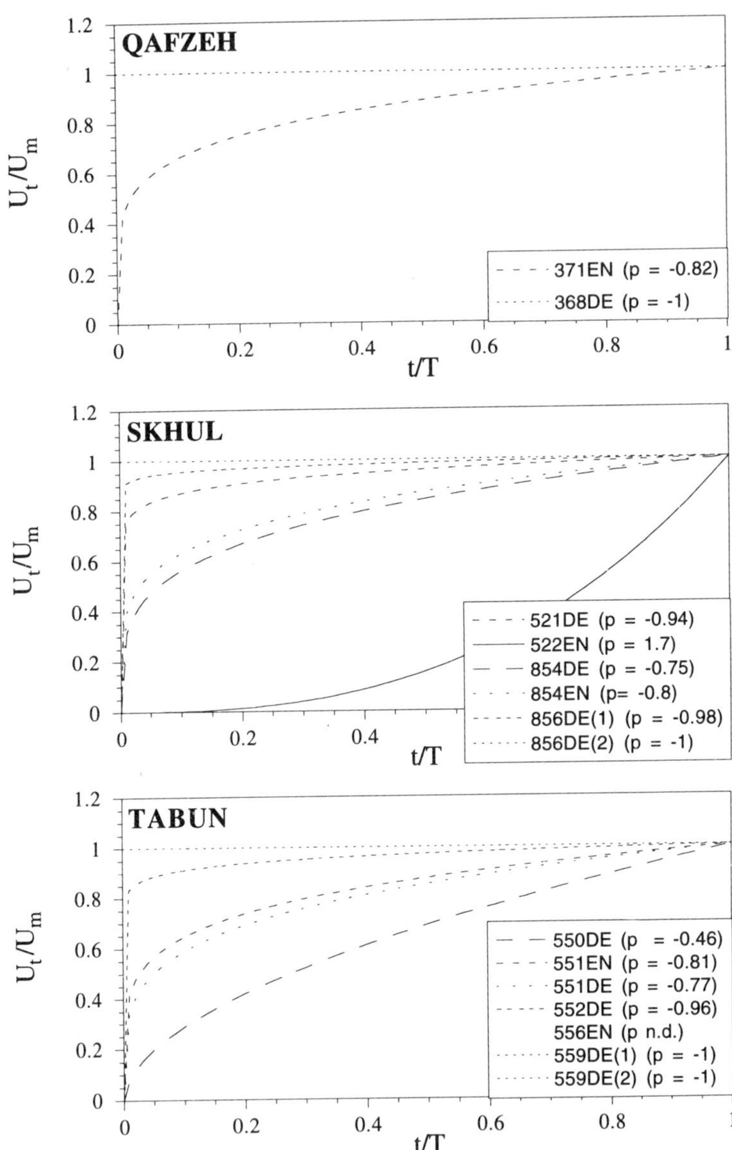

Figure 8.15. U-uptake models for samples from the sites of Qafzeh (top), Skhul (middle) and Tabun (below). Early U-uptake results (p = -1) in a straight horizontal line (as e.g., sample 368DE, Qafzeh) while linear U-uptake (p=0) would correspond in a straight line between (x=0, y=0) and (x=1, y=1); see Figure 11(top). Most samples show a uranium uptake history lying between early and linear models (p-values between -1 and -.5), except sample 522EN (Skhul) which indicates a sub-linear U-accumulation.

It can immediately be seen that the relative chronology based on advances in the production of lithic artifacts is basically duplicated with the ESR results: Tabun C corresponds to Qafzeh; Tabun B relates to Skhul. If the hypothesis is correct that Skhul B contains two distinct faunal elements, but only lithic assemblages of type Tabun B, the latter assemblage would represent a long time span and there would be no problem with (i) relating the results of Tabun B, Kebara and Skhul and (ii) claiming that Tabun B represents a late Mousterian industry. Unfortunately, the uncertainty of the age of layer B at Skhul makes it more difficult to establish the antiquity of the hominid remains of the site.

To summarise, the relative sequence of lithic industries and their correlation with other sites is basically substantiated by the ESR results. The original absolute chronology of these lithic phases (Jelinek 1982a, 1982b) which was based on circumstantial evidence and ^{14}C results, is significantly younger than the ESR results. On the other hand, some of the age assignments based on micro fauna (e.g., Tabun layer E, Qafzeh) agree fairly well with the ESR data. The problem of correlating Qafzeh with a period earlier than Tabun D seems intrinsically limited to the interpretation of the microfaunal analysis.

Other problems arise from the TL dating results of Tabun by Mercier (1992). His results on burnt flint indicate ages of about 150 to 300 ka for layer C, 240 to 350 ka for layer D and about 250 to 400 ka for layer Ea to Ed. This data set will be the subject of future discussions of how these results can be reconciled with the ESR and U-series data as well as the dating results and relative chronologies from the other hominid sites in the Levant.

The implications of the ESR and TL dating results on our understanding of human evolution is summarised in Figure 8.16 (from Grün and Stringer 1991): in Europe early modern humans are younger than about 35 ka whereas Neanderthals are older than about 35 ka. This palaeoanthropological transition is mirrored by the change of lithic industries. The Châtelperronian industry which constitutes a transitional phase between the Middle Palaeolithic (Mousterian) and Upper Palaeolithic (Aurignacian) was first dated at Arcy-sur-Cure by radiocarbon to 33,860±250 BP (Vogel and Waterbolk 1967). Subsequently, Mercier *et al.* (1991) provided TL age estimates of 36.3±2.7 ka for the Châtelperronian at St. Cèsaire where this lithic industry is associated with Neanderthal remains. In Israel, the transition between the Middle and Upper Palaeolithic has been dated to about 45 ka at Boker Tachtit (Marks 1981). However, as long as anatomically modern humans used Middle Palaeolithic tools which are indistinguishable from those found with Neanderthal remains, both hominid groups share the same geographical area. This is not to say that they necessarily lived contemporaneously side by side. With the development of a new stone industry which may be accompanied by new sociological structures, the Neanderthals vanish from the archaeological record in the Levant as well as in Europe.

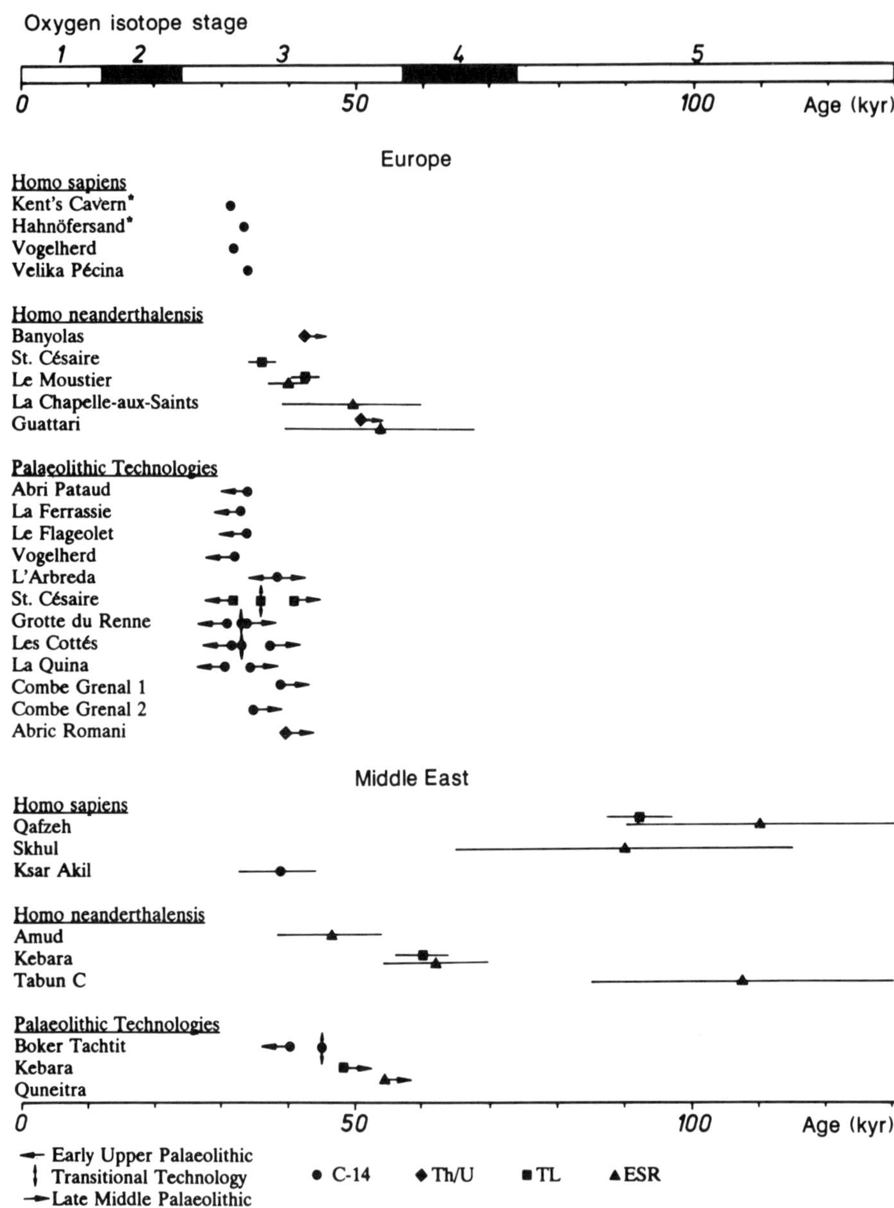

Figure 8.16. Selected age estimates for *Homo sapiens*, *Homo neanderthalensis* and Palaeolithic industries. For source references see Stringer and Grün 1991. An asterisk identifies sites with directly measured specimen.

Conclusions

ESR dating of teeth has turned out to be a valuable tool for establishing archaeological chronologies. Further development is aimed towards analysing very small samples which will then permit the direct age analyses of hominid dental remains (Grün 1995). This approach will overcome one of the main problems in the interpretation of dating results in palaeoanthropological contexts, namely the precise relationship between the samples that have been dated and the hominid specimen whose age is to be determined. Certainly, the best dating strategy is to analyse the human remains themselves.

ESR DATING OF SPELEOTHEMS

Dating of speleothems was the first application of ESR dating (Ikeya 1975). For some time it was thought that this application was particularly promising because relatively small samples could be measured very rapidly, which is a great advantage over radiocarbon and U-series dating. Additionally, a dating range of a few thousand to about a million years seemed possible. However, few systematic ESR dating studies have been carried out on speleothems and it has not been possible to prove the reliability of ESR age estimates beyond the U-series limit of about 350,000 years. Mass spectrometric U-series dating now allows high precision dating on very small samples to about 400,000 years (see Edwards *et al.* 1987a, 1987b), although such analyses have not yet been carried out in archaeological contexts.

The Determination of D_E in Speleothems

The signal at g=2.0005 (see Figure 8.17: upper spectrum) is most commonly used for dating speleothems. The signal also occurs in other secondary carbonates such as aragonitic mollusc shells and corals. For a comprehensive review of this signal at g=2.0005, the reader is referred to Barabas *et al.* (1992a, 1992b). The broad line shown in Figure 8.17 (lower spectrum) has also been used for dating. The use of this ESR signal *may* lead to severe age over-estimations (Grün 1985, 1989a) especially when dating spring deposited travertines (Grün *et al.* 1988b). In some cases, however, reliable age estimates of speleothems can be obtained using this broad line (Wieser *et al.* 1985).

The Determination of $\dot{D}$ in Speleothems

The internal dose rate of speleothems is nearly exclusively controlled by the uranium content (Th and K are usually negligible). The uranium concentrations are usually very low and the contribution from the internal dose rate

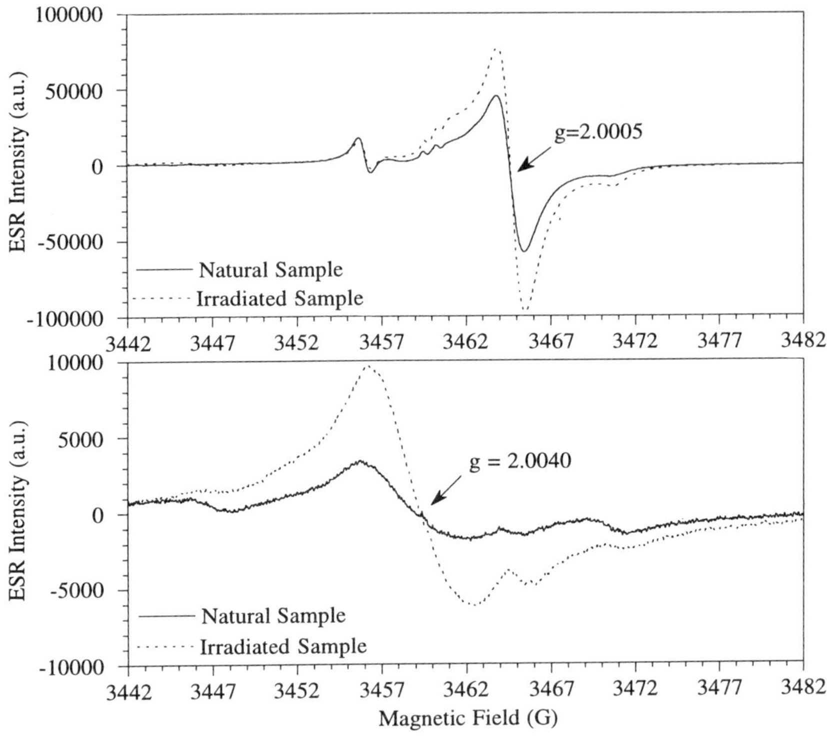

Figure 8.17. ESR spectra of speleothems. The upper figure shows the ESR line around g=2.0005 which has been successfully used for dating. The broad line around g=2.0040, shown in the lower diagram, may lead to ESR age over-estimations.

is usually very small. Lyons and Brennan (1991) determined a value of 0.052±0.026 for the alpha efficiency of speleothem calcite.

The external dose rate is generated by a multitude of sources in a cave. It is not possible to assume this value and it is necessary to determine the external gamma dose rate *in situ* with a thermoluminescence dosimeter or a portable gamma spectrometer. Any assumptions may lead to very erroneous results. The cosmic dose rates is usually negligible in caves.

Case Study: Multiple Studies for Dating the Petralona Hominid

The controversial results on speleothems relating to the Petralona hominid (see Poulianos *et al.* 1982) are the probably the best known ESR dating studies (Ikeya 1980; Hennig *et al.* 1981). There are five distinctive units that have been dated: (i) the red-brown calcite encrustation of the skull, (ii) a thin laminated brown reddish layer on top of the flowstone that underlies the skull,

(iii) a pale grey top layer of the flowstone, (iv) thick white flowstone below this re layer and (v) bone fragments of the skull. The first two units are supposedly younger than the skull whilst units 3 and 4 are older (for details see Grün 1996).

Figure 8.18 summarises the dating results of these units. U-series analyses of the encrustation seemed difficult because of "bone contamination" (Liritzis 1980) or a very low $^{230}Th/^{232}U$ ratio of about 1 (Shen and Yokoyama 1984). Liritzis (1980) reported a non-corrected U-series result of $84^{+46}/_{-32}$ ka which he corrected into an age of about 130 to 150 ka. Shen and Yokoyama (1984) did not carry out any age calculation on their sample. However, the un-corrected isotopic mean values would result in an age of about 82 ka. According to the first group of U-series analyses, the age of the skull is in the range of about 150

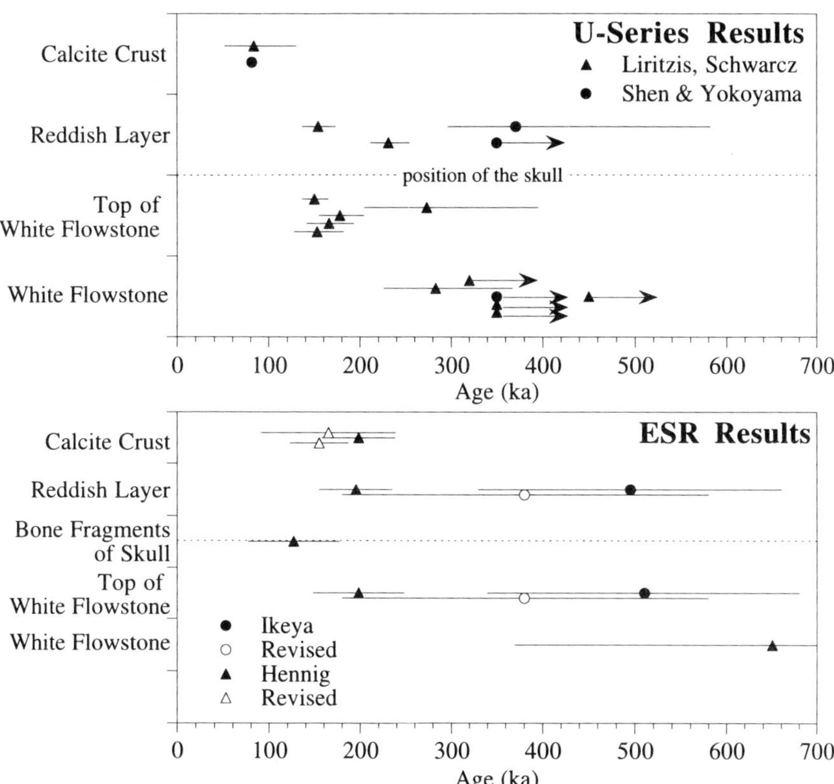

Figure 8.18. Dating results of samples relating to the Petralona hominid. Upper: U-series results of samples from Petralona. The first group of U-series results, triangles, were published by Liritzis (1980, 1982), Schwarcz *et al.* (1980) and Latham and Schwarcz (1992). The second group, circles, were published by Shen and Yokoyama (1984). The arrows indicate infinite U-series results. Lower: ESR dating results from Ikeya (1980) and Hennig *et al.* (1982) with revisions of Grün (1996).

to 200 ka whereas the data of Shen and Yokoyama (1984) suggest an age of greater than 300 ka.

The two samples dated by Ikeya (1980) using ESR relate to the cranium, one from above the skull, which may relate to either unit 1 or 2, and one from the underlying flowstone (unit 3 or 4). The original results of about 350 ka were later doubled to about 700 after re-assessing the dose rate (Poulianos 1980, 1981). Hennig *et al.* (1981) obtained ESR results of about 200±40 ka for the speleothem layers directly over- and underlying the skull and, additionally, an age of 127±35 ka for bone splinters from the hominid specimen. Grün (1996) carried out a re-assessment of the ESR analyses and concluded that the results from Ikeya (1980) translate into an age range of 175 to 580 ka and the ones of Hennig *et al.* (1981) would represent an age range of 90 to 240 ka.

The results of Hennig *et al.* (1981) are in remarkable agreement with one group of U-series results (circles in Fig. 8.18) whereas the ESR age estimates of Ikeya (1980) agree well with the other set of U-series results. The discrepancies between the ESR as well as the U-series laboratories may point to the problem that the samples cannot be related to each other. It may well be that there are several reddish-brownish layers with distinct ages. With respect to the age of the Petralona cranium, Grün (1996) concluded: (i) The cranium has a minimum ESR age of 126±35 ka (ESR of the bone splinters which have to be considered as age underestimations, see remarks on ESR dating of bones), (ii) the crust covering the skull is well within the range of U-series dating, but it may be difficult to determine precise age assessments due to contamination problems, (iii) all U-series studies on the white layer immediately under the reddish top layer of the floor travertine give finite U-series age assessments (i.e., <300 ka), and, (iv) all U-series results on the deeper white travertine are infinite (i.e., >300 ka).

Although this does not allow precise age estimation, the results imply that the age of the Petralona hominid is well within the range of U-series dating, i.e. it is younger than 350,000 years. If it is accepted that the age of the hominid is bracketed by the crust on the cranium (giving the lowest possible age) and the thin white layer immediately under the reddish brown top layer of the floor travertine (giving the upper age), the most likely age of the Petralona hominid is in the range of 150 to 250 ka.

Conclusions

ESR dating of speleothems has been capable of producing comparable results to U-series dating (using α-spectrometry), though with somewhat larger uncertainties. It may be doubted, however, whether there will be many applications of ESR dating on speleothems in the near future. The main reason lies in advances that have been made in U-series dating with the introduction of mass spectrometry enabling high precision dating on very small samples to about 400,000 years. Even the best ESR age estimates will be associated with errors that are at least 5 times larger.

ESR DATING OF SPRING DEPOSITED TRAVERTINES

Spring deposited travertines have often been the focal point of human activities in prehistoric times. Important palaeoanthropological travertine sites spring to mind such as Weimar-Ehringsdorf (Steiner 1975, 1979, Grün *et al.* 1988b), Bilzingsleben (Mania *et al.* 1980; Schwarcz *et al.* 1988a), Verteszöllös (Thoma 1972, Schwarcz and Latham 1984) or Banyolas (Julià and Bischoff 1991).

Dating of spring deposited travertines has been difficult beyond the range of radiocarbon dating because these calcite formations are open systems for uranium, often making U-series dating impossible (e.g. Cherdyntsev *et al.* 1975). ESR dating is severely limited by the fact that the line at g=2.0005 (as used in dating speleothems) occurs only in a small number of samples. The broad line around g=2.0045 cannot be used for dating because large intensities of this line have been measured in recent samples (Grün *et al.* 1988b), hence, the most basic principle for ESR dating, that the ESR intensity is zero at the time of sample formation, is violated.

Determination of D_E in Spring Deposited Travertines

The ESR signals in spring deposited travertines are the same as in speleothems. Successful dating can only be carried out via the signal at g=2.0005. When collecting samples in the field, dense calcite crusts are more likely to contain the signal at g=2.0005 than randomly collected samples (Grün *et al.* 1988b). For the discussion of the ESR lines see the speleothem section.

Determination of $\dot{D}$ in Spring Deposited Travertines

The internal dose rate of spring deposited travertines originates from two sources, (i) uranium in the calcite and (ii) U, Th and K in clay minerals dispersed in the calcite. When collecting dense calcite crusts, the clay mineral contents is negligible (Grün *et al.* 1988b). As with speleothems the U-concentration is very low. The alpha efficiency is the same.

The external dose rate is also usually low. For the calculation of the external gamma dose rate, disequilibria in the U-decay chains have to be considered. It is necessary to measure the external gamma dose rate *in situ* with a portable gamma spectrometer. The cosmic dose rate has to be carefully considered as it may constitute a large part of the total dose rate.

Case Study: Weimar Ehringsdorf

The carbonate deposits at Weimar-Ehringsdorf have been subdivided into two units, the Lower and the Upper Travertine, separated by a loessic deposit, the so-called "Pariser" horizon. Excavations of the Lower Travertine revealed several archaeological strata which also contained the fossil remains of several human remains (Behm-Blancke 1960). In particular, the cranial fragments represent a mixture of modern and Neanderthal characteristics (see Cook *et al.* 1982). The fauna of the travertines are fully interglacial whereas the Pariser horizon represents a cold climate.

Numerous U-series dating studies gave somewhat contradictory results: Cherdyntsev *et al.* (1975) recognised that travertines represent an open system for uranium and therefore suggested averaging the analytical measurements resulting in an age of 115±30 ka for the site. Brunnacker *et al.* (1983) as well as Blackwell and Schwarcz (1986) faced the open system problem which basically leads to a very large scattering of U-series age estimates (see Figure 8.19). The U-series results suggested, however, that the Upper Travertine is of last interglacial age whilst the deeper deposits of the Lower Travertine correspond to the penultimate glaciation, around 200 to 240 ka. Blackwell and Schwarcz (1986) speculated that the higher layers of the Lower Travertine may have been deposited during a glacial period (stage 6) at about 160 ka.

The samples of the study of Brunnacker *et al.* (1983) were also analysed using ESR (Grün *et al.* 1988b, Schwarcz *et al.* 1988a). Only a small number of samples showed the line at g=2.0005 which can be used for ESR dating. Figure

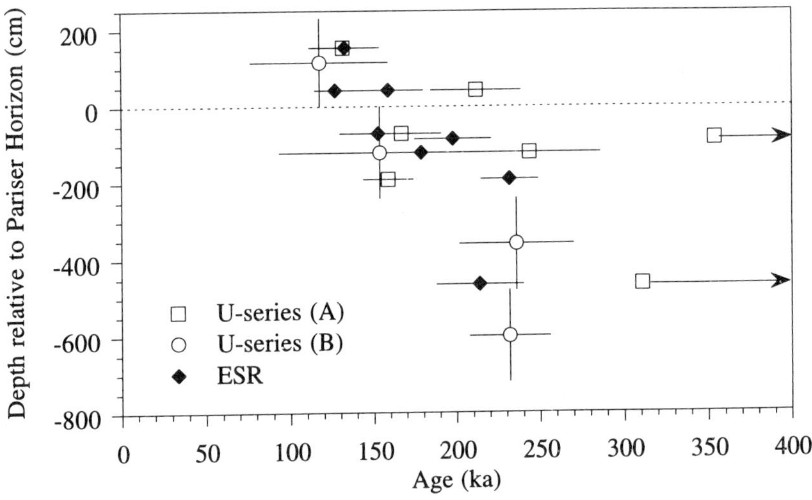

Figure 8.19. Dating results for the travertines at Weimar-Ehringsdorf. The ESR and U-series results (U-series A: Brunnacker *et al.* 1983) were carried out in the same samples. The arrows on the U-series results indicate infinite age results. The second set of U-series results (U-series B: Blackwell and Schwarcz 1986) gives averages for several samples for the Upper Travertine and three subdivisions of the Lower Travertine. The age results imply that the lower part of the Upper Travertine and the upper part of the Lower Travertine may have been deposited during cold stage 6. However, the scatter of the data does not allow any definite statements to be made in this respect.

8.19 shows re-evaluated ESR and U-series age estimates. There is a clear indication that the Upper Travertine was deposited around 100 to 150 ka, very likely corresponding to the last interglacial climatic optimum and that most of the Lower Travertine relates to the penultimate interglaciation. The ESR data are not good enough to support the speculation of Blackwell and Schwarcz (1986) that about the upper third of the Lower Travertine was deposited during the cold stage 6.

Conclusions

ESR dating of travertines is strongly affected by the lack of suitable ESR signals in the majority of samples. Furthermore, spring deposited travertines usually show open system behaviour with respect to uranium, but also with respect to crystallisation processes. Meaningful ESR results can only be obtained in conjunction with detailed studies of the sedimentology, fauna and flora as well as other dating methods.

ESR DATING OF SHELLS

Although shells occur abundantly in archaeological deposits, few ESR dating studies have been carried out in archaeological contexts. Most studies were focussed on the establishment of chronologies for coastal deposits (e.g., Ikeya and Ohmura 1981, Radtke *et al.* 1985, Radtke 1989, Molodkov 1988, 1993, Imai and Shimokawa 1993, Skinner and Shawl 1994) yielding promising dating results. Some ESR studies have also been carried out on ostrich egg shells, a material that is particularly well suited for amino acid racemisation dating (Brooks *et al.* 1990, 1993, Miller *et al.* 1992). However, ESR studies resulted in serious age underestimations (Wendorf *et al.* 1987), which may be attributable to a very low thermal stability of the ESR signals.

Determination of D_E in Shells

The ESR spectra of shells are quite complicated (Figure 8.20, top) Spectra of aragonitic shells show the signal at g=2.0005, however, it is interfered with by other signals, which are thermally unstable. There have been several approaches to define a dating signal (Figure 8.20, bottom), however, it cannot yet be concluded which one leads to the most reliable dating results.

Regardless of measurement conditions, Katzenberger and Willems (1988) reported that the dose response of mollusc shells is very complicated and shows inflexion points (see Figure 8.21, top). In some samples, this effect is not very pronounced, in others it may be very strong and can lead to serious ambiguities (Figure 8.21, bottom).

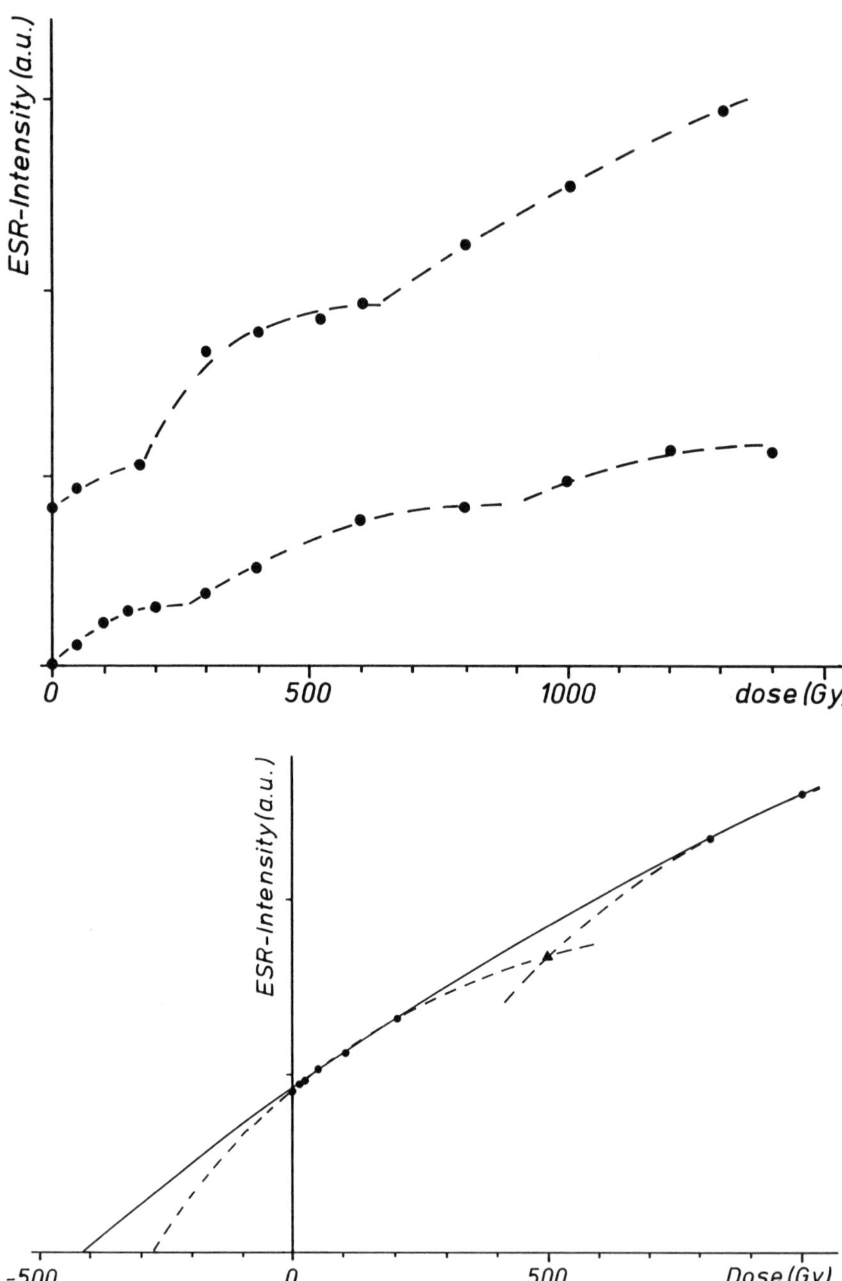

Figure 8.20. ESR spectra of aragonitic mollusc shells (solid lines: natural sample, dotted lines: irradiated sample). These samples do not have a clearly defined dating signal. Spectra A: Radtke *et al.* (1985) suggested using a signal intensity as indicated in the upper spectra. Spectra B: Katzenberger *et al.* (1988) could separate a clearly defined signal by measuring at 145°K (-130°C). Spectra C: Molodkov (1988) suggested use of very high microwave powers which suppress the sharp, unstable signals (base).

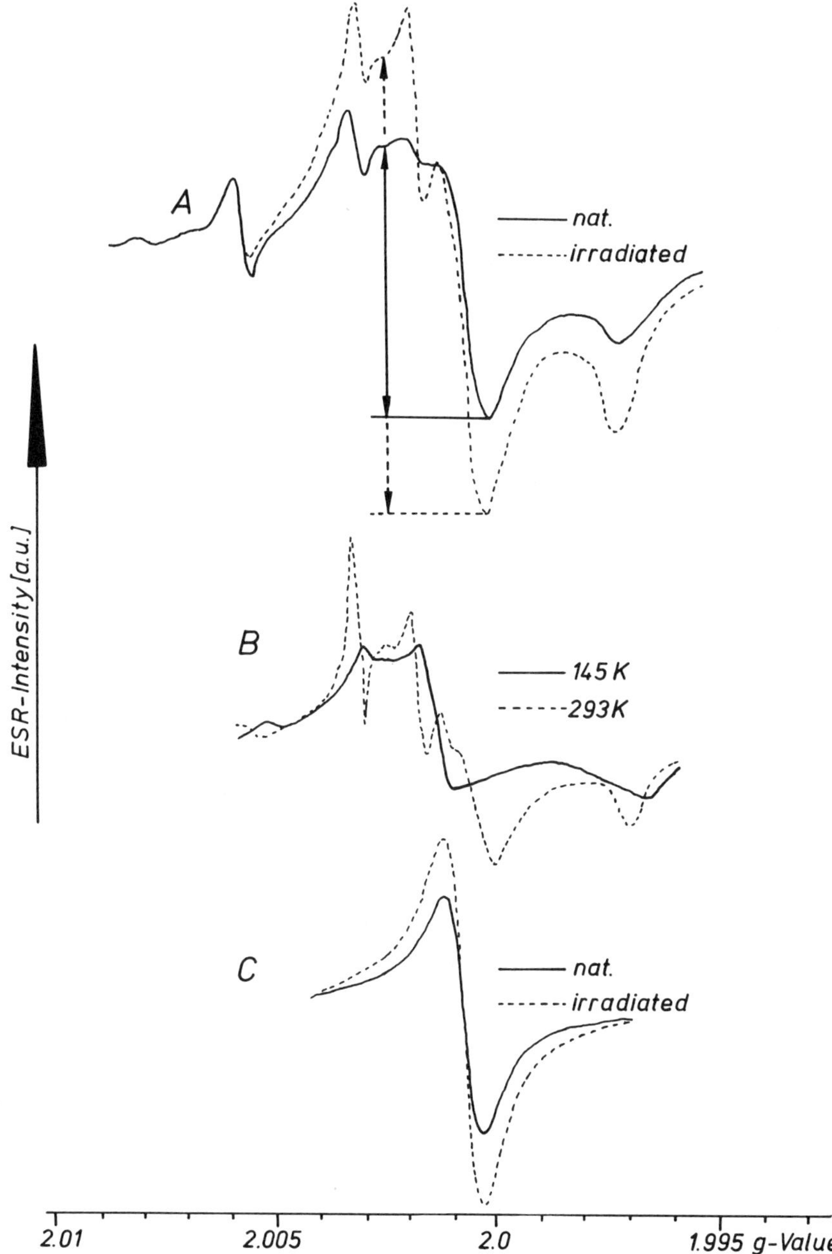

Figure 8.21. (Upper): Dose response curves of a Pleistocene and a recent mollusc sample (after Katzenberger and Willems 1988). The dose response cannot be described by a simple mathematical model and precise accumulated dose estimation is difficult. (Lower): Interpretation of a hypothetical data set. The triangle may be an outlier and the accumulated dose value would result from the solid line. On the other hand, the triangle may indicate a more complex dose response, as above, and the correct accumulated dose value would result from the dotted lines. Correct assessments cannot be made without further measurements.

Determination of $\dot{D}$ in Shells

Shells are usually thin walled. While it is possible to remove about 50 μm from each side for the elimination of the volume that has received external alpha rays, it is often not possible to remove 2 mm from each side to eliminate the influence of external beta rays. Therefore, the sediment of the immediate surroundings has to be collected and analysed for the calculation of the external beta dose rate. The external gamma dose rate should be measured *in situ*. Shells are usually free of Th and K and therefore need only be analysed for U. The U-decay chains are in disequilibrium and an α-efficiency of 0.1 has been measured by Radtke *et al*. (1985).

Case Study: Batadomba Cave, Sri Lanka

Abeyratne *et al*. (1997) have carried out a multi dating study on Batadomba Cave, Sri Lanka. The cave was first excavated from 1937 to 1940 and several human remains were found (Deraniyagala 1940). Further excavations were carried out and the whole sequence was analysed by radiocarbon dating (Kennedy and Deraniyagala 1989). The archaeological deposits are of particular importance because human remains were found in clear association with geometric microliths and dated to about 28,500 B.P. Such stone tools occur in Europe at much later times.

Sediment samples for OSL dating were collected *in situ* whereas the shells for ESR dating, all but one of the snail species *Paludomus*, originated from the earlier excavations at the site and were curated by the Department of Archaeology, University of Colombo. Unfortunately, no shell samples were available from the lower layers. Figure 8.22 shows the results of the dating study (Abeyratne *et al*. 1997). The previously established charcoal chronology shows a more or less regular age increase with the strata at the site, spanning from about 10,000 for layer 3 to about 28,500 B.P. for layer 7C. The OSL ages seem to have a tendency towards younger age estimates whereas the shells seems to result in somewhat older age estimates, and also showing one large outlier. The main problem of shell ESR age estimations lies in the recognition of inflexion points (Figure 8.21). Because there is always some scatter of the data points, less pronounced inflexion points are hardly visible. It may well be that the outlier in Layer 5 can be attributed to such an effect. Bard *et al*. (1993) showed that in the time range of 10,000 to 20,000 years, radiocarbon produces age estimates that are increasingly too young (1000 years at about 10,000 years and 3500 years at about 20,000 years), due to an increased production of ^{14}C in the upper atmosphere. Some of the differences between the radiocarbon and ESR age estimates can be attributed to this effect (see discussion in Chapter 3, Radiocarbon Dating). The study shows that the systematic application of ESR dating on mollusc shells may provide reasonable chronologies for archaeological sites. However, outliers can only be

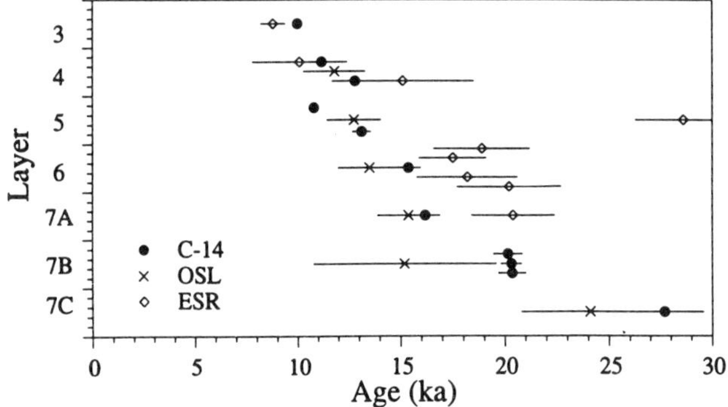

Figure 8.22. Dating results on various materials from Batadomba Cave, Sri Lanka (from Abeyratne *et al.* 1997). The radiocarbon charcoal results indicate a depositional history of between about 10,000 and 28,000 B.P. The OSL results seem to have a trend towards younger ages whereas the ESR shell results show older ages compared to the radiocarbon results. In the range of 10,000 to 20,000 years, radiocarbon results may underestimate the correct age between 1,000 and 3,000 years (Bard *et al.* 1993).

recognised if multiple samples are analysed from each layer. As it is generally the case, reliable chronologies can only be established through the application of several, independent dating methods.

Conclusions

At many archaeological sites, shells are the only material that can be dated. ESR dating can be carried out relatively quickly on small samples. In some cases ESR can be used for the investigation of reworking processes. ESR dating of shells seems to be underutilised in archaeological studies.

ESR DATING OF BURNT FLINT

Burnt flint can be found at many prehistoric human occupation sites. Thermoluminescence dating of burnt flint has greatly contributed to our understanding of modern human evolution (e.g., Mercier *et al.* 1995). The first ESR investigations on flint were related to the heating history of the specimens (Griffiths *et al.* 1982, 1983). So far, there have been only a few dating studies on flint (e.g., Porat 1991, Porat *et al.* 1994).

Determination of D_E in Flint

There are two signals that have been used for the measurement of the DE value of burnt flint, the E′ centre at room temperature, and the Al- centre at liquid nitrogen temperature (about - 200°C). There are two problems related to the precise measurement of these centres: Porat and Schwarcz (1995) show that the thermal stability of the E′ centre is very low (less than 100 years). Although this very low thermal stability is in contradiction to the measurement of geological E′ dose values in a variety of samples (Porat and Schwarcz 1991, Porat *et al.* 1994), the use of the E′ centre seems to lead to systematic age underestimations which have been attributed by Toyoda and Schwarcz (1996) to a superimposed, unstable signal. The Al- centre, on the other hand, is strongly superimposed by an isotropic signal (C), probably due to amorphous carbon. Two ways of eliminating this carbon signal have been outlined by Porat and Schwarcz (1991) and Walther and Zilles (1994) by using subtraction techniques. All of these studies have in common that the data points often show a very significant scatter and errors in the range of 15 to 30% in the estimation of the DE value are common.

Determination of the $\dot{D}$ in Flint

For the estimation of the dose rate, the internal U, Th and K concentrations have to be measured. In TL studies it has been noticed that the α-efficiency may vary from sample to sample by a factor of three (Mercier *et al.* 1995), generally being in the range of 0.05 to 0.15 (Aitken 1985). So far, no ESR α-efficiency value has been determined. Usually, 2 mm can be removed from the outside of the sample so that only the external gamma dose rate has to be measured and the cosmic dose rate has to be assessed.

Case Study: Kebara

The fossil hominid site of Kebara has been subject to a variety of dating studies (see above). Porat *et al.* (1994) carried out a dating comparison between TL and ESR (see Figure 8.23). As pointed out above, the use of the E′ centre results in a trend of age underestimations. However, the large scatter of the data does not permit the clear conclusion that use of the Al centre results in any better age estimates.

Conclusions

The advantage of ESR over TL lies in the fact that the ESR signals are not light sensitive and therefore sample preparation and measurement can be carried out in ambient light environments. However, there is only limited information in the ESR spectrum to show that the samples were sufficiently heated and all previously acquired ESR intensity was zeroed with the ancient firing. This is a distinct advantage of TL (see Mercier *et al.* 1995). Future efforts must focus on obtaining more precise D_E determinations.

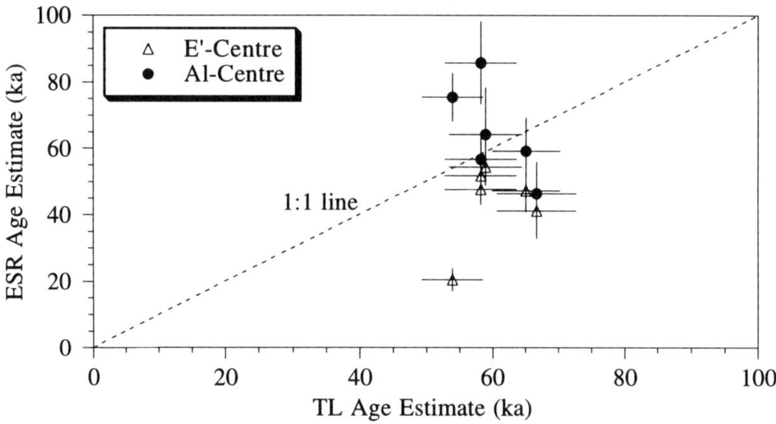

Figure 8.23. Dating results on flint samples from Kebara (data from Porat *et al.* 1994). The ESR results using the E′ centre are all younger than the TL age estimates on the same samples. The results obtained from the Al-centre seem to show a normal distribution around the 1:1 line. Both ESR data sets show a significantly larger age spread than the TL results.

FUTURE DEVELOPMENTS

ESR dating is still in a rapid phase of development. Every year new applications and materials are investigated for ESR dating. Presently there are only about five laboratories in the world working on ESR dating of tooth enamel which is probably the most complicated application of ESR dating. So far, the ESR dating procedures and citation criteria have not been standardised (see Grün 1992).

The new procedure of ESR-U-series dating promises age estimates within the last 300,000 years, probably with a precision of 10% or somewhat less. The analytical procedures are very tedious and can only be carried out by a few laboratories worldwide and these have very little measuring time available. In the foreseeable future combined ESR-U-series dating studies will therefore rarely be carried out.

GENERAL CONCLUSIONS

The application of ESR dating of speleothems in an archaeological context is still not well established. ESR age estimates from the early eighties have to be regarded as less accurate than was claimed in the original publications. ESR dating of tooth enamel is mainly limited by the unknown uranium uptake history. The combination of ESR and U-series analysis may provide archaeology with a powerful tool to extend chronologies well beyond the limit of radiocarbon dating. ESR dating of mollusc shells seem to have potential for archaeological applications and has so far been underutilised.

ACKNOWLEDGMENTS

I wish to thank C.B. Stringer, Natural History Museum, London, for comments and J. Papps and F. M. Grün, Canberra, for corrections on the manuscript.

REFERENCES

Abeyratne, M., Spooner, N., Grün, R., and Head, J. 1997 A multi-dating study on Batadomba Cave, Sri Lanka. *Quaternary Geochronology (Quaternary Science Reviews)* 16: 243–255.

Aitken, M.J. 1985 *Thermoluminescence dating*. New York, Academic Press.

Aitken, M.J. 1990 *Science-based Dating in Archaeology*. London, Longman.

Aitken, M.J. and Xie, J. 1990 Moisture correction for annual gamma dose. *Ancient TL* 8: 6–9.

Barabas, M., Mudelsee, M., Bach, A., Walther, R. and Mangini, A. 1992a General properties of the paramagnetic centre at g=2.0006 in carbonates. *Quaternary Science Reviews* 11: 165–171.

Barabas, M., Mudelsee, M., Walther, R. and Mangini, A. 1992b Dose response and thermal behaviour of the ESR signal at g=2.0006 in carbonates. *Quaternary Science Reviews* 11: 173–179.

Bard, E., Arnold, M., Fairbanks, R.G., and Hamelin, B. 1993 ^{230}Th-^{234}U and ^{14}C ages obtained by mass spectrometry on corals. *Radiocarbon* 35: 191–199.

Bar-Yosef, O. 1989 Geochronology of the Levantine Middle Paleolithic. In Mellars, P. and Stringer, C.B., eds, *The human revolution: Behavioural and biological perspectives on the origins of modern humans, Vol. I*. Edinburgh, Edinburgh University Press: 589–610.

Bar-Yosef, O. and Vandermeersch, B. 1981 Notes concerning the possible age of the Mousterian layers in Qafzeh Cave. In Cauvin, J., and Sanlaville, P., eds, *Préhistoire du Levant*. Paris, CNRS: 281–286.

Behm-Blancke, G. 1960 Altsteinzeitliche Rastplätze im Travertingebiet von Taubach, Weimar, Ehringsdorf. *Alt-Thüringen* 4: 1–246.

Blackwell, B.A. and Schwarcz, H.P. 1993 ESR isochron dating for teeth: a brief demonstration in solving the external dose calculation problem. *Applied Radiation and Isotopes* 44:243–252.

Blackwell, B. and Schwarcz, H.P. 1986 U-series analysis of the lower travertine at Ehringsdorf, DDR. *Quaternary Research* 25: 215–222.

Bowdler, S. and Cavalli-Sforza, L.L. 1992 Fourth Day's Discussion. In Akazawa, T., Aoki, T. and Kimura, T., eds, *The Evolution and Dispersal of Modern Humans in Asia*. Tokyo, Hokusen-Sha: 625–638.

Bowman, S.G.E. 1976 *Thermoluminescence dating, the evaluation of radiation dosage*. Unpublished PhD Thesis, Oxford, University of Oxford.

Brooks, A.S., Hare, P.E., and Kokis, J.E. 1993 Age of early anatomically modern human fossils from the cave of Klasies River Mouth, South Africa. *Yearbook of the Carnegie Institution of Washington* 92: 80–85.

Brooks, A., Kokis, J.E., Miller, G.H., Ernst, R.E., and Wendorf, F. 1990 Chronometric dating of Pleistocene sites: Protein diagenesis in ostrich eggshell. *Science* 248: 60–64.

Brumby, S. 1992 Regression analysis of ESR/TL dose-response data. *Nuclear Tracks* 20: 595–599.

Brunnacker, K., Jäger, K.D., Hennig, G.J., Preuss, J. and Grün, R. 1983 Radiometrische Untersuchungen zur Datierung mitteleuropäischer Travertinvorkommen. *Ethnographisch-Archäologische Zeitschrift* 24: 217–266.

Callens, F.J., Verbeeck, R.M.H., Matthys, P.F.A., Martens, L.C. and Boesman, E.R. (1987) The contribution of CO_3^{3-} and CO_2^- to the ESR spectrum near g=2 of powdered human tooth enamel. *Calcified Tissues International* 41: 124–129.

Chen, T.M., Yang, Q. and Wu, E. 1994 Antiquity of Homo sapiens in China. *Nature* 368: 55–56.

Cherdyntsev, V., Senina, N. and Kuzmina, E.A. 1975 Die Altersbestimmung der Travertine von Weimar-Ehringsdorf. *Abhandlungen des zentralen Geologischen Instituts* 23: 7–14.

Cook, J., Stringer, C.B., Currant, A.P., Schwarcz, H.P. and Wintle, A.G. 1982 A review of the chronology of the European Middle Pleistocene hominid record. *Yearbook of Physical Anthropology* 25: 19–65.

DeCanniere, P., Debuyst, R., Dejehet, F., Apers, D. and Grün, R. 1986 ESR dating: A study of ^{210}Po-coated geological and synthetic samples. *Nuclear Tracks* 11: 211–220.

Deraniyagala, P.E.P. 1940 The Stone Age and cave men of Ceylon. *Journal of the Royal Asiatic Society (Ceylon Branch)* 34: 351–373.

Driessens, F.C.M. 1980, The mineral in bone, dentin and tooth enamel. *Bulletin de la Societe Chimique de Belgique* 89: 663–689.

Edwards, R.L., Chen, J.H., Ku, T.L. and Wasserburg, G.J. 1987a Precise timing of the last interglacial period from mass spectrometric determination of thorium-230 in corals. *Science* 236: 1547–1553.

Edwards, R.L., Chen, J.H. and Wasserburg, G.J. 1987b ^{238}U-^{234}U-^{230}Th-^{232}Th systematics and the precise measurement of time over the past 500,000 years. *Earth and Planetary Science Letters* 81: 175–192.

Griffiths, D.R., Robins, G.V., Chandra, H., McNeil, D.A.C. and Symons, M.C.R. 1982 Trapped methyl radicals in chert. *Nature* 300: 435–436.

Griffiths, D.R., Seeley, N.J., Chandra, H. & Symons, M.C.R. 1983 ESR dating of heated chert. *PACT* 9: 399–409.

Grine, F.E. 1988 *Evolutionary History of the Robust Australopithicines'*. New York, Aldine d'Gruyter.

Grün, R. 1985 Beiträge zur ESR-Datierung. *Sonderveröffentlichungen des Geologischen Instituts der Universität zu Köln* 59: 1–157.

Grün, R. 1986 Beta dose attenuation in thin layers. *Ancient TL* 4: 1–8.

Grün, R. 1989a Electron spin resonance (ESR) dating. *Quaternary International* 1: 65–109.

Grün, R. 1989b *Die ESR-Altersbestimmungsmethode*. Berlin-Heidelberg, Springer: 132 p.

Grün, R. 1992 Suggestions on minimum requirements for reporting ESR age estimates. *Ancient TL* 10: 37–41.

Grün, R. 1995 Semi non-destructive, single aliquot ESR dating. *Ancient TL* 13: 3–7.

Grün, R. 1996 A Re-analysis of ESR dating results associated with the Petralona hominid. *Journal of Human Evolution* 30: 227–241.

Grün, R., Beaumont, P. and Stringer, C.B. 1990 ESR dating evidence for early modern humans at Border Cave in South Africa. *Nature* 344: 537–539.

Grün, R. and Brumby, S. 1994 The assessment of errors in the past radiation doses extrapolated from ESR/TL dose response data. *Radiation Measurements* 23: 307–315.

Grün, R. and McDermott, F. 1994 Open system modelling for U-series and ESR dating of teeth. *Quaternary Geochronology (Quaternary Science Reviews)* 13: 121–125.

Grün, R., Mellars, P. and Laville, H. 1991a ESR chronology of a 100,000-year archaeological sequence at Pech de l'Aze II, France. *Antiquity* 65: 544–551.

Grün, R. and Schwarcz, H.P. 1987 Some remarks on "ESR dating of bones." *Ancient TL* 5: 1–9.

Grün, R., Schwarcz, H.P. and Chadam, J.M. 1988a ESR dating of tooth enamel: Coupled correction for U-uptake and U-series disequilibrium. *Nuclear Tracks* 14: 237–241.

Grün, R., Schwarcz, H.P., Ford, D.C. and Hentzsch, B. 1988b ESR dating of spring deposited travertines. *Quaternary Science Reviews* 7: 429–432.

Grün, R., Schwarcz, H.P. and Zymela, S. 1987 ESR dating of tooth enamel. *Canadian Journal of Earth Sciences* 24: 1022–1037.

Grün, R. and Stringer, C.B. 1991 ESR dating and the evolution of modern humans. *Archaeometry* 33: 153–199.

Grün, R., Stringer, C.B. and Schwarcz, H.P. 1991b ESR dating of teeth from Garrod's Tabun cave collection. *Journal of Human Evolution* 20: 231–248.

Hassan, A.A., Termine, J.D. and Haynes, Jr., C.V. 1977 Mineralogical studies on bone apatite and their implications for radiocarbon dating. *Radiocarbon* 19: 364–374.

Hennig, G.J., Herr, W., Weber, E. and Xirotiris, N.I. 1981 ESR-dating of the fossil hominid cranium from Petralona Cave, Greece. *Nature* 292: 533–536.

Ikeya, M. 1975 Dating a stalactite by electron paramagnetic resonance. *Nature* 255: 48–50.

Ikeya, M. 1980 ESR dating of carbonates at Petralona Cave. *Anthropos (Athens)* 7: 143–150.

Ikeya, M. 1982 A model of linear uranium accumulation for ESR age of Heidelberg, Mauer, and Tautavel bones. *Japanese Journal of Applied Physics* 21: L690-L692.

Ikeya, M. 1993 *New Applications of Electron Spin Resonance-Dating, Dosimetry and Microscopy*. Singapore, World Scientific.

Ikeya, M. and Ohmura, K. 1981 Dating of fossil shells with electron spin resonance. *Journal of Geology* 89: 247–251.

Imai, N. and Shimokawa, K. 1993 ESR ages and trace elements in a fossil mollusc shell. *Applied Radiation and Isotopes* 44: 161–165.

Jelinek, A.J. 1982a The Middle Paleolithic in the Southern Levant with comments on the appearance of modern man (*Homo sapiens*). In Ronen, A., ed, *The Transition from Lower to Middle Paleolithic and the Origin of Modern Man*. BAR Int. Series 151: 57–101.

Jelinek, A.J. 1982b The Tabun Cave and Paleolithic man in the Levant. *Science* 216: 1369–1375.

Julia, R. and Bischoff, J.L. 1991 Radiometric dating of Quaternary deposits and the hominid mandible of Lake Banyolas, Spain. *Journal of Archaeological Science* 18: 707–722.

Katzenberger, O., Debuyst, R., DeCanniere, P., Dejehet, F., Apers, D. & Barabas, M. 1989 Temperature experiments on mollusc samples: an approach to ESR signal definition. *Applied Radiation and Isotopes* 40: 1113–1118.

Katzenberger, O. and Willems, N. 1988 Interferences encountered in the determination of AD of mollusc samples. *Quaternary Science Reviews* 7: 485–489.

Kennedy, K.A.R. and Deraniyagala, S.U. 1989 Fossil remains of 28,000-year-old hominids from Sri Lanka. *Current Anthropology* 30: 394–399.

Latham, A.G. & Schwarcz 1992 The Petralona hominid site: Uranium-series re-analysis of "Layer 10" calcite and associated palaeomagnetic analyses. *Archaeometry* 34: 135–140.

Liritzis, Y. 1980 ^{230}Th/^{234}U dating of spelaeothems in Petralona. *Anthropos* 7: 215–241.

Liritzis, Y. 1982 Petralona Cave dating controversy. *Nature* 299: 280–181.

Lyons, R.G. and Brennan, B.J. 1991 Alpha/gamma effectiveness ratios of calcite speleothem. *Nuclear Tracks* 18: 223–227.

Mania, D., Toepfer, V., and Vlek, E. 1980 *Bilzingsleben I. Homo erectus - seine Kultur und seine Umwelt*. Veröffentlichungen des Landesmuseums für Vorgeschichte in Halle, Berlin.

Marks, A.E. 1981 In: Cauvin, J. and Sanlaville, P., eds, *Prehistoire du Levant*, Paris, CNRS: 287–298.

Martinson, D.G., Pisias, N.G., Hays, J.D., Imbrie, J., Moore, T.C. and Shackleton, N.J. 1987 Age dating and the orbital theory of the ice ages, Development of a high-resolution 0 to 300,000-year chronostratigraphy. *Quaternary Research* 27; 1–29.

Maurer, C.A. 1980 *Electron spin resonance spectroscopy: a potential technique for dating ancient ceramics*. Unpublished Ph.D. thesis, University of Illinois, Urbana.

McDermott, F., Grün, R., Stringer, C.B. and Hawkesworth, C.J. 1993 Mass-spectrometric U-series dates for Israeli Neanderthal/early modern hominid sites. *Nature* 363: 252–255.

McKinney C.R. 1991 *The determination of the reliability of uranium series dating of enamel, dentine and bone*. Unpublished PhD thesis, Southern Methodist University.

Mercier, N. 1992 Apport des méthodes radionucléaires de datation á l'étude du peuplement de l'Europe et du Proche-Orient au cours du Pléistocène moyen et supérieur. Unpublished Ph.D. thesis, University of Bordeaux.

Mercier, N., Valladas, H., Bar-Yosef, O., Vandermeersch, B., Stringer, C. and Joron, J.L. 1993 Thermoluminescence date for the Mousterian burial site of Es-Skhul, Mt. Carmel. *Journal of Archaeological Science* 20: 169–174.

Mercier, N., Valladas, H., Joron, J.L., Reyss, J.L., Lévêque, F. and Vandermeersch. B. 1991 Thermoluminescence dating of the late Neanderthal remains from Saint-Césaire. *Nature* 351: 737–739.

Mercier, N., Valladas, H., and Valladas, G. 1995 Flint thermoluminescence dates from the CFR laboratory at Gif: Contributions to the study of the chronology of the Middle Palaeolithic. *Quaternary Geochronology (Quaternary Science Reviews)* 14: 351–364.

Miller, G.H., Beaumont, P.B., Jull, A.T. and Johnson, B.J. 1992 Pleistocene geochronology and palaeothermometry from protein diagenesis in ostrich eggshells: Implications for the evolution of modern humans. *Philosophical Transactions of the Royal Society of London*, B337: 149–157.

Molodkov, A. 1988 ESR dating of Quaternary shells: recent advances. *Quaternary Science Reviews* 7: 477–484.

Molodkov, A. 1993 ESR-dating of non-marine mollusc shells. *Applied Radiation and Isotopes* 44: 145–148.

Nambi, K.S.V. and Aitken, M.J. 1986 Annual dose conversion factors for TL and ESR dating. *Archaeometry* 28: 202–205.

Newesely, H. 1989 Fossil bone apatite. *Applied Geochemistry* 4: 233–245.

Oduwole, A.D. and Sales, K.D. 1991 ESR signals in bones: Interference from Fe^{3+} ions and a new method of dating. *Nuclear Tracks* 18: 213–221.

Ostrowski, K., Dziedzic-Goclawska, A., Stachowicz, W., and Michalik, J. 1974 Accuracy, sensitivity, and specificity of electron spin resonance analysis of mineral constituents of irradiated tissues. *Annals New York Academy of Sciences* 238: 186–200.

Porat, N. 1991 ESR dating of burned flint. Department of Geology, McMaster University, *Technical Memo* 91.1

Porat, N. and Schwarcz, H.P. 1991 Use of signal subtraction methods in ESR dating of burned flint. *Nuclear Tracks* 18: 203–212.

Porat, N. and Schwarcz, H.P. 1995 Problems in determining lifetimes of ESR signals in natural and burned flint by isothermal annealing. *Radiation Measurements* 24: 161–167.

Porat, N., Schwarcz, H.P., Valladas, H., Bar-Yosef, O., and Vandermeersch, B. 1994 Electron spin resonance dating of burned flint from Kebara Cave, Israel. *Geoarchaeology* 9: 393–407.

Poulianos, A.N. 1980 The postcranial skeleton of the *Archanthropus europaeus petraloniensis*. *Anthropos (Athens)* 7: 13–29.

Poulianos, A.N. 1981 Pre-sapiens man in Greece. *Current Anthropology* 22: 287–288.

Poulianos, A.N., Liritzis, Y., Ikeya, M., Hennig, G.J., Herr, W., Weber, E. and Xirotiris, N.I. 1982 Petralona cave dating controversy. *Nature* 299: 280–282.

Prescott, J.R. and Hutton, J.T. 1988 Cosmic ray and gamma ray dosimetry for TL and ESR. *Nuclear Tracks and Radiation Measurement* 14: 223–227.

Prescott, J.R. and Stephan, L.G. 1982 The contribution of cosmic radiation to the environmental dose for thermoluminescence dating-latitude, altitude and depth dependencies. *PACT* 6: 17–25.

Radtke, U. 1989 Marine Terrassen und Korallenriffe-das Problem der quartären Meeresspiegelschwankungen erläutert an Fallstudien aus Chile, Argentinien und Barbados. *Düsseldorfer Geographische Schriften* 27: 1–246.

Radtke, U., Mangini, A., and Grün, R. 1985 ESR dating of fossil marine shells. *Nuclear Tracks* 10: 879–884.

Schwarcz, H.P. 1985 ESR studies of tooth enamel. *Nuclear Tracks* 10: 865–867.

Schwarcz, H.P., Buhay, W.M., Grün, R., Valladas, H., Tchernov, E., Bar-Yosef, O. and Vandermeersch, B. 1989 ESR Dating of the Neanderthal Site, Kebara Cave, Israel. *Journal of Archaeological Science* 16: 653–659.

Schwarcz, H.P., Grün, R. and Tobias, P.V. 1994 ESR dating studies of the Australopithecine site of Sterkfontein, South Africa. *Journal of Human Evolution* 26: 175–181.

Schwarcz, H.P., Grün, R., Latham, A.G., Mania, D. & Brunnacker, K. 1988a The Bilzingsleben archaeological site: New dating evidence. *Archaeometry* 30: 5–17.

Schwarcz, H.P., Grün, R., Vandermeersch, B., Bar-Yosef, O., Valladas, H. and Tchernov, E. 1988b ESR dates for the hominid burial site of Qafzeh in Israel. *Journal of Human Evolution* 17: 733–737.

Schwarcz, H.P. and Latham, A.G. 1984 Uranium-series age determination of travertines from the site of Vertesszöllös, Hungary. *Journal of Archaeological Science* 11: 327–336.

Schwarcz, H.P., Liritzis, Y. and Dixon, A. 1980 Absolute dating of travertines from Petralona Cave, Khalkidiki-Greece. *Anthropos (Athens)* 7: 152–167.

Shen, G. & Yokoyama, Y. 1984 Th-230/U-234 dating of Petralona spelaeothems. *Anthropos* 11: 23–32.

Skinner, A.R. and Shawl, C.E. 1994 ESR dating of terrestrial Quaternary shells. *Quaternary Geochronology (Quaternary Science Reviews)* 13: 679–684.

Steiner, W. 1975 Zur stratigraphischen Stellung des Travertinprofils von Ehringsdorf bei Weimar. *Alt-Thüringen* 13: 7–15.

Steiner, W. 1979 *Der Travertin von Ehringsdorf und seine Fossilien*. Wittenberg, A. Ziemsen Verlag.

Stringer, C.B., Grün, R., Schwarcz, H.P. and Goldberg, P. 1989 ESR dates for the hominid burial site of Es Skhul in Israel. *Nature* 338: 756–758.

Tchernov, E. 1988 Biochronology of the Middle Paleolithic and dispersal events of hominids in the Levant. In Otte, M., ed, *L'Homme de Neanderthal, Vol. 2: L'Environnement*, Liége: 153–168.

Thoma, A. 1972 On Vertesszöllös man. *Nature* 236: 464–465.

Toyoda, S. and Schwarcz, H.P. 1996 Counterfeit E1' signal in quartz. *Radiation Measurements*, in press.

Tuross, N., Behrensmeyer, A.K., Eanes, E.D., Fisher, L.W. and Hare, P.E. 1989 Molecular preservation and crystallographic alterations in a weathering sequence of wildebeest bones. *Applied Geochemistry* 4: 261–270.

Valladas, H., Reys, J.L., Joron, J.L., Valladas, G., Bar-Yosef, O. and Vandermeersch, B. 1988 Thermoluminescence dating of Mousterian 'Proto-Cro-Magnon' remains from Israel and the origin of modern man. *Nature* 331: 614–616.

Valladas, H., Joron, J.L., Valladas, G., Arensburg, B., Bar-Yosef, O., Belfer-Cohen, A., Goldberg, P., Laville, H., Meignen, L., Rak, Y., Tchernov, E., Tillier, A.M. and Vandermeersch, B. 1987 Thermoluminescence dates for the Neanderthal burial site at Kebara in Israel. *Nature* 330: 159–160.

Vogel, J.C. and Waterbolk, H.T. 1967 Gröningen radiocarbon dates VII. *Radiocarbon* 9: 107–155.

Walther, R. and Zilles, D. 1994 ESR studies on flint with a difference-spectrum method. *Quaternary Geochronology (Quaternary Science Reviews)* 13: 635–639.

Wendorf, F., Close, A.E., Schild, R., Gautier, A., Schwarcz, H.P., Miller, G.H., Kowalski, K., Krolik, H., Bluszcz, A., Robins, D., Grün, R. and McKinney, C. 1987 Chronology and stratigraphy of the Middle Paleolithic at Bir Tarfawi, Egypt. In: Clark, J.D., ed. *Cultural Beginnings* Hablet, Bonn: 197–208.

Wieser, A., Göksu, H.Y. and Regulla, D.F. 1985 Characteristics of gamma-induced ESR spectra in various calcites. *Nuclear Tracks 10*: 831–836.

Chapter 9

Protein and Amino Acid Diagenesis Dating

P. E. HARE, D. W. VON ENDT, AND J. E. KOKIS

ABSTRACT

This chapter reviews the general biogeochemical principles underlying the use of various protein and amino acid diagenetic processes as a means of assigning relative and chronometric ages to various sample materials including bone, shell and teeth. The focus of this discussion is on racemization and epimerization processes and their application to archaeological materials and related Quaternary geological, climatic, or environmental contexts. The factors influencing accuracy and precision of the age estimates based on the measurement of the rates of amino acid racemization and modeling of factors influencing these rates are discussed.

INTRODUCTION

Calcified tissues or biominerals such as shell, bone, and teeth are composed of a mineral phase in association with an organic matrix consisting largely of protein material. These proteins may undergo a number of chemical reactions, which, in principle, may be used to estimate the age since the living

P. E. HARE • Geophysical Laboratory, Carnegie Institution of Washington, DC, 20015, USA. **DAVID W. VON ENDT** • Conservation Analytical Laboratory, Smithsonian Institution, Washington, DC, 20015, USA. **JULIE E. KOKIS** • Geophysical Laboratory, Carnegie Institution of Washington, Washington, DC, 20015, USA.

Chronometric Dating in Archaeology, edited by Taylor and Aitken.
Plenum Press, New York, 1997.

animal produced the biominerals. The most widely used chemical reactions employed for chronometric applications in both marine and terrestrial environments have been amino acid racemization and the related process, epimerization. Other approaches utilize the decomposition or degradation of amino acids. Earlier versions of this approach measured nitrogen or collagen levels in bone. A study of biominerals is of special interest to archaeologists because these materials can be preserved through long periods of time and form a substantial part of the fossil record.

Much of the pioneering research concerning the occurrence and stability of proteins and amino acids in fossils was undertaken by Abelson (1954a, 1954b, 1955, 1956, 1963). He noted the importance of water in considering the reactions proteins and amino acids may undergo over geological time and speculated on the possible usefulness of amino acid reactions for geochronology. Building on the initial work of Abelson, Hare and his collaborators provided data indicating that the epimerization of isoleucine could be used as an indicator of age in shell and deep-sea core foraminifera (Hare and Mitterer 1967, 1969; Hare and Abelson 1968; Wehmiller and Hare 1971). This was the first use of amino acid diagenesis to estimate the age of fossils.

The application of various amino acid racemization (AAR) reactions for dating various materials of archaeological relevance has exhibited an uneven development and differential success. Rutter *et al.* (1985) notes that both cautious and speculative uses of AAR data to provide chronometric interpretations are characteristic of the literature. The most difficult applications have been with bone. With other materials, e.g., marine shell and avian eggshell, AAR has been much more successfully employed. For archaeologists, AAR techniques offered the possibility of obtaining age inferences on samples which are too old for effective ^{14}C-based age estimates (Bada and Deems 1975). Also, required sample sizes are far less than that required for conventional decay counting ^{14}C applications and, until recently at least, generally, even less than that required with AMS-based ^{14}C measurements. Several other factors have contributed to continued research on the development of AAR dating techniques: the preparation of samples for AAR analysis is less involved, and consequently less expensive, than for ^{14}C measurements; the measuring devices are much less expensive to purchase and maintain than radionuclide equipment; rapid results are possible, and many individual samples can be measured for each stratigraphic level.

Summaries of earlier research can be found in Hare (1969, 1974a), Wyckoff (1972), Kvenvolden (1975), Bada and Schroeder (1975), Schroeder and Bada (1976), Williams and Smith (1977), Davis and Treloar (1977), Von Endt (1979), Bada (1982, 1984, 1985, 1987), Smith and Evans (1980), Wehmiller (1982, 1984), Rutter *et al.* (1985), and the chapters contained in *Biogeochemistry of Amino Acids* (Hare *et al.* 1980). Recent general summaries of various aspects of amino acid racemization and diagenesis of fossil materials include Wehmiller (1986), Masters (1986), Wehmiller and Miller (1990, in press), Elster *et al.* (1991), Kaufman and Miller (1992), Murray-Wallace (1993), Rutter and Blackwell (1996) and Johnson and Miller (1997). Hare *et al.* (1985), Engel and Hare (1985) and Murray-Wallace (1993) have provided summaries of the analytical methods used in the analysis of amino acids.

GENERAL PRINCIPLES

Proteins are complex biopolymers built from specific sequences of amino acids in which the acid part (carboxyl group, COOH) of one amino acid is bound to the amino group (NH_2) of a second amino acid by a linkage known as a peptide bond. Peptide bonds arise by elimination of the elements of water from the carboxyl group of one amino acid and an amino group of the next. There are about 20 different amino acids involved in the biosynthesis of proteins (Table 9.1). However, the possible combinations of sequence and length comprising protein molecules is virtually unlimited. The variety of life

Table 9.1. Amino Acids of Calcified Tissue

Amino acid	3-letter code	1-letter code
alanine	Ala	A
arginine	Arg	R
aspartic acid	Asp	D
asparagine	Asn	N
cysteine	Cys	C
glutamic acid	Glu	E
glutamine	Gln	Q
glycine	Gly	G
histidine	His	H
hydroxylysine[a]	Hyl	-
hydroxyproline[b]	Hyp	-
isoleucine	Ile	I
leucine	Leu	L
lysine	Lys	K
methionine	Met	M
phenylalanine	Phe	F
proline	Pro	P
serine	Ser	S
threonine	Thr	T
tryptophan	Trp	W
tyrosine	Tyr	Y
valine	Val	V

[a] Synthesized from lysine.
[b] Synthesized from proline.

forms found today, as well as the even richer variety of extinct life forms recovered in the fossil record, are, in large part, a consequence of the large number of proteins synthesized by biological systems.

Amino Acid Diagenesis Processes

When a living organism dies, protein synthesis ends and the proteins begin their diagenetic breakdown. There are several reactions involving amino acids that could potentially be used to estimate the age of fossil bones, shells, or teeth (Fig. 9.1). The initial reactions involve the hydrolysis of the proteins to produce free amino acids, peptides, and various fragments of the degraded proteins. Hydrolysis occurs as water reacts with the intact proteins and breaks apart the peptide bonds which hold the constituent amino acids in place. As discussed in the next section, racemization and epimerization of the amino acids involves structural alteration. Other reactions that are of potential interest in the study of amino acid diagenesis and dating are decarboxylation to form amines and deamination to form carboxylic acids.

Although many of the amino acids from recent fossils and archaeological materials are still linked in the form of proteins and peptides, older fossils contain increasing amounts of "free" or unbound amino acids as peptide bonds are progressively hydrolyzed. Typically, the total concentration of amino acids in

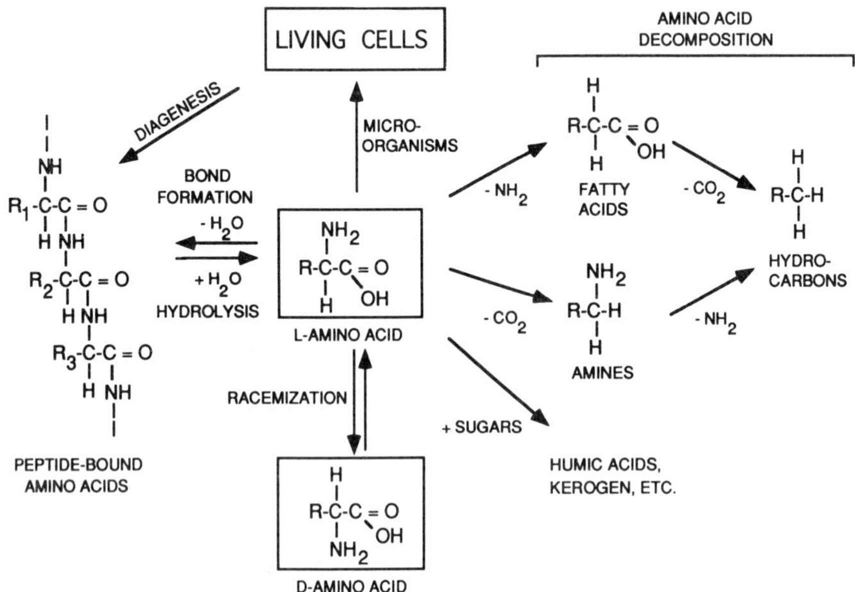

Figure 9.1. Illustration of types of diagenetic biogeochemical reactions observed in fossil materials.

a fossil matrix decreases dramatically as free amino acids and peptides are removed from the fossil by ground water action or other environmental processes. These effects are slowed in low temperature environments—for example, in the arctic or high altitude environments—or where the exclusion of water has occurred. Examples of such situations are in bone impregnated with tar or in egg shells due to their tight physical matrix (Hare 1980; Brooks *et al.* 1990).

Early studies determined that different amino acids manifested varying stabilities (Abelson 1954a, 1954b, 1959). The results of these studies led to the prediction that some amino acids could remain intact at ambient temperatures for millions of years. It also established a list of predicted stabilities for amino acids, e.g., *relatively stable* (glycine, alanine, valine, leucine, isoleucine, glutamic acid, proline) *relatively less stable* (aspartic acid, phenylalanine, lysine) and *least stable:* (threonine, serine, tyrosine, arginine). The variability in the stability of different amino acids indicated that amino acids might be useful as markers in studies concerning the geologic fate of biological organisms, and that older fossils would be enriched in the stable amino acids while containing little or none of the least stable. Vallentyne (1964, 1968, 1969) provided confirmation of the above order of amino acid thermal stability. He also discovered that some ancient amino acids had decomposed and given rise to a series of products commonly found in fossils. Table 9.2 lists some of the reaction products formed from the decomposition of amino acids.

Table 9.2. Examples of Reaction Products from the Thermal Decomposition of Amino Acids (after Vallentyne 1964; Hare 1969; Von Endt 1979)

amino acid	product[a]
aspartic acid	beta-alanine, malic acid
cystine	cysteic acid
glutamic acid	alpha-amino butyric acid [AABA], gamma-amino butyric acid [GABA]
glycine	methylamine
alanine	ethylamine, proprionic acid
threonine	glycine
serine	glycine, alanine
methionine	glycine, alanine, methionine sulfoxide, methionine sulfone
arginine	ornithine, proline, citrulline, urea

[a] Also, deamination of amino acids produces ammonia, decarboxylation produces amines, and the organic matrix of shells produces glucosamine and galactosamine.

One of these decomposition products is ammonia (NH_3) which is derived from the amino group of an amino acid. The concentration of NH_3 was shown to increase in older fossil shells (Florkin *et al.* 1961, Florkin 1969). In addition, as noted in Table 9.2, some reaction products are other amino acids. For instance, serine and threonine may decompose to the more stable glycine. Other amino acids may decarboxylate—lose their acid group—to produce primary amines such as methylamine, while others may lose their amine group (deamination) and produce organic acids such as propionic acid. Clearly, the organic material content of fossils is a complex mix that represents the results of a complicated series of diagenetic reactions. As a result, fossil amino acids represent remnants of the original matrix protein and its constituent amino acids, as well as the decomposition products of other amino acids that may have been originally present but no longer exist, or exist in much reduced concentrations.

Racemization and Epimerization Processes

The diagenetic chemical processes most often employed to infer relative or chronometric temporal relationships in fossil shells and bones are racemization and epimerization. The basis on which this occurs is illustrated in Fig. 9.2. Glycine, the simplest amino acid, has two hydrogens, an amine group (NH_2), and a carboxylic acid group (COOH) attached to the same carbon. What are termed *chiral carbons* have four different atoms or groups bonded to the carbon. Since glycine has only three different groups (two are hydrogens) attached to the same carbon atom, it cannot be chiral, but all other amino acids are. Other groups of atoms may substitute for one of these two hydrogens, forming a series of amino acids which differ in chemical properties. This is illustrated by the other amino acids in the figure, where one of the hydrogens of glycine has been substituted to form two other amino acids found in proteins. In Fig. 9.2, the carbon atom which is starred is the one at which substitution occurs.

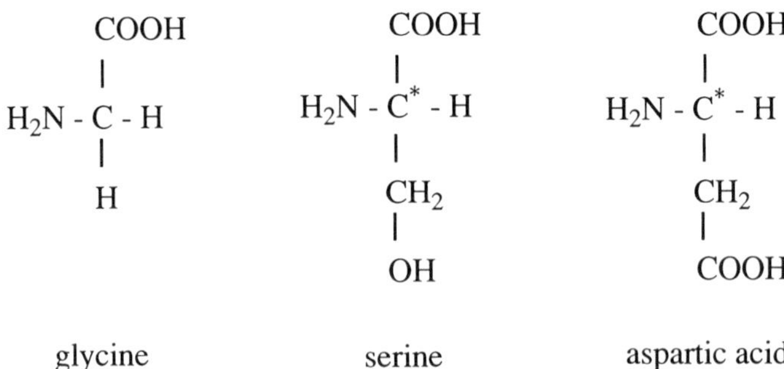

Figure 9.2. Structure of glycine, serine, and aspartic acid. Starred carbon atom (*chiral* carbon) is substitution site for other groups.

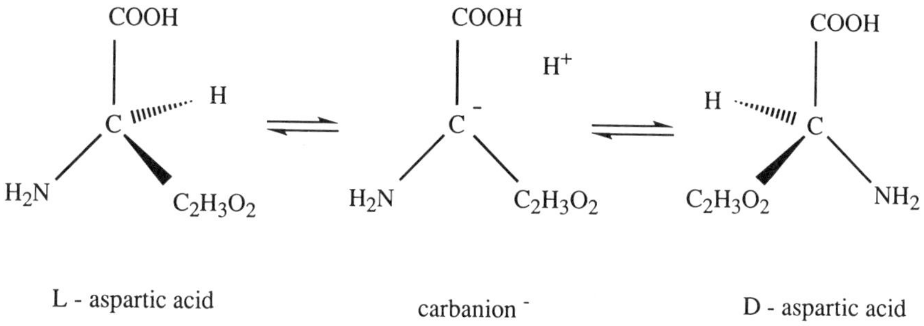

Figure 9.3. Representation of formation of D-enantiomer from L-enantiomer of aspartic acid.

In Fig. 9.3, the three dimensional nature of molecules is emphasized by using solid, triangular shapes to connect atoms or groups that project forward from the plane of the paper, while solid lines represent bonds which lie in the plane of the paper, and dashed lines connect atoms or groups lying behind the plane. These are standard line conventions, used because many of the covalent bonds to carbon are formed at an angle of about 120° with respect to each other. The amino acid depicted in Fig. 9.3 is aspartic acid, one of the two most common amino acids used in geochronological applications. The arrangement of groups of atoms around the second carbon from the acid end of aspartic acid is unique. Removal of these groups of atoms from the second or beta carbon, and their rearrangement in all possible ways yields only two non-equivalent forms, the naturally occurring L-(*levo*) isomer, and its mirror image, the D-(*dextro*) isomer. Thus the two forms are chemically equivalent but structurally different.

With few exceptions (e.g., the cell walls of some bacteria), living organisms contain only the L- form of aspartic acid and other amino acids, whereas fossils organisms tend to accumulate increasing amounts of the D- amino acid as a function of their age. The interconversion of these L- and D- forms is termed *racemization*. When an amino acid such as isoleucine, the other common amino acid used for dating, has two or more chiral carbons, the interconversion process—involving only one of the chiral carbons—is known as *epimerization*.

A necessary condition for racemization and epimerization is that the carbon atom must have attached to it four atoms or groups of atoms that are different from each other. Assymetric carbon centers such as these are termed *chiral centers*. Aspartic acid has one such center and can exist as either of the isomers L- or D- aspartic. Isoleucine has two such centers and can thus exist as a D- and L- isoleucine pair, or as the closely related *epimers* D- and L-alloisoleucine. The chiral centers in Fig. 9.4 are the 2nd and 3rd carbons from the acid (COOH) end of the molecules. The rearrangement of atoms and groups of atoms about the chiral 2nd carbon of isoleucine results in the formation of

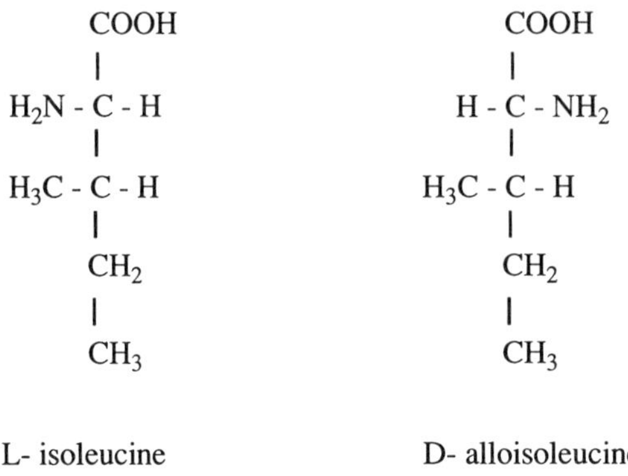

Figure 9.4. Isoleucine and alloisoleucine.

the non-protein amino acid, D-alloisoleucine, the amino acid that forms during protein diagenesis.

It should be noted that the racemization process involves the production of intermediate forms as illustrated with aspartic acid in Fig. 9.3. The labile (easily removable) hydrogen atom on the chiral second carbon is removed. At this point a negatively charged, intermediate carbanion (carbon anion) is formed (identified by the negative sign in Fig. 9.3) and the carbon center presents two approximately equivalent surfaces for hydrogen reattachment. If hydrogen reattachment occurs on the side opposite to that from which it was removed, the D- enantiomer will form. Because there is an approximately equal chance for hydrogen reattachment on either side, a solution of exclusively L-amino acid will eventually become an equal mixture of D- and L- forms. At this point, as many L- amino acid molecules are changing to D- as are converting from D- to L-. At equilibrium, the mixture is said to be racemic.

The rate of racemization is dependent on the ease with which the hydrogen atom can be removed and reattached to the chiral carbon. The principal factor affecting the interconversion rate is temperature; the application of energy to a chemical system as heat will speed the racemization process. In addition, the presence of chemicals that enhance or retard the removal of hydrogen from the chiral carbon also affects the speed of the reaction. For instance, chemicals having alkaline properties promote racemization by forming tenuous bonds with the hydrogen attached to the chiral carbon, enhancing its ability to be removed.

Racemization/Epimerization Rates

Many of the predictions of the occurrence of diagenetic products in fossils were based on laboratory simulations using higher temperatures. To model these processes, assumptions were made that would fit experimental data as a function of effective temperature. Inferences based on higher temperature simulations could then be extrapolated to ambient temperatures experienced by living systems. Goodfriend and Meyer (1991) tested these assumptions with respect to racemization kinetics, and concluded that heating experiments do accurately model natural processes and give good predictions of kinetic patterns in relation to time.

For example, first order rate expressions assume that the rate of appearance of products formed in a chemical reaction is dependent on the concentration of reactant at any given time. However, since the first order rate equation is rather rigidly defined, and the changes that proteins and amino acids undergo in fossils are complicated, "pseudo-first-order" is a term better suited to describe the complex series of reactions that proceed simultaneously in ancient calcified tissue.

The first-order rate expression is:

$$dx/dt = k(a - x) \qquad (1)$$

where dx is the change in reactant, dt is the change in time, and k is a constant defining the slope of the curve. The term a-x thus represents the difference between the original concentration of a at time zero, and the amount, x, that has reacted at time t. Since changes in the reactant are proportional to the amount remaining, the initial change is greatest, with subsequent changes occurring at a progressively slower rate.

To more easily interpret experimental results when using the first-order rate expression, the equation can be adjusted to compensate for the logarithmic relationship between variables x and t by using the integrated form:

$$ln\ [a/(a - x)] = kt \qquad (2)$$

where ln is the natural logarithm. This equation is the formula for a straight line, and implies that for a given temperature a reaction will proceed at a constant logarithmic rate until the reactant is exhausted. The linearity expressed in equation (2) has been an important assumption for archaeological dating techniques, and has been used to predict how long it would take for an observed chemical change to occur. However, if the relationship is shown to be non-linear, then the reactions are not even "pseudo-first-order," but rather more complex, and, as a result, the use of this equation cannot lead to predictive results.

As noted, equations (1) and (2) are typically used to describe reactions taking place at high temperatures in laboratory experiments designed to generate calibration curves that allow the calculation of rates of change at a constant temperature. The rates can then be used to infer the time required, for example, to change the ratio of L- and D- forms of one or more amino acids. In equation (2), the data from a series of laboratory experiments conducted at different temperatures then can be used to calculate the ratio $a/a - x$. When the data are projected to the time it would take to reduce the ratio 63%, to a value of 2.72, the natural logarithm acquires a value of 1. The projected values can then be fitted into the conventional Arrhenius equation:

$$k = Ae - E/RT \tag{3}$$

The natural log form of which is:

$$\ln k = -[E/RT] + \ln A \tag{4}$$

which, as before, is a log-linear relationship. A and R are constants; E is the activation energy of the reaction, T represents temperature (°K), and k is the amount of time necessary for $a/a\text{-}x$ to acquire the value 2.72. This equation describes the effect of temperature on the course of the reaction and may be used to predict the rate at which a reaction would proceed at a different temperature, such as the ambient temperature of an archaeological site.

In order to apply the above equations to amino acid racemization and epimerization, account must be taken of the reversible nature of these processes as illustrated in (5).

$$\text{L-amino acid} \underset{k_2}{\overset{k_1}{\rightleftharpoons}} \text{D-amino acid} \tag{5}$$

For racemization reactions, the assumed first-order rate constants for the conversion of L- to D-, as well as the reverse, are usually equal to each other. However, for the epimerization of isoleucine to alloisoleucine, the rate constants are not equal, and the mixture at equilibrium contains slightly more alloisoleucine than isoleucine.

The rate expressions for these laboratory simulation or calibration studies have appeared in the literature in several different, but equivalent forms. The degree of D- to L- racemization may be expressed as a fraction of the completed reaction whose integrated form is:

$$\ln (X_e - X)/X_e = -(k_1 + k_2) \cdot t \tag{6}$$

where X_e is the amount of D- isomer expected at equilibrium (usually 0.5 for racemization reactions), X is the amount of D- formed by time t, and has the value D/D+L which is, in effect, the D/L ratio. Using equation 6, for allo-isoleucine/isoleucine (aIle/Ile or A/I) epimerization, X_e (aIle) has a value of about 0.56, and the ratio is about 1.27 (Wehmiller and Hare 1971). Bada and Protsch (1973) stated the expression in an alternate form for racemization reactions:

$$\ln\,[1 + (D/L)/1 - (D/L)]_t - \ln\,[1 + (D/L)/1 - (D/L)]_{t=0} = 2 \cdot \mathrm{k} \cdot \mathrm{t} \qquad (7)$$

The *t=0* term was required by the experimental arrangement for the measurement of D/L ratios, in which laboratory hydrolysis created a measurable amount of racemization in modern bone. This value was determined to be 0.14 for aspartic acid in bone by Bada and his co-workers (Bada and Protsch 1973). For isoleucine epimerization, Bada and Schroeder (1972) modified the equation to take into account the greater amount of allo-isoleucine at equilibrium:

$$\ln\,[1+(D/L)/1 - k\,(D/L)]_t - \ln\,[1 + (D/L)/1 - k\,(D/L)]_{t=0} = (1 + k)2 \cdot k \cdot t \qquad (8)$$

Here k is the A/I ratio at equilibrium and was determined to be 1.38 for bone and 1.4 for marine sediments, while Wehmiller and Hare (1971) arrived at a value of 1.25 for marine shell. Variations in k suggest that the precise equilibrium ratio of allo-isoleucine to isoleucine is probably matrix dependent.

AMINO ACID RACEMIZATION APPLICATIONS

Bone

The initial examination of fossil bone AAR data discussed in Hare (1969, 1974a, 1974b, 1980) found it generally to be a problematical sample material because of its porosity and the resultant potential effects of leaching and loss of reactants and products by ground water action. During this early period, Bada and his co-workers proposed methods using the racemization of isoleucine (Bada 1972, 1987) and aspartic acid (Bada *et al.* 1973) to obtain AAR-inferred chronometric ages for bone.

In the early 1970s, Bada and Protsch (1973) described a "calibration method" of evaluating the *in situ* average temperature to which a bone had been exposed by first measuring the degree of racemization in aspartic acid of a known age—usually ^{14}C dated—bone. They suggested that this bone could serve as a calibration of the average temperature experienced by all bone samples from the same site or region. Using this aspartic acid D/L ratio and the presumed known age of a calibration sample, an apparent *in situ* first order rate constant (k_{asp}) could be calculated. An aspartic acid AAR-deduced age could then be calculated for other bones from the same temperature regime using this calculated k_{asp} and the relationship expressed in equation (6). Aspartic acid was chosen, in part, because it has one of the fastest rates of racemization of any of the stable amino acids. Bada and Schroeder (1975) calculated that at 20°C, the D/L_{asp} "half-life" (i.e., the time it takes the D- to L-ratio to reach 0.33) is about 15,000 years.

Section A of Table 9.3 illustrates the calibration procedure on bone samples, in this case on bone taken from the Olduvai Gorge region of East Africa. Bada (1974, 1981) argued that for non-contaminated bones which had not been exposed to anomalous heating, the only two critical variables that affect amino acid racemization in bone were time and environmental temperature. In the early 1980s, he commented that AAR-inferred ages had been assigned to fossil bones from over 40 sites throughout the world and reported that "in almost all instances the ages obtained from aspartic acid racemization are in excellent agreement with the other independent age estimates." (Bada 1982). Later, in reporting on isoleucine epimerization-based age determinations on bone and tooth samples from Olduviai and Zhoukoudian, China, Bada (1987) noted that, at least for the Olduvai samples, there were problems with contamination perhaps carried as a component of humic acids being transported by percolating ground waters. He noted that the best results were obtained on tooth enamel and suggested that bone should be used only when tooth enamel was not available. Rutter and Blackwell (1996) have compiled a list of the archaeologically- and paleoanthropologically-related sites for which AAR-deduced ages have been obtained.

While isoleucine epimerization and aspartic acid AAR-deduced ages on bone from a number of Old World localities were reported by some to be

Table 9.3. Illustration of the Calculation of Amino Acid Racemization Age Estimates on Bone by the Calibration Method

Site	Level/ description provenience	^{14}C age (yr BP)	D/L_{asp}	k_{asp} (yr^{-1})	AAR age (yr BP)
		A. *Illustration of method* (Bada and Protsch 1973)			
Olduvai	Naisiusiu Beds	17,500±1000	0.32	$1.48x10^{-5}$	Calibration
Olduvai	Ndutu Beds	-	0.72	$1.48x10^{-5}$	56,000±3500
Lake Eyasi	Eyasi I hominid	-	ca. 0.5	$1.48x10^{-5}$	ca. 34,000
		B. *New World example* (Bada *et al.* 1974)			
Laguna	-	17,150±1470	0.25	$1.08x10^{-5}$	Calibration
Del Mar	-	-	0.53	$1.08x10^{-5}$	48,000
		C. *Revised example* (Ennis *et al.* 1986)			
Laguna	-	5100±500[a]	0.25	$3.64x10^{-5}$	Calibration[b]
Del Mar	-	(5400±120)[a]	0.53	$3.64x10^{-5}$	14,300

[a] Bada *et al.* 1984.

[b] Bada (1985) proposed a k_{asp} value of $6.0 \pm 2x10^{-5}$ yr^{-1} for skeletons from this area in which the preservation of the amino acids is poor and $1.5x10^{-5}$ yr^{-1} where the preservation is good to excellent.

acceptable, the application of the calibration approach using aspartic acid by Bada to purported Pleistocene New World human skeletal samples yielded a series of highly disputed age assignments. Most notable was an aspartic acid deduced AAR age of about 70 ka assigned to a morphologically fully modern human skeleton from Sunnyvale, California (Bada and Helfman 1975). Another controversial age determination was 48 ka assigned to the Del Mar skeleton from the San Diego region of California (Bada *et al.* 1974). The calibration value for the Del Mar bone was based on a ^{14}C analysis by conventional decay counting on a human skeleton from Laguna Beach, California. The basis on which the aspartic acid AAR-based age inferences were calculated are presented in Section B of Table 9.3.

With the advent of AMS-based ^{14}C analysis, it became practical to obtain ^{14}C age determinations directly on various organic fractions of many of the California human bone samples for which AAR-deduced ages had been obtained (Taylor 1983; Taylor *et al.* 1983, 1985; Stafford *et al.* 1984, 1990). In each case examined, it was determined that the original AAR-deduced age was significantly in excess of that indicated by the ^{14}C value—by as much as an order of magnitude in some cases. As a result of these AMS-based ^{14}C measurements, there is currently no directly dated human skeleton from North America with well-established ^{14}C ages in excess of 11 ka BP. This includes the Laguna skeleton which had originally been used as the calibration sample to infer the AAR-deduced age of the Del Mar skeleton. The revised AMS-based ^{14}C age determination on the Laguna specimen was 5100±500 BP. Assuming that the AMS-based age for the Laguna sample is correct and calculating a revised k_{asp} value in the same manner as originally proposed by Bada and Protsch (1973), the revised AAR-inferred age of the Del Mar skeleton (14,300 yr BP) is still inflated by more than a factor of 2 from that obtained by a direct ^{14}C analysis (5400±120 BP) (Section C of Table 9.3). By this time, it was clear that other factors, in addition to an incorrect calibration value, were responsible for the anomalous AAR-based age inferences for the California skeletons.

Over the previous decade, several researchers in addition to Hare (1974a, 1974b), including Bender (1974), Williams and Smith (1977), Smith *et al.* (1978), Kessels and Dungworth (1980), Von Endt (1979, 1980) and Matsu'ura and Ueta (1980), Blackwell *et al.* (1989), Saint-Martin (1991), Elster *et al.* (1991), Child *et al.* (1993), and Child (1996) have examined factors other than time and temperature that could account for the AAR values found in bone. Some of their concerns included (1) the influence of the chemical state of the amino acids on racemization kinetics, (2) the improbability of the requirement that a calibration sample and a sample to be dated have experienced essentially identical temperature histories, (3) the effects of algal, bacterial and other types of contamination including the precipitation of secondary minerals such as calicite and dolomite, (4) the effects of variable geochemical conditions, e.g. the presence of various metals and minerals, in the surrounding soil matrix, (5) the actual D/L ratio at time zero in the racemization process in different bones, and (6) the homogeneity of D/L ratios in fossil bone from the same skeleton or from skeletons with identical age and temperature histories (Ennis *et al.* 1986).

In AAR analysis, one implicit assumption has been that a sample bone has not been subjected to any major heating event. Recent studies have shown that, for bone, very high NH_3 levels and a non-collagen-like amino acid pattern are associated with thermal effects (see Fig. 9.5; Taylor *et al.* 1995). However, since diagenetic processes can also produce these characteristics, more unique thermal markers for bone are currently being examined that would be similar to the alpha and gamma amino butyric acid signals which are indicators of heating for eggshell (Brooks *et al.* 1991; Hare *et al.* 1993).

Several studies have pointed to the fact that significant variability in D/L ratios can be introduced in bone of similar age and temperature history as a function of the degree to which intact collagen is retained. This reflects the observation that free amino acids racemize at different rates than peptide-bound amino acids (Prior *et al.* 1986; Kessels and Dungworth 1980; Matsu'ura and Ueta 1980). Masters (1987) also reported that racemization rates of collagen and non-collagen proteins in the same bone were very different. Fig. 9.5 illustrates this effect in a suite of bone samples of similar age in which there appears to be an inverse relationship in bone between D/L_{asp} and amino acid nitrogen content—as nitrogen content decreases, D/L_{asp} values generally increase. Nitrogen content is one index of the degree of retention of the original collagen-like structure in bone (Taylor *et al.* 1989).

Studies undertaken within the last decade have generally supported the view that the chemical state of the amino acids has a decisive effect on the ability to use racemization in bone to infer chronological age. Elster *et al.* (1991) reported a generally good correlation between time and degree of aspartic AAR in a suite of recent to Mousterian age bones retaining significant amounts of collagen, whereas no such correlation existed for those bones exhibiting trace amounts of collagen. Kimber and Hare (1992) found a wide range in D/L_{asp} values from various peptide and molecular weight fractions of the same bone. They concluded that valid D/L_{asp} comparisons could be made only using similar stable peptide fractions.

Saint-Martin and Julg (1991) reported that AAR-inferred ages of fossil bones from La Caune de l'Arago, France were approximately 250 ka, whereas stratigraphic comparison and U-series age estimates indicated age for the bones of 400–450 ka. At La Chaise-de-Vouthon, France, using experimentally-derived rate constants for alanine, leucine, aspartic acid and glutamic acid, AAR-inferred ages on bone and teeth were also in serious disagreement with the U-series inferred age values as well. Although some of the bone was degraded in terms of collagen content, this could not explain the major age disconcordance in almost all samples. In the words of the investigators, "not only were most dates extremely low compared to the known ages, only

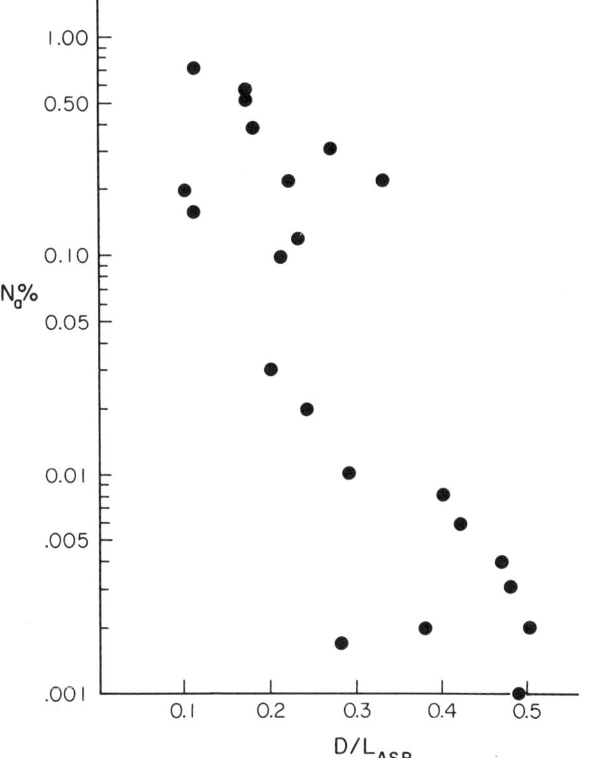

Figure 9.5. Relationship between amino acid nitrogen content (N_a) and D/L_{asp} in total hydrolystate of bones of similar Late Holocene age (Taylor *et al.* 1989).

geologically improbable temperatures resulted in dates close to the known ages (Blackwell *et al.* 1990:142). Clearly, a complex set of factors was responsible for the major anomalies observed in AAR values exhibited in these samples.

Despite the earlier acceptance by some of AAR-based age estimates on bone for archaeological purposes (e.g., Skeleton 1983), current evidence suggests that obtaining accurate chronometric age estimates on bone based on AAR data *alone* remains generally problematical. In our view, an example of an appropriate use was reported by Rae *et al.* (1987) where ^{14}C, uranium-series and aspartic acid AAR data resulted in concordant age estimates for well-preserved bones from a cave environment. Although we view few of the published stand-alone AAR age inferences on bone to be reliable, the many laboratory experiments and field tests involved in the search for a reliable AAR dating method applied to bone has provided valuable information concerning the effects of various diagenetic processes on AAR values observed in bone samples.

Studies of amino acid racemization and epimerization in teeth have shown teeth dentine and enamel to be more promising than bone in providing reliable results (Hare *et al.* 1978; Bada 1981, 1987). Unlike bone, the enamel and dentine of teeth do not turn over at an appreciable rate during the life of the animal. Diagenetic reactions, therefore take place in teeth while the animals are still living. Attempts have been made to use these reactions for deriving the biological age at death of the animal. However, reaction rates are generally so slow that it is very difficult to resolve the biological diagenetic reactions from the laboratory induced reactions (Helfman and Bada 1975, 1976).

Shell

In contrast to the difficulties encountered with bone in terrestrial environments, the use of amino acid ratios to provide temporal placement in oceanographic, marine geology and archaeological contexts for shell samples of various types has proved to be much more reliable and generally useful and thus has become widely applied. For carbonates, isoleucine and leucine are the most frequently employed amino acids for geochronological purposes. Both have relatively slow racemization rates, are not created by decomposition of other amino acids, and are not often found as contaminants (Miller and Brigham-Grette 1989)

Miller and his collaborators (Miller *et al.* 1979; Miller and Hare 1980; Miller 1982) coined the word "aminostratigraphy" to distinguish the use of amino acid ratios in mollusks as a regional correlation tool. Relative dates could be applied to strata, and correlations between disjunct layers could be made. Using this technique, regional chronostratigraphies and paleoclimatic interpretations have been devised for a number of regions. A primary geological use of this approach has been the reconstruction of Quaternary (Pleistocene/Holocene) sea levels. Isoleucine epimerization has also been applied to questions relating to interglacial high sea stands (Oxygen Isotope Stages 1, 3, 5e and 7), tectonic histories, and paleotemperature estimates.

Aminochronology

Calibration with ^{14}C or another radiometric technique such as uranium/thorium on associated corals (Corrado *et al.* 1986) provides what Wehmiller (1993) calls an "aminochronology" chronometric technique. Over the past 15 years, good regional calibrations have been developed. For example, AAR data for the Mediterranean region has been calibrated with uranium-series ages on corals (Hearty *et al.*, 1986). Recently, Hollin *et al.* (1993) detected a 1°C difference between sea caves and regional current mean annual temperatures (CMAT). This correction is important for regional Pleistocene temperature estimates as uranium series ages on speleothems from such caves in northwest Europe have been used as regional calibrations for AAR dating in the Northeast Atlantic region.

Because of the complexity of epimerization kinetics and a general lack of information on the actual temperature history of fossil material, a temperature proxy can be derived by calibrating the site or region with radiometric methods. By combining calibration sample ages with their alloisoleucine/isoleucine (A/I) ratios and solving the kinetic expressions, an "effective diagenetic temperature" (EDT) for a locality can be provided (Miller 1985). This is not the same as the "mean annual temperature" (MAT) over the geologic time period in question but rather it is weighted toward the warm periods of the warm-cold oscillations of the Pleistocene-Holocene. This is because the rate of a chemical reaction such as racemization is exponentially related to an increase in temperature. The EDT can then be incorporated into a kinetic equation along with a series of racemization (or epimerization) ratios to solve for the age of each sample analyzed. Clusters of ratios can thus define the age of a stratigraphic level.

When possible, a ^{14}C calibration of about 30 ka is preferred. This is because, when employed in kinetic equations, the calibrated rate constant will be based on approximately equal parts Holocene (0 to 10–12 ka) and last glacial maximum (13–25 ka with a peak at 18 ka) and the associated interstadials with their intermediate temperatures. The EDT derived from such a calibration is assumed to be representative of the period from about 30 ka to 75 ka. The period from about 75 ka to 130 ka may be more closely represented by a Holocene EDT. Current calculation of thermal histories for the Last Interglacial use both Pleistocene "cold" EDT and Holocene "warm" EDT extrapolations to "bound" calculated dates. They give maximum and minimum age estimates respectively.

The temperature curves used in such calculations are based on $^{18}O/^{16}O$ ratios in foraminifera in deep sea cores as well as high sea level terrace records dated by ^{14}C and uranium disequilibrium (Martinson *et al.* 1987; Chappell and Shackleton 1986; Shackleton and Opdyke 1973, 1976). Although paleotemperatures are less well known for terrestrial regions, recent data suggest that the temperature depression during the last glacial maximum in Southern Africa was between 4–6°C (Deacon and Lancaster 1968). Miller *et al.* (1997) have also derived a MAT decrease of 6–9°C between 45 and 16 ka BP in Southern Australia, based on isoleucine epimerization of emu eggshell.

The depth of burial is another factor believed to affect amino acid ratios in shell, as it would in bone. Samples which spend periods of time in the "kinetically-active" soil zone, the upper 30 cm., will be subject to daily and yearly temperature fluctuations and experience accelerated racemization as a result (Wehmiller 1977). Miller and Brigham-Grette (1989) determined that the depth to which samples are affected by these temperature fluctuations extends to one meter. Goodfriend (1987a, 1991) and others (Ellis *et al.* 1996) however, found no trend with depth although the surface (the upper 20 to 30 cm.) will often produce mixed AAR values due to bioturbation and other natural and anthropogenic factors.

Increased racemization values induced by artificial heating, surface exposure, or residence in the "kinetically active" soil zone are factors which limit reliable quantification of errors in age estimates based on D/L values. The amplitude of their effect can be reduced by identifying artificially heated samples as well as excluding the upper 20 to 30 cm. of an archaeological excavation from AAR analysis. Although not as severe as in bone, leaching of the original amino acids in older fossils is perhaps the most important physical process affecting the amino acid concentration in fossil shells (Mitterer 1993: 751).

Alternative Kinetic Models

As long as the reaction follows a pseudo first-order rate reaction, a simple linear extrapolation of the kinetic expression can be used to estimate ages of fossils with high ratios. For molluscs, this range is 0.3–0.5, for avian eggshell it is approximately 1.0 (see discussion below). To expand the range of values that follow a linear, predictive, rate constant, Mitterer and Kriausakul (1989) developed a model using parabolic kinetics. This model uses the square root of time and the ratio of D- to L- epimers as follows:

$$t = [(D/L)_s/m_c]^2 \tag{9}$$

where: t= age in years; $(D/L)_s$ is the D/L ratio of the fossil and m_c is the slope ($= (D/L)/t^{1/2}$) derived from the calibration samples. Using this model, A/I values of up to 1.0 for molluscs can be utilized in geochronological investigations. The advantage of this approach is that it overcomes the limiting values applicable to pseudo-first-order kinetic models by providing a kinetic model which is valid over the range of A/I ratios encountered, and which extends the age range for which AAR dating is applicable (Murray-Wallace and Kimber 1993; Goodfriend 1991).

Parabolic kinetics has been used to develop a chronostratigraphy in Bermuda (Hearty *et al.* 1992), to correlate North American midcontinental loess deposits (Mirecki and Miller 1994), to investigate Australian marine strata (Murray-Wallace *et al.* 1993), to date British late pleistocene sea stands (Hollin *et al.* 1993), and to define Alaskan Pliocene/Pleistocene high sea stands (Kaufman 1992).

Several caveats need to be considered when working with amino acid racemization ratios derived from mollusks. First, separate genera may be characterized by different rate constants. Therefore, laboratory kinetic experiments should be undertaken for each new genus of mollusk utilized in isoleucine epimerization or aspartic acid racemization analysis. This effect is assumed to be due to unique proportions or combinations of proteins within the shell and is supported by the fact that distinct genera exhibit different amino acid compositions. The proteins themselves, however, have not yet been fully characterized (Lajoie *et al.* 1980; Lowenstam and Weiner 1989; Weiner and Traub 1984; Weiner 1983, 1979). Second, variability in amino acid ratios is affected by the particular layer of the shell as well as the particular shell part sampled (Hearty *et al.* 1986; Goodfriend *et al.* 1997). Intrashell variability can be controlled by consistency in sampling the shell layer on each valve (Miller and Hare, 1980; Miller and Brigham-Grette 1989). Because of these problems, Meyer (1991) has suggested that geochronological inferences in shell should be based on several amino acids and the practice of using only isoleucine should be abandoned. Alternatively, Goodfriend (1991) argues that aspartic acid provides the best resolution for young samples whereas isoleucine can accomplish this best for older samples, as the analysis of more than one amino acid generally gives redundant information.

Archaeological Applications

Archaeological applications incorporating aminostratigraphic correlations have had a somewhat less successful history than geologic ones. Early studies ran into difficulty because of the complex thermal histories of archaeological sites. For example, the human use of fire is ubiquitous. Certain cooking techniques and even proximity to a heat source such as a campfire combined with complex burial histories can be reflected in variations in the rate of racemization in a given fossil material. Even subtle heating events can compromise dating scenarios. Mollusks collected as grave goods, or as personal ornamentation (jewelry or decorations on clothing) may have a more straightforward temperature history.

Masters and Bada (1977) studied mollusks in California shell middens and hypothesized that prehistoric cooking had accelerated the racemization rates and that this was the reason for the discordance between the AAR and ^{14}C dates at these sites. Wehmiller (1977) analyzed the same data as Masters and Bada but concluded that high ground surface temperatures produced the observed discrepancies. Other workers (Kvenvolden *et al.* 1979) noted that the amino ages calculated for an Alaskan midden site were too high in comparison with ^{14}C dates because of variability in the site EDT history.

In some cases, there are ambiguous results from the application of racemization/epimerization analysis. For example, the archaeological site of Boxgrove, Sussex, situated on Britain's southern coastal plain, is considered to be one of the most securely dated middle Pleistocene localities in Europe based on geomorphology as well as microtine rodent biostratigraphy (Klein 1989; Gamble 1994). A hominid tibia, designated *Homo heidelbergensis* (Roberts *et al.* 1994) was discovered in a level which has been assigned to OIS stage 13 (524 ka to 478 ka), a temperate period just before the Anglian glaciation. Bowen and Sykes (1994) utilized isolelucine epimerization ratios from 27 Boxgrove marine gastropods (mean A/I = 0.29±0.025) from sands underlying the tibia to assign it to OIS Stage 11 (423 ka to 462 ka) based on equivalent ratios from Stage 11 elsewhere. However, an earlier model of AAR and OIS correlations places this mean ratio in OIS Stage 13 (Bowen and Sykes 1988). This discordance in interpretation has yet to be resolved (Roberts 1994).

Using AAR combined with ^{14}C data, Cann *et al.* (1991) studied mollusks from a Holocene shell-midden site along the Australian coast and confirmed a date of 7.9 to 8.3 ka for this Early Horizon aboriginal shell midden. The data also provides support for a major Early Holocene transgression.

Non-marine Mollusks

Preliminary evaluations of freshwater molluscs (Miller and Hare 1980, Rutter *et al.* 1980, Miller *et al.* 1979) demonstrated their utility for stratigraphic correlations and relative dating as long as generic differences in racemization rates were considered. Harmon *et al.* (1983) were the first to work with land snails to establish an absolute dating framework. Their study involved the dating of high sea stands during the middle to late Pleistocene in Bermuda (see also Hearty *et al.* 1992).

Freshwater and terrestrial mollusks have also become an increasingly important material over the last 10 years for non-marine, continental Quaternary (Holocene/Pleistocene) chronostratigraphy (Bowen *et al.* 1989) as well as Central European loess deposits (Oches and McCoy 1989, 1995, 1996). Deep-lake cycles in Pleistocene Lake Bonneville (McCoy 1987a) as well as long-distance correlations between Mississippi Valley loess deposits and glacial tills (Clark *et al.* 1989, 1990; Alford 1990; Forman *et al.* 1992; Mirecki and Miller 1994) have been documented. North American midcontinental paleotemperature estimates of about –8°C to –12°C for the last glacial maximum (18–20 ka) have also been derived (Oches and McCoy 1989).

Isoleucine epimerization or aspartic acid racemization analysis combined with ^{14}C determinations on land snails (Goodfriend 1987b, 1989; Goodfriend and Mitterer 1993, Goodfriend *et al.* 1994, Ellis *et al.* 1996, Ellis and Goodfriend 1994) provides both an absolute chronology and a method for study of the extent of age distribution of samples or degree of mixing *within* a deposit. This combination of methods provides an extensive characterization of the "chronology of sedimentation" because it enables the investigator to analyze numerous individual samples per level. This technique is cost-effective, requires small amounts of material, and provides relatively rapid results. In addition, this integrative approach demonstrates that, as fossil assemblages are often age-mixed, bulk ^{14}C dates will overestimate the age of a unit, because they will time-average the individuals making up the sample (Goodfriend and Stanley 1996; Goodfriend 1989).

Because of its high initial rate of racemization, aspartic acid analysis of mollusks is an excellent method for dating the last 350 years (Goodfriend 1992a; Goodfriend *et al.* 1991, 1996; Goodfriend and Stanley 1996). Post-A.D. 1650 materials are particularly interesting because ^{14}C does not generally provide enough precision in this time range. Goodfriend and his co-workers (Goodfriend 1992a, Goodfriend *et al.* 1994) have demonstrated a 1% change in D/L aspartic values every 20 years in land snails and a 1% change per 35 years in ostrich eggshell. This method can provide good resolution for the last 350 yr time period, which is not adequately covered by ^{14}C because of the natural and man-made atmospheric variation in ^{14}C levels. Aspartic acid racemization can also be used to date corals (Goodfriend *et al.* 1992) and can provide annual resolution of the growth bands on deep water gastropods (Goodfriend *et al.* 1995).

An example of an archaeological application of AAR analysis of terrestrial mollusks includes the dating of sites in the Negev desert which contain "Gaza Ware," a pottery style believed to be less than 200 years old. A/I and aspartic acid AAR dating of associated land snail shells demonstrated an age of about AD 1700, an instance where ^{14}C data would not be a precise chronometric indicator (Rosen and Goodfriend 1993).

A large number of prehistoric sites were analyzed using amino acid epimerization of land snails combined with AMS ^{14}C determinations at Fort Hood, Texas (Ellis *et al.* 1996; Abbott *et al.* 1995; Ellis and Goodfriend 1994; Abbott *et al.* 1996). In this area, land snails are often the only plentiful fossil organic materials. In this case, the purposes of the study were to provide a rapid and inexpensive means of screening a series of sites for possible detailed excavation, assess the stratigraphic integrity of the deposits, and provide data on the rate of sediment deposition in a cost effective way (about 10% of the cost of AMS ^{14}C dating) for contract or cultural resource management archaeology. The study indicated that a majority of the sites had questionable archaeological integrity as their land snail assemblages were of mixed age. Land snails have also been utilized to track climatic change and localized extinctions resulting from human habitat disturbance (Goodfriend and Mitterer 1988; Cook *et al.* 1993; Goodfriend *et al.* 1994; Goodfriend 1992b).

Avian Eggshell

Ratites (large flightless birds) and fossil ratite eggshell are commonly found in the arid and semi-arid regions of Africa, Australia, Asia, South America and the Middle East. The birds have had a close association with humans, as the eggs were employed as a food source and the intact shell was then used for water containers or the fabrication of eggshell beads. Due to these uses, many archaeological assemblages in these regions have fossil eggshell fragments (Sampson 1994; Brooks *et al.* 1990).

The calcium carbonate matrix of eggshell is in the form of microscopic calcite crystals, which are more stable than aragonite or the bone mineral hydroxyapatite. Thus the protection of indigenous protein in eggshell is more efficient. The organic and inorganic matrix are bound so tightly that a nearly closed system is formed in which possible contaminants are excluded and the original protein is retained for an extended period (Johnson 1995; Brooks *et al.* 1990; Kokis 1988; Ernst 1989). The resistance of eggshell to leaching has been amply demonstrated in laboratory heating experiments (Kokis 1988; Ernst, 1989; Miller *et al.* 1990; Brooks *et al.* 1990).

Ostrich eggshell (OES), the first ratite shell analyzed (Hare *et al.* 1984), shows a relatively high protein content (about 3%) and thus a sample weight of 6–7 mg is large enough for ion-exchange HPLC analysis. This very small sample size allows individual fragments to be dated (Johnson 1995; Miller *et al.* 1992). The "pseudo-first-order" kinetics are remarkably regular in that the log transformation of the epimerization reaction is linear (i.e. predictive) up to a value of about 1.0 (Kokis 1988, Ernst 1989, Brooks *et al.* 1990, Miller *et al.* 1992), a value much higher than that shown by other materials (Miller and Beaumont 1989) such as mollusk shell, which becomes non-linear at values from 0.3 to 0.5 (Mitterer and Kriausakul 1989; Kaufman 1992).

Stratigraphic admixture of artifacts, as well as associated datable materials in archaeological sites, can occur for a whole host of reasons including bioturbation, deflation in arid regions, as well as the instability of sediments such as sands and sandy soils (Van Strydonck *et al.* 1995). Anthropogenic disturbances can also be a major factor. In such cases it is especially important not to use bulk samples for ^{14}C dating. Ostrich eggshell has sufficient organic content to allow simultaneous AAR and AMS ^{14}C (plus stable isotope) samples to be run on the same 100 mg fragment if desired. This multiple analytic property can be used to clarify mixed assemblages. In order to assess the amount of vertical displacement at a given site, multiple samples (10 to 20) per level should be analyzed in order to determine which samples are in their original context. Because of the time and expense involved in ^{14}C dating, generally age estimates for a series of levels will be based on one ^{14}C sample per layer and age mixing will show as stratigraphic anomalies (Goodfriend 1989). The number of samples that can be analyzed using isoleucine epimerization or aspartic acid racemization is limited more by the number available from a site than by any analytical or cost limitations. By analyzing 10–20 fragments per level, stratigraphic admixture is demonstrated by the presence of mixed populations of aspartic acid or A/I ratios within a level.

For example, at the archaeological site of ≠Gi, Botswana, OES fragments with A/I values close to 1.0 are found in levels less than 30 ka old. Radiocarbon dating of one of these fragments yielded an age of > 37.2 ka (AA-3303). These anomalous fragments are found in an area of the site which is characterized by extensive pit digging by the Late Stone Age inhabitants and most certainly are derived from the older Middle Stone Age habitation levels, where the A/I values range from 0.9 to 1.1 (Brooks *et al.* 1990).

Artificial heating of shell increases the A/I ratio resulting in an anomalously old age for these samples when analyzed. This happens because shells are dropped in or near a campfire, for example. Intense heating is easy to recognize because it decomposes the amino acids leaving only an ammonia signal when analyzed (Fig. 9.6). Cooking eggs is generally not the cause of this heating effect. The boiling of an egg occurs too rapidly to have a significant effect, as laboratory samples heated in water for a week at 100°C do not show

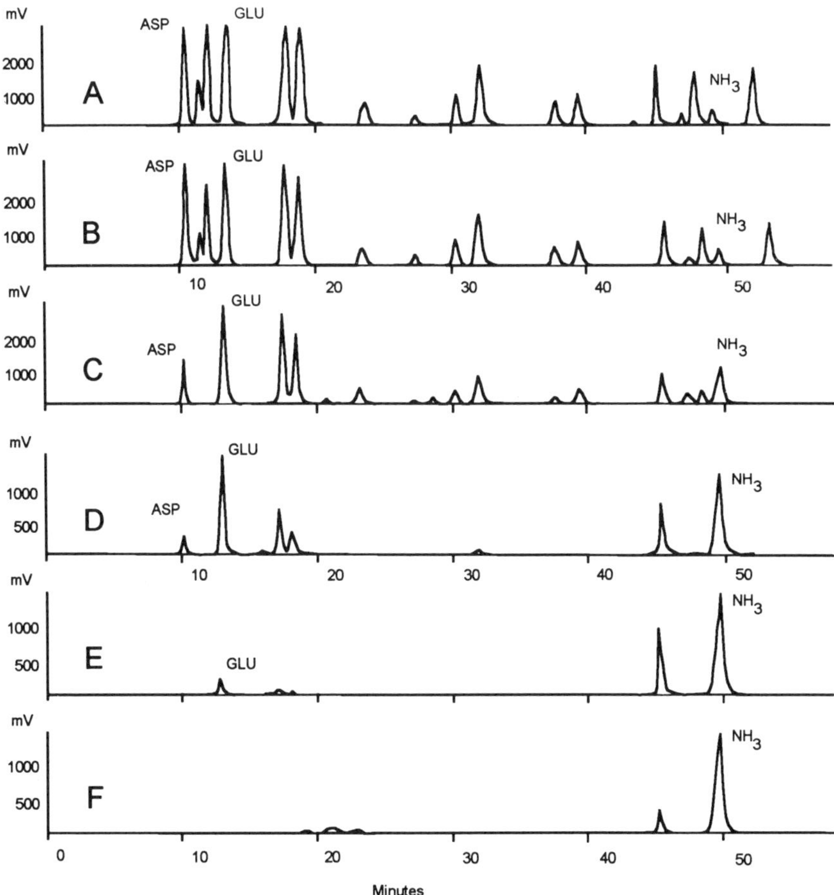

Figure 9.6. Chromatograms of series of heating experiments to simulate amino acid diagenesis in modern ostrich egg shell. Asp=aspartic acid, Glu=glutamic acid, NH_3= ammonia. A = fresh, unheated shell; B=1hr@160°C; C=1hr@240°C; D=1hr@280°C; E=1hr@320°C; F=1hr@360°C.

an elevated A/I ratio. Also, in the case of the !Kung of the Kalahari desert, they do not subject the shell to heat at all, for they blow out the liquid contents of the egg to preserve the shell. Thus, the shell itself is not heated but saved for more valuable uses such as water containers and beads (A. Brooks, personal communication, 1996). However, the !Kung do their work and socializing around a campfire, so it is possible that worked fragments would be subject over time to subtle heating.

Leucine hydrolysis (Miller *et al.* 1992) can be used as an objective basis for the identification of burnt samples. Since there is about a 10% difference in activation energy, the simultaneous solution of rate equations for leucine hydrolysis and isoleucine epimerization gives a site simultaneous temperature with a ±10°C error. Although this error is too large to use for establishing ambient site temperatures, for effective temperatures (EDT) well above site temperature, as would be the case in burned samples, the technique can give good results. Also, as a general rule, when amino acid ratios within a level differ by 10% or less, anomalous heating can be excluded and the mean value can be considered both the age of the shell and the enclosing sediment.

Changes in the pattern of amino acid composition and the formation of characteristic decomposition products (amines, alpha amino butyric acid, gamma amino butyric acid) are other indicators of burning (Hare *et al.* 1993; Brooks *et al.* 1991). Also, amino acid concentrations are often lower in heated shell. Lightly heated shell may exhibit variable A/I ratios within a single fragment. This pattern has been demonstrated in land snails (Abbott *et al.* 1996) and can be expected in eggshell as well.

At Boomplaas, a site in the Republic of South Africa, two samples in the third level from the top of the stratigraphic sequence (BLD) showed anomalous A/I ratios (0.37, 0.26) which were greater than the ratio (0.24) from the level near bedrock (OCH). To decide if these samples were heated or stratigraphically admixed, their amino acid patterns were compared to the sample from level OCH. The BLD samples show depleted serine, threonine, methionine, histidine and arginine and enriched ammonia. Also, there is a clear signal from the presence of gamma-amino butyric acid [GABA] as well as methyl, ethyl and butyl amine peaks in the BLD samples which demonstrates that the samples from BLD were heated and those near bedrock were not. One of the anomalous samples (A/I = 0.37) was ^{14}C dated to 5219±72 ka (AA-6087), which is concordant with previously acquired ^{14}C dates (Kokis *et al.* 1990, Deacon 1979) for that level. The two levels above BLD contain vitrified sheep dung which indicates that the cave had been a sheep paddock and was burned seasonally to control parasites (Deacon 1979). Thus, the prolonged heating in the top two members had accelerated the epimerization reaction in level BLD.

Amino acid racemization/epimerization data has also been applied to the question of the emergence of anatomically modern humans (AMH). Between

40 and 200 ka, AMH remains appear for the first time in Africa and the Near East. The precise chronology, however, remains controversial (Klein 1995; Minugh-Purvis 1995). Uncertainty exists concerning both the dating and stratigraphic provenience of key hominid fossils and artifacts in both geographic areas, although it is generally agreed that these fossils are beyond the range of radiocarbon (Klein 1995). Stratigraphy, biostratigraphy and paleoenvironmental reconstruction provide correlations with oxygen isotope or recognized glacial stages.

Epimerization in ostrich eggshell provides an additional method for constructing chronologies in hominid evolution (Brooks *et al.* 1990). For example, in Africa, early human remains classified as AMH are usually found in association with Middle Stone Age (MSA) tool industries. This term refers to the use of the prepared core technique to make flake tools of different types. With few exceptions, the MSA in Africa ended prior to 40 ky. This fact, coupled with problems of stratigraphic disturbance, makes dating the MSA difficult (Kokis 1988; Brooks *et al.* 1990; Klein 1977, 1983, 1989, 1994; Volman 1984, Vogel and Beaumont 1972).

Epimerization in ostrich eggshell has been used to date the MSA levels at Klasies River Mouth, South Africa, which contain the remains of early AMH, to approximately 75 to 125 ka (Hare *et al.* 1993; Brooks *et al.* 1993). The strata which contain AMH remains at the South African site of Border Cave have estimated amino ages of > 70 ka (Miller and Beaumont 1989; Miller *et al.* 1992).

Two Levantine Mousterian rockshelters in southern Jordan were dated to ca. 69 ka using isoleucine epimerization of ostrich eggshell (Henry and Miller 1992). Modern human remains at Qafzeh, Israel have been recently dated by thermoluminescence (Aitken and Valladas 1992; Valladas *et al.* 1988) to approximately 90 ka. Similarly, the uranium series and electron spin resonance techniques provide a date of 100±5 ka (McDernott *et al* 1993; Schwarcz *et al* 1988). Due to a lack of a calibration sample within the ^{14}C range, isoleucine epimerization utilizing ostrich eggshell has not been able to provide an exact date of occupation by AMHs. However, this technique provides evidence that Qafzeh was occupied over many thousands of years rather than in a brief pulse (Gibbons 1992). In these two instances, AAR is being used to address the issue of Neanderthal/AMH interactions in the Middle East: a "crossroads" for human migrations.

The MSA at ≠Gi, an open-air site in the Kalahari Desert, Botswana, includes a number of behaviors typically attributed to Upper Paleolithic archaeological contexts such as points modified for hafting, the hunting of dangerous prey and the use of grindstones. However at ≠Gi, these behaviors are associated with an epimerization age of 65 to 85 ka. Support for this early date is provided by a thermoluminescence (TL) date of 77±11 ka on the same level (Hare *et al.* 1984; Brooks *et al.* 1990). Katanda, in the Semliki River Valley of Zaire, has yielded barbed bone points (harpoons) which have been dated by several methods, including AAR on freshwater mollusk shell, to about 90 ka (Brooks *et al.* 1995; Yellen *et al.* 1995). These dates support an African behavioral as well as anatomical origin of early modern humans.

Geological episodes which would have affected human migration and settlement patterns in Africa have also been addressed. Using uranium disequilibrium for calibration, three lacustrine episodes in the Eastern Sahara have been dated by AAR on OES (Miller *et al.* 1991). The most recent occurred about 100 ka BP. This wetter period would have been more conducive to movement across northeastern Africa and correlates well with the earliest appearance of Anatomically Modern Humans in the Middle East.

Other Materials

Additional materials from archaeological sites can potentially be used for AAR determinations. Kinetic experiments have shown that otoliths, the calcified ear bones of fish, are second only to eggshell in retention of their indigenous amino acids. However, like molluscs, samples for analysis must be consistently taken from the same physical location on the bone. With that caution, A/I ratios are predictive to 0.75, a value intermediate between the limiting linear kinetic values for molluscs and eggshell (Miller and Rosewater 1995). Other promising materials include mollusc opercula, speleothems (Lauritzen *et al.* 1994), soils (Kimber *et al.* 1994; Milnes *et al.* 1987), and hair (Morell 1994; Taylor *et al.* 1995). There has also been an examination of the use of aspartic acid AAR for stratigraphic correlations of fossil wood (Zumberge *et al.* 1980; Rutter and Crawford 1984; Rutter and Vlahos 1988).

CONCLUSION

The use of chemical reactions such as racemization or epimerization to obtain chronological inferences involves the measurement or estimation of initial and final concentrations of reactants and products as well as estimates of rates of conversion of initial reactants to final products. For ratios of initial and final concentrations to be converted into temporal inferences, a number of assumptions must be made, especially assumptions about reaction rates. These are highly dependent on temperature and other chemical environmental factors, including, in a number of cases, the often unique chemical state of a sample. In many cases, only relative age inferences are possible.

Chronometric (time placement) ages can be reliably inferred in cases where detailed knowledge of effective temperature calibration is possible and where the parameters controlling chemical reaction rates have been critically examined. This often must be done on a sample-by-sample and site-by-site basis. An understanding of these parameters is still, unfortunately, incomplete and may, in many cases, be valid for only some sample types, e.g., various types of shell, and a limited number of site types where annual average effective temperature fluctuations are minimized. For terrestrial applications, these conditions may only occur in special environments, e.g., caves and rockshelters.

The technical aspects of AAR dating continue to be refined. The isolation of individual amino acids as well as high molecular weight fractions (Kaufman and Miller 1992; Kaufman and Sejrup 1995) will decrease the effect of diagenetic change on amino acid ratio variability. Study of the complete diagenetic process, including hydrolysis and decomposition will provide an opportunity for making various types of protein diagenesis dating independent of calibration processes since the variation in activation energies among these reactions will provide the ability to solve for both age and temperature history by looking at the simultaneous changes in two or more reactions (Miller *et al.* 1992; Hare *et al.* 1993).

REFERENCES

Abbott, J.T., Ellis, G. L., and Goodfriend, G.A. 1995 Chronometric and integrity analyses using land snails. *In* Abbott, J.T. and Trierweiler, W.N., eds., NRHP Significance Testing of 57 Prehistoric Archeological Sites on Fort Hood, Texas, Volume II. *United States Army Fort Hood Archaeological Resource Management Series Research Report* No. 34: 801–814.

Abbott, J.T., Goodfriend, G.A., and Ellis, G.L. 1996 Landsnail investigations. *In* Trierweiler, W.N., ed., *Archaeological Testing at Fort Hood: 1994–95*. Volume II. United States Army Fort Hood Archaeological Resource Management Series Research Report No. 35: 619–636.

Abelson, P.H. 1954a Organic constituents of fossils. *Carnegie Institution of Washington Yearbook* 53: 97–101.

_____ 1954b Amino acids in fossils. *Science* 119: 576.

_____ 1955 Organic constituents of fossils. *Carnegie Institution of Washington Yearbook* 54: 107–109.

_____ 1956 Paleobiochemistry. *Scientific American* 195: 83–92.

_____ 1959 Geochemistry of organic substances. *In* Abelson, P.H., ed., *Researches in Geochemistry*. New York, Wiley and Sons: 79–103.

_____ 1963 Geochemistry of amino acids. *In* Berger, I.A., ed., *Organic Geochemistry*. New York, Macmillan: 431–455.

Aitken, J.J. and Valladas, H. 1992 Luminescence dating relevant to human origins. *Philosophical Transactions of the Royal Society of London* B337: 139–144.

Alford, J.J. 1990 Quaternary aminostratigraphy of Mississippi Valley loess: discussion and reply. *Geological Society of America Bulletin* 102: 1136–1138.

Bada, J.L. 1972 The dating of fossil bones using the racemization of isoleucine. *Earth and Planetary Science Letters* 15: 223–231.

_____ 1974 Reply to Bender. *Nature* 252: 379–381.

_____ 1981 Racemization of amino acids in fossil bones and teeth from the Olduvai Gorge Region, Tanzania, East Africa. *Earth and Planetary Science Letters* 55: 292–298.

_____ 1982 Racemization of amino acids in nature. *Interdisciplinary Science Reviews* 7: 30–46.

_____ 1984 Racemization of amino acids. *In* G.C. Barrett, ed., *Chemistry and Biochemistry of the Amino Acids*. London, Chapman and Hall: 399–414.

_____ 1985 Amino acid racemization dating of fossil bones. *Annual Review of Earth and Planetary Science* 13: 214–268

_____ 1987 Paleoanthropological applications of amino acid racemization dating of fossil bones and teeth. *Anthropologisch Anzeiger* 45: 1–8.

Bada, J.L. and Deems, L. 1975 Accuracy of dates beyond the ^{14}C dating limit using the aspartic acid racemization reaction. *Nature* 255: 218–219.

Bada, J.L., Gillespie, R., Gowlett, J.A.J. and Hedges, R.E.M. 1984 Accelerator mass spectrometry: radiocarbon ages of amino acid extracts from Californian paleoindian skeletons. *Nature* 312: 442–444.

Bada, J.L. and Helfman, P. M. 1975 Amino acid racemization dating of fossil bones. *World Archaeology* 7: 160–173.

Bada, J.L, Kvenvolden, F. A. and Peterson, E. 1973 Racemization of amino acids in bones. *Nature* 245: 308–310.

Bada, J.L. and Protsch R. 1973 The racemization reaction of aspartic acid and its use in dating fossil bones. *Proceedings of the National Academy of Science*, USA 70: 1331–1334.

Bada, J.L. and Schroeder, R.A. 1972 Racemization of isoleucine in calcareous marine sediments: kinetics and mechanism. *Earth and Planetary Science Letters* 15: 1–11.

_____ 1975 Amino acid racemization reactions and their geochemical implications. *Naturwissenschaften* 62: 71–79.

Bada, J.L., Schroeder, R.A. and Carter, G.F. 1974 New evidence for the antiquity of man in North America deduced from aspartic acid racemization. *Science* 184: 791–793.

Bender, M.L. 1974 Reliability of amino acid racemization dating and paleotemperature analysis on bones. *Nature* 252: 378–379.

Blackwell, B., Rutter, N.W. and Last, W.M. 1989 Effects of fossilization on amino acid racemization in recent mammalian bones and teeth from saline lakes, Australia and Saskatchewan. *Geological Society of America Abstracts* 21: A210.

Blackwell, B., Rutter, N.W. and Debenath, H. 1990 Amino acid racemization analysis of mammalian bones and teeth from La Chaise-de Vouthon (Charente), France. *Geoarchaeology* 5: 121–147.

Bowen, D.Q., Hughes, S., Sykes, G.A. and Miller, G.H. 1989 Land-sea correlations in the Pleistocene based on isoleucine epimerization in non-marine molluscs. *Nature* 340: 49–51

Bowen, D.Q. and Sykes, G.A. 1988 Correlation of marine events and glaciations on the northeast Atlantic margin. *Transactions of the Royal Society of London* 318B: 619–635.

_____ 1994 How old is "Boxgrove Man"? *Nature* 371: 751.

Brooks, A.S., Hare, P.E., Kokis, J. Miller, G.H., Ernst, R. D. and Wendorf, F. 1990 Dating Pleistocene archeological sties by protein diagenesis in ostrich eggshell. *Science* 248: 60–64.

Brooks, A.S., Hare, P.E., and Kokis, J. 1993 Age of early Anatomically Modern Human fossils from the cave of Klasies River Mouth, South Africa. *Carnegie Institution of Washington Year Book* 92: 95–96.

Brooks, A.S., Hare, P.E., Kokis, J.E. and Durana, K. 1991 A burning question: differences between laboratory-induced and natural diagenesis in ostrich eggshell proteins. *Annual Report of the Director, Geopysical Laboratory, 1990–1991*. Washington D.C.: Geophysical Laboratory, Carnegie Institution of Washington: 176–179.

Brooks, A.S., Helgren, D.M., Cramer, J.S., Franklin, A., Hornyak, W., Keating, J.M., Klein, R.G., Rink, W.J., Schwarcz, H., Smith, K.N.L., Stewart, K., Todd, N.E. Verniers, J., Yellen, J.E. 1995 Dating and context of three Middle Stone Age sites with bone points in the Upper Semliki Valley, Zaire. *Science* 268: 548–553.

Cann, J.H., De Deckker, P. and Murray-Wallace, C.V. 1991 Coastal aboriginal shell middens and their palaeoenvironmental significance, Robe Range, South Australia. *Transactions of the Royal Society of South Australia* 115: 161–175.

Chappell, J. and Shackleton, N.J. 1986 Oxygen isotopes and sea level. *Nature* 324: 137–140.

Child, A.M. 1996 Amino acid racemization and the effects of microbial diagenesis. *In* M.V. Orna, ed., *Archaeological Chemistry Organic, Inorganic and Biochemical Analysis*. Washington, D.C., American Chemical Society: 366–377.

Child, A.M, Gillard, R.D., and Pollard, A.M. 1993 Microbially-induced promotion of amino acid racemization in bone: isolation of the microorganisms and the detection of their enzymes. *Journal of Archaeological Science* 20: 159–168.

Clark, P.U., Nelson, A.R., McCoy, W.D., Miller, B.B., and Barnes, D.K. 1989 Quaternary aminostratigraphy of Mississippi Valley loess. *Geological Society of America Bulletin* 101: 918–926.

_____ 1990 Quaternary aminostratigraphy of Mississippi Valley loess: discussion and reply. *Geological Society of America Bulletin* 102: 1136–1138.

Cook, L.M., Goodfriend, G.A. and Cameron, R.A.D. 1993 Changes in the land snail fauna of eastern Madeira during the Quaternary. *Philosophical Transactions of the Royal Society of London* B339: 83–103.

Corrado, J.C., Weems, R. E., Hare, P.E. and Bambach, R.K. 1986 Capabilities and limitations of applied aminostratigraphy, as illustrated by analyses of *Mulinia lateralis* from the late Cenozoic marine beds near Charleston, South Carolina. *South Carolina Geology* 30: 19–46.

Davis, W.E. and Treloar, F.E. 1977 The application of racemisation dating in archaeology: a critical review. *The Artifact* (The Journal of the Archaeological and Anthropological Society of Victoria) 2: 63–94.

Deacon, H.J. 1979 Excavations at Boomplaas Cave—a sequence through the Upper Pleistocene and Holocene in South Africa. *World Archaeology* 10: 241–255.

Deacon, H.J. and Lancaster, N. 1988 *Late Quaternary Environments of Southern Africa*. Oxford, Clarendon Press.

Ellis, G.L., Goodfriend, G.A., Abbott, J.T., Hare, P.E., and Von Endt, D.W. 1996 Assessment of integrity and geochronology of archaeological sites using amino acid racemization in land snail shells: examples from Central Texas. *Geoarchaeology* 11: 189–213.

Ellis, G.L. and Goodfriend, G.A. 1994 Chronometric and site-formation studies using land snail shells: preliminary results. *In* W.N. Trierweiler, ed., *Archeological Investigations on 571 Prehistoric Sites at Fort Hood, Hell and Coryell Counties, Texas* United States Army Fort Hood Archeological Resource Management Series Research Report 31: 183–201.

Elster, H., Emanuel, G., and Weiner, S. 1991 Amino acid racemization of fossil bone. *Journal of Archaeological Science* 18: 605–617.

Engel, M.H. and Hare, P.E. 1985 Gas liquid chromatographic separation of amino acids and their derivatives. *In* G.C. Barrett, ed., *Chemistry and Biochemistry of Amino Acids*. London, Chapman and Hall: 462–479.

Ennis, P., Noltman, E.A., Hare, P.E., Slota, P.J., Payen, L.A., Prior, C.A., and Taylor, R.E. 1986 The use of AMS ^{14}C analysis in the study of problems in aspartic acid racemization-deduced age estimates on bone. *Radiocarbon* 28: 539–546.

Ernst, R.D. 1989 Reaction kinetics of protein hydrolysis, amino acid decomposition and isoleucine epimerization in eggshell of the African ostrich, *Struthio camelus*. M.A. thesis, Department of Geoscience, University of Arizona: 150 pp.

Florkin, M. 1969 Fossil shell "Conchiolin" and Other Preserved Biopolymers. *In* G. Eglinton, and M.T.J. Murphy, eds., *Organic Geochemistry—Methods and Results*. Berlin, Springer Verlag: 498–520.

Florkin, M., Gregoire, C., Bricteux-Gregorie, S. and Schofeniels, F. 1961 Paleobiochimie—Conchiolines de Nacres Fossiles. *Academie des Sciences, Comptes Rendus* 252: 440–442.

Forman, S.L., Bettis, E.A., Kemmis, T.J., and Miller, B.B. 1992 Chronologic evidence for multiple periods of loess deposition during the late Pleistocene in the Missouri and Mississippi Valley, United States, implications for the activity of the Laurentide ice sheet. *Palaeogeography, Palaeoclimatology, Palaeoecology* 93: 71–83.

Gamble, C. 1994 Time for Boxgrove Man. *Nature* 369: 275–276.

Gibbons, A. 1992 Paleoanthropologists launch a society of their own: following a trail of old ostrich eggshells. *Science* 256: 1281–1282.

Goede, A. and Bada, J.L. 1985 Electron spin resonance dating of Quaternary bone materials from Tasmanian Caves: a comparison with ages determined by aspartic acid racemization and ^{14}C. *Australian Journal of Earth Sciences* 32: 155–162.

Goodfriend, G.A. 1987a Chronostratigraphic studies of sediments in the Negev Desert, using amino acid epimerization analysis of land snail shells. *Quaternary Research* 28: 374–392.

_____ 1987b Evaluation of amino-acid racemization/epimerization dating using radiocarbon-dated fossil land snails. *Geology* 15: 698–700.

_____ 1989 Complementary use of amino-acid epimerization and radiocarbon analysis for dating of mixed-age fossil assemblages. *Radiocarbon* 31: 1053–1059.

_____ 1991 Patterns of racemization and epimerization of amino acids in land snail shells over the course of the Holocene. *Geochmica et Cosmochimica Acta* 55: 293–302.

_____ 1992a Rapid racemization of aspartic acid in mollusc shells and potential for dating over recent centuries. *Nature* 357: 399–401.

_____ 1992b The use of land snail shells in paleoenvironmental reconstruction. *Quaternary Science Reviews* 11: 665–685.

Goodfriend, G.A., Cameron, R.A.D., and Cook, L.M. 1994 Fossil evidence of recent human impact on the land snail fauna of Madeira. *Journal of Biogeography* 21: 703–715.

Goodfriend, G.A. and Mitterer, R. M. 1988 Late Quaternary land snails from the north coast of Jamaica: local extinctions and climatic change. *Paleogeography, Palaeocoimatology, Paleoecology* 63: 293–311.

Goodfriend, G.A., Von Endt, D.W., and Hare, P. E. 1991 Rapid racemization of aspartic acid in mollusk and ostrich egg shells: a new method for dating on a decadal time scale. *Annual Report of the Director, Geophysical Laboratory, Carnegie Instiution of Washington, 1990–1991*: 172–176.

Goodfriend, G.A. and Meyer, V.R. 1991 A comparative study of amino acid racemization/epimerization kinetics in fossil and modern mollusk shells. *Geochmica et Cosmochimica Acta* 55: 3355–3367.

Goodfriend, G.A. Hare, P.E. and Druffel, E.R.M. 1992 Aspartic acid racemization and protein diagenesis in corals over the last 350 years. *Geochimica et Cosmochimica Acta* 56: 3847–3850.

Goodfriend, G.A. and Mitterer, R.M. 1993 A 45,000-yr record of a tropical lowland biota: the land snail fauna from cave sediments at Coco Ree, Jamaica. *Geological Society of America Bulletin* 105: 18–29.

Goodfriend, G.A., Kashgarian, M., and Harasewych, M.G. 1995 Use of aspartic acid racemization and post-bomb ^{14}C to reconstruct growth rate and longevity of the deep-water slit shell *Entemnotrochus adansonianus*. *Geochimica et Cosmochimica Acta* 59: 1125–1129.

Goodfriend, G.A. and Stanley, D.J. 1996 Reworking and discontinuities in Holocene sedimentation in the Nile Delta: documentation from amino acid racemization and stable isotopes in mollusk shells. *Marine Geology* 129: 271–283.

Goodfriend, G.A., Cameron, R.A.D., Cook, L.M., Courty, M.-A., Fedoroff, N., Livett, E., and Tallis, J. 1996 The Quaternary eolian sequence of Madeira: stratigraphy, chronology, and paleoenvironmental interpretation *Palaeogeography, Palaeoclimatology, Palaeoecology* 120: 195–234.

Goodfriend, G.A., Flessa, K.W. and Hare, P.E. 1997 Variation in amino acid epimerization rates and amino acid composition among shell layers in the bivalve *Chione* from the Gulf of California. *Geochimica et Cosmochimica Acta* 61: 1487–1493.

Hare, P.E. 1969 Geochemistry of proteins, peptides and amino acids. *In* Eglinton, G. and Murphy, M.T.J., eds. *Organic Geochemistry*. Berlin, Springer-Verlag: 438–463.

_____ 1974a Amino acid dating—a history and an evaluation. *Museum Applied Science Center for Archaeology Newsletter* 10: 4–7.

_____ 1974b Amino acid dating of bone—the influence of water. *Carnegie Institution of Washington Yearbook* 73: 576–81.

_____ 1980 Organic geochemistry of bone and its relation to the survival of bone in the natural environment. *In* Behrensmeyer, A.K. and Hill, A.P., eds., *Fossils in the Making: Vertebrate Taphonomy and Paleoecology*. Chicago, University of Chicago Press: 208–19.

Hare, P.E. and Abelson, P.H. 1968 Racemization of amino acids in fossil shells. *Carnegie Institution of Washington Yearbook* 66: 526–528.

Hare, P.E., Brooks, A.S., Helgren, D.M. Kokis, J.E. and Kuman, K. 1984 Aminostratigraphy: the use of ostrich eggshell in dating the Middle Stone Age at #Gi, Botswana. *Geological Society of America Abstracts with Programs* 16: 529.

Hare, P.E., Goodfriend, G.A., Brooks, A.S., Kokis, J.E. and Von Endt, D.W. 1993 Chemical clocks and thermometers: diagenetic reactions of amino acids in fossils. *Yearbook of the Carnegie Institution of Washington* 92: 80–85.

Hare, P.E., Hoering, T.C., and King, K., Jr. 1980 *Biogeochemistry of Amino Acids*. New York, John Wiley & Sons.

Hare P.E. and Mitterer, R.M. 1967 Nonprotein amino acids in fossil shells. *Carnegie Institution of Washington Yearbook* 65: 363–364.

_____ 1969 Laboratory simulation of amino-acid diagenesis in fossils. *Carnegie Institution of Washington Yearbook* 67: 205–211.

Hare, P.E., St. John, P.A. and Engel, M.H. 1985 Ion exchange separation of amino acids. *In* G.C. Barrett, ed., *Chemistry and Biochemistry of Amino Acids*. Chapman and Hall, London: 415–425.

Hare, P.E., Turnbull, H.F. and Taylor, R.E. 1978 Amino acid dating of Pleistocene fossil materials: Olduvai Gorge, Tanzania. *In* Freeman, L.G., ed., *Views of the Past: Essays in Old World Prehistory and Paleoanthropology*. Mouton, The Hague: 7–12.

Harmon, R.S., Mitterer, R.M., Kriausakul, N., Land, L.S., Schwarcz, H.P., Garrett, P., Larson, G.J., Vacher, H.L, and Rowe, M. 1983 U-series and amino-acid racemization geochronology of Bermuda: implications for eustatic sea-level fluctuations over the past 250,000 years. *Palaeogeography, Palaeoclimatology, Palaeoecology* 44: 41–70.

Hearty, P.J., Miller, G.H., Sterns, C.E. and Szabo, B.J. 1986 Aminostratigraphy of Quaternary shorelines in the Mediterranean basin. *Geological Society of America Bulletin* 97: 850–858.

Hearty, P.J., Vacher, H.L and Mitterer, R.M. 1992 Aminostratigraphy and ages of Pleistocene limestones of Bermuda. *Geological Society of America Bulletin* 104: 471–480.

Helfman, P.M. and Bada, J.L. 1975 Aspartic acid racemization in tooth enamel from living humans. *Proceedings of the National Academy of Sciences* 72:2891–2894.

_____ 1976 Aspartic acid racemization in dentine as a measure of aging. *Nature* 262:279–281.

Henry, D.O. and Miller, G.H. 1992 The implications of amino acid racemization dates of Levantine Mousterian deposits in southern Jordan. *Paleorient* 18: 45–52.

Hollin, J.T., Smith, F.L, Renouf, J.T. and Jenkins, D.G. 1993 Sea-cave temperature measurements and amino acid geochronology of British Late Pleistocene sea stands. *Journal of Quaternary Science* 8: 359–364.

Johnson, B.J. 1995 Stable isotope biogeochemistry of ostrich eggshell and its application to Late Quaternary paleoenvironmental reconstruction in South Africa. Ph.D. dissertation, University of Colorado.

Johnson, B.J. and Miller, G.H. 1997 Archaeological applications of amino acid racemization: A review. *Archaeometry* 39: 265–288.

Kaufman, D. S. 1992 Aminostratigraphy of Pliocene-Pleistocene high-sea-level deposits, Nome coastal plain and adjacent nearshore area, Alaska. *Geological Society of America Bulletin* 104: 40–52.

Kaufman, D.S. and Miller, G.H. 1992 Overview of amino acid geochronology. *Comparative Biochemistry and Physiology* 102B: 199–204.

Kaufman, D.S. and Sejrup, H.P. 1995 Isoleucine epimerization in the high-molecular-weight fraction of Pleistocene *Arctica*. *Quaternary Science Reviews (Quaternary Geochronology)* 14: 337–350

Kessels, H.J. and Dungworth, G. 1980 Necessity of reporting amino acid compositions of fossil bones where racemization analyses are used for geochronological applications: inhomogeneities of D/L amino acids in fossil bones. *In* Hare, P.E., Hoering, T.C., and King, K. Jr., eds., *Biogeochemistry of Amino Acids*. New York: Wiley and Sons: 527–542.

Kimber, R.W.L. and Griffin, C.V. 1987 Further evidence of the complexity of the racemization process in fossil shells with implications for amino acid racemization dating. *Geochimica et Cosmochimica Acta* 51: 839–846.

Kimber, R.W.L., Kennedy, N.M. and Milnes, A.R. 1994 Amino acid racemization dating of a 140,000 year old tephra-loess-palaeosol sequence on the Mamaku Plateau near Rotorua, New Zealand. *Australian Journal of Earth Sciences* 41: 19–26.

Kimber, R.W.L., Griffin, C.V. and Milnes, A.R. 1986 Amino acid racemization dating: evidence of apparent reversal in aspartic acid racemization with time in shells of *Ostrea*. *Geochimica et Cosmochimica Acta* 50: 1159–1161.

Kimber, R.W.L and Hare, P.E. 1992 Wide range of racemization of amino acids in peptides from human fossil bone and its implications for amino acid racemization dating. *Geochimica et Cosmochimica Acta* 56: 739–743.

Klein, R. G. 1977 The ecology of early man in southern Africa. *Science* 197: 115–126.

_____ 1983 The stone age prehistory of Southern Africa. *Annual Reviews in Anthropology* 12:25–48.

_____ 1989 *The Human Career: Human Biological and Cultural Origins*. Chicago, University of Chicago Press.

_____ 1994 Southern Africa before the Iron Age. *In* Corruccini, R.S. and Ciochon, R.L., eds., *Integrative Paths to the Past: Paleoanthropological Advances in Honor of F. Clark Howell*. Englewood Cliffs, New Jersey, Prentice Hall: 471–519.

_____ 1995 Anatomy, behavior, and modern human origins. *Journal of World Prehistory* 9: 167–198.

Kokis, J.E. 1988 Protein diagenesis dating of ostrich (*Struthio camelus*) eggshell: an Upper Pleistocene dating technique. M.A. thesis, George Washington University.

Kokis, J.E., Brooks, A.S. and Hare, P.E. 1990 Chronology and aminostratigraphy of Middle and Late Stone Age sites from Sub-saharan Africa: a comparison of protein diagenesis and radiocarbon dating of ostrich eggshell. *Geological Society of America Abstracts with Programs* 22: A145–146.

Kvenvolden, K.A. 1975 Advances in the geochemistry of amino acids. *Annual Review of Earth and Planetary Science* 3: 183–212.

Kvenvolden, K.A., Blunt, D.J., Robinson, S.W., and Bacon, G. 1979 Amino-acid dating of an archaeological site on Amaknak Island, Alaska. *Geological Society of America Abstracts with Programs* 11: 462.

Lajoie, K.R., Wehmiller, J.F. and Kennedy, G.L. 1980 Inter- and Intrageneric trends in apparent racemization kinetics of amino acids in Quaternary mollusks. *In* Hare, P.E., Hoering, T.C. and King, K. Jr., eds., *Biogeochemistry of Amino Acids*, New York, John Wiley: 305–340.

Lauritzen, S.E., Haugen, J.E., Lovlie, R., and Gilje-Nielsen, H. 1994 Geochronological potential of isoleucine epimerization in calcite speleothems. *Quaternary Research* 41: 52–58.

Lowenstam, H. and Weiner, S. 1989 *On Biomineralization*. New York, Oxford University Press.

Martinson, D.G., Pisias, N.G., Hays, J.D., Imbrie, J.E., Moore, T.C., Jr. and Shackleton, N.J. 1987 Age dating and orbital theory of the ice ages: Development of a high-resolution 0–300,000 years chronostratigraphy. *Quaternary Research* 27: 1–29.

Masters, P.M. 1986 Amino acid racemization dating. *In* Zimmerman, M.R. and Angel, J.L., eds., *Dating and Age Determination of Biological Materials*. London, Cromm, Helm, Longwood: 39–58.

Masters, P.M. 1987 Preferential preservation of noncollagenous protein during bone diagenesis: implications for chronometric and stable isotope measurements. *Geochimica et Cosmochimica Acta* 51: 3209–3214.

Masters, P.M. and Bada, J.L. 1977 Racemization of isoleucine in fossil molluscs from Indian middens and interglacial terraces in Southern California. *Earth and Planetary Science Letters* 37: 173–183.

Matsu'ura, S. and Ueta, N. 1980 Fraction dependent variation of aspartic acid racemization age of fossil bone. *Nature* 286: 883–884.

McCoy, W.D. 1987a Quaternary aminostratigraphy of the Bonneville Basin, Western United States. *Geological Sociegty of America Bulletin* 98: 99–112.

_____ 1987b The precision of amino acid geochronology and paleothermometry. *Quaternary Science Reviews* 6: 43–54.

McDernott, F., Grun, R., Stringer, C.B. and Hawkesworth, C.J. 1993 Mass-spectrometric U-series dates for Israeli Neanderthal/Early Modern hominid sites. *Nature* 363: 252–255.

Meyer, V.R. 1991 Amino acid racemization: a tool for dating? *In* Ahuja, S., ed., *Chiral Separations by Liquid Chromatography*. Washington, D.C.: American Chemical Society: 217–227.

Miller, B.B., McCoy, W.D., Wayne, W.J., Brockman, C.S. 1992 Ages of the Whitewater and Fairhaven Tills in southwestern Ohio and southeastern Indiana. *In* Clar, P.U. and Lea, P.D., eds. *The Last Interglacial-Glacial Transition in North America*. Geological Society of America Special Paper 270: 89–98.

Miller, G.H. 1982 Quaternary depositional episodes, western Spitsbergen, Norway: aminostratigraphy and glacial history. *Arctic and Alpine Research* 14: 321–340.

_____ 1985 Aminostratigraphy of Baffin Island shell bearing depostis. *In* Andrews, J.T., ed., *Quaternary Environments: the Eastern Canadian Arctic, Baffin Bay and Western Greenland*. Boston, Allen and Unwin: 394–427.

Miller, G.H. and Beaumont, P.B. 1989 Dating the Middle Stone Age at Border Cave, South Africa, by the epimerization of isoleucine in ostrich eggshell. *Geological Society of America Abstracts with Programs* 21: A235.

Miller, G.H., Beaumont, P.B., Jull, A.J.T., and Johnson, B. 1992 Pleistocene geochronology and palaeothermometry from protein diagenesis in ostrich eggshells: implications for the evolution of modern humans. *Philosphical Transactions of the Royal Society of London* 337: 149–157.

Miller, G.H., and Brigham-Grette, J. 1989 Amino acid geochronology: Resolution and precision in carbonate fossils. *Quaternary International* 1: 111–128.

Miller, G.H., and Hare P.E. 1980 Amino acid geochronology: integrity of the carbonate matrix and potential of molluscan fossils. *In* Hare, P.E., Hoering, T.C., and King, K. Jr., eds., *Biogeochemistry of Amino Acids*. New York, John Wiley: 425–443.

Miller, G.H., Hollin, J.T. and Andrews, J.T. 1979 Aminostratigraphy of U.K. Pleistocene deposits. *Nature* 281: 539–543.

Miller, G.H., Johnson, B.J., and Ernst, R.D. 1990 Modeling amino acid racemization and decomposition and protein hydrolysis in ratite eggshells. *Geological Society of America Abstracts with Programs* 22: A145.

Miller, G.H., Magee, J.W., and Jull, A.J.T. 1997 Low-latitude glacial cooling in the Southern Hemisphere from amino-acid racemization in emu eggshells. *Nature* 385: 241–244.

Miller, G.H. and Rosewater, A. 1995 The potential of isoleucine epimerization in fish otoliths to date Pleistocene archaeological sites. *Geological Society of America Abstracts with Programs* 27: A415.

Miller, G.H., Wendorf, F., Ernst, R., Schild, R., Close, A.E., Friedman, I., and Schwarcz, H.P. 1991 Dating lacustrine episodes in the eastern Sahara by the epimerization of isoleucine in ostrich eggshells. *Palaeogeography, Palaeoclimatology, Palaeoecology* 84: 175–190.

Milnes, A.R., Kimber, R.W., and Phillips, S.E. 1987 Studies in calcareous aeolian landscapes of southern Australia. *In* Liu, T., ed., *Aspects of Loess Research*. Hong King, China Ocean Press: 130–139.

Minugh-Purvis, N. 1995 The Modern Human origins controversy: 1984–1994. *Evolutionary Anthropology* 4: 140–147.

Mirecki, J.E. and Miller, B.B. 1994 Aminostratigraphic correlation and geochronology of two quaternary loess localities, Central Mississippi Valley. *Quaternary Research* 41: 289–297.

Mitterer, R.M. 1993 The diagenesis of proteins and amino acids in fossil shells. *In* Engel, M.H, and Macko, S.A., eds., *Organic Geochemistry Principles and Applications*, New York, Plenum: 739–753.

Mitterer, R.M. and Kriausakul, N. 1989 Calculation of amino acid racemization ages based on apparent parabolic kinetics. *Quaternary Science Reviews* 8: 353–357.

Morell, V. 1994 Pulling hair from the ground. *Science* 265: 741.

Murray-Wallace, C.V. 1993 A review of the application of amino acid racemisation reaction to archaeological dating. *The Artifact* (The Journal of the Archaeological and Anthropological Society of Victoria) 16: 19–26.

Murray-Wallace, C.V., Belperio, A.P., Gostin, V.A. and Cann, J.H. 1993 Amino acid racemization and radiocarbon dating of interstadial marine strata (oxygen isotope stage 3) Gulf of St. Vincent, South Australia. *Marine Geology* 110: 83–92.

Murray-Wallace, C.V. and Bourman, R.P. 1990 Direct radiocarbon calibration for amino acid racemization dating. *Australian Journal of Earth Sciences* 37: 365–367.

Murray-Wallace, C.V. and Kimber, R.W.L. 1987 Evaluation of the amino acid racemization reaction in studies of Quaternary marine sediments in South Australia. *Australian Journal of Earth Sciences* 34: 279–292.

_____ 1993 Further evidence for apparent 'parabolic' racemization kinetics in Quaternary molluscs. *Australian Journal of Earth Sciences* 40: 313–317.

Oches, E.A. and McCoy, W.D. 1989 Amino acid paleotemperature estimates for the Last Glacial Maximum, Lower Mississippi Valley. *Geological Society of America Abstracts with Programs* 21: A210.

_____ 1995 Aminostratigraphic evalution of conflicting age estimates for the "Young Loess" of Hungary. *Quaternary Research* 44: 160–170.

_____ 1996 Amino acid geochronology applied to the correlation and dating of Central European loess deposits. *Quaternary Science Reviews* 14: 767–782.

Prior, C.A., Ennis, P.J., Noltmann, E.A., Hare, P.E. and Taylor, R.E. 1986 Variations in D/L aspartic acid ratios in bones of similar age and temperature history. *In* Olin, J.S. and Blackman, M.J., eds., *Proceedings of the 24th International Archaeometry Symposium*. Washington, D.C., Smithsonian Institution: 487–498.

Rae, A.M., Ivanovich, M., Green, H.S., Head, M.J. and Kimber, R.W.L. 1987 A comparative dating study of bones from Little Hoyle Cave, South Wales, U.K. *Journal of Archaeological Science* 14: 243–250.

Roberts, M.B. 1994 How old is "Boxgrove Man"? Reply. *Nature* 371: 751.

Roberts, M.B., Sringer, C.B. and Parfitt, S.A. 1994 A hominid tibia from Middle Pleistocene sediments at Boxgrove, UK. *Nature* 369: 311–313.

Rosen, S.A. and Goodfriend, G.A. 1993 An early date for Gaza Ware from the Northern Negev. *Palestine Exploration Quarterly* 125: 143–148.

Rutter, N.W. and Blackwell, B. 1996 Amino acid racemization dating. *In* Rutter, N.W. and Catto, N.R., eds., *Pleistocene Dating Methods: Problems and Applications*. Edmonton, Geoscience Canada: 1–40.

Rutter, N.W. and Crawford, R.J. 1984 Utilizing wood in amino acid dating. *In* Mahaney, W.C., ed. *Quaternary Dating Methods*. Amsterdam, Elsevier: 195–209.

Rutter, N.W., Crawford, R.J. and Hamilton, R.D. 1985 Dating methods of Pleistocene deposits and their problems: IV. Amino acid racemization dating. *In* Rutter, N.W., ed., *Dating Methods of Pleistocene Deposits and Their Problems*. Edmonton, Geoscience Canada Reprint Series 2: 23–30.

Rutter, N.W., Crawford, R.J., and Hamilton, R.D. 1980 Correlation and relative age dating of Quaternary strata in the continuous permafrost zone of northern Yukon with D/L ratios of aspartic acid of wood, freshwater molluscs, and bone. *In* Hare, P.E., Hoering, T.C., and King, K. Jr., eds., *Biogeochemistry of Amino Acids*. New York, John Wiley: 463–475.

Rutter, N.W. and Vlahos, C.K. 1988 Amino acid racemization kinetics in wood: applications to geochronology and geothermometry. *In* Easterbrook, D.J., ed. *Dating Quaternary Sediments*. Geological Society of America Special Paper 227: 51–67.

Saint-Martin, B. 1991 Étude des influences géochimiques sur la vitesse de racémisation des acides aminés dans les ossements fossiles. *C. R. Académie des Sciences, Paris* 313: 655–660.

Saint-Martin, B. and Julg, A. 1991 Influence of the interaction between asymmetry centers on the kinetics of racemization. *Journal of Molecular Structure* 251: 375–383.

Sampson, C.G. 1994 Ostrich eggs and Bushman survival on the northeast frontier of the Cape Colony. *Journal of Arid Environments* 26: 383–399.

Schroeder, R.A. and Bada, J.L. 1976 A review of the geochemical applications of the amino acid racemization reaction. *Earth Sciences Review* 12: 347–391.

Schwarcz, H.P., Grun, R., Vandermeersch, B., Bar-Yosef, O., Vallada, H., and Tchernov, E. 1988 ESR dates for the hominid burial site of Qafzeh in Israel. *Journal of Human Evolution* 7: 733–737.

Shackleton, N.J. and Opdyke, N.D. 1973 Oxygen isotope and paleomagnetic stratigraphy of equatorial Pacific core V28–238: oxygen isotope temperatures on a 10^5 and 10^6 year time scale. *Quaternary Research* 3: 39–55.

_____ 1976 Oxygen isotope and paleomagnetic stratigraphy of Pacific core V28–239: Latest Micocene to Latest Pleistocene. *Geological Society of America Memoirs* 145: 449–463.

Skeleton, R.R. 1982 A test of the applicability of amino acid racemization dating for Northern California. *American Journal of Physical Anthropology* 57: 228–229.

Smith, G.G. and Evans, R.C. 1980 The effect of structure and conditions on the rate of racemization of free and bound amino acids. *In* Hare, P.E., Hoering, T.C., and K. King, Jr., eds., *Biogeochemistry of Amino Acids*. New York, John Wiley & Sons: 257–282.

Smith, G.G., Williams, K.M. and Wonnacott, D.M. 1978 Factors affecting the rate of racemization of amino acids and their significance to geochronology. *Journal of Organic Chemistry* 43: 1–5.

Stafford, T.W. Jr., Jull, A.J.T., Zabel, T.H., Donahue, D.J., Duhamel, R.C., Brendel, K., Haynes C.V., Jr., Bischoff, J.L., Payen, L.A. and Taylor, R.E 1984 Holocene age of the Yuha burial: direct radiocarbon determinations by accelerator mass spectrometry. *Nature* 308: 446–447.

Stafford, T.W. Jr., Hare, P.E., Currie, L., Jull, A.J.T., and Donahue D.J. 1990 Accuracy of North American human skeleton ages. *Quaternary Research* 34: 111–120.

Taylor, R.E. 1983 Non-concordance of radiocarbon and amino acid racemization deduced age estimates on human bone. *Radiocarbon* 25: 647–654.

Taylor, R.E., Ennis, P.J., Slota, P.J. Jr., and Payen, L.A. 1989 Non-age-related variations in aspartic acid racemization in bone from a radiocarbon-dated late Holocene archaeological site. *Radiocarbon* 31: 1048–1056.

Taylor, R.E., Hare, P.E., and White, T.D. 1995 Geochemical criteria for thermal alteration of bone. *Journal of Archaeological Science* 22: 115–119.

Taylor, R.E., Hare, P.E., Prior, C.A., Kirner, D.L., Wan, L. and Burky, R.R. 1995 Radiocarbon dating of biochemically characterized hair. *Radiocarbon* 37: 319–330.

Taylor, R.E., Payen, L.A. and Gerow, B., Donahue, D.J., Zabel, T.H., Jull, A.J.T., and Damon, P.E. 1983 Middle Holocene age of the Sunnyvale human skeleton. *Science* 220: 1271–1273.

Taylor, R.E., Payen, L.A., Prior, C.A., Slota, P.J., Gillespie, R., Gowlett, J.A.J., Hedges, R.E.B., Jull, A.J.T., Zabel, T.H., Donahue, D.J., and Berger, R. 1985 Major revisions in the Pleistocene age assignment for North American human skeletons by ^{14}C accelerator mass spectrometry: none older than 11,000 ^{14}C years B.P. *American Antiquity* 50: 136–140.

Valladas, H., Reyss, J.L., Joron, J.L., Valladas, G., Bar-Yosef, O., and Vandermeersch, B. 1988 Thermoluminescence dating of Mousterian "Proto-Cro-Magnon" remains from Israel and the origin of modern man. *Nature* 331: 614–616.

Vallentyne, J.R. 1964 Biogeochemistry of Organic Matter: II. Thermal reaction kinetics and transformation products of amino compounds. *Geochimica et Cosmochimica Acta* 28: 157–188.

_____ 1968 Pyrolysis of proline, leucine, arginine and lysine in aqueous solution. *Geochimica et Cosmochimica Acta* 32: 1353–1356.

_____ 1969 Pyrolysis of amino acids in Pleistocene *Mercenaria* shells. *Geochimica et Cosmochimica Acta* 33: 1453–1458.

Van Strydonck, M.J.Y., Van Roeyen, J-P., Minnaert, G. and Verbruggen, C. 1995 Problems in dating Stone-age settlements on sandy soils: the Hof Ten Damme Site near Melsele, Belgium. *Radiocarbon* 37: 291–297.

Vogel, J.C. and Beaumont, P.B. 1972 Revised radiocarbon chronology for the stone age in South Africa. *Nature* 237: 50–51.

Volman, T.P. 1984 Early prehistory of southern Africa. *In* Klein, R.G., ed., *Southern African Prehistory and Paleoenvironments*. Rotterdam, A.A. Belkema: 169–220.

Von Endt, D.W. 1979 Techniques of amino acid dating. *In*: Humphrey, R.L. and Stanford, D., eds., *Pre-Llano Cultures of the Americas: Paradoxes and Possibilities*. Washington, D.C., The Anthropological Society of Washington: 71–100.

_____ 1980 Protein hydrolysis and amino acid racemization in sized bone. *In* Hare, P.E., Hoering, T.C., and King, K. Jr., eds., *Biogeochemistry of Amino Acids*. New York, John Wiley: 297–304.

Wehmiller, J.F. 1977 Amino acid studies of the Del Mar, California, midden site: apparent rate constants, ground temperature models and chronological implications. *Earth and Planetary Science Letters* 37: 184–196.

_____ 1982 A review of amino acid racemization studies in Quaternary mollusks: stratigraphic and chronological applications in coastal and interglacial sites, Pacific and Atlantic coast, United States, United Kingdom, Baffin Island, and tropical islands. *Quaternary Science Reviews* 1: 83–120.

_____ 1984 Relative and absolute dating of Quaternary molluscs with amino acid racemization: evaluation, applications and questions. *In* Mahaney, W.C., ed., *Quaternary dating methods*. Amsterdam, Elserview Science Publishers: 171–193.

_____ 1986 Amino acid racemization geochronology *In*: A.J. Hurford, A.J., Jager, E., and Tencate, J.A., eds., *Dating Young Sediments*. Bangok, United Nations CCOP Technical Publications: 139–158.

_____ 1993 Applications of organic geochemistry for Quaternary research: aminostratigraphy and aminochronology. *In* Engel, M.H. and Macko, S.A. eds., *Organic Geochemistry*. New York, Plenum Press: 755–783.

Wehmiller, J. and Hare, P.E. 1971 Racemization of amino acids in marine sediments. *Science* 173: 907–911.

Wehmiller, J.F. and Miller, G.H. 1990 Amino acid racemization geochronology. *In* Edwards, T.W.D., ed., *Examples and Critiques of Quaternary Dating Methods*. AMQUA/CANQUA Short Course 3: 1–72.

_____ in press Amino acid racemization. *In* Noller, J.S., Sowers, J.M. and Lettis, W.F., *Quaternary geochronology: applications in Quaternary geology and paleoseismology*. Washington, DC, United States Regulatory Commission, NUREG/CR 5562: 307–361.

Weiner, S. 1979 Aspartic acid-rich proteins: major components of the soluble organic matrix of mollusk shells. *Calcified Tissue International* 29: 163–167.

_____ 1983 Mollusk shell formation: isolation of two organic matrix proteins associated with calcite deposition in the bivalve *Mytilus californianus*. *Biochemistry* 22: 4139–4145.

Weiner, S. and Traub, W. 1984 Macromolecules in mollusc shells and their functions in biomineralization. *Philosophical Transactions of the Royal Society of London* B304: 425–434.

Williams, K.M. and Smith, G.G. 1977 A critical evaluation of the application of amino acid racemization to geochronology and geothermometry. *Origins of Life* 8: 91–144.

Wyckoff, R.W.G. 1972 *The Biochemistry of Animal Fossils*. Bristol, Scientechnica.

Yellen, J.E., Brooks, A.S., Cornelissen, E., Mehlman, M.J., Stewart, K. 1995 A Middle Stone Age worked bone industry from Katanda, Upper Semlike Valley, Zaire. *Science* 268: 553–556.

Zumberge, J.E., Engel, M.H. and Nagy, B. 1980 Amino acids in Bristlecone pine: an evaluation of factors affecting racemization rates and paleothermometry. *In* Hare, P.E., Hoering, T.C. and King, K, Jr., eds., *Biogeochemistry of Amino Acids*. New York, John Wiley & Sons: 503–525.

Chapter 10

Obsidian Hydration Dating

IRVING FRIEDMAN, FRED W. TREMBOUR, AND
RICHARD E. HUGHES

ABSTRACT

A freshly-made surface of obsidian (volcanic glass of rhyolitic composition) will absorb water which slowly penetrates by diffusion into the body of the artifact. Although the depth of penetration can be measured by various methods, it is generally determined by microscopic examination on thin sections of the artifact cut normal to the surface. The rate of penetration of water is dependent upon several factors, primarily the chemical composition of the glass and the temperature at which the hydration occurred. Discussions are given of techniques for measuring the hydration thickness, measurement (or estimates) of ambient hydration temperature, chemical composition of the obsidian, and the conversion of hydration thickness to dating the time of manufacture of the artifact. Comparisons are made between the results of obsidian hydration and other dating methods.

INTRODUCTION

Obsidian is a glassy volcanic rock of rhyolitic composition (70–78% SiO_2; 11–16% Al_2O_3; 0.1–5% Fe_2O_3; 0.1–4% FeO; 0.1–1% MgO; 0.1–5% CaO; 2–6% Na_2O; 1–5% K_2O). It is formed when molten lava of the appropriate composi-

IRVING FRIEDMAN • Laboratory of Isotope Geology, United States Geological Survey, Denver, Colorado 80225, USA. **FRED W. TREMBOUR** • Laboratory of Isotope Geology, United States Geological Survey, Denver, Colorado 80225, USA. **RICHARD E. HUGHES** • Geochemical Research Laboratory, Portola Valley, California 94028, USA.

Chronometric Dating in Archaeology, edited by Taylor and Aitken.
Plenum Press, New York, 1997.

tion is rapidly cooled by eruption onto the earths surface, or when hot volcanic ash is compacted and welded into a dense, transparent glass (welded tuff or ignimbrite). Obsidian is extremely resistant to both physical and chemical weathering, and possesses remarkable flaking properties. In all areas of the world where geologic obsidian deposits occur ancient peoples employed it extensively to fashion a wide variety of tools.

The dating of obsidian by hydration was first published by Friedman and Smith (1960). The technique makes use of the fact that an obsidian surface, as soon as it is created, will adsorb water from the atmosphere to form an adherent hydrated layer or rind which thickens with time as the water slowly diffuses into the glass. The hydrated layer has a higher density and refractive index than the original glass (Ross and Smith 1955) and can be observed and measured under the microscope on thin sections cut normal to the surface (Fig. 10.1A).

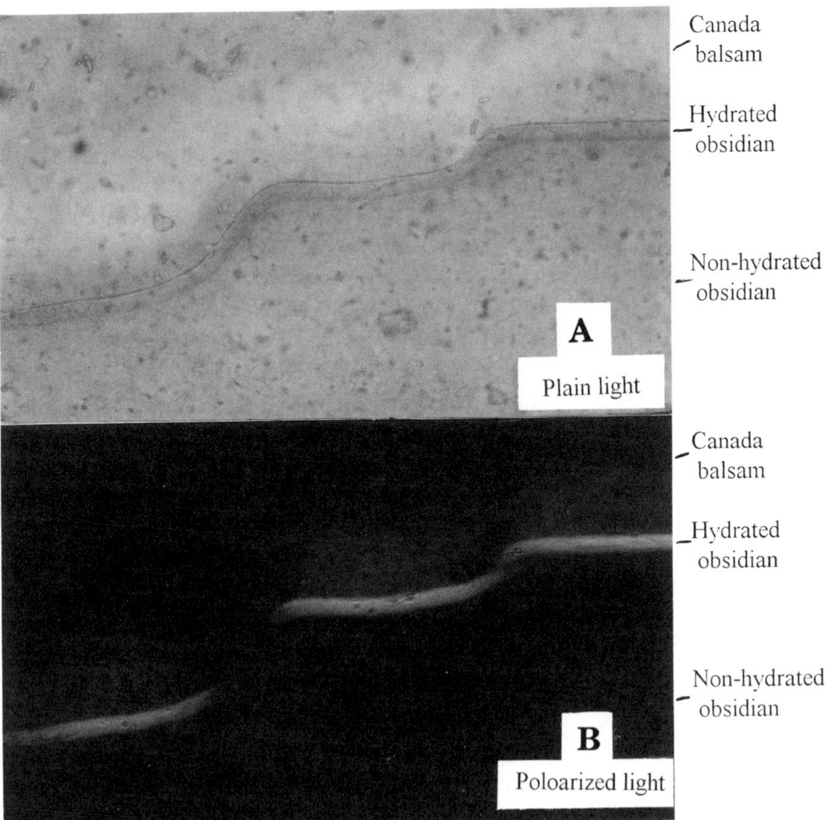

Figure 10.1. Photomicrographs of thin section of an obsidian artifact showing hydration rind, viewed in (A) plain light and (B) crossed polarized light (Friedman and Smith 1960).

The rate of hydration is dependent on the temperature, on the chemical composition of the glass, and on the relative humidity (rH) of the environment. Often measurable hydration is formed in a few hundred years, and continues for a million or more years to a depth of 50 to 100 micro-meters (μm), after which the hydration layer spalls off and a new layer begins to form. Although obsidian is very resistant to alteration by weathering, chemical alteration or removal of the hydrated layer has been observed in some samples buried in acid tropical soils, as well as in calcareous soils developed in arid climates.

The establishment in 1989 of the International Association for Obsidian Studies (IAOS) testifies to the rapid expansion of the use of this dating tool (see Meighan and Scalise 1988; Skinner and Tremaine 1993 for extensive bibliographies). This expansion has tended to create problems relating to the proliferation of differing techniques of measuring hydration thickness and converting these measurements to relative or to absolute ages. We define a relative age as an age given in relation to another sample, while an absolute age is a chronologic age that expresses the time, in years, between the present and the manufacture of the artifact. We will discuss these problems and, where possible, suggest solutions.

To derive an absolute age for obsidian artifacts, information is needed about the environment of the archaeological site (temperature) as well as the chemical composition of the obsidian. To calculate relative ages, it is necessary to know only the chemical composition of the artifacts.

Morgenstein and Felsher (1971) proposed that the alteration of basaltic glass proceeded at a linear rate and could be used for dating. Because of the very different chemical composition of basaltic glass as compared to rhyolite glass, this alteration process, which might include a hydration step, is not equivalent to the hydration of rhyolitic glass and is more akin to the rusting of iron. During the alteration process ions are transported in and out of the basaltic glass, and therefore the rate of alteration depends on the availability of various ions in the environment where alteration is occurring. This might explain the observation that alteration dating reversals have been observed where basaltic glass higher in a stratified deposit produced thicker alteration rinds than lower ones in the sequence, thus placing in doubt this method of dating basaltic glass. (Graves and Ladefoged 1991; Rosendahl *et al.* 1987; Schilt 1984; Welch 1989).

Since the early 1980s an interest in glass hydration research has developed in the field of nuclear waste disposal in synthetic glasses (Bates *et al.* 1982). Comparative laboratory studies on obsidian vs. synthetic glasses have helped in understanding the kinetics of hydration (Bates *et al.* 1988; Ebert *et al.* 1991).

Studies carried out on obsidian are used in a number of fields including archaeology and geology. An information flow chart (Fig. 10.2) illustrates the interrelationships between obsidian sample sources and the final data output that can be used in a number of ways.

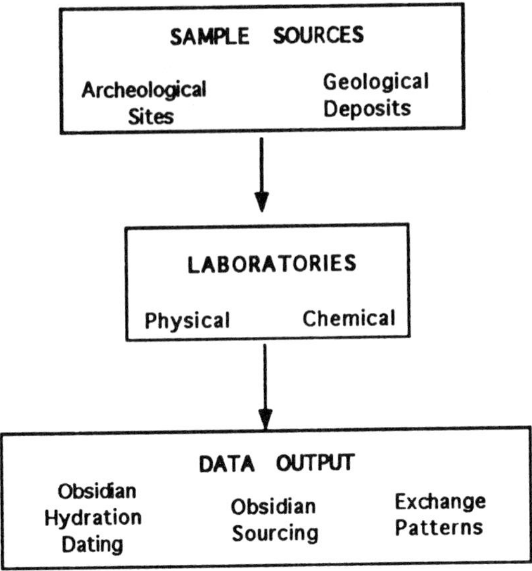

Figure 10.2. Information flow chart showing pathways between sample sites and the products of obsidian analysis. It demonstrates the interrelations between the different data outputs.

LABORATORY TECHNIQUES

Thin Section Techniques

The preparation of the thin section has changed little since the original description in Friedman and Smith (1960). Although many investigators perform the grinding of the required thin sections by hand, using a glass plate and fine abrasive, we have expedited the process as follows: First a 0.5 to 1 mm thick slice of obsidian is cut normal to the hydrated surface using a thin continuous-rim blade charged with diamond powder of 400 mesh or finer (Fig. 10.3A). Then the obsidian slice is cemented to a glass microscope slide, using either Canada Balsam or Lakeside resin (Fig. 10.3B), and it is ground on a rotating metal lap charged with 10 micron-sized abrasive until its thickness has been reduced to about one half of its original thickness (Fig. 10.3C). The slice is removed from the glass slide, inverted and recemented with the previously ground surface in contact with the slide (Fig. 10.3D). Grinding is resumed until the thickness has been reduced to 0.08 to 0.10 mm (0.003 to 0.004 inches) or less, depending on the opacity of the obsidian (Fig. 10.3E). Finally, a glass cover slip is cemented to the ground obsidian sample with Canada Balsam or Lakeside resin (Fig. 10.3F).

Grinding of the surfaces of the obsidian that contains the saw cuts is necessary to remove the edge material that has been chipped by the saw blade. We have found that the use of jigs to hold the glass microscope slide containing

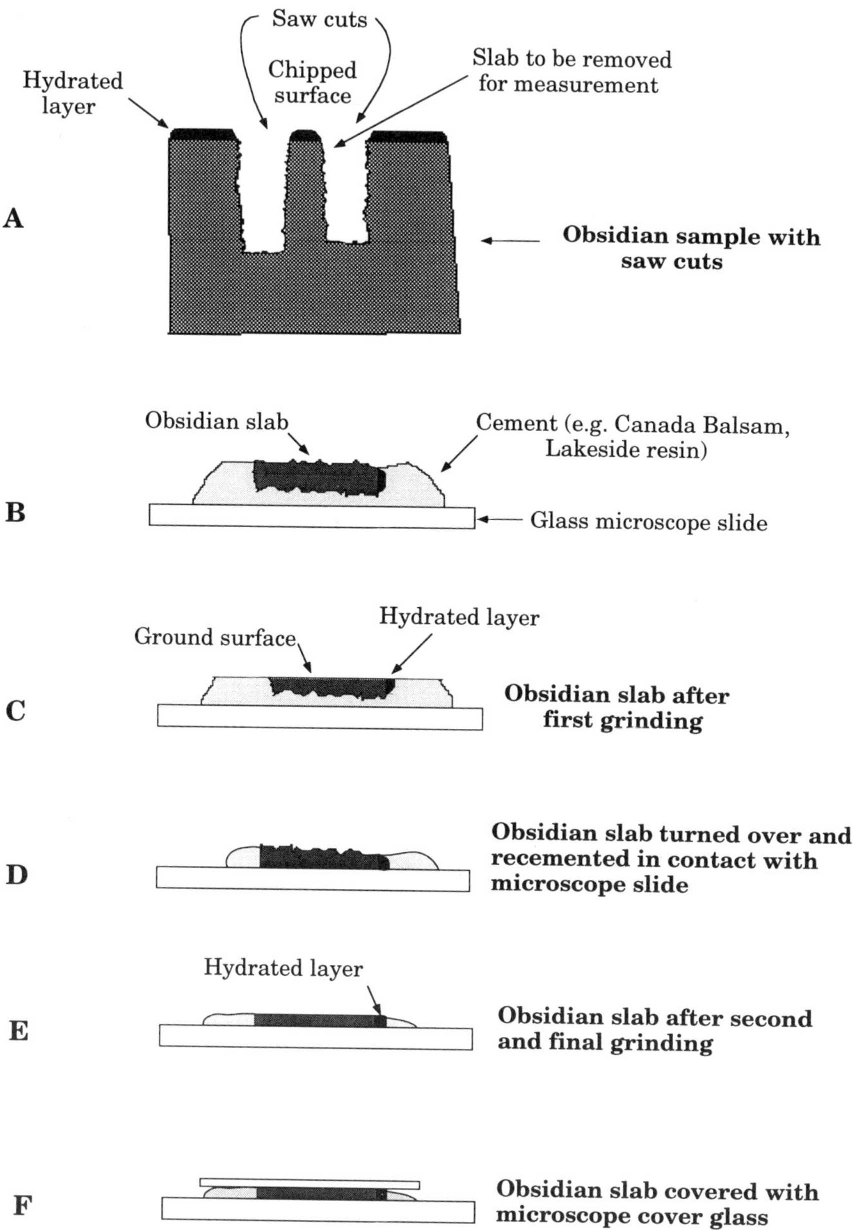

Figure 10.3. A sketch showing the stages in the preparation of the thin section used for the measurement of hydration thickness. (A) Obsidian sample that has been cut with diamond-charged blade showing edges of obsidian damaged by saw during cutting. It is necessary to grind away the chipped material in order to reach undamaged hydrated surface on both sides of slab. (B) Obsidian slab removed from sample and cemented to microscope slide. (C) View microscope slide after first grinding. (D) View after the obsidian slab has been removed, turned over, and recemented with previously ground side in contact with microscope slide. (E) View after grinding to final thickness. (F) View after microscope cover glass has been cemented to obsidian slab. Slide is now ready for measurement of hydration thickness. Note that thicknesses shown are not to scale.

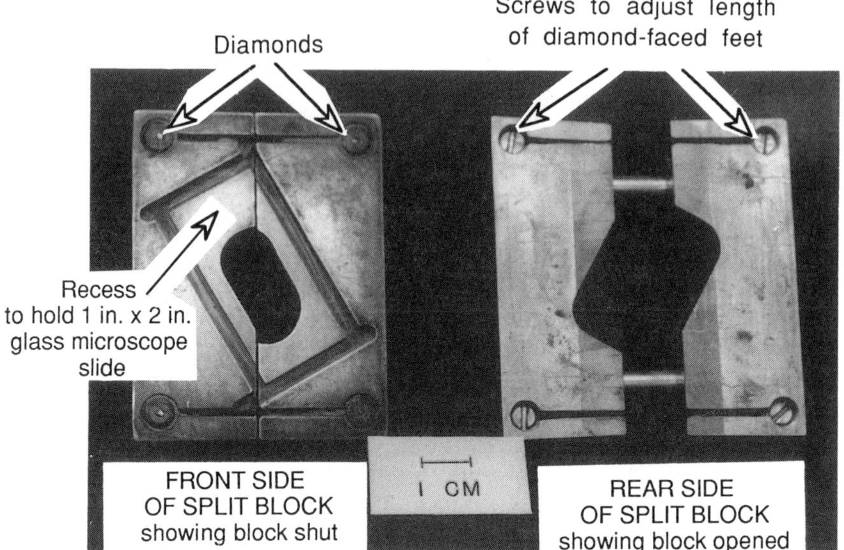

Figure 10.4. Photograph of split slide holder used in grinding of sections to final thickness showing adjustable industrial diamond-faced feet and recess to hold slide.

the obsidian thin section during grinding facilitates this operation. The jigs have four diamond-faced feet whose length is adjusted so that the diamonds contact the abrasive-charged grinding plate, and stop further thinning of the obsidian, when the required thickness has been reached (Fig. 10.4). The use of these grinding jigs requires that the glass microscope slides be preselected for thickness.

Measurement of Hydration Thickness

The differing refractive indices of the hydrated and unhydrated glass result in a demarcation between these two that is visible as a thin line when ordinary light passes through the thin section. Originally the measurement of the thickness of the hydration rind was made under the microscope using ordinary light. The hydrated portion of the obsidian has a higher density than the remainder of the obsidian, resulting in the development of strain in the glass. The strain causes rotation of the plane of polarization of the transmitted light, making the rind visible as a bright band when viewed between crossed polarizers (Fig. 10.1B). This effect is useful in detecting the hydrated layer during examination of a thin section, because the strain-image as seen under crossed polarizers is brighter and easier to detect than the interface between the hydrated and non-hydrated glass when viewed under

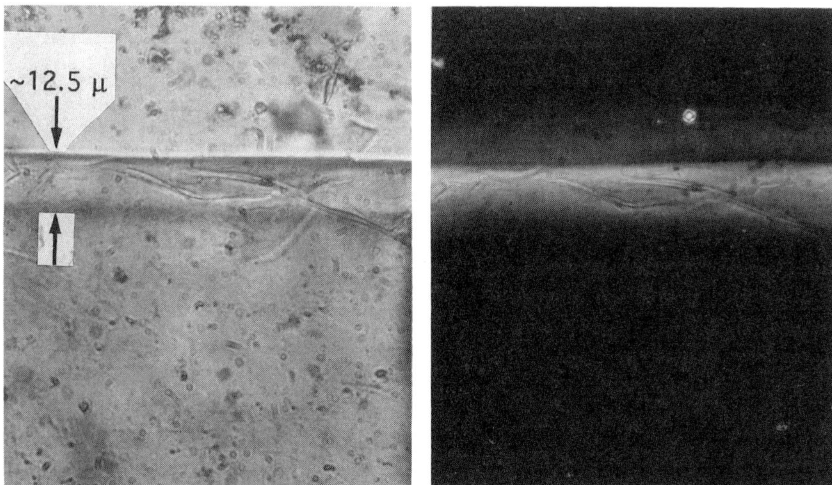

Figure 10.5. Photomicrographs of a thin section of obsidian from American Falls, Idaho. The sample was hydrated in the laboratory at 245°C and demonstrates the diffuse nature of the inner boundary of the hydrated layer produced by such procedure. Natural hydration produces a thin sharp line in plain light. Compare the image taken under plain light (A) with that taken under crossed polarizers (B).

ordinary light. However, this strain will propagate into the non-hydrated glass, and measurement of the strain-caused bright object is not equivalent to measurement of the actual hydration thickness as determined from the interface between the hydrated and non-hydrated glass (Fig. 10.5). Nevertheless, a number of investigators use measurements made under crossed polarizers. Other investigators do not always report the method used to make their measurements.

Many obsidian samples contain cracks that originated at the surface and penetrated the obsidian for a short distance. These cracks were generated by the percussion event that created the surface, and water vapor has penetrated the cracks resulting in hydration along both sides of the crack (see Pierce *et al.* 1976: Fig. 2; Ambrose 1994: Fig. 2). As has been pointed out by Ambrose (1994), these cracks often provide hydration that has not been altered or removed by chemical erosion caused by materials present in the soil in which the sample was buried.

Another kind of superficial cracks (or crazing) on obsidian is attributed to exposure to fire after manufacture (Friedman and Trembour 1983). Although hydration within these cracks has been observed, care should be exercised before using these measurements because an appreciable time interval may exist between artifact manufacture and the creation of the fire-crazing.

Measurement Devices

Optical Methods

The measurement of hydration thickness using a simple filar micrometer eyepiece, which requires reading numbers on an external drum, is slow, and often requires two people, one looking at the object through the microscope, and the other simultaneously reading the micrometer dial and recording the data. A filar micrometer eyepiece that utilizes internal readings facilitates the measurements because the observer does not have to change his viewpoint in order to read the micrometer displacement. The image-splitting eyepiece designed by Dyson (1960) allows one person to make measurements rapidly, with some gain in precision. Findlow and De Atley (1976) suggested measuring the hydration on an enlarged photomicrograph. Although this technique may facilitate measurement, the claimed precision of measurement of less than 0.05 µm is not possible (see discussion below). Recently, video imaging devices attached to the microscope have been adapted for thickness measurement (IAOS 1989, 1993; Ambrose 1994) with excellent results.

Nonoptical Methods

The need for alternatives to the microscope and thin sections has arisen when dealing with very thin rinds (< ca. 1 µm) or when seeking a non-destructive test. Lee *et al.* (1974) developed a nuclear reaction technique to measure the diffusion profile of the hydrogen in the water that diffused into silicate glasses. Leach and Naylor (1981) noted the lack of reliable obsidian hydration dating techniques for New Zealand and described a similar method for measuring very thin hydration rinds. Leach (1977) assessed the potential of several measurement methods and foresaw some promise for electron microscopy, ion spectroscopy, and argon milling, if research was pursued further. Lowe *et al.* (1984) published a radio-chemical method of obsidian rind measurement: it involves exchange of tritiated water with the rind water and back exchange of the tritiated water. The procedure was considered especially useful for young glasses.

Measurement Precision

The precision of measurement is limited by the resolution of the microscope, which, under ideal conditions, is limited to 1/4 of the wavelength of the light used for measurement. For visible light this translates to approximately 0.1 µm. The Dyson image-splitting eyepiece theoretically could increase measurement accuracy. However, under the conditions under which it is used to measure hydration thickness (sub-stage condenser iris diaphragm partially shut and low object contrast), the increased accuracy is not achieved (Stevenson and Scheetz 1989: 29). In spite of this physical restriction on the maximum resolution of the optical microscope, some investigators routinely report measurements to 0.01 μm under the mistaken belief that the image-splitting eyepiece allows such precision, and that averaging many measurements increases the precision. For an example, where claims of high measurement precision have resulted in controversial conclusions, see Hatch *et al.* (1990); Hughes (1992a); and Stevenson *et al.* (1992). In Fig. 10.6 we have replotted the data, measured on the same slides, by Hatch *et al.* (1990) and by Stevenson *et al.* (1987). Note the large difference between the two data sets. Fig. 10.7 are plots of the data of Hatch *et al.* (1990) together with the data reported by Friedman and Smith (1960) from the same sites (but not the same samples). Recently, one of the authors (I.F.) recut and remeasured the same samples used in

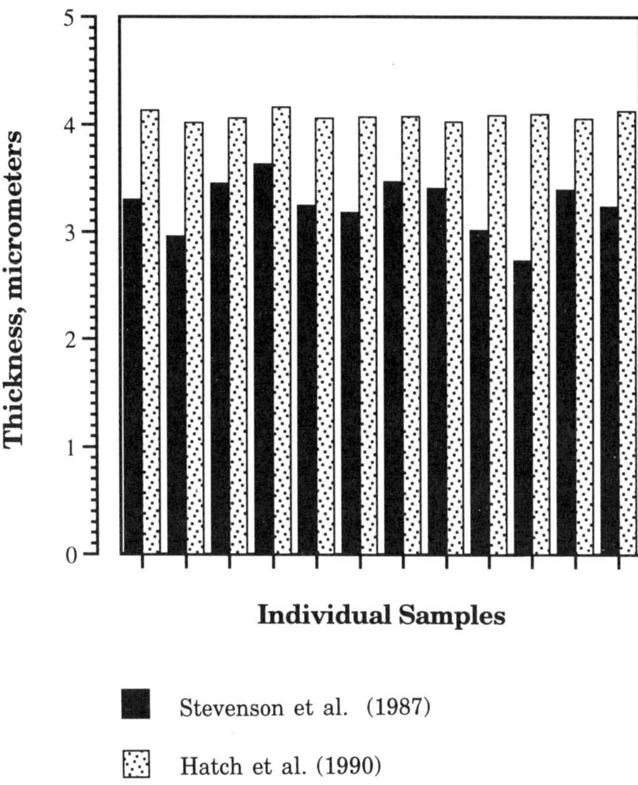

Figure 10.6. Plot of hydration thickness measurements made on the same samples by Stevenson *et al.* (1987) and Hatch *et al.* (1990). The precision of measurement given by the authors is 0.25 μm (Stevenson) and 0.10 μm (Hatch). Note that the systematic as well as between-sample differences are much larger than the estimates of error.

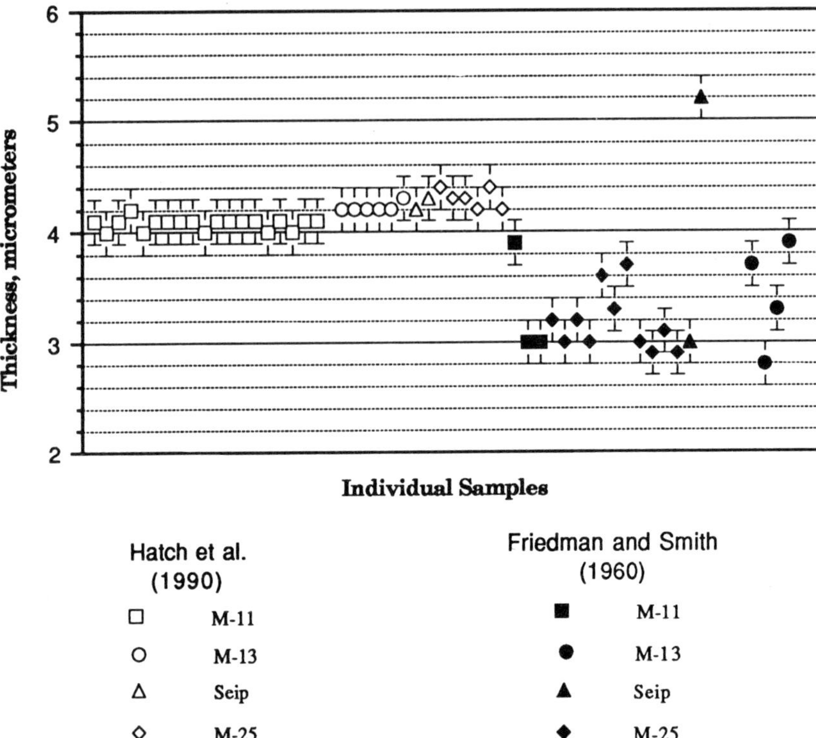

Figure 10.7. Plot of the hydration thickness measurements from samples from the same four Hopewell sites as reported by Friedman and Smith (1960) and Hatch *et al.* (1990). The measurement precision for both sets of measurements is given as 0.1 µm. The width of the plot symbols is equal to ±2 sigma. Recently we have recut and measured the samples used by Friedman and Smith (1960). The results agree with the original 1960 measurements, except that the two data points for Mound 25 which had thicknesses of 3.6 µm and 3.7 µm, were found to be in error. The new measurements reduced these to 3.0 µm and 3.3 µm. There are obvious differences, which are presently unexplained, between the measurements made by Hatch *et al.* and those of Friedman and Smith as confirmed by the present authors (see text under Measurement Precision).

Friedman and Smith (1960). In spite of the different measuring devices used (filar micrometer in 1960, image splitting eye piece in 1995) in making the two sets of measurements 35 years apart, the sets agreed remarkably well. The 15 samples measured in 1995 yielded an average of 3.15 µm (standard deviation = 0.16) while the same samples (with sample 2–2A eliminated) averaged 3.20 mm (standard deviation = 0.30) in 1960 (Table 10.1).

It is interesting to note that these two sets of measurements agree with those of both Hughes (1992a), and Stevenson *et al.* (1992), but are in serious disagreement with those reported by Hatch *et al.* (1990). We have no explana-

Table 10.1. Comparison of Measurements Made 35 Years Apart on Identical Samples from Hopewell Burials

Sample Number[a]	Burial Mound	1960 measurements, micrometers[b]	1995 measurements, micrometers[c]
2-1B	11	3.0	3.1
2-2A	13	1.2[d]	3.1
2-2B	13	3.7	3.1
2-2D	13	2.8	2.9
2-2E	13	3.3	3.4
2-3A	25	3.2	3.2
2-3B	25	3.0	3.3
2-3C	25	3.2	3.1
2-3D	25	3.0	3.0
2-3E	25	3.6	3.0
2-3F	25	3.3	3.3
2-3G	25	3.7	3.4
2-3H	25	3.0	3.0
2-3I	25	2.9	3.3
2-3J	25	3.1	3.0
		average = 3.20 standard deviation = 0.30	average = 3.15 standard deviation = 0.16

[a] Sample numbers in Friedman and Smith, 1960, Table 1.
[b] Measurements made using filar micrometer
[c] Meassurements made using image splitting eyepiece
[d] This data point not included in average.

tion for this disagreement, but the weight of the evidence suggests an error in the measurements reported in Hatch *et al.* (1990).

CONVERSION TO AGE

To convert hydration thickness to age, the functional dependence of the equation relating hydration thickness to time must be known. In addition, the constants of the hydration rate equation must be determined.

Hydration Rate Equation

Based on the use of obsidian artifacts of known age and the relationship between obsidian hydration and molecular diffusion, Friedman and Smith (1960) determined the relation:

$$\text{age} = k\ (\text{thickness})^2 \tag{1}$$

where k is a constant (discussed below) Later, experimental evidence (Friedman and Long 1976; Ebert *et al.* 1991; Mazer *et al.* 1991) confirmed that the hydration proceeds as the square-root of time. No published experimental data suggests other than a square root rate. However, based on archaeological evidence, Meighan *et al.* (1968) proposed a linear rate:

$$\text{age} = \text{k (thickness)} \tag{2}$$

At present, Meighan and his students tend to favor a linear rate of increase of hydration thickness with time rate equation (2) (Meighan 1983; Meighan and Scalise 1988), while most other researchers use a square-root of time rate equation (1). Friedman and Evans (1968) pointed out that over short time periods the use of a linear rate produces ages that approximate those calculated using a square-root relationship between thickness and time. This is illustrated in Fig. 10.8 where the curve is a plot of equation (1), while the two straight lines are plots of equation (2). Point A is a calibration point

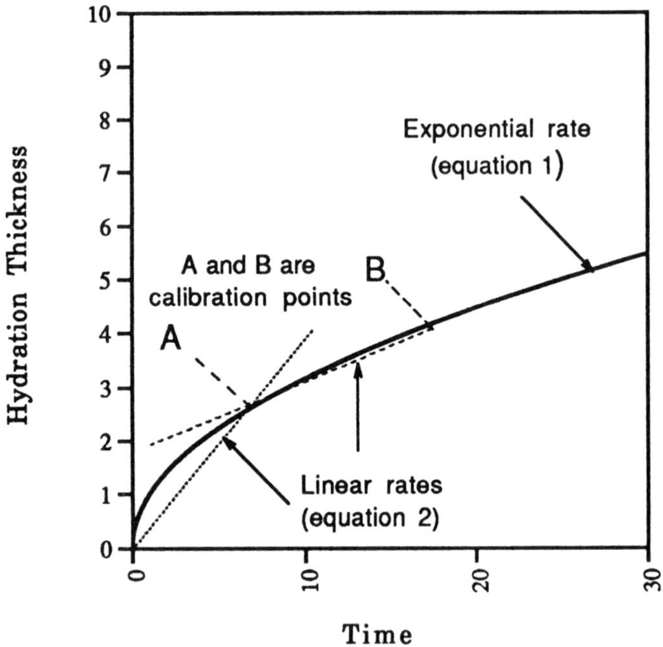

Figure 10.8. Plot showing the development of hydration as a function of time. The curved line is for an exponential rate, while the dotted lines are for linear rates. A and B are calibration points usually determined from radiocarbon ages. The dotted line is drawn from the origin to a calibration point, while the dashed line is drawn between two calibration points. This figure illustrates the extent of error introduced by the use of linear rather than exponential hydration rates.

that is derived using an independent method of age determination, such as a radiocarbon date, and assuming that the hydration thickness must be zero at zero time. Line A-B was drawn using two calibration points (A and B), but ignoring the requirement that the hydration thickness must be zero at zero time. Our examination of the published literature suggests that most archaeologists that use linear rates ignore this essential requirement. Assuming that the square-root relationship is the valid one, then the degree to which the straight line deviates from the curve defines the error of ages calculated using a linear rate. Also note that extrapolation of the linear rate beyond the time period defined by the calibration point(s) can cause large errors in the calculated ages.

Rate Equation Constant

The constant (k) of the rate equation depends on temperature, chemical composition of the glass, and relative humidity (rH) of the environment. Laboratory investigations of these hydration rate constants were made by two different techniques. The first, by Friedman and Long (1976), measured the induced hydration of 12 chemically different obsidians exposed to water vapor at elevated temperatures (95° to 245°C) for varying lengths of time. Because the hydration rate at ambient temperature is so low that it would require about 100 years for measurable hydration to develop (see Origer 1989 for an informative test), it was necessary to increase the rate by experimentally hydrating obsidian samples at elevated temperatures between 95° and 245°C. The measurements were made on thin sections in the usual manner. The other method, suggested by Ambrose (1976), was the measurement of weight-change experienced by powdered obsidian samples exposed to water vapor at temperatures below 100°C.

Temperature

Suzuki (1973), using the Emiliiani (1966) tropical ocean temperature fluctuation curve, discussed the effect on the hydration rate of temperature variations caused by climate change over the past 15,000 years. An experimental investigation of the effect of temperature on hydration rate was conducted by Friedman and Long (1976). In general, the rate doubles for every 6°C (11°F) rise in temperature. The relationship between hydration rate and temperature is given by the Arrhenius equation:

$$k = Ae^{-E/RT} \tag{3}$$

where k is the hydration rate (micrometers squared per thousand years), A is a constant, E is the activation energy of the hydration process (calories per mole), R is the gas constant (calories per degree per mole), T is the absolute temperature (Kelvin), and e is the base of natural logarithms.

As can be seen from equation (3), the rate of diffusion of water into obsidian depends nonlinearly on temperature. A positive temperature change will speed it up more than an equivalent negative temperature change will slow it down. Therefore if the obsidian, while hydrating, is exposed to a fluctuating temperature, the hydration depth will be the same as if the obsidian was exposed to a constant temperature that is higher than the arithmetic mean temperature. This temperature is referred to as the effective hydration temperature EHT (Norton and Friedman 1981), and is dependent on the activation energy of the process (E in equation (3)). For the case of a sinusoidally varying temperature, the EHT also depends on the temperature range—the difference between the highest and lowest temperature.

In order to secure hydration temperature data at specific archaeological sites, Ambrose (1976) and Trembour *et al.* (1986; 1988) devised simple plastic cells that integrate temperature over long periods of time. These devices require no power or servicing in the field, and they work on the principle of water diffusion through plastic. The rate of diffusion is determined in the laboratory by measuring weight change of the cells, which is dependent on temperature and the chemical activity of water. Normally these cells are emplaced for a year to integrate the annual temperature cycle, and they yield a value quite similar to EHT. Ideally, ground temperature data should be acquired for several years. The temperatures that are derived from these cells are integrated temperatures that approximate the EHT for obsidian. The difference between the EHT for obsidian and the temperature measured using Ambrose-type cells is usually small, and can be corrected by using the graphs in Norton and Friedman (1981). Six years of field experience using Trembour cells at sites where the integrated annual ground temperatures varied from 4° to 7°C resulted in data having a variation of ±0.5°C, compared to the ±0.2° expected from laboratory studies (Trembour *et al.* 1988). If this difference between field and laboratory conditions is extrapolated to higher temperatures, then we can expect that these cells will yield precisions of ±0.3°C in field studies where the integrated ground temperatures are higher and vary from 7 to 25°C.

If it is not possible to obtain temperature data using diffusion cells, an estimate of the EHT can be made using either daily maximum-minimum air temperatures measured at (or close to) the site, or ground temperatures determined twice a year at the archaeological find-site, measured at the depth of burial of the artifacts (Friedman 1976). Redfield (1965a; 1965b) discussed the measurement of mean-annual ground temperatures using two ground temperature measurements taken 182 days apart. With this calculated mean-annual ground temperature and the temperature range determined from the two measured ground temperatures (taken as close to the annual minima and maxima as possible), it is possible to estimate the EHT with an accuracy of about ±2°C.

Another method of calculating EHT at a specific site where independently well-dated obsidian artifacts are available, is to make use of equation (3), solving it for temperature. To carry out the calculation, it is necessary to know the constants in equation (3), which are source-specific and therefore requires a knowledge of the obsidian source and the activation energy of hydration of this obsidian. The latter is usually determined in the laboratory. This approach removes the problem of the unknown paleoclimate at the artifacts findspot because the hydration rind has integrated a record of this variable in its accumulated thickness. The resulting EHT determination is useful for the absolute dating of unassociated obsidian recoveries in the region.

Chemical Composition of the Glass

Obsidian is a complex alumino-silicate glass that is mainly composed of the major elements; O, Si, Al, Na, K, Ca, Mg, and Fe as well as a large number of other elements in minor or trace proportions (Macdonald *et al.* 1992). The effect of these various constituents on the hydration rate of rhyolitic obsidian was investigated by Friedman and Long (1976), and by Stevenson *et al.* (1993). Disagreement exists between these two groups as to the relative importance on the hydration rate of several of the major constituents of the glass, including the original water content. Stevenson *et al.* (1993) determined the water content of their glass samples using infra-red absorption. It is presently unclear, however, how water percentages determined by infra-red absorption compare to determinations made by other methods, including the direct measurement of water released by melting of the glass under vacuum. Additional work is necessary in this area. Suzuki (1973: 446) explored the rates of hydration of rhyolite vs. dacite glass, and found that the rates were related to the K_2O/Al_2O_3 ratio in these chemically distinct glasses.

In general, the chemical composition of a single obsidian flow, based on the amounts of the 10 most abundant constituents (major elements) that determine the hydration rate, is uniform (Bacon *et al.* 1981). The constituents present only in small amounts (minor or trace elements) in a single flow are useful in fingerprinting the obsidian (Bacon *et al.* 1981; Hughes 1993). However the major and minor element composition varies from flow-to-flow within a volcanic province (Gordus *et al.* 1968), and ratios of various minor elements differ sufficiently to distinguish separate flows or sources of archaeological material.

Although one obsidian source usually has only one hydration rate, we should point out that sequential removal (or tapping) of a chemically zoned magma chamber coupled with magma mixing and roof and wall contamination (Bowman *et al.* 1973; Hughes and Smith 1993: 85) could alter the major element chemistry within a source enough to affect the hydration rate, as well as its trace element profile.

As has been pointed out by Hughes and Smith (1993), obsidian formed by the compaction and welding of volcanic ash can show greater chemical variability than obsidian formed by the cooling of a lava flow. This could result in greater variability of the rates of hydration for these glasses. Although welded-tuff deposits often cover large areas, few of them produce glass of artifact quality. An even less common type of obsidian, rhyolite agglutinate, formed by the welding of pyroclastic spatter, can also yield artifact-grade obsidian, but a single deposit may have varying chemical composition (Hughes and Smith, 1993).

There are usually relatively few sources of obsidian in a region, and once the hydration rates of obsidian from specific volcanic flows (sources) of distinctive chemical composition have been determined, then the trace element composition of individual flows can be compared to that of specific artifacts. When a match is found, then the hydration rates of the artifact and flow are equal. Since the trace element composition can be determined nondestructively and cheaply, this simplifies the assignment of hydration rates to specific artifacts.

Another method of correlating artifacts with flows by comparing the refractive indices of the glasses was used by Boyer and Robinson (1956) on samples from the Jemez Mountains of New Mexico (also see Trembour 1992). Recent advances in techniques to measure refractive indices on small powdered samples under the microscope have facilitated the use of such measurements. These include the focal masking technique (Wilcox 1983) and the use of high dispersion immersion liquids (Wilcox 1964).

Trace Elements

It is clear that varying concentration of major elements of the glass most directly influence the rate at which obsidian hydrates. However, it is unique combinations of trace elements that are the most useful for determining the geologic provenance of obsidian artifacts. Two principal instrumental methods have been employed to chemically characterize the trace element composition of obsidians: x-ray fluorescence (XRF)—both wavelength and energy dispersive techniques—and instrumental neutron activation analysis (INAA). Although each method provides data on many elements, XRF analysts typically report abundances of the elements Ba, Fe, Mn, Nb, Rb, Sr, Ti, Y, Zn, and Zr, while INAA analysis provides data on Ba, Ce, Co, Cs, Dy, Eu, Fe, Hf, K, La, Lu, Mn, Na, Rb, Sb, Sc, Sm, Ta, Tb, Th, U, Yb, and Zn. Despite the large number of elements measured, it is usually possible to select a distinctive subset and to employ bivariate scatter plots or ternary diagrams to illustrate contrasts among obsidian sources and the degree of correspondence with archaeological artifacts (Hughes 1994; Fig. 2; Jack 1976: Fig. 11.1a; Nelson 1985: Figs. 3 and 4).

In practice once the chemical characteristics—the major and trace elements—of an obsidian source have been determined, various combinations of trace elements are employed as proxies for major element composition in hydration dating. This is an important point since, as discussed previously, it is the major element composition, in concert with temperature, which appears to have the most dramatic effect on the rate at which water is absorbed into glass. Following the establishment of unique chemical profiles for sources in a region, "source-specific" hydration rates are constructed on the explicit assumption that homogeneity of trace element composition monitors homogeneity in major element composition. Thus it is assumed that all obsidian from one source will hydrate at the same rate (Hughes 1982, 1988b).

However, it is important to appreciate another dimension of the relationship between trace element and major element chemistry in hydration dating. Archaeologists sometimes assume that each distinctive trace element group has its own hydration rate; for example, if five different trace element varieties of obsidian are identified in an archaeological assemblage, the existence of five different hydration rates may be postulated. However, it is possible that obsidians of different trace element composition may have the same major element composition and thus hydrate at the same rate.

Relative Humidity

Based on evidence from archaeological material, Friedman and Smith (1960) determined that relative humidity (rH) had little or no effect on hydration rate. Later experimental work by Ambrose (1976); Friedman *et al.* (1990); Mazer *et al.* (1991); Ebert *et al.* (1991), and Friedman *et al.* (1994) indicated that rH is an important variable in the hydration process. Ambrose (1976) reported that the effect of lowered rH was only significant below about 50% rH. On the other hand, Michels (1965;1967) found no significant difference in hydration thickness between deeply buried obsidian artifacts and similar material exposed at or near the earths surface at the same site. Origer and Wickstrom (1982) and Hall and Jackson (1989) also observed no statistical differences in the distribution of hydration values between surface and subsurface artifacts. Thus, presumed differences in the rH at different soil levels had no effect on hydration rates in these instances.

However, as was pointed out by Trembour (in Leach and Hamel 1984) and by Friedman *et al.* (1994), the measured mean relative humidity of most desert soils at soil depths below 20 cm is generally 100%, and this high humidity often occurs at even higher levels in the soil. Therefore, in most buried settings, this constancy of rH eliminates it as a variable in calculating ages. In the case of surface-collected artifacts, these may have been drier over time (lowering the rate), but hotter due to insolation (raising the rate) than those buried at the same site. The opposite effect of the two variables on the rate tends to cancel, and the two sets of artifacts may develop similar hydration rind thicknesses. In view of these considerations, we believe that for most samples, humidity is not an important variable, and may be only of minor importance for surface samples because of offsetting effects (Friedman *et al.* 1994).

The cells that are used to measure temperature can also be used to integrate relative humidity over long time periods (Ambrose 1980; Trembour *et al.* 1986; 1988), so that rH data is easily acquired, and in the event that the relative humidity at a site is not 100%, humidity corrections can be made to the age equation (Friedman *et al.* 1994).

Errors in Age Determination

Errors in Assigning Relative Age

It is not necessary to determine the hydration rate when comparing the relative age of artifacts from a single site where all of the samples were exposed to the same environmental conditions during hydration. In this case, the only variable that affects the relative ages is the major-element composition of the artifacts. In the event that several artifacts can be shown, on the basis of their minor-element composition or refractive index (Trembour 1992), to be from the same source and therefore have the same chemical composition, then the relative ages of these artifacts will be proportional to the square of their hydration thicknesses. Thus, the only error that can affect these relative ages is the thickness-measurement error, and therefore one can say with confidence that artifact A is x times older, or younger, than artifact B (Suzuki 1973; Trembour 1983; Tremaine and Fredrickson 1988).

Errors in Assigning Absolute Age

The accuracy to which the absolute age can be calculated is determined by (1) the error of measurement of hydration thickness and (2) the error in determining the constant (k) of the hydration rate equation (equation (1)). The value of this constant is determined by the chemical composition of the obsidian and the temperature at which the hydration occurred. Where the relative humidity was appreciably less than 100%, an additional correction to the constant must be made. As mentioned previously, the constant k can be evaluated by using the hydration thickness and a date for the artifact as determined by another dating method such as associated radiocarbon. The constant so determined is only applicable to the specific EHT at the site.

Another way of determining k is by experimentally inducing hydration in obsidian at a constant, but elevated, temperature, as was done by Friedman and Long (1976). As was discussed in Friedman and Long (1976), the higher the temperature at which the samples were hydrated, the more diffuse is he interface between the hydrated and non-hydrated glass (Fig. 10.9), and the greater the error of measurement of the hydration thickness. Nevertheless,

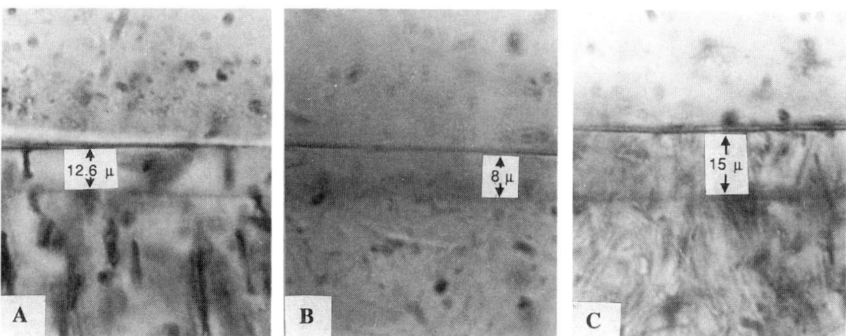

Figure 10.9. Photomicrographs showing obsidian sample from Coso Hot Springs, California. The two end photos (A and C) are of obsidian that has hydrated in nature under surficial conditions, while the center photo (B) is of the same material hydrated in the laboratory at 150°C. Note the indistinct boundary between the unhydrated and hydrated material in (B), as compared to the other two companion photomicrographs.

others who have conducted experimental hydration at elevated temperatures claim high precision for their measurements (see Michels 1981–1988; Mazer *et al.* 1991). Hughes (1989:10; 1992b) noted that in some cases significantly different laboratory-induced hydration rates have been advanced for obsidian from the same source. Stevenson *et al.* (1989: 195) pointed out that a number of investigators have used liquid water rather than water vapor in the experimental hydration, which had caused solution of constituents from the glass, thereby changing its chemical composition and resulting in invalid rates. They suggested that silica gel be added to the water used for induced hydration to prevent silica dissolution from the glass surface. However, this does not prevent the leaching of other constituents such as sodium, potassium, etc. from the glass, that can also change the hydration rate.

Ambrose (1976) and Ebert *et al.* (1991) measured the weight gain caused by the hydration of samples of powdered obsidian exposed to water vapor at temperatures below 100°C. To convert these weight-changes to rates, it is necessary to measure the surface area of each sample. The measurement of powder surface area to the necessary precision is very difficult, and has limited the usefulness of this method.

COMPARISONS OF DATING METHODS

A number of investigators have used obsidian hydration dating in conjunction with other techniques of dating, usually radiocarbon. A few selected examples follow:

Scarborough (1989) reported the use of three dating methods, archeomagnetism, radiocarbon, and obsidian hydration in dating a Late Pithouse-Early Pueblo Period excavation in New Mexico. Although insufficient basic information to assess the data was given, all three methods yielded compatible dates.

Hammond (1989) published absolute obsidian dating and radiocarbon results from Maya Tecep Phase occupation at Nohmul, Belize. The two radiocarbon dates were several hundred years older than the 16 obsidian results. The author suggested that the difference may have been due to an intrusive burial of the obsidian. In addition he noted that the EHT used to calculate the obsidian hydration ages was assumed from atmospheric measurements at two distant locations. The use of the questionable EHT might explain part or all of the difference between the two dating techniques.

Michels *et al.* (1983) employed three independent strategies to estimate the hydration rate for Sardinian obsidian—induced hydration, chemical index, and correlation with archaeological age estimates. They derived good agreement of the values and a useful rate for these samples of Sardinian obsidian.

Webster and Freter (1990) and Freter (1992) have applied obsidian hydration dating to 200 Maya sites at Copan, Western Honduras. The results dating of over 2000 obsidian artifacts showed that the obsidian hydration dates are in excellent agreement with the ceramic phasing, radiocarbon, and archaeomagnetic dates, the long count dates, internal site stratigraphy, paleodemographic reconstructions, palynologyical data, paleoethnobotanical data, and computer simulations of the agricultural system. What the hydration dates have provided is a more detailed understanding of the least known phase of occupation in the valley, the postmonument Coner period.

In a paper by Hatch *et al.* (1990), the authors cited recent radiocarbon dates for the burials at two Hopewell mounds and compared these with associated obsidian dates. They obtained exceptional agreement between the two methods.

In Western Idaho, source-specific obsidian hydration dating on Timber Butte obsidian suggested an age of ca. 4500–4000 BP for Western Idaho Archaic Burial Complex sites (Pavesic 1985), about 1,000 years later than the single radiocarbon date available for one of the sites in the complex. The hydration dates were consistent with an age of ca. 4500 BP based on projectile point typological cross-dating.

We wish to emphasize that radiocarbon-obsidian hydration calibration can be dramatically influenced by incorrect archaeological linkage between radiocarbon dates and the obsidian artifacts used to establish the hydration rate(s). This is due, in part, to the fact that the obsidian hydration method dates the actual cultural object, while the radiocarbon dates carbonaceous material hopefully associated with the cultural context represented by the obsidian. In practice, radiocarbon-obsidian hydration rate calibrations have been proposed from widely differing archaeological contexts, ranging from those coupling midden charcoal radiocarbon dates and hydration rim measurements on obsidian artifacts found at the same depth, to truly direct associations such as radiocarbon dating of wooden foreshafts on which obsidian points are still hafted. Given the importance of association between the carbonaceous material and the obsidian, it is imperative that only bona fide associations be used to avoid constructing inaccurate rates.

CONCLUSIONS

In order to increase the precision and usefulness of obsidian hydration dating, we suggest that the following researches should be carried out: (1) The development of a technique for the measurement of hydration rind thicknesses of less than 1.5 μm that does not require the use of expensive equipment. (2) The determination of the hydration rate on obsidian samples from a large variety of sources and of varying chemical composition. These determinations must be as error-free as possible and should not suffer from the difficulties discussed in this paper. The chemical compositions of the samples used for rate determination should be analyzed by the most precise state-of-the-art methods, rather than the quick-but imprecise techniques often used. (3) A quick, precise, and non-destructive method of rind thickness measurement should be developed. If the current labor-intensive thin sectioning and slide preparation phases can be eliminated or drastically reduced, this would not only increase the number of samples routinely available to archaeologists for interpretation, but would open the door to more thoroughgoing obsidian dating research on artifacts in existing museum collections. Many curators currently are extremely reluctant to have "museum-quality" specimens defaced (or destroyed altogether) regardless of the potential scientific payoff. Sourcing research on artifacts in museum collections is often possible only because a method is non-destructive; a non-destructive method for obsidian hydration dating would simultaneously allay the understandable concerns of museum conservators and be responsive to archaeology's explicit conservation ethic. (4) Standardization of all laboratory procedures involved in the hydration analysis and sourcing of cultural obsidian. Until this is achieved it will be difficult to evaluate and compare results from different laboratories.

REFERENCES

Ambrose, W. 1976 Intrinsic hydration rate dating of obsidian. *In* Taylor, R.E., ed., *Advances in Obsidian Glass Studies*. Park Ridge, New Jersey, Noyes Press: 81–105.

Ambrose, W. 1980 Monitoring long-term temperature and humidity. Institute for the Conservation of Cultural Material. *Bulletin* 6: 36–42.

Ambrose, W.R. 1994 Obsidian hydration dating of Pleistocene age site from the Manus Islands, Papua, New Guinea. *Quaternary Geochronology (Quaternary Science Reviews)* 13: 137–142.

Bacon, C.R., Macdonald, R., Smith, R.L. and Baedecker, P.A. 1981 Pleistocene high-silica rhyolites of the Coso Volcanic Field, Inyo County, California. *Journal of Geophysical Research* 86 (B11): 10,223–10,241.

Bowman, H.R., Asaro, F. and Perlman, I. 1973 On the uniformity of composition in obsidians and evidence for magmatic mixing. *Journal of Geology* 81: 312–327.

Bates, J,K., Jardine, L.J. and Steindler, M.J. 1982 Hydration aging of nuclear waste glasses. *Science* 218: 51–53.

Bates, J.K., Abrajano, T.A., Ebert, W.L., Mazer, J.J. and Gerding, T.J. 1988 Experimental hydration studies of natural and synthetic glasses. *Materials Research Society Symposium Proceedings* 123: 237–244.

Boyer, W.W. and Robinson, P. 1956 Obsidian artifacts of Northwestern New Mexico and their correlation with source material. *El Palacio* 63: 333–345.

Dyson, J. 1960 Precise measurement by image-splitting. *Journal of the Optical Society of America* 50: 754–757.

Ebert, W.L., Hoburg, R.F. and Bates, J.K. 1991 The sorption of water on obsidian and a nuclear waste glass. *Physics and Chemistry of Glasses* 32: 133–137.

Emiliani, C. 1966 Isotopic paleotemperatures. *Science* 154: 857–881.

Findlow, F. J. and De Atley, S.P. 1976 Photographic measurement in obsidian hydration dating. *In* Taylor, R.E. ed., *Advances in Obsidian Glass Studies*. Park Ridge, (New Jersey), Noyes Press: 165–172.

Freter, A. 1992 Chronological Research at Copan. *Ancient Mesoamerica* 3: 117–133.

Friedman, I. 1976 Calculations of obsidian hydration rates from temperature measurements. *In* Taylor, R.E., ed., *Advances in Obsidian Glass Studies*. Park Ridge, (New Jersey), Noyes Press: 173–182.

Friedman, I. and Evans, C. 1968 Obsidian dating revisited. *Science* 162: 813–81.

Friedman, I. and Long, W. 1976 Hydration rate of obsidian. *Science* 191: 347–352.

Friedman, I. and Smith. R.L. 1960 A new dating method using obsidian. Part 1, the development of the method. *American Antiquity* 25: 476–493.

Friedman, I. and Trembour, F.W. 1983 Obsidian hydration dating update. *American Antiquity* 48:544–547.

Friedman, I., Trembour, F. and Smith, F. 1990 Obsidian hydration rates as a function of relative humidity (Abstract). *International Association for Obsidian Studies Newsletter* 3:8.

Friedman, I., Trembour, F.W., Smith, F.L. and Smith, G.I. 1994 Is obsidian hydration dating affected by relative humidity? *Quaternary Research* 41:185–190.

Gordus, A.A., Wright, G.A. and Griffin, J.B. 1968 Obsidian sources characterized by neutron-activation analysis. *Science* 161: 382–384.

Graves, M.W. and Ladefoged, T.N. 1991 The disparity between radiocarbon and volcanic glass dates: new evidence from the island of Lana-i, Hawaii. *Archaeology in Oceania* 26: 70–77.

Hall, M.C. and Jackson, R.J. 1989 Obsidian hydration rates in California. *In* Hughes, R.E., ed., Current Directions in California Obsidian Studies. *Contributions of the University of California Archaeological Research Facility* 48: 31–58.

Hammond, N. 1989 Obsidian hydration dating of Tecep Phase occupation at Nohmul, Belize. *American Antiquity* 54: 513–521.

Hatch, J.W., Michels, J.W., Stevenson, C.M., Scheetz, B.E. and Geidel, R.A. 1990 Hopewell obsidian studies; Behavioral implications of recent sourcing and dating research. *American Antiquity* 55: 461–479.

Hughes, R.E. 1982 Age and exploitation of obsidian from the Medicine Lake Highland, California. *Journal of Archaeological Science* 9: 173–185.

_____ 1988a Archaeological signifidance of geochemical contrasts among southwestern New Mexico obsidians. *Texas Journal of Science* 40: 297–307.

_____ 1988b The Coso Volcanic Field reexamined: implications for obsidian sourcing and hydration dating research. *Geoarchaeology* 3: 253–265.

_____ 1989 A new look at Mono basin obsidians. *In* Hughes, R.E., ed., Current Directions in California Obsidian Studies. *Contributions of the University of California Archaeological Research Facility* 48: 1–12.

_____ 1992a Another look at Hopewell obsidian studies. *American Antiquity* 57: 515–523.

_____ 1992b Northern California obsidian studies: some thoughts and observations on the first two decades. *Proceedings of the Society for California Archaeology* 5: 113–122.

_____ 1993 Trace element geochemistry of volcanic glass from the Obsidian Cliffs flow, Three Sisters Wilderness, Oregon. *Northwest Science* 67: 199–207.

_____ 1994 Intrasource chemical variability of artefact-quality obsidians from the Casa Diablo area, California. *Journal of Archaeological Science* 21: 263–271.

Hughes, R.E. and Smith, R.L. 1993 Archaeology, geology, and geochemistry in obsidian provenance studies. *In* Stein, J.K. and Linse, A.R. eds., *Effects of Scale on Archaeological and Geoscientific Perspectives*, Geological Society of America Special Paper 283: 79–91. Boulder, Colorado.

IAOS 1989 *International Association for Obsidian Studies Newsletter* 1:1–14.

IAOS 1993 *International Association for Obsidian Studies Newsletter* 8: 12–13.

Jack, R.N. 1976 Prehistoric obsidian in California I: geochemical aspects. *In* Taylor, R.E., ed., *Advances in Obsidian Glass Studies: Archaeological and Geochemical Perspectives*. Park Ridge, New Jersey, Noyes Press: 183–217.

Leach, B.F. 1977 New perspectives on dating obsidian artifacts in New Zealand. *New Zealand Journal of Science* 20: 123–138.

Leach, B.F. and Naylor, H. 1981 Dating New Zealand obsidians by resonant nuclear reactions. *New Zealand Journal of Archaeology* 3: 33–49.

Leach, B.F. and Hamel, G.E. 1984 The influence of archeological soil temperatures on obsidian hydration in New Zealand. *New Zealand Journal of Science* 27: 399–408.

Lee, R.R., Leich, D.A., Tombrello, T.A., Ericson, J.E. and Friedman, I. 1974 Obsidian hydration profile measurements using a nuclear technique. *Nature* 250: 44–47.

Lowe, J.P., Lowe, D.J., Hodder, A.P.W. and Wilson, A.T. 1984. A tritium exchange method for obsidian hydration shell measurement. *Isotope Geosciences* 2: 351–363.

Macdonald, R., Smith, R.L. and Thomas, J.E. 1992 Chemistry of the subalkalic silicic obsidians. *U.S. Geological Survey Professional Paper* 1523. Washington, D.C., U.S. Government Printing Office.

Mazer, J.J., Stevenson, C.M., Ebert, W.L. and Bates, J.K. 1991 The experimental hydration of obsidian as a function of relative humidity and temperature. *American Antiquity* 56: 504–513.

Meighan, C.W. 1983 Obsidian dating in California: theory and practice. *American Antiquity* 48: 600–609.

Meighan, C.W., Foote, L.J. and Aiello, P.V. 1968 Obsidian hydration dating in west Mexico archeology. *Science* 160: 169–175.

Meighan, C.W. and Scalise, J.L. 1988 A compendium of the obsidian hydration determinations made at the UCLA obsidian hydration laboratory: Obsidian Dates IV. *Monograph XXIX. Institute of Archeology*, University of California, Los Angeles: 473–511.

Meighan, C.W. and Scalise, J.L., eds., *Obsidian Dates IV 1988 A compendium of the obsidian hydration determinations made at the UCLA obsidian hydration laboratory*. Monograph XXIX, Los Angeles, Institute of Archaeology, University of California.

Michels, J.W. 1965 Lithic serial chronology through obsidian hydration dating. Ph.D. dissertation, University of California, Los Angeles.

_____ 1967 Archeology and dating by obsidian hydration. *Science* 158: 211–214.

_____ 1981–1988 *MOHLAB Technical Reports*: 1–86. MOHLAB, State College, Pennsylvania.

_____ 1982 Bulk element composition versus trace element composition in the reconstruction of an obsidian source system. *Journal of Archaeological Science* 9: 113–123.

Michels, J.W., Atzeni, E., Tsong, I.S.T., and Smith, G.A. 1983 Sardinian archeology and obsidian dating, *In* Balmuth, M.S., ed., *Studies in Sardinian Archeology*. Ann Arbor, University of Michigan Press.

Morganstein, M. and Felsher, M. 1971 The origin of manganese nodules: A combined theory with special reference to palagonitization. *Pacific Science* 25: 301–307.

Nelson, F.W. 1985 Summary of the results of analysis of obsidain artifacts from the Maya Lowlands. *Scanning Electron Microscopy* 2: 631–649.

Norton, D.R. and Friedman, I. 1981 Ground temperature measurements: Part I, Pallman Technique. *U.S. Geological Professional Paper* 1203: 1–12.

Origer, T.M. 1989 Hydration analysis of obsidian flakes produced by Ishi during the Historic period. *In* Hughes, R.E., ed., Current Directions in California Obsidian Studies. *Contributions of the University of California Archaeological Research Facility* 48: 69–77.

Origer, T.M. and Wickstrom, B.P. 1982 The use of hydration measurements to date obsidian materials from Sonoma County, California. *Journal of California and Great Basin Anthropology* 4: 123–131.

Pavesic, M.G. 1985 Cache blades and Turkey Tails: piecing together the Western Idaho Archaic Burial Complex. *In* Plew, M.G., Woods, J.C. and Pavesic, M.G., eds., *Stone Tool Analysis: Essays in Honor of Don E. Crabtree*. Albuquerque, University of New Mexico Press: 55–89.

Pierce, K.L., Obradovich, J.D. and Friedman, I. 1976 Obsidian hydration dating and correlation of Bull Lake and Pinedale Glaciations near West Yellowstone, Montana. *Geological Society of America Bulletin* 87: 703–710.

Redfield, A.C. 1965a Terrestrial heat flow through salt-marsh peat. *Science* 148: 1219–1220.

Redfield, A.C. 1965b The thermal regime in salt marsh peat at Barnstable, Massachusetts. *Tellus* 18: 246–259.

Rosendahl, P.H., Haun, A.E., Halbig, J.B., Kaschko, M. and Allen, M.S. 1987 Kahoolawe excavations, 1982–83 data recovery project, island of Kahoolawe, Hawaii: draft report. Hilo, Hawaii, Paul H. Rosendahl Inc..

Ross, C.S. and Smith, R.L. 1955 Water and other volatiles in volcanic glasses. *American Mineralogist* 40: 1071–1089.

Scarborough, V.L. 1989 Site structure of a village of the Late Pithouse-Early Pueblo Period in New Mexico. *Journal of Field Archaeology* 16: 405–425.

Schilt, R. 1984 Subsistence and conflict in Kona, Hawaii: An archeological study of the Kuakini highway realignment corridor. *Departmental Report Series* 84–1. Honolulu, Department of Anthropology, B.P. Bishop Museum.

Shackley, M.S. 1988 Sources of archaeological obsidian in the Southwest: an archaeological, petrological, and geochemical study. *American Antiquity* 53: 752–772.

Skinner, C.E. and Tremaine, K.J. 1993 Obsidian: An interdisciplinary bibliography. *International Association for Obsidian Studies Occasional Paper* No. 1. San Jose, California: 1–174.

Stevenson, C.M. and Scheetz, B.E. 1989 Induced hydration rate development of obsidians from the Coso Volcanic Field: A comparison of experimental procedures. *In* Hughes, R.E. ed., Current Directions in California Obsidian Studies. *Contributions of the University of California Archaeological Research Facility* 48: 23–30.

Stevenson, C.M., Carpenter, J. and Scheetz, B.E. 1989 Obsidian Dating: Recent advances in the experimental determination and application of hydration rates. *Archaeometry* 31: 193–206.

Stevenson, C.M., Scheetz, B.E. and Hatch, J.W. 1992 Reply to Hughes. *American Antiquity* 57: 524–525.

Stevenson, C.M., Knaus, E., Mazer, J.J. and Bates, J.K. 1993 Homogeneity of water content in obsidian from Coso Volcanic field: Implications for obsidian hydration dating. *Geoarchaeology* 8: 371–384.

Suzuki, M. 1973 Chronology of prehistoric human activity in Konto, Japan. *Journal of the Faculty of Science, The University of Tokyo* No. IV, Sec. V, Part 3: 241–318.

Tremaine, K.J. and Fredrickson, D.A. 1988 Induced obsidian hydration experiments: An investigation in relative dating. *In* Sayre, E., ed., *Materials Issues in Art and Archeology*. Materials Research Society Symposium Proceedings 123: 271–278.

Trembour, F.W. 1983 Obsidian hydration study of prismatic blade fragments from the Cambio site; Appendix 10-A, *In* Sheets, P., ed., *Archeology and Volcanism in Central America*. Austin, University of Texas Press: 224–226.

Trembour, F., Friedman, I., Jurceka, F. J. and Smith, F.L, 1986 A simple device for integrating temperature, relative humidity, and salinity over time. *Journal of Atmospheric and Oceanic Technology* 3: 186–190.

Trembour, F., Smith, F.L. and Friedman, I. 1988 Cells for integrating temperature and humidity over long periods of time. *In* Sayre, E., ed., *Materials Issues in Art and Archeology Materials*, Materials Research Society Symposium Proceedings 123: 245–251.

Trembour, F.W. 1992 Hydration dating of obsidian artifacts from the Sacred Cenote, Chichen Itza; Appendix 6.A, *In* Coggins, C.C., ed., *Artifacts from the Cenote of Sacrifice, Chichen Itza, Yucatan*. Cambridge, Harvard University Press: 179–181.

Webster, D. and Freter, A. 1990 Settlement history and classic collapse at Copan: A redefined Chronological perspective. *Latin American Antiquity* 1: 66–85.

Welch, D.J. 1989 Archeological investigations at Pauoa Bay (Ritz-Carlton Mauna Lani Report) South Kohala, Hawaii. Honolulu, International Archeological Research.

Wilcox, R.E. 1964 Immersion liquids of relatively strong dispersion in the low refractive index range (1.46 to 1.52). *American Mineralogist* 49: 683–688.

Wilcox, R.E. 1983 Refractive index determination using the central focal masking technique with dispersion colors. *American Mineralogist* 68: 1226–1236.

Chapter **11**

Archaeomagnetic Dating

ROBERT S. STERNBERG

ABSTRACT

Archaeomagnetic dating is based on the comparison of directions, intensities or polarities with master records of change. Archaeomagnetic direction and archaeointensity dating are regional pattern-matching techniques, whereas magnetic reversal dating is a global pattern-matching method. Secular variation dating using archaeomagnetic directions and archaeointensities has been used for Neolithic and younger cultures. Directional dating can sometimes be as good as ±25 years. Magnetic reversal stratigraphy has been useful in dating hominid sites for paleoanthropologists, with precisions of about ±0.01 Ma, or 10 ka. Besides reviewing the basic principles of these methods, this article describes a number of applications, emphasizing explication of the method and solution of particular archaeological problems.

INTRODUCTION

Archaeomagnetism is a subfield of paleomagnetism which utilizes archaeological materials or rocks that have been magnetized during archaeological time. Paleomagnetism is concerned with the history of the Earth's magnetic field during geologic time, and applications to geological and geophysical problems. Archaeomagnetism involves the study of the Earth's magnetic field during archaeological time, and the application of paleomagnetic techniques and principles to archaeological features and artifacts (Tarling 1983).

ROBERT S. STERNBERG • Department of Geosciences, Franklin and Marshall College, Lancaster, Pennsylvania 17604, USA.

Chronometric Dating in Archaeology, edited by Taylor and Aitken.
Plenum Press, New York, 1997.

Archaeomagnetism includes three major phenomena concerning temporal variations of the geomagnetic field. First, the direction of the magnetic field undergoes secular variation, whereby the direction of the field at any point on the earth's surface changes irregularly at rates of about 1° every one to two decades, with maximum changes of about 20° around the average. Second, the strength (or intensity, paleointensity, or archaeointensity) of the field undergoes secular variation with changes of several percent of the field strength every century, with maximum changes of about 50%.

Secular variation involves changes occurring on a time scale between several decades and several millennia. Third, the polarity of the field occasionally flips over, with north and south magnetic poles reversing. Reversals occur randomly, on the average once every 250 ka, lasting about 10 ka. Secular variation patterns are congruent only out to distances of several thousand kilometers because of the regional nature of the geomagnetic non-dipole field, whereas polarity reversals of the geomagnetic dipole field are globally synchronous.

Along with temporal variations of the field, the other major phenomenon making archaeomagnetic studies possible is the ability of certain ferromagnetic minerals in rocks to acquire a permanent (remanent) magnetization. The most important such minerals are magnetite and hematite. As igneous rocks and baked clays cool from above (or close to) the Curie temperature of their ferromagnetic minerals (580°C for magnetite, 680°C for hematite), they become magnetized parallel to the magnetic field, thereby acquiring a thermoremanent magnetization, or TRM. Archaeomagnetism of baked clays in hearths, ceramics, burned walls and floors has an advantage over ^{14}C in that the event being dated, the firing of the clay feature, is usually a cultural event of archaeological interest.

Sediments can also be magnetized with a depositional or post-depositional remanent magnetization (DRM and PDRM, respectively)—ferromagnetic grains align with the ambient magnetic field during sedimentation or re-align in pore spaces after deposition. This phenomenon is relevant for dating of archaeological sediments and for recording of magnetic reversals in geologic sediments associated with hominid remains and artifacts. Sedimentary records have been shown to be congruent with contemporaneous archaeomagnetic data from the same geographic area (Barton and Barbetti 1982; Verosub 1988; Cong and Wei 1989).

Archaeomagnetism is often referred to as an absolute dating method, but Aitken (1990: 2) makes a useful distinction in referring to it as a "derivative" dating method. That is to say, a pattern of change for the relevant phenomenon must first be established, and dating is done by matching the archaeomagnetic measurement to this pattern. This type of dating has also been termed a "correlation method" (Colman *et al.* 1987). Sternberg (1990) classifies dating methods according to two dimensions: (1) whether they are "clocks," or whether they involve matching of patterns, and (2) whether they are applicable globally or regionally/locally. Archaeomagnetic directional and intensity secular variation dating are regional pattern-matching methods, whereas magnetic reversal stratigraphy is a global pattern-matching method. Field and lab procedures are well established in archaeomagnetism, but as in any of the pattern-matching methods, investigators have used different procedures for the compilation of the patterns and comparison of features to be dated against the pattern. Standardization of such procedures, as has occurred with radiocarbon calibration, only occurs when the number of practitioners and users demands that it be done. This has not yet occurred in archaeomagnetic dating.

Basic principles of the three types of archaeomagnetic dating will be outlined below; the reader is also referred to more complete explications of these methods oriented towards the archaeologist: Tarling (1983, 1985, 1991), Wolfman (1984), Parkes (1986), Aitken (1990), and Eighmy and Sternberg (1990). Although many interesting archaeomagnetic results and their dating implications can be found in archaeological reports, references herein are to primary journals and to published conference proceedings, with a preference for more recent literature. Several applications of the major types of archaeomagnetic dating will be presented. The focus will be on the archaeological and chronometric implications of the results, with an emphasis on North America, and the approach will be to review the conclusions in the papers cited. Methodological and paleomagnetic aspects of these studies will be left for the interested reader to pursue in the original publications. The reader should also bear in mind that archaeomagnetism has other possible nonchronometric applications to archaeology, as summarized by Tarling (1983).

PRINCIPLES OF ARCHAEOMAGNETIC (DIRECTIONAL) DATING

Most often, the term "archaeomagnetic dating" refers to the use of secular variation of direction for the determination of absolute (i.e., derivative) dates. These dates can only be inferred if a master curve of secular variation has already been established, since the secular variation pattern is not predictable. In the absence of a master curve, it is possible to use archaeomagnetic directions to evaluate contemporaneity of different features. Although most archaeomagnetic studies are done on baked clays, archaeological and geological sediments and igneous rocks have been used as well.

Field and laboratory work parallels procedures for a typical paleomagnetic study. Oriented samples must be collected from *in situ* features, usually baked clays such as hearths, kilns, burned walls and floors (Eighmy 1990), but burned stones can also be used (Barbetti *et al.* 1980; Atkinson and Shaw 1991b). Typically, 8–12 oriented samples, each with a volume of several cubic centimeters, are collected per feature, allowing statistical analyses to be performed on the results. Samples are oriented by enclosing them in cubes of plaster of paris, or by adhering a plastic disk onto the sample. Depending on the nature of the material, it may take anywhere from a couple of hours to a day to collect the requisite number of samples. Orientation is done with a transit, pocket transit, or sun compass. Although collection procedures are not difficult in principle, Lange and Murphy (1990) have shown that inexperienced collectors can be responsible for poor results.

In the laboratory, the direction and strength of the natural remanent magnetization (NRM) are measured with either a spinner or cryogenic magnetometer. The known field orientation of the sample allows the determination of the magnetization direction in field coordinates, hence the direction of the ancient magnetic field. The stability of the magnetization must be assessed by demagnetizing the sample, using either thermal or alternating (magnetic) field demagnetization. These analyses are used to remove unstable secondary components of magnetization (e.g., accumulation of viscous remanence over time, a partial TRM due to later heatings, or an isothermal remanence due to lightning strikes) in order to retrieve the primary magnetic direction of interest.

Archaeomagnetic directions can be represented as either the direction of the field at the site of interest, or the location of the equivalent virtual geomagnetic pole (VGP). The former is specified by two angles—declination is the angle between the horizontal component of the magnetic field (magnetic north) and geographic north, and inclination is the dip of the magnetic field vector below horizontal. The VGP is a mathematical transformation of the magnetic direction from a particular site location to the latitude and longitude where the equivalent dipole axis intersects the Earth's surface, assuming no nondipole field. For a single site, results can be represented either by directions or VGPs for comparison with each other. Over an archaeomagnetic region, e.g., the American Southwest, VGPs will cluster better than magnetic directions because of the geographical variation of dipole field directions which is removed by the VGP transformation. Directions from different sites within a region can also be transformed through the VGP to an equivalent site location. Ultimately, even a VGP secular variation curve is consistent over only a limited geographic area because of the variation of the nondipole field. The mean angular error of archaeomagnetic directions is typically 5° per 1000 km if the dipole correction is not made, and 2° per 1000 km after the dipole correction has been made (Noel and Batt 1990). If we accept a typical accuracy of archaeomagnetic directions of 5° (Eighmy and Hathaway 1987; Tarling and Dobson 1995), and we wish the geographic dipole effect to be no more than 50% of this, the secular variation curve is only valid over a geographic radius of about 2.5°/(2° per 1000 km) = 1250 km.

Paleomagnetic direction vectors require different statistical treatment than scalar quantities. It is customary to use the Fisher distribution and Fisher statistics (Tarling 1983: 111–130). This distribution is analogous to a two-dimensional Gaussian distribution, with the precision of the population of vectors characterized by the precision parameter k, which increases from zero as the vectors are clustered more closely. Mean sample directions are calculated as vector means. The reliability of the sample mean is quantified by the α_{95}, which is the angular radius of the cone of confidence about the sample mean such that there is a 95% probability that the true direction lies within this cone of confidence.

Construction of a secular variation master curve for a region involves several challenges: collecting and measuring of sufficient samples; determining when these samples acquired their magnetization; and deriving a curve from the data. Collection of archaeomagnetic samples is "opportunistic" because, in most cases, choosing samples according to their quality and age is subject to their availability. Independent dating of these samples is also potentially problematic. What is needed is the date of the last substantial firing of the feature, which is often not a directly dated event (Dean 1978). Thus, the estimated date of firing of these features is usually a combination of chronometric dates and archaeological inference. Nonetheless, adequate secular variation curves are now available for a number of regions around the world (Creer *et al.* 1983; Wolfman 1984). Improvement of existing curves and generating master curves for new regions requires an ongoing collaboration between archaeomagnetists and archaeologists (Eighmy 1990; Sternberg 1990; Blackwell and Schwarcz 1993). Compilations of archaeomagnetic data are becoming better documented through published catalogs (Burlatskaya 1986; Clark *et al.* 1988; LaBelle and Eighmy 1995) and computerized databases (Tarling and Dobson 1995; Sternberg *et al.* 1997).

Methods of curve construction are discussed in some detail by Sternberg and McGuire (1990b). In archaeomagnetism, secular variation curves have been derived using graphical (Wolfman 1982; Rolph *et al.* 1987; Wolfman 1990a, 1990b), semi-quantitative (Holcomb *et al.* 1986) and quantitative methods (Sternberg and McGuire 1990b). Graphical methods are appropriate and necessary when data are too sparse for quantitative methods. Graphical methods for curve construction use the independent ages as a guideline, but also utilize stratigraphic/relative dating relationships and the serial correlation of magnetic directions in order to constrain the secular variation curve. The quantitative methods have sometimes been called "statistical"; these methods are not necessarily statistically rigorous, although presumably reasonable as a method of data treatment.

Interpreting archaeomagnetic dates then becomes a process similar to calibrating a radiocarbon date (Sternberg and McGuire 1990b). To infer a date, a measured quantity related to the object to be dated must be compared with a temporally varying pattern. The situation in archaeomagnetism is more complicated than with ^{14}C because the quantities of interest are vectors. Like radiocarbon dating, archaeomagnetic dating can yield several dates for the same archaeomagnetic direction. Dates can only be obtained for the time period covered by the secular variation curve. Use of different secular variation curves, or revisions of an existing curve, will yield different dating interpretations for the same archaeomagnetic result (Eighmy and Doyel 1987; Sternberg and McGuire 1990b; Baker and Eighmy 1993).

PRINCIPLES OF ARCHAEOINTENSITY DATING

Unoriented as well as oriented materials can be used for paleointensity studies, an advantage because potsherds are very abundant at many archaeological sites. Paleointensity studies have most often been done with samples carrying a TRM, which theory and experiment indicate is linearly proportional to the strength of the magnetizing field. Thus:

$$TRM_{paleo} = k_{TRM} B_{paleo}$$

$$TRM_{lab} = k_{TRM} B_{lab} \qquad (1)$$

and, if k_{TRM} is constant,

$$B_{paleo} = B_{lab} \times TRM_{paleo} / TRM_{lab} \qquad (2)$$

where TRM_{paleo} is the strength of thermoremanent magnetization acquired in the paleomagnetic field having paleointensity B_{paleo}, TRM_{lab} is the strength of magnetization acquired in the laboratory field B_{lab}, and k_{TRM} is the susceptibility to TRM acquisition. Equation (2) implies that the paleointensity can be determined by measuring TRM_{paleo}, heating the sample in the known B_{lab}, and then measuring the resulting TRM_{lab}. In practice, the experiment is more complicated and time consuming. It is quite possible that the magnetic minerals will have altered either *in situ* since the feature/artifact was originally fired or during the laboratory heatings. Thus, k_{TRM} would not be constant. In the classic Thellier method (Thellier and Thellier 1959), this can be analyzed by heating the sample to a series of increasing temperatures, up to the Curie temperatures of the magnetic minerals. Two heatings at each temperature separate the remaining original TRM left in the sample, and the new laboratory TRM acquired up to that temperature. When the remaining NRM is plotted against the acquired TRM, the paleointensity is equal to the slope of the linear portion of the graph multiplied by the laboratory field B_{lab}. Much time is consumed by the numerous heating steps, and if no preselection is done, many samples may not yield acceptable results. Points frequently fall off the best-fit line at low and high temperatures, most likely due to viscous remanence in the original remanence of the samples and mineralogical changes during the experimental heatings, respectively. A variety of reliability tests during the experiment enhances the likelihood of selecting the best temperature range and making a valid interpretation.

Other variations of the paleointensity method are designed to save time or increase chances for experimental success (Thomas 1983). The most prevalent alternative to the Thellier method is the Shaw method (Shaw, 1974; Yang *et al.* 1993), which uses alternating-field demagnetization instead of thermal demagnetization of the original and laboratory TRMs. Another new, promising technique also tries to minimize thermal alteration during the experiment by using microwave demagnetization (Shaw *et al.* 1996). Cui and Verosub (1995) suggest an alternative approach—preselecting samples with rock magnetic properties that identify those samples as good candidates for the paleointensity experiment. Among the many commendable papers using these paleointensity techniques are the applications to Roman ceramics by Hedley and Wagner (1991) and to bricks from Greek churches by Aitken *et al.* (1989).

Archaeointensities themselves are scalars, representing the length of the archaeomagnetic vector; together with the archaeomagnetic direction, the archaeointensity describes the complete archaeomagnetic vector. In principle, using the intensity as well as the direction could reduce the ambiguity of archaeomagnetic dates, especially when there are multiple dating options. The experimental difficulties in obtaining archaeointensities has dissuaded most archaeomagnetists from doing this on a routine basis. Other independent dating methods such as thermoluminescence, also set by the firing of a feature, could also be used to reduce this ambiguity (Becker *et al.* 1994).

APPLICATIONS

Quantitative Curve Construction: American Southwest

One type of quantitative curve construction technique is the moving-window method (Sternberg 1989b). This technique uses weighted averages of all data that fall within windows of time. Each point is weighted by the product of its paleomagnetic precision parameter k and its fractional overlap with the time window of interest. For example, if an averaging window extends from AD 1000–1100, a feature that dates AD 1000–1100 or AD 1025–1075 would have the maximum fractional overlap of 1.0; a feature that dates AD 1100–1200 would have the minimum fractional overlap of 0.0; a feature that dates AD 1050–1150 or AD 950–1150 would have a fractional overlap of 0.5. The calculated secular variation curve consists of an average pole position with confidence limits (both precision parameter and α_{95}, the polar equivalent of α_{95}) for each window of time. Connecting these points gives the appearance of a curve. Thus, the quantitative curve-fitting method accounts for errors in the individual data points and yields a curve with a measure of uncertainty assigned to it. Each point is treated independently, so relationships (e.g., stratigraphic) between them are not accounted for. Any smoothing method, including this one, will smooth out higher frequency variations in the magnetic field (Eighmy *et al.* 1986).

Fig. 11.1 shows a recent version of the secular variation curve for the American Southwest (Eighmy 1991). This curve is based on 206 archaeomagnetic results, selected to include only well-dated results with independent dates of 50 years or better. Each result has an error bar associated with its age and an error bar associated with the sample mean direction. The moving-window method was applied to these data to generate the secular variation curve in Fig. 11.1, as tabulated in Eighmy (1991, Table 2). Window lengths are 40 years, at 25-year intervals. The general patterns on the curve are similar to other

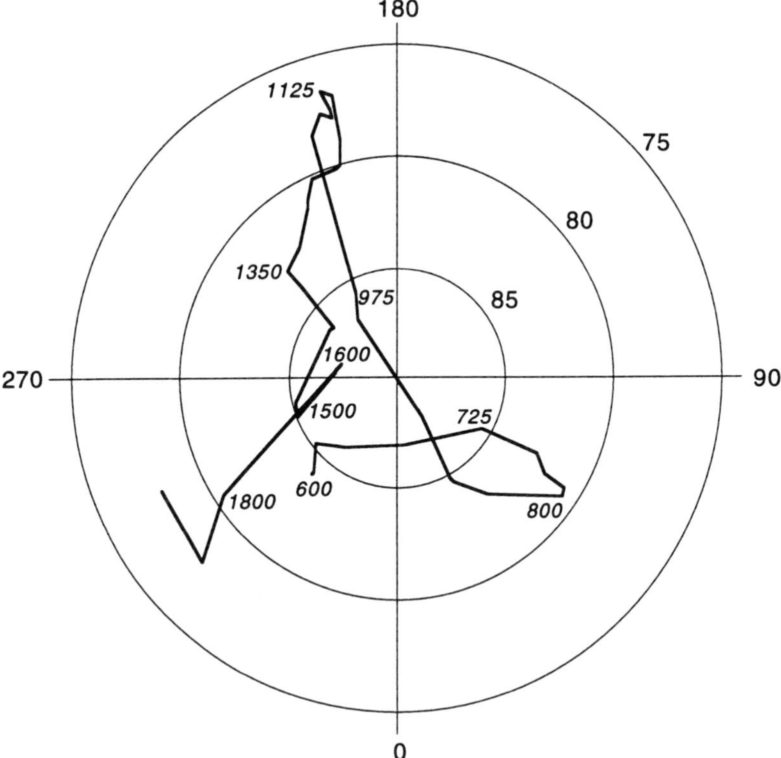

Figure 11.1. Archaeomagnetic secular variation curve for the American Southwest (after Eighmy 1991). Plot of VGPs, with the north geographic pole at the center of the figure. Longitudes 0°, 90°, 180°, and 270°, and latitudes 75°, 80° and 85° are indicated. The ages of several points in years AD are indicated; points are at 25-year intervals.

Southwestern secular variation curves using different data sets and curve construction methods (DuBois 1975, 1991; Sternberg 1989b; Sternberg and McGuire 1990a).

Secular variation rates can be quantified by taking the angular differences between subsequent points. For the 45 points on the curve, secular variation rates of the VGP location have an average of 1° every 15 years, and a median of 1° every 22 years. This curve shows that a particular direction is non-unique as the pole position wanders back and forth, which can lead to multiple options for archaeomagnetic dates. The curve has endpoints, so that archaeomagnetic dates cannot be determined beyond those end points, although these dates may be mistakenly aliased onto an existing portion of the curve.

Quantitative Date Interpretation: Sunset Crater

Discrete secular variation curves of the moving-window type allow statistical comparisons to be made between each point on the secular variation curve and a direction to be dated (Sternberg 1989b; Sternberg and McGuire 1990b). With a null hypothesis that these directions are the same, the archaeomagnetic date will thus be the range of time corresponding to those points on the curve for which the null hypothesis cannot be rejected. A 5% significance level F-test is used, as is common in paleomagnetic work. With this test, the uncertainty in the curve as well as the point to be dated is accounted for. The highest precision dates occur when a VGP dates to only one point on the curve, corresponding to one window length.

Sternberg (1989b) used this method to infer archaeomagnetic dates for igneous rocks from the Sunset Crater volcanic field of northern Arizona. Five paleomagnetic pole positions for these rocks (Champion 1980) are plotted along with a version of the Southwest VGP secular variation curve (Sternberg 1989b) in Fig. 11.2. As the directions are transformed to the VGP, the α_{95} of each direction is transformed to an oval of confidence.

Table 11.1 compares the dates interpreted by Sternberg (1989b) using the quantitative method with those interpreted by Champion (1980) based on the secular variation curve of DuBois (1975) and using a graphical method. The re-interpreted archaeomagnetic dates are consistent with the AD 1065–1067 dendrochronological age of tree-rings in the area showing stunted growth, presumably due to one of these volcanic eruptions (Breternitz 1967). In any case, this example points out how an archaeomagnetic date depends on which secular variation curve is used. Note that the Kana-a VGP plots so far from the secular variation curve that the null hypothesis is rejected for all points on the curve, and no date is interpreted with the quantitative method. Because of the uncertainty in the curve (not shown on Fig. 11.2), the Bonito flow dates even though its VGP direction does not fall right on the curve, and Vent 512 gives one age range including the age range that falls outside of the oval of confidence.

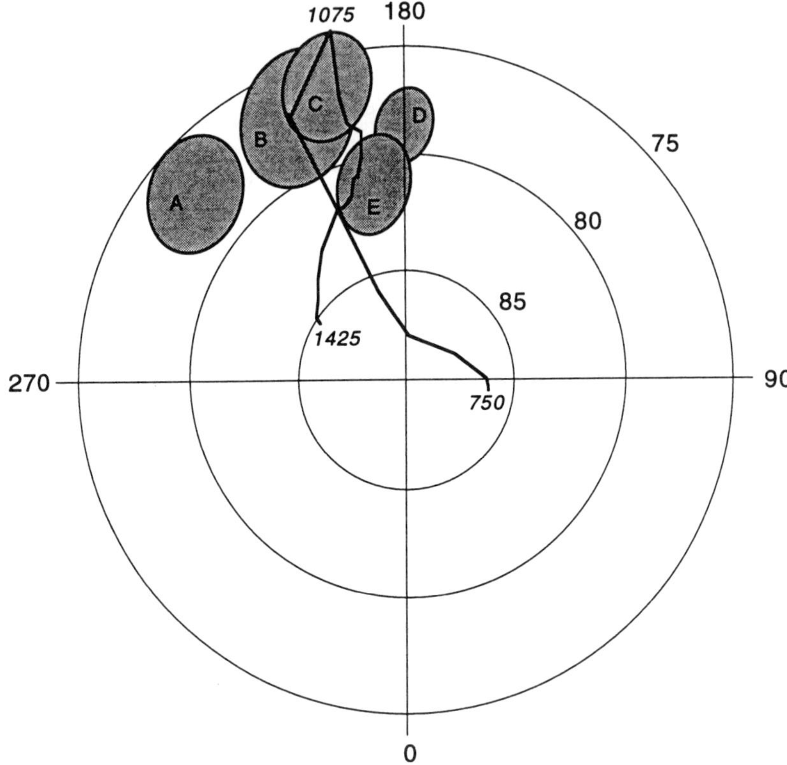

Figure 11.2. Archaeomagnetic dating of Holocene lavas in the American Southwest. Plot of VGPs using same format as Fig. 11.1. The ages of several points in years AD are indicated along the secular variation curve; points are at 50-year intervals from AD 750–1000, and 25 years thereafter. The ovals of confidence are shown for the results to be dated. Letters are identified in Table 11.1. After Sternberg (1989b) and Sternberg and McGuire (1990a).

Table 11.1. Archaeomagnetic Dates for Five Lava Flows near Sunset Crater, Arizona, from Comparison to Two Different Secular Variation Curves. Letters in Parentheses Refer to Labels in Fig. 11.2

Flow	Age (AD) Sternberg (1989b)	Age (AD) Champion (1980)
Kana-a (A)	none	1150
Vent 512 (B)	1000-1175	1190
Gyp Crater (C)	1000-1175	1190
Bonito (D)	1100-1175	1230
Sunset Crater (E)	100-1325	1250

Graphical Curve Construction and Date Interpretation: Arkansas

Wolfman (1982, 1990c) describes a method using VGPs to construct a secular variation curve, and then in turn using that curve to derive archaeomagnetic dates. There is a tendency with this method to emphasize the accuracy of the archaeomagnetic directions, which may not be warranted (Eighmy and Hathaway 1987; Tarling and Dobson 1995). Arguments for and against the graphical method are put forward in Wolfman (1990c) and Sternberg and McGuire (1990b).

Wolfman (1982) used 35 results with $\alpha_{95} < 4.0°$ from Arkansas, USA, and border areas to construct a secular variation curve for AD 1200–1500 (Fig. 11.3). The curve is drawn graphically, using the VGP positions as a guide. Independent dates are taken into account, but are not necessarily given

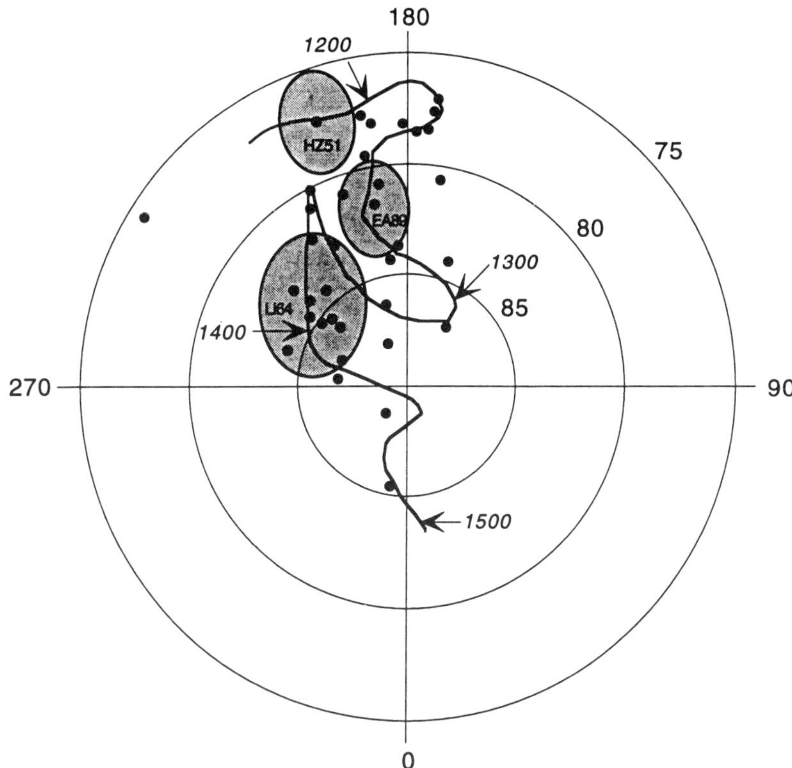

Figure 11.3. VGP secular variation curve for Arkansas, graphically constructed from the VGPs shown as dots. Several ages in years AD are shown along the curve. The cones of confidence for three VGPs archaeomagnetically dated by comparison to the curve are also shown. After Wolfman (1982).

Table 11.2. Independent and Archaeomagnetic Dates for Three VGPs from Arkansas (Wolfman 1982)

Feature	Independent Years AD	Archaeomagnetic Years AD
HZ51	1100-1350	1180±20
EA89	1100-1450	1270±20
LI64	1200-1400	1335-1425

precedence over the pole position. The drawn curve is subjective, but tends to minimize variance of the pole positions about the curve. When the Arkansas data are subjected to the moving-window method, the secular variation curve is similar to the Southwest curve, but systematically displaced by about 1.5°. This could be due to the 1500 km geographic separation between sites, and the variation of the nondipole field over that distance (Sternberg 1989b).

Fig. 11.3 also shows how some of these same points are then used for archaeomagnetic dating. The age range is determined by dividing the semi-major axis of the oval of confidence by a typical secular variation rate of 0.1°/year, with adjustments to account for the relation of a particular point to the curve (Wolfman 1982, 1984, 1990c). Table 11.2 lists both the independent and the archaeomagnetic dates for these three features. The independent and archaeomagnetic age ranges overlap for each of the three features. Although all three features have similar independent ages because of their assignment to the same archaeological period, the archaeomagnetic dates are differentiated by the different locations of the VGPs along the secular variation curve.

Eighmy *et al.* (1993) has suggested using the quantitative dating method with adjustments based on the graphical method to account for anomalies that can arise in the strict application of the quantitative method. These ideas warrant further investigation.

Graphical Curve Construction and Date Interpretation: Mt. Etna

Paleomagnetic methods can also be applied to volcanic rocks, including those that have erupted during archaeological time (Holcomb *et al.* 1986), and at archaeological sites (Tarling and Downey 1990). Rolph *et al.* (1987) sampled 45 lava flows of Mt. Etna, Sicily, that had been historically dated between AD 1169 and 1983. Paleomagnetic directions were determined for 37 flows from which oriented samples were collected, and the paleointensity experiment was successful for 37 flows (not the same 37 as for directions). As in the previous example, these results were used to construct a secular variation curve, but also used to assess the degree to which the assigned ages were reasonable. Figure

11.4 shows the directions on a stereographic projection (as is often used to display paleomagnetic directions), with the declination easting clockwise around the perimeter, and the inclination steepening from the outside inwards. Fig. 11.4 also shows the secular variation curve drawn to best fit these directions; a quantitative method gave a very similar curve (T. C. Rolph, personal communication, 1996). The smoothing of the curve does not exactly fit every point, and the directions are sometimes honored above the dates in ordering the points along the curve.

Eight flows were of doubtful age based on their magnetic directions or intensities, or on geologic grounds; the directions with confidence limits (square symbols with ovals) for these points are shown in Fig. 11.4. The directions for six flows (points 2, 3, 5, 6, 7 and 8 in Fig. 11.4) are inconsistent with the curve for the assigned historical ages; it was concluded that the assigned historical dates were wrong, and the archaeomagnetic directions were correct. The archaeomagnetic date for point 1 is consistent with the historical date, even though this flow has distinct petrographic characteristics. The directions for points 4 and 5 are different from each other, even though they were originally assigned the same date of AD 1536. This also demonstrates how archaeomagnetism can be used to evaluate the contemporaneity of two features by comparing their directions to each other. Intensity alone is often not able to resolve dates: two flows assigned historical dates of AD 1651 had indistinguishable intensities, yet very different directions.

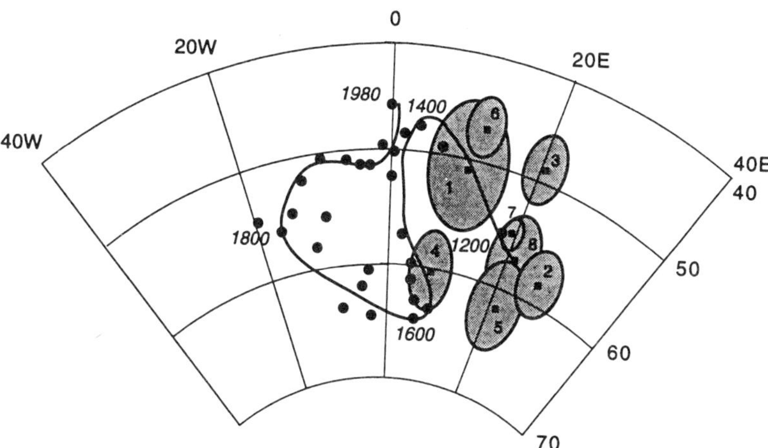

Figure 11.4. Stereographic projections of paleomagnetic directions from Mt. Etna igneous rocks. Declination easts clockwise around the perimeter; inclination steepens towards the center. The secular variation curve was drawn to fit the directions. Ages of several points along the curve are shown. Directions for questionable results are shown as squares with ovals of confidence. After Rolph *et al.* (1987).

Holcomb *et al.* (1986) applied a somewhat similar approach to lava flows from Hawaii. Results from 67 sites of known age (historic and ^{14}C) were used to construct a secular variation curve for the past 2500 years. Dates were inferred for 68 additional sites of unknown age using what the authors call a semi-quantitative method. Directions were first grouped using geologic criteria, ^{14}C dates, and magnetic directions. Next the groups were ordered, using geologic evidence, ^{14}C dates, and a preference towards less complicated sequences. The directions of these ordered groups were used to refine the secular variation curve based on the dated flows.

Further interesting applications of paleomagnetic results from lava flows to absolute and relative dating and volcanology problems are given by Kuntz *et al.* (1986), Donnelly-Nolan *et al.* (1990), Champion and Donnelly-Nolan (1994), and Hagstrum and Champion (1994).

Graphical Date Interpretation with Intensity: Bulgaria

Archaeointensity studies have been most often carried out to elaborate the secular variation of geomagnetic field strength (Creer *et al.* 1983). In some areas, investigators have carried out directional and paleointensity studies in parallel (Sternberg 1989a; Sternberg 1989b). However, only Kovacheva's research program in Bulgaria has routinely used paleointensity along with directions for all archaeomagnetic dating results (Kovacheva 1986, 1989, 1991). Kovacheva's dating program is also remarkable in the extension of the secular variation record from the present back into the early Neolithic, ca. 6000 BC, providing this region with the oldest archaeomagnetic dates in the world. This record provides a useful frame of reference for other studies on older material in Europe and the Middle East.

Results for the dating of a Neolithic site at Popovo, Bulgaria are shown in Fig. 11.5 (Kovacheva 1991). Kovacheva treats the declination, inclination, and archaeointensity results as independent scalar quantities, unlike other investigators who treat the declination and inclination together as a direction or VGP (e.g., Sternberg and McGuire 1990b). Kovacheva's presentation of separate components is similar to the paleomagnetic declination, inclination and intensity logs often shown for sedimentary records. The band for each component represents the secular variation pattern along with its uncertainty, due to dating and paleomagnetic uncertainties in the points on which the curves are based. Results for Popovo are declination = 6.6°, inclination = 58.6°, α_{95} = 1.9°, paleointensity = (0.815±0.027) × (present-day field strength). The direction is the average of 39 samples; the intensity result averages five samples. The means are shown as straight lines on each graph in Fig. 11.5. Dating options are determined by the intersection of these lines with the envelope of the curves; multiple options are possible for each curve. The dating options for each curve are shown as the hatched areas on the time axes in the figures, and listed in Table 11.3. The single declination option rules out the earliest of the

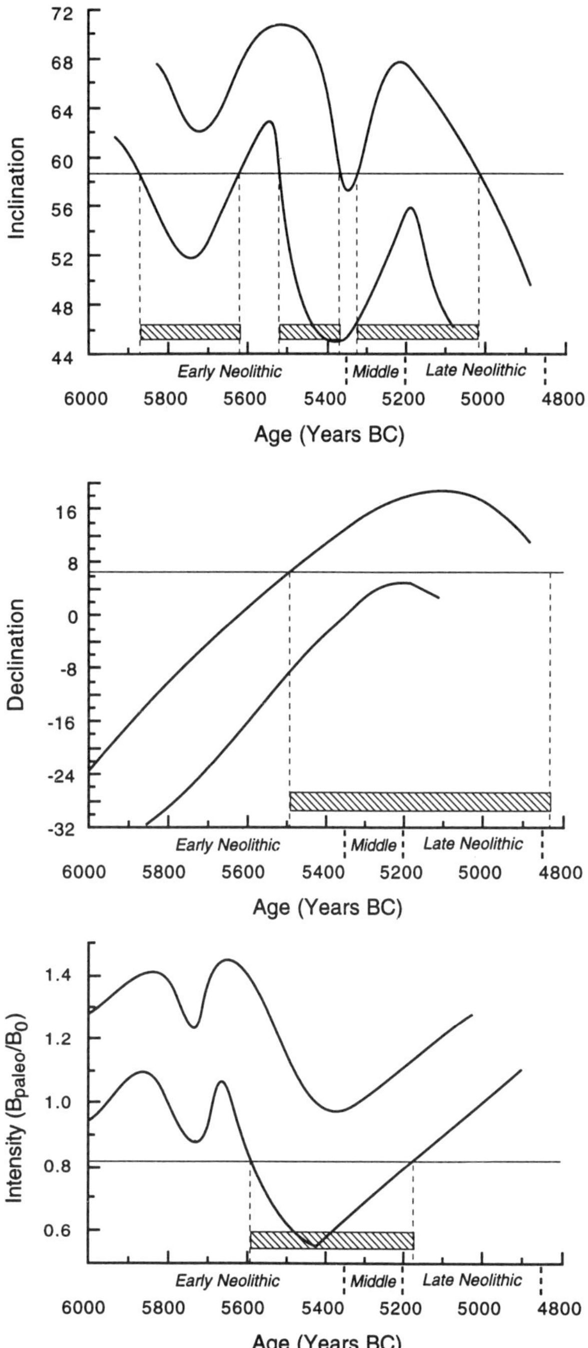

Figure 11.5. Neolithic secular variation curves for Bulgaria, and archaeomagnetic results from Popovo (horizontal lines). The hatched areas on the time axes show the dating options for each element. After Kovacheva (1991).

Table 11.3. Archaeomagnetic Dating Options in Years BC for Popovo, Bulgaria (Kovacheva 1991)

	Option 1	Option 2	Option 3
Inclination	5880-5620	5530-5380	5330-5020
Declination	5490-4830		
Intensity	5590-5180		

three inclination options. The intensity result is consistent with both the remaining inclination options, but the recent option is more reasonable based on archaeological grounds, yielding a preferred archaeomagnetic date of 5330–5180 BC. The archaeomagnetic dates for Popovo and five other newly excavated Neolithic sites suggest a sequence of use covering approximately 800 years during the sixth millennium BC.

CASE STUDIES

Directions from a Single Site: Las Colinas, Arizona

A number of archaeomagnetic studies have focused on the dating of a single feature, or just a few features from one site. These studies include sites in Denmark (Abrahamsen and Breiner 1991), Scotland (Gentles and Tarling 1988), England (Zhaoqin and Noel 1989), The Netherlands (Langereis and Kars 1990), France (Langouet and Goulpeau 1984; Lanos 1987; Dearden and Clark 1990), Spain (Parés *et al.* 1992), Gėrmany (Schurr *et al.* 1984), Switzerland (Hedley et al. 1983), and Turkey (Saribudak and Tarling 1993). Although not in the primary literature, there are a number of archaeomagnetic dating reports by the Ancient Monuments Laboratory, English Heritage.

When a large number of archaeomagnetic features are analyzed from a single site, the results can give insight into the statistics of archaeomagnetic results. Sternberg *et al.* (1991) analyzed 168 archaeomagnetic results on baked clays from the Hohokam culture site of Las Colinas, in the present-day city of Phoenix, Arizona, USA. Dates were interpreted for 143 features, an 85% "success" rate. Thirty-eight of these features (28% of the datable features) had two dating options and one feature had three options. A histogram of the age ranges interpreted using the "statistical" method at the 5% significance level shows a median age range of 200 years (roughly equivalent to ±100 years), with an interquartile range of 140–340 years (Figure 11.6, upper plot). This compares favorably with 95%-confidence-interval calibrated ^{14}C dates from the Hohokam culture area, shown in Figure 11.6, lower plot (data from Schiffer

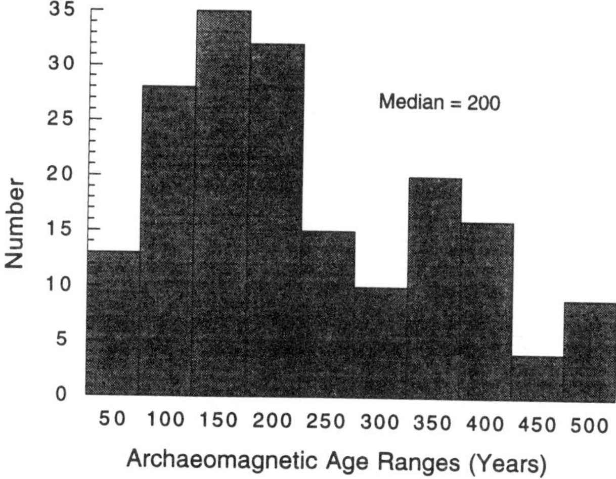

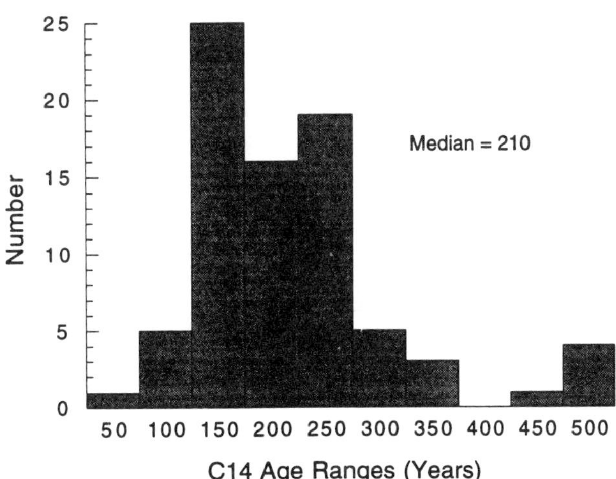

Figure 11.6. Histograms of archaeomagnetic age ranges from Las Colinas, Arizona (upper plot), and calibrated ^{14}C dates from the Hohokam culture area (lower plot). ^{14}C data from Schiffer and Staski (1982). After Sternberg *et al.* (1991).

and Staski 1982). The Hohokam ^{14}C dates have a median age range of 210 calendrical years, and an interquartile range of 154–260 years.

Ten features at Las Colinas were dated by both archaeomagnetism and ^{14}C. For seven of the pairs, the archaeomagnetic and ^{14}C dates were not significantly different. No archaeomagnetic date was interpreted for two pairs. For one pair the dates were different; archaeologically the ^{14}C date was more reasonable. One should resist the temptation to automatically regard ^{14}C dates as the correct benchmark in such a comparison, but the comparison of these dates is generally supportive of both methods.

Perhaps the most interesting aspect of this study was an assessment of what affected the precision of the archaeomagnetic dates. Somewhat surprisingly, the precision of the archaeomagnetic direction (α_{95}) to be dated was not the major factor. The ten features with the largest archaeomagnetic age ranges did have poor precision, but for the remaining samples there was no significant correlation. However, when the archaeomagnetic age range is plotted against the midpoint of the age range, striking patterns emerge (Fig. 11.7). These patterns can be explained by considering the nature of the secular variation curve that was used (Fig. 11.2), and the α_{95}s of the features being dated. The "digital" appearance of Fig. 11.7 is partly because the age ranges are rounded off to 10-year increments. The smallest age ranges, when the dated feature is only compatible with a short section of the secular variation curve, occur when secular variation is faster (ca. AD 1325), or when there is a bend in the secular variation curve (ca. AD 1075). As the dates approach the endpoints of the finite secular variation curve, the age ranges tend to decrease because the age range can only extend to the end of the curve. These age ranges are really open-ended. The largest age ranges occur when two conditions co-exist: the feature being dated has a large α_{95}, and the feature dates between AD 1000 and AD 1300 when the secular variation curve loops back on itself. These conditions allow the feature direction to be compatible with a longer segment of the curve

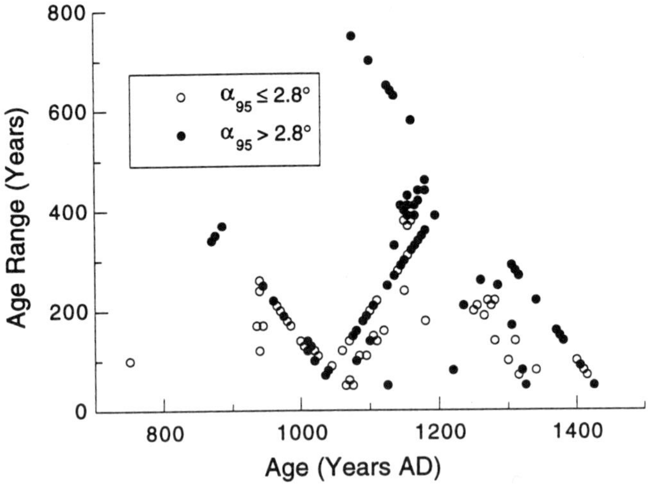

Figure 11.7. Age ranges of the archaeomagnetic dates at Las Colinas, as a function of the age. Open symbols are for features with α_{95} at or below 2.8° (the median value), and solid symbols are for α_{95} greater than 2.8°. After Sternberg *et al.* (1991).

covering both sides of the secular variation loop. The minimum age range possible is 50 years (±25 years), when the direction to be dated is only compatible with one 50-year window of the secular variation curve. My opinion is that this value realistically represents nearly the best possible precision for a single archaeomagnetic date, allowing for the uncertainty in both the master curve and the direction of the feature to be dated.

Eighmy and Mitchell (1994) studied 174 features at Pueblo Grande, another Hohokam site within the city limits of modern Phoenix. Las Colinas and Pueblo Grande may be the two most intensively sampled sites for archaeomagnetism that have been reported in the literature. Some similar conclusions were drawn at Pueblo Grande as in the previous example: (1) A high proportion (80%) of Southwestern hearths yield archaeomagnetic dates; (2) for quantitative dating, the median age range for archaeomagnetic dates is 175 years, with an interquartile range of 50–200 years; (3) about 20% of the archaeomagnetic dates do not agree with dates based on associated ceramics, but 90% agree with ^{14}C dates; 4) the precision of archaeomagnetic dates is independent of α_{95} when α_{95} varies from 1.0–5.0°; (5) although increasing the number of samples decreases α_{95} somewhat, dating accuracy is not highly dependent on the number of samples.

Directions from a Culture Area: Hohokam Culture, Arizona

In the American Southwest, archaeomagnetism has become a routine dating method (Eighmy and Sternberg 1990); the secular variation curve has been calibrated by tree-ring dating at the higher elevations of the Colorado Plateau, after which archaeomagnetic dating can be applied in the nearby Sonoran desert where tree rings are too complacent for dendrochronology. The Hohokam chronology has long been controversial. The preservation of wood in the desert environment where the Hohokam lived means that tree-ring or ^{14}C dates may significantly pre-date the archaeological date of interest when the wood was used. As a result, archaeomagnetic dating has been an important method in Hohokam archaeology and chronology building.

Eighmy and McGuire (1989) reviewed over 700 archaeomagnetic results from the Hohokam culture area in the American Southwest. They selected a subset of 312 reliable archaeomagnetic results that could be assigned (usually by ceramics) to Hohokam culture phases or phase transitions. Of the total, 241 were from the Phoenix (Arizona) Basin, and 71 were from the Tucson Basin, approximately 150 km away. The results from the two basins were separated in order to evaluate the relative timing of the phases between the two areas. Mean VGPs were calculated for each phase. The means fall close to the secular variation curve at times consistent with some of the previous Hohokam time scales, and track around the curve in the correct stratigraphic order (Eighmy and McGuire 1989: Figs. 6–7).

Archaeomagnetic dates were interpreted for each feature. There was considerable overlap between the archaeomagnetic dates from the Rincon and Tanque Verde phases, a pattern also seen in most of the phases for the Phoenix Basin. Eighmy and McGuire (1989) interpret this as due to actual temporal overlap of the use of pottery styles assigned to different culture phases. They conclude that (Hohokam) chronology building could benefit from increased attention to the reliability of ceramic phase assignments, and to the site formation processes that produce ceramic floor assemblages.

Finally, Eighmy and McGuire (1989) use the extreme endpoints of the archaeomagnetic dates within each phase to define the phase durations in both the Phoenix and Tucson Basins. Boundaries themselves are difficult to delineate (in fact, sharp boundaries may not really exist, as indicated in the previous paragraph), and are sometimes determined by halving the difference between the phase means. Nonetheless, the results (Eighmy and McGuire 1989: Fig. 8) indicate that there is no clear temporal relationship between the phases in the two basins. They do not begin or end simultaneously, nor is there any consistent lag of one phase sequence behind the other. The archaeomagnetic data thus suggest that the phase changes (and cultural evolution) in each area should be viewed in terms of the internal dynamics particular to each area.

Dean (1991) similarly reviewed the long-standing Hohokam chronology problem, focusing on the independent chronometry provided by ^{14}C and archaeomagnetic dates. Archaeomagnetic dates included those considered by Eighmy and McGuire (1989), plus additional dates. Elimination of anomalous dates left 443 dates used in the analysis. Dean also found: (1) dates for contexts assigned to different phases overlap; (2) the traditional cultural phases appear to represent distinct temporal and cultural units; (3) the trend from early to late phases corresponds to accepted sequences for both the Phoenix and Tucson basins; (4) the chronology could not be refined beyond what was already known.

Deaver and Ciolek-Torrello (1995) also included archaeomagnetic dates in their analysis of the Early Formative period (AD 1–800) in the Tucson Basin. Thirteen results from six sites were used, although two results did not date and two pre-dated the beginning of the curve. Like the other Hohokam archaeomagnetic cultural syntheses, but unlike conventional archaeomagnetic dating in the Southwest, the objective was to identify sets of features that represented occupational components, and then to assign dates to the components rather than the individual archaeomagnetic features. Deaver and Ciolek-Torrello (1995) also make the interesting observation that, in a large group of archaeomagnetic directions, secular variation should show up as a trend rather than as directions randomly oriented about a mean. Such a trend could be used as a sort of wiggle-matching dating method, as is used with ^{14}C in floating tree-ring sequences.

Case Study for Many Features from a Culture Area: Mesoamerica

Wolfman (1990b) begins his review of archaeomagnetic dating in Mesoamerica with a discussion of other dating methods that have been used in that region. Most chronometric studies have utilized ^{14}C dating. Even though this method is often used as a benchmark, Wolfman points out that problems with calibration, sample collection, treatment and contamination can have a significant impact on chronology development. Calendars were ubiquitous in Mesoamerica, but Wolfman also notes that correlating those calendars with the Christian calendar does not have a unique solution. Increased use of other chronometric methods, such as archaeomagnetism, has the potential to answer some outstanding questions.

Wolfman (1990b) used the graphical methods of curve construction and dating with over 200 Mesoamerican archaeomagnetic results. These archaeomagnetic dates had several archaeological implications. First, and most simply, two results from Huapalcalco provide the first direct dates for the Xometla phase in central Mexico, from the mid-eighth to mid-ninth centuries AD.

Second, the archaeomagnetic dating for the central Mexican Xolalpan phase at Teotihuacan, AD 350–600, has this phase beginning as much as 150 years earlier than other models. Eight archaeomagnetic features collected near the center of the city were all burned in the conflagration that occurred in either the Xolalpan or the succeeding Metepec phase. The archaeomagnetic results suggest they could have all been heated simultaneously at either AD 310 or 475, with the two possibilities due to two dating options on the secular variation curve. The uncertainty about the phase in which the conflagration occurred and which of the two dating options is correct leads to several possible interpretations. One possibility is that the burning of the city center occurred many years before the rest of the site was abandoned. In any case, these archaeomagnetic results imply that the timing of the late Preclassic and Classic periods at Teotihuacan are in need of reevaluation.

A third implication of the Mesoamerican archaeomagnetic dates is the relative dating of the occupation at Teotihuacan in the Valley of Mexico, and Kaminaljuyu in the Mayan highlands. The archaeomagnetic dates for the major burning at Teotihuacan ca. AD 475–500 are earlier than the archaeomagnetic dates for the middle and late Esperanza phase (Valley of Guatemala chronology) at Kaminaljuyu, ca. AD 525–585. These results suggest that the Teotihuacan influence on Kaminaljuyu, which began in the early Esperanza phase before the conflagration at Teotihuacan, lasted for another century thereafter. More samples from before the fire might better clarify the relationship between these two important sites.

A fourth significant use of Mesoamerican archaeomagnetic dates would be addressing the several proposed correlations of the Mayan calendar to the Christian calendar. A feature was sampled from beneath five meters of volcanic ash deposited by the Ilopango eruption in San Salvador. The most likely archaeomagnetic dating option of AD 75–135 brackets the proposed date for this eruption of AD 119 from tree-ring evidence (LaMarche and Hirschboek 1984). Migrations into the Petén peninsula due to this eruption would be consistent with this date and the G-M-T (Goodman-Martínez-Thompson) Correlation, although this correlation is not uniquely satisfactory.

Other regional syntheses of archaeomagnetic data include those for the United Kingdom (Aitken 1970; Clark *et al.* 1988), France (Thellier 1981; Bucur, 1994), Italy (Evans and Mareschal 1989), Thailand (Barbetti and Hein 1989) and the southeastern U.S. (Wolfman 1990a).

Case Study for Relative Dating in a Culture Area: Minoan Thera and Crete

A wide variety of dating methods have been applied to the destruction of the Mediterranean volcanic island Thera, or Santorini (Hardy and Renfrew 1989; Manning 1990), ca. 1500 BC. Tarling and Downey (1990; see also Downey and Tarling 1984) used archaeomagnetic results in an attempt to correlate destruction of Minoan structures on Crete with igneous eruptions on Thera, 120 km to the north. This application is noteworthy in that it is an example of the use of archaeomagnetism as a relative dating technique. That is, even in the absence of a master curve of secular variation, magnetic directions can be compared as essentially a test of contemporaneity (Hurst 1962; Becker 1979). If features were heated and magnetized at the same time, they should have the same direction of magnetization. This test is somewhat confounded by the rate of secular variation, which varies in space and time.

Paleomagnetic samples were collected from four volcanic units on Thera at ten different localities; different units were sampled at several localities. Archaeomagnetic samples were collected from a hearth at the archaeological site of Akrotiri on Thera and from 18 archaeological structures at ten localities on Crete, of which nine sites provided reliable archaeomagnetic directions. Most of the Cretan samples were mud brick that had been intensely heated during the Late Minoan I period destruction of these localities. Archaeointensities were also determined for the archaeomagnetic samples, another novel aspect of this study.

The archaeomagnetic directions on Crete were grouped into two clusters, according to whether they were from the eastern or western part of the island. The mean directions for these two clusters and the hearth from Akrotiri are shown in Fig. 11.8. Several geomagnetic, rock magnetic, and mechanical possibilities for these directional differences were considered, but it was concluded that they were most likely due to heating at different times when the magnetic field had different directions. Thus, the destruction at sites in Akrotiri, eastern Crete and western Crete was interpreted to occur at three

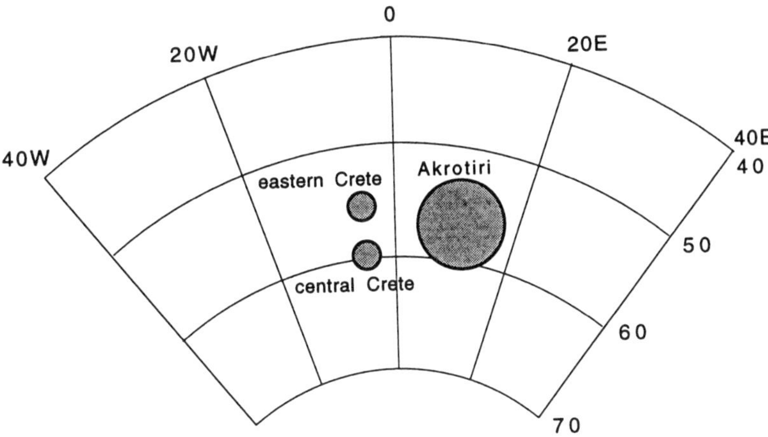

Figure 11.8. Archaeomagnetic directions from Thera and Crete (Tarling and Downey 1990).

different times. Using the angular differences between these directions along with a typical modern rate of secular variation, the time span represented by these three directions could be as short as a couple of decades or as long as a couple of centuries. This argument is supported by the different archaeointensities for Akrotiri, central Crete (10% higher than Akrotiri), and eastern Crete (18% higher than central Crete).

Although other interpretations of these data have been suggested (Liritzis 1985; Sparks 1985; Evans and Mareschal 1988), this study stands as an excellent example of the use of archaeomagnetic results from hearths and igneous rocks at different localities, using both directions and paleointensities, to answer questions concerning synchroneity and relative dating.

Case Study of Archaeointensity for Dating and Ceramic Authenticity Testing: Glozel

An interesting application of paleointensity considered the age and authenticity of ceramics from the enigmatic Glozel site in France (Renfrew 1976; Jones 1990: 301–303). It has been suggested that the very unusual ceramics and mixtures of styles found at Glozel may be fakes; one element of this argument is the inconsistency of different dating methods, including ^{14}C and thermoluminescence.

Barbetti (1976) used six samples of baked clay tablets and other ceramics for a paleointensity study. Because the Thellier paleointensity method involves sequential heating, firing temperatures can be estimated where the points begin to deviate from the linear relationship predicted by equation (2). Most

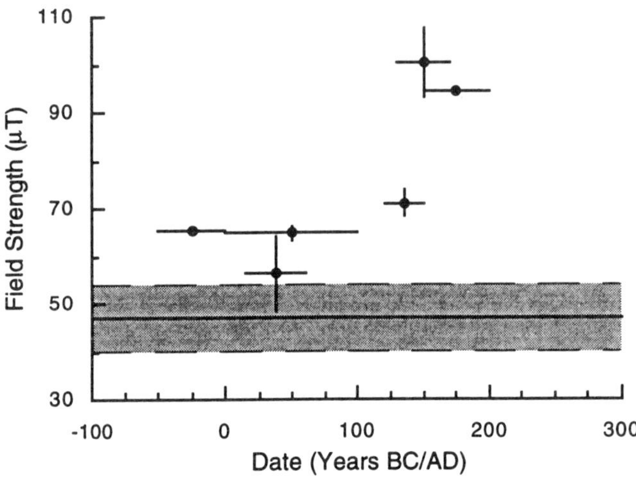

Figure 11.9. Secular variation of archaeointensity in Europe (crosses), and the mean (solid line) and standard error (dashed lines, with shading) for the ceramic archaeointensities from Glozel. After Shaw (1979) and Barbetti (1976), respectively.

Glozel samples were heated above 500°C according to these magnetic analyses. Three of these samples exhibited distinct non-linearity in their paleointensity diagrams. The two most reliable remaining results had paleointensity confidence intervals of 44–49 and 44–48 μT (microteslas). This is quite similar to the present-day field strength in France (hence not inconsistent with a modern forgery!), but considerably lower than the 60–75 μT field strength during the interval of 700 BC-AD 100 (Glozel age according to thermoluminescence dates then available) according to the secular variation curve used at that time. However, based on additional paleointensity results from other well-dated ceramics, Shaw (1979) concluded that the paleointensity in Europe varied more rapidly between 100 BC and AD 300 than was previously thought, with a field strength as low as 50 μT about AD 25. This would not be inconsistent with a Glozel paleointensity date of about 50 BC-AD 100 (Fig. 11.9). Although it did not completely resolve the Glozel controversy, this study demonstrates the potential application of archaeointensity dating to unoriented ceramics. Like the direction study of Eighmy and Doyel (1987) cited earlier, this study also illustrates an important archaeomagnetic (or general chronometric) principle: if the secular variation curve (master pattern) is revised, the original basic paleomagnetic results on the dated object can be re-interpreted to give a new date in accordance with the latest pattern.

The application of archaeointensities to dating for individual sites has also been described by Ramaswamy and Duraiswamy (1990).

Some Other Approaches

Now that archaeomagnetic procedures have become more commonplace and standardized, several investigators are looking at other materials and methods. Among the materials, one of the most promising are archaeological sediments. Sedimentary magnetization has proven important for a number of paleomagnetic and environmental problems (Thompson and Oldfield 1986). Sedimentary records can be used to build up quasi-continuous secular variation curves, although these can suffer from dating errors and smoothing of the paleomagnetic signal. Sediments deposited in various archaeological contexts can be dated against archaeomagnetic master curves. This can be done for stratigraphic sections of sediments that can then be matched to the master curves using their "wiggles" (Clark 1992) or by using discrete sediment samples analogously to conventional archaeomagnetic dating (Batt and Noel 1991; Eighmy and Howard 1991). These recent efforts are reminiscent of earlier and continuing work on cave sediments (Creer and Kopper 1974; Kopper and Creer 1976; Gale *et al.* 1984; Noel and Thistlewood 1989).

Atkinson and Shaw (1991a) have considered whether viscous remanent magnetization could be used to date the age of an object. Viscous remanence builds up logarithmically with time, but depends in a complicated fashion on the magnetic mineralogy in a material. This method was first suggested by Heller and Markert (1973), who used the construction of the Roman Hadrian's Wall in northern England to check the feasibility of this approach.

Finally, the orientation of buildings with magnetic north might be used as an indicator of secular variation of declination, and conversely as a magnetic dating method. This approach has been discussed for the Maya in Mesoamerica (Carlson 1977; Beyer 1991), and for medieval churches in Europe (Abrahamsen 1992). This method presupposes existence and use of the magnetic compass in these regions at these times (Abrahamsen 1992; Carlson 1975).

MAGNETIC REVERSAL DATING

Principles

Another type of field variation which is useful in paleoanthropology is the geomagnetic reversal: occasionally the magnetic field reverses polarity as the north and south magnetic poles exchange positions. The present day polarity of the field is by convention termed normal; the opposite polarity is reversed. This important geophysical event has occurred in a random fashion at least 23 times in the past 5 Ma, the last indisputable reversal being at 780 ka years ago (Fig. 11.10, left segment). True geomagnetic reversals are globally synchronous.

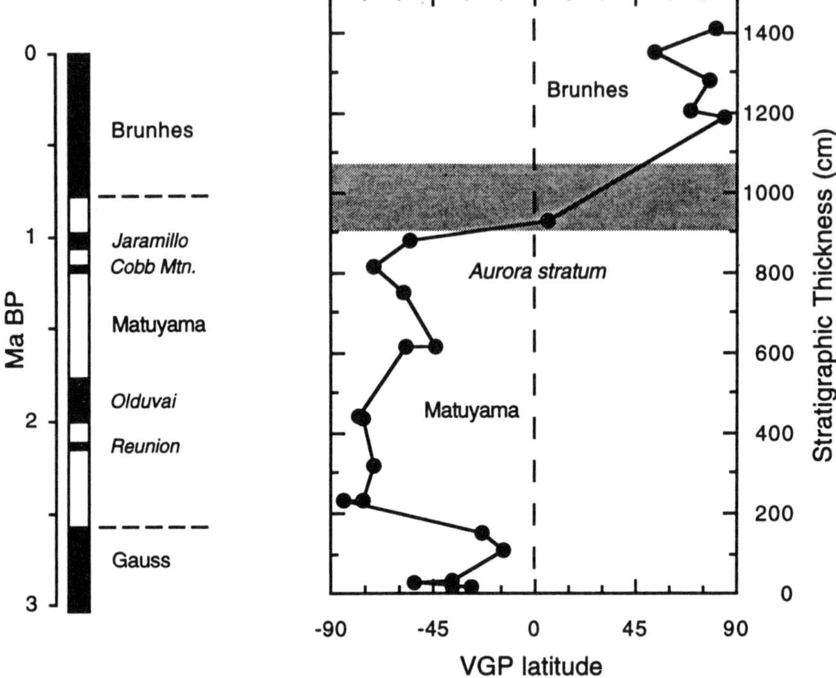

Figure 11.10. Left segment: The geomagnetic polarity (reversal) time scale, back to 3 Ma, using revised ages of Baksi (1995: Table 2), and Turrin *et al.* (1994) for the Cobb Mountain subchron. Brunhes, Matuyama and Gauss chrons are shown, along with several shorter subchrons. As is convention, shaded areas indicate normal polarity, and blank areas represent reversed. Right segment: Magnetic pole latitudes from sediments of the Gran Dolina section at Sierra de Atapuerca (Parés and Pérez-Gonzalez 1995). Shaded area indicates the Brunhes-Matuyama polarity transition. Hominid finds are in the Aurora stratum at a stratigraphic thickness of about 800 cm. in the Matuyama chron.

Magnetic reversal dating is also a "derivative" dating method in the sense of Aitken (1990), although the pattern of reversals is global and does not need to be separately worked out for each region, as is the case for secular variation. Layers of normally and reversely magnetized rocks carrying a DRM can be found in a quasi-continuous sedimentary record of the paleomagnetic field. Such a sequence of normal and reversed magnetozones are usually needed to match the thicknesses of these zones to the temporal duration of the various magnetochrons. Independent estimates of age, such as a radiometric date, may facilitate the match to the reversal time scale. A zone of reversed magnetization by itself implies that the rock must be at least 780 ka old, unless it was magnetized during a more recent short-lived event. Although the resolution of magnetic reversal dating is not as high as for the type of archaeomagnetic directional dating described above, the coarser resolution is appropriate for examining problems of hominid evolution, as opposed to post-Mesolithic cultural evolution (Blackwell and Schwarcz 1993).

Case Study of Early Hominids in Asia: Lantian Fossils

A major problem in paleoanthropology is the nature and timing of the dispersal of *Homo erectus* from Africa. Finds of *Homo erectus* fossils in Asia have been rare. One such find is the site of Lantian, China, where a *H. erectus* cranium and mandible were found within loess. An underlying concretionary marker bed was correlated with a similar bed within a 140 m-thick loess section 10 km away. Shaw *et al.* (1991) attempted to date the Lantian site by comparing the magnetic reversal stratigraphy of this 140 m section with other magnetostratigraphic results from the Chinese loess plateau. The situation at Lantian is reminiscent of what is sometimes encountered in conventional archaeomagnetism, especially in the construction of secular variation curves—not only should the archaeologist or paleoanthropologist be concerned with the chronometric results, but also with the association between the material actually dated (Pleistocene loess in this example) and the object of interest, in this case a cranium (Dean 1978).

Paleomagnetic results for the section showed the most recent Brunhes normal polarity epoch, the Matuyama reversed polarity chron with the Jaramillo, Cobb Mountain, Olduvai, and Réunion 1 and 2 normal subchrons, and the top of the Gauss normal chron. The stratigraphic position of the Lantian cranium is just below the Cobb Mountain subchron (Fig. 11.10, left segment), which was then dated at 1.12 Ma. The estimated date for the cranium and mandible was thus 1.13 Ma. This date agrees with the magnetostratigraphic date of 1.15 Ma inferred by Zhisheng and Kun (1989) from a less detailed study in the section where the fossils were found. Lantian is thus the oldest well-dated site for *Homo erectus* fossils in China. Paleomagnetic dating of earlier representatives of genus *Homo* in China to nearly 2 Ma is discussed by Wanpo *et al.* (1995).

The date for the Cobb Mountain event has since been revised to 1.186 Ma based on $^{40}Ar/^{39}Ar$ dating (Turrin *et al.* 1994), which would make the Lantian cranium about 0.066 Ma older. Revision of the pattern, in this case the reversal time scale, leads to a revision in dates just as in secular variation dating.

Case Study of Early Hominids in Europe: Sierra de Atapuerca, Spain

Another ongoing problem in hominid evolution and dispersal is the arrival of various hominid groups in Europe. Modern *Homo sapiens* arrived more than 40 ka, and Neandertals about 127 ka. When did the first hominids arrive? Both long and short chronologies have been offered for hominid arrival in Europe, somewhat reminiscent of the debate over the Hohokam long- and short-count chronologies. The short chronology has the hominids arriving after 500 ka (Roebroeks and van Kolfschoten 1994). Evidence for older hominid arrival is debated on the basis of either chronology or the artifactual character of assemblages.

New evidence favoring a long chronology comes from the Gran Dolina site in Atapuerca, northern Spain. The Aurora stratum within level TD6 at this site yielded more than 30 hominid fossils and 100 lithic objects (Carbonell *et al.* 1995). The fossils may be a primitive form of *Homo heidelbergensis*, or possibly a new species. Paleomagnetic data from the sedimentary rocks at the site indicate that the transition from the Brunhes to Matuyama chrons occurs at a stratigraphic thickness of 900–1000 cm, about 100 cm above the Aurora stratum (Fig. 11.10, right segment; Parés and Pérez-Gonzalez 1995). This suggests an age for the fossils as somewhat greater than 780 ka, the age of the Brunhes-Matuyama transition. Archaeological remains, and a ^{234}U/^{232}Th date of 350 ka from higher up in the section constrain the age to the Pleistocene, so that the reverse-to-normal polarity transition must represent the Matuyama-Brunhes boundary. No Matuyama subchrons were identified, either because the sampling interval was too coarse, there was a hiatus in sedimentation, or the oldest levels sampled are younger than the Jaramillo subchron.

A number of other references to magnetic reversal dating of hominid sites including Africa can be found in Parkes (1986) and Aitken (1990).

SUMMARY

Archaeomagnetic dating has been useful in many parts of the world. Secular variation of archaeomagnetic direction and archaeointensity has been used for Neolithic and younger cultures, with a precision sometimes as good as ±25 years. Magnetic reversal stratigraphy has been useful in dating hominid sites for paleoanthropologists, with precisions of about ±0.01 Ma, or 10 ka. The best dates will be obtainable only as a result of ongoing collaboration between archaeomagnetists and archaeologists (or geologists) for the development of master curves of secular variation (or reversals), and collaboration during individual studies for the sites of interest. As a derivative dating method, the success of archaeomagnetic dating ultimately depends on the complementary success of other chronometric methods.

ACKNOWLEDGMENTS

I wish to thank the editors for assembling this volume, for having patience with at least one rather tardy author, and for suggestions which I hope have led to the improvement of this contribution.

REFERENCES

Abrahamsen, N. 1992 Evidence for church orientation by magnetic compass in twelfth-century Denmark. *Archaeometry* 34: 293–303.

Abrahamsen, N. and Breiner, N. 1991 Magnetic investigations of a mediaeval tile kiln near Kalø, Denmark. *In* Pernicka, E. and Wagner, G.A., eds., *Archaeometry '90*. Basel, Birkhäuser Verlag: 657–666.

Aitken, M.J. 1970 Dating by archaeomagnetic and thermoluminescent methods. *Philosophical Transactions of the Royal Society of London* A 269: 77–88.

_____1990 *Science-based Dating in Archaeology*. London, Longman.

Aitken, M.J., Allsop, A.L., Bussell, G.D. and Winter, M. 1989 Geomagnetic intensity variations during the last 4000 years. *Physics of the Earth and Planetary Interiors* 56: 49–58.

Atkinson, D. and Shaw, J. 1991a Magnetic viscosity dating. *In* Pernicka, E. and Wagner, G.A., eds., *Archaeometry '90*. Basel, Birkhäuser Verlag: 533–540.

_____1991b Red fired sandstone: A good recorder of ancient geomagnetic field? *In* Budd, P., Chapman, B., Jackson, C., Janaway, R. and Ottaway, B., eds., *Archaeological Sciences 1989*. Oxford, Oxbow Books: 217–224.

Baker, K.A. and Eighmy, J.L. 1993 DAP archaeomagnetic dates reconsidered. *Southwestern Lore* 59: 1–25.

Baksi, A.K. 1995 Fine tuning the radiometrically derived geomagnetic polarity time scale (GPTS) for 0–10 Ma. *Geophysical Research Letters* 22: 457–460.

Barbetti, M. 1976 Archaeomagnetic analyses of six Glozelian ceramic artifacts. *Journal of Archaeological Science* 3: 137–151.

Barbetti, M. and Hein, D. 1989 Palaeomagnetism and high résolution dating of ceramic kilns in Thailand: a progress report. *World Archaeology* 21: 51–70.

Barbetti, M., Taborin, Y., Schmider, B. and Flude, K. 1980 Archaeomagnetic results from Late Pleistocene hearths at Etiolles and Marsangy, France. *Archaeometry* 22: 25–46.

Barton, C.E. and Barbetti, M. 1982 Geomagnetic secular variation from recent lake sediments, ancient fireplaces and historical measurements in southeastern Australia. *Earth and Planetary Science Letters* 59: 375–387.

Batt, C.M. and Noel, M. 1991 Magnetic studies of archaeological sediments. *In* Budd, P., Chapman, B., Jackson, C., Janaway, R. and Ottaway, B., eds., *Archaeological Sciences 1989*. Oxford, Oxbow Books: 234–241.

Becker, H. 1979 Archaeomagnetic investigations in Anatolia from prehistoric and Hittite sites (first preliminary results). *Archaeo-Physika* 10: 382–387.

Becker, H., Göksu, H.Y. and Regulla, D.F. 1994 Combination of archaeomagnetism and thermoluminescence for precision dating. *Quaternary Science Reviews* 13: 563–567.

Beyer, M.A.B.F. 1991 Veränderungen des "magnetischen Nordpols" und die Orientierung der Bauten im Zapotekenzentrum Monte Alban. *Das Altertum* 37: 175–180.

Blackwell, B.A. and Schwarcz, H.P. 1993 Archaeochronology and scale. *In* Stein, J.K. and Linse, A.R., eds., Effects of Scale on Archaeological and Geoscientific Perspectives. Boulder, *Geological Society of America, Special Paper* 283: 39–58.

Breternitz, D.A. 1967 The eruption(s) of Sunset Crater. *Plateau* 40: 72–76.

Bucur, I. 1994 The direction of the terrestrial magnetic field in France, during the last 21 centuries. Recent progress. *Physics of the Earth and Planetary Interiors* 87: 95–109.

Burlskaya, A. 1986 *Archaeomagnetic Determinations of Geomagnetic Field Elements*. Moscow, World Data Center.

Carbonell, E., Bermúdez de Castro, J.M., Arsuaga, J.L., Díez, J.C., Rosas, A., Cuenca-Bescós, G., Sala, R., Mosquera, M. and Rodríguez, X.P. 1995 Lower Pleistocene hominids and artifacts from Atapuerca-TD6 (Spain). *Science* 269: 826–830.

Carlson, J.B. 1975 Lodestone compass: Chinese or Olmec primacy? *Science* 189: 753–760.

_____1977 The case for geomagnetic alignments of Precolumbian Mesoamerican. *Katunob* 10: 67–88.

Champion, D.E. 1980 Holocene geomagnetic secular variation in the western United States: implications for global geomagnetic field. *U.S. Geological Survey Open-File Report* 80–824: 1–326.

Champion, D.E. and Donnelly-Nolan, J.M. 1994 Duration of eruption at the Giant Crater lava field, Medicine Lake volcano, California, based on paleomagnetic secular variation. *Journal of Geophysical Research* 99: 15,595–15,604.

Clark, A.J. 1992 Magnetic dating of alluvial deposits. *In* Needham, S. and Macklin, M.G., eds., *Alluvial Archaeology in Britain*. Oxford, Oxbow: 37–42.

Clark, A.J., Tarling, D.H. and Noël, M. 1988 Developments in archaeomagnetic dating in Britain. *Journal of Archaeological Science* 15: 645–667.

Colman, S.M., Pierce, K.L. and Birkeland, P.W. 1987 Suggested terminology for Quaternary dating methods. *Quaternary Research* 28: 314–319.

Cong, Y.S. and Wei, Q.Y. 1989 Study of secular variation (2000 BC–1900 AD) based on comparison of contemporaneous records in marine sediments and baked clays. *Physics of the Earth and Planetary Interiors* 56: 69–75.

Creer, K.M. and Kopper, J.S. 1974 Paleomagnetic dating of cave paintings in Tito Bustillo Cave, Asturias, Spain. *Science* 186: 348–350.

Creer, K.M., Tucholka, P. and Barton, C.E., eds, 1983 *Geomagnetism of Baked Clays and Recent Sediments*. Amsterdam, Elsevier.

Cui, Y. and Verosub, K.L. 1995 A mineral magnetic study of some pottery samples: Possible implications for sample selection in archaeointensity studies. *Physics of the Earth and Planetary Interiors* 91: 261–271.

Dean, J.S. 1978 Independent dating in archaeological analysis. *In* Schiffer, M.B., ed., *Advances in Archaeological Method and Theory*. New York, Academic Press: 223–265.

_____1991 Thoughts on Hohokam chronology In Gumerman, G.J., ed., *Exploring the Hohokam*. Dragoon, Arizona, Amerind Foundation: 61–149.

Dearden, B. and Clark, A. 1990 Pont-de-l'Arche or Pîtres? a location and archaeomagnetic dating for Charles the Bald's fortifications on the Seine. *Antiquity* 64: 567–571.

Deaver, W.L. and Ciolek-Torrello, R.S. 1995 Early Formative period chronology for the Tucson Basin. *Kiva* 60: 481–529.

Donnelly-Nolan, J.M., Champion, D.E., Miller, C.D., Grove, T.L. and Trimble D.A. 1990 Post-11,000-year volcanism at Medicine Lake volcano, Cascade Range, northern California. *Journal of Geophysical Research* 95: 19,693–19,704.

Downey, W.S. and Tarling, D.H. 1984 Archaeomagnetic dating of Santorini volcanic eruptions and fired destruction levels of Late Minoan civilization. *Nature* 309: 519–523.

DuBois, R.L. 1975 Secular variation in southwestern United States as suggested by archaeomagnetic studies. *In* Fisher, R.M., Fuller, M., Schmidt, V.A. and Wasilewski, P.J., eds., *Takesi Nagata Conference-Magnetic Fields: Past and Present*. Greenbelt, Goddard Space Flight Center: 133–144.

_____1991 Archeomagnetic results from southwest United States and Mesoamerica, and comparisons with some other areas. *Physics of the Earth and Planetary Interiors* 56: 18–33.

Eighmy, J.L. 1990 Archaeomagnetic dating: Practical problems for the archaeologist. In Eighmy, J.L. and Sternberg, R.S., eds., *Archaeomagnetic Dating*. Tucson, University of Arizona Press: 33–64.

_____1991 Archaeomagnetism: New data on the South-West U.S.A. master virtual geomagnetic pole curve. *Archaeometry* 33: 201–214.

Eighmy, J.L. and Doyel, D.E. 1987 A reanalysis of first reported archaeomagnetic dates from the Hohokam Area, Southern Arizona. *Journal of Field Archaeology* 14: 331–342.

Eighmy, J.L. and Hathaway, J.H. 1987 Contemporary archaeomagnetic results and the accuracy of archaeomagnetic dating. *Geoarchaeology* 2: 49–61.

Eighmy, J.L., Hathaway, J.H. and Henderson, T.K. 1986 Secular change in the direction of the geomagnetic field, A.D. 900 to 1100: New U.S. Southwest data. *MASCA Journal* 4: 81–85.

Eighmy, J.L. and Howard, J.B. 1991 Direct dating of prehistorical canal sediments using archaeomagnetism. *American Antiquity* 56: 88–102.

Eighmy, J.L. and McGuire, R.H. 1989 Dating the Hohokam phase sequence: An analysis of archaeomagnetic dates. *Journal of Field Archaeology* 16: 215–231.

Eighmy, J.L. and Mitchell, D.R. 1994 Archaeomagnetic dating at Pueblo Grande. *Journal of Archaeological Science* 21: 445–453.

Eighmy, J.L. and Sternberg, eds., 1990 *Archaeomagnetic Dating*. Tucson, University of Arizona Press.

Eighmy, J.L., Taylor, R.S. and Klein, P.Y. 1993 Archaeomagnetic dating on the Great Plains. *Plains Anthropologist* 38: 21–50.

Evans, M.E. and Mareschal, M. 1988 Secular variation and magnetic dating of fired structures in Greece. *In* Farquhar, R.M., Hancock, R.G.V. and Pavlish, L.A., eds., *Archaeometry-Proceedings of the 26th International Symposium*. Toronto, University of Toronto: 75–79.

_____1989 Secular variation and magnetic dating of fired structures in Southern Italy. *In* Maniatis, Y., ed., *Archaeometry-Proceedings of the 25th International Symposium*. Amsterdam, Elsevier: 59–68.

Gale, S.J., Hunt, C.O. and Southgate, G.A. 1984 Kirkhead Cave: Biostratigraphy and magnetostratigraphy. *Archaeometry* 26: 192–198.

Gentles, D.S. and Tarling, D.H. 1988 Archaeomagnetic directional dating and magnetic analyses with special reference to a Scottish vitrified dun. *In* Slater, E.A. and Tate, J.O., eds., *Science and Archaeology, Glasgow 1987:* Proceedings of a Conference on the Application of Scientific Techniques to Archaeology. London, BAR: 647–667.

Hagstrum, J.T. and Champion, D.E. 1994 Paleomagnetic correlation of Late Quaternary lava flows in the lower east rift zone of Kilauea Volcano, Hawaii. *Journal of Geophysical Research* 99: 21,679–21,690.

Hardy, D.A. and Renfrew, A.C., eds., 1989 *Thera and the Aegean World III: Volume 3-Chronology*. Proceedings of the Third International Conference. London, The Thera Foundation.

Hedley, I.G., Sennhauser, H.-R. and Wagner, J.-J. 1983 Étude archéomagnétique d'un moule de cloche de l'église de Sainte-Marie, Disentis (Grisons). *Arch. Sc. Geneve* 36: 351–360.

Hedley, I.G. and Wagner, J.J. 1991 A magnetic investigation of Roman and pre-Roman pottery. *In* Pernicka, E. and Wagner, G.A., eds., *Archaeometry '90*. Basel, Birkhäuser Verlag: 275–284.

Heller, F. and Markert, H. 1973 The age of viscous remanent magnetization of Hadrian's wall (Northern Ireland). *Geophysical Journal of the Royal Astronomical Society* 31: 395–406.

Holcomb, R., Champion, D. and McWilliams, M. 1986 Dating recent Hawaiian lava flows using paleomagnetic secular variation. *Geological Society of America Bulletin* 97: 829–939.

Hurst, J.G. 1962 Post-Roman archaeological dating and its correlation with archaeomagnetic results. *Archaeometry* 5: 25–27.

Jones, M., ed. 1990 *Fake? The Art of Deception*. University of California Press, Berkeley.

Kopper, J.S. and Creer, K.M. 1976 Paleomagnetic dating and stratigraphic interpretation in archeology. *MASCA Newsletter* 12: 1–4.

Kovacheva, M. 1986 Archaeomagnetism: results from southeast Europe, their use as dating technique, difficulties. *Acta Interdisciplinaria Archaeologica* 4: 137–147.

_____1989 Archaeomagnetic studies as a dating tool and some considerations on the archaeomagnetic methodology. *In* Maniatis, Y., ed., *Archaeometry-Proceedings of the 25th Annual Symposium*. Amsterdam, Elsevier: 35–43.

_____1991 Prehistoric sites from Bulgaria studied archaeomagnetically. *In* Pernicka, E. and Wagner, G.A., eds, *Archaeometry '90*. Basel, Birkhäuser Verlag: 559–567.

Kuntz, M.A., Champion, D.E., Spiker, E.C. and Lefebvre, R.H. 1986 Contrasting magma types and steady-state, volume-predictable, basaltic volcanism along the Great Rift, Idaho. *Geological Society of America Bulletin* 97: 579–594.

LaBelle, J.M. and Eighmy, J.L. 1995 Additions to the List of Independently Dated Virtual Poles and the Southwest Master Curve,. Boulder, Colorado State University, Department of Anthropology, Archaeometric Laboratory, Technical Series No. 7: 1–59.

LaMarche, V.C. and Hirschboek, K.K. 1984 Frost rings in trees as records of major volcanic eruptions. *Nature* 307: 121–126.

Lange, R.C. and Murphy, B.A. 1990 A discussion of collection factors affecting the quality of archaeomagnetic results. *In* Eighmy, J.L. and Sternberg, R.S., eds., *Archaeomagnetic Dating*. Tucson, University of Arizona Press: 65–80.

Langereis, C.G. and Kars, H. 1990 Archaeomagnetic dating of a limestone kiln at Nijmegen (The Netherlands). *Geologie en Mijnbouw* 69: 319–326.

Langouet, L. and Goulpeau, L. 1984 La datation archéomagnétique du temple du Haut-Bächerel a Corseul. *Rev. Archéol. Ouest.* 1: 85–88.

Lanos, P. 1987 The effects of demagnetized fields on thermoremanent magnetization acquired by parallel-sided baked clay blocks. *Geophysical Journal of the Royal Astronomical Society* 91: 985–1012.

Liritzis, Y. 1985 Archaeomagnetism, Santorini volcanic eruptions and fired destruction levels on Crete. *Nature* 313: 76.

Manning, S.W. 1990 The Thera eruption: The Third Congress and the problem of the date. *Archaeometry* 32: 91–100.

Noel, M. and Thistlewood, L. 1989 Developments in cave sediment palaeomagnetism. *In* Lowes, F.J., Collinson, D.W., Parry, J.H., Runcorn, S.K. and Tozer, D.C., eds., *Geomagnetism and Palaeomagnetism*. Dordrecht, Kluwer Academic Publishers: 91–106.

Noel, M. and Batt, C.M. 1990 A method for correcting geographically separated remanence directions for the purpose of archaeomagnetic dating. *Geophysical Journal International* 102: 753–756.

Parés, J.M., Jonge, R.D., Pascual, J.O., Bermúdez, A., Tovar, C.J., Luezas, R.A. and Maestro, N. 1992 Archaeomagnetic evidence for the age of a Roman pottery kiln from Calahorra (Spain). *Geophysical Journal International* 112: 533–537.

Parés, J.M. and Pérez-Gonzalez, A. 1995 Paleomagnetic age for hominid fossils at Atapuerca archaeological site, Spain. *Science* 269: 830–832.

Parkes, P.A. 1986 *Current Scientific Techniques in Archaeology*. New York, St. Martin's Press.

Ramaswamy, K. and Duraiswamy, D. 1990 Archaeomagnetic studies on some archaeological sites in Tamil Nadu, India. *Physics of the Earth and Planetary Interiors* 60: 278–284.

Renfrew, C. 1976 Glozel and the two cultures. *Antiquity* 49: 219–222.

Roebroeks, W. and van Kolfschoten, T. 1994 The earliest occupation of Europe: a short chronology. *Antiquity* 68: 489–503.

Rolph, T.C., Shaw, J. and Guest, J.E. 1987 Geomagnetic field variations as a dating tool: Application to Sicilian lavas. *Journal of Archaeological Science* 14: 215–225.

Saribudak, M. and Tarling, D.H. 1993 Archaeomagnetic studies of the Urartian civilization, eastern Turkey. *Antiquity* 67: 620–68.

Schiffer, M.B. and Staski, E. 1982 Radiocarbon dates from southern Arizona pertaining to the post-Archaic prehistory. *In* McGuire, R.H. and Schiffer, M.B., eds., *Hohokam and Patayan: Prehistory of Southwestern Arizona*. New York, Academic Press: 521–528.

Schurr, K., Becker, H. and Soffel, H.C. 1984 Archaeomagnetic study of medieval fireplaces at Mannheim-Wallstadt and ovens from Herrenchiemsee (southern Germany) and the problem of magnetic refraction. *Journal of Geophysics* 56: 1–8.

Shaw, J. 1974 A new method of determining the magnitude of the palaeomagnetic field: Application to five historic lavas and five archaeological samples. *Geophysical Journal of the Royal Astronomical Society* 39: 133–141.

Shaw, J. 1979 Rapid changes in the magnitude of the archaeomagnetic field. *Geophysical Journal of the Royal Astronomical Society* 58: 107–116.

Shaw, J., Hongbo, Z. and Zisheng, A. 1991 Magnetic dating of early man in China. *In* Pernicka, E. and Wagner, G.A., eds, *Archaeometry '90*. Basel, Birkhäuser Verlag: 589–595.

Shaw, J., Walton, D. and Share, J.A. 1996 Microwave archaeointensities from Peruvian ceramics. *Geophysical Journal International* 124: 241–244.

Sparks, R.S.J. 1985 Archaeomagnetism, Santorini volcanic eruptions and fired destruction levels on Crete. *Nature* 313: 74–75.

Sternberg, R.S. 1989a Archaeomagnetic paleointensity in the American Southwest during the past 2000 years. *Physics of the Earth and Planetary Interiors* 56: 1–17.

_____1989b Secular variation of archaeomagnetic direction in the American Southwest, A.D. 750–1425. *Journal of Geophysical Research* 94: 527–546.

_____1990 The geophysical basis of archaeomagnetic dating. *In* Eighmy, J.L. and Sternberg, R.S., eds., *Archaeomagnetic Dating*. Tucson, University of Arizona Press: 5–28.

Sternberg, R.S., Deaver, W.L., Kuter, E.A. and Kiley, A.L. 1997 A North American archaeomagnetic database. *Journal of Geomagnetism and Geoelectricity* 49: 519–522.

Sternberg, R.S., Lange, R.C., Murphy, B.A., Deaver, W.L. and Teague, L.S. 1991 Archaeomagnetic dating at Las Colinas, Arizona, USA. *In* Pernicka, E. and Wagner, G.A., eds., *Archaeometry '90*. Basel, Birkhäuser Verlag: 597–606.

Sternberg, R.S. and McGuire, R.H. 1990a Archaeomagnetic secular variation in the American Southwest, A.D. 700–1450. *In* Eighmy, J.L. and Sternberg, R.S., eds., *Archaeomagnetic Dating*. Tucson, University of Arizona Press: 199–225.

_____1990b Techniques for constructing secular variation curves and for interpreting archaeomagnetic dates. *In* Eighmy, J.L. and Sternberg, R.S., eds., *Archaeomagnetic Dating*. Tucson, University of Arizona Press: 109–134.

Tarling, D.H. 1983 *Palaeomagnetism: Principles and Applications in Geology, Geophysics, and Archaeology*. London, Chapman and Hall.

_____1985 Archaeomagnetism. *In* Rapp, Jr., George and Gifford, John A., eds., *Archaeological Geology*. New Haven, Yale University Press: 237–263.

_____1991 Archaeomagnetism and paleomagnetism. *In* Göksu, H.Y., Oberhofer, M. and Regulla, D., eds., *Scientific Dating Methods*. Dordrecht, Kluwer: 217–250.

Tarling, D.H. and Dobson, M.J. 1995 Archaeomagnetism: An error assessment of fired material observations in the British directional database. *Journal of Geomagnetism and Geoelectricity* 47: 5–18.

Tarling, D.H. and Downey, W.S. 1990 Archaeomagnetic results from Late Minoan destruction levels on Crete and the "Minoan" tephra on Thera. *In* Hardy, D.A., eds., *Thera and the Aegean World III: Volume 3 Chronology*, Proceedings of the Third International Conference. London, The Thera Foundation: 146–159.

Thellier, E. 1981 Sur la direction du champ magnetique terrestre, en France, durant les deux derniers millenaires. *Physics of the Earth and Planetary Interiors* 24: 89–132.

Thellier, E. and Thellier, O. 1959 Sur l'intensité du champ magnétique terrestre dans le passé historique et géologique. *Annales de Géophysique* 15: 285–376.

Thomas, R. 1983 Review of archaeointensity methods. *Geophysical Surveys* 5: 381–393.

Thompson, R. and Oldfield, F. 1986 *Environmental Magnetism*. London, Allen and Unwin.

Turrin, B.D., Donnelly-Nolan, J.M. and Hearn, Jr., B.C. 1994 40Ar/39Ar ages from the rhyolite of Alder Creek, California: Age of the Cobb Mountain Normal-Polarity Subchron revisited. *Geology* 22: 251–254.

Verosub, K.L. 1988 Geomagnetic secular variation and the dating of Quaternary sediments. *Geological Society of America Special Paper* 227: 123–138.

Wanpo, H., Ciochon R., Yumin G., Larick R., Qiren F., Schwarcz H., Yonge C., de Vos, J. and Rink W. 1995 Early Homo and associated artefacts from Asia.*Nature* 378: 275–278.

Wolfman, D. 1982 Archeomagnetic dating in Arkansas and the border areas of adjacent states. *In* Jeter, M. and Trubowitz, N., eds., *Arkansas Archeology in Review*. Fayetteville, Arkansas Archeological Survey (Research Series No. 15): 277–300.

_____1984 Geomagnetic dating methods in archaeology. *Advances in Archaeological Method and Theory* 7: 363–458.

_____1990a Archaeomagnetic dating in Arkansas and the border areas of adjacent States-II. *In* Eighmy, J.L. and Sternberg, R.S., eds., *Archaeomagnetic Dating*. Tucson, University of Arizona Press: 237–260.

_____1990b Mesoamerican chronology and archaeomagnetic dating, A.D. 1–1200. *In* Eighmy, J.L. and Sternberg, R.S., eds., *Archaeomagnetic Dating*. Tucson, University of Arizona Press: 261–308.

_____1990c Retrospect and prospect. *In* Eighmy, J.L. and Sternberg, R.S., eds., *Archaeomagnetic Dating*. Tucson, University of Arizona Press: 313–364.

Yang, S., Shaw, J. and Wei Q.Y. 1993 A comparison of archaeointensity results from Chinese ceramics using Thellier's and Shaw's palaeointensity methods. *Geophysics Journal International* 113: 499–508.

Zhaoqin, M. and Noel, M. 1989 Archaeomagnetic evidence for the age and duration of firing of mediaeval hearths from Coffee Yard, York. *Geophysical Journal* 97: 357–359.

Zhisheng, A. and Kun, H.C. 1989 New magnetostratigraphic dates of Lantian Homo erectus. *Quaternary Research* 32: 213–221.

Chapter **12**

Surface Dating Using Rock Varnish

JOAN S. SCHNEIDER AND PAUL R. BIERMAN

ABSTRACT

Rock varnish, a dark-colored, magnesium-, iron-, and silica-rich coating that forms on exposed rock surfaces over time, especially in arid and semi-arid regions, has been used as a chronometric dating tool in both archaeology and geology. The methods most commonly employed are cation-ratio dating, using differential leaching of cations in the varnish coating, and accelerator mass spectrometry-based radiocarbon dating of organic material contained within or trapped beneath the varnish coating. The premises, supporting assumptions, and limitations involved in using each of these methods for dating archaeological surfaces using rock varnish seriously call into question any chronological conclusions derived from either method. Rock-varnish dates should be considered unreliable at this time.

INTRODUCTION

Rock varnish is a dark-colored, Mn-, Fe-, and Si-rich coating that develops, over time, on exposed rock surfaces and is particularly prevalent in arid and semiarid regions. Despite decades of research, mechanisms of its formation are still not fully understood. Rock varnish is made up of micron-scale laminar

JOAN S. SCHNEIDER • Department of Anthropology, University of California, Riverside 92521, USA. **PAUL R. BIERMAN** • Department of Geology, University of Vermont, Burlington, Vermont 05405, USA.

Chronometric Dating in Archaeology, edited by Taylor and Aitken.
Plenum Press, New York, 1997.

and botryoidial (i.e., having the form of a bunch of grapes) structures that are primarily composed of oxides of Mn, Fe, Al, and Si (all > 5% by weight) within a matrix of clay minerals. In most cases, the clay portion, which typically makes up about 70% of the varnish matrix, appears to be derived from wind-blown dust (Potter and Rossman 1977; Perry and Adams 1978). Other varnish constituents include percent-level amounts of Mg, Ba, Ti, Ca, K, and various other trace elements (Potter and Rossman 1977; Allen 1978; Dorn and Oberlander 1982; Reneau *et al.* 1992). It is now generally agreed that, at least in desert areas, these components are derived solely from the external environment and not from the immediate rock substrate since it has been determined that the specific chemical composition of a given varnish at any one locus is independent of the underlying rock (Potter and Rossman 1977; Allen 1978; Perry and Adams 1978; Bierman and Gillespie 1994).

The physical character of the underlying rock, however, does apparently affect varnish formation. Because varnish does not develop in an uniform layer, but starts in depressions on the rock surface and expands in all directions from

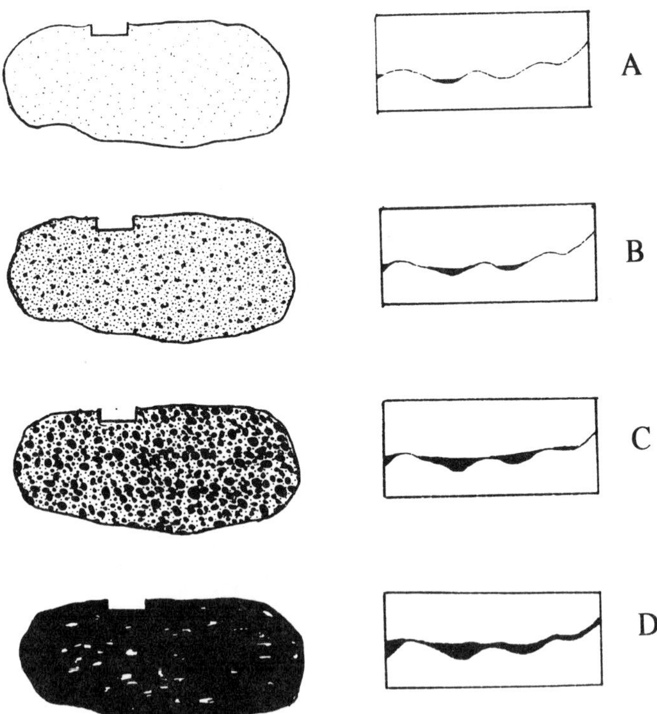

Figure 12.1. Schematic representation of the growth of rock varnish on the exposed surface of a clast; seen in plan view as the extent of varnish coating on the clast (left) and by a magnified view of varnish growth on the surface of the clast (right). A: an approximation of < 25% coverage; B: 25 to 49% coverage; C: 50 to 74% coverage; D: 75 to 100% coverage.

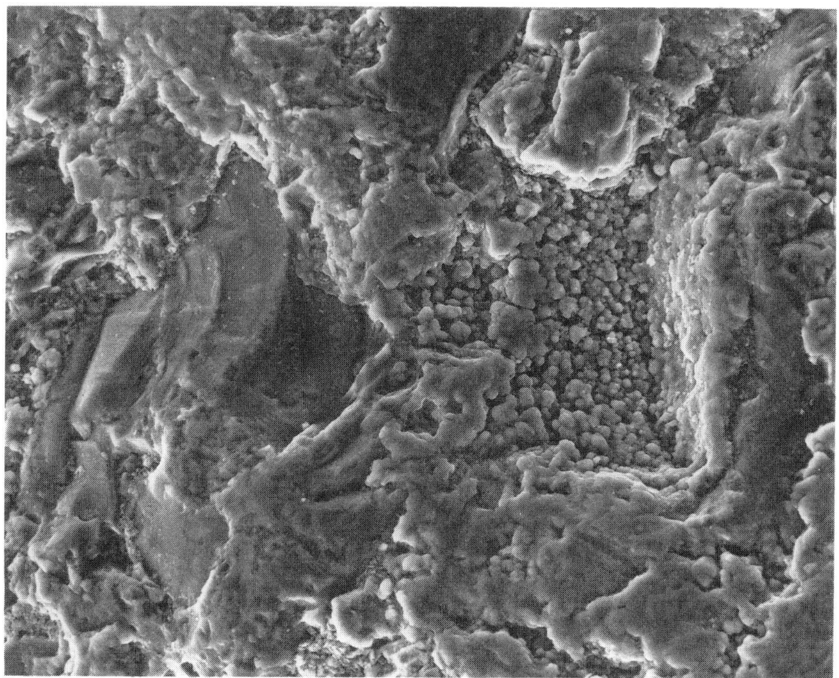

Figure 12.2. SEM photograph of rock varnish on the surface of a quartz grain in granite from the Owens Valley, California. Note the filling of depression on the surface and the laminated and botyroidal structures. Width of image approximately 500 μm.

a "nucleation center," rocks with relatively rough surfaces (i.e., extreme microtopography), such as basalts and andesites, encourage the rapid development of varnish (Figs. 12.1 and 12.2). Rough surfaces have minute depressions that retain moisture for longer periods of time and act as traps for dust-borne particles, thus maintaining an optimal environment for varnish "growth" (Raymond and Harrington 1989; Bierman and Harry 1992; Reneau *et al.* 1992; Harry 1995). Rocks with relatively smooth surfaces (i.e., mimimal microtopography), such as chert and crystalline quartz, do not encourage varnish development. Moreover, apparent time differences between surface exposure and the onset of varnish formation in different areas on the same substrate surface make attempts to sample the lowest (*oldest*?) varnish layer (i.e., next to the rock substrate) extremely problematic.

Because of the spreading nature of varnish growth, some investigators have suspected that a biological process similar to bacterial colonization is involved (Perry and Adams 1978; Raymond and Harrington 1989; Dorn and Oberlander 1982; Dorn 1983; Reneau *et al.* 1991, 1992). In this model, there is Mn enhancement due to microbial agents preferentially fixing Mn in accreted clays from desert dust. Other investigators believe that the process is a strictly physicochemical one in which a sixty-fold Mn enrichment above ambient levels takes place by mobilization from desert dust by pH-Eh fluctuations and precipitation events (Elvidge and Iverson 1983; Smith and Whaley 1988; Jones 1991). In addition to the character of the underlying rock, apparently the size of the clast also affects the rate of varnish growth. Clasts of relatively smaller size (< 10 cm diameter) on a given landform surface have a heavier varnish coating. The reasons are unclear, but a sheltered (by larger clasts and by having minimal relief from the ground surface) microenvironment may encourage varnish growth and provide less exposure to eolian erosion (Reneau 1993:311–312). Many other variables have been hypothesized to affect the formation of and growth of varnish including, but not limited to: exposure to sunlight, daily and seasonal temperature variation, precipitation, wind direction and velocity, atmospheric dust, geographical location, and direction of exposure.

Archaeological Relevance

Rock varnish is important to archaeologists because it coats many surface artifacts and features (Figs. 12.3 and 12.4) and therefore has been seen as a possible means of chronological control for surface phenomena. Geologists and

Figure 12.3. An example of a varnish-coated andesite artifact, a prehistoric metate (lower grinding stone), broken during manufacture, at a quarry in eastern California. Note the heavily varnished upper surface (not worked) and the light varnish on the lower surfaces (worked). Hand-tape case is 5 cm. long. Photograph by Joan S. Schneider.

geomorphologists, too, have investigated the potential of rock varnish to determine relative exposure ages of geological surfaces (e.g., Dorn *et al.* 1986, 1987b; Wells *et al.* 1987; McFadden *et al.* 1989). Stability of certain landforms in arid regions of the world, in particular the deserts of the southwestern United States, central Australia, coastal and Andean South America, and the Middle

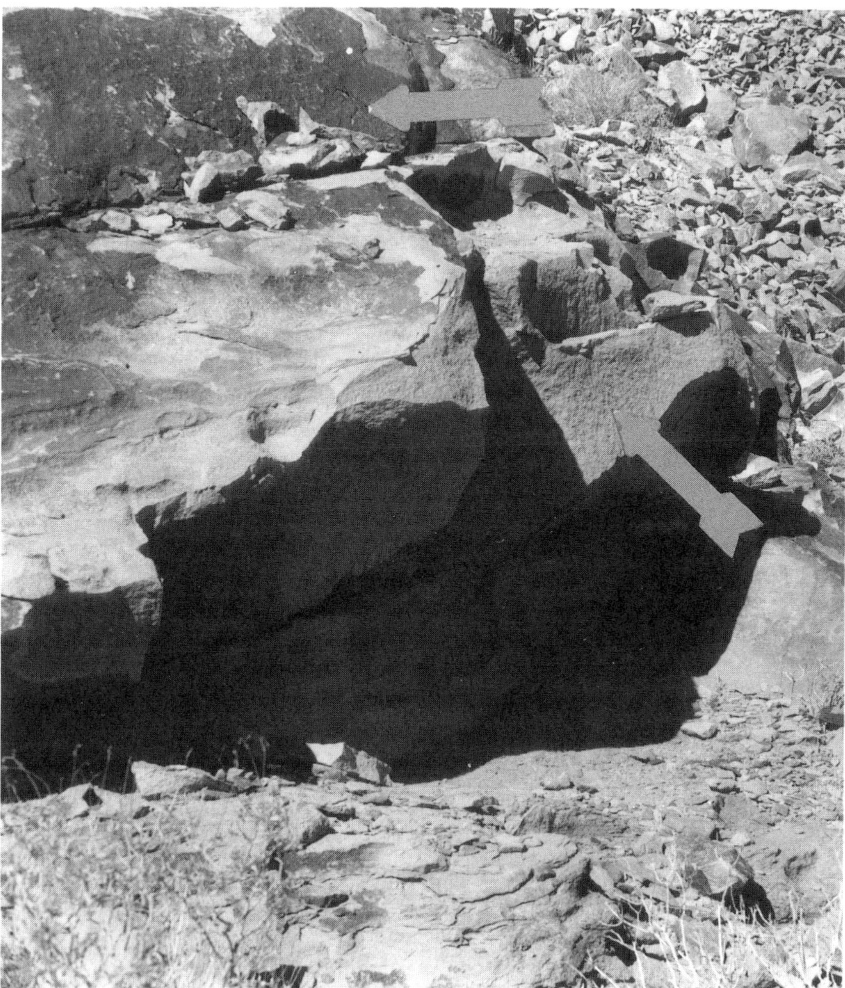

Figure 12.4. Rock varnish on a sandstone bedrock outcrop at a milling-implement quarry on the Gila River in Arizona. Aboriginal quarrying of the outcrop has exposed fresh surfaces. Quarry is hypothesized to have been used from the early Archaic period through the historic era (Schneider 1993, 1996). Quarrying debris covers the surface (foreground). Note the extent of rock varnish on nonquarried portions of the outcrop (top arrow) as compared with the quarried portions (lower arrow). Photograph by Joan S. Schneider.

East has promoted the occurrence of archaeological sites and artifacts of a wide temporal range in surface contexts. In other environmental and cultural situations, remains of human activity may be buried by colluvium, alluvium, or other subsequent cultural or natural events (e.g., building debris, intentional burial and/or destruction, flood, earthquake). These events, whether they be catastrophic or gradual, result in buried (and sometimes stratified) deposits. Where landforms are stable and cultural and/or natural events have not buried archaeological surfaces, archaeological sites and materials may remain on the surface from the time of their deposition until they are found and studied by archaeologists. Assigning chronological context to features and artifacts in this situation has continued to frustrate scientists. In the desert West of the United States, for example, there are archaeological materials that have been candidates for "early" (i.e., pre-Clovis) occupation of the New World; many of the sites and/or artifacts are surface occurrences and lack any stratigraphy.

Spectacular surface archaeological features such as giant ground figures, because of their visibility, uncertainty of age, and indeterminate cultural affiliation, have generated a great deal of interest, both scientific and sensational. Other surface cultural features may or may not be spectacular, but continue to be temporal enigmas. These include, but are not limited to, features such as: rock art (especially petroglyphs [carving into rock]); ground figures of immense to small scale (known as intaglios, geoglyphs, earthen art, rock alignments); possible cultural features incorporated into desert pavement surfaces (cleared areas sometimes known as "sleeping circles"); prehistoric and historic structures of stone and masonry (dwellings, hunting blinds, rock cairns, stone burial mounds and tombs, fortifications, and various monuments); isolated hearths, artifacts comprising site assemblages at temporary or permanent living or activity areas; stone quarries of various types; and other surface archaeological features composed of materials nondatable by ^{14}C or other accepted dating methods (Beck 1994).

Varied approaches have been used to place surface archaeological materials within a chronological context. One approach assumes association between nearby securely dated features and undated surface sites or artifacts. Another popular method is dependent on "time-sensitive" artifact types. For example, chronological schemes have been developed based on apparently temporally diagnostic artifacts such as projectile points (e.g., Thomas 1981), shell beads and ornaments (e.g., Bennyhoff and Hughes 1987) or ceramic vessel design. Still another approach characterizes site artifact assemblages, features, elements of construction, and/or topographic features and other factors and compares them to other sites or paleoevents for which dates have been established by radiometric or other accepted dating methods. In the Mojave Desert of western North America, for example, a characteristic artifact assemblage has been associated with high shorelines surrounding remnant playas of lakes, marshes, and drainages of late Pleistocene/Early Holocene times. The assemblages (sometimes lumped together as the Western Pluvial Lakes Tradition) include characteristic projectile point types known as Lake Mojave and Silver Lake, leaf-shaped percussion-flaked tools, large core and flake tools often of microcrystalline quartz, crescent-shaped artifacts, and few or no milling tools (Moratto 1984: 92–103). This assemblage (or most elements of it), if found in an appropriate geographical context and judged to be of appropriate technological level, would probably be chronologically placed in the Early Holocene.

The above methods (assuming validity) of placing surface archaeological materials in chronological contexts are limited because (1) they depend on the presence of time-sensitive artifacts, (2) many types of artifacts and features are not necessarily temporally diagnostic, and (3) continuity of cultural behaviors has promoted site assemblages, features, and artifacts that have changed little or not at all over millennia.

Many surface artifacts and features that have been exposed to the atmosphere for varying periods of time, particularly in arid regions of the world, share one characteristic: coatings of rock varnish. Archaeologists and other scientists have used several methods exploiting the characteristics of varnish in attempts to solve the problems of dating surface phenomena.

Chronological Uses of Rock Varnish

A variety of techniques have been proposed for using rock varnish as either a relative or calendrical dating tool including: relative varnish intensity, neutron activation analysis, cation-ratio dating, and accelerator mass spectrometry (AMS)-based ^{14}C analyses of various types. Each technique is discussed below.

Relative Intensity

Relative degree of varnish darkness, intensity, and/or thickness has long been used as a method to place archaeological materials in a relative chronological sequence (e.g., Heizer and Baumhoff 1962); darker-colored, thicker, and more complete varnish coatings are considered older than lighter-colored, thinner, and partial varnish coatings, with an entire spectrum of intermediate levels between the two extremes. This method has limited chronological resolution. Degree of overall surface darkening is still used as a relative age indicator by archaeologists and geomorphologists.

Neutron Activation Analysis and X-Ray Fluorescence

James Bard (1979), as part of his dissertation research, made an attempt to use neutron-activation and X-ray fluorescence trace analyses on varnish to date Great Basin petroglyphs. Although Bard (1979: 380–386) could measure subtle and minor chemical and elemental differences in the constituents of rock varnish, his attempt to use $^{230}Th/^{226}Ra$ ratios to develop a chronological scheme was not successful; he suggested that a relative dating scheme using Ba abundance might be a possibility.

Cation-Ratio and Chemical Characteristics

A method of dating landforms and archaeological features and artifacts, based on chemical composition of rock varnish, was first proposed more than a decade ago (Dorn 1983). The technique, termed "cation-ratio dating" (C-R) by its originator, was based on the hypothesis that "mobile" cations such as Na, Ca, and K are leached more quickly from rock varnish matrix than "stable" cations such as Ti. The C-R is derived from the formula: (Ca+K)/Ti. Ca and K are hypothesized to leach preferentially from varnish over time; therefore, a low ratio supposedly indicates that varnish has been exposed to leaching (time of exposure of the surface) for a significant period of time. A number of C-R curves have been developed and calibrated using a variety of dating techniques: potassium-argon (K-Ar) dates, archaeologically and geomorphologically associated ^{14}C determinations, ^{14}C analysis of varnish constituents, and historical dates (Dorn 1983, 1988b, 1989; Dorn *et al.* 1986, 1987a, 1987b, 1988; Bamforth and Dorn 1988; Nobbs and Dorn 1988; Pineda *et al.* 1988; Francis *et al.* 1993). The C-R dating hypothesis is subject to many assumptions, some of which are discussed below.

Accelerator Mass Spectrometry-Based Radiocarbon Measurements

The advent of accelerator mass spectrometry (AMS) for radiocarbon (^{14}C) analyses made feasible the direct dating of organic matter contained within rock varnish in that it allowed dating of extremely small samples. Dorn employed this technology as a means of obtaining ^{14}C values directly on Pleistocene and later surfaces that were varnish-coated. Age determinations on the deepest (i.e., presumed oldest) varnish layers were used to calibrate a number of C-R curves (e.g., Dorn *et al.* 1986, 1987a, 1987b; Nobbs and Dorn 1988; Dorn *et al.* 1989). Later, Dorn used dated organic materials from the interface between the varnish coating and rock substrate (e.g., Clarkson and Dorn 1995). The source and nature of the organic matter that was being ^{14}C- dated has never been determined (Reneau and Harrington 1988; Watchman 1989). The failure to identify the source of carbon, and therefore the characteristics of the dated material, is a major uncertainty in interpreting AMS-based ^{14}C determinations used to date directly varnish layers or to calibrate C-R curves for rock varnish.

Both C-R and ^{14}C dating of rock varnish have been controversial. At present (1997), most geologists, geochemists, and geomorphologists have reevaluated the validity and applicability of C-R dating of surface geological exposures; little research is currently being conducted. Archaeologists are in the process of doing the same (e.g. Bierman and Harry 1992; Harry 1995). The following sections contain a short history of rock-varnish dating methods and the surrounding controversies.

CATION-RATIO DATING

Underlying Assumptions of Cation-Ratio Dating

The basic assumption of cation-ratio dating is that the ratio (Ca+K)/Ti decreases through preferential leaching of less stable cations of Ca and K throughout the time of varnish exposure while Ti is retained in the varnish coating. The basic premise depends on a number of assumptions. First, that leaching is a process that takes place in varnish and, if it does take place, the process is regular throughout the varnish.

Second, that the rock-surface (i.e., substrate surface) is assumed to be stable at the micron scale over periods of time ranging from thousands to millions of years. This assumption cannot be demonstrated; in fact, recent measurements of cosmogenic nuclides demonstrate that even the most stable rock surfaces are eroding at rates of tens of cm to meters every million years (Bierman 1994; Bierman and Turner 1995). Rocks continually weather by an interaction of chemical and physical processes from the time of their formation. Different rock types weather at different rates in different climates.

Third, it is assumed that the initial cation ratio is known. As far as we are aware, the cation ratio of freshly formed rock varnish has never been measured. One hundred years of surface exposure has been proposed (Dorn and Whitley 1984) as the time span necessary for varnish development, but this has subsequently been modified (Dorn and Meek 1995).

Fourth, it is assumed that varnish deposition is time-transgressive. Varnish is thought to be laid down in layers over time. However, there is no documentation regarding the regularity of this process or if and what diagenic processes take place within varnish layers after formation and/or how substrate weathering and other environmental factors affect varnish formation, growth, and stability.

Fifth, it is assumed that the processes of varnish accretion are well known. Unfortunately, researchers have not yet fully documented the processes of varnish formation. A number of processes may be involved. Processes of accretion may vary with the environment and substrate.

Sixth, it is assumed that varnish is both an open- and closed-system. Cation leaching requires an open system. If cations of K and Ca are preferentially leached, the varnish system is open. AMS-based ^{14}C determinations that are used to calibrate C-R curves require the system to be closed to carbon exchange (Dean 1997).

Seventh, it is assumed that environments do not change over time. Varnish appears to be derived from environmental substances (i.e., wind-blown dust). It is known that changes in climatic patterns (e.g., wind, dust, moisture) have occurred frequently in the past. How does this affect the regularity of accretion and compositions of varnish?

Historical Perspective

Despite fifteen years of intensive research, there is still no agreement in the rock-varnish community regarding the reliability of C-R dating (see Bamforth 1997; Harry 1997). Dorn and his colleagues continue to use and argue for validity and reliability of C-R dates (Dorn 1995; Whitley and Dorn 1993). Workers at the University of Washington have produced several data sets which suggest strongly that rock varnish C-R dating is unreliable (Bierman and Gillespie 1991a; Bierman and Gillespie 1991b; Bierman and Gillespie 1994) while researchers at Los Alamos National Laboratory are split in their opinions, with Harrington (Harrington and Whitney 1995) supporting revised use of rock varnish-dating applications and Reneau (Reneau and Raymond 1991) questioning the fundamental tenets of the methods.

In this discussion, we illustrate the development of C-R rock varnish dating and the diversity of opinions by reviewing some of the more important and controversial studies which have been published. Because the literature is so extensive and so diverse in opinion, we strongly encourage interested readers to review the original papers critically and make their own independent judgement based on published data and methodologies.

Initial Developments

Quantitative rock-varnish dating was first proposed by Dorn (1983). In that paper, Dorn presents graphically results from three study sites where the relative age of geomorphological features was constrained and where samples had been collected and the C-R ratio of rock varnish had been measured by XRF or PIXE. Dorn also presents data from a fourth site, the Coso volcanic field, for which K/Ar ages were available for many flows. In each case, the varnish C-Rs appear to decrease with the relative age of the geomorphological surface or lava flow although the statistical uncertainty in C-Rs for many samples is quite large. It is important to note that for some dated Coso samples, differing by an order of magnitude or more in K/Ar-based age, the measured C-Rs are indistinguishable at 1 sigma (Fig. 12.5).

What is most striking about this paper, and about many of Dorn's papers which followed in the next five years, is the absence of: (1) data tables presenting chemical analyses of the samples from which the C-Rs were calculated, (2) detailed analytical methodology, and (3) information regarding

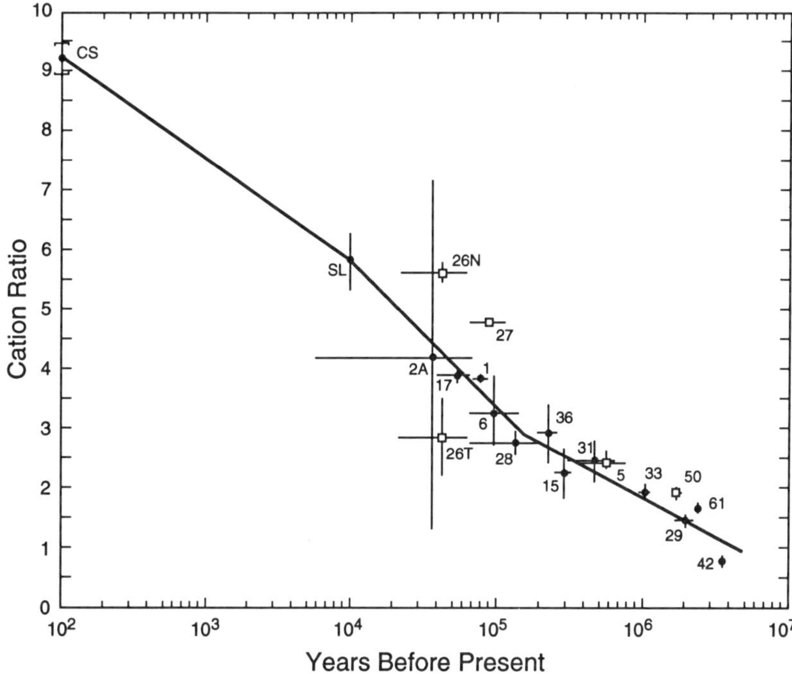

Figure 12.5. Varnish K+Ca:Ti cation-leaching curve for the Coso region, southern California. Points represent K/Ar-dated volcanic deposits of the Coso volcanic field. Open squares (5, 26N, 26T, 27, 50) represent volcanic surfaces that probably do not accurately represent K/Ar radiometric ages according to Dorn 1983. The point labeled SL is the varnish ratio for late Pleistocene high stand of Searles Lake. The point CS is the ratio for the clay-sized Coso Soil material from all 16 volcanic sites. The horizontal bars extending from each point represent the K/Ar age uncertainties (1σ); the vertical bars represent the uncertainties (1σ) of varnish cation ratios. The brackets on either side of the CS point on the left margin of the graph indicate 1σ of all 16 soil samples. The lines are semilog regressions, and they indicate the rate of varnish-cation leaching in the Coso Range and vicinity, based on the volcanic rocks (indicated by the points) and the SL and CS ratios. (Adapted, with permission, from Dorn 1983, Fig. 7).

substrate lithology and sample collection sites. The absence of these data from the public domain has prevented replication of much of Dorn's work and has fueled many of the on-going controversies (Bierman *et al.* 1992; Bierman and Gillespie 1992a; Bierman and Gillespie 1992b; Cahill 1992; Dorn 1992a; Dorn 1992b). The thesis in which Dorn developed C-R dating contains no tables of chemical data nor does it contain a detailed methodology describing how the chemical analyses were made (Dorn 1982).

During the mid-1980's, C-R dating was applied by Dorn and his co-workers to several sites in the arid western United States and Australia (Dorn 1988b; Dorn *et al.* 1986, 1987a; Nobbs and Dorn 1988). In some cases, the resulting

C-R ages proved controversial, particularly when the ages were used to overturn previously accepted chronologies (Bamforth and Dorn 1988; Dorn *et al.* 1988). During this time, two separate research groups (one at Los Alamos National Laboratory and the other in South Africa) reproduced Dorn's finding that rock varnish C-R appeared to decrease with increasing substrate age (Harrington and Whitney 1987; Pineda *et al.* 1988). Both groups, however, employed different analytical methods, both of which were different from those employed by Dorn and both of which were later shown to be inaccurate (Bierman and Gillespie 1991a; Bierman and Gillespie 1992a; Harrington *et al.* 1991). By the late 1980s, the first methodological questions began to be raised regarding the underlying premises of C-R dating and the first disagreements began to appear in the literature, polarizing the scientific community.

Revisionist Perspectives

The first scientific paper questioning the validity of C-R dating was published in 1988 (Reneau and Harrington 1988) in response to C-R dating of Australian rock art (Dorn *et al.* 1988; Nobbs and Dorn 1988). In their comment, Reneau and Harrington question the validity of assuming a 100-year age for the initial C-R and point out that C-R age uncertainties appear to have been systematically underestimated by Nobbs and Dorn. Later comments on the statistical validity of the Nobbs and Dorn paper were more pointed (Lanteigne 1989; Lanteigne 1991) stating that the statistical treatment of the data employed by Nobbs and Dorn was inherently flawed and that many of the conclusions they reached were not statistically significant. At the same time, Dorn published two long papers; the first (Dorn 1989) summarized his work through the 1980s and presented a long list of sampling criteria many of which were based on only several chemical analyses and, as a result, were statistically insignificant; the second was a rêport to the State of Nevada which strongly criticized the work of Los Alamos researchers (i.e., Harrington) and presented for the first time, a table of chemical data (Dorn 1988a). This data table showed that most of Dorn's samples from Yucca Mountain appeared to contain no Ba, a finding which would have great significance in the following years.

During the late 1980s and early 1990s, fundamental questions began to be raised regarding the accuracy of rock-varnish analyses used to generate C-R dates. In particular, Harrington *et al.* (1991) suggested that most previous rock-varnish chemical analyses were inaccurate because Ba (undetected by many XRF methods) masqueraded as Ti, artificially lowering measured C-Rs. A blind test of analytical laboratories showed that the PIXE laboratory, which had generated most of the C-Rs used by Dorn for dating, could not detect Ba in material similar in composition to rock varnish (Fig. 12.6). Comments by Dorn and Thomas Cahill, his collaborator who was responsible for the chemical analysis, contested the conclusions of Bierman and Gillespie (1991a) but

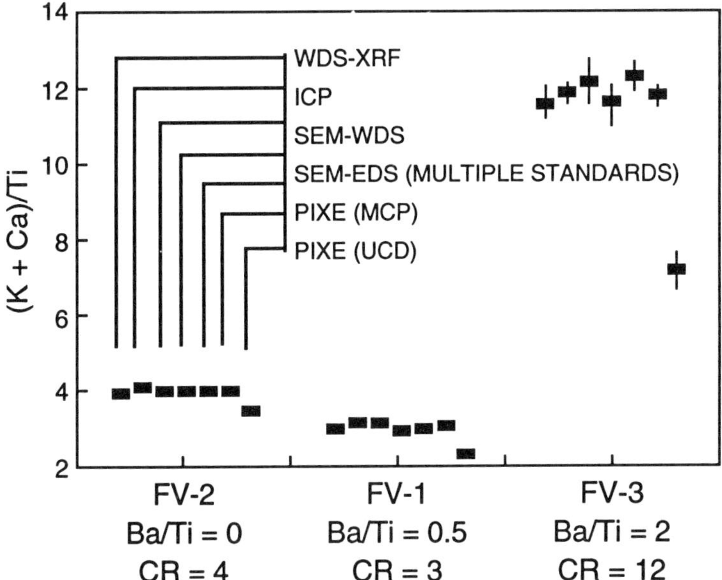

Figure 12.6. Analysis of synthetic varnish standards indicate that SEM-EDS cation ratios are accurate and comparable to those measured by all other methods except PIXE UCD which was used by Dorn to make most C-R measurements. PIXE UCD error increases with Ba/Ti ratio, suggesting that Ba, included in Ti abundances, lowers cation ratios. Uncertainties, calculated according to Bierman *et al.* (1991), are shown if they exceed the width symbol. Ratios in the same order for FV-1 and FV-3 as for FV-2. CR = cation ratio (K+Ca)/Ti. (Reproduced with permission from Bierman and Gillespie 1991a, Fig. 2).

admitted that during the time many of Dorn's rock-varnish analyses were made, Ba could not be detected by the PIXE analytical system (Cahill 1992; Dorn 1992a). Earlier, Dorn *et al.* (1990) had presented data at odds with both his and Cahill's comments, data which suggest that in some cases, PIXE appeared to have measured accurately the abundance of Ba in rock varnish. In this same paper, earlier C-R rock-varnish dates for glaciation in Owens Valley (Dorn et al. 1987b) were revised (by some 50%) so that they more closely matched new ^{36}Cl dates (Phillips *et al.* 1990).

Current Status

Since the early 1990s, few rock-varnish data have appeared in the geological literature and interest in rock-varnish chronologies appears to have shifted to the archaeological community (Clarkson and Dorn 1991, 1995; Clarkson 1992, 1994; Dorn *et al.* 1992; Francis *et al.* 1993; Whitley and Dorn 1993; Von Werlhof 1995). For example, the last rock-varnish-related abstract submitted by Dorn and his colleagues to a national meeting of the Geological Society of America was in 1989.

In the 1990s, there have been several publications examining some of the assumptions underlying C-R dating of rock varnish. Dragovich (1988) investigated within-varnish leaching trends to determine if lower layers were more leached and found no patterning. Dorn and Krinsley (1991) performed accelerated leaching experiments in the laboratory, experiments which indicated that when varnish is immersed in water, concentrations of K and Ca in solution are higher than concentrations of Ti. The relationship of this observation to field conditions is uncertain. Reneau and Raymond (1991) suggest that K and Ca are not preferentially leached from varnish over time. They base this conclusion on the lack of observed changes in K:Si and Ca:Mn ratios in varnish, changes which might be expected if leaching were occurring. Reneau and Raymond (1991) suggest that observed time-dependent changes in apparent C-Rs result from incorporation of substrate in the sample upon which the chemical analyses were performed.

It is possible that many of the published rock-varnish analyses are inaccurate, to varying degrees, due to the difficulty of measuring Ti accurately in the presence of Ba. For example, Dorn repeatedly cites a list of studies which support the use and accuracy of C-R dating (Dorn 1992a, 1995). Yet, when one examines these studies more closely (Bierman *et al.* 1992; Bierman and Gillespie 1992a; Bierman and Gillespie 1995) it becomes clear that many of the studies cited by Dorn have not measured C-Rs accurately because of the Ba interference with Ti determination (Bull 1991; Dethier *et al.* 1988; Harrington and Whitney 1987; Pineda *et al.* 1988; Whitney and Harrington 1993), or provide no information regarding the substrate (Bull 1991). One study cited by Dorn in support of C-R dating actually finds no meaningful trend in C-Rs at all (Glazovskiy 1985).

There is, to our knowledge, only one study to date which has been made on rock varnish which used demonstratably accurate analytical techniques and for which substrate incorporation can play no role in C-R measurements (Bierman and Gillespie 1994; Bierman and Harry 1992; Harry 1995). This study of artifacts and varnished bedrock from the Mojave Desert shows that chemical analyses of rock varnish underlain by chert (a non-contaminating, Si substrate) show no systematic change in C-R with increasing relative substrate age (Fig. 12.7). This finding supports the assertion of Reneau and Raymond (1991) that previously observed C-R trends may have been the result of inadvertent substrate inclusion in the sample subjected to chemical analysis (see Bamforth 1997; Harry 1997).

Perhaps the best summary of the current status of rock-varnish dating was made in 1990 by Robert Bednarik, an Australian archaeologist, after a two-day workshop in which Dorn presented his methodology for rock-varnish analysis to 25 Australian archaeologists, geomorphologists, and geochemists.

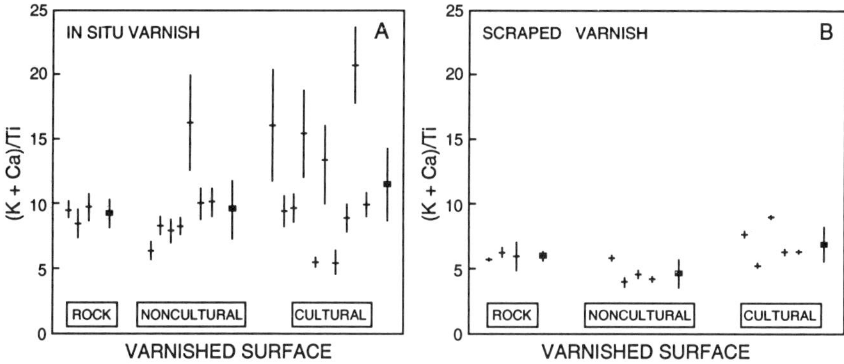

Figure 12.7. No statistical differences are observed in varnish C-Rs between cultural and noncultural surfaces on chert substrate. Mean and grand mean cation ratios for individual samples and for populations of *bedrock*, *noncultural*, and *cultural* varnish samples analyzed *in situ* and after scraping. Thin horizontal lines are means for individual samples. Squares represent grand mean calculated from sample means. Error bars represent 90% confidence intervals (t statistic, n-1 df) about both the sample and grand means. *Rock* refers to bedrock samples. *Noncultural* refers to both varnish on pieces of unworked rock and varnish on unworked cortical portions of mixed samples. *Cultural* refers to both varnish on pieces of worked rock and varnish on the worked faces of mixed samples. (A) *In situ* varnish, (B) Scraped varnish fused into glass. (Reproduced with permission from Bierman and Gillespie 1994, Fig. 4).

> The seminar, conducted on the first day, proved to be rather unproductive because debate of the crucial issues remained elusive. The workshop of the second day . . . was far more effective in tackling the critical questions. The result was an increase in the skepticism of most participants. It is appropriate for research funding agencies to reconsider funding strategy in this field, and to more closely examine alternative dating methods. [Bednarik 1990:3]

As Bednarik (1995: 11) would later comment, "If replicability is not assured, scientific credibility is impaired."

RADIOCARBON DATING ROCK VARNISH

It is assumed that the reader is familiar with the basic premise and the underlying assumptions of radiocarbon dating (refer to Chapter 3, this volume, or to Taylor 1987). Conventional decay-counting ^{14}C determinations on organic archaeological materials associated with varnished artifacts were first used to calibrate C-R curves in early studies, along with K/Ar dates for surfaces outside the lower radiocarbon age span (i.e., earlier than about 40,000 years B.P.) and historical dates for surfaces outside the upper radiocarbon age span (i.e., surfaces younger than about 300 years B.P.). With the advent of AMS technology applied to ^{14}C analysis in the 1980s, direct dates on much smaller samples of organic material were now possible including the feasibility of directly dating the organic components of rock varnish. Hypothetically, the method could be used to date individual varnish layers without relying on calibrated C-R curves (Dorn *et al.* 1989). AMS determinations, however, are costly. There are also practical limitations of securing multiple direct AMS-based ^{14}C determinations on archaeological materials, limitations imposed by required sample size (see below). These factors encouraged the continuation of the use of ^{14}C-calibrated C-R curves (e.g., Dorn *et al.* 1988; Nobbs and Dorn 1988; Clarkson and Dorn 1991, 1995; Clarkson 1992, 1994; Dorn *et al.* 1992; Francis *et al.* 1993; Whitley and Dorn 1993; Von Werlhof 1995). Table 12.1 presents selected radiocarbon data that have been derived from rock-varnish research.

Trace amounts of organic material (1–2%) have been reported as being present in rock varnish (Dorn and DeNiro 1985; Dorn *et al.* 1986, 1989), but we understand that there can be significant variation in these values, with some varnish samples having a much-reduced carbon content (Timothy Jull, personal communication, 1997). Preliminary work at the UC Riverside Radiocarbon Laboratory on varnish samples from a variety of locations in eastern California has produced yields of organics ranging from 0.15 to 0.62% (Richard Burky, personal communication, 1997). Moreover, to date, analytical data have not been presented to characterize the organic component(s) of varnish that have been ^{14}C dated. Suggested organic sources include microorganisms within the varnish and on the underlying rock, their remnants or their products; airborne plant particles; airborne pollens and other plant parts; and remnants of lichens, fungal mats, and algae (Dorn *et al.* 1989; Nagy *et al.* 1990; Adams *et al.* 1992). There may be, in fact, a wide range of ^{14}C ages represented in organic components of rock varnish at the time of formation due to heterogeneous sources of carbon (Raymond and Harrington 1989; Watchman 1989, 1992; Dorn 1996; 1997). It is also possible that young carbon may be introduced after the varnish is formed depending on regional and local environmental conditions.

Studies are needed that statistically can (1) demonstrate that discrete varnish-layer sampling can be reproduced (Clarke 1989; Raymond and Harrington 1989; Lanteigne 1989; Bierman *et al.* 1991; Reneau *et al.* 1991; Harry 1995); (2) demonstrate that one or more specific organic components of the varnish matrix in a wide range of depositional environments generally exhibit ^{14}C ages that are temporally consistent in terms of known-age relationships (Dorn 1996); (3) demonstrate that older varnish at the bottom of depressions produces ^{14}C dates older than younger varnish that forms on the edges of the depression and elevations on the same rock surface. As far as the authors and others (Towner 1996: 397) are aware, such data have not yet been obtained for rock varnish. In the absence of such data, the use of ^{14}C age estimates to directly date rock varnish or to provide calibration for C-R leaching curves is highly problematic.

Table 12.1. Selected Published AMS Radiocarbon Dates on Rock Varnish from Archaeological Contexts. Radiocarbon Dates Expressed in Uncalibrated Radiocarbon Years

ARCHAEOLOGICAL CONTEXT	SAMPLE LOCATION	SAMPLE ID	DATE B.P.	1 σ	LAB NUMBER	REFERENCE (by date)	COMMENTS
Cima basalt flow clasts, Mojave Desert, USA	basal varnish layer	uncertain, but $\delta^{13}C$ same as nearby plants	14,600	±800	AA-356	Dorn et al. 1986	TAMS dates on geomorphological features used to calibrate cation leaching curve for artifacts in Mojave River Basin. 167 artifacts from 6 surface sites.
Alluvial-fan clasts near Silver Lake, USA	"	"	13,100	±500	AA-671	"	"
Shoreline clasts, Manix Lake, USA	"	"	16,800	±700	AA-670	"	"
Alluvial-fan clasts, East Cronise Basin, USA	"	"	16,100	±800	AA-741	"	"
Alluvial-fan clasts, East Cronise Basin, USA	"	"	9,700	±430	AA-937	"	"
Alluvial-fan clasts, East Cronise Basin, USA	"	"	1,370	±360	AA-938	"	"
Australian geomorphological surfaces with cation ratios similar to the petroglyph cation ratios	basal varnish layer (lower 10% of varnish)	none; "organic matter"	2,120	no σ	ETH-2804	Nobbs and Dorn 1988 Dorn et al. 1988	used to calibrate petroglyph cation ratio curves
"	"	"	21,550	"	ETH-2941	"	"
"	"	"	34,590	"	ETH-2940	"	"
Petroglyph, Mojave Desert, USA	basal varnish layer (lower 10% of varnish)	microorganisms, pollen, organic decay fall, adsorbed organic matter; $\delta^{13}C$ indicate organic matter from nearby plants	3,760	±50	AA-2233	Dorn et al. 1989	

Table 12.1. *(Continued)*

ARCHAEOLOGICAL CONTEXT	SAMPLE LOCATION	SAMPLE ID	DATE B.P.	1 σ	LAB NUMBER	REFERENCE (by date)	COMMENTS
Ayers Rock, Australia	organic inclusions encapsulated in accreting varnish	unknown; possibly nearby plant material	27,100	±400	Beta-19893 ETH-2809	Dorn et al. 1992	outcrop surface near rock art
Llama geoglyph on hillside (T1), Peru	"	"	1,400	±80	TO-1495	"	
Bird geoglyph on Nazca pampa (T2), Peru	"	"	1,520	±60	TO-1614	"	
Linear geoglyph on Nazca pampa (T3), Peru	"	"	1,460	±60	TO-1615	"	
Linear geoglyph Center #1 (T4), Peru	"	"	1,670	±70	TO-1616	"	
Linear geoglyph Center #2 (T5), Peru	"	"	1,720	±50	TO-1617	"	
Linear geoglyph Center #2 (T6), Peru	"	"	1,680	±50	TO-1618	"	
Trapezoid geoglyph Center #2 (T7), Peru	"	"	2,100	±50	TO-1619	"	
Linear geoglyph on Pampa Gorda (T8), Peru	"	"	1,720	±50	TO-1620	"	
Orca geoglyph on Nazca pampa (T9), Peru	"	"	1,500	±50	TO-1621	"	
CRG-1 Colorado River Anthropomorphic geoglyph, USA	"	"	1,060	±65	ETH-6572 Beta-37033	"	
CRG-2 Colorado River Anthropomorphic geoglyph, USA	"	"	1,195	±65	ETH-6574 Beta-37035	"	
CRG-3 Colorado River Quadruped geoglyph, USA	"	"	1,145	±65	ETH-6575 Beta-37036	"	

Table 12.1. *(Continued)*

ARCHAEOLOGICAL CONTEXT	SAMPLE LOCATION	SAMPLE ID	DATE B.P.	1 σ	LAB NUMBER	REFERENCE (by date)	COMMENTS
Mojave Desert quarry artifact 85-16, corer, USA	"	"	3,690	±65	ETH-6573 Beta-37034	"	
Mojave Desert quarry artifact 85-8, biface, flake scar 1, USA	"	"	14,840	±115	ETH-6577 Beta-37038	"	
Mojave Desert quarry artifact 85-8, biface, flake scar 2, USA	"	"	13,655	±105	AA-6547	"	
Mojave Desert quarry artifact 85-12, primary flake, USA	"	"	26,070	±360	ETH-4478 Beta-27774	"	
South Australia petroglyph K15, Curved Line	"	"	12,650	±150	NZA-1369	"	abundant silica glaze interbedded with rock varnish
South Australia petroglyph K21, Bird Track	"	"	22,480	±340	NZA-1366	"	
South Australian petroglyph K23, Curved Line	"	"	30,230	±770	NZA-1378	"	
South Australian petroglyph K24, "Abstract" motif	"	"	12,970	±150	NZA-1414	"	
South Australian petroglyph K26, Curved Line superimposed by motif K23	"	"	31,230	±920	NZA-1370	"	
South Australian petroglyph WH1, possible Drominorthid Track	"	"	14,910	±180	NZA-1367	"	abundant silica glaze interbedded with rock varnish
South Australian petroglyph WH5, Oval	"	"	36,400	±1700	NZA-1356	"	

Table 12.1. *(Continued)*

ARCHAEOLOGICAL CONTEXT	SAMPLE LOCATION	SAMPLE ID	DATE B.P.	1 σ	LAB NUMBER	REFERENCE (by date)	COMMENTS
Olary petroglyph K28A, Hand Print, Australia	mixture of organics from varnish/rock interface and weathering rind	organic carbon within varnish; microcolonial fungi, bacteria, other organisms	9,125	±100	AA-6910	"	
Olary petroglyph K29, Foot Print, Australia	varnish/rock interface	charcoal or organic mat at base of varnish	9,980	±85	AA-6910	"	
Olary petroglyph K30, Foot Print, Australia	weathering rind	organic matter in weathering rind	20,105	±185	AA-6548	"	
Olary petroglyph K32, Track, Australia	varnish/rock interface	charcoal or organic mat at base of varnish	21,195	±220	AA-6905	"	
Olary petroglyph YS1, Complex Curvilinear, Australia	mixture of organics from varnish/rock interface and weathering rind	organic carbon within varnish; microcolonial fungi, bacteria, other organisms	13,950	±110	AA-6914	"	
Olary petroglyph YS2, Large Macropod Track, Australia	weathering rind	organic matter in weathering rind	7,365	±85	AA-6909	"	
Olary petroglyph YS3, Barred Circle, Australia	weathering rind	organic matter in weathering rind	1,510	±50	AA-6906	"	
Olary petroglyph YS4, Abraded Grooves, Australia	mixture of organics from varnish/rock interface and weathering rind	organic carbon within varnish; microcolonial fungi, bacteria, other organisms	6,355	±85	AA-6551	"	
Olary petroglyph WH2, Footprint, Australia	"	"	18,485	±165	AA-6918	"	
Olary petroglyph WH5, Oval, Australia	weathering rind	organic matter in weathering rind	35,530	±650	NZA 2361	"	

Table 12.1. *(Continued)*

ARCHAEOLOGICAL CONTEXT	SAMPLE LOCATION	SAMPLE ID	DATE B.P.	1 σ	LAB NUMBER	REFERENCE (by date)	COMMENTS
	varnish/rock interface	charcoal or organic mat at base of varnish	36,400	±1,700	NZA-1356		
	"	"	37,890	±820	NZA-2180		
	"	"	>42,000		AA-6907		
Olary petroglyph PN4, Circles with Spiral	not given	not given	5,635	±90	AA-6549	"	sample used for calibration of cation ratio curve
Olary petroglyph PN5, Complex Curvilinear	weathering rind	organic matter in weathering rind	3,795	±65	AA-6903	"	"
	varnish/rock interface	charcoal or organic mat at base of varnish	3,575	±65	AA-6913		
Olary petroglyph PN6, Curved Line(upper)	mixture of organics from varnish/rock interface and weathering rind	organic carbon within varnish; microcolonial fungi, bacteria, other organisms	43,140	±3,000	AA-6898	"	"
	"	"	>43,100		AA-6920		
Petroglyphs on stable talus boulders CM-8, Coso Range, USA	weathering rind	lichen remnants, charcoal, fungal mats, cyanobacteria, endolithic algae, pollen, plant remains, nonidentified material	14,070	±130	NZA-2364	Whitley and Dorn 1993	
Petroglyphs on stable talus boulders PEFO-7, Petrified Forest National Park, USA	mixture of organics from varnish/rock interface and weathering rind	organic carbon within varnish; microcolonial fungi, bacteria, other organisms	18,180	±190	NZA-2115	"	
	"	"	16,600	±120	NZA-2191		

Table 12.1. *(Continued)*

ARCHAEOLOGICAL CONTEXT	SAMPLE LOCATION	SAMPLE ID	DATE B.P.	1 σ	LAB NUMBER	REFERENCE (by date)	COMMENTS
Primary flake, 5j, from stable desert pavement at the Baker site, USA	weathering rind	lichen remnants, charcoal, fungal mats, cyanobacteria, endolithic algae, pollen, plant remains, nonidentified material	12,820	±100	NZA-1919	"	
Biface chopper, #85-8, from Manix Lake Quarry stable desert pavement, USA	varnish/rock interface	charcoal or organic mat at base of varnish	14,840	±115	ETH-6577 Beta-37038	"	Flake scar 1
			13,655	±105	AA-6547		Flake scar 2
Blade-like flake, #85-12, from Manix Lake Quarry stable desert pavement, USA	"	"	26,070	±360	ETH-4478 Beta-32774	"	
Artifact #1, Lot 96, SBr-2100, Locus 70 from Manix Lake Quarry stable desert pavement, USA	weathering rind	lichen remnants, charcoal, fungal mats, cyanobacteria, endolithic algae, pollen, plant remains, nonidentified material	26,590	±230	NZA-2637	"	
Petroglyph panel at 48HO469, sample WP-90-1, Bighorn Area, USA	subvarnish organic matter	charcoal?	225	±60	AA-6545	Francis et al. 1993	
Petroglyph panel at Coal Draw, sample WP-90-2, Bighorn Area, USA	"	"	325	±70	AA-6535	"	
Petroglyph panel at 48HO4, sample WP-90-4, Bighorn Area, USA	"	"	5,775	±80	AA-6536	"	
Petroglyph panel at Legend Rock, sample WP-90-4, Bighorn Area, USA	"	"	6,005	±105	AA-6552	"	second date on same sample run at later date
Petroglyph panel at Legend Rock, sample WP-90-17, Bighorn Area, USA	"	"	295	±55	AA-6542	"	

Table 12.1. *(Continued)*

ARCHAEOLOGICAL CONTEXT	SAMPLE LOCATION	SAMPLE ID	DATE B.P.	1 σ	LAB NUMBER	REFERENCE (by date)	COMMENTS
Petroglyph panel at 48FR372, sample WP-90-20, Bighorn Area, USA	"	"	1,820	±65	AA-6538	"	
Petroglyph panel at 48BH499, sample WP-90-21, Bighorn Area, USA	"	"	325	±70	AA-6541	"	
Petroglyph panel at Medicine Lodge Creek, sample WP-90-22, Bighorn Area, USA	"	"	70	±60	AA-6540	"	
Petroglyph panel at 24CB602, sample WP-90-28, Bighorn Area, USA	"	"	1,250	±65	AA-6544	"	
Geomorphic surface of arenite sandstone in Petroglyph Canyon, sample WP-90-30, Bighorn Area, USA	"	"	15,695	±135	AA-6537	"	
Petroglyph panel at 24CB1090, sample WP-90-32, Bighorn Area, USA	"	"	1,470	±75	AA-6539	"	
Bear Shield petroglyph, sample WP-90-35, Bighorn Area, USA	"	"	1,595	±60	AA-6543	"	
Tool in association with geoglyph, Eastern California, USA	not given	not identified	8,000	not given	not identified	Von Werlhof 1995	reference is a newsletter from Imperial Valley Community College Museum
Dressed lintel stone of Peruvian puquio (hydralic system), Nazca, Peru	interface between varnish and "newly" exposed stone surface	cyanobacteria, fungi, lichens	1,460	±50	TO-1622	Clarkson and Dorn 1955	information on methods not provided
"	"	"	1,430	±60	TO-1623	"	"

ARCHAEOLOGICAL APPLICATIONS: CURRENT ISSUES AND PROBLEMS

Elsewhere in this chapter, we have focused on the assumptions involved in using rock varnish as a dating material and the problems involved in laboratory and field methods. Here, we focus on the ways that the assumptions and problems are further exaggerated by limitations imposed by the very fact that materials being dated are archaeological.

Chronological Limitations

It is well-documented that human populations were in the New World by at least 11,500 radiocarbon years BP (Haynes 1992; Taylor *et al.* 1996). There have been many claims of earlier occupation of the New World (e.g., Dillehay 1989), but very few have been widely accepted for a variety of reasons that are beyond the scope of our discussion here. In the Old World, the archaeological record is much longer, reaching back to at least the early Pleistocene. At least for the late Quaternary (i.e., terminal Pleistocene and Holocene) in the New World, archaeologists deal with a relatively narrow span of time, as currently viewed, whereas geologists and Quaternary geomorphologists work with much larger segments of the geological time scale. The narrowness of the archaeological range, particularly in the New World, confounds the basic problems of adequate sampling and statistical significance. Archaeologists, for the most part, want to establish as "tight" a date as possible, so that the dates can be used in the development of models and schemes of cultural continuity and change. For example, the inherent variability in varnish chemistry and its apparent change over time in some studies often negates the value of any C-R age determination for archaeological purposes, i.e., there is too much uncertainty for the calibrated ages to be meaningful.

Interpretive Limitations

In our view, interpreting the age of a cultural surface remains unsolved, even if we *know*: (1) the deepest (i.e., hypothetically the oldest) layer of rock varnish is being dated and (2) the organic material on which the date is obtained are coincident in origin with the beginning of varnish formation (Dorn *et al.* 1992). It is possible only to state that the fresh surface existed before the onset of varnish formation. Little is known about the time-interval lapse between the exposure of a fresh surface (e.g., by flake removal, removal of an old varnish coating to create a design element in a petroglyph, the setting of a newly quarried stone in a structure, or removal of an old surface at a quarried outcrop) and the beginning of microscopic/macroscopic development of new varnish. One hundred years had been suggested as the interval (Dorn and Whitley

1984), but this has never been tested and the interval between exposure and varnish formation must vary if the varnish coating forms in a time-transgressive manner. Recent observations suggest that the interval between exposure and varnish development may be much shorter than one hundred years (Dorn and Meek 1995), but observed limitations in time-lapse intervals between surface exposure and initiation of varnish growth suggest that it may be impossible to ever accurately predict that interval. Due to limitations of obtaining sufficient organic material from very young surfaces, even for AMS-based ^{14}C determinations, this problem may never be overcome.

Sample Size Limitations

Two factors limit adequate sampling of rock varnish on archaeological surfaces: the destructive nature of securing samples and the limited size of most archaeological surfaces. In the first case, archaeological features and artifacts are nonrenewable. Acquiring varnish samples from artifact surfaces or rock-art surfaces constitutes destructive analyses. There is great reluctance for archaeologists and the public to harm archaeological resources. Although permission to collect samples is sometimes granted, it is granted with reluctance and with legal restrictions. As a result, few archaeological samples are taken, thus limiting adequate tests of methods and statistical significance.

In the second case, the carbon content of rock-varnish matrix is reported to be in a range of 1 to 2%. A sizeable area would have to be removed, even for a sample intended for AMS-based ^{14}C measurement. At 1 to 2%, approximately 300 mg. of varnish would be needed to produce enough organic fraction to carry out appropriate HPLC and spectrometric analyses in addition to a sample with sufficient carbon content (e.g., a few hundred micrograms), for an AMS-based ^{14}C determination (Christine Prior, personal communication, 1995). If samples are removed only from the lower laminations or from areas between the varnish coating and the underlying rock, acquiring samples would be a very destructive process. In addition, consistently separating lower varnish laminations from the total varnish by scraping away 90% of the upper varnish (e.g., separating 10 µm from a 100 µm coating) is problematic. In some cases, a square meter of varnish would have to be removed to get a sample of sufficient size for a single date. Most artifacts do not have a surface of this size that has been exposed to varnish development. Many petroglyph surfaces (i.e., the area within the scraped motif) have the same limitations. It would seem that only redundant and abundant cultural surfaces would be feasible sources of adequate sample size (Harry 1995).

Comparability Limitations

Varnish growth appears to be dependent upon a number of variables (Dorn 1983: 56; Bednarik 1988; Reneau *et al.* 1992; Reneau 1993). For archaeological materials, perhaps the most important are lithology, environment, and surface stability.

Lithology

The growth of varnish is indirectly dependent on lithology (Raymond and Harrington 1989; Raymond *et al.* 1991). While most investigators recognize that the substrate (underlying rock) does not chemically contribute to varnish formation, the rate of varnish growth appears to depend on microtopography of the rock surface. Varnish first starts to form in depressions on the substrate surface. This is likely due to the entrapment and retention of airborne particles and recurrent moisture in the depressions (Raymond and Harrington 1989). The accretionary processes of varnish growth are more rapid on rocks with rough and uneven surfaces.

Prehistoric stoneworkers often preferred microcrystalline quartz, fine-grained volcanics, and obsidian (volcanic glass) for tool stone, rocks that have characteristics that make them easier to control when flaking than other rock types, but rocks that also have relatively smooth surfaces, not conducive to rapid varnish growth. On the other hand, rough-textured sandstones and volcanics (especially rhyolites, andesites, and basalts) were often preferred for milling and processing tools. The latter rock types appear to encourage rapid varnish growth in appropriate environments. Since archaeological materials vary both between rock types and by degree of granularity within rock types, temporal comparisons using C-R or AMS-based ^{14}C measurements on rock varnish would be difficult without tight control of these lithological and textural variables (Bierman and Harry 1992; Bierman and Gillespie 1994; Harry 1995).

Temporal assignments of features such as rock alignments or geoglyphs that are based on analyses of individual rocks, cobbles, boulders, or artifacts composing or within those features would be highly suspect unless it could be assured that all rocks or boulders were of the same lithology and of comparable surface texture. Petroglyph panels present a similar dilemma. One would need to determine the comparability of the underlying bedrock outcrop or boulders in order to insure any comparability of the results of varnish analyses.

Environment

The rates of varnish growth and subsequent removal or degradation appear to be environmentally dependent. It has been assumed that environmental variables are especially significant for C-R analysis (Dorn 1983, 1986; Reneau 1993). Control of these variables would seem to be particularly crucial for archaeological purposes because of the "tight" dates desired. Variability of slope, exposure, and microenvironment confound the comparability of varnish on specimens and features between sites and within sites (see Reneau 1993).

Stability

Surface stability and continuous surface exposure must be established in order for rock-varnish dating of artifacts to be reliable. Furthermore, the stability of individual archaeological materials on a documented stable surface (Wells *et al.* 1994) must be considered. With the exception of features occurring on bedrock outcrops or desert pavement, such stability is extremely difficult to establish. To get a meaningful date, it would be necessary to document that once the primary archaeological despositional event occurred, no subsequent events disturbed the material in any way. Minimum dates might still be acquired from artifacts that were subsequently reused or used as elements of a feature for example, artifacts that were recycled, redeposited by sheet wash, moved by eolian forces, seismic events, or bioturbation, altered by fire, intentionally buried and/or exhumed, or moved by visitors to a site. Since both prehistoric and historic cultural activities often involve movement of archaeological materials, stability would be very difficult to establish. Personal field observances noted that artifacts have been relocated or reworked at various times during their depositional histories because variations in the degree of varnish development can often be seen on the same artifact.

SUMMARY

At the present time, the meaning of C-R and ^{14}C varnish dates is uncertain. C-R dating appears to have been little used since the controversy of the early 1990s. However, many critical questions affecting the validity of ^{14}C dating remain unanswered. Among the unanswered questions are: (1) What is the source and nature of ^{14}C-dated organic material? (2) What is the reproducibility of ^{14}C values derived from the same rock-varnish sample? (3) How do ^{14}C values on rock varnish relate to ages of surfaces? (4) How does the origin and the composition of the organic matter relate to the ^{14}C dates derived from it? Bednarik (1995: 11) noted that there is a "a need for distinguishing between direct methods of dating rock art that relate to variable indices on the one hand, and those using uniform indices on the other." In other words, archaeologists are forced to make a compromise between reliability and precision. "In all cases, we should be biased in favour of methods that offer statistically meaningful numbers of measurements" (Bendarik 1995: 11).

ACKNOWLEDGMENTS

The authors are indebted to R. E. Taylor, Charles D. Harrington, Karen G. Harry, and A.J.T. Jull, who commented on earlier drafts of this chapter. Richard Burky and Karen Selsor conducted a preliminary analysis of the organic content of a variety of rock varnishes from eastern California. As always, all errors of omission and commission are our own responsibility.

REFERENCES

Adams, J.B., Palmer, F., and Staley, J.T. 1992 Rock weathering in deserts: Mobilization and concentration of ferric Iron by microorganisms. *Geomicrobiology Journal* 10: 99–114.

Allen, C.C. 1978 Desert varnish of the Sonoran Desert-optical and electron probe microanalysis. *Journal of Geology* 86: 743–752.

Bamforth, D.B. 1997 Cation-ratio dating and archaeological research design: Response to Harry. *American Antiquity* 62(1): 121–129.

Bamforth, D.B. and Dorn, R.I. 1988 On the nature and antiquity of the Manix Lake Industry. *Journal of California and Great Basin Anthropology* 10(2): 209–226.

Bard, J.C. 1979 *The Development of a Patination Dating Technique for Great Basin Petroglyphs Utilizing Neutron Activation and X-ray Fluorescence Analyses*. Ph.D. dissertation, University of California, Berkeley.

Beck, C. 1994 *Dating in Exposed Surface Contexts*. Albuquerque, University of New Mexico Press.

Bednarik, R.G. 1988 Comments. *Rock Art Research* 5(2): 124–126, 139.

Bednarik, R.G. 1990 Summary of seminar and workshop by R.I. Dorn on geochemical methods for dating of rock art. *Australian Rock Art Research Association Newsletter* 7: 3.

Bednarik, R.G. 1995 Only time will tell: a review of the methodology of direct rock art dating. *Archaeometry* 38(1): 1–13.

Bennyhoff, J.A. and Hughes, R.A. 1987 Shell bead and ornament exchange networks between California and the Western Great Basin. *Anthropological Papers of the America Museum of Natural History* 64(2).

Bierman, P.R. 1994 Using in-situ produced cosmogenic isotopes to estimate rates of landscape evolution: a review from a geomorphic perspective. *Journal of Geophysical Research* 99: 13,885–13,896.

Bierman, P.R. and Gillespie A.R. 1991a Accuracy of rock varnish chemical analyses: Implications for cation ratio dating. *Geology* 19: 196–199.

Bierman, P.R. and Gillespie A.R. 1991b Range fires: a significant factor in exposure-age determination and geomorphic surface evolution. *Geology* 19: 641–644.

Bierman, P.R. and Gillespie A.R. 1992a Replies to comments on accuracy of rock varnish chemical analyses: Implications for cation ratio dating. *Geology* 20: 469–472.

Bierman, P.R. and Gillespie A.R. 1992b Reply to comment on range fires: a significant factor in exposure-age determination and geomorphic surface evolution. *Geology* 20: 283–285.

Bierman, P.R. and Gillespie A.R. 1994 Evidence suggesting that methods of rock-varnish cation ratio dating are neither comparable nor consistently reliable. *Quaternary Research* 41: 82–90.

Bierman, P.R. and Gillespie A.R. 1995 Reply to comment on evidence suggesting that methods of rock-varnish cation ratio dating are neither comparable nor consistently reliable. *Quaternary Research* 43: 274–276.

Bierman, P., Gillespie, A., Harrington, C., Raymond, R., McFadden, L., and Wells, S. 1992 Throwing rocks. *American Scientist* 80: 110–112.

Bierman, P.R., Gillespie, A.R., and Kuehner, S. 1991 Precision of rock-varnish chemical analyses and cation-ratio ages. *Geology* 19: 135–138.

Bierman, P.R. and Harry, K. 1992 Rock varnish cation-ratios may not be a reliable method for dating lithic artifacts. *In* Vandiver, P.J., Wheeler, G., and Freestone, I., eds., *Material Issues in Art and Archaeology III, Materials Research Society Proceedings* 267: 165–178.

Bierman, P. and Turner, J. 1995 ^{10}Be and ^{26}Al evidence for exceptionally low rates of Australian bedrock erosion and the likely existence of pre-Pleistocene landscapes. *Quaternary Research* 44: 378–382.

Bull, W. 1991 *Geomorphic Responses to Climatic Change*. New York, Oxford University Press.

Cahill, T. 1992 Comment on accuracy of rock varnish chemical analyses: Implications for cation ratio dating. *Geology* 20: 469.

Clarke, J. 1989 Comment on age determinations for rock varnish formation within petroglyphs. *Rock Art Research* 6(1): 63–65.

Clarkson, P.B. 1992 Absolute chronometric dates of the Nazca geoglyphs: Applications of radiocarbon dating in the Nazca region, Department of Ica, Peru, 1991. Report submitted to the Instituto Nacional de Cultura, Peru.

Clarkson, P.B. 1994 The Cultural insistence of geoglyphs: the Andean and Southwestern phenomena. *In* Ezzo, J.A. ed., *Recent Research Along the Lower Colorado River*, pp. 149–177. Technical Series No. 5. Tucson, Statistical Research.

Clarkson, P.B. and Dorn, R.I. 1991 Nuevos datos relativos a la antiquedad de los geoglifos y Pukious de Nazca, Peru. *Boletin de Lima* 13/78:33–45.

Clarkson, P.B. and Dorn, R.I. 1995 New chronometric dates for the Puquios of Nasca, Peru. *Latin American Antiquity* 6(1): 56–69.

Dethier, D.P., Harrington, C.D., and Aldrich, M.J. 1988 Late Cenozoic rates of erosion in the Western Espanola Basin, New Mexico: Evidence from geologic dating of erosion surfaces. *Geological Society of America Bulletin* 100: 928–937.

Dillehay, T.D.1989 *Monte Verde, a Late Pleistocene Settlement in Chile*. Washington, DC, Smithsonian Institution.

Dorn, R.I. 1982 *Dating Rock Varnish*. M.S. thesis, University of California, Berkeley.

Dorn, R.I. 1983 Cation-ratio Dating: a new rock varnish age determination technique. *Quaternary Research* 20: 49–73.

Dorn, R.I. 1988a *A Critical Evaluation of Cation-dating of Rock Varnish and Evaluation of its Application to the Yucca Mountain Repository by the Department of Energy and its Subcontractors*. Nevada Bureau of Mines and Geology.

Dorn, R.I. 1988b A rock varnish interpretation of alluvial-fan development in Death Valley, California. *National Geographic Research* 4: 56–73.

Dorn, R.I. 1989 Cation-ratio dating of rock varnish: a geographic assessment. *Physical Geography* 13: 559–596.

Dorn, R.I. 1992a Comment on accuracy of rock varnish chemical analyses: Implications for cation ratio dating. *Geology* 20: 470–471.

Dorn, R.I. 1992b Comment on range fires: a significant factor in exposure-age determination and geomorphic surface evolution. *Geology* 20: 283–284.

Dorn, R.I. 1995 Comment on evidence suggesting that methods of rock-varnish cation ratio dating are neither comparable nor consistently reliable. *Quaternary Research* 43: 272–273.

Dorn, R.I. 1996 A change of perception. *La Pintura* 23(2): 10–11.

Dorn, R.I. 1997 Constraining the age of the Côa Valley (Portugal) engravings with radiocarbon dating. *Antiquity* 71: 105–115.

Dorn, R.I., Bamforth, D., Cahill, T., Dohrenwend, J.C., Turrin, B.D., Donahue, D.J., Jull, A.J.T., Long, A., Macko, M.E., and Weils, E.B. 1986 Cation-ratio and accelerator radiocarbon dating of rock varnish on Mojave artifacts and landform surfaces. *Science* 231: 830–833.

Dorn, R.I., Cahill, T.A., Eldred, R.A., Gill, T.E., Kushko, B.H., Bach, A.J., and Elliot-Fiske, D.L. 1990 Dating rock varnish by the cation ratio method with PIXE, ICP, and electron microprobe. *International Journal of PIXE* 1: 157–195.

Dorn, R.I., Clarkson, P.B., Nobbs, M.F., Loendorf, L.L., and Whitley, D.S. 1992 New approach to the radiocarbon dating of rock varnish, with examples from drylands. *Annals of the Association of American Geographers* 82(1): 136–151.

Dorn, R.I. and DeNiro, M.J. 1985 Stable isotope ratios of rock varnish organic matter: a new paleoenvironmental factor. *Science* 231: 1472–1474.

Dorn, R.I., Jull, A.J.T., Donahue, J.D., Linick, T.W., Toolin L.J. 1989 Accelerator mass spectrometry radiocarbon dating of rock varnish. *Geological Society of America Bulletin* 101: 1363–1372.

Dorn, R.I. and Krinsley, D.H. 1991 Cation leaching sites in rock varnish. *Geology* 19: 1077–1080.

Dorn, R.I. and Meek, N. 1995 Rapid formation of rock varnish and other rock coatings on slag deposits near Fontana, California. *Earth Surface Processes and Landforms* 20: 547–560.

Dorn, R.I., Nobbs, M., and Cahill T.A. 1988 Cation-ratio dating of rock engravings from the Olary Province of arid South Australia. *Antiquity* 62: 681–689.

Dorn, R.I. and Oberlander, T.M. 1982 Rock varnish. *Progress in Physical Geography* 6: 317–367.

Dorn, R.I., Tanner, D., Turrin, B.D., and Dohrenwend, J.C. 1987a Cation ratio dating of Quaternary materials in the east-central Mojave Desert, CA. *Physical Geography* 8: 72–81.

Dorn, R.I., Tanner, D., Turrin, B.D., and Dohrenwend, J.C. 1987b Radiocarbon and cation-ratio ages for rock varnish on Tioga and Tahoe morainal boulders of Pine Creek, Eastern Sierra Nevada, California and their paleoclimatic implications. *Quaternary Research* 28: 38–49.

Dorn, R.I. and Whitley, D.S. 1984 Chronometric and relative age determination of petroglyphs in the Western United States. *Association of American Geographers Annals* 74: 308–322.

Dragovich, D. 1988 A Preliminary electron probe study of microchemical variations in desert varnish in Western New South Wales, Australia. *Earth Surface Processes and Landforms* 13: 259–270.

Elvidge, C.D. and Iverson, R.M. 1983 Regeneration of desert pavement and varnish. *In* Webb, R.H. and Wilshire, H.G. eds., *Environmental Effects of Off-Road Vehicles: Impacts and Management in Arid Regions*. New York, Springer-Verlag: 225–243.

Francis, J.E., Loendorf, L.L., and Dorn, R.I. 1993 AMS radiocarbon and cation-ratio dating of rock art in the Bighorn Basin of Wyoming and Montana. *American Antiquity* 58(4): 711–737.

Glazovskiy, A.F. 1985 Rock varnish in the glaciated Pamirs. *Data of the Glaciological Studies (Moscow)* 54: 136–141.

Harrington, C.D. and Whitney, J.W. 1987 Scanning electron microscope method for rock varnish dating. *Geology* 15: 967–970.

Harrington, C.D. and Whitney, J.W. 1995 Comment on evidence suggesting that methods of rock-varnish cation ratio dating are neither comparable nor consistently reliable. *Quaternary Research* 43: 268–271.

Harrington, C.D., Krier, D.J., Raymond, R., and Reneau, S.L. 1991 Barium concentrations in rock varnish: Implications for calibrated rock varnish dating curves. *Scanning Microscopy* 5: 55–62.

Harry, K. 1995 Cation-ratio dating of varnished artifacts: Testing the assumptions. *American Antiquity* 60(1): 118–130.

Harry, K. 1997 Reply to Bamforth. *American Antiquity* 62(1): 130–138.

Haynes, C.V. Jr. 1992 Contributions of radiocarbon dating to the geochronology of the peopling of the New World. *In* R.E. Taylor, A. Long, and R.S. Kra, eds., *Radiocarbon After Four Decades: an Interdisciplinary Perspective*. New York, Springer-Verlag: 355–374.

Heizer, R.F. and Baumhoff, M.A. 1962 *Prehistoric Rock Art of Nevada and Eastern California*. Berkeley, University of California Press.

Jones, C.E. 1991 Characteristics and origin of rock varnish from the hyperarid coastal deserts of Northern Peru. *Quaternary Research* 35: 116–129.

Lanteigne, M. 1989 Comment on age determinations for rock varnish formation within petroglyphs. *Rock Art Research* 6: 145–149.

Lanteigne, M. 1991 Comment on age determinations for rock varnish formation within petroglyphs. *Rock Art Research* 8: 127–130.

McFadden, L.D., Ritter, J.H., Wells, S.G. 1989 Use of multiparameter relative-age methods for age estimation and correlation of alluvial fan surfaces on a desert pavement, eastern Mojave Desert, California. *Quaternary Research* 32: 276–290.

Moratto, M.J. 1984 *California Archaeology*. Orlando, Academic Press.

Nagy, B., Nagy, L.A., Rigali, M.J., Jones, W.D., Bilodeau, W.K., Krinsley, D.H., Schram, K.H., and Baker, P.F. 1990 Sedimentological processes affecting the development of rock varnish. Abstract 09137. *Geological Society of America Abstracts*. Dallas, Geological Society of America.

Nobbs, M. and Dorn, R.I. 1988 Age-determinations for rock varnish formation within petroglyphs: Cation-ratio dating of 24 motifs from the Olary Region of arid South Australia. *Rock Art Research* 5: 108–146.

Perry, R.S. and J.B. Adams 1978 Desert Varnish: Evidence for the cyclic deposition of Manganese. *Nature* 276: 489–491.

Philips, F.M., Zreda, M.G.,Smith, S.S, Elmore, D., Kubik, M.W., and Sharma, P. 1990 Cosmogenic Chlorine-36 chronology for glacial deposits at Bloody Canyon, eastern Sierra Nevada. *Science* 248: 1529–1532.

Pineda, C.A., Peisach, M. and Jacobson, L. 1988 Ion beam analysis for the determination of cation-ratios as a means of dating Southern African rock art. *Nuclear Instruments and Methods in Physics Research* 5: 141–142.

Potter, R.M. and Rossman, G.R. 1977 Desert varnish: the Importance of clay minerals. *Science* 196: 1146–1448.

Raymond, R. and Harrington, C.D. 1989 Lithologic controls on rock varnish formation as determined by SEM. *In* Russell, P.E. ed., *Microbeam Analysis*. San Francisco, San Francisco Press: 567–570.

Raymond, R. Jr., Reneau, S.L., Harrington, C.D. 1991 Elemental relationships in rock varnish as seen with scanning electron microscopy and energy dispersive X-ray elemental line profiling. *Scanning Microscopy* 5(1): 37–46.

Reneau, S.L. 1993 Manganese accumulations in rock varnish on a desert piedmont, Mojave Desert, California, and application to evaluating varnish development. *Quaternary Research* 40: 309–317.

Reneau, S.L., Hagan, R.C., Harrington, C.D., and Raymond, R. 1991 Scanning electron microscopic analysis of rock varnish chemistry for cation-ratio dating: an examination of electron beam penetration depths. *Scanning Microscopy* 5(1): 47–54.

Reneau, S.L. and Harrington, C.D. 1988 Comment on age determinations for rock varnish formation within petroglyphs. *Rock Art Research* 5: 141–142.

Reneau, S.L. and Raymond, R. 1991 Cation-ratio dating of rock varnish: Why Does it Work? *Geology* 16: 937–940.

Reneau, S.L., Raymond, R., and Harrington, C.D. 1992 Elemental relationships in rock varnish stratigraphic layers, Cima Volcanic Field, California: Implications for varnish development and the interpretation of varnish chemistry. *American Journal of Science* 292: 684–723.

Schneider, J.S. 1993 *Aboriginal Milling Implement Quarries in Eastern California and Western Arizona: a Behavioral Perspective*. Ph.D. dissertation, University of CAlifornia, Riverside.

Schneider, J.S. 1996 Quarrying and production of milling implements at Antelope Hill, Arizona. *Journal of Field Archaeology* 23: 299–311.

Smith, B.J. and Whaley W.B. 1988 A Note on the characteristics and possible origins of desert varnish from Southeast Morocco. *Earth Surface Processes and Landforms* 13: 251–258.

Taylor, R.E. 1987 *Radiocarbon Dating: an Archaeological Perspective*. San Diego, Academic Press.

Taylor, R.E., Haynes, C.V., Jr., and Stuiver, M. 1996 Clovis and Folsom age estimates: Stratigraphic context and radiocarbon calibration. *Antiquity* 70: 515–525.

Thomas, D.H. 1981 How to classify the projectile points from Monitor Valley, Nevada. *Journal of California and Great Basin Anthropology* 3(1): 7–43.

Towner, R.H. 1996 Review of dating in exposed and surface contexts. *Journal of Field Archaeology* 23(3): 396–398.

Von Werlhof, J. 1995 New dating on Imperial County earthen art. *Imperial Valley College Desert Museum Society Newsletter* XVIV [sic] (3): 5.

Watchman, A. 1989 Comments on age determinations for rock varnish formation within petroglyphs: Cation-ratio dating of 24 Motifs from the Olary Region. *Rock Art Research* 6(1): 65–66.

Watchman, A. 1992 Comment on cation-leaching sites in rock varnish. *Geology* 20: 1050–1051.

Wells, S.G., McFadden, L.D., and Dohrenwend, J.C. 1987 Quaternary climatic changes on geomorphic and pedogenic processes on a desert piedmont, eastern Mojave Desert, California. *Quaternary Research* 27: 130–146.

Wells, S.G., McFadden, L.D., Olinger, C.T., and Poths, J. 1994 Use of cosmogenic ^{3}He to understand desert pavement formation. *In* McGill, S.F. and Ross, T.M., eds., *Geological Investigations of an Active Margin, Geological Society of America, Cordilleran Section Guidebook*. Redlands, San Bernardino County Museum Association: 201–205.

Whitley, D.S. and Dorn, R.I. 1993 New perspectives on the Clovis vs. pre-Clovis controversy. *American Antiquity* 58(4): 626–609.

Whitney, J.W. and Harrington, C.D. 1993 Relict colluvial boulder deposits as paleoclimatic indicators in the Yucca Mountain Region, southern Nevada. *Geological Society of America Bulletin* 105: 1008–1018.

About the Editors

R. E. Taylor is Professor of Anthropology, Research Anthropologist in the Institute of Geophysics and Planetary Physics, and Director, Radiocarbon Laboratory, at the University of California, Riverside. His research focuses on the application of dating and analytical techniques in archaeology (archaeometry) with an emphasis on radiocarbon dating. He received his Ph.D. in anthropology at the University of California, Los Angeles (UCLA) in 1970 in the Isotope Laboratory of the late Willard F. Libby and was a NSF Postdoctoral Fellow with Daniel Kivelson, Department of Chemistry, UCLA.

M. J. Aitken is now Emeritus Professor of Archaeometry at Oxford University. He received his D.Phil in 1954 for research in nuclear physics, also at Oxford University, and shortly afterwards joined the Research Laboratory for Archaeology—newly-formed under the directorship of E.T. Hall through the joint initiative of Christopher Hawkes and Viscount Cherwell. His principle areas of research were in Magnetic Prospection, Archaeomagnetism, and Luminescence Dating. In 1983, he was elected a Fellow of the Royal Society of London. In 1992, he received the Gemant Award of the American Institute of Physics.

Index

ISBN 0-306-45715-6